INDIANA
LAND ENTRIES

Volume 2, Part 1

Vincennes District

1807-1877

All of Daviess, Gibson,
Knox, Martin & Pike Counties
About Half of Monroe and Lawrence Counties

*(Excluding the Donation, Canal, Swamp, Saline,
and School lands not sold at the Vincennes government land office)*

MARGARET R. WATERS

Southern Historical Press, Inc.
Greenville, South Carolina

This volume was reproduced
from a personal copy located in
the Publishers private library

Please direct all correspondence and book orders to:
SOUTHERN HISTORICAL PRESS, Inc.
PO Box 1267
Greenville, SC   29602-1267

Originally printed: Indianapolis, IN. 1948
ISBN #978-1-63914-123-4
Printed in the United States of America

CONTENTS

Map of Vinconnes District   1

Plat of Township and Section Divisions   2

To the Searcher   3

Daviess County   9-51

Gibson County   52-95

Knox County   96-122

Lawrence County   123-150

Martin County   151-184

Monroe County   185-210

Pike County   211-234

Index   235-274

MAP ILLUSTRATING
THE PIONEER PERIODS IN INDIANA

S — DATE OF FIRST WHITE SETTLERS

O — DATE OF ORGANIZATION AS A COUNTY

C — DATE WHEN FIRST COURT CONVENED

L — DATE OF FIRST LAND ENTRY

+ — EARLIER THAN

HEAVY BLACK LINES INDICATE BOUNDARIES OF THREE PIONEER PERIODS — THE HEAVY FIGURES — 1, 2, 3 INDICATE THE PIONEER PERIOD IN THE COUNTIES GROUPED WITHIN THE BOUNDARIES

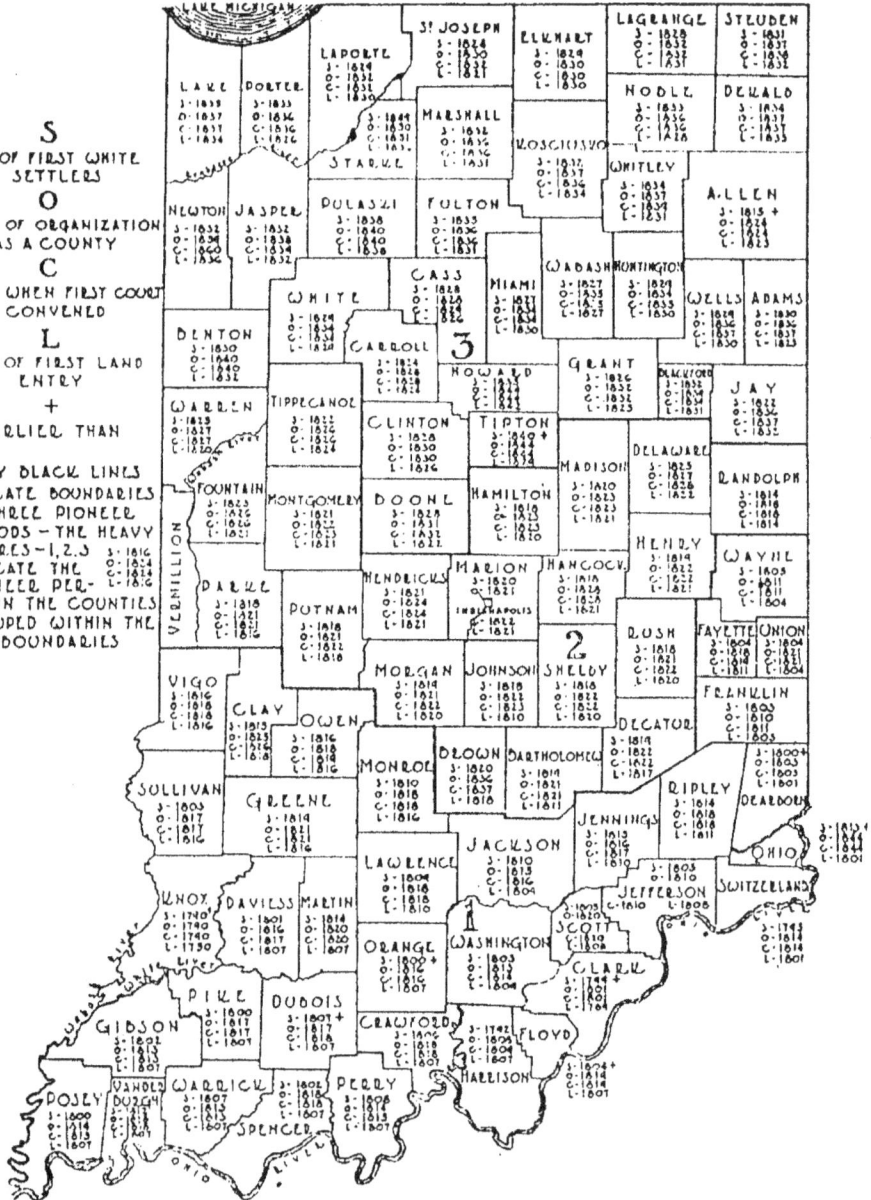

COMPILED BY CHARLES NEBEKER THOMPSON FOR THE 1932 YEAR BOOK OF THE SOCIETY OF INDIANA PIONEERS

U. S. GOVERNMENT LAND DISTRICTS

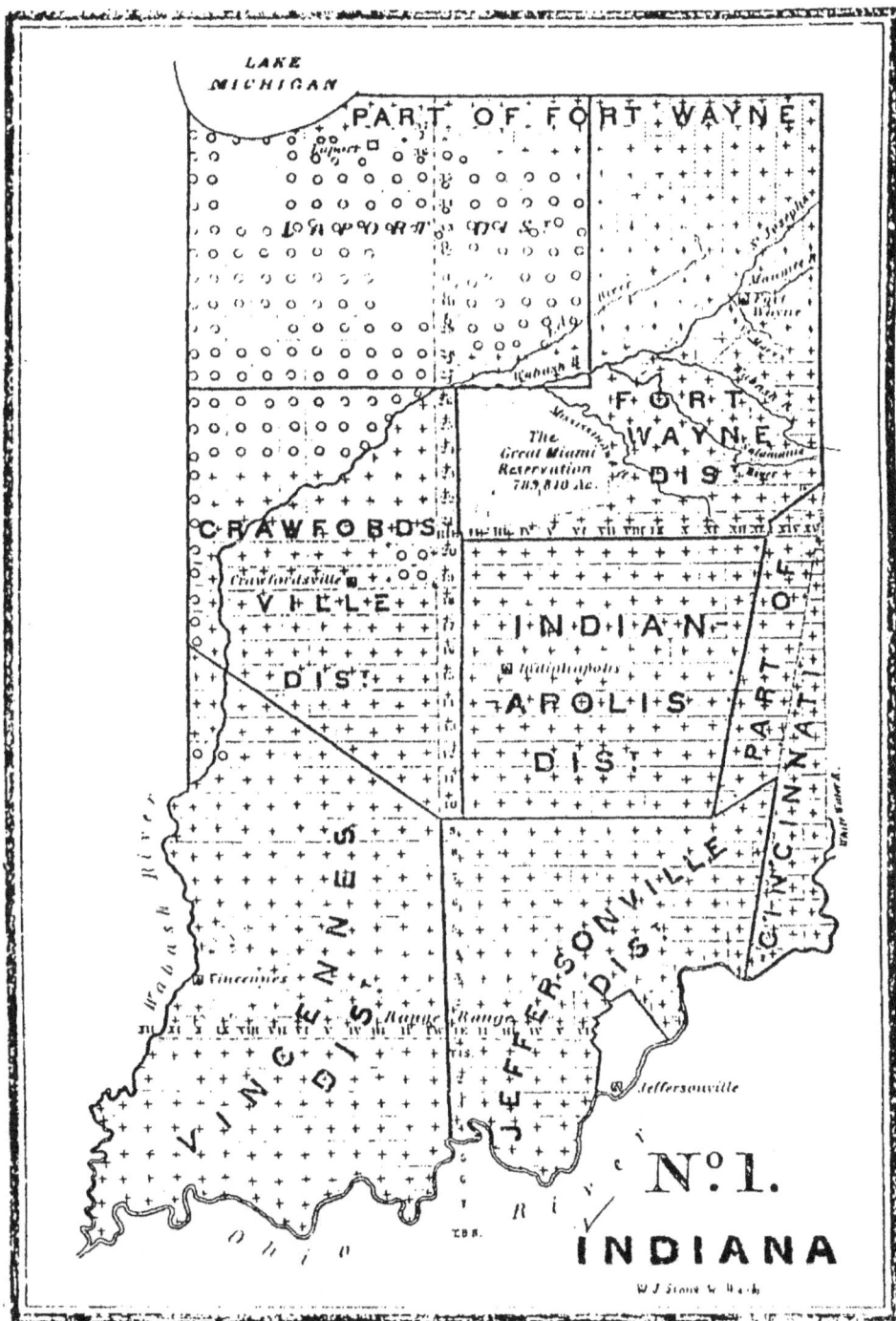

LAKE MICHIGAN

PART OF FORT WAYNE

FORT WAYNE DIS

The Great Miami Reservation 749,810 Ac.

CRAWFORDS VILLE DIST

INDIANAPOLIS DIST

PART OF CINCINNATI

VINCENNES DIST

JEFFERSONVILLE DIST

Jeffersonville

Vincennes

Crawfordsville

Ohio River

Wabash River

No. 1.

INDIANA

FOREWORD

Sharp, spirited, and steadfast, all deserving traits of a good genealogist, also highlight a description of Margaret R. Waters.

Miss Waters has been tracing family trees for over 40 years. A retired English teacher, she first became interested in genealogy when she had to write an autobiography for her high school English class. After the completion of her formal education by receiving degrees from Butler and Northwestern Universities, Miss Waters began her genealogical investigations with her own Waters family. Becoming one of the first professional genealogists in the country, she has since helped many other persons with their family history search.

Miss Waters has compiled several outstanding genealogical resource aids including *Revolutionary Soldiers Buried in Indiana*, Supplement.

This lovely lady who has given so much to the field of genealogy is not only an ardent supporter of the Indiana State Library but also a personal friend.

Carolyne L. Miller

Head Librarian, Genealogy Division

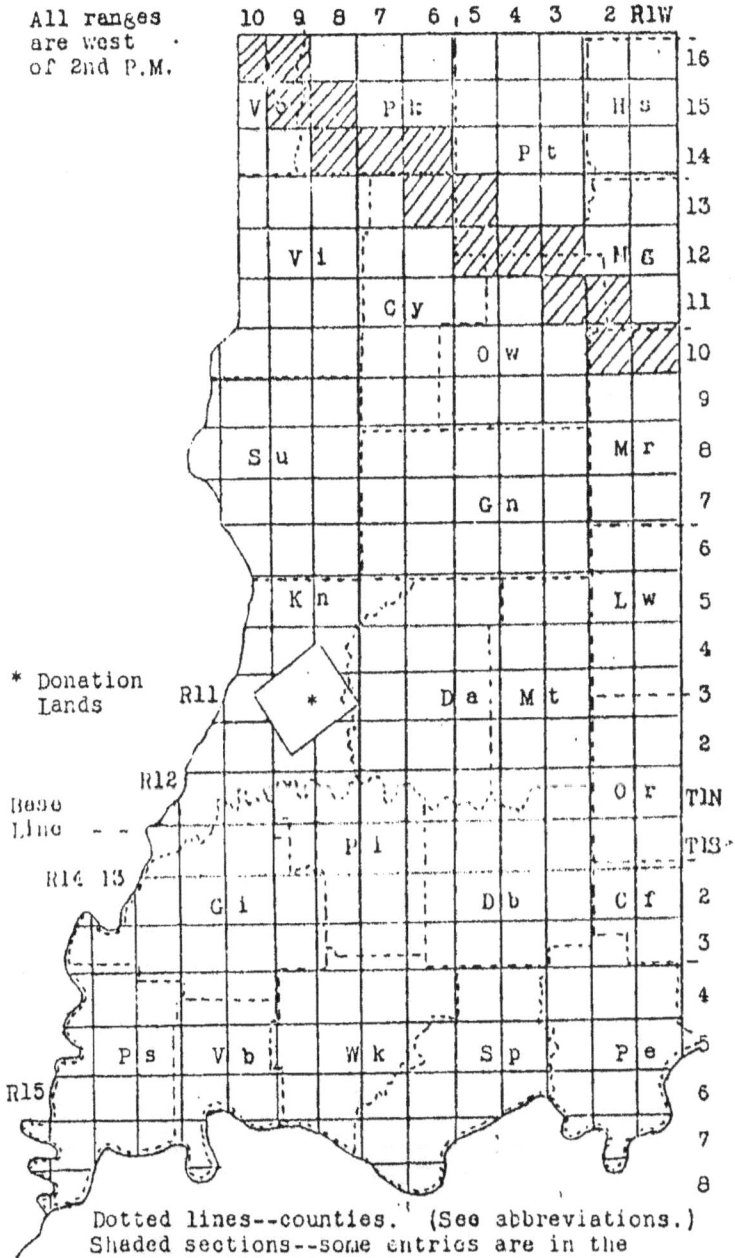

All ranges are west of 2nd P.M.

10 9 8 7 6 5 4 3 2 R1W

* Donation Lands

R11
R12
Base Line
R14 13
R15

Dotted lines--counties. (See abbreviations.)
Shaded sections--some entries are in the
Crawfordsville District.

6	5	4	3	2	1
7	8	9	10	11	12
18	17	16	15	14	13
19	20	21	22	23	24
30	29	28	27	26	25
31	32	33	34	35	36

Arrangement of sections in a
"perfect" township, 36 sq. mi.

	40 NW$\frac{1}{4}$-NE$\frac{1}{4}$	40 NE$\frac{1}{4}$-NE$\frac{1}{4}$
W$\frac{1}{2}$ 320	S$\frac{1}{2}$-NE$\frac{1}{4}$ 80	
	SE$\frac{1}{4}$ 160	

Typical acreage divisions of a
"perfect" section:
  1 Section-640 ac., 1 sq. mi.
  W$\frac{1}{2}$ - 320 ac.
  SE$\frac{1}{4}$ - 160 ac.
  S$\frac{1}{2}$-NE$\frac{1}{4}$ - 80 ac.
  NE$\frac{1}{4}$-NE$\frac{1}{4}$ - 40 ac.
Acreage of fractional parts are
in tract book or plat book only
-2-

An article in the Indiana History Bulletin for December 1947, published by the Indiana Historical Bureau, Indianapolis, and quoted by permission, gives an excellent account of the status of the public domain in Indiana Territory, created May 7, 1800.

"Prior to 1800 the only land owned by individuals in Indiana was either in and around Vincennes, where titles went back to French and Indian grants, or in Clark's Grant opposite the present Louisville, which had been allotted to the men who had served with George Rogers Clark in his Revolutionary War campaign against the British.

"Indian title to all lands in Indiana was recognized at least nominally by the Federal government; and before any particular area was opened for sale, negotiations were opened with the chiefs of the tribes that claimed the land. Treaties were made whereby the Indians gave up their claims and accepted goods and money in exchange. The negotiations might be prolonged, but in the end the government always won out.

"The first such treaty affecting Indiana land was held in 1795, when the Indians ceded lands east of a line drawn from Fort Recovery in Ohio to a point on the Ohio River opposite the mouth of the Kentucky River. A triangular strip in what is now southeastern Indiana was thus opened for settlement; but it was not until six years later after the land had been surveyed and a land office was opened at Cincinnati, that it could be purchased. In the meantime, many settlers moved in and 'squatted' on the land, hoping to purchase their preferred site when the area was opened for sale.

"During the first two decades of government land sales in Indiana, purchasers had to buy at least 320 acres and pay a minimum of $2.00 per acre. Four years were allowed in which to complete payments. Land auctions were held when new areas were opened, and the land was sold to the highest bidder. Any tracts not sold at auction could be purchased at the land office for the minimum price. Many purchasers were forced to forfeit their lands when hard times came and payments could not be made. In 1820 a new law was passed which placed the minimum price at $1.25 an acre and allowed purchasers to buy as little as 80 acres. The credit system was abolished in favor of cash payments. At the auction sales, choice land often sold for three and four times the minimum price. In the 1830's and 1840's, pre-emption acts were passed by Congress to give the 'squatter' who had settled and improved a piece of land the opportunity to purchase it at the minimum price before the public sale.

"The rectangular system of land surveys was used for the first time in what is now Ohio in the 1790's. The system was conceived by Thomas Hutchins in 1764 while on an expedition against the Indians."

- - - - -

The tract books for the several land offices in Indiana are deposited in the office of the Auditor of State, Indianapolis, and are in the care of the State Land Clerk. Eventually, it is my plan to copy all of these records according to the chronological opening of the various land offices up to the closing of the offices and the transfer of the records of the remaining, unsold lands in each district to the then-called General Land Office in Washington, D.C.

These records have been copied solely for genealogical purposes to enable a searcher to learn if an ancestor did locate in Indiana; if so, where and when. Consequently, to save time and space, I have omitted giving the acreage and the final certificate numbers. Reference to my page 2 will give the acreage except in the case of fractional sections; and if anyone particularly cares for the final certificate number, he would probably want a signed letter from the Bureau of Land Management in Washington, D.C.

The land records for Indiana have never been published, copied, nor indexed by names. Therefore, they have been completely useless to searchers unless they knew the exact, or at least a close approximate, location of the land on which they suspected ancestors might have settled.

Since the 1820 Census is the first for Indiana, these records will serve, in a way, as a substitute for earlier censuses. The fact that a person entered land, however, does not necessarily mean that he ever actually lived on it. Also, some "squatter" residents may never have bought their land before they migrated to other places. These records will also serve as a partial index to the 1820 through 1880 Censuses, inclusive, in that they will locate a man in a definite township and county.

In copying the records, I have done so exactly as they appear in the originals --- by location. By this, searchers may be able to identify other members of the family from nearby entries made by people of the same surname; also there is the possibility of a clue to neighboring families into which daughters might have married. When a man entered several locations in the same township, I have listed these together after his name to save repeating it later --- providing I have caught the multiple entries in time.

After copying by locations, I have then re-arranged all those in one county together. Some years ago, a member of the State Board of Accounts, interested in the records, labeled the county names on the original pages. In most cases, these were easy for me to check. However, in the case of fractional sections bordering county lines, it is very hard to verify these; in such cases, I have accepted his labels although I do not guarantee them.

The searcher is warned against assuming, without other proof, that Sr. and Jr. necessarily mean father and son. In the early days, this often literally meant the "elder" and the "younger"---sometimes a man and his nephew, occasionally two unrelated men of the same name, coincidentally. A given name or middle name resembling a surname does not always positively indicate a relationship to that family. Children were often given the name of a neighbor. Of course, such names as George Washington Brown or Lorenzo Dow Green are self-explanatory!

-4-

In old handwriting, J and I were made identically. One can, of course, interpret Jones or Isaac; but where this letter is used as a middle initial, it is impossible to determine which is meant. I have copied such middle initials as J since in the various styles of handwriting that can be easily interpreted, J appears as a middle initial more often than I. It is hard sometimes to tell whether M is a middle initial or a name like McAdams. I have found difficulty in interpreting Lemuel and Samuel; also, I may have miscopied Jas. and Jos. although I have never seen Joseph abbreviated Jos.

Whimsical spelling has been given exactly as it appears. In the text itself, I have included all middle names and initials. However, in the index, to save space, I have used only the first name with the assumption that most men were called by it. If the searcher suspects that his ancestor might have used his middle name (and this is especially true of Germans), it would be wise to look up all given names listed under a surname. All entries under the same given and surname have been combined in the index; this does not necessarily mean that they are all for the same man.

In the index, I have occasionally made an attempt to standardize or modernize the spelling to make the names more easily found. Also I have combined similar-sounding names such as Meyer-Meier-Myers. However, my interpretation of the handwriting may be faulty; so the searcher is advised to "look around" the alphabet. Names beginning with L-S-T, for instance, look much alike in some script. Also, remember that German names were often spelled interchangeably: B-P, C-G, C-K, D-T, F-P, G-C, G-K, K-N, K-G, N-K, P-B, P-F, S-Z, T-D, V-W, V-F, W-V, Z-S.

Volume 1 of the Indiana Land Entries covered the Cincinnati District, 1801-1840. These records were contained in one small and one large book.

For the Vincennes District, there are 13 large books (some of which are partial duplicates) and one small. I think that it will take at least three books of the size which I am able to publish in order to cover the whole district. At the present time, I have divided the counties contained in this region into three approximately equal parts. This division has no significance other than to suit my convenience. Part 1 comprises all of the present counties of Daviess, Gibson, Knox, Martin, and Pike; and over half of Monroe and Lawrence; this is roughly the central third of the region.

There are in Indiana two Principal Meridians---the first at the Ohio-Indiana State Line at approximately 84 degrees and 49 minutes longitude, the second about two-thirds of the way across the state to the west at approximately 86 degrees and 28 minutes longitude. All ranges in the Vincennes District are west of the 2nd P.M. The Base Line in Indiana is located in the southern part of the state at approximately 38 degrees and 28 minutes latitude. Townships in the Vincennes District are both north and south of the Base Line.

Many entries in the Vincennes District will not be included
here (and in Parts 2 and 3) because much of this land was set aside
to be sold by the state as Wabash & Erie Canal Lands, Swamp Lands,
and Saline Lands. (There are no Michigan Road Lands in this region.
The entries for these are available; but they are contained in so
many different volumes and in such scattered fashion that to copy
them now and attempt to correlate the locations with the counties
would prevent the early publication of this and succeeding volumes.
Consequently, I shall copy all of the regular land offices first and
later copy these other records. The searcher must keep in mind that
if he does not find his ancestor in the region in which he is said
to have lived, the man may show up later in the Swamp Lands records,
for instance. Or, additional entries by the same man may show up in
several records. In other words, the Vincennes Land Office records
do not cover all the sales of lands in its area. Likewise, in a few
cases, locations in the Vincennes District are listed as having been
sold from the Jeffersonville District. Book 3 of the Vincennes records includes a few locations in the Jeffersonville District, namely
T 7 N, R 3 E; T 8 N, R 10 E - R 13 E, incl.; and T 9 N, R 1 E -
R 13 E, incl.; these I am holding over until I copy the Jeffersonville District. Some entries in an over-lapping area on the north
(see map on page 1) will be found in the Crawfordsville District, to
be copied later.

By Act of Mar. 26, 1804, the Vincennes Land Office opened on
Apr. 27, 1807, although the earliest entries in Part 1 are dated
May 15, 1807. The office, discontinued on Apr. 12, 1840, re-opened
on order of Apr. 20, 1853, and finally closed on Dec. 20, 1861, although I find entries in years not included here and as late as on
Sept. 4, 1877. Some of the dates in the 1870's I have suspected to
be poorly written 50's, but I have no way of verifying this here.

Fortunately for the searcher, most entries list the present or
former place of residence. To save space, I have used an asterisk *
after a man's name to indicate that he is given as a resident of the
county at the top of the page. Out-of-state places of residence are
given in full. Residence in Indiana counties other than the one at
the top of the page is abbreviated as follows:

Ad	Adams	Dk	DeKalb	Hy	Henry	Mn	Marion
Al	Allen	Dw	Delaware	Ho	Howard	Ms	Marshall
Ba	Bartholomew	Du	Dubois	Ht	Huntington	Mt	Martin
Be	Benton	El	Elkhart	Jk	Jackson	Mm	Miami
Bk	Blackford	Fa	Fayette	Js	Jasper	Mr	Monroe
Bo	Boone	Fd	Floyd	Jy	Jay	My	Montgomery
Br	Brown	Fo	Fountain	Jf	Jefferson	Mg	Morgan
Cr	Carroll	Fr	Franklin	Jn	Jennings	Ne	Newton
Cs	Cass	Fu	Fulton	Jo	Johnson	No	Noble
Ck	Clark	Gi	Gibson	Kn	Knox	Oh	Ohio
Cy	Clay	Gt	Grant	Ko	Kosciusko	Or	Orange
Cn	Clinton	Gn	Greene	Lg	Lagrange	Ow	Owen
Cf	Crawford	Hm	Hamilton	Lk	Lake	Pk	Parke
Da	Daviess	Hn	Hancock	Lp	LaPorte	Pe	Perry
Dr	Dearborn	Hr	Harrison	Lw	Lawrence	Pi	Pike
Dr	Decatur	Hs	Hendricks	Mi	Madison	Pr	Porter

Ps	Posey	Sc	Scott	To	Tippecanoe	Wn	Warren
Pu	Pulaski	Sh	Shelby	Tn	Tipton	Wk	Warrick
Pt	Putnam	Sp	Spencer	Un	Union	Ws	Washington
Ra	Randolph	Sk	Starke	Vb	Vanderburgh	Wy	Wayne
Ri	Ripley	St	Steuben	Ve	Vermillion	We	Wells
Ru	Rush	Su	Sullivan	Vi	Vigo	Wi	White
Sa	St.Joseph	Sz	Switzerland	Wb	Wabash	Wt	Whitley

The fact that a man is listed at an early date as a resident of a certain county does not necessarily mean that the county concerned is the present county of that name. A resident of a certain county in one year might find himself residing in another county the next year---without having moved! The last county line changes in the Vincennes District were not completed until 1868.

Some names are followed by MLW, which means Military Land Warrant. I have included these. Correspondence with the National Archives concerning several of these picked at random indicates that the majority are for service in the War of 1812, with some for the Black Hawk War and the Mexican War. Some entries are followed by LW. I suspect that these are for military service; but as I am not sure, I have omitted them.

All dates refer to the 1800's, 4-3-31 meaning April 3, 1831. One date after several entries means that all were entered on the same date.

I have omitted ½ and ¼ in the description since one capital letter always means a ½ section and two capital letters always means a ¼ section. Example:

    N-SE   north half of south-east quarter
    E-N   east half of north half
    NW-SW north-west quarter of south-west quarter

Note the difference between NE-NW-S2 and NE, NW-S2. The former means the NE¼ of the NW¼ of Section 2 (or 40 acres); the latter means the NE¼ and also the NW¼ (a total of 320 acres) in Section 2. See page 2 for typical divisions of a whole section.

There is one slim book of Relinquishments. I feel sure that it does not include all of the entries which were relinquished for non-payment as there are many names in the 13 books after which a final certificate number does not appear and as the latest relinquishments are dated only through 1831. Relinquished lands were sometimes sold to a new purchaser or were sometimes bought back later by the original entrant, in full or in part. One date after a Relinquishment means the date of entry; in a few cases, the date of relinquishment follows as a second date.

Joint entries in the original records are listed as Richard and Henry Jones. I have copied and indexed these as Richard Jones and Henry Jones. However, some joint entries are listed as John Gray and James Carter Jones. I do not know whether this means John Gray or John Gray Jones. I have copied such entries exactly but have indexed them both ways.

Special mention must be made of Knox County as it was the very earliest part of the state to be settled. Knox County is an abstracter's nightmare since very little of the county is surveyed in townships; the "square" covers most of the land. In 1814 a courthouse fire destroyed all records. The present deed indexes start in 1814. For earlier records, the abstracters consult Vols. 1-2-7 of the American State Papers. Vol. 2, pp. 285-287 list the heads of families residing there in 1783 who were entitled to the Donation lands, often called the French Grants. In the "square" (a small part of which is now in Daviess County) were laid off 160 lots of 400 acres each. These were found to be insufficient; so 96 more lots were laid off surrounding the "square". An excellent account of the matter can be found on pp. 94-146 of Goodspeed's 1886 History of Knox and Daviess Counties, Indiana.

The Militia Donations were 128 grants of 100 acres each to men who were enrolled in the Militia at Vincennes on Aug. 1, 1790, and who had done military duty but who had not received a donation. In Knox County originally, these grants are now in Gibson County.

Near Vincennes 5,400 acres were granted to the inhabitants of the city as a "common". These were later divided into square lots of 5-10-20 acres called Divisions A-B-C.

Private claims were not considered in the laying out of the Donation Lands and Military Donations. Claimants were permitted other locations, irregularly shaped, of from just a few acres to 400; these claims were called Locations.

For still other claimants, irregularly shaped surveys were made and allotted; such claims were called Surveys. For lists of all these grants, see Goodspeed's history.

Abbreviations used in the text are:

T	township	MLW	Military Land Warrant
R	range	BLW	Bounty Land Warrant
S	section	fr	fraction
P.M.	Principal Meridian (2nd)	pt	part
n.d.	no date	cor	corner
decd.	deceased	assee.	assignee

December 27, 1947
to
June 2, 1949

Margaret R. Waters
20 N. Bosart Avenue
Indianapolis 1, Ind.

George R. Patton W-NE-S3; 2-22-20
James F. Allen NW & SW-S3; 7-26-19
William Kelso* NE-SE-S3; 8-1-39
Michael Abel* SE-SE-S3; 4-23-38
David McCord* NW-SE-S3; 5-26-40
Charles Allen SE-NE, SW-NE, & W-SE-S4; 1-16-50. MLW 48404
George Fraim, Mt NE-NW-S4; 10-15-40
Joseph Allen* SE-NW-S4; 1-28-39; SW-NW-S4; 9-8-52; NE-NE-S5;
   4-25-38. MLW 25347
Susannah Allen* NW-NW-S4; 3-1-45
Michael Gibney, Kn SE-SW-S4; 5-1-41; SE-SE-S5; 5-1-40
Philander McCardle E-SE-S4; 9-19-51. MLW 2992
Patrick Fatherston* SE-NE & NE-SE-S5; 5-11-44
William S. Turner W-NE & E-NW-S5; 10-5-52. MLW 18942
Robert Snodgrass, Jefferson Co., O. W-NW-S5; 3-15-39
Luke McAvoz* NE-SW-S5; 2-18-51
George Washington Cochran* SE-SW-S5; 4-27-38; SW-SW-S5; 1-4-39
Charles Donoho, Hamilton Co., O. NW-SW-S5; NE-SE-S6; 11-6-40
Turance Riley* NW-SE-S5; 11-2-44
Jacob Hedrick* SW-SE-S5; 4-25-38
Robert Snodgrass, Jefferson Co., O. E-NE-S6; 3-15-39
James Porter, Jefferson Co., O. W-NE & E-NW-S6; 3-30-38
John McAdam* W-NW-S6; 3-25-37
Charles Riley* NE-SW-S6; 3-23-40
Samuel Chadd* SE-SW-S6; 1-31-39
Michael Rirdon* SE-SE-S6; 8-22-40
John Rirdon* SW-SE-S6; 12-9-39; NE-NE-S14; 1-4-39
George Washington Hedrick* NE-SE-S7; 12-14-44
Trice Stafford NW-S7; 12-8-15; SW-S7; 6-20-14
Caleb Brock NE-S7; SE-S10; NW-S15; 8-30-16
William Ballow SE-S8; 4-29-15
Jos. H. McClesky NE-S8; 6-2-18
Thomas Scales SW-S8; 4-29-15
James W. Blair NW-S9; 12-16-19
Edmund Adams SW-S9; 4-4-16
William D. Allen* SW-NE-S10; 10-16-37
George Alexis Burch* SE-SW-S10; 7-16-39
Henry Foster W-SW-S10; 10-1-16
Joseph Kelso NW-S10; 1-4-17
John Tucker, Mr SE-NE-S11; 11-13-32
William Cochran* SW-NW-S11; 6-5-38
Thomas Patton SW-S11; 11-24-17; NW-S14; 2-2-18
Richard Gibson, Mt SE-SE-S13; 6-13-53
Reuben Mathis NW-SE-S13; 2-17-52. MLW 27152
Isaac Hollingsworth E-SW-S14; 4-19-16
Benjamin Hawkins E-SE-S14; 4-19-16
Joseph Hays SW-S15; 2-23-16
George Gregory SE-S15; 4-19-16
William Ballow Nfr-S17; 9-18-15
Thomas Morehead & Robert Taylor, Jr. NE-Nfr-S17; SE-Nfr-S18;
   Nfr-S19; 10-13-18
Thomas Scales* NE-NW-Nfr-S17; 9-19-37; W-NW-Nfr-S17; 7-3-37

Samuel White* SE-NW-Nfr-S17; 8-17-52
William J. Demoss* NE-SW-Nfr-S18; 12-7-50
Jacob Reeder Nfr-S20; Nfr-S21; 11-24-15
Thomas Patton Efr-S22; Nfr-S27; 9-30-16
Joshua Reeve Nfr-S23; 4-13-12

(See p. 16 for
Relinquishments
omitted here.)

T 1 N, R 6 W

Samuel Chadd* NE-NE-S1; 1-7-39
Joseph Chadd* SE-NE-S1; 1-21-39; SW-NW-S1; 10-18-39
Thomas Deering* E-NW-S1; 10-16-39
James Brown* NE-SW & NW-SE-S1; 11-5-39   12-30-36
Thomas Allen* NE-SE-S1; 11-28-48; SE-SE-S1; 10-2-50; SE-NW-S4;
John Gay E-SW-S2; 3-6-52. MLW 27171
William S. Turner SW-SW-S2; 4-8-52. MLW 23153
Caleb Brock NW-S2; 8-30-16
John Liverman* NE-NE-S3; NW-NE-S3; 1-14-39
Zachariah Risley* NW-NW-S3; 10-28-39
Matthew Risley* SW-NW-S3; 1-12-39; NE-SE-S4; 12-9-40
Alexander Miller E-SW-S3; 3-9-18
James Allen* NW-SW-S3; 4-2-39; SW-SW-S3; 8-1-37
Peary Poachee* E-SE-S3; 1-28-39
Levi Davis Colbert* NW-SE-S3; 1-19-39
Justus Pearson Chapman* NE-NE-S4; 1-12-39
William Smith Wallis* SW-NE-S4; 10-28-40
Samuel Anderson* SW-NW-S4; 7-21-43
Peter Wilson* NE-SW-S4; 2-16-36; SE-SW-S4; 6-12-32
William Baldwin* W-SW-S4; SE-NE-S5; 7-11-37; SE-NW-S5; 5-20-39
William Chapman W-SE-S4; 2-3-18
Campbell Vance* NE-NE-S5; 11-17-38
James Shrader Stafford* NW-NE-S5; 6-20-36
John Simpson Baldwin* SW-NE-S5; 4-26-37
John Baldwin* NE-NW & SE-SE-S5; 6-23-37; W-NW & W-SW-S5; 1-2-30;
    Wfr-Nfr-S8; 6-14-33
Thomas Jones* NE-SE-S5; 12-30-36
Jesse Baldwin* NW-SE-S5; 4-26-37; SW-SE-S5; 6-7-37
Frances Baldwin E-NE-S6; 10-7-18; SW-NE-S6; 7-30-32
Daniel Baldwin* NW-NE-S6; 2-4-39
Isaac Gregory, Union Dist., S.C. E-NW-S6; 6-16-37
John DePauw W-NW-S6; 7-26-15
John Gregory" NE-SW-S6; 7-3-37
Josiah Wallace Morgan* SE-SW-S6; 11-5-36
Joseph Jones* NW-SW-S6; 11-14-36
John Lorenzo Caldwell, Pi SW-SW-S6; 3-27-39
Elias Stone E-SE & W-SE-S6; 11-25-14
Joseph Case Nfr-S7; 2-8-14   1-1-17
George Belue & Elijah Hammond NEfr-Nfr & SE-Nfr-S8; Nfr-S17;
Clayton Rogers NE-S9; 7-1-19
Daniel Clifft NW-S9; 3-8-15
Robert Hays SW-S9; 9-22-14
George W. Clifft SE-S9; 3-8-15
Edward Jordan Kirk* NE-NE & NW-NE-S10; 6-13-38
Ulysses E. Jackson* NW-SW-S10; 11-17-38

David L. Coleman NW-S10; 1-24-18
Samuel Comer SE-S10; 11-10-17
John Ellis* SW-NE-S11; 1-19-37
Coleman Carlisle Wallace* SW-SE-S11; 3-4-37
Caleb Brook NW & SW-S11; 8-30-16
Thomas Moorehead & John Moorehead NE-S12; 10-13-18
Thomas Haley, Hamilton Co., O. SE-NW-S12; 2-17-40
William Jones W-NW-S12; 3-1-20
John Davisson Nfr-S13; 4-15-16
Elisha Hyatt & William Holphasine SE-NE, SW-NE, & E-NW-Nfr-S14;
    10-19-50. MLW 39216
John Ralph* NW-NE-Nfr-S14; 11-2-38   5-23-18
Jacob Drake & Robert Taylor, Jr. SW-Nfr & SE-Nfr-S14; Nfr-S23;
Hylic Burk & Elisha Burk Nfr-S15; 7-22-18
A. G. Heylman, Washington, D.C. Nfr-S17; 9-26-76
John Davisson Nfr-S24; 4-15-16

RELINQUISHMENTS

James Gregory SE-S5; 7-26-15; 7-4-29
John Wallis SW-S6; 9-2-14; 7-4-29
John DePaul SW-S5; 7-26-15; E-NW-S6; 7-26-15
Francis Baldwin W-NE-S6; 10-7-18
Hulick Burk & Elisha Burk SW-S10; 1-16-19
John Allen, Jr. NE-S11; 8-12-19
James Allen, Sr. E-SE & W-SE-S11; 8-6-19
Thomas Moorhead & John Moorhead SE-S12; 10-13-18
Alexander Miller W-SW-S3; 3-9-18
Daniel Clifft SW-S4; 7-30-18
William Chapman E-SE-S4; 2-3-18
George Belue & Elijah Hammond Wfr-Nfr-S8; 1-1-17
William Jones E-NW-S12; 3-1-20
Jacob Drake & Robert Taylor, Jr. NE-Nfr & NW-Nfr-S14; 5-23-18
Charles Dewey & Peleg R. Allen Sfr-S14; 1-5-18
Andrew Coan SE-S3; 2-16-19
John Baldwin W-NW-S5; 10-14-18
William Coan NE-S10; 2-16-19

T 1 N, R 7 W

William Jones NE-S1; 2-20-30
Jonathan Morgan E-NW-S1; 11-10-17
Moses Morgan S-NW-S1; 3-21-37
James Horrell SW-S1; 10-24-17
Joseph Wilmore, Kn NW-SE-S1; 8-4-37. Of *, SW-SE-S1; 11-13-38
William Chapman E-NE-S2; 9-1-17
John Holland* NW-NE-& NE-NW-S2; 12-9-37
William Richardson Morgan* SW-NE-S2; 6-28-36
Thomas Horrell* SW-NW-S2; 3-19-38; SE-SE-Nfr-S3; 3-8-36
Henry Scudder* NE-SW & SW-SW-S2; 11-5-36
John Case, Pi SE-SW-S2; 11-5-36
Tolever Colbert E-SE-S2; 1-24-18
George Gregory* W-SE-S2; 10-27-36

DAVIESS COUNTY

Elias White* NE-NE-Nfr-S3; 12-19-42
William Horrall* SE-NE-Nfr-S3; 2-18-37; SW-NE-Nfr-S3; 1-9-36
Alexander Leslie NW-NE-Nfr-S3; 5-9-54. MLW 97171
Hiram Barber* E-W & W-W-Nfr-S3; 6-20-31
Abner Davis & Alfred Davis, Da NE-SE-Nfr-S3; 3-22-37
John Wesley Horrall* W-SE-Nfr-S3; 2-27-35; Nfr-S13; Nfr-S14; 12-
Harrison Wallace* Nfr-S4; 1-11-38   12-14
John Scudder* NEfr-NW-S5; 5-23-32
John Peck* E-NWfr-Nfr-S5; 9-8-35
David Lyle Colman* NW-NWfr-Nfr-S5; 9-1-35
Hezekiah Jackson* SW-NWfr-Nfr-S5; 9-1-35. Of Pi, NW-NE-Nfr-
    S6; 9-1-35
Jason Horrell* Lots 5,8-SWfr-Nfr-S5; 1-11-36
Aaron Arnold, Pi SEfr-Nfr-S6; 7-18-29
John Wise, Kn NE-NE-Nfr-S6; 4-20-30
William Glenn Horrall* SE-NE-Nfr-S6; 1-19-35
George Tefortilar* Lot 3-W-Nfr-S6; 1-25-36
James Jackson* Lot 2-W-Nfr-S6; 1-14-36
William Kinman, Jr., Pi Efr-S10; 3-7-36
Hugh McCain, Pi S-SEfr-Nfr-S11; 2-24-36
John Jones* Lot 1-E-E-Nfr-S12; 12-22-35
Green McCafferty* Lot 4-E-E-Nfr-S12; 8-31-35
William Jones, Jr.* NE-NW-Nfr-S12; 4-3-37
Abbott Levi Todd* SE-NW-Nfr & SW-NW-Nfr-S12; 3-10-37
Josiah W. Morgan* NW-NW-Nfr-S12; 3-6-37
Friend Spears S-Nfr-S12; 1-8-18

RELINQUISHMENTS

Jesse Colbert NE-S1; 12-11-17
Jonathan Morgan W-NW-S1; 11-10-17
Elijah Chapman SE-S1; 3-5-18; W-NE-S2; 5-16-18; Nfr-S4; 3-6-19
Friend Spears Efr-Nfr & NW-Nfr-S12; 1-8-18

T 2 N, R 5 W

William Houghten NE-S2; 9-19-18
James Summers* NE-NW-S2; 10-3-36
Patrick Connell, Mt NE-NE-S3; 10-13-40
John Stafford* NW-NE-S3; 9-9-36
Lewis Davis, Mt NE-NW-S3; 8-25-36
John Ewing, Kn W-NW-S3; 8-20-38
William George E-NE-S4; 10-1-16
William Burtch & William Jones Herberd, Kn NW-NW-S4; 2-16-35
Robert M. Davis NW-S5; 12-26-15
Robert Chester E-SW-S5; 10-20-19
James Coughlan, Jefferson Co., Ky. SE-SE-S5; 10-13-42
James Mullin* W-SE-S5; 10-2-39
Francis Riley* NE-NE-S6; 11-2-44
Daniel Dickerson* SE-NE & SW-NE-S6; 1-29-38
Henry Hill* NW-NE-S6; 1-11-44
John Johnson NW-S6; 12-2-16. Of *, SE-SW-S7; 11-14-32
Matthew Walton Kyle* E-SW-S6; 8-19-36; W-SW-S6; 8-5-36

John Graves* SE-SE-S6; 8-26-36; SW-SE-S6; 12-5-38
Owen Traynor* NW-SE-S6; 10-9-43
Samuel Reynels Beckett* NE-NE-S7; 6-30-37; SW-SE-S7; 1-4-39
William Beckett* SE-NE-S7; 1-4-39; NW-NE-S7; 1-8-42
John Beckett* SW-NE-S7; 9-25-37; NW-SE-S7; 4-4-36
Richard Peed NW-S7; 10-7-18
John Becket* NE-SW-S7; 4-4-36
George Brewer* NW-SW-S7; 2-9-36; SW-SW-S7; 11-29-33
Lawrence Noland, Hamilton Co., O. E-SE-S7; 2-27-40
John Hunter* NE-NE-S8; 11-24-38
Henry Fegan* SE-NE-S8; 1-11-41
James Mattingly* NW-NE-S8; 11-26-38
William Cahill, Mt SW-NE-S8; 12-2-39
Patrick Hart, Ws E-NW-S8; 9-2-40
Samuel Reynolds Beckett* W-NW-S8; 6-8-40   7-10-39
Patrick Madigan* NE-SW-S8; 7-10-39; NW-SW-S8; 11-4-43; NW-SE-S8;
Michael Connelly* SE-SW-S8; 12-25-37; SW-SW-S8; 3-27-38
John Hunter* NE-SE-S8; 6-4-44; W-SW-S9; 5-21-18
William H. Robinson* NW-NE-S9; 2-4-39
Henry Fegan* SW-NE & NW-S9; 4-1-40
Charles Norris* SE-SW-S9; 1-17-37
Michel Egan* NE-SE & SW-SE-S9; 9-5-43
James Somers* NW-NE-S10; 8-30-41
Patrick Tully, Hamilton Co., O. SW-NE-S10; 10-5-39
Joseph Totten* NE-SW-S10; 12-18-43
Peter Burrass* SW-SW-S10; 2-22-44
Martin Patterson SE-SE-S10; 12-25-37
John Cole, Mt SE-NE-S11; 12-19-50
Richard Summors* SW-NE-S11; 8-25-38
Martin Patterson NE-NW-S11; 6-28-52; NW-SW-S11; 7-17-48. MLW
John Summers* SE-NW-S11; 4-16-39   44777
Thomas Burriss* NW-NW-S11; 10-29-38
Felix Timothy* SE-SW-S11; 4-20-40
John Downey* SW-SW-S11; 7-14-41
John Riley, Mt E-SE-S11; 8-18-38
Samuel Lutte* NW-SE-S11; 7-14-41
Charles Summers* SW-SE-S11; 10-21-39
Samuel Fitzgerell NE-S14; 8-17-18
Thomas Conlin, Mt NW-S14; 8-24-39
Nicholas Kelly* SW-S14; 5-7-39
Henry Fegan* E-SE-S14; 4-1-40
Joseph Patterson* NE-NE-S15; 3-16-39
Thomas Somers* SE-NE-S15; 2-12-40
Rodolphus Somers* SW-NE-S15; 3-6-40
Joshua O. Arvin* SE-NW-S15; 7-13-44
Thomas Summers, Sr., Mt NE-SW-S15; 11-19-38; SE-SW-S15; 1-10-38
John Burris* W-SW-S15; 11-25-41
Samuel Swift* SE-SW-S15; 1-9-44
William Somers, Mt NW-SE-S15; 3-6-39
James Raney, Mt SW-SE-S15; 5-24-41
Joseph Stockton W-NE-S17; 4-2-19
John Darr* E-NW-S17; 9-6-37
Robert Noland, Hamilton Co., O. W-NW-S17; 2-6-40
John McBride* E-SE-S17; 4-3-40

Thomas Flinn* E-NE-S18; 2-27-40
Lawrence Noland, Hamilton Co., O. NW-NE-S18; 2-27-50 (40?)
Edward Noland, Hamilton Co., O. SW-NE-S18; 2-27-40
Samuel Reynolds Beckett* NW-NW-S18; 7-21-36
Thomas McDonald* W-SW-S18; 10-2-43
Patrick Lyons* W-SE-S18; 6-28-38
Enis McMullin, Jn E-NE & NW-NE-S19; W-NW-S20; 9-16-37
Henry Fegan* SW-NE, W-SW, & NW-SE-S19; 8-19-37
John Cahan, Hamilton Co., O. NE-NW-S19; 6-28-38
Rowland Beamon Sutton* SE-NW-S19; 12-9-37; NW-NW-S19; 8-30-37
Rowland Sutton* SW-NW-S19; 6-6-36
James Flanigan, Hamilton Co., O. NE-SW-S19; 3-18-40
Terry Reillay* SE-SW-S19; 11-15-43
John Castles, Jr E-SE-S19; NW-SW-S20; 9-16-37
Micheel Naylon* E-NE-S20; 11-13-39
Patrick Naylon* W-NE-S20; 11-13-39
Dennis Naylon* E-NW-S20; 11-13-39
Ann Williams, E. A. Williams, E. Williams, C.L. Williams, F.D.
     Williams, D. Williams, S. Williams, Thomas S.(L.?) Williams, &
     David Williams SE-SW & SW-SW-S20; 10-17-37
Peter McKanna* W-SE-S20; 3-11-39
John Burriss* NE-NE-S21; 11-25-39
Christopher Murray* SE-NE-S21; 11-17-41
James Grinnon, Hamilton Co., O. W-NE-S21; 3-4-40
Patrick Grinon, Hamilton Co., O. E-NW-S21; 3-4-40
Alexander McCune* W-NW-S21; 11-13-39
William Henry Weber* NE-SW-S21; 10-15-38
James Horen* SE-SW & SW-SW-S21; 2-21-40; E-NE-S22; 3-25-42
Bernard McHugh* NW-SW-S21; 3-5-45
George Courtney Hays* NE-SE & SE-SE-S21; SW-S22; 3-15-39
Michael Shea & James Shea, Hamilton Co., O. W-SE-S21; 3-10-40
John Downey* NE-NW-S22; 7-4-44
Jeremiah Lyons* W-NW-S22; 9-2-41
Valentine Bernerd Montgomery* SE-S22; 6-15-39
Peter North, Hamilton Co., O. E-NW-S23; 5-24-41
Hugh Parks* W-NW-S23; 11-7-40
John H. Kannaday* W-SW-S23; 6-21-39
Philip Berlitz* NE-S26; 6-24-39
James Gold* SE-NW-S26; 2-26-45
Jeremiah Prater* NE-SW & NW-SW-S26; 6-24-39
James Gilley* SW-SW-S26; SE-NE-S27; 10-9-40
John Chandler* SW-NE-S27; 10-30-44
Michael Shea, Hamilton Co., O. NE-NW-S27; 3-13-40
Michael White* NW-NW-S27; 2-6-39
James Shea* SW-NW-S27; 12-19-40
John Gold* SE-SW & SW-SW-S27; 6-4-40
William Gold* NE-SE-S27; 2-10-45
Thomas Downey, Wabash Co., Ill. SE-SE & SW-SE-S27; 12-15-38
John Welsh, Hamilton Co., O. NE-NE & NW-NE-S28; 3-10-40
John Kelly* SE-NE & SW-NE-S28; 11-16-41; NE-SE-S28; 3-18-42
David Lonergan, Hamilton Co., C. E-SW-S28; 2-19-40
Patrick Murphy* NW-SW-S28; 8-5-44; SW-SW-S30; 6-13-40
John Jones, Hamilton Co., O. W-SE-S28; 12-21-40
John Hughes & Edward Hughes* W-NE-S29; 3-11-39

Peter McKanna* E-NW-S29; 3-11-39
Daniel Linn* W-NW-S29; 3-11-39
Edward Beatty* NE-SW-S29; 8-22-38; SE-SW-S29; 8-17-38
William Whiteside* W-SW-S29; 10-15-38; NE-SE-S30; 10-18-39
James Conley, Hamilton Co., O. E-SE-S29; 2-19-40
Cornelius O'Brien, Hamilton Co., O. W-SE-S29; 2-19-40
Andrew McFadin, Jn E-NE-S30; 9-16-37
Overton Burress* SW-NE-S30; 4-2-39; SE-NW-S30; 9-22-38
Terry Reilley* NE-NW-S30; 11-15-43
Peter Soda, Fd W-NW-S30; 6-12-37
James Gilley* E-SW-S30; 10-5-38
Rice Burress* NW-SW-S30; 4-23-39
James McCord, Or E-NE-S31; 11-23-39
James McMahon, Or W-NE-S31; 11-23-39
John Barr* E-NW-S31; 1-3-38
Francis Wilson* W-NW-S31; 11-23-39
Calvin Porter, Jefferson Co., O. E-SW-S31; 3-30-38; E-SE-S31;
    3-15-39; W-SE-S31; 3-30-38
John Aikman* W-SW-S31; 1-9-39
Thomas Seals* SE-NE-S32; 11-11-39
Overton Cosby, Jr.* NE-NW-S32; 8-5-39
Morgan Johnson* SE-NW-S32; 8-14-40
Isaac Johnson* NW-NW-S32; 4-4-40
John Rodenburry* SW-NW-S32; 1-29-38
James Fitzsimons* E-SW-S32; 8-22-39
Terry Doneho* W-SW-S32; 8-22-39
Charles Allen* NE-SE-S32; 2-16-37
James Donohoe* SE-SE & SW-SE-S32; 4-21-41   6-4-40
Thomas Harmon* NW-SE-S32; 10-12-39; E-NW-S33; 8-20-40; SW-NW-S34;
William Demoss* NE-NE-S33; 7-13-40
Jacob Hedrick* SW-NE-S33; 6-2-40
Richard Archdeacon, Warren Co., O. E-SW-S33; 10-15-40
Nicholas Archdeacon, Warren Co., O. W-SW-S33; 10-15-40
George Washington Gilley* NE-NE-S34; 9-5-40
James Alford* SE-NE-S34; 2-10-45
James Gilly & Job Hammond W-NE-S34; 8-18-19
Franklin Alford* E-NW-S34; 12-30-39
James Barres, Boone Co., Ky. E-SW-S34; 6-2-40
James Alford SE-S34; 2-12-19
George W. Alford* SE-NE-S35; 5-27-39
Harrison Allen* SE-NW-S35; 5-30-43
James Gilley* NW-NW-S35; 10-9-40
Gilbert White* NE-SW-S35; 9-7-44
John Collins* SW-SW-S35; 5-30-43
Wayne Alford* SE-SE-S35; 1-23-50; SW-SE-S35; 6-15-44

RELINQUISHMENTS

Fred Shotts & James G. Reed NW-S4; 10-30-17
Robert Akester W-SW-S5; 10-20-19
Presley Day SW-S6; 10-22-18
William G. Hunt NE & SE-S11; 6-17-18
Joseph Stockston E-NE-S17; 4-2-19
James Gilly & Job Hammond E-NE-S34; 8-18-19

John C. Wenzel SE-S3; NW & SW-S11; 5-14-19
John M. Prentiss SW & SE-S4; 7-8-19
Ezekiel Benjamin NW-S3; 5-20-19
Peter Ammerman SW-S3; 11-16-19
William George W-NE-S4; 10-1-16
Robert Johnson W-SE-S5; 11-26-19
John Johnson NE-S6; 9-24-17
John Hunter NW-& E-SW-S9; 5-21-18
John Gold SW-S27; 4-19-19
Robert M. Davis NW-S5; 12-26-16; 7-4-29

T 1 N, R 5 W
RELINQUISHMENTS
(omitted from p. 10)

George R. Patton E-NE-S3; 2-22-20
Henry Foster E-SW-S10; 10-1-16
Isaac Hollingsworth W-SW-S14; 4-19-16
Benjamin Hawkins W-SE-S14; 4-19-16
Robert Gilley W-SW-S5; 8-18-19
Samuel Comer NE-S11; 5-27-17
Littleton Baker NE-S14; 5-30-18
Thomas Morehead & Robert Taylor, Jr. NW-Nfr & SW-Nfr-S18; 10-13-18
Thomas Abeall SE-S3; 8-25-19

T 2 N, R 6 W

Richard McCrackin* E-NE & N-NE-S1; 11-28-31; E-NW-S1; 2-3-37
William McCracken* SE-SW-S1; 2-3-37; W-SW-S1; 6-18-36
Presley Day SE-S1; 10-17-18
Solomon Weber* NE-NE-S2; 2-3-37; SE-NE-S2; 6-18-36
James Welch, Hamilton Co., O. NE-NW-S2; 9-7-37
Jesse Megehee* SE-NW-S2; 1-21-53
Jesse Harris* NW-NW-S2; 12-2-44
Patrick McManus, Hamilton Co., O. SW-NW-S2; 9-7-37
John McCracken* NE-SE-S2; 2-29-36; SE-SE-S2; 2-14-37
Alexander Stephenson NE-S3; 8-12-17
George Smith Farr, Vb NW-S3; 8-25-36
William E. Meads* SW-SW-S3; 5-11-40
Essick Hopkins SE-S3; 10-13-18
John Fulton NE-S4; 1-8-18
Robert Logan* NE-SE-S4; 2-21-45
James Carnahan W-SE-S4; 1-28-18
Samuel Aikman SW-S4; 1-28-18
John Cochren, Clark Co., O. W-NE-S5; 11-30-38
Thomas Elliott Meads* NE-NW-S5; 1-22-39
Robert Morehead* SE-NW-S5; 8-12-33
Bryan McCabe* E-SW-S5; 10-28-41
Robert Fryer Carnahan* NW-SW-S5; 9-12-36; W-NW-S5; 5-13-28
Adam Wise* SW-SW-S5; 8-28-39
Philip Sincon, Clark Co., O. E-SE-S5; 11-30-38
William Salmon* NW-SE-S5; 6-11-40

Henry Solomon* SW-SE-S5; 9-12-36
Caly Hawkins NE-S6; 10-26-18
Thomas Golden NW-S6; 9-9-18
Thomas Field, Philadelphia Co., Pa. E-SW & SE-SE-S6; 8-22-41
Watson Williams* NW-SW-S6; 6-2-37
John Logan Brattain* SW-SW-S6; 11-24-36
Wilson Carnahan* NE-SE-S6; 5-3-37
Samuel Murry* NW-SE-S6; 12-26-36
Robert A. Kester* SW-SE-S6; 5-30-37; NE-NE-S18; 12-15-35; W-NE-
    S18; 9-22-31; NW-SE-S18; 5-1-39. Akester.
John Johnson NE-S7; 10-24-18
Abraham Wise* NE-NW-S7; 6-5-37; W-NW-S7; 8-25-18
John Wise* SE-NW-S7; 6-3-36   9-1-38
John Arthur* NE-SW-S7; 11-21-32; SE-SW-S7; 9-12-36; SW-SE-S7;
Enoch Davis* NE-SE-S7; 5-11-36; NW-SE-S7; 12-5-36
Seth Reddick* SE-SE-S7; 1-21-39
James Arthur W-SW-S7; 5-12-18
Edward Horace Johnson* NE-NE-S8; 6-2-37; NW-NE-S8; 8-28-36
Morgan Wise SE-NE-S8; 4-1-40
James Peaches* SW-NE-S8; 2-3-40
Adem Wise* NE-NW-S8; 3-13-39; NW-NW-S8; 8-28-39
Bruce Wellman Fields* SE-NW-S8; 3-23-39
Willson Carnahan* SW-NW-S8; 1-29-39
John McAdow, Jr. SW-S8; 10-14-18
William Carter Hays* E-SE-S8; 2-21-38
William Henry Cross* SW-SE-S8; 6-29-42
David Logan* NE-NE-S9; 8-30-36
Thomes Greenwood* SE-NE-S9; 11-28-37; NE-SW-S9; 8-5-37
Robert McBay, P1 SE-NW-S9; 11-15-38
Morgan Wise* NW-NW-S9; 4-2-39
William Meeds* SE-SW-S9; 1-15-38; NE-NW-S10; 4-25-40. Meads
William Carter Hays* NW-SW-S9; 2-21-38
John Green* SW-SW-S9; 6-2-37
Robert Farr, Vb E-SE-S9; 8-25-36
William Farr, Vb W-SE-S9; 9-10-36
Samuel Stephenson E-NE-S10; 6-14-18
John Farr, Vb W-NE-S10; 8-25-36
James Henry* SE-NW-S10; 7-3-37
Eseck Hopkins* W-NW-S10; NW-S11; 10-13-21   11-21-37
Owen Reilly* NE-SW-S10; 5-1-39. Of Lycoming Co., Pa., SE-SW-S10;
Patrick Reilly, Lycoming Co., Pa. W-SW-S10; 11-21-37
Francis Bradley* SE-S10; 2-6-37; SW-SE-S11; 5-9-36
John Mollon* NE-S11; 7-14-37
James Tully, Jr NE-SW & W-SW-S11; 8-9-37
Jemes Galvin* SE-SW-S11; 9-9-37
Patrick Bradley* E-SE & NW-SE-S11; 10-10-35
Richard Peed NE-S12; 10-17-18
Daniel Harriss* NE-NW-S12; 10-17-42; W-NW-S12; 2-22-33
Joseph Warder Allison* SE-NW-S12; 10-17-42
Thomas Wilson SW-S12; NW-S13; 10-14-18
George Brewer* NE-SE-S12; 2-1-37
William Beckett* SE-SE-S12; NE-NE-S13; 5-18-36
Michael McGovran, Hamilton Co., O. NW-SE-S12; 8-2-38   2-9-29
John Walker* SW-SE-S12; 9-3-35; SE-NE-S13; 12-31-36; W-NE-S13;

Mark Brewar* E-SW & NW-SE-S13; 6-13-38
Arthur Hughes* W-SW-S13; 2-20-38
Anthony Sheridan, Jr E-SE & SW-SE-S13; 9-19-37
Edward Lamb, Hamilton Co., O. NE-NE & NW-NE-S14; 6-17-36
Wesley McClelland* SE-NE-S14; 5-25-36
Patrick Bradley* SW-NE-S14; 9-18-37
James Galvin* NE-NW-S14; 9-9-37
Peter Clarke* SE-NW-S14; 11-11-36; SW-NW-S14; 11-29-36
Bornheart Hiebler+ NW-NW-S14; 5-16-37; NE-NE-S15; 5-16-37. Heibler
James Downing* E-SW-S14; 2-3-38
Thomas Loughlin* W-SW-S14; 2-6-37
Duncan McCoy+ NE-SE-S14; 2-15-42. Of Jr, SE-SE & W-SE-S14; 2-6-38
Anthony Deser* SE-NE-S15; 8-16-36; SW-NE, SE-NW, W-NW-S15; 12-30-
    36; NE-SW-S15; 6-22-37
John McGuire* NW-NE-S15; 2-6-37
James Smith* NE-NW-S15; 8-17-36
William Conway Berry* SE-SW & SW-SE-S15; 5-11-36
Henderson Hill* NW-SW-S15; 8-30-36; SW-SW-S15; 12-5-36
Raphael Smith* NE-SE-S15; 8-17-36
William Moore, Hamilton Co., O. SE-SE & NW-SE-S15; 9-9-36
Timothy O'Neil* NE-NE-S17; 9-19-37; SW-NE-S17; 4-13-40
James Campbell* SE-NE-S17; 10-26-39
Zelek Hopkins* NW-NE-S17; 12-13-38
Ephraim Wilson NW-S17; 10-14-18
Hiram Martin Johnson* NE-SW-S17; 6-14-36; SE-SW-S17; 12-14-38
James Cosby* NW-SW-S17; 12-10-38
John Murphy* SW-SW-S17; 11-9-41
John Arthur* E-SE-S17; 5-11-37
Jesse D. Marmaduke* SE-NE-S18; 3-5-38
John Allen NW-S18; 4-25-18
Overton Cosby* NE-SW-S18; 8-5-34; W-SW-S18; 6-16-31
Jacob Cosby* SE-SW-S18; 11-7-36
Thomas Tibbs Young* SW-SE-S18; 12-11-44
John Thomas Coleman* SE-NE-S19; 8-28-44
Abner Cosby* NW-NE-S19; 12-22-38
Delilah Lashly* SW-NE-S19; 5-31-41
Stephen Johnson, Union Dist., S.C. E-NW & E-SW-S19; 10-27-36
Isaac Gregory, Union Dist., S.C. W-NW-S19; 10-27-36; W-SW-S19;
Green McCafferty* SE-SE-S19; 10-31-3 (illegible)   6-16-37
John Edwards* E-NE-S20; 5-18-38; W-NE-S20; 2-7-40; E-SE-S20;
    2-9-28; NW-SE-S20; 9-28-33; SW-SE-S20; 2-7-40
William Swann* NE-NW-S20; 12-30-35
Elias Allen* SE-NW-S20; 7-8-39; NE-SW-S20; 4-1-43
Hiram Martin Johnson* NW-NW-S20; 2-20-43
John Leander Murphy* SW-NW- & NW-SW-S20; 5-3-41
David Lyle Coleman* SE-SW-S20; 8-28-44
Robert Grigry* SW-SW-S20; 11-2-35
James French Smith* NE-NE & NW-NE-S21; 12-15-38
William Payne Smoot* SE-NE & SW-NE-S21; 4-5-36; NE-SE-S21; 1-1-38
John H. Shanklin NW-S21; 10-31-18
William Foster* NE-SW-S21; 6-13-39
John Lindsey Alexander* SE-SW-S21; 4-10-37
Elijah Griffith Robinson* NW-SW-S21; 9-21-38
Elijah Nash Robinson* SW-SW-S21; 6-4-41

Anderson Arms* SE-SE-S21; 8-17-36; NE-NE-S28; 3-6-37
William Jett* NW-SE-S21; 1-2-37
John Pennington* SW-SE-S21; 10-29-38
John McGuire* NE-NE-S22; 2-6-37
John Cassidy* SE-NE-S22; 1-19-38; SE-NW-S22; 1-18-38
Raphael Smith* W-NE-S22; 9-9-36
John Smith* NE-NW-S22; 10-13-37
Hugh Edwards, Kn SW-NW-S22; 8-19-36; NW-NW-S22; 8-23-36
Sylvester Mattingly* NE-SW-S22; 10-12-37
Philip Cramer, Columbiana Co., O. SE-SW & W-SE-S22; 10-26-36
Michael Martin, Jf W-SW-S22; 12-7-37
William Molloy, Hamilton Co., O. E-SE-S22; 9-9-36
William Beckett & John Beckett* E-NE-S23; 1-20-37
Samuel Aikman* W-NE-S23; 12-29-31
John Fox, Alleghany Co., Pa. NE-NW-S23; 9-21-40
Hugh Barr* SE-NW & NE-SE-S23; 1-25-37
Anthony Mulheron, Hamilton Co., O. W-NW-S23; 5-9-38
John Horen* E-SW-S23; 5-16-38
Robert Cruise, Hamilton Co., O. W-SW-S23; 6-28-38
Jesse Burress* SE-SE-S23; 3-17-37
Robert Barr* NW-SE-S23; 6-17-37
Michael Kattall, Jf SW-SE-S23; 8-9-37
Rowland Sutton* NE-NE-S24; 6-6-36
Rowland Beaman Sutton* SE-NE-S24; 12-31-36; SW-NE-S24; 9-13-36;
    SE-NW-S24; 1-24-37
James Calvin, Jf NW-NE-S24; 9-19-37
Mark Brewer* NE-NW-S24; 9-12-36; W-NW-S24; 1-26-37
Francis Riley, Fd SW-S24; 6-12-37
Matthew Deen, Jf E-SE & NW-SE-S24; 8-9-37
Thomas Owens, Fd E-NE-S25; 6-12-37
Philip Soda, Fd NW-NE, NE-NW, SE-NW-S25; 6-12-37
Thomas Owens & Peter Soda, Fd SW-NE-S25; 6-12-37
James Mattingly* NW-NW-S25; 9-23-36
Hugh Aikman* SW-NW-S25; 4-15-37
Patrick McDonald* NE-SW-S25; 6-22-40; NE-SE-S25; 3-21-40
Isaac Johnson* SE-SW-S25; 1-7-39; SW-SE-S25; 10-19-37
Thomas McCaffry, Hamilton Co., O. W-SW-S25; 10-14-39
Andrew Johnson* SE-SE-S25; 11-1-37; NW-SE-S25; 9-9-36
Hugh Aikman* NE-NE-S26; 8-30-37; SE-NE-S26; 4-15-37
Michael Kallett, Jf NW-NE-S26; 8-9-37
Peter Molloy* SW-NE & E-NW-S26; 11-15-37
Dennis Ochler, Columbiana Co., O. W-NW & NW-SW-S26; 10-26-36
Arthur McDonald, Tc E-SW-S26; 9-24-38; E-SE-S26; 10-5-39
James Gilley* NW-SE-S26; 10-31-37
John Barr* SW-SE-S26; 10-19-37
William Molloy, Hamilton Co., O. NE-NE & NW-NE-S27; 9-9-36;
    W-NW-S27; 12-1-37
Pierce Cavenaugh, Hamilton Co., O. SE-NE & SW-NE-S27; 8-29-38
Michael O'Connor* NE-NW-S27; 8-7-40; SE-NW-S27; 9-8-38
Michael Condron, Alleghany Co., Pa. E-SW & W-SE-S27; 9-24-38
Campbell Vance* W-SW-S27; 6-28-37
Michael Cain, Hamilton Co., O. NE-SE-S27; 12-3-60
James Armes* SE-NE & NW-NE-S28; 6-19-40
Patrick Duffy* E-NW-S28; 2-12-39

James Randal Delk* NW-NW-S28; 11-7-32
Michael Molloy* SW-NW-S28; 12-20-44; NW-SW-S28; 10-29-38
Campbell Vance* E-SW & W-SE-S28; 10-8-38; E-SE-S28; 6-28-37;
    SW-NW-S31; 10-11-37
George Major* SW-SW-S28; 10-29-38
John Williamson Clark* NE-NE-S29; 7-24-44
Thomas Abeall NW-S29; E-NE-S30; 8-25-19
Stephen Johnson* W-SW-S29; 9-18-38; W-NE-S30; 6-16-37. Of Union
    Dist., S.C., E-NW-S30; 10-26-36; NE-SE-S30; 6-16-37
James Hughes, Philadelphia Co., Pa. E-SE-S29; 12-3-38
Salem Sinks* SW-SE-S29; 5-17-31
George Gregory* W-NW-S30; 10-27-36
Joseph Hollingsworth* NE-NE-S31; 4-24-37
Isaac Gregory, Union Dist., S.C. NW-NE-S31; 10-8-38   6-17-37
Parmenas Jones* SW-NE-S31; 10-3-36; SE-NW-S31; 11-10-38; NW-SE-S31;
Josiah Evrett* NE-NW-S31; 8-16-36
Charles Cosby* NW-NW-S31; 8-4-36
Jeremiah Raymond SW-S31; 2-28-22
Jonathan Gregory, Union Dist., S.C. E-SE & SW-SE-S31; 10-8-38
Mason Palmer* NE-NE-S32; 1-12-26
John Campbell Steen* SE-NE-S32; 6-28-37; SW-NE & SE-NW-S32; 11-17-
    38; NE-SW, E-SE, NW-SE-S32; 6-28-37
William Banks* NE-NW-S32; 8-3-38   5-5-38
Jonathan Gregory, Union Dist., S.C. W-NW-S32; 6-16-37; NW-SW-S32;
James Lett* SE-SW & SW-SW-S32; 5-22-37
William Baldwin* SW-SE-S32; 5-19-37
Joshua Wilder NE-S33; 3-3-19
John Rowan* NE-NW-S33; 11-1-43
Reazon Smith Chapman* SE-NW-S33; 5-27-48; SW-NW-S33; 12-5-36
Mason Palmer* NW-NW-S33; 1-12-26
James McCarty* SW-SW-S33; 5-10-37
Celestine R. L. De la Hailandiere, Kn NE-NE-S34; 8-20-40
Philip Keal* SE-NE-S34; 6-6-36
Michael Stafford* W-NE-S34; 12-6-38; NW-SE-S34; 12-6-38. Of Jf,
    SE-SW-S34; 6-18-38
Michael Condron, Alleghany Co., Pa. NW-S34; 9-24-38
John Batthus, Kn NE-SW-S34; 5-18-37; W-SW-S34; 3-7-37
Isaac Johnston* SE-SE-S34; 1-9-39
Jacob Wycokk & George Kauffman* SW-SE-S34; 1-11-39
Patrick Delleany, Hamilton Co., O. E-NE-S35; 9-5-39
Patrick Made, Hamilton Co., O. W-NE-S35; 9-5-39
Matthew Leavy, Hamilton Co., O. E-NW-S35; 11-13-39
Samuel Potts* SW-NW-S35; 10-18-37
Coleman Carlisle Jones* NW-SW-S35; 1-15-39
Thomas Jones* SW-SW-S35; 9-22-37
John Toy, Alleghany Co., Pa. E-NE-S36; 9-21-40
Thomas McLaughlan* NW-NE & NE-NW-S36; 6-10-40. Says Daviess Co.,
    Pa., but the Pa. is surely an error from the line above.
Timothy Donovan, Hamilton Co., O. W-NW-S36; 9-4-39
Thomas Deering* SE-SW-S36; 10-16-39
Philip Garigan* NE-SE-S36; 1-15-42
John Willemen* SE-SE-S36; 3-25-37
Morgan Johnson* SW-SE-S36; 8-14-40

DAVIESS COUNTY

RELINQUISHMENTS

Catherine Hawkins & Thomas Goulden SE-S6; 3-4-19
Ephraim Wilson SE-S11; 10-14-18
Thomas Wilson NW-S12; 10-14-18; SE-S12; 10-17-18; NE-S14; 10-14-18
John Allen NE-S17; 10-14-18
John H. Shanklin E-NE-S20; NE-S21; 10-31-18
John Johnson SW-S21; NW-S28; 10-31-18
James F. Allen SW-S28; NE-S29; 10-31-18
William Stephenson SE-S7; 9-4-18
John Barkshire E-SE-S10; 9-19-19
Nicholas Kile NE-S11; 10-14-18
Joseph Edwards SE-S20; 12-26-16
Trice Stafford SE-S25; 10-21-18
Wesley Wallis W-SW-S33; 2-3-18
Joseph Culbertson NE-S1; 12-31-16
James Carnahan E-SE-S4; 1-28-18
Samuel Finney SW-S17; 9-29-18
James Arthur SW-S18; 4-25-18; SW-S7; 5-12-18
Thomas S. Brothers NE-S22; 12-15-19; W-NE & E-NW-S23; 12-15-19
Peter Peterson SE-S22; 11-23-19
Peter Ham NW-S3; 12-11-17
Samuel Stephenson W-NE-S10; 6-4-18
Robert Agland SW-S6; 12-11-19
John Kennedy SE-S17; 10-19-18; 3-3-30
Amos Cervis NE-S18; 10-10-18; 7-4-29
Thomas Abeall E-NE-S30; 8-25-19; 7-4-29

T 2 N, R 7 W

William Perry* E-NE-S1; 12-20-36
James G. Reed & Charles R. Brown W-NE-S1; 6-15-18
William Batchelor NW-S1; 1-23-18
Daniel Ward* E-SW-S1; 3-22-36
Thomas B. Donaldson W-SW-S1; 8-22-18
James Allen SE-S1; 4-1-18
John Wallis E-NE-S2; 4-10-18
John Smith* W-NE-S2; 6-15-29
Joseph Hobbs NW-S2; 12-7-16
William Sample SW-S2; 7-10-17
John Stringer E-SE-S2; 4-14-18
Josiah Wallis W-SE-S2; 2-23-18
Jeremiah Lucas NE-S3; 9-18-13
Ebenezer Jones NW-S3; 8-5-11
Friend Spears SW-S3; 12-13-08
Thomas Golden SE-S3; 10-7-16
Thomas Aikman NE-S4; 5-5-10
Hezekiah Ragsdale NW-S4; 4-29-11
Richard Steen SW-S4; 5-20-08
Daniel Comer SE-S4; 5-16-08
Thomas Jones NE-S5; 6-12-07
Joseph Culbertson NW-S5; 6-2-08
Abraham Rodarmel SW-S5; 6-10-07
John McDonald SE-S5; 6-18-07; NE & NW-S8; 5-30-07

Eli Hawkins Efr-S6; 5-20-08
John Tranter Efr-S7; 11-15-14
George W. Stilwell, Mm Wfr-S7; 2-3-70
Simon Nicholson SW-S8; 8-29-08
Daniel Gregory SE-S8; 11-25-09
John Wallace NE-S9; 4-28-09
William Bellew NW-S9; 4-28-09
William Horral SW-S9; 10-13-10. Or *, E-NE-S11; 7-20-31
Thomas Horral SE-S9; 10-13-10
William Chapman NE & SE-S10; 10-7-16; SW-S11; 8-23-17
Vance Jones NW-S10; 12-11-11
John Aikman SW-S10; 12-14-11
John Graham* NW-NE-S11; 2-19-36; SW-NE-S11; 11-23-33
Orms Thomas NW-S11; 11-10-07
Leonard Dickerson Stringer* NE-SE-S11; 2-4-37; NW-SE-S11; 1-5-36;
   NW-NW-S13; 6-13-49; E-NE-S14; 12-6-37; NW-NE-S14; 1-13-38
Benjamin Fitzgerald* SE-SE & SW-SE-S11; 5-17-38
Abram Wise* NE-NE-S12; 9-27-36
Abraham Wise* SE-NE-S12; 12-5-36
John Shanks, Fayette Co., Pa. NW-NE, NE-NW, W-SW-S12; 12-29-38
Esek Hopkins Stringer* SW-NE-S12; 2-20-39; NE-SW-S12; 11-14-44;
   SE-SW-S12; 6-16-49
Thomas Brown Donaldson* SE-NW-S12; 1-7-37
James Allen W-NW-S12; 4-25-18
Ephraim Wilson SE-S12; 8-25-18
Michael Rupert, Kn NE-NE-S13; 7-9-33
Overton Cosby* SE-NE-S13; 1-10-39
Charles Cosby W-NE-S13; 3-11-37
Michael Simmons E-NW-S13; 8-28-18
Henry Smith* SW-NW-S13; 2-20-39
Elijah Johnson SE-S13; 8-28-18
Elijah Summers E-SW-S13; 8-28-18
Jacob Dillon Crabs* NW-SW-S13; 9-23-33
Milton Crabs* SW-SW-S13; 5-5-37
David Hogshead* SW-NE-S14; 12-28-37
Daniel Ward & James Williams* NE-NW-S14; 3-29-50
Overton Cosby, Jr.* SE-NW-S14; 7-27-40
Benjamin Fitzgerald* W-NW-S14; 7-23-38
John Anderson Scudder E-SW-S14; 10-30-18. Or *, SW-SW-S14; 11-15-
Elijah Chapman SE-S14; 6-23-17; NW-S15; 12-3-14   33
Jason Horrell* NE-NE-S15; 10-3-35; SW-NE-S15; 12-29-38
John Horrall* SE-NE-S15; 6-27-37
Moses Allen* NW-NE-S15; 10-1-35
Joseph Warner E-SW-S15; 3-25-18
Fenwick Scudder* NW-SW-S15; 10-17-36
Thomas Turman Ragsdale* SW-SW-S15; 10-9-40
Edward McKinley SE-S15; 8-11-18
William Wallis NE-S17; 2-23-10
James C. Veale NW-S17; 10-31-07; SW-S17; 6-24-07; SE-S17; 12-11-15
Amos Rogers Efr-S18; 12-28-08
James Arrell Efr-S19; 12-1-12
John Edwards NE-S20; 12-13-15
Henry Edwards NW-S20; 12-23-08
John Smith SW-S20; 7-6-08

James Lott SE-S20; 9-7-09; W-SW-S21; 10-19-32
Samuel Hughey, Jr. NE-S21; 4-24-16
Parmenas Palmer NW-S21; 12-21-15
John Peck* NE-SW-S21; 5-26-35
John D. Tate SE-SW & SW-SE-S21; 3-5-49; MLW 24491
Rennesson Tisdale* NE-SE-S21; 2-15-36
William Thomas Veale* SE-SE-S21; 2-27-49
John Pry* NW-SE-S21; 5-11-37
Moses Morgan NE-S22; 9-18-17
John Rodarmel* NE-NW-S22; 7-27-35; SW-SW-S22; 2-15-36
Jesse Crabs* SE-NW-S22; 7-14-32; W-NW-S22; 2-13-32
James Carnahan E-SW-S22; 11-14-18
John Scudder* NW-SW-S22; 1-9-39
George Houts E-SE-S22; 11-5-17. Of *, NW-SE-S22; 8-5-34
Aden Barber* SW-SE-S22; 3-21-37
John Johnson* NE-NE-S23; 8-5-34
John Linsey Johnson* SE-NE-S23; 9-20-36
Elijah Chapman* NW-NE-S23; 7-3-33
James Chapman* SW-NE-S23; 1-27-37
John Anderson Scudder E-NW-S23; 10-30-18. Of *, NW-NW-S23; 11-15-
Thomas Horrall* SW-NW-S23; 4-24-37   33
Henry Alpius Edwards* NE-SE-S23; 8-23-36
John Frederick Franklin* SE-SE-S23; 6-26-44
William Traylor W-SE-S23; 2-16-19
U. Frederick Shenick SW-S23; 3-11-18
Coleman Carlisle Wallace* NE-NE-S24; 12-1-35
Jonathan Gregory, Union Dist., S.C. SE-NE-S24; 10-27-36
David Yancey Ellis* W-NE-S24; 12-11-44
Elijah Johnson NW-S24; 8-28-18
Isaac Gregory, Union Dist., S.C. E-SW-S24; E-NE-S25; 6-16-37;
    E-SE-S24; W-NE-S25; 10-27-36
Thompson Wallace* NW-SW-S24; 5-11-43
John Frederick Franklin* SW-SW-S24; 6-26-44
John Boyd* SW-SE-S24; 3-29-37
John Wesley Wallace* NE-NW-S25; 3-5-37
John Wilson Crooks* W-NW-S25; 3-5-37
Samuel White* SE-SW-S25; 1-26-37
Henry Alpheus Edwards* NW-SW-S25; 3-15-37
William Traylor NE-S26; 3-7-15
Trueman Shell NW-S26; 3-9-18
Laban Johnson* NE-SW-S26; 6-6-39
Thomas Johnson* SE-SW-S26; 10-22-39; NW-SW-S26; 2-18-37
William Boardman SE-S26; 11-26-17
George Houts* E-NE-S27; 3-9-39
Abner Blackwell Alexander* NW-NE-S27; 3-24-46
Ashbury Alexander* SW-NE-S27; 4-10-37
Arm Jackson* SE-NW-S27; 1-15-51
Haley Tisdale* E-SW-S27; 8-23-31
John Edwards W-SW-S27; 5-7-16
Lloid SE-S27; 11-4-18. May be first name or surname.
William Hardin* SE-NE-S28; 9-28-37
John D. Tate W-NE-S28; 3-5-49. MLW 24491
James Gray Reed, Ck E-NW & SW-NW-S28; 11-29-36
Thomas Pry* NW-NW-S28; 10-12-35

William Pry* NE-SW-S28; 11-30-36
Clement Evans* W-SW-S28; 2-11-37
Elijah Chapman E-SE-S28; 3-12-19
Haley Tisdale, Sr.* SW-SE-S28; 10-12-37
Robert Hays NE-S29; 2-11-11
William Smith NW-S29; 9-22-08
Christopher Coleman & Samuel Conner SW-S29; 8-5-13
Alexander Hays SE-S29; 12-9-15
Jonathan Morgan & Abraham Tevenbaugh Efr-S30; 2-25-15
William Sullivan, George W. Pratt, & George M. Thacher NE, SE,
    SE-SW, W-SW-S31; 2-25-37; W-NW, E-SW, NE-SE, NW-SE-S32; 2-25-37
Booker Boman, Spartanburgh Dist., S.C. Lot 1-NWfr-S31; 8-9-36
Christopher Coleman* Lot 2-NWfr-S31; 1-5-36
Thomas Beard & John B. Coleman* NE-SW-S31; 1-18-36
George W. Stibbins, Kn Wfr-NW(W of R)-S31; 2-9-70
William Veale NE-S32; 5-23-17
Christian Dedrick E-NW-S32; 1-9-18
James G. Read, Ck W-SW-S32; 6-20-36
John Scudder* SE-SE-S32; 12-29-35; SW-SE-S32; 5-5-36
John Cannon* NE-NW- & NE-SW-S33; 4-1-36
Haley Tisdale, Sr.* SE-NW-S33; 10-12-37
John Case, Pk SE-SW-S33; 11-11-36; NW-SW-S33; 3-29-37
William Pry* SW-SW-S33; 1-1-36
Haley Townsend Tisdale* E-SE-S33; 5-8-37
James Buckner, Db W-SE-S33; 3-24-37
James Batchelor* NE-NE-S34; 5-18-37
James Steveson NE-NW & NW-NW-S34; 5-5-52. MLW 19052
William Martin Tisdale* SE-NW-S34; 7-12-36
Ellen F. Crabs* SW-NW-S34; 2-28-54
Ashbury Alexander* SE-SW-S34; 4-10-37
James Willison Stevenson* NE-SE-S34; 1-31-37
George Houts* SW-SE-S34; 8-5-34
James Boardman NE-S35; 11-26-17
James Aikman NW-S35; 2-7-17
William Chapman E-SW-S35; 8-23-17; SE-S35; 1-31-17
Stephen Johnson* NE-NE-S36; 9-18-38; SW-NE-S36; 6-16-37
Thomas Baldwin* SE-NE-S36; 4-25-36
Jonathan Bartholomew Johnson* NW-NE-S36; 9-18-38
Samuel White, Gi NE-NW-S36; 5-30-36; E-SE-S36; 3-6-37
Hardin Paine Wheeler+ SE-NW & W-SW-S36; 3-24-37; SW-NW-S36; 3-26-
Elijah Banks* NW-NW-S36; 1-6-37   37
John Wallis* NE-SW-S36; 1-26-37
William Jones, Sr.* SE-SW-S36; 4-3-37
Allen Barber* W-SE-S36; 10-6-37

RELINQUISHMENTS

James G. Reed & Charles R. Brown E-NE-S1; 6-15-18
Thomas B. Donaldson E-SW-S1; 8-22-18
John Wallis W-NE-S2; 4-10-18
John Hawkins E-NE & W-NE-S11; 2-18-18
John Wheatley NE-S12; 8-28-18
James Allen E-NW-S12; 4-25-18
Michael Summers W-NW-S13; 8-28-18

Elijah Summers W-SW-S13; 8-28-18
John A. Scudder W-SW-S14; 10-30-18
Joseph Warner W-SW-S15; 3-25-18
James Carnahan W-SW-S22; 11-14-18
George Houts W-SE-S22; 11-5-17
Elijah Chapman E-NE-S23; 4-29-19; W-SE-S28; 3-12-19
Thomas Horrell W-NW-S23; 2-19-18
John Edwards E-SW-S27; 5-7-18
John Pry NW-S28; 11-19-18
Christian Deadrick W-NW-S32; 1-9-18
William Jones E-NW-S33; 4-10-18
Thomas Golden SE-S34; 11-2-14
William Chapman W-SW-S35; 8-23-17; E-SW & W-SW-S36; 2-3-18
Amos Garvis NW-S36; 3-31-18
Samuel Fitzgerrell SE-S36; 9-2-18
John Stringer E-SE-S2; 4-14-18; 7-4-29
William Chapman SW-S11; 8-23-17; 7-4-29
Polly Glasgow NE-S13; 4-25-18; 7-4-29
James Brawdes NW-S22; 5-16-18; 7-4-29
Elijah Chapman W-NE-S23; 2-18-19; 7-4-29

T 2 N, R 8 W

Andrew Lillie* Lot 1-SEfr-S1; 2-29-36. Of Kn, Nfr-S12; 10-24-35
Franis Cassidy* Lot 2-SEfr-S1; 7-26-38
Amos Rogers Efr-S13; 1-28-08
Clayton Rogers Efr-S24; 9-7-09
Jonathan Morgan & Abraham Tevenbaugh Efr-S25; 2-25-15

T 3 N, R 5 W

James Bradley* NE-NE-S2; 3-9-43
Presley Nevel Prence* SE-NE-S2; 12-20-37
William Berry, Mt W-NE-S2; 11-17-24
George Padgett, Ve NE-NW-S2; 6-18-36
Benedict Padget* SE-NW-S2; 3-25-39
Ignatius Spalding* W-NW-S2; 8-30-38. Of Mt, E-NE-S3; 9-30-22.
    W-NE-S3; 11-13-38
Bernard Norris* NE-SW-S2; 1-17-37
John Dennis Norris* SE-SW & SW-SW-S2; 2-27-38
Isaac Burgen E-SE-S2; 6-6-18
John F. Henry & Thomas M. McClung W-SE-S2; 9-23-18
Harvy Sharum* NE-SW-S3; 8-3-48
Michael Cleary, Mt SE-SW-S3; 2-9-50
Thomas Melton* W-SE-S3; 10-14-24
William Paget* NE-NE-S4; 1-30-37
Edward Hopkins* NW-NW-S4; 2-18-45
Michael Cunningham* SW-S4; 9-8-40; NW-SE-S4; 9-9-47
Luke Reiley, Hamilton Co., O. SW-SE-S4; 6-13-40
Hiram Allen, Lw E-NE-S5; 12-9-36
Raphael Ash* NW-NE & NE-NW-S5; 11-16-38
Westley Satterfield* NW-NW-S5; 10-25-44

Solomon Satterfield* NE-NE-S6; NE-NE-S7; 3-12-40; W-NE-S7; 12-21-
Joseph Wilson* SE-NE-S6; 10-16-39   33
Harvey Harmon Jones* NW-NE-S6; 9-4-43
Michael Wyne* E-NW & NW-NW-S6; 12-6-42
John Tahan* NE-SW & NW-SW-S6; 12-4-37
Michael Tahan* SE-SW-S6; 6-10-38; W-SE-S6; 6-19-38
Samuel Satterfield* E-SE-S6; 11-3-37
John Perkins* NE-NW-S7; 12-21-33; SE-NW-S7; 8-10-36; W-NW-S7;
John Lennon, Washington Co., Md. E-SW-S7; 5-9-38   11-13-38
Patrick Lennon* NW-SW-S7; 11-13-38
Alexander McCall* SW-SW-S7; 4-10-37
Michael Wiles SE-S7; 9-3-17
James Clark* E-NE-S8; 11-20-39
John Hughes, Jefferson Co., Ky. W-NE & E-NW-S8; 6-28-37; SW-NW &
    NW-SE-S8; 10-13-37; W-SW-S9; 1-2-39
James Riel, Baltimore Co., Md. E-SW & SE-SE-S8; 4-23-38
Patrick Reilley, Lycoming Co., Pa. W-SW-S8; 10-26-37
Patrick Brady* NE-SE-S8; 12-8-38
Michael Royal, Vb SW-SE-S8; 4-23-38
Michael Reilly, Jr NE-S9; 9-11-37
Michael Mathews, Jr E-NW-S9; 9-11-37
John James O'Brine, Mt W-NW-S9; 10-2-43
George McAtee* NE-SE-S9; 3-18-44   12-16-28
Daniel McAtee* SE-SE-S9; 7-21-37; E-SW-S10; 6-2-37; W-SW-S10;
Simon Gabriel Brute, Kn E-NE-S10; 7-20-37; W-NE-S10; 10-12-37
Calistus Melton* NE-NW-S10; 7-1-40
Michael Grannan* SE-NW-S10; 6-26-40
Enoch Cox SE-S10; 5-17-19
William C. Love, Mt NE-NE-S11; 9-14-39
Henry Walker, Mt SE-NE-S11; 3-1-43
Bernard Norris* NE-NW-S11; 12-8-37
Richard Norris* W-NW-S11; 8-24-30
Thomas Treakle SW-S11; 5-17-19
Levin Bramble* NE-SE-S11; 10-20-37
Charles Medley Strange, Mt NW-SE-S11; 10-26-38
John Fitzgerald, Mt NE-NE-S14; 6-16-40
John Dennis Norris* E-NW & SW-NW-S14; 1-11-40
Robert Riney* NW-NW-S14; 2-28-37
James Ambrose Sideell* NE-SW-S14; 2-28-45
William Walker* SE-SW-S14; 5-27-39
Silas Gootee* NW-SW-S14; 9-6-36
John Walker* SW-SW-S14; 2-28-37
Eneas Clutter NE-S15; 5-17-19
Henry Mattingly* NE-NW-S15; 9-7-36; SE-NW-S15; 12-14-38
William Bowling* W-NW-S15; 3-18-39
Joseph Elliott Salding, Sr.* NW-SW-S15; 5-29-44
James Dant* SW-SW-S15; 12-9-37
James S. Cissell* NE-SE-S15; 12-14-38
Robert Raney* SE-SE-S15; 4-1-39
Patrick Hopkins, Mt NW-SE-S15; 10-2-43
Michael Royl, Vb NE-NE-S17; 4-23-38
James Riel, Baltimore Co., Md. NW-NW-S17; 4-23-38
John Logan SW-S17; 7-12-19
James McCall NE-S18; 3-26-19

Elisha Perkins* NE-NW-S18; 3-18-37
Matthew McInnorny* SE-NW & SW-NW-S18; 4-22-39
Patrick Lennon* NW-NW-S18; 4-20-39
Zachariah Walker* SE-SW-S18; 7-11-39
John Sharum* SW-SW-S18; 8-2-42
David Hefren, Pi NE-SE-S18; 6-28-39
Ignatius Gough* SE-SE-S18; 2-28-37
Lawrence Hefren* W-SE-S18; 6-3-39
Michael Martin* NE-NE-S19; 10-12-37; NW-NW-S20; 10-12-37
Catherine McNally* SE-NE & NE-SE-S19; 10-26-37
James Kennedy* SW-NE-S19; 6-17-39; SE-SE-S19; 9-27-39
Cornelius Ketty* E-NW-S19; 6-4-27
Thomas Meehan, Pi W-NW-S19; 6-20-39
Patrick Brady* NE-SW-S19; 6-26-37
Nicholas Wathen* SE-SW & W-SW-S19; 12-2-36
James McCracken* NW-SE & SW-SE-S19; 2-1-43
John Pluck, Pi E-NE-S20; 4-3-39
Robert Bratton W-NE-S20; 3-9-19
James Kidwell* E-NW-S20; 7-15-22
William McNally* SW-NW & NW-SW-S20; 3-31-37
Dennis Keffe, Mi E-SW-S20; 6-16-37; W-NE & E-NW-S29; 6-16-37
Andrew McCracken* SW-SW-S20; 2-1-43
Thomas Gilleace, Jefferson Co., Ky. SE-S20; 6-13-37; NW-SW-S21;
John Clare* NE-NE-S21; 6-16-43   10-2-43
William Buchanan Gibson* E-NW-S21; 9-15-27; NW-NW-S21; 7-11-37
James Donoghue, Or SW-SW-S21; 10-13-37
Thomas Gardiner, Washington Co., Ky. NW-S22; 3-29-22
Thomas Shircliff* NE-SW-S22; 2-11-34; NW-NE-S26; 2-16-37; NE-NW-
Robert Shircliff* SE-SW-S22; 9-5-43   S26; 9-10-47
Joseph Carrico* NW-SW-S22; 8-28-38; W-SE-S22; 7-7-43
Isaac Burgin NE-S23; 6-1-15
Joseph Elzear Spaulding SW-S23; 3-13-50. MLW 46767
Hugh Freel* NE-SE & NW-SE-S23; 10-12-49
Mathew Clark, Mt SE-SE-S23; 12-14-48
John Gates, Mt NE-NE-S26; 4-1-39
Philip Hager* SE-NE-S26; 6-17-37
John T. Raney, Mt SW-NE-S26; 2-12-40
Thomas Williams, Mt SE-NW-S26; 11-23-49; NW-SE-S26; 8-14-49
Matthew Raney* NW-NW-S26; 3-18-54
Benjamin Summers, Mt NE-SE-S26; 2-21-37; SE-SE-S26; 11-22-49
Clement Raney, Mt NE-NE-S27; 9-11-37
Joseph Carrico, Mt NE-NW-S27; 1-27-51
Charles Martin, Mt SE-NW-S27; 11-19-50
John Christopher Montgomery* SW-NW-S27; NE-SE-S28; 3-30-39
Philip Hager* NW-SE-S27; 9-6-47
Patrick Farrell* E-SW-S28; 9-29-42
James Donoghue, Or NE-NE-S29; 10-13-37
Augustin Mattingly* W-NW-S29; 6-7-37; W-SE-S29; 6-26-37
Henry J. Cooper SW-S29; 10-28-18
Peter Burruss E-SE-S29; 12-21-18
Peter Spaulding NE-S30; 10-28-18
Patrick Brady* NE-NW-S30; 6-26-37; NW-NW-S30; 2-12-39
Andrew McCracken* NE-SW-S30; 2-1-43
James Studeville Morgan* SE-SW-S30; 1-9-37

James Hughes, Philadelphia Co., Pa. NE-SE & NW-SE-S30; 12-3-38
John Wesley Kyle* SE-SE & SW-SE-S30; 10-12-37
Nathan Harris* NE-NE-S31; 1-11-37; W-NE-S31; 3-14-32
Cornelius Berkshire, Mt SE-NE-S31; 12-18-38
Jesse Morgan NW-S31; 10-9-17
William Peterson SW-S31; 10-21-16
James Barr SW-S31; 3-18-16
Matthew Walton Kyle' NE-NE-S32; 9-6-37; NW-NE-S32; 8-30-37;
    W-NW-S33; 9-3-36
Alva Clark* SW-NE-S32; 9-28-39
Charles Donahew Morgan* NE-NW-S32; 8-25-37
William Coleman Elliott, Kn SE-NW-S32; 10-9-37; W-NW-S32; 9-29-37
Alexander Bruce SW-S32; 11-1-17
Morgan Day SE-S32; 8-27-18
Thomas Ruble Foyles* SE-NE-S33; 10-10-42
Frederick Shotes & James G. Reed W-SW-S33; 11-3-17
James Coughlan, Jefferson Co., Ky. E-SE-S33; 9-3-42
John Wise, Samuel Wise, William Jacob Wise, & Thomas J. Brooks
    NE-S34; 12-17-38
Philip Davis, Mt NE-SW-S34; 12-25-38; SW-SW-S35; 3-24-37
Lewis Davis, Mt SE-SW-S34; 8-25-36
George Frain, Mt W-SW-S34; 3-19-36
Timothy Hurley, Mt SE-SE-S34; 10-13-40
Elisha Davis* SW-SE-S34; 9-8-40
Ambrose Somers* SE-NE-S35; 1-8-39; SW-NE-S35; 9-8-37
Benjamin Davis, Mt E-SW-S35; 9-23-36
Thomas Somers* E-SE-S35; 8-13-31
Cornelius Ridge W-SE-S35; 5-5-18

RELINQUISHMENTS

John F. Henry & Thomas M. McClung NE, NW, SW-S2; 9-23-18
John Wingate SW-S7; 11-4-18
John Perkins NW-S7; 11-5-18
Peter Burruss NE-S29; 12-21-18; W-SE-S29; 12-21-18; 7-4-29
Peter Spalding NW-S29; 10-28-18
Cornelius Ridge W-NW-S36; 5-5-18; E-SE-S35; 5-5-18
Elisha Perkins NW-S18; 11-5-18
Stephen Donaldson & John Donaldson SE-S20; 7-4-19
Jesse Morgan E-SW-S30; 8-27-18
Christopher Stafford SE-S30; 8-11-19
Charles D. Morgan NW-S32; 9-13-19
Frederick Shotts & James G. Reed E-SW-S33; 11-3-17
James Bratton NW-S15; 4-19-19
Samuel Harris NE-S31; 11-4-17; 7-4-29

T 3 N, R 6 W

Roseberry Perkins* NE-NE-S1; 5-19-43. Asbury? --- see below
Martin Gottlieb Flankler* NE-NW-S1; 5-4-43
Francis Knable* NW-NW-S1; SW-NW-S2; 12-28-38
William Parsons* SW-NW-S1; 9-8-47
John Asbery Wilson* NE-SW-S1; 7-20-43; NW-SE-S1; 12-18-44

Alexander McCall* NE-SE-S1; 10-25-44
Asberry Perkins* E-NE-S2; 8-15-39; W-SE-S2; 1-11-51. Roseberry?
Moses Bennington* SE-NW-S2; 1-24-51; NW-NE & NE-NW-S4; 1-26-37
Aaron A. Freeland NE-SW-S2; 1-28-54; SE-SW-S2; 6-15-53. MLW 58949
Matthias Shole* W-SW-S2; 7-18-39
Michael McCall* NE-SE-S2; 3-20-51; SE-SE-S2; 2-13-49
Elijah Edds* NE-NE-S4; 12-22-38
Joseph Doherty* NW-NW-S4; 4-15-39
James McKnight* SW-SE-S4; 9-13-47
John Allen* SW-NW-S5; 7-23-39
Daniel Sparks* SE-SW-S5; 2-26-33; SW-SW-S5; 3-6-37
William Allen* SW-SE-S5; 12-20-44
George Doddick* SE-SW-S6; 8-15-36. Roddick? see below
Cephas McDonald* SW-SW-S6; 6-17-36
James McDonald* SW-SE-S6; 3-29-37
Thomas Murphy* SW-NE-S7; 1-16-44
Patrick Egan* E-NW-S7; 1-5-37; W-SE-S7; 1-13-38
Seth Roddick & George Roddick* W-NW & NW-SW-S7; 7-15-36
George McLin* SW-SW-S7; 6-17-36
Robert Elsey* NE-SE-S7; 6-3-37
Elisha Perkins E-NE-S8; 11-28-16; SW-NE-S8; 3-21-36
William Allen, Jr.* NW-NE-S8; 10-26-47
James McDonald E-NW-S8; 11-25-16. Of *, W-NW-S8; 2-27-37
Levi Madon SW-S8; 10-3-17
Julius Nicholas Emanuel Muret, Sz E-SE-S8; 3-20-38
John Harsha* W-SE-S8; 8-9-27
James C. Allen* NE-NE-S9; 9-30-39
Aaron Hart* SE-NE-S9; 11-22-34
John G. Burch W-NW-S9; 9-26-17
Francis McDonald SW-S9; 11-25-16
George A. Waller SE-S9; 6-4-17
John Albert* NE-NW-S10; 9-16-39
Asahel Gibbens* SE-NW-S10; 1-19-48
Aaron Ruggles* NW-NW-S10; 3-21-37
Henry Rumsour, Kn NE-SW-S10; 2-24-37; NW-SE-S10; 4-10-37
Isaac Feagins* SE-SW-S10; 11-23-44; SE-SE-S10; 11-27-35
Valentine Routt W-SW-S10; 6-4-17
Levi McGibbens* SE-SE-S10; 12-3-44
Patrick Reilley, Lycoming Co., Pa. SE-NE-S11; SW-NW-S12; 10-26-37
Alfred Perkins* SW-NE-S11; 12-21-33; NE-NW-S11; 9-7-47; SE-NW-
Joseph Alton, Kn SW-SW-S11; 11-30-48   S11; 10-31-37
Charles Sefrit* W-SE-S11; 7-29-31; NE-NE-S14; 1-26-37
Thomas Mahee* SW-NE-S12; 12-8-41
Patrick Lennon* SE-SE-S12; 4-20-39
Elisha Perkins, Sr.* E-NE-S13; 11-15-21
Omy Parsons* SW-NE-S13; 12-12-40
William McCormick E-SW-S13; 10-17-18
Simon Petit Lalumiere* W-SW-S13; 9-29-37
Matthew McInnerry* NE-SE & NW-SE-S13; 4-23-39
John Maher* SE-NE-S14; 11-22-41
Mr. Seifreit W-NE-S14; 5-5-18. No given name
Obadiah Fagins* SE-SW-S14; 2-6-37; W-SW-S14; 9-14-18
John Mahew* NE-SE-S14; 8-1-49
Corridon Parsons* SE-SE-S14; 1-15-51

Mark Perkins* NW-SE-S14; 8-31-47
Walter Warder Feagins* SW-SE-S14; 6-3-39; NE-NW-S23; 11-18-34; NW-
James Moore* NE-NW-S15; 2-29-36   NW-S23; 11-21-34
Samuel Thompson Osmon* NW-NW-S15; 11-21-36
John Rankin Kendall* NE-SW-S15; 1-9-36; SE-SW-S15; 11-17-35
Thomas D. Brewer & John Shepherd W-SW-S15; 12-22-29
Caleb Tarleton SE-S15; 10-28-18
Dennis Clark NE-S17; 9-26-17
George H. Keith E-NW-S17; 9-12-17
Zachariah Wood* NW-NW-S17; 4-2-39
Melville Wiley, Sz E-SW-S17; 3-20-38
Elijah Eads* W-SW-S17; 7-18-31; SW-NE-S20; 8-7-34
James Honey SE-S17; 8-30-17
Patrick Egan* NW-NE & NE-NW-S18; 1-13-38
Henry Cobbs* SW-NE-S18; 5-27-39; SE-NW-S18; 3-16-36
Isaac Milton Osmon* NW-NW-S18; 1-26-36
Reuben Perkins* SW-NW-S18; 1-20-38
Hugh Barr* E-SW-S18; 2-5-38
Hugh Barr, Jr.* NW-SW-S18; 11-30-35
Stephen Belding* SW-SW-S18; 11-10-35
William Allen* E-SE-S18; 12-22-21; E-NE-S19; 9-19-22
John McElcarny* NE-NW-S19; 9-17-41
James Ketty* SE-NW-S19; 8-4-36
Abraham Perkins W-NW-S19; 9-2-16
William Perkins* E-SW-S19; 9-22-47; SW-SW-S19; 2-20-36
Robert Darlington Major* NW-SW-S19; 2-15-36
John S. Allen* E-SE-S19; 9-10-22
John McKinley E-NE-S20; 1-22-17
John Allen NW-S20; 9-12-17
Benjamin Small* E-SW-S20; 5-15-21
Robert Burress E-SE-S20; 1-11-17
Thomas D. Brewer* W-SE-S20; W-NE-S21; 12-22-29
Isaac Feagins* E-NE-S21; 11-17-35
Mary Ammerman* NW-S21; 10-21-36
Benjamin Brattain SW-S21; 1-16-17
Isaac Dickerson* NE-SE-S21; 12-9-36
William Dickerson* NW-SE-S21; 10-10-36
James Peachee* SW-SE-S21; 7-11-42
Francis Bradley* NE-NE-S22; 6-22-35
Joseph Feagins* SE-NE-S22; SW-NW-S23; 11-18-34
John Shepard W-NE-S22; 10-15-18
John Mauzy & Thomas Mauzy NW-S22; 9-17-17
James Madison Brown* NE-SW-S22; 8-11-35; NW-SW-S22; 8-10-35
John Henry Boury* SE-SW-S22; 8-14-35
Thomas Cahill* SW-SW-S22; 8-12-39
Joseph Brown SE-S22; 1-24-18
William Wilson* NE-NE-S23; 11-3-40
James Montgomery* SE-NE-S23; 12-11-38; SE-SE-S23; 7-18-37; W-SE-
    S23; NE-S26; 10-25-16
David Reisinger, Cumberland Co., Pa. W-NE & SE-NW-S23; 5-23-37
Augustin Mattingly* NE-SW-S23; 8-10-35
Joseph Benedict Quigley* SE-SW-S23; 8-13-35
Susannah Quigley* W-SW-S23; 11-5-31
Bearned Grannon, Jr NE-SE-S23; 11-8-37; W-SW-S24; 10-3-37

James Dant* E-NE-S24; 7-10-37
William Junier Smith* SW-NE & NE-SW-S24; 10-5-36
Michael Connor* E-SE & SW-SE-S24; 5-25-38; NE-NE-S25; 2-11-39
John Shaum* NW-SE-S24; 1-17-37
Francis McNally* SE-NE-S25; 7-25-37
James Kennedy* SW-NE-S25; 9-27-39
William Dant NW-S25; 6-13-18; NE-S27; 12-3-17
William G. Folks & William Coleman Elliott SE-SW, NW-SE, SW-SE-
William McNally* E-SE-S25; 9-28-35   S25; 10-12-37
Nicholas Kidwell NW-S26; 10-25-16
John Hutson SW-S26; 2-7-16
James Campbell* E-SE-S26; 12-9-37
Shadrach Bowman, Nicholas Co., Ky. W-SE-S26; 9-5-25
George Courtney Hays E-NW-S27; 10-27-17. Of * NW-NW-S27; 9-21-
   35; SW-S27; 2-3-17; SE-SE-S28; 11-28-35
Benjamin Hays* SW-NW-S27; 1-9-37
John McCracking SE-S27; 11-4-17
Thomas Cahill* SE-NE-S28; 10-9-37; W-SW-S28; 8-20-19. Cahale
Mary Ann Shepherd* E-NW-S28; 12-22-29
Benjamin Peachy* W-NW-S28; 12-30-31; NE-SW-S28; 10-14-43. Peachee
Charner Hawkins* SE-SW-S28; 9-23-37
Joseph Hays* NE-SE-S28; 10-24-40
Charner Hawkins & William W. Potts* W-SE-S28; 9-23-37
Moses Knight, Kn NE-NE-S29; 1-6-34
James G. Read, Ck SE-NE-S29; 11-11-36; W-NW-S33; 6-15-18
Joseph Miller W-NE-S29; 10-30-17
Hillary Mattingly* E-NW & NW-NW-S29; 5-7-36
John Smith Allen* SW-NW-S29; 10-11-32
Samuel Chamness SW-S29; 10-24-16
William Williams SE-S29; 11-1-15; NE-S32; 10-7-16
James Gray Read, Ck SE-NE-S30; 6-14-37. Of *, SE-S30; 12-22-29
Patrick Fitzpatrick, Columbiana Co., O. W-NE & E-NW-S30; 3-12-40
William H. Route W-NW-S30; 3-28-17
James McKinley SW-S30; 11-11-15
Calvin Butler* NE-NE-S31; 4-30-36; SE-NE-S31; 7-30-36
James Morehead* W-NE-S31; 9-22-31; W-SE-S31; 9-26-17
James Carnahan NW-S31; 10-22-17. Of*, NE-SW-S31; 7-11-37
John Aikman, Jr. W-SW-S31; 10-24-17
Michael Gaffney* NE-SE-S31; 6-8-42
Mary Woods* SE-SE-S31; 5-7-42
William Meeds* NE-NW & NW-SE-S32; 10-7-35; NW-SW-S32; 7-10-39
Alfred Davis* SE-NW-S32; 1-22-39
Joel Chamness* NW-NW-S32; 6-25-35
Shadrach Elliott & William Meeds E-SW-S32; 12-14-19
Thomas Elliott Meads* SW-SW-S32; 6-22-39
Robert McBay, Pi E-SE-S32; 11-18-38; SW-SE-S32; 11-15-38
William Allison* NE-NE-S33; 8-27-32; SE-NE-S33; 5-11-38
Hugh Barr* NW-NE-S33; 9-12-37; NW-S35; 11-7-17
Joseph Warder Allison* SW-NE-S33; 10-17-42
James McClelland* NE-NW-S33; 3-29-33
George Thomas Hays* SE-NW-S33; 1-24-39; NE-SW-S33; 6-21-36; NW-
Thomas Greenwood* SE-SW-S33; 1-17-37   SW-S33; 11-8-36
Patrick Bradley* SW-SW-S33; 12-5-34
Robert Barr NE-S34; 10-25-16

James C. Reed, Frederick Shotts, & Alexander Bruce   NW-S34; 2-3-17
Abigail Bunnell* NW-SW-S34; 11-17-36
Samuel Healy* SW-SW-S34; 8-24-43
Daniel Harris* SE-SE-S34; 12-2-44
James McEvoy* NW-SE-S34; 1-6-38; SW-SE-S34; 12-27-37
Solomon Weber* E-NE-S35; 7-16-31
Thomas Moore* NW-NE-S35; 4-7-36
Henry Hill* SW-NE & NW-SE-S35; 3-18-44; E-SE-S35; 11-16-38
John Tolbert Summers, Kn NE-SW-S35; 6-2-40
Adam Boyd Aikman* SE-SW & SW-SW-S35; 5-5-40
Andrew Jackson Summers, Kn NW-SW-S35; 5-12-40
John Megehee* SW-SE-S35; 8-9-44
Ephraim Wilson E-NE-S36; 10-31-19
William G. Folks & William Coleman Elliott, Kn NW-NE-S36; 2-28-38
Charles McLear NW-S36; 5-12-19
Joseph Walker* SW-NE-S36; 9-18-32
Ignatius Walker* NE-SW-S36; 2-15-36; SE-SW-S36; 1-3-39
Thomas McCracken* NW-SW-S36; 2-29-36
Joseph Miller E-SE-S36; 7-24-18. Of*, W-SE-S36; 12-17-31

RELINQUISHMENTS

Daniel Colbert W-SW-S7; 4-9-17
William McCormick NW-S13; 10-17-18
Moses Allen SE-S21; 9-12-17
Stephen P. Striker SW-S22; 10-17-17
Robert Hill NE-S23; 10-28-18
Rachel Allen E-NW-S29; 9-12-17
James Moorhead W-SE-S31; 9-26-18
Shadrach Elliott & William Meeds NW-S32; 12-14-19
James G. Reed & William Batchelor SW-S36; 10-24-17
Solomon Satterfield & E. Perkins SW-S5; n.d.
James McDonald W-NW-S8; 11-25-16
John Tucker SE-S8; 4-9-17
John G. Burch E-NW-S9; 9-26-17
Valentine Routt NW-S10; 9-30-17; E-SW-S10; 6-4-17
George Soifriet E-NE-S14; 5-5-18
Daniel Pender NW-S15; 8-15-18
George McKinley W-NE-S20; 1-22-17
Thomas Burruss NW-S28; 10-2-18
Charles McLear NE-S35; 5-12-19
Elisha Perkins W-NE-S8; 11-28-16
William Chadd SW-S15; 8-26-18; NE-S21; 8-30-17
George H. Keith W-NW-S17; 9-12-17
Abraham Perkins E-SW & W-SW-S19; 10-24-16; E-NW-S19; 9-2-16
Robert Burruss W-SE-S20; 1-11-17
John Shephard E-NE-S22; 10-15-18
Obadiah Fagins NW-S23; 9-14-18; E-SW-S14; 9-14-18
James Montgomery E-SE-S23; 10-25-16
Thomas Cahale E-SW-S28; 8-26-19
Joseph Miller E-NE-S29; 9-30-17
Robert Burruss, Jr. NE-S28; 10-2-18
William H. Routt E-NW-S30; 3-28-17
George McKinley SE-S30; 8-26-17

William Allison NE-S33; 8-25-18
John Bennington, Sr. SW-S33; 8-17-19
James G. Reed E-NW-S33; 8-15-18
Ephraim Wilson W-NE-S36; 10-31-18
Joseph Miller W-SE-S36; 7-24-18; NE-S30; 10-27-17; NE-S31; 10-27-17
Joseph Parks SW-S17; 8-26-17; NW-S21; 1-24-18
George C. Hays W-NW-S27; 10-27-17
Dennis Clark NE-S9; 9-20-17
John Aukman, Jr. E-SW-S31; 10-24-17. Aikman?
Jesse Rubel SW-S23; 11-2-18
William McCormick W-SW-S13; 10-17-18; 7-4-29
John Allen W-NW-S20; 9-12-17; 7-4-29
S. Elliott & William Meads W-SW-S32; 12-14-19; 7-4-29

T 3 N, R 7 W

Stephen Masten, Sr.* W-NW-S2; 2-6-36
James Hart* NE-SW-S2; 2-9-36; E-SW-S4; 2-9-36; W-NE-S9; 2-9-36
Jonathan Hawkins* SE-SW-S2; 2-8-36
Frederick Killion* W-SW-S2; 3-14-31
John Shepard* SW-SE-S2; 4-4-38
William Sullivan, George W. Pratt, & George M. Thacher NE, E-NW,
    SW-NW, E-SW, NW-SW, E-SE, SW-SE-S3; E-NE, SW-NW, NE-SW,
    SW-SW, W-SE-S9; 3-6-37
Hugh Cotter* NW-NW-S3; 9-5-36
Peter Heddrick* SW-SW-S3; 11-9-36
Joseph Williams* NW-SE-S3; 11-29-36
Ralph Hart* NE-NE-S4; 1-3-35
Levi Willemin* SE-NE & SE-NW-S4; 2-10-36
Daniel Emerson* W-NE-S4; 8-22-39
Joseph Allender* NE-NW-S4; 12-22-35
Philip Karns* SW-NW-S4; 12-14-35; NW-SW-S4; 10-17-35; E-SE-S5;
James Armstrong Karns* SW-SW-S4; 2-20-36   12-29-35
John Willemin* NE-SE-S4; 4-23-36
Thomas Newton Lett* SE-SE-S4; 4-30-44
Anderson Hart* W-SE-S4; 12-15-35
Thomas B. Graham E-SW, NW-SW, SW-SW-S5; 8-11-54. MIW 10503,42234,
Orms Thomas* NE-NE-S6; 2-4-39; W-NE, E-NW-S6; 7-2-20   78967
David Warner Snyder* NE-SW-S6; 5-5-36; NW-SW-S6; 6-24-37
Samuel Snyder* SW-SW-S6; 5-18-39
Charles Butler, New York City W-NW-S7; 7-4-36
George Engle* NE-NE-S8; 8-2-36; NW-NW-S9; 8-2-36
Simon Osmun, Adams Co., O. NW-NE-S8; NE-NW-S8; 9-26-36
Thomas M. Lett* Lot 3-SWfr-S8; 11-26-50; Lot 5-SWfr-S8; 8-26-54;
    NE-NW-S10; 1-11-51
Samuel Hollingsworth* Lot 4-SWfr-S8; 12-11-35; SW-SE & SE-SW-S8;
Jonathan Hawkins* Lot 2-SEfr-S8; 3-4-37   8-28-33
Anthony Benham* Lot 1-SEfr-S8; 3-4-37; SW-NE-S10; 2-20-33
Anderson Hart* E-NW-S9; 2-15-36
Ezekiel York* SE-SW-S9; 12-11-35; NW-SW-S9; 4-2-36
Thomas Rees* E-SE-S9; SW-S10; 7-6-21
Mishack Porter* E-NE-S10; 7-18-31
Hiram Lewis Willemin* NW-NE-S10; 12-20-38

James Houston* SE-NW-S10; 12-15-35
Jacob Bunnel* NW-NW-S10; 12-15-35
James Wilkins* SW-NW-S10; 4-17-37
Emanuel Vantrees* E-SEfr-S10; 12-22-21; W-NEfr-S17; 8-7-21; W-SE-
Elam Hart & Ralph Hart* W-SEfr-S10; 4-23-28   S20;8-15-21
James Peachee* NEfr-S11; 7-5-21
George Henson Keith* E-NW-S11; 2-9-36
Joseph Bradford* W-NW-S11; 7-18-31
Charles Osmon* SWfr-S11; 8-18-31
Henry Gulick* SEfr-S11; 9-3-21
William Major, Da Lot 1-NE-NEfr-S12; 2-20-36
Robert Darlington Major, Da Lot 4-SE-NEfr-S12; 2-15-36; SEfr-S12;
Richard Lambert, Da Lot 2-W-NEfr-S12; 9-8-42   7-16-36
John Williams, Da Lot 3-W-NEfr-S12; 2-17-36
John Ross, Mason Co., Ky. NWfr-S12; 8-16-22
Stephen Bolding, Da Lot 2-FrS13; 6-30-35
John Allen* NWfr-S14; 9-3-21
Hugh Barr* SEfr-S14; 10-5-21
Milton Taylor Givens* Lot 1-N-N-FrS15; 4-23-36; Lot 4-S-N-FrS15;
John M. Berry Lot 2-N-N-FrS15; 7-26-52   5-6-35
George Bradford* Lot 3-S-N-FrS15; 7-2-36
Richard Mattingley* N-S-FrS15; 12-5-32
John Whalen* S-S-FrS15; 7-13-21
Buck Ballow* E-NEfr-S17; 7-31-35; E-SE-S17; 8-1-29
John Allen* Lot 29 in Fr. Secs. 10-11-14-15; 9-1-34. Aug. 28,
    1835. Receipt No. 7847 issued to William Bradford for the undi-
    vided half of Lot 292 but the marks are delayed until John
    Allen withdraws his entry and gets a new receipt for the other
Seth Roddick & George Roddick* E-NWfr-S17; 10-2-35   pay.
John Hawkins* W-NWfr-S17; 8-14-21; Lot 5-E-NWfr-S18; 10-24-35
Jesse Lucas* SWfr-S17; 7-24-30; SEfr-S18; 11-15-21
Amos Hawkins* W-SE-S17; 6-13-36   36
Isaac Hollingsworth* Lot 1-N-NEfr-S18; 12-11-35; S-NEfr-S18;8-15-
Samuel Anderson* Lot 2-N-NEfr-S18; 7-8-39; Lot 3-E-NWfr-S18;6-3-
William Hawkins* W-NWfr-S18; 6-8-36   39
Jeremiah Gregory* SWfr-S18; 1-17-22
Josiah Culbertson* E-NE-S19; 7-2-21
William Sullivan, George W. Pratt, & George M. Thacher W-NE-S19;
    SW-SW-S20; 3-6-37
Moses Hawkins* Lot 1-NWfr-S19; 10-20-35; Lot 2-NWfr-S19; 6-1-44
Thomas Samply* Lot 4-SWfr-S19; 11-15-42
Wiley Right* Lot 5-SWfr-S19; 9-8-35
Burrille Coleman* E-SE, NW-SE-S19; 3-7-35
William Booker* E-SE & SW-SE-S19; 6-20-35
Jacob Hawkins* E-NE-S20; 4-13-31; SW-NE-S20; 8-5-34
Smith Scott* NW-NE-S20; 2-22-34; SW-NW-S21; 6-27-36
Francis Cassiday* E-NW-S20; 6-7-38
Richard Palmer* W-NW-S20; 7-2-21
Robert Scott Underwood* NE-SW-S20; 10-12-35; NW-SW-S20; 8-23-33
Edmund Thomas* SE-SW-S20; 9-22-35
William Wood & Richard Wood E-SE-S20; 9-20-22
Henry Clifton* E-Efr-S21; 10-7-21
Thomas Tuning* W-Efr-S21; 2-24-23
Thomas Meredith* NE-NW, NW-NW-S21; 6-14-36

Nathan Clifton* SE-NW-S21; 1-11-36
Lewis Jones* NE-SW-S21; 6-7-36; SE-SW-S21; 9-15-32; W-SW-S21; 2-
William Bradford* NEfr-S22; 7-2-21   11-32
George Lashley, Jr.* N-NWfr-S22; 1-25-22
Peter Headrick* S-NWfr-S22;.12-7-30
Christian Bruner, Jessamine Co., Ky. SWfr-S22; 10-1-21
Nathan Reed* E-NEfr-S23; 8-29-22
George A. Weller* W-NEfr-S23; 8-28-21
George Fausett* W-SWfr-S23; 7-28-21
John Bradford* E-SWfr-S23; 7-2-21
George Brunner* E-SE-S23; 11-15-22. Of Jessamine Co., Ky.,E-SE-
Benedict Shody* W-SE-S23; 9-6-21   S29; 11-5-21
James H. Karnes, Da Efr-S24; 10-9-21
Robert D. Major, Da Wfr-S24; 10-16-30
Robert Raper, Da Lot 1-E-NEfr-S25; 12-22-35
William Bratton, Da Lot 2-E-NEfr-S25; 12-22-35
Elijah N. Robinson, Da W-NEfr-S25; 7-2-21; SWfr-S25; 6-18-21
John Shepard, Da E-NWfr-S25; 9-9-31
William Chadd* W-NWfr-S25; 4-14-23
Grandison Thomas, Da SE-S25; 7-21-21; E-NWfr-S36; 8-7-28
Emanuel Vantrees* E-NEfr-S26; 11-24-21; SEfr-S26; 6-19-21
Samuel J. Kelso* W-NEfr-S26; 7-2-21
Elijah N. Robinson* NWfr-S26; SEfr-S28; 6-18-21; E-SW-S28; 9-19-21
James H. McDonald* SWfr-S26; 6-18-24
Jacob Freeland* NEfr-S28; 9-30-21
Stephen Masten* E-NW-S28; 7-2-21
William Wood & Richard Wood W-NW-S28; 9-20-22
Peter Hedrick* W-SW-S28; 7-2-21   4-9-37
Solomon Thomas* E-NE-S29; 8-6-31; NE-NW-S29; 2-15-34; NE-SW-S29;
Patrick Mulcahy Brett* W-NE-S29; 7-23-36; SE-NW-S29; 8-1-36
Francis Cassiday* W-NW-S29; 6-7-38
Francis Xaverius Spink* SE-SW-S29; 3-25-36; SW-SE-S29; 10-5-35;
   NEfr-S32; 10-9-21
Edmund Thomas* W-SW-S29; 1-4-36; E-SE-S30; 12-8-30
Jacob Hawkins* NW-SE-S29; 6-15-36
William Booker* NE-NE-S30; 1-9-36; NWfr-S30; 11-14-36
Wiley Wright* SE-NE-S30; 6-28-32
William Sullivan, George W. Pratt, & George M. Thacher W-NE, NW-SE-
   S30; 3-6-37
Philip Barton & Barton Peck* Lot 1-E-SW-S30; 2-6-36
John Thompson* Lot 2-E-SW-S30; 9-15-35
Eli Hawkins* Lot 3-W-SW-S30; 12-23-34
William Hawkins* SW-SE-S30; 2-24-33; Nfr-S31; 10-10-21; NWfr-S33;
Michael R. Boos* NWfr-S32; 7-8-22   6-18-21
John Reiley* E-SE-S34; 7-5-21   Samuel Chamness*
James Wilkins* E-SW-S35; 12-24-33   W-SW-S36;5-9-22
Hiram Dye, Mason Co., Ky. W-SW-S35; 9-25-22
Emanuel Vantrees* E-SE-S35; 12-3-21   Robert Raper*
Samuel Arnold* W-SE-S35; 8-6-23   NE-SE-S36;6-12-37
Richard Merrell, Da NE-S36; 8-20-21
Jos. (Jas.?) Warner & Seth Rodick* W-NWfr-S36; 6-18-21
Amos Jarvis* NE-SW-S36; 12-16-34; W-SE-S36; 7-31-21. Gervis
David Morris Hixson* SE-SW-S36; 12-5-34
Patrick Tracy, Jefferson Co., Ky. SE-SE-S36; 3-7-38

T 3 N, R 8 W

Josiah Lawrence, William Oliver, & Lucius Barber NE-Fr$\frac{1}{4}$ & NW-Fr$\frac{1}{4}$
    & SE-S1; 5-11-36
Joseph Hogue, Kn Lot 3-W-SWfr-S1; 4-14-36; Lot 4-W-SWfr-S1; 3-21-
    36; Efr-S11; 3-18-33
Charles Butler, New York City NE & E-NW-S12; 7-4-36.
Isaac Harrel* NW-NW-S12; 5-3-36
John Hogue, Kn SW-NW-S12; 7-23-36   Jacob Hawkins*
William Gilmore, Kn NE-SWfr-S12; 5-29-39.   Lot 1-N-NEfr-Nfr-
Zebulon Hogue, Kn Lot 1-W-SWfr-S12; 5-14-39.   S25;9-22-35;
Francis Cassidy* E-NEfr-S13; 5-18-39.   S-NEfr-Nfr-S25;
Harrison Bions* Lot 3-SEfr-S13; 3-9-37.   9-4-35.
Jesse Lucas* Lot 4-SEfr-S13; Nfr-D24; 8-15-36.
James Smith* Sfr-S24; 4-21-46
Moses Knight* NWfr-Nfr-S25; 8-26-29   (Lot 2-N-NEfr-
Eli Hawkins* Lot 4-SEfr-Nfr-S25; 6-20-35   (Nfr-S25;2-13-
Calvin Butler* Lot 3-SEfr-Nfr-S25; 7-16-36   (36;SWfr-Nfr-
Michael Murphy, Jefferson Co., Ky. Efr-S36; 6-20-21;(S25;8-21-35

T 4 N, R 5 W

Jacob Williams* SE-NE, SW-NE-S2; 11-4-51; N-SW, Sfr-S2; 11-26-44
Stephen Wooden, Lw E-Sfr-S3; 5-20-40   38
Simpson Kilgore* E-W-Sfr-S3; 12-7-36 ;SW-SE-S9; SW-NW-S11; 10-20-
Ozias Crooke* W-W-Sfr-S3; 6-17-36; SE-SE-S4; 12-10-36   39
William Herron* S-NEfr, N-SEfr-S3; 10-26-44; Of Lw, SW-NW-S4;6-17-
Peter Ragle* SE-NE-S4; 1-3-51; NE-SW-S4; 2-11-45; NE-SE-S4; 9-23-
John Lee* N-NWfr-S3; 9-28-47   36
William Flinn, Lw S-NWfr-S3; 11-14-44
James Watt* SE-SW-S4; 1-31-37
Lewis Beck, Lw W-SW-S4; 6-25-36
James Owens, Lw W-SE-S4; 10-29-32
Reuben Kilgore* SE-NE-S5; 11-29-36; NE-SE-S5; 2-25-37
Elijah Montgomery* W-NE-S5; 5-3-37
Nicholas Osburn, Lw W-NW-S5; E-NE-S6; 9-28-36
Samuel Owens* SE-SE-S5; 7-4-36; NE-NE-S8; 10-30-33
Susannah Overton* SW-SE-S5; 2-13-45
Pleasant Franklin* SW-NE-S6; 2-8-39; NE-SW-S6; 8-12-44
David Florer E-NW-S6; 8-11-19
Peter Arb* SW-NW-S6; 11-2-40; SE-SW, W-SW-S6; NW-S7; 8-1-40
John Fisher, Or SW-NE-S7; 2-19-39
Henry Stigall, Or E-SW, W-SE-S7; 2-19-39
John Dougherty, Lw W-SW-S7; 2-3-37
Andrew McClelland, Lw SE-NE-S8; 6-25-39
Samuel Crawford, Lw W-NE-S8; 10-16-37
Moses Osborn, Lw SE-NW-S8; 5-23-37; W-NW-S8; 1-27-37; NW-NE-S9;
    5-30-37; NW-NW-S9; 11-12-38
Samuel Graham* NE-SE-S8; 12-7-36
Francis Peterson* SE-SE-S8; 11-16-32
Ozias Crooke* NE-NE-S9; 2-15-37
Willet Galbreth, Lw SE-NE-S9; 9-21-39
Peter Ragle* SW-NE-S9; 9-23-36

Hiram Kilgour* NE-NW-S9; 7-6-36; NW-NW-S11; 11-29-36
Stephen Kilgore* SE-SW-S9; 12-16-44; E-NW-S10; 6-21-36; NW-NW-S10;
    12-7-36; SE-SE-S11; 11-16-32
Charles Killgore* SW-SW-S9; 11-18-33
Jonathan Wooden* NW-SW-S10; 1-29-40. Of Lw, E-SE-S9; 12-7-39
John Wesley Wadsworth* NW-SE-S9; 6-8-37
Francis Cassidy* E-SE, W-SE-S10; 4-20-39
Moses Woodruff* SE-NE, NE-SE-S11; 11-16-32
Austin Hendrixson* SW-NW-S14; 12-22-46
Jonathan Dilly Calvin, Mt NE-SE-S14; 6-21-47
James S. Stranges* SE-SE-S14; 3-31-46
John Gibson* SW-NE-S15; 2-11-47
Aaron Hendrixson* NE-NW-S15; 12-22-46
John Steel, Lw SE-NW-S15; 5-26-40
Tyre Kinser* W-NW-S15; 4-18-46
John Hendrixson* NE-SW-S15; 8-12-46; NW-SW-S15; 10-7-46
James King* SE-SW-S15; 6-27-39
Samuel Graham* SW-SW-S15; 12-7-36; E-NW-S22; 12-7-36
Robert King* SE-SE-S15; 6-27-39; NE-NE-S22; 3-18-39
Cyrus Allen* SW-SE-S15; 2-22-47
William Peterson* W-SW-S17; 9-9-22
Jonathan Wright, Or SE-SW-S17; 3-18-36
Thomas Poteet Fulkerson* NE-SE-S17; 9-1-36
Lemuel Coulter, Lw NE-S18; 6-26-39
Henry Stigall, Or NE-NW-S18; 2-19-39
John Gabbert* NE-SW, NW-SW-S18; 6-3-39
John Vest Coulter* SE-SE-S18; 3-4-44
Alexander Nichols Jamison, Lw W-NW-S19; 12-5-37
William Killian, Jr.* SE-SW-S19; 8-16-39
William Cook* SE-SW-S20; 12-27-37
Willis Cook* NW-SE-S20; 11-13-37; SE-NW-S21; 7-15-36
Samuel McBride* SW-SE-S20; 11-16-32
Matthew Borland, Lw E-NE, NE-NW-S21; 4-18-37
Sion Cavness* SW-NW-S21; 12-26-44
William McBride* NE-SW, NW-SE-S21; 2-16-38
Abel Starr, Lw E-SE-S21; 1-31-38; W-SW-S22; 1-31-38
Gustavus Clark, Lw SW-SE-S21; 10-8-49
James King* SE-NE-S22; 6-27-39
Gottlob Byer* SW-NE-S22; 9-29-37; NW-SE-S22; 5-25-40
Charles Kilgore, Sr.* W-NW-S22; 4-21-36
Reuben Kilgore* NE-SW-S22; 10-24-37
Thomas Edwards, Jr.* NE-SE-S22; 1-22-39
Thomas Edwards* SE-SE-S22; 9-10-36
James Strange, Mt NW-SW-S23; 8-10-42
William Clements* SW-SW-S23; 2-5-45
John James O'Brien, Mt E-SE-S23; 8-9-44
Charles Ash* NE-NE-S26; 1-3-51
Presley A. Prince, Mt SE-NE-S26; 2-13-49
Philip Strange, Mt SW-NE-S26; 1-22-51
William Lents, Mt SW-NW-S26; 5-30-50. Of*, SW-NE-S27; 2-20-39
Bridget Dunn, Mt NE-SW-S26; 1-13-51
John Doyle, Mt SE-SW-S26; 9-6-50; SW-SW-S26; 8-23-48
Thomas Dunn, Mt NW-SW-S26; 1-4-51
John Strange* NE-SE-S26; 6-6-39

Charles Strange* SE-SE-S26; 10-22-38; SW-SE-S26; 10-4-36
Samuel Lundy, Mt NW-SE-S26; 1-13-51
Nicholas Lents* SE-SW-S27; 2-20-39
Jacob Lentz* NW-SW-S27; 12-13-37
Nelson Lents* SE-NE-S28; 2-20-39
Presley Nevel Prence* SW-NE-S28; 12-20-37; E-SE-S28; 12-13-37
William Cook* NE-NW-S28; 12-7-36
Horatio Jeter, Lw NW-NW-S28; 1-23-57; NE-NE-S29; 6-13-35
Charles Cootee* SE-SW-S28; 10-4-36; NE-NW-S33; 11-22-36
Edward Gilliam, Jr W-SE-S28; 12-20-37
Samuel McBride* NW-NE-S29; 12-18-35
Joshua McBride* NE-NW-S29; 6-23-36
Willis Cook* SE-NW-S29; 2-22-38
Hiram Allen* E-SW, W-SE-S29; 11-4-36
William Patterson* SW-SW-S29; 8-10-39   83426
William S. Turner* SE-NW-S30; 5-27-57; NW-NW-S33; 7-16-53. MLW /
Gilbert Patterson, Jr.* SW-NW-S30; 8-28-39; SW-SE-S30; 10-4-36
Jabez Osmon* SE-SW-S30; 1-20-37; NE-NW-S31; 9-20-36
William Baker W-NW-S31; 11-13-18
Greenberry Patterson, Lw NE-SE-S31; 8-10-39
Hiram Miller* SE-S32; 11-4-36
John Lents* NE-NE-S33; 6-19-40; SE-NE-S33; 7-4-37; NW-NE-S33;
    5-30-50. Of Mt, SE-NW-S33; 12-30-47
Stephen Melton* SW-NW-S33; 5-21-49
Washington Drury* NE-SW-S33; 1-16-48; W-SE-S33; 11-4-48
William Paget* SE-SW-S33; 1-30-37
John Seals* SW-SW-S33; 8-3-48
Hillery Spalding, Mt NE-SE-S33; 6-19-40
William Seal* NE, SE-NW, NE-SE, NW-SE-S34; NW-SW-S35; 2-20-39;
    Of Mt, NE-SW-S35; 11-18-40
Thomas M. Spaulding* NE-NW-S34; 7-4-37
Vincent Lents, Mt NW-NW-S34; 12-30-50
William Bryant Padget* E-SW-S34; 2-18-48. Of Mt, NW-SW-S34;
George Padget* SE-SE-S34; 10-30-38   12-4-50
John B. Spalding* SW-SE-S34; 5-23-50
John Doyle* NE-NE-S35; 3-16-48; NE-NW, NW-NW-S35; 11-16-46
Patrick Patridge, Hamilton Co., O. SE-NE, W-NE-S35; 3-4-40
•Ezekiel Miller* SE-NW-S35; 10-22-38; SE-SW-S35; 3-25-39. Of
    Mason Co., Ky., W-SE-S35; 10-3-22
James Dunn* SW-NW-S35; 11-11-48
Benedict Padget* SW-SW-S35; 1-13-51
James Berry, Mt E-SE-S35; 11-17-24

RELINQUISHMENTS

William Baker E-NW-S31; 11-13-18
William Williams NE-S6; 8-11-19
David Florer W-NW-S6; 8-11-19

T 4 N, R 6 W

Hosea H. Nunnally* SE-NE, SW-NE-S1; 12-17-38
Moses Woody* SW-NW-S1; 6-5-37
Jonas Brooks Wood* NE-SW-S1; 8-26-37
Jonathan Casto* SE-SW-S1; 4-13-39
Christopher Frederick Hammer* W-SW-S1; 10-5-36
Peter Arb* E-SE-S1; 8-1-40
Noah Casto* NW-SE-S1; 4-13-39
Joel Carter, Mr SE-NE-S2; 6-11-49
Daniel Myers* E-SW-S2; 5-27-36
Elihu Allen, Lw E-SE, NW-SE-S2; 1-25-37
John Head, Or SW-SE-S2; 8-26-36
William Stone, Or NW-NE-S3; 2-2-37
Joshua Moore* W-SW-S3; SW-NE, SE-S4; 7-12-38
Jacob Killion* NE-SW-S4; 8-12-36
Mathias Killion* W-SW-S4; W-SW-S5; W-NE-S6; 12-14-22
Lewis Gibson* SE-NE-S5; 2-8-37
Charles Franklin Wells* SW-NE-S5; 1-31-38; SW-NE-S7; 7-27-35;
    W-SE-S7; 7-18-31
Andrew Jackson Wells* E-NE-S6; 11-6-44
Adam Killion E-NW-S6; 3-26-27
William Samples NW-S7; 6-22-49. MLW 52280
Joseph Summers E-SE-S7; 6-30-17; SW-S7; 7-2-17
Thomas Cobb* SE-NE-S8; 2-15-34
John Beneficl E-NW, SW-S8; 8-14-17
Nathan Green Robertson* W-NW-S8; 6-4-31
John Anderson SE-S8; 8-28-17
Jonas Killion* SE-NE-S9; 7-22-40
Joshua Moore* NW-NE-S9; 7-12-38
Frederick Killion* SW-NE-S9; 10-23-37
John Myers* SE-NW-S9; 11-9-35
William McChan SW-S9; 9-10-18
John Bray* NE-SE-S9; 9-27-38
Charles W. Reynolds* SE-SE-S9; 7-5-50
Samuel Stewart W-SE-S9; 1-22-19
John Bowers* SE-SW-S10; 1-10-39
Lewis Gibson* NE-NE-S11; 2-17-36
Henry Banta Shively, Or SE-NE-S11; 8-26-36
William Head* NW-NE-, SE-NW-S11; 10-21-39
Jacob Ellis* SW-NE-S11; 11-24-36
William McGuire* SE-SE-S11; 1-9-38
John Dougherty, Lw E-NE-S12; 2-3-37; E-SE-S12; 2-3-37
Allen Smith, Or W-NE-S12; 11-11-39
Elihu Allen, Lw NE-NW, W-NW-S12; 1-25-37
Andrew Ellis* SE-NW-S12; 12-9-36
Jacob Ellis* SW-S12; 12-9-36
Clement Sapp & Samuel F. Irwin W-SE-S12; 8-15-39
Evan Wade, Lw W-NE, E-NW, E-SW, W-SE-S13; 7-18-36
Levi Fidler, Lw W-NW-S13; 9-4-39. Of *, NW-SE-S14; 2-5-45
Henry Fidler* SW-SW-S13; 9-10-41
John McGuire, Or NE-NE, NW-NE-S14; 12-13-36
William Fidler, Lw SE-NE-S14; 8-15-39; SW-NE-S14; 8-16-39
Peter Yunt* NE-NW, W-NW-S14; 5-27-36

Joseph Miars* NW-NE-S15; 12-28-36
Abraham Snyder* SW-NE-S15; 2-26-35
John Rumner* E-NW-S15; 4-12-32
Andrew Bemount* SE-SW-S15; 11-3-37
Daniel Matthewson* NW-SW-S15; 2-9-37
John Myars, Jr.* SE-SE-S15; 3-9-39
Joseph Miers* W-SE-S15; 9-4-30
Franklin Wilhite* NE-NE-S17; 7-29-37
John Myers* SE-NE-S17; 11-9-35; SE-NW-S23; 10-22-38
John Anderson W-NE-S17; SE-S18; 8-28-17
John Benefiel NW-S17; 8-14-17
John Simpson Pringle* NE-SW-S17; 10-13-37
Michael Robertson W-SW-S17; 12-21-16; W-NE-S18; 9-29-18; E-NE-
    S19; 3-14-18. Roberson. W-NW-S20; 12-21-16
Amsted B. Tommy* E-SE-S17; 3-14-31
John Crantom Burch* NE-NE-S18; 3-24-34
Charles Franklin Wells* SE-NE-S18; 3-8-37
Abraham Lester* NE-NW-S19; 7-16-36
Smallwood Cawood E-SW-S19; 12-4-17
Elias Myers* SW-SW-S19; 1-9-38
Alexander English* E-SE-S19; 11-13-28
Daniel Myers* SW-SE-S19; E-NE-S20; 2-13-49; NE-NW-S20; 10-23-37;
    SE-NW-S20; 12-11-38
Abraham Perkins* NE-SW-S20; 1-18-36
Frederick Myers* SE-SW-S20; 10-12-36; W-SE-S20; 6-30-31
Mathew H. Blackburn W-SW-S20; 7-7-18
Catherine Goldman* NE-NE-S21; 8-21-39
Frederick Ruminer* SE-NE-S21; 11-5-36; E-SE-S21; 9-5-31; NW-SE-
Elias Myers* NE-NW-S21; 10-4-50   S21; 8-21-39
Amsted Bracher Tommy* SW-NW-S21; 2-9-37; NW-SW-S21; 7-3-37
Marion McDonald Garrett* SE-SW-S21; 9-17-47
George Washington Tommy* NE-NE-S22; 5-27-36
George Burget* SW-NW-S22; 9-3-38
James Gadberry* NE-SW-S22; 8-18-38; W-SW-S22; 9-5-31
David Henkel* SE-SW-S22; 11-8-37; SW-SE-S22; 10-4-50. Hinkel
Charles Grove* SE-NE-S23; 11-14-38
Henry Fairchild W-NW, W-SW-S23; 3-31-49. MW 42488
Levi Nunnally* NE-NE, NW-NE-S24; 10-26-35
Alexander Nichols Johnson, Lw SE-NE-S24; 8-30-38
John Humphries, Lw SW-NW-S24; 2-18-40; E-NW-S24; 9-9-36
William Litten* W-NW-S24; 11-4-36
John Grooms, Adams Co., O. E-SW, NW-SW-S24; 10-25-39
William Killian* NE-SE-S24; 8-16-39   48020
Charles M. Norris SE-NE, SW-NE, NE-SE, NW-SE-S25; 12-29-49. MLW /
Augustus F. Bugher, Lw SE-NW, W-NW, SE-SW, SW-SW-S25; 8-8-50. MLW
William S. Turner SE-SE, SW-SE-S25; 5-5-53   67381
John H. Grove* SE-NE-S26; 11-4-50
Job Denning, Adams Co., O. E-SW-S26; 10-25-39
Zachariah Grooms, Adams Co., O. W-SW-S26; 10-25-39
John Turner, Harrison Co., Ky. E-SE-S26; 1-3-22
Robert Lillie, Kn SW-SE-S26; 12-12-39
Jesse Wilson* SW-NE-S27; 4-12-37
William H. Grove* NE-NW-S27; 2-6-51
Josiah Jacob Tommy* SE-NW-S27; 8-1-48

Thomas Bolder Graham* NE-SW-S27; NE-SW, NE-SE, NW-SE-S28; 12-9-
   50. MLW 53309(once); MLW 53305(Twice). See James Bolder Graham
Wyley Killion* NW-SW-S27; 10-4-51   below
Judier Osmon* SE-SE-S27; 7-26-37; NE-NE-S34; 6-24-39. Joedier
Perry Peachee* NW-NE-S28; 2-28-43
Thomas Nicholas Browning* NE-NW-S28; 9-2-47
William Jasper Carell* NW-NW-S28; 1-21-43
Henry Fidler* SE-SW-S28; 11-22-48
James Bolder Graham NW-SW-S28; 12-9-50. MLW 53305. See above
James Connelly, Jr SW-SW-S28; 10-6-38; NW-NW-S33; 10-6-38
Robert Finley Likes* NE-NE-S29; 2-9-37
Frederick Miars* NW-NE-S29; 10-31-38
Jacob Tommy NW-S29; 3-20-18
Daniel Myers* NW-SW-S29; 5-10-50
John G. Burch NE-S30; 10-9-17
Elias Myers E-NW-S30; 1-28-18; W-NW-S30; 4-9-36; E-SW-S30; 5-23-17
Thomas Faith* NW-SW-S30; 9-4-38; SW-SW-S30; 10-13-37
David Killion* NE-SE-S30; 10-18-37; W-SE-S30; 2-12-18
Daniel Rumner NW-S31; 8-24-18
William Killion* E-SW-S32; 12-20-20
Joseph Doherty* SE-SE-S32; 4-15-39
Michael Maker Ryan, Jr NE-NE, NW-NE, E-NW-S33; 10-6-38
John Weeks* SE-NE-S33; 5-7-39; Of Jr, W-NW-S34; 10-6-38
John Bennington* SW-NW-S33; 1-26-37; NW-SW-S33; 2-12-39
Richard Lehearty* SE-SW, SE-SE-S33; 2-14-39
Aaron Heart* SW-SW-S33; 5-28-36
Wiley Roten Jones* NW-SE-S33; 4-15-39; SW-SE-S33; 1-21-39
Patrick Rush, Trumbull Co., O. NW-NE, E-NW-S34; 10-19-38
Michael Gribbins* SE-SW-S34; 6-25-42
Patrick Weeks* NW-SW-S34; 12-2-50
James Conley* SW-SW-S34; 4-14-40
John Garland* SE-SE-S34; 10-12-42
James Lillie, Kn NE-NE, NW-NE-S35; 10-17-39
William Devern Clary* NE-SW-S35; 11-16-39
Reuben Bennington* SW-SE-S35; 2-23-49
Jabez Osmon, Jr. E-NE-S36; 1-24-18
Augustus F. Bugher NE-NW, NW-NW-S36; 8-8-50. MLW 67381
Martin Fleisher* E-SW-S36; 5-25-39
Asberry Perkins* SW-SW-S36; 4-7-48
Jabez Osmon, Sr. SE-S36; 4-6-18

RELINQUISHMENTS

Adam Killion W-NW-S6; 10-27-19
John Benefiel NE-S8; 9-25-18; W-NW-S8; 8-14-17
Samuel Stewart E-SE-S9; 1-22-19
Smallwood Cawood W-SW-S19; 12-4-17; SE-S19; 8-14-18; E-SW-S20;
Jabez Osmon, Jr. W-NE-S36; 1-24-18   3-13-18
John Anderson E-NE-S17; 8-28-17
John T. Purington E-SW-S29; 8-28-18. Bennington?
Elias Myers W-NW-S30; 1-27-18; W-SW-S30; 5-23-17
Michael Roberson E-NE-S18; 9-29-18; E-NW-S20; 12-21-16; W-NE-S19;
   3-14-18; E-SW-S17; 12-21-16
Abraham Luster NW-S19; 8-14-18. Lester?

Frederick Myars W-SE-S20; 1-16-19
A. Tommy & Daniel Myers E-SE-S30; 11-23-18
Joseph Summers W-SE-S7; 6-30-17; 7-4-29
John T. Purington W-SW-S29; 8-28-18; 7-4-29. Bennington?
Daniel Harsha W-SW-S33; 12-29-18; 7-4-29
Jabus Osmon, Sr. SE-S36; 4-6-18; 7-4-29

T 4 N, R 7 W

Alexander Killion* NE-NE-S1; 10-4-48
Enoch Grimsly* NW-NE-S1; 6-28-37
John Bray* NE-NW-S1; 2-15-36
James Barnes* W-NW-S1; 1-9-38
Eldad Stibbins, Hampshire Co., Me. SW-S1; 3-31-36
William Sullivan, George W. Pratt, & George M. Thacher NE-NE,
   W-SW, SE-SE-S2; 3-6-37
William Cobbs* SE-NE-S2; 11-30-35; NE-SE-S2; 7-16-35
John Graham* W-NE-S2; 11-30-35; NE-NW-S2; 2-29-36
Kirtley Waymon* SE-NW-S2; 2-9-36; E-SW-S2; 7-12-31; W-SE-S2; 1-2-
John Walker* W-NW-S2; 11-6-35   29
William Walker* E-NE-S3; 7-23-29
Robert Lester* W-NE-S3; 12-20-32; NW-SE-S2; 4-8-39
William Lester* E-NW-S3; 7-23-29
Joseph Lester* SW-NW-S3; 3-9-39; W-SW-S3; 9-3-25
Adam McCormick* E-SW-S3; 6-9-29
Andrew Jones Hannah* NE-NE-S3; 3-29-36
Isaac Hedden SE-SE-S3; 10-10-51. MLW 15688
Andrew McCormick* SW-SE-S3; 1-21-36
Joseph Hall McClesky* Lot ?-NE-Sfr-S4; 8-31-35; Lot 1-NE-Sfr-S4;
   6-24-36; NW-Sfr-S4; 3-29-33
John McCormick* NE-SW-S4; 12-20-34
William Johnson* SE-SW-S4; 8-8-35; Lot 4-E-E-Nfr; Lot 5-W-E-Nfr-
Matthew H. Blackburn* W-SW-S4; 12-24-25   S6; 1-16-43
William Summers* NE-SE-S4; 6-2-35; SW-SE-S4; 12-29-35
James Killion* SE-SE-S4; 8-5-34
John Dickey McClesky* NW-SE-S4; 3-16-35
James Goodman* N-Sfr-S5; 1-5-36
John Kuykendall* SW-Sfr-S5; 3-21-26
Nathan Ashby* SE-Sfr-S5; 7-6-29
Henry Cook* NE-SW-Sfr-S6; 9-4-37
William Buckels, Kn SW-SW-Sfr-S6; 2-6-37
Nicholas Hoover, Fr SE-SW-Sfr-S6; 10-26-37
Josiah Lawrence, William Oliver, & Lucius Barber E-E-Sfr-S6; 5-11-
Abraham Hoover* W-E-Sfr-S6; 5-5-36   36
Alfred Bicknell* E-NE-S7; 3-28-27
Leonard Skinner Cox* NW-NE-S7; 11-5-38; NE-NWfr-S7; 12-17-38
William Hargis* SW-NE, SE-NWfr-S7; 6-16-35
Alexander Rankin Hinds, Kn NW-NWfr-S7; 1-26-36
William Canada Sandage* SW-NWfr-S7; 10-28-35
Joseph Hollingsworth, Kn SWfr-S7; 12-7-25
Edmund Hulen* NE-SE-S7; 6-29-35; NW-SE-S6; 12-23-34
Isaiah Simonson* SE-SE-S7; 4-20-35
Martin Lucas* Pt-W-SE-S7; 8-5-34; Pt-W-SE-S7; 11-3-35

William Morris* NE-NE, NW-NE-S8; 8-5-34
Anderson Faris* SE-NE-S8; 2-22-36
Lucas Dedrick* SW-NE-S8; 4-29-35. Lucas and Dedrick? see below
Nicholas Hoover* E-NW-S8; 4-23-28; E-NW-S9; 4-23-38
Lewis Reeves* W-NW-S8; 4-4-26
Jonathan Farmer* NE-SW-S8; 2-27-34
William Tigert* SE-SW-S8; 12-23-34; SW-SE-S8; 10-2-35
Obadiah F. Patrick, Kn W-SW-S8; 3-23-36
Hiram Hulen* NE-SE-S8; 10-3-36; NW-SW-S9; 3-17-36
Lucas Dedrick* SE-SE-S8; 3-29-36. Lucas and Dedrick? see below
Andrew Faris* NE-S9; 6-7-36
John Lucas & Parker Dedrick W-NW-S9; 1-4-26. See above
Ebenezer Lester* NE-SE-S9; 8-5-34; E-SW-S10; 11-19-35
Abraham Lester* SE-SE-S9; 3-9-39
Robert Henderson Lester, Su NW-SE-S9; 1-4-36
Thomas Hulen* SW-SE-S9; 12-20-50
Rufus Breed NE-S10; 5-19-49. MLW 47610
William Walker* NE-NW-S10; 11-6-35
Joseph Lester* NW-NW-S10; 7-21-35
Thomas McCormick* SW-NW-S10; 8-23-37; NE-NW-S15; 11-28-35
Franklin Summers* NW-SW-S10; 9-30-39
Elijah Allen* SW-SE-S10; 1-6-36
Andrew Jonas Hannah* NE-NE-S11; 3-29-36
Moses Eckert* W-NE-S11; 11-8-22
Eldad Stibbins, Hampshire Co., Me. E-NW-S11; 3-31-36
William Sullivan, George W. Pratt, & George M. Thacher SW, SE-S11;
  3-6-37; NE, NW-S14; 3-6-37
Jacob Leap NE-S12; 6-20-49. MLW 21912
John C. Conrad, assee. of John M. Conrad NE-S13; 3-13-48. MLW 5893
Robert Arnold Perkins* NE-SW-S13; 3-11-43
John Cawood* NE-NE, W-NE-S15; 7-13-35
Abraham Hoover, Sr.* SE-NW, SW-NW, NW-SE-S15; 5-21-38; SE-SE,SW-SE-
Andrew Dawson Faris* NW-NW-S15; 11-18-35   S18; 5-21-38
Anthony Hinkle, Jr.* NE-NE-S17; 3-8-36
Jonah Seaman Applegate, Hamilton Co., O. SE-NE-S17; 11-9-37
Anthony Hinkle* NW-NE-S17; 6-27-36; NE-NW-S17; 6-17-35
David Peter Zoliff* SW-NE-S17; 8-10-37. Of Cataraugus Co., N.Y.,
Philip Hinkle* SE-NW-S17; 3-8-36   SE-SW-S17; n.d.
Edmund Herrington* NW-NW-S17; 1-9-36
David Hincle* NE-SW-S17; 9-16-36
John Simason* SW-SW-S17; 4-27-36
Charles Burriss* NE-SE, NW-SE-S17; 10-29-38; E-NE-S20; 11-2-38
John Hoover, Jr.* NE-NE-S18; 5-26-35; SE-NE-S18; 4-18-37
John Hoover* NW-NE-S18; 4-20-35; SW-NE-S18; 8-5-34
Thomas Hargis, Pe NWfr-S18; 11-28-28
Peter Hoover* NE-SW-S18; 4-20-35. Of Kn, NW-SE-S18; 7-20-32
George Herrington* SE-SW-S18; 7-5-36
John Harrington* NW-SW-S18; 1-23-36
William Calffly* SW-SW-S18; 11-10-35
William Hoover* NE-SE-S18; 6-7-36
Alfred Simoson* NE-NE-S19; SW-NW-S20; 1-11-36
Moses Cawood* SE-NE-S19; 11-6-38; W-NE-S19; 1-11-36
Alfred Bascom* NE-NW-S19; 1-15-36
Josiah Simonson* NW-NW-S19; 12-26-37

James Coslutt, Ba SW-NW-S19; 7-19-39
John Eagle* NE-SW-S19; 4-3-40; NW-SE-S19; 12-29-35
Nicholas Hoover* SW-SW-S19; 10-16-39
Jesse Fowler* NE-SE-S19; 1-19-36
Andrew Coutchman* W-NE-S20; 6-18-21; E-NW-S20; 7-2-21
Abraham Case, Kn E-SW, W-SW-S20; 6-18-21
Isaac Dunn Bruce, Kn NE-SE-S20; 1-12-36
William Bruce, Kn SE-SE-S20; 5-6-37
Alexander R. Hinds* W-SE-S20; 6-18-21
John A. Everett* NW-SW-S21; 1-11-51
William Sullivan, George W. Pratt, & George M. Thacher SE-S21;
    3-8-37; NE, SE-S22; NE, SW, SE-S27; NE, SE-S33; NW, SW-S34;
Jacob Bunnel* E-NW-S22; 2-12-59   3-6-37
Wiley Killion* E-NE, SE-SE-S23; 2-20-37; NE-SE-S23; 10-31-53;
    E-SW-S24; 2-20-37; W-SW-S24; 11-5-28; NW-NW-S25; 6-13-36; E-SW-
John Hoover* W-SE-S23; 8-4-38   S25; 2-16-39
David Elrod Ellis* SW-NE-S24; 9-20-47
Elias Miars* E-NE-S25; 11-10-25
Matthias Killion* E-SE-S25; 11-19-22
Anthony Hinkel* W-SE-S25; 11-24-28
James Killion* NW-NE-S26; 1-15-35
Charles Butler, New York City NW-S27; NE-S28; 6-20-36
Moses Cawood, Jr.* NE-NE-S29; 7-25-35
Josiah Culbertson* W-NE-S29; 8-10-21
Benjamin Coutchman* E-NW-S29; 6-18-21
Squire Bruce* NW-NW-S29; 4-6-35; NW-SE-S29; 5-4-35. Spier? see
Moses Cawood* NE-SW-S29; 4-1-35; W-SE-S30; 3-20-30   below
Elias Bedle, Kn W-SW-S29; 6-19-21; E-SE-S30; 7-2-21
John Andrew Holmes, Kn SW-SE-S29; 12-28-35; NE-NW-S32; 9-22-35
Squire Bruce & William Bruce NWfr-S30; 1-21-36
William Williams* SE-SW-S30; 5-19-36; NW-NW-S32; 10-17-35
James Wilkins* W-SW-S30; 4-17-37
John Ritchey* E-NE-S31; 7-20-21
James Williams* E-NW-S31; 5-22-35; SW-NW-S31; 9-26-36; SW-NW-S32;
Richard Raleigh, New York City NE-SW-S31; 7-28-42   7-16-39
Orms Thomas* SE-SW-S31; 5-5-36; W-SE-S31; 7-3-21
John J. Copus* NW-SW-S31; 11-18-39
George Coutchman* E-SE-S31; 6-30-21
Joseph Williams* NW-NE-S32; 12-24-35
Spier Spencer Bruce* SW-NE-S32; 1-2-36; NE-SE-S32; 11-5-35. Squire?
John Scroggins* SE-NW-S32; 2-20-36   see above
Stephen Masten, Jr* W-SE-S32; 12-24-35
Milton Hinkle* NW-NE-S35; 8-23-48
Venson Ebenezer Jones* NE-NW-S35; 6-13-36
Alexander McClelland, Tc E-SW, SE-S35; 8-21-38
Stephen Masten, Sr.* NW-SW-S35; 8-9-36; SW-SW-S35; 2-6-36
Elias Myer* E-NE-S36; 7-6-21
Levi Sparks, Jr., Ck W-NE-S36; 8-12-39
William Killion* E-NW-S36; 11-19-22; W-NW-S36; 2-16-39; NE-SW-S36;
    6-29-38
John Williams* SW-SW-S36; 1-10-38
Fanny Myer* NW-SE-S36; 3-18-37

DAVIESS COUNTY

T 4 N, R 8 W

Samuel Tomlinson, Vincennes, Kn Efr-S12; 11-6-33
Josiah Lawrence, William Oliver, & Lucius Barber Sfr-S13; 5-11-36;
   NE-Efr, NW-Efr-S24; 5-11-36
Wyley Killion* SEfr-Efr-S24; 3-18-51
John Henry, Brook Co., Va. N-Efr-S36; 5-21-35
John J. Copus* Lots 5-6-N-S-Efr-S36; 11-5-39
William Williams* S-S-Efr-S36; 12-29-35

T 5 N, R 5 W

Fielding Lewis O'Donold, Gn N-E-NE-S1; 6-3-36
Little Berry Vest, Sr., Ow NW-NE-S1; 8-25-36
John Miller* SW-NE-S1; 11-26-38; SE-NW-S1; 3-12-47; NE-SW-S1;
   6-18-36; SE-SE-S1; 10-5-35
George W. Vest, Gn NE-NW-S1; 11-19-38
Philip Miller* W-NW-S1; 6-6-36; E-NE-S2; 7-15-26; NW-NE-S2;
   4-24-37; E-SE-S2; 4-10-39
Nathaniel Ledgerwood* SE-SW-S1; 1-15-44
Jacob Elswick* NW-SW-S1; 4-16-44; SE-NW-S2; 1-14-37
William O'Donald* SW-SW-S1; 1-14-37
Henry Ruebotham, Lw NE-SE-S1; 1-21-39
Mark Cheney* SW-NE-S2; 4-20-37
William Ledgerwood* NE-NW-S2; 2-10-37. Of Mt, NW-NW-S2; 11-21-36
William Chaney* SW-NW-S2; 6-19-37
William Davis* NE-SW-S2; 6-7-36; SW-NE-S3; 11-6-37
James Allen* SE-SW-S2; 2-18-37
Elijah Chaney* NW-SW-S2; 2-15-37. Of Gn, NE-NE-S3; 5-31-36
David Ledgerwood* SW-SW-S2; 5-13-36
Calvin Allen* NW-SE-S2; 10-16-43
Andrew Miller* SW-SE-S2; 2-28-54
John Chaney* SE-NE-S3; 4-5-37
William Porter, Jr.* NE-NW-S3; 6-29-35
Robert Clark* SE-NW-S3; 5-13-36; E-SW, W-SE-S3; 3-21-36
William Roach* NW-NW-S3; 4-1-36
James Madison O'Neall* SW-NW-S3; 3-8-48; NW-SW-S3; 2-15-37
William Perkins* SW-SW-S3; 1-15-38; SE-SE-S4; 6-27-36
David Ledgerwood* E-SE-S3; 2-18-37
Samuel Hughen, Gn NE-S4; 10-20-21
Zebulon Jenkins* E-NW-S4; 5-19-21
Nathan Chandler, Gn W-NW-S4; 6-6-30; SE-NE-S5; 6-18-36
Joseph Burns Vanmatre* NE-SW-S4; 3-10-36; NW-SW-S4; 6-18-36
Henry O'Neall* NE-SE-S4; 2-16-36
Robert Evans, Sr.* W-SE-S4; 8-20-21
Samuel O'Neal* NE-NE-S5; 6-25-49
William Denton Osborn, Mt NE-SW-S5; 11-9-35
James Hamersly* SE-SW-S5; 4-1-39; NW-SW-S5; 7-5-38
James Osborn* SW-SW-S5; 3-21-38
Wilson Gadberry* SW-NE-S6; 4-2-39
Hugh O'Neal* NE-NW-S6; 5-22-39
George W. Sherrow* SE-NW-S6; 10-27-47
David Manning* NW-NW-S6; 6-24-37

John Shields* NE-SW-S6; 8-11-37. Of Mt, SW-NW, NE-NW-S8; 9-3-36
John Gadberry* SE-SW-S6; 4-30-36
James Gadberry* NW-SW-S6; 4-30-36
Daniel Harmon* SW-SW-S6; 6-23-36
Nicholas Feltner+ SE-SE-S6; 9-4-47; SW-SE-S6; 7-15-44; E-SE, NW-
Joseph Robison* NW-SE-S6; 4-1-39   -SE-S7; 2-19-39
Joshua Manning* E-NW-S7; 10-21-29
James Hamersly* NW-NW-S7; 10-19-48; SW-NW-S7; 7-15-40
Lorenzo Dow Sharrow* NE-SW-S7; 12-22-43
Joseph Delinger, Gn SE-SW, NW-SW-S7; 4-19-37
James S. Courtney* SW-SE-S7; 8-16-39
Jesse Richey & Sarah Rebecca Richey E-NE, SW-NE; NE-SE-S8; 7-19-
Winfield Smeltser* NW-NE-S8; 4-23-49   51. MLW 62467
James Roberts Shields* SE-NW-S8; 8-11-37
Henry Shields* NW-SW-S8; 2-2-39
Robert Baker, Ru SE-SE-S8; 9-22-37
Abner Ward* NW-SE-S8; 11-14-44
John Wilson* SW-SE-S8; 10-24-51
John B. Vanmatre, Ws E-NE-S9; 4-7-29
Lanford Webster* NE-NW-S9; 7-8-36
Zedekiah Robison* SE-NW, SW-NW, NE-SW, NW-SW-S9; 4-23-49. MLW
Gideon Baker, Ru SE-SW, SW-SW-S9; 6-6-37
Rosana Winfield NE-S10; 3-24-49. MLW
Charles Ledgerwood* NE-NW-S10; 2-23-36
John Gullet* SE-NW-S10; 4-20-40
John York* NW-NW-S10; 2-13-49
George Willis* SE-SW-S10; 2-15-39
Leroy Wilson* SW-SW-S10; 2-24-36
John Wingfield* SW-SE-S10; 10-31-36
Silas Phillips, Gn NE-NE-S11; 9-20-48
Hiram Bricker* SE-NE-S11; 7-8-53
Elswick Hays Ledgerwood* NE-NW-S11; 2-27-45; NW-NW-S11; 2-22-45
John Ross NE-SW, NW-SW-S11; 10-30-51. MLW
Joseph Carlisle, Alleghany Co., Pa. SE-SW, SW-SW-S11; 12-7-53. MLW
John Miller SE-S11; 8-14-48. MW
George Ledgerwood NE-NE, NW-NE-S12; 10-22-52
John Philips, Jr., Mt SE-NE-S12; 6-18-51
Frederick Baugh, Jr., Gn SW-NE-S12; 6-24-53
John Allen+ NE-NW-S12; 8-7-48
John York* SE-NW-S12; 10-23-57
William Ledgerwood* NW-NW-S12; 2-22-45
William Phillips, Gn SW-NW-S12; 9-20-48
Thomas Barker SW-S12; 7-26-48. MW
Joseph Knight, Gn NE-SE-S12; 5-3-55
Henry Rubottom* SE-SE-S12; 5-13-48; NW-SE-S12; 11-21-53
Asa M. Helphinstine* SW-SE-S12; 2-18-58
Reuben Mullis, Gn NE-NE-S13; 1-22-53
Henry V.M. Fisher SE-NE, W-NE, NW-NE-S13; 3-24-49. MW
William S. Turner SW-NW-S13; SE-NE-S14; 7-26-53
James Osburn Slumaker* NW-SW-S13; 6-13-49; NE-SW-S13; 6-18-49
Benjamin Potter Phipps* SW-SW-S13; 4-7-49
John R. Gibson* NE-SE-S13; 10-27-49. MLW
William J. Morgan* SE-SE, SE-SW, SW-SE-S13; 10-2-54
Pierson Wagley NE-NE-S14; 2-7-53

Dawson Elliott W-NE-S14; 10-18-51. MLW
Jesse Morgan* NE-NW, NW-NW-S14; 10-2-54
Solomon York* SE-NW-S14; 12-31-38
Jesse Robertson* SW-NW-S14; 3-11-36
William Gatewood* NE-SW-S14; 4-19-37
John Wilson* SE-SW, NW-SW-S14; 2-11-52; SE-SW-S15; 4-18-39; NE-NE-
Solomon Soalberry York* SW-SW-S14; 2-13-45   S17;10-24-51
Robert Gatewood* SE-SE-S14; 12-28-38; NW-SE-S14; 3-11-36
Moses Shumaker* SW-SE-S14; 11-25-39
John York* SE-NE-S15; 1-26-44
James Wooden Clawson, Mt NW-NE-S15; 3-11-39
Leroy Wilson* NW-NW-S15; 12-24-35
George Wilson* SW-NW-S15; 3-4-37; NE-NE-S21; 8-4-35
Emsle Odell* NE-SW-S15; 3-15-45
William Cunningham* SW-SW-S15; 8-16-39
Samuel Brummit, Gn SE-SE-S15; 10-15-36
William Brummit* SW-SE-S15; 6-9-49; W-NE-S22; 11-22-38
John Kitchen Dawson, Ru SW-NE, W-SE-S17; 9-30-37
Jacob Osborn* E-NW, NW-NW-S17; 3-18-36
George Osborn* SW-NW-S17; 11-25-38
Lewis Vales* NE-SW, NW-SW-S17; 10-6-36
Wilson Webster* SE-SW-S17; 1-19-39; NE-SW-S20; 2-20-36
Reuben Rainey, Lw E-SE-S17; 12-2-35. Of*, NE-NE-S20; 2-11-37
William Baker, Jr.* NE-NE-S18; 1-17-39
William Simpkins* SE-NE-S18; 9-21-44
James S. Courtney* NW-NE-S18; 6-12-40
William Perkins* SW-NE-S18; 2-11-47
John Cetchem* SE-NW-S18; 1-8-39
Lewis Phipps* W-NW-S18; 9-9-44
Elizabeth Smiley* NE-SW-S18; 1-1-39
David Washington Hum* SE-SW, SW-SE-S18; 6-16-37
James Moore SW-SW-S18; 5-18-37
Joseph Young* NE-SE-S18; 11-11-38
Benjamin L. Perkins* NW-SE-S18; 10-19-47
James Long* NE-NE-S19; 1-13-36
Baldwin Howard* SE-NE-S19; 1-24-36; SW-NW-S20; 1-15-36   20-36
John Ragle* NW-NE-S19; 12-5-36; SE-NW-S19; 7-16-47; NW-SE-S20; 2-
Alfred Heacox, Starke Co., O. SW-NE, SE-S19; W-SW-S20; 6-8-36
George W. Sherrow* NE-NW-S19; 5-3-47
Jesse Franklin Phipps* W-NW-S19; 9-17-47
Henry F. Earnest, Ru SE-NE-S20; 7-29-40
John Townsend* SW-NE-S20; 5-4-36
Joseph Young* NW-NW-S20; 3-29-36
Philip Keck* SE-SW-S20; 3-11-36
Amos Townsend, Starke Co., O. E-SE-S20; 6-8-36
Jacob Ketchem* SW-SE-S20; 4-1-46
William Travis Baloy* SE-NE-S21; 5-31-39; NW-NE-S21; 3-18-36;
    SW-NE-S21; 12-18-38
Baldwin Howard* E-NW-S21; 9-19-36; SE-SW-S21; 12-16-36; W-SW-S21;
Michael Razar* SW-NW-S21; 1-21-37   8-17-36
Daniel Rasar* NE-SW-S21; 9-19-36
Thomas Cunninghem, Ck NE-SE-S21; 12-9-39
Joseph John Sumner, Ck W-SE-S21; 8-16-39
Joseph Reaney* NE-NE-S22; 9-13-36

-47-

Littleton Jackson* NE-NW-S22; 4-18-39
Jonathan Cunningham, Ck SE-NW-S22; 9-13-48
William Cunningham, Ck W-NW-S22; 9-9-37. Of*, NW-SW-S22; 6-13-48
Andrew Hammersly* NE-SE-S22; 10-15-36. Of Or, SW-SW-S23; 3-18-36
Lorenzo Dow Sherrow* SE-SE-S22; 12-15-38
Benjamin Phipps* NE-NE-S23; 4-8-40. Of Lw, NE-NW-S24; 8-10-39;
Silas Roberts* SE-NE-S23; 2-1-39   W-NW-S24; 2-31-39
Michael Fisher* W-NE-S23; 1-23-39
William Gatewood* NE-NW-S23; 12-28-38
James Garten, Lw SE-NW, SE-SW, NW-SE-S23; 2-13-39; SW-NW-S23;
Paulser Smelser* NW-NW-S23; 3-11-36   10-2-39
John Bryner, Or NE-SW-S23; 3-18-36
Jacob Osborn* NW-SW-S23; 3-3-36
James Woodward* E-SE-S23; 11-1-38. Of Mr, SW-SW-S24; 12-11-38
Solomon Osburn Atchley* SW-SE-S23; 7-15-36
Joseph Gillis Loughlin W-NE, SE-NW, NW-SE-S24; 5-15-49. MLW
William McBride, Lw E-SE-S24; 12-28-38
John McBride, Lw SW-SE-S24; 2-5-39
William G. Harklet NE-NE-S25; 1-22-53
James Osborn* NW-NW-S25; 12-24-38
Solomon Osborn* SW-NW-S25; NE-SE-S26; 2-8-36
Daniel Ketcham, Cr SE-SW-S25; 7-15-59
Moses M. Carter* NW-SW-S25; 11-20-38
Robert Clark, Mr SW-SE-S25; 4-11-37
Thomas Nichols* E-NE-S26; 7-27-38
Simpson Woodward, Mr E-NW-S26; 12-11-38
George Reaney* W-NW-S26; 9-21-32; SE-NE-S27; 2-19-39
Jonas Baker, Mr E-SW, SW-SW, W-SE-S26; 4-9-39
James Hamersly* NW-SW-S26; 4-9-39
William Garten* NW-NW-S27; 10-25-44
William Hubbard, NE-SW, W-SW, NW-SE-S27; 5-18-49. MLW
Joseph Lafferty* SE-SW-S27; 4-15-39
Wesley Hubbard* NE-SE-S27; 4-23-50
Balden Howard* NW-NE-S28; 3-15-45; W-NW-S28; 8-17-36. Baldwin
William Rasar* SW-NE-S28; 12-30-44; SE-NW-S28; 2-11-43
Robert Field* NE-SW-S28; 7-15-36
Joseph Rainey* SE-SW-S28; 6-14-39
John Adams* NW-SE-S28; 10-26-44   6-8-36
Amos Townsend* E-NE-S29; 8-17-36. Of Starke Co., O., W-NE-S29;
John Townsend, Kn E-NW-S29; 4-4-36; Of*, W-NW, E-SW, W-SE-S29;
Leroy Wilson* W-SW-S29; 8-24-31   5-21-36
Joseph Hastings* NE-SW-S30; 2-25-45; E-NE-S31; 3-30-42
Phineas Cox* NW-SW-S30; 7-9-50
Jesse Trueblood, Lw SW-SW-S30;.1-13-51
Benjamin Coombs, Sz E-SE-S30; 8-20-23
William Gilmore, Sz W-SE-S30; 8-26-22
John Roddick* E-SE-S31; 6-29-31
Isaiah Johnston & Jonathan Johnston E-NE-S32; 6-28-36
William Farris* NW-NE-S32; 6-20-36
Isaiah Hastings* NW-SW-S32; 2-22-45   SW-S33; 10-26-39
Moses Overton* SE-SE-S32; 12-11-44. Of Lw, E-SW-S33; 6-14-39; SW-
Joseph McReynolds* NE-NW-S33; 8-20-39; NW-NW-S33; 1-12-37
Mathis Hams* SE-SE-S33; 7-19-44
Paul Fisher* SW-SE-S34; 8-22-39

John Nichols, Mr NE, NE-SE-S35; 4-9-39
Josias Baker, Mr NE-NW-S35; 4-9-39
Andrew Lee* SE-NW-S35; 10-21-33
Moses McCarter, Mr SE-SE-S35; 3-30-37; NW-S36; 3-25-37
John Kutch, Mr NE-S36; 4-11-37; SW-S36; 11-7-36
John Ketcham, Mr NE-S36; 3-28-37; NW-S36; 3-25-37
Philip Keck & Christian Keck SW, SE-S36; 11-7-36

                    RELINQUISHMENTS
Zebulon Jenkins SW-S4; 5-24-20

                    T 5 N, R 6 W

Daniel Harmon* NE-NE-S1; 4-2-39. Of Ws, E-SE-S1; 8-21-21
Isaac A. Chandler, Mr SE-NE-S1; 2-28-48
John Westley Ragsdale, Mr NW-NE-S1; 2-28-48
Robert M. Courtney* SW-NE-S1; 6-16-51
Samuel Pearson* E-NW-S1; 7-25-21
Joseph B. Vanmetre* NW-NW-S1; 1-28-48
Mathias Bennett* SW-NW-S1; 5-29-37
Thomas Brant Graham* SW-SE-S1; 4-10-39
William Sullivan, George W. Pratt, & George M. Thacher NE, NW,
    SE-S2; 3-6-37; SW-S2; 2-25-37; E-NW, SW, SE-S3; 7-16-36; NE-NE-
    S9; 3-6-37; W-NE-S9; 7-16-36; SE-S9; E-NE, NW-NW, E-SW, W-SE-
    S10; 2-25-37; E-SE-S17; E-E-Sfr-S19; S20; S21; NE, NW, SE-S30;
    7-16-36
Zepheniah Dunn, Gn E-NE-S3; 11-29-21; W-NE-S3; 11-1-22
Thomas Cobb* W-NW-S3; 7-7-29
Rezin Elmore* E-NEfr-S4; 4-23-28
Cary Tate* NW-NEfr-S4; 1-9-36
Jesse Cobb* SW-NEfr-S4; 8-12-36
Robert Mitchell, Lw Lot 1-NWfr-FrS4; 4-20-36
John Storms* Lot 2-NWfr-FrS4; 2-10-36
William Dillon* Lot 3-NWfr-FrS4; 4-15-36; NW-NW-S8; 6-4-35
Isaac Elmore SWfr-S4; 10-5-18; SE-NW-S9; 9-1-35--- of *
Jacob Wesner* NE-SEfr, NW-SEfr-S4; 6-25-32
Samuel Hensley McCullah SE-SEfr-S4; 11-8-33; SW-SEfr-S4; 11-17-32
Isaiah Johnston Lot 1-N-S-Efr-S7; 2-15-36
Richard Fulton Lot 2-N-S-Efr-S7; 2-6-36. Of Ow, S-S-Efr-S7; 3-16-
William Paddock & Solomon Dixon SW-S8; 9-18-16   31
Emanuel Vantrees SE-S8; SW-S9; 9-19-16
Beverly W. Dennis* SE-NE-S9; SW-NW-S10; 2-10-36
Stephen Elmore* NE-NW-S9; 2-15-36; W-NW-S9; 4-23-30
Andrew J. Fritts, Fl W-NE, E-NW-S10; 11-4-36
John Murphey* W-SW-S10; 1-7-31
Jacob Smiley* E-SE-S10; 10-29-36
John Autery SE-NE, W-NE, NW-SE-S11; 8-7-39
Silas Cetcham* SW-NW-S11; 1-31-37; NW-SW-S11; 2-10-34
Solomon Cetcham* NE-SW-S11; 2-10-34; SE-SE-S12; 3-7-37; NW-SE-S12;
Moses Ritter E-SE-S11; 3-8-20   3-31-46
William Moore* SW-SE-S11; 2-13-33; SW-SE-S12; 1-31-37
Nicholas Feltner* NE-NE-S12; 7-15-44
John Cadberry* SE-NE-S12; 4-2-39

Gideon Baker* NW-NE-S12; 3-26-50
John Smiley* SW-NE-S12; 8-10-47
James Robison* E-SW-S12; 7-24-27; E-NE-S14; 8-9-26; NE-NW-S13;
William Batchellor W-SW-S12; 10-12-16   6-6-33
Jonathan Smiley* NE-SE-S12; 5-23-37
James Moore* SE-NE-S13; 4-17-37; NE-SW-S13; 11-28-44
Joseph Robison* NW-NE-S13; 8-2-39
Elizabeth Smiley & James Sterling Autrey SW-NE-S13; 6-25-36
John K. Long* SE-NW-S13; 2-6-36
Edward Tate* W-NW-S13; 12-30-29
James S. Autrey* SE-SW-S13; 2-2-37; W-SW-S13; 10-29-38
John Murphey* W-NE-S14; 9-18-28
Isaac Dillon* SE-NW-S14; 11-12-34
Andrew Hannah* NE-SW-S14; 11-17-38; E-SE-Efr-S18; 9-29-24
Beverly W. Dennis* NE-SE-S14; 11-30-38
Cary Tate* SE-SE-S14; 3-18-36; W-NE-S23; 1-19-20
William Baker Dillon* W-SE-S14; 2-11-37
Marshall Cetcham* NE-NE-S15; 10-22-38
Nathan Hannah* NW-NE-S15; 8-17-38; Lot 1-NWfr-Efr-S18; 1-21-36
John Langden Allard, Jr., Fl NW-S15; 11-4-36
Edward Johnston NE, SW-S17; 9-19-16
Joseph Taylor NW-S17; 9-18-16
Jonathan Johnson* W-SE-S17; 6-17-31
Christopher Johnston & Isaiah Johnston E-NE-Efr-S18; 4-27-25
Christopher Johnston* W-NE-Efr-S18; 8-19-29
Jesse Cobbs* Lot 2-NWfr-Efr-S18; 2-11-36; Lot 2-E-W-Nfr-S19;
Thomas Cobb* N-SW-Efr-S18; 1-20-30   4-23-36
John Bray* S-SW-Efr-S18; 12-29-25
William Cobbs* W-SE-Efr-S18; 10-14-24
Winthrop Foot* Lots 1,4-E-E-Nfr-S19; 4-16-36
William Benham, Gn W-E-Nfr-S19; 6-30-26
Thomas Jefferson Singleton Lot 3-E-W-Nfr-S19; 1-11-39
Mary Hannah* W-W-Nfr-S19; 4-16-36
William Hannah Lot 8-W-E-Sfr-S19; 8-5-35
Eldad Stibbins, Hampshire Co., Me. Lot 9-W-E-Sfr; Lots 7,10-E-W-
    Sfr-S19; 3-31-36
Michael Yount* Lot 11-W-W-Sfr-S19; 4-14-36
Daniel Killon* Lot 6-W-W-Sfr-S19; 2-9-39
William Hastings* NE-NE-S23; 3-7-45; SE-NE-S23; 8-23-47
John Rogers Long* NE-SE-S23; 8-3-47; NW-SW-S24; 8-18-47
Phineas Cox SE-SE-S23; SE-SW, SW-SW-S24; NE-NW-S25; 9-23-50
Alexander Hannah NE-NE-S24; 9-5-44
Jacob Cetcham* NE-NW-S24; 1-8-34
Joseph V. Harrison* W-NW-S24; 2-24-30
Alexander Lamb SW-S25; 7-15-48
Wesley Elkins SE-S25; 6-13-48
Rufus Breed E-NE, E-SE-S29; E-NE, W-NW, W-SW; E-SE-S32; 5-19-49
John English* NE-SW-S30; 4-5-36; SE-SW-S30; 11-5-35
Alexander English* W-SW-S30; 10-24-25
Smith Cawood* NE-NW-S31; 4-5-36; NW-NW-S31; 8-25-34
Andrew J. Wells* SW-SE-S32; 2-6-50; SW-NE-S34; 3-5-49; E-SW,
    SE-SE, W-SE-S34; 2-28-49
John Denison Noble & Simpson Kilgore NE-NE-S34; 2-28-48
John Hastings* SE-NE, SE-NW-S34; 3-24-49

DAVIESS COUNTY

Jacob S. Grove* NE-SE-S34; 4-2-38
Joel Charles Dougherty, Lw SE-SW, SW-SW-S35; 2-3-37
Moses Jones, Mg E-SE-S35; 10-10-39
Benson Millian E-NE-S36; 10-17-51
Lewis Francis W-NE-S36; 10-17-51
James Dum NE-SE-S36; 10-17-51
Jeremiah Powell SE-SE-S36; 10-17-51

RELINQUISHMENTS

Moses Ritter W-SE-S11; 3-8-20
Edward Johnson E-SE, W-SE-S17; 9-18-16
:Robert Bratten E-W-Sfr, W-W-Sfr-S19; 4-1-16
Lazarus Ritter E-NW, W-NW-S24; 3-8-20
Isaac Elmore NEfr, NWfr-S4; SEfr-S4; Efr-S5; NW-S9; 10-5-18
James Ball NW-S8; 10-25-16
William Batchelor E-SW-S12; 10-12-16

T 5 N, R 7 W

John Langdon Allard, Fl Efr-S12; 11-4-36
Matthias Killion* SWfr-Efr, Efr-S23; S-SEfr-Efr-S24; 8-28-26;
   NWfr-Efr-S25; 3-1-26   (/ 12-3-25)
William Haynes* Lot 2-Nfr-S24; 6-29-36
John English* Lots 7-8-N-SEfr-Efr-S24; 2-8-36
J. (I.?) B. Homan Lots 1,3-Nfr-S24; 10-2-69. Might be in Kn Co.
David Snyder* E-SW-Efr-S25; 6-1-29; W-SW-Efr-S25; 1-4-26
Alexander English* E-SE-Efr-S25; 8-27-24; W-SE-Efr-S25; 1-4-26
Michael O'Connor* NE-NE-Efr-S25; 1-23-50
.James Barnes Lot 3-Nfr-S26; 4-28-36
William Killion Lots 4-5-NW-Sfr-S26; 4-4-36
Martin Grimsley* S-E-SW-Sfr-S26; 2-10-36
Jesse Buckner* SW-SW-Sfr-S26; 3-14-36
John Bray* Lot 7-E-E-Sfr-S26; 2-15-36
Thomas Cobb* Lot 8-E-E-Sfr-S26; 2-11-36.   W-SW-S36;10-6-29
Alexander English Lot 6-W-E-Sfr-S26; 9-21-36; NE-NE-S36;2-23-36;
·Andrew English Lot 9-W-E-Sfr-S26; 2-10-36
Joseph Marlatt* NE-SW-Sfr, NW-SW-Sfr-S26; 11-8-44; Lots 1-2-N-Efr,
· Lots 6-7-S-Efr-S27; 2-1-43
James Barnes Lots 3,12-NEfr-Sfr-S34; 2-12-36
Abraham Hoover NWfr-Sfr-S34; 7-19-36
William Lester* E-SW-Sfr, W-SW-Sfr-S34; 4-28-36
Alfred Simoson* NE-SE-Sfr, NW-SE-Sfr-S34; 10-1-38
John Lester* SE-SE-Sfr-S34; 7-11-32
John Lester & James Barnes SW-SE-Sfr-S34; 12-5-33
Eldad Stibbins, Hampshire Co., Mo. NE-NE-S35; 3-31-36   35
Daniel Miller* SE-NE-S35; 6-1-33; W-NE-S35; 4-23-36; NE-SE-S35;7-21
John Graham* E-NW-S35; 11-30-35
Henry Griffin* W-NW-S35; 12-7-35; E-NW-S36; 10-15-21.   10-27-32
,Nancy Ann & Louisa Jane Willis, heirs of Jesse Willis, decd. SW-S35;
William Sullivan,George W.Pratt,George M.Thacher SE-NE,W-NE,E-SW,
David Snyder, Kn W-NW-S36; 7-16-21   SE-S36;2-25-37
Jesse Buckner* SE-SE-S35; 5-17-36; SW-SE-S35; 1-1-38

T 1 N, R 10 W.

John Catt* Lot 2-Sfr-S17; 3-6-37
John G. Crow, Kn Lot 1-Sfr-S17; 5-20-37
Sparling Young* Wfr-S19; 6-20-36
Andrew Purcell, Kn Lots 3-4-Efr-S20; 4-17-37
Henry Sullivan* Lot 2-Efr-S20; 2-4-39
John Sullivan* Lot 1-N-N-Wfr-S21; 8-5-34; Lots 3-4-W-FrS27, N-Sfr-
Lewis Catt* Lot 2-N-N-Wfr-S21; 1-11-36   S30; 8-25-36
Henry O'Neill* S-N-Wfr-S21; 1-4-36; Lot 2-Efr-S28; 9-22-37
Adam Miller* Sfr-S21; 12-23-35; Lot 5-E-W-Sfr-S22; 10-2-37; Lot 7-
   W-W-Sfr-S22; 5-28-39; Lot 1-Efr-S28; 3-7-39
Andrew Cunningham* E-Sfr-S22; 8-22-38
James Sutphen Lot 8-E-W-Sfr-S22; 11-1-52. MLW 68319
Jarret Watkins* Lot 6-W-W-Sfr-S22; 9-22-37
Ransom Decker* NEfr-Efr-S23; 1-11-38
William Sullivan* NE-SEfr-Efr-S23; 1-7-57
James Oliphant, Pi SE-SEfr-Efr-S23; 11-6-49
Payton Phillips* W-SEfr-Efr-S23; Lot 2-Wfr-S24; Lot 1-FrS25;5-1-37
Elizabeth Decker* Lot 1-Wfr-S24; 1-16-36
Edwin Phillips* NE-NE-S26; 10-20-54
Andrew Phillips* SE-NE-S26; 10-31-36
Benjamin Hayes* NE-NW-S26; 10-13-51; NW-NE-S26; 7-21-52. MLW 6983
Roda Phillips* SW-NE-S26; 10-20-54; SE-NW-S26; 11-27-53; SWfr-S26;
Elias Sutphen, Vb NW-NW-S26; 10-27-54   12-27-56
James S. Hays* SW-NW-S26; 12-20-53; Lot 2-SEfr-S26; 3-3-54
Thomas J. Decker, Plaquemine Parish, La. E-Efr-S27; 6-12-52; Lot 2-
   W-Efr-S27; 6-3-52
Green Cunningham* Lot 5-W-Efr-S27; 9-18-37
James Dick, Kn Wfr-S28; 5-9-54
Thomas Westfall & Samuel Emison Nfr-S29; 1-20-35
John McGowen, Kn Nfr-S30; 4-30-36
John Brown* N-S-Sfr-S30; 7-11-35; Lots 3-4-S-S-Sfr-S30; 5-8-37;
   Lot 1-Nfr-S31; 1-12-35
William Brown* Lot 2-Nfr-S31; 11-3-35
Stephen Freeman* Lot 3-Sfr-S31; 1-23-37; Lot 4-Sfr-S31; 1-16-36
Joseph Manifold, Morgan Co., O. Sfr-S36; 5-28-39

T 1 N, R 11 W

Harrison Warth, Kn Lot 4-Efr-S24; 3-24-37
William Brown* Lot 11-S-Efr-S25; 11-3-35
John Brown* N-N-Efr-S36; 8-9-25; NW-SE-Efr-S36; 6-13-33
Henry Reel & Abel Stewart S-N-Efr, SWfr-Efr-S36; 4-6-18
Sparling Young* E-SE-Efr-S36; 4-28-25
Stephen Freeman* SW-SE-Efr-S36; 1-22-38

T 1 S, R 8 W

William Sullivan, George W. Pratt, & George M. Thacher SW, SE-
   S31; 10-16-36

Joseph Davisson & Elijah H. Davisson E-NE-S6; 8-21-17
Fielding Colvin* W-NE-S6; 4-4-35; SE-SE-S6; 5-7-39
Richard Colvin* NE-NW-S6; 10-26-35
Stephen Lewis* SE-NW-S6; 11-4-37
Joseph Manifield, Morgan Co., O. W-NW-S6; 5-28-39
John Jones* E-SW-S6; 11-3-37
James Bullard, Gennessee Co., N.Y. W-SW-S6; 6-20-37
Miles Yager* NE-SE-S6; 11-17-51
John McClelland Jones* E-NE-S7; 2-6-37
James Neely Phillips* SE-NW-S7; 2-13-37; NW-NE-S19; 10-26-37
John O'Naile* SW-S7; 8-28-17
Samuel Cunningham* NE-SE-S7; 10-11-38
Andrew Harvey* SE-SE-S7; 1-25-39   3-14-36
William Phillips* NW-SE-S7; 2-13-37; SW-S18; 10-4-13; SW-SE-S18;
John Phillips* SW-SE-S7; 1-12-39; SW, SE-S19; 9-3-18
Hugh Harris, York Dist., S.C. NE-S17; 9-7-36
William Moffatt, Chester Dist., S.C. NW-S17; 9-7-36
Jonathan Dillon* NE-SW-S17; 9-23-47
Hugh White Gardner* SE-SW-S17; 1-16-37; W-SW-S17; 5-18-36
Reuben Pemberton* E-SE, NW-SE, SW-SE-S17; 10-26-18
Alexander Harvey NE-S18; 9-3-13
Thomas Sullivan NW-S18; 4-17-13
Richard Mason Kirk* E-SE-S18; 9-6-36; W-NE, E-NW-S21; 8-20-36;
    E-SW-S21; 8-26-36; E-NE-S29; 4-16-33; W-NE-S29; 10-11-32;
    NE-NW, W-NW-S29; 3-15-36; SE-NW-S29; 4-16-33
William Harvey Phillips* NW-SE-S18; 2-13-37
William Paul* E-NE-S19; 5-20-37; W-NW, W-SW-S20; 5-17-37
William T. Coleman* SW-NE-S19; 10-16-37
George Bowman* NW-S19; 2-12-08
James Lessley NE-S20; 12-12-17
Samuel Caldwell Baldridge* E-NW-S20; 5-16-37
Edmund Kirk* NE-SW-S20; 11-9-36; W-SW-S21; 4-1-36
James Crow Kirk* SE-SW-S20; 4-1-36
William Robinson* SE-S20; 12-28-14
Jason H. Crow* NE-NE-S21; 3-29-47
William Routt* SE-NE-S21; 2-13-37
James Turner, Ru SE-S21; 7-20-36
William Richardson* NE-NE-S28; 12-1-34; SE-NE-S28; 12-11-35
Wiley Jones* W-NE-S28; 12-11-35; NW-SE-S28; 4-11-36; NE-NE-S30;
Elijah Smith* NE-NW-S28; 8-26-36   8-5-34
William Miller SE-NW, E-SW-S28; 10-11-49
Amzi Price* W-NW-S28; 7-5-36
Daniel Kirk W-SW-S28; 5-20-19
Calvin O'Neal* NE-SE-S28; 10-31-33
Thomas Jones* SE-SE-S28; 10-13-32; NE-NE-S33; 4-15-37
John Gardner* NE-SW-S29; 3-14-36
Henry Crow* NW-NE-S30; 4-9-36; SE-NW-S30; 8-31-48; NW-NW-S30;
    5-18-35; NE-NE-S31; 11-13-49
James Hussey* NE-NW-S30; 3-14-38
William Kurtz* E-SW-S30; 3-17-54
Demps Grigsby* E-SW-S32; 1-2-36

RELINQUISHMENTS

Jos. (Jas.?) Davisson & Elijah H. Davisson W-NE-S6; 8-21-17;
   4-8-25
William Norris E-SW-S17; 10-30-18; 8-25-21; W-SW-S17; 10-30-18;
Daniel Kirk E-SW-S28; 5-20-19; 9-10-21   9-22-24
William Robinson NE-S29; 12-28-14; 7-4-29

T 1 S, R 10 W

John Zimmerman* Lots 1-2-N-Nfr-S1; 9-20-36; Lot 3-S-Nfr-S1; 2-13-
William Wallace Wright, Pi Lot 5-N-Sfr-S1; 8-29-39   37
Benniah Cullick Mitchell* Lot 6-N-Sfr-S1; 9-20-37
William Ballenger, Mason Co., Ky. S-Sfr-S1; 3-22-24
Reuben Fields* Lot 1-N-FrS6; 1-27-37
Jonathan Walk* Lot 2-N-FrS6; 12-20-34
Elizabeth Hedges* S-FrS6; 11-17-28
George Humphreys* FrS7; 10-15-23; Nfr, NE-SWfr-S17; 8-14-44
William Price* Lots 1-2-N-Nfr-S12; 9-30-37
Auzi Price*Lot 4-S-Nfr-S12; 3-14-38
John Eanis* Lot 3-S-Nfr-S12; 2-6-37. Eaves? Ennis?
John Robinson* S-FrS12; 12-27-33
Alexander Nixon* Lot 1-N-FrS13, Lot 5-N-Sfr-S13; 9-12-36
Robert Nixon* Lot 2-N-FrS13;/Lot 3-N-FrS13, NEfr-S14; 8-21-34
     9-9-36
John A. Cullick* Lot 4-N-Sfr, NW-SW-S13; NE-SEfr-S14; 2-14-37
Jonathan Cullick* SW-SW-S13; SE-SEfr-S14; 9-12-36
Joseph Markle, Westmoreland Co., Pa. SEfr-S13; 5-21-38
Robert Kirk SWfr-S14; 3-19-36
Dickson Kirk* W-SEfr-S14; 9-7-36
Robert Philips* Lots 1-2-FrS15; 3-25-36; W-SEfr-S22; 9-12-28
Alexander Philips* Lot 3-FrS15; 9-19-48; Lots 1-2-N-Nfr-S21;
   Lots 2-3-NWfr-S22; 4-9-36
Shadrach Duncan* SE-SWfr-S17; 3-18-41; NE-NWfr-S20; 8-5-34; W-NWfr-
Joseph Humphreys* W-SWfr-S17; 8-5-34   S20; 1-6-38
Azza Harrison* SEfr-S17; 7-10-33
Elijah Humphreys* NEfr-S18; 4-22-24
Smith Miller* NWfr-S18; 8-5-34
David Milburn* E-SWfr-S18; 7-5-30; SW-SE-S18; 5-27-33; Efr-S19;
   6-14-36; Wfr-S19; 5-30-51
Hugh McFarland Griggs* W-SWfr-S18; 5-27-33
Nehemiah Fisher Pierce, Mason Co., Ky. E-SE-S18; 12-9-31
William Key, Jr.* NW-SE-S18; 8-5-34
Waitman Trippet* NEfr-S20; 10-14-39; S-Sfr-S21; 2-4-34; NE-NE-S28;
Archibald Spain* SE-NWfr-S20; 3-12-38   8-15-34
Linzey Hargrove* S-SWfr-S20; 1-11-37
John Tomson* Lots 3-4-S-Nfr-S21; 8-5-34
Alexander Trippet* N-Sfr-S21; 12-2-33; NE-SWfr-S22; 11-28-36;
   NW-NW-S27; 8-15-34
John Camm Moore* SE-SWfr-S22; 12-19-32; W-NE-S27; 9-18-37; NE-NW-
Henry Thompson* W-SWfr-S22; 7-18-29   S27; 5-23-36
John Lance* E-SEfr-S22; 10-14-34
Robert Falls* SE-NEfr-S23; 6-17-36

John Marshall* SW-NE-S23; 12-2-36
John Ames* NE-NWfr-S23; 11-5-39
James Mills* SE-NWfr, SW-NWfr-S23; 6-25-32; NW-SWfr-S23; 2-8-36
William Turpin* SW-SWfr-S23; 2-23-36
Andrew Lewis W-SEfr-S23; 12-13-53
Demps Grigsby* SE-SW, SW-SW-S25; 4-6-36
Robert Steven* NW-SW-S25; 3-28-36. Slavin? see below
Isaac Slavin* SE-SE-S25; 1-9-39. Steven? see above
John Zimmerman* SW-SE-S25; 7-2-32; E-NEfr-S32; 2-16-26
John Hall Finney* SW-NW-S26; 12-12-36
James Mekemson, St.Clair Co., Ill. SW-S26; 9-14-24
Joseph Wilks* E-SE-S26; 8-26-30
Henry Anderson McCartney* W-SE-S26; 12-3-31
Anson White* E-NE-S27; 3-22-31
Stewart Cunningham* SE-NW, SW-NW-S27; 1-26-39
Milo Townsend* E-SW-S27; 3-23-30; E-NW-S34; 4-11-36
Susan Townsend* NW-SW-S27; 5-27-39
Erastus Townsend & Milo Townsend SW-SW-S27; 9-15-34
John Carter, New York SE-S27; 7-5-21
Caleb Trippet* SE-NE-S28; 11-8-38
Daniel Kirk* W-NE-S28; 9-17-22
Edward Moore* E-NWfr-S29; 8-6-35
James Hudleson* W-NWfr-S28; 8-15-35
Robert Brownlee* NE-SW-S28; 3-15-50
Erastus Dean Townsend* SE-SW-S28; 6-25-28; W-SW-S28; 8-12-31
Samuel Shannon* E-SE-S28; 3-9-25   10-31-28
Erastus Townsend* W-SE-S28; 7-21-27; E-NE-S33; 7-26-27; W-NE-S33;/
Samuel Ayers Stewart* NEfr-S29; 8-5-34; E-NWfr-S29; 9-26-31
Linzey Hargrove* Lot 1-W-NWfr-S29; 9-6-39
William Leathers* Lot 2-W-NWfr-S29; 2-15-39; SWfr-S29; 1-23-35
John Hargrove* Nfr-S30; 6-15-35
John Berlin* Sfr-S30; 10-9-26
James Lynn* N-NEfr-S31; 7-26-28
Joseph R. Brown* S-NEfr-S31; 10-14-28
William Lethom* Wfr-S31; 7-12-26
George Brownlee* SEfr-S31; SWfr, SEfr-S32; 6-29-21
Andrew J. Crawford, Wk W-NE-S32; 7-20-26; E-NW-S32; 11-12-27;
    of*, W-NWfr-S32; 6-29-21
John Munford, Wk E-NW-S33; 11-19-25
Robert Farr* NW-NW-S33; 9-14-33
Daniel Zimmerman* SW-NW-S33; 4-22-36
Nancy Boswell* E-SW-S33; 8-24-29
James Boswell* W-SW-S33; 8-8-29
William Boswell* SE-S33; 7-18-28
Joseph Mekemson* E-NE-S34; 1-6-36   11-23-37
John Christy, Washington Co., Pa. W-NE-S34; 3-15-38; E-SW-S34;
Benjamin Whitsett* NW-NW-S34; 9-9-46; SW-NW-S34; 12-10-44
Hugh McMullin* W-SW-S34; 3-10-29
Richard Daniel* E-SE-S34; 1-12-22
Andrew Carrithers* NW-SE-S34; 2-4-37
Henry Boswell* SW-SE-S34; 2-19-36; NW-SW-S35; 2-11-36
Thomas Hosack, Wk E-NE-S35; SW-NW-S36; 6-15-36; of*, NW-NW-S36;
Henry Anderson McCartney* W-NE-S35; 12-3-31   9-10-33
William Turpin* E-NW, SW-NW-S35; 3-23-36

William Storment* NW-NW-S35; 6-28-36
Eli Alexander Williams* NE-SW-S35; 3-5-34
George Humphreys, Jr.* SE-SW-S35; 4-11-36
John Lance* SW-SW-S35; 9-5-32
Isaac Slevin* NE-SE-S35; 9-9-35
Thomas Harbison* SE-SE-S35; 6-23-38
William Terry* W-SE-S35; 6-23-26
Michael Redburn* NW-NE-S36; 6-10-36; SW-NE-S36; 4-8-36
Shelton Dawson* NE-NW-S36; 4-15-39
John Doson* SE-NW, NE-SW-S36; 6-17-36
Smith Dawson* SE-SW-S36; 7-10-37
William Redburn* NW-SW, NW-SE-S36; 6-8-36
Simeon Lemaster* SW-SW-S36; 12-15-35
George Grigsby* SW-SE-S36; 11-2-36

T 1 S, R 11 W

Peter Snyder Miller* N-E-NE-Efr-S1; 1-11-36
William A. Hood SE-NE-Efr-S1; 5-6-52   see
Abraham Fields* W-NE-Efr-S1; 3-12-36; NWfr-Efr-S1; 3-14-37 # below
Keen Field* Lot 5-S-SW-Efr-S1; 7-5-36
William Martin* Lot 7-S-SW-Efr-S1; 3-2-48
John Leach* Lot 6-S-SW-Efr-S1; 5-16-36; NEfr-Sfr-S10; 9-12-31
Keen W. Field* SW-SEfr-S1; 6-21-55
John Brown* Efr-S2; 3-15-36
Joseph Shields, Kn Sfr-S5; 11-18-53
Scoby Stewart, Wabash Co., Ill. Efr-S7; 1-28-37
Ezekiel Field* Lot 1-E-NE-Efr-S8; 7-14-36
Samuel & Emanuel Meisenhelter, Adams Co., Pa. Lots 3-4-E-NE-Efr-
Joseph Devin* Lot 8-E-NE-Efr-S8; 12-9-53.   S8; 12-5-53;
Cary Allen Milburn* Lot 6-E-NW-Efr-S8;   Emanuel of Kn
   12-29-35; Lot 5-W-NW-Efr-S8; 12-29-35.
John Milburn* NE-SW-Efr-, Lot 9-SW-Efr-S8; 11-2-35
Patrick Payne* SE-SW-Efr-S8; 4-22-35; SW-SE-Efr-S8; 11-9-36
William Daniel* NEfr-Sfr, Lots 1-2-E-SEfr-Sfr-S9; 4-29-37; W-W-
   Sfr-S10; 6-6-36
Nathaniel Prince* SE-SW-Sfr, SW-SW-Sfr-S9; 7-21-37
Samuel Hall* SW-SEfr-Sfr-S9; 12-20-38
Stephen Lewis Field* Lot 3-E-W-Sfr-S10; 5-19-38
George Cornwell, Orange Co., N.Y. Lot 6-E-W-Sfr-S10; 2-24-54
Uriah Humphreys* E-SE-Sfr-S10; 1-11-38; Lot 3-E-SWfr-Sfr, NW-SWfr-
Hugh McFarlin Griggs* Lot 1-E-E-Sfr-S11; 2-4-37.(Sfr-S11;7-4-36.
Daniel Catlin* Lot 6-E-E-Sfr-S11; 11-14-37.
Reuben Fields* NWfr-Sfr-S11; 3-20-30. (#Lot 4-N-SW-Efr-S1;3-18-36;
Lucy Brittonham* W-SW-Efr-S17; 8-8-31. (SE-SEfr-S1;3-12-36;
William Howe* SE-SE, SW-SE-S17; 2-18-36. (W-SEfr-S1;8-30-47.)
Robert Steen* NE-SE, NW-SE-S17; 6-6-36.   see above#
Samuel Gordon Sfr-S18; 4-9-12
Robert Lucas, Sr., Wabash Co., Ill. N-NE-S19; 5-18-33
John Lucas* NE-NW-S19; 5-9-33
William Gordon W-NW-S19; 2-24-19
Adam Orr* NW-SW-S19; 2-16-50
William Greathouse, Vb E-NE-S20; 6-23-36

John Miller, Vb W-NE-S20; 10-10-36
Abner Landsdown & Thomas Sanders Evans NE-NW-S20; 3-11-36
Cornelius McCullom, Clermont Co., O. W-NW-S20; 7-24-20
William P. Witherspoon* NE-NE-S21; 10-27-48
John Ulm* NW-NE-S21; 4-11-36
Thomas Alvis* NE-NW-S21; 3-14-36
William Burtch, Kn SE-NW-S21; SW-NE-S22; 1-4-54
William Greathouse, Vb W-NW-S21; 6-23-36
James Adams* NE-NE, NW-NE-S22; 5-21-32
Richard Sloan* SE-NE-S22; 12-14-36
Meredith Jones Bracher* NE-SE-S22; 4-23-39
Thomas Martin* NE-NE-S23; 10-12-32; NW-NE-S23; 5-11-35
Abraham Bruner* SE-NE-S23; 10-15-36
Sylvester J. Jerauld* SW-NE-S23; 1-6-52
Andrew Culbertson* E-NW-S23; 11-19-28
Abel Stewart* NW-NW-S23; 4-22-33
Robert Steen* SW-NW-S23; 1-6-36
John Bruner E-SW-S23; 1-5-18
Charles Evins* NW-SW-S23; 7-20-36
Thomas Sanders Evans* SW-SW-S23; 4-25-39
George Humphreys* E-SE-S23; 8-29-31; NE-S25; 10-13-12; SW-S25;1-28-
Frederick Brunner W-SE-S23; 4-21-15   14
Robert Mosely NE-S24; 5-18-07
Nathaniel Ewing NW-S24; 4-17-13
Samuel Adams SW-S24; 2-18-08
John A. Miller SE-S24; NW-S25; NE-S26; 5-18-07; NE-S35; 5-18-07
William Lathom SE-S25; 4-19-13
Andrew Nixon* E-NW-S26; 2-2-37
Mordecai Price* NW-NW-S26; 8-9-37
William Johnson* SW-NW-S26; 4-30-39; NE-SW-S26; 8-5-34
James Lynn* SE-SW-S26; 3-14-33
John Decker* NW-SW-S26; 2-11-37; SW-SW-S26; 3-16-37
Alexander Devin E-SE-S26; 4-17-13
Isum Lynn* NW-SE-S26; 2-15-36; SW-SE-S26; 6-4-32
John Decker & William Miln* E-SW-S27; 3-16-37
Wesley Jones* SE-SE-S27; 1-30-50
Charles Harrington* SW-SE-S27; 3-10-37
John Riley* SE-NE-S28; 8-6-47
Thomas McDaniel* SE-SW-S28; 11-22-50
John Lagow* SW-SE-S29; 11-28-50
Patrick Mumey, Orleans Co., La. N-NW-NW-S31; 2-1-51. Mooney?
John W. Morris* SE-NE-S32; 11-27-50
Alexander King* NE-SE-S32; 11-23-50; NW-SE-S32; 11-3-50
Elias Roberts, Ps NE-NE, NW-NE-S33; 10-21-47; SW-NE-S33; 1-22-48
Thomas McMullen* SE-NE-S33; 4-10-47; NE-SE-S33; 9-5-48; SW-NW,
    SE-SW, W-SW-S34; 4-10-47
Joseph Deim* SE-NW-S33; 11-28-50. Devin?
Wiley Day* NW-NW-S33; 11-13-50
Mark Day* SW-NW-S33; 11-13-50
Alexander King* NW-SW-S33; 12-3-50
George Humphreys NE-S34; 3-7-08; NW-S35; 1-12-08
David Stormont* NE-NW-S34; 10-21-47
Thomas Manning* SE-NW-S34; 12-11-35
Calvin Minnis* SE-S34; 2-14-15

GIBSON COUNTY

Robert Stormont SW-S35; 10-19-13
Walter Taylor SE-S35; 5-20-07
John Fisher NE-S36; 5-18-07
Absolam Lynn NW-S36; 5-18-07
William Hargrove SW-S36; 5-18-07
Jeremiah Harrison SE-S36; 6-2-07

RELINQUISHMENTS

Joseph Humphreys E-NE-S14; 10-29-18; 7-30-21; W-NE-S14; 10-29-18;
William Gordon E-NW-S19; 2-24-19; 2-1-25   1-29-27
Rodom Kinnar E-NE-S23; 10-5-18; 6-4-27
Robert Mosely NW-S23; 12-17-16; 10-22-24
Frederick Bruner E-SE-S23; 4-24-15; 4-9-25
George Ish SW-S26; 6-20-16; 9-9-29
Alexander Devin W-SE-S26; 4-17-13; 9-5-21
James Breading E-NW, W-NW, SW, W-SE-S12; 10-5-16; 9-28-21; W-NE,
    E-SE-S12; 10-5-16; 12-16-26

T 1 S, R 12 W

Conrad Crum Sfr-S13; 10-16-17; FrS24; 10-16-17
Thomas L. Hinde & William McDowell Efr-S21; Lot 1-Sfr-S22; 3-4-17
James Pleasant Terrel Lot 2-Sfr-S22; 10-13-32
Walter & James Pleasant Terrel Lot 3-Sfr-S22; 11-12-31
Robert C. Hatton, Wabash Co., Ill. Lot 4-Sfr-S22; 5-17-32
George Humphreys NW-S25; 10-24-16
William Moore* NE-SW-S25; 6-13-40
Jacob Johnson* SE-SW-S25; 11-15-42; NW-SW-S25; 10-23-37;SW-SE-S26;
John Sharp* SW-SW-S25; 11-11-35   9-28-35
Philip Smith* SE-NW, NE-SW-S26; 1-18-36
Ephraim Wonzer* SE-SE-S26; 10-8-35
Thomas Key* NE-NE-S27; 10-15-36; NW-NE-S27; 7-14-36
Mary Taylor* E-NW-S27; 10-22-36   11-17-35
Scoby Stewart, Wabash Co., Ill. NW-NW-S27; 11-11-35; SW-NW-S27;/
Harvey Batenline* NW-SW-S27; 10-22-36; SW-SW-S27; 12-2-44. Balen-
James Sproul, Su N-Efr-S28; 10-3-28   .   tine
Harvey Balentine, D.T. Cavanaugh, & T.S. Hinde N-S-Efr-S28;1-10-31
Harvey Balentine* Lots 1-2-3-S-Efr-S28; 8-5-34; NWfr-S33; 10-19-35
Thomas Gwin* FrS32; 2-13-22
Joseph Diven* NE-NEfr-S33; NW-NW-S34; 10-14-47. Devin?
William Sharp, Jr.* SE-NEfr-S33; 1-11-36; SW-NW-S34; 1-29-39
Scoby Stewart & Abraham Russell W-NEfr-S33; 10-8-36
Charles Clark Kneipp, Wabash Co., Ill. E-SWfr-S33; 5-24-37
Mary Taylor* NW-SW-S33; 6-1-36
John Mock* E-SEfr-S33; 9-5-34
John Black* NW-SEfr-S33; 8-8-36
Harris Sharp* NE-SW-S34; 9-24-34
James Sharp* SE-SW-S34; 10-17-32; NW-SW-S34; 5-31-33
Hiram Bell, Wabash Co., Ill. SW-SW-S34; 5-27-33
George Humphreys, Sr. NE-S55; 11-6-19
John Burket* NE-NW-S35; 9-14-35
James Moore Sharp, Wabash Co., Ill. SE-NW-S35; 1-14-36

William Hamilton, Hopkins Co., Ky. E-NW-S36; 10-17-42
Elijah Melton* NW-NW-S36; 4-14-37

RELINQUISHMENTS

T.S. Hinde & W. McDowell Efr side-S22; FrS28; 3-4-17; 9-1-21

T 2 S, R 8 W

Page Coleman, Pi SE-NE-S5; 4-4-36
William Kurtz* NW-NE-S5; 2-20-53
John Ore¹ SW-NE-S5; 2-10-53
Henry O. Babcock & Horatio Q. Wheeler E-SW-S5; E-NW-S8; 7-16-53
William & Alvin Bacon Carpenter W-SW-S5; 10-20-38
Joseph Rutledge Brown* E-SE-S5; 4-11-36; E-NE-S7; 4-8-36; W-NW-
   S8; 4-6-36
William Sullivan, George W. Pratt, & George M. Thacher NE-S6;
   10-14-36; W-NE, W-SE-S7; 3-6-37
James Washington Cockrum* NE-NW-S6; 6-6-36; SW-S6; 4-23-36; E-SE-
   S6; 10-26-36; W-SE-S6; 4-26-36; E-SE-S7; SW-SW-S8; 4-19-36;
   W-NE-S17; 4-23-29; NW-SW-S17; 4-18-36; W-NE, NE-SW, W-SW, NE-SE-
Columbus Cockrum* SE-NW, SW-NW-S6; 4-26-36.   S18; 4-19-36
David Barnes* NW-NW-S6; 4-23-36
John T. Walker NW-S7; 4-21-48; NE-S29; 4-21-48
Joseph Howe Montgomery* SE-NE-S8; 4-11-36; NE-SE-S8; 4-15-36
Joseph P. Elliott W-NE-S8; 7-30-53
Harrison Lathom* NW-SW-S8; 3-25-36
Jacob Warrick Hargrove* SE-SE-S8; 12-6-53; E-NE-S17; 7-25-53
William Hargrove* NE-NW-S17; 10-5-36; SE-NW-S17; 6-2-35; W-SE-S17;
   5-24-37
Martin Gnat Clark Hargrove* (2 men?) W-NW-S17; 2-13-36; SW-SW-
   S17; 5-24-37. Marsten, not Martin, in 2nd entry
Elisha Embree* NE-NE-S8; E-SW-S17; E-NE, W-SE-S18; E-SE-S19; 4-18-
Isaac Montgomery* NW-S18; 11-17-19; S20; 2-19-19.   36
Richard Miles Barrett* SE-SW-S18; 8-9-33
Holly Crawford* NE-NE-S19; 10-30-50; SE-NE-S19; 8-15-49
John Nichol, Gn W-NE-S19; 3-26-39
John Nichol Johnson, Belmont Co., O. SW, W-SE-S19; 3-26-89
Thomas Watt, Gn E-NW-S29; 11-5-39
James Mason, Pi NE-SW-S29; 2-19-40
David Mason, Pi SE-SW, SW-SE-S29; 6-1-39
Rufus Breed NE-SE-S29; 6-6-49. MLW 51462
David Farris* SE-SE-S29; 10-23-47
Willis Howe* NW-SE-S29; 6-24-36
Thomas Collins* NE-NE-S30; 9-14-49; NW-NE-S30; 8-15-49
Albert Loomis* SE-NE-S30; 9-13-47
William Nossett* SW-NE-S30; 9-13-47
Matthew Kell* NE-SW-S30; 4-7-37; SE-SW-S30; 6-17-36
James Kell* NW-SW-S30; 6-7-47
Archibald Kell* NE-NE-S31; 4-7-37
William Cravens* NW-NE-S31; 6-8-36; NE-NW-S31; 2-2-37; |NW-NE-S32;
Lucy Mitchell SW-NW-S31; 7-31-51. MLW 9659.   4-16-47
William Reynolds, Alleghany Co., Pa. SW-S31; 5-13-37

George Menoun Watt, Green Co., O. E-SE-S31; NW-SW-S32; 11-23-38
Isaac Farmer* SW-SE-S31; 5-18-37
Johnson Wheeler* NE-NE-S32; 3-3-48; SE-NE-S32; 4-13-49
James Minnis* SW-NE-S32; 5-17-50
Hugh Watt, Greene Co., O. E-SW, W-SE-S32; 11-23-38
Philemon Dill* SW-SW-S32; 11-18-36
Thomas Bell* E-SE-S32; 8-9-39

RELINQUISHMENTS

Isaac Montgomery SW-S18; 2-19-19; 3-28-25
Timothy Mayhall & James Lessley W-NW-S19; 3-5-19; 9-8-21; E-NW-
    S19; 3-5-19; 3-28-25
David Huddleston, Jr. NE-S31; 10-19-19; 3-28-25
John J. Mors E-SE-S8; 7-26-17; 2-14-25
James Cockrum SW-S17; 2-1-19; 3-28-25
Michael Melton W-SE-S17; 2-8-19; 1-29-27   21
William B. Dimick NE-S19; 8-17-18; 3-28-25; SE-S19; 8-17-18; 9-13-
John Fleener & John Devin SE-S30; W-NE-S31; 12-5-18; 9-8-21

T 2 S, R 9 W

William A. McDowell NE, SW-S1; 7-30-50. MLW
James Washington Cockrum* E-SE-S1; 4-28-36
Solomon Dill* SE-SW-S2; 11-29-50
Josephus Potter* SW-SW-S2; 1-7-50
William Reans, Jr. SW-S3; 6-20-49. MLW. Undoubtedly Reavis
Thomas Potter* SE-S3; 6-15-36
Fleming Farmer* NE-SW-S4; 11-14-38; SW-SW-S4; 1-14-35
Craven Boswell* SE-SW-S4; 7-11-33
William Farmer* NW-SW-S4; 5-18-35
Samuel Moore* SE-NE-S5; 5-18-35
David Johnson* SW-NE-S5; 4-17-33; E-NW-S5; 10-28-39; W-NW-S5;
    9-5-49; NE-SW-S5; 5-18-35; SE-S5; 7-26-17
Miles Terry* W-SW-S5; 2-3-37; NW-NW-S9; 3-4-33
William Embree* W-NW-S6; 6-17-36
George Humphreys, Jr.* SE-SW-S6; 2-4-36
William Lawrence, Green Co., O. W-SW-S6; 9-24-32
Randolph West SE-S6; NW-S7; 10-13-18
Simeon Lemasters* NW-NE-S7; 2-19-36; E-SW-S8; 10-6-38
Purnell Truitt* NE-SW-S7; 9-21-36; NW-SW-S7; Aug. - 34
Willard Carpenter SE-SW, SW-SW-S7; 6-20-53
James McClellan* NE-SE-S7; 1-3-51; of Green Co., O., E-NE, SW-NE-
Lewis Johnson* SE-SE-S7; 10-20-32   S8; 10-22-38.
Nancy Barber* SW-SE-S7; 7-18-36
William Graham Taylor* NW-NE-S8; Dec. - 34; E-NW-S8; 6-8-26
Joseph McClellan* SW-SW-S8; 6-16-36.
William Lathom* E-SE-S8; 3-14-36
John J. Mors W-SE-S8; 7-26-17
William Kurtz* SW-NE-S9; 4-4-55
Henry Fin Coleman* NE-NW-S9; 12-8-34
James Finney, Jr.* NW-SW-S9; 9-26-38
Absalom Potter* NE-NE, NW-NE-S10; 8-30-36

Elisha Embree* SW-NE-S10; 6-2-38; E-SW, W-SE-S10; 4-22-36; E-SW,
Robert Rowe* E-NW-S10; 8-5-36   W-SE-S11; 5-11-36
Fleming Farmer* NW-SW-S10; 7-19-47; SW-SW-S10; 4-2-49
Eli Bigham* E-SE-S10; 6-2-38
Francis Borland* E-NE-S11; W-NW-S12; 6-26-38; of Bristol Co.,
    Mass., SW-S12; W-NE, NW, E-SW, W-SE-S13; 6-19-37; of*, W-SW-S13;
Thomas Harper* SW-NE-S11;12-13-48;SE-NW-S11;10-12-39.   8-17-37
John Harper* NW-NW-S11; 12-7-38
William Griffith* SE-SE-S11; NE-NE-S14; 6-5-41
James Washington Cockrum* E-NE-S13; 4-19-36
Solomon Dill* SE-NE-S14; 3-8-47
Charles F. Elwyn* NW-NE-S14; 9-27-47
Calvin Minis* SW-NE-S14; 7-19-47; NW-SE-S14; 9-5-44
Farris Farmer* SW-SW-S14; 10-18-39; NE-NE-S22;8-4-49;SE-NE-S22;
William Jarrel, Jr.* NE-SE-S14; 8-5-39   2-13-47
William Stewart Duncan* SE-SE-S14; 1-30-40
Sanford Ramay Parker* NE-NE-S15; 6-30-47; NW-NE-S15; 3-2-50
William Graham Taylor* NE-NE-S17; 11-14-38
Alexander Dill* SE-NE-S17; 7-15-48
John Hoge* W-NE-S17; 3-1-37
James R. Utley* NW-S17; 9-5-49
Seth C. Eggleston* NE-SW-S17; 9-5-37; SE-SW-S17; 7-24-37
Thomas Burchfield* SW-SW-S17; 1-20-36; NW-SE-S19; 3-19-36
Michael Melton E-SE-S17; 2-8-19
James McClellan SW-SE-S17; 12-2-34
Joseph McClellan* NE-S18; 10-19-33
James Moore Wilson, Alleghany Co., Pa. SE-NW, SW-NW-S18; 5-19-36
John McConnell* E-SW-S18; 11-17-35; of Gn, SW-SW-S18; 6-11-35
Daniel Mills* NW-SW-S18; 10-17-32
Jonathan Curry* NE-SE-S18; 6-27-36; NW-SE-S18; 12-22-35
John Perkins* SE-SE-S18; 9-26-50
Joseph Rutledge Brown* SW-SE-S18; 5-2-36
James White Dorrell* NE-NE-S19; 7-1-33; NW-NE-S19; 4-22-33; see
    note after following entry
Thomas Burchfield* SE-NE, SW-NE-S19; 8-5-34. .Note at bottom of
    page: S-NE-S19 entered on Aug. 31, 1836 by James White Dorrell,
    who proved a pre-emption to said tract, which proof was approved
    by the Comr. See his letter of July 14, 1836. (152)
William Foster, Green Co., O. E-NW, SE-SW, SW-SW-S19; 2-19-36
William Reavis* W-NW-S19; 4-5-36; NE-SW, NW-SW-S19; 1-20-36;SW-SE-
Hardy Beasley* E-SE-S19; 8-15-34.   S19; 5-19-36
Joseph Manning NE-S20; 11-27-19
James Cockrum NW-S20; 8-15-18
William Harrington SW-S20; 9-15-18
John H. Vickers* NE-SE-S20; 3-19-40
Commodore Perry Brown* NW-SE-S20; 3-10-49
Francis Marion Manning* SW-SE-S20; 3-10-49
William Manning* SW-NE-S21; 11-27-37
James McGrady Downey, Vb NE-NW, NW-NW-S21; 12-20-47
Joseph M. Duff* SE-NW-S21; 1-4-51
Andrew Duncan, Green Co., O. SW-NW, E-SW-S21; 3-16-39
John Cox* NW-SW-S21; 4-25-36; SW-SW-S21; 7-16-33
William Skelton* NW-NE-S22; 10-10-50
James Sampson Wallace* SW-NE-S22; 9-28-47

John T. Walker SW-S22; 4-21-48. MLW. Wallace? see below
William Reavis, Jr. E-NE-S23; 2-7-53. MLW
John Taylor Wallace* NW-NE-S23; 7-11-49; SW-NE-S23; 3-15-47; see
Thomas Minnis* SE-NW-S23; 6-20-36   Walker above
James Minnis* SW-NW-S23; 6-24-39
Calvin Minnis* NE-SW-S23; 6-24-39   11-1-36
Robert Harper* W-SW-S23; 6-19-39; SE-NE-S26; 4-7-37; SW-NE-S26;
Rufus Breed* NE-S24; NE-S25; NE-S27; 6-6-49. MLW 45665
Henry Coleman* NE-NW-S24; 10-14-48
William Stewart Duncan* NW-NW-S24; 1-30-40
Andrew Gudgel* NE-SW-S25; 9-7-49; W-SW-S25; 9-16-47
Robert Steele* NW-NE-S26; 4-1-37
William Dill* NE-SW-S26; 6-7-49; NW-NW-S26; 2-13-47; SW-NW-S26;
William Harper* SE-NW-S26; 7-30-49   7-15-48
Samuel McDill* SW-S26; 4-1-37
John Arbuthews NE-SW-S27; 9-18-51. MLW 16135
William Chesterfield Barrett* NW-SW-S27; 3-8-50
Lucinda Barrett* SW-SW-S27; 5-7-40; NE-SE-S28; 4-1-37
James B. McGarrah E-SE-S27; 11-7-17
Samuel G. Barrett* SE-NE-S28; 8-29-51
Nathan Breedlove* NE-NW-S28; 2-18-39
William Hamilton* W-NW-S28; E-NE-S29; 11-3-38
Jonathan Curry* E-SW, W-SE-S28; 11-17-36
Ann Wilson* W-SW-S28; E-SE-S29; 11-10-36
William Barrett* SE-SE-S28; 4-8-36; NE-NE-S33; 7-20-33
John Davis* NE-NW-S29; 8-21-39
Hardy Beasley* SE-NW-S29; 10-24-49
John Devin* E-SW-S29; 9-14-31
Thomas Beasley* W-SW-S29; 8-15-36; W-SE-S29; 10-26-36; NW-NE-S32;
William Wood* NE-NE-S30; 7-13-47; SW-NE-S30; 1-9-50.   1-29-39
George Hederick* SE-NE-S30; 12-14-50
William Reavis* E-NW-S30; 3-3-36; W-NW-S30; 1-8-18; W-SW-S30;
Jordan Perseley Cockrum, Vb SE-SE, SW-SE-S30; 8-18-36.   8-18-36
John Fleener & James Devin E-NE-S31; 12-5-18
James Devin* W-NE-S31; 9-14-31
James Skelton, Sr.* SE-NW-S31; 6-17-36
James Skelton* W-NW-S31; 6-19-26; NE-SW-S31; 2-9-36
Tabitha Reavis* SE-SW-S31; 10-12-36
Thomas Childress* SW-SW-S31; 2-9-36
John T. Walker, assoc. of Joseph Hewey SE-S31; 12-20-47. MLW
William Wilson* SW-NE-S32; 8-17-38
James Wilson* E-NW-S32; 11-10-36
David Barber* NW-NW-S32; 9-5-36
William Reavis, Jr. NE-SE, W-SE-S32; 6-20-49. MLW 57916. W-SW-
    S33; 8-4-49; SW-S33; 10-19-50
James McConnell* SE-SE-S32; 10-14-39
William Skelton, Jr.* SE-NE-S33; 8-17-49
Ellen Wilson* W-NE, E-NW-S33; 11-10-36
Joseph Pringal Sterrett* E-SW-S33; 7-16-42
Joseph R. Brown NE-S34; 1-7-17
John Farmer* E-NW-S34; 7-11-39; NE-SE-S34; 11-9-35; NW-SE-S34;
    11-7-36; W-NW-S35; 3-23-37
John Washington Barrett* NW-NW-S34; 11-9-36
William Williams* SW-NW, SE-SW, W-SW-S34; 8-17-48. MLW

Samuel Hall* NE-SW-S34; 10-4-47
Elijah Walton Harper* NE-NE-S35; 3-6-50
Elihu McCulloch* SE-NE-S35; 9-27-36
Adam Brown Harper* W-NE-S35; 4-1-37
Robert Steel* NE-NW-S35; 4-1-37
John Crawford White* SE-NW-S35; 6-5-49
Jane P. McCulloch* E-SE-S35; 9-27-36
William Harvey Harper* SE-NW-S36; 6-19-38; SW-NW-S36; 7-8-39
Willard Carpenter NW-NW-S36; 6-21-53. MLW
Robert McConnell, Alleghany Co., Pa. E-SW, W-SE-S36; 12-6-36
Margaret McCulloch* W-SW-S36; 9-27-36
Elijah Coulter, Jr., Washington Co., Pa. E-SE-S36; 5-13-37

RELINQUISHMENTS

William Terry E-SW-S4; 3-2-19; 9-18-21; W-SW-S4; 3-2-19; 10-28-26
John J. Mors E-SE-S8; 7-26-17; 2-14-25
James Cockrum SW-S17; 2-1-19; 3-28-25
Michael Melton W-SE-S17; 2-8-19; 1-29-27   21
William B. Dimick NE-S19; 8-17-18; 3-28-25; SE-S19; 8-17-18; 9-13-
James Kell W-SE-S26; 11-2-16; 9-29-21; E-SE-S26;11-2-16;3-28-25.
John Fleener & John Devin SE-S30; W-NE-S31; 12-5-18; 9-8-21
James B. McGarrah W-SE-S27; 11-7-17; 9-22-21
James Lessley NE-S33; 3-5-19; 9-8-21

T 2 S, R 10 W

Jacob Hartin NE-S1; 12-10-18
Isaac Ferris NW-S1; 1-2-19
Joshua Stapleton SW-S1; 2-2-16
William Lawrence, Green Co., O. E-SE-S1; 9-24-32
Margaret Hartin* NW-SE-S1; 11-2-36
John Davidson* SW-SE-S1; 11-17-35; E-NE-S3; 7-25-32
Henry Hopkins E-NE-S2; 1-29-18
John Lagow* NW-NE-S2; 1-28-50; SE-SE-S9; 8-27-36
George Humphreys, Jr.* SW-NE-S2; 5-21-33; W-SW-S2; 12-19-17
George Humphreys NW-S2; 12-18-16
George Hartin E-SW-S2; 8-27-18
William Hanks E-SE-S2; 1-29-18
Samuel Lawrence* W-SE-S2; 11-7-33
Joseph Davisson* W-NE-S3;.4-6-33
John Christy, Washington Co., Pa. NE-NW-S3; 11-23-37
Samuel Whitsett* SE-NW-S3; 10-5-36; W-NE-S4; 9-17-29
John Whitsett W-NW-S3; 8-18-19
James Stormont* NE-SW, SW-SW-S3; 9-5-32; SE-SW-S3; 3-2-36
Benjamin Whitsett* NW-SW-S3; 5-25-36
Alexander Kell SE-S3; 8-27-18
Joseph Whitesides E-NE-S4; 5-3-17
Samuel Hogue, Sr. NW-S4; 2-21-14
James B. McCall SW-S4; 2-3-16
Samuel Hall* E-SE-S4; 4-29-30; NW-SE-S4; 5-2-32
Willis Howe & Joseph Jackson Kirkman SW-SE-S4; 7-2-36
William Hargrove NE-S5; 1-20-16; NW-S5; 10-19-16

Jonathan Lathom SW-S5; 2-13-14; SE-S6; 5-15-07
George W.L. Jones & Bazil Brown SE-S5; 1-31-16
Isaac Montgomery NE-S6; 4-14-13
John A. Miller NW, SW-S6; 5-15-07
Robert M. Evans NE, SE-S7; 2-12-14
Henry Hopkins NW-S7; 12-10-11; SW-S7; 10-21-08
James W. Jones NE-S8; 1-26-16
Hazael Putnam NW-S8; 3-20-13
William Harrington SW-S8; 2-12-14
James Leslie SE-S8; 8-8-15
William Stormont* NE-NW-S9; 8-5-34
Purnell Fisher* SE-NW-S9; 10-5-32; W-NW-S9; 7-9-17; W-NW-S10;
Solomon D. King SW-S9; 7-22-17   10-22-17
John McWilliams* NE-SE-S9; 8-5-34; NW-SW-S10; 5-16-36
Robert Stormont* W-SE-S9; 8-5-34
John Orr Sprowl* NE-NE-S10; 5-28-35; W-NW-S11; 6-28-36
John Sprowl* SE-NE-S10; 6-28-36
Joshua Stapleton W-NE-S10; 2-10-19
John Orr, Green Co., O. E-NW-S10; 5-7-33; E-SE-S10; 10-24-38
Alexander McWilliams* E-SW, SW-SE-S10; 10-12-36; SW-SW-S10; 11-21-
David Cherry McWilliams* NW-SE-S10; 12-14-36   36
James Mills NE, SE-S11; 8-9-19
Matthew Clark* E-NW-S11; 6-17-36
Robert Casbolt* NE-SW-S11; 12-13-37
Zachariah Hussey* SE-SW-S11; 5-19-37
William Rowe* NW-SW-S11; 11-13-37
Polly Casbolt* SW-SW-S11; 6-7-41
Joseph Mitchell Davidson* NE-NE-S12; 3-11-36
John Davidson* NW-NE-S12; 11-17-35
Martin McKissick, Mr SW-NE, NW-SE-S12; 9-28-36
William Lawrence* NE-NW-S12; 3-16-36; SE-NW-S12; 11-17-35
Samuel Leprone Boicourt* W-NW-S12; 8-10-31
Richard Hussey* NE-SW-S12; 1-6-36; W-SW-S12; 8-17-30
William Martin* SE-SW-S12; 9-28-36; of Mr, NE-SE-S12; 9-28-36
Thomas Johnston* SE-SE-S12; 8-9-43
William George Guirey* SW-SE-S12; 7-8-39. Guirey? Quincy?
Sarah Barber* SE-NE-S13; 12-22-35
Samuel Whitsett* NW-NE-S13; 6-11-47
Samuel Murphy* SW-NE-S13; 12-1-34
William Crow NW-S13; 10-6-18
James Wilson* NE-SW-S13; 12-1-34; SE-SW-S13; 11-17-35
William Chittendon W-SW-S13; 8-7-18
Robert McConnell Wilson, Greene Co., O. E-SE-S13; 3-10-34; of *
    SW-SE-S13; 11-17-35
William Wilson, Greene Co., O. NW-SE-S13; 3-10-34
James Mills NE-S14; 8-18-19
Hugh Murphy* NE-NW-S14; 7-9-39
John K. Harten* SE-NW-S14; 11-24-47
George Hartin SW-S14; 12-3-18
Joseph Rutledge Brown* SE-S14; 4-25-36
John Ewing & Robert Milburn NE, E-NW, NW-SE-S15; 1-9-37
William B. Dimick W-NW, SW-S15; 8-7-18
Edward Pinney* E-SE-S15; 4-7-37
Isaac Reynolds SW-SE-S15; 7-15-36

William Parvin NE-S17; 3-11-14
William Harrington & James McClure NW-S17; 3-21-14
James McClure SW-S17; 2-17-14; SW-S20; 10-3-16
James Lessley SE-S17; 1-10-17
John D. Hay NE-S18; 2-12-14
John Barker NW-S18; 2-5-10
John Braselton SW-S18; 12-14-11
Robert M. Evans SE-S18; 10-6-13
Samuel T. Scott NE-S19; 4-16-13
Daniel Putman NW-S19; 3-10-13
Joseph Woods SW-S19; 11-15-15
Thomas T. Johnson SE-S19; 11-16-16
Alexander Devin NE-S20; 3-15-13
Zachariah Skelton NW-S20; 4-28-13
Joseph Haynes Reynolds* NE-SE-S20; 12-6-34; SE-SE-S20; 11-18-35
John Orr, Green Co., O. W-SE-S20; 5-7-33
Erastus Townsend E-NE-S21; 9-12-18
Samuel H. Shannon* W-NE-S21; 12-1-34; NW-NW-S22; 2-10-36; SW-NW-
James W. Hoge* NE-NW-S21; 8-27-36.   S22; 3-15-34
Harvey O'Neal* SE-NW-S21; 8-5-34
Vincent Woods W-NW-S21; 12-10-18
Wyett Smith* NE-SW-S21; 4-5-33; NW-NE-S23; 1-31-37
John Sterns* SE-SW-S21; 9-24-36; SW-SW-S21; 12-24-36
William Hune Hogue* NW-SW-S21; 3-16-33
Eli Bigham* NE-SE-S21; 12-10-33; SE-SE-S21; 8-5-34
James Bigham W-SE-S21; 8-5-34
Lewis Kolb* NE-NE-S22; 9-9-36
John Sprague Maxam* SE-NE-S22; 8-5-34
Sylvester Maxam W-NE, E-NW, E-SW-S22; 8-7-18
John Lewis Bittrolff* NW-SW-S22; 2-17-36; SW-SW-S22; 8-5-34
James Wood* NE-SE-S22; 5-30-35; NW-SE-S22; 8-5-34
Hosea Ashmead* SE-SE-S22; 9-19-36
Frederick Huther* SW-SE-S22; 10-6-34
James Hartin* NE-NE-S23; 12-26-37
Eli Williams* SE-NE-S23; 3-6-39
John Hargrove* SW-NE-S23; 4-8-37
Thomas Chapman E-NW-S23; 12-22-18; W-NW-S23; 12-30-18
Martin Schmoll, Vb E-SW, SW-SW-S23; 12-6-37
William Lose* NW-SW-S23; 1-11-37
Joseph Hanes Reynolds & William Reavis E-SE-S23; 12-6-38
Joseph Hanes Reynolds* W-SE-S23; 3-23-37
Joseph Rutledge Brown* E-NE, NW-NE-S24; 9-23-36; SW-S24; 9-9-36;
    W-SE-S24; 4-25-36
Daniel Spencer* SW-NE-S24; 2-25-36; SE-NW-S24; 9-26-33
Samuel Lawrence* NE-NW, NW-NW-S24; 11-17-35
Samuel T. Spencer* SW-NW-S24; 3-2-36
John N. Trusdale E-SE-S24; 9-26-18
William Reavis* E-NE-S25; 4-5-36; E-NW-S25; 10-30-18
Joseph Logan Reavis NW-NE-S25; 3-2-36; NE-SW-S25; 4-8-37
Tabiths Reavis* SW-NE-S25; 3-3-36; SE-SW-S25; 6-21-37; NW-SW-S25;
John McCray* W-NW-S25; 8-19-28; NE-NE-S26; 3-30-36.   2-9-36
Alexander Devin Reavis* SW-SW-S25; 3-23-37
Isham Reavis W-SE-S25; 2-3-16
Nicholas Jasper Hargrove* SE-NE-S26; 4-1-36

John T. Walker, Vb NW-NE, E-NW-S26; 7-28-47
Joseph G. Crow, Kn SW-NE-S26; 5-20-37
Robert Milburn* W-NW-S26; 10-22-38   S35; 3-1-37
William Sullivan, George W. Pratt, & George M. Thacher SW-S26;W-NW-
Elisha Embree & Samuel Hall E-SE-S26; 2-6-36
James Perry Drake, Kn NW-SE-S26; 2-27-37
Isaac Strickland* SW-SE-S26; 9-20-36
Nuttall Smith* NE-NE-S27; 12-31-33
Wilay Smith* SE-NE-S27; 5-2-36
Adam Huther* W-NE-S27; 10-6-34
Sophia Geise* NE-NW-S27; 5-7-38
George Weller* SECNW, SW-NW-S27; 6-22-36
John Fisher* NW-NW-S27; 4-4-38
Cornelius Clark* NE-SW-S27; 10-27-35
Samuel Henderson Davis* SE-SW-S27; 10-27-35
Frederick Hasselbrink* NW-SW-S27; NE-SE-S28; 4-4-38
Samuel Mitchell* SW-SW-S27; SE-SE-S28; 12-13-33
William Wood* NE-SE-S27; 7-6-36
Samuel H. Shannon* SE-SE-S27; 11-15-36
James Wood* W-SE-S27; 2-9-36
Henry Klusman* E-NE-S28; 4-20-39
John Orr, Greene Co., O. W-NE-S28; 10-24-38; NW-S28; E-NE-S29;
Isaac Ferris SW-S28; 5-26-19   10-15-38
Johnson Wheeler* NW-SE-S28; 5-10-38
John George Ratze* SW-SE-S28; 2-8-36; NW-SE-S32; 6-10-35
Hugh Parkinson* W-NE-S29; 1-19-38
Alexander Abercrombie E-SW-S29; 8-6-19
Norman Chambers* NW-SW-S29; 11-9-35
Joseph Chambers* SW-SW-S29; 5-18-32.
Thomas E. Sumner SE-S29; NE-S33; 12-13-16
William Brazelton* E-NE-S30; 6-24-28
Robert Kingsbury* W-NE-S30; 6-21-28
John J. Neely NW, SW, SE-S30; 11-15-15
Isaac Hudspeth* E-NE-S31; 7-26-31; W-NE-S31; 7-19-31
John Arbuthnot NW-S31; 7-10-17
Elias Barker SW-S31; 2-24-16
James Ferguson SE-S31; 10-4-17
Isaac Ferris NE-S32; 2-9-19
John Byers NW-S32; 10-24-18
Payton Wheeler SW-S32; 12-20-16; SW-S32; 2-29-36
Stacey Mitchell* E-SE-S32; 12-28-21; NW-SE-S33; 6-17-33
James Wheeler NW-S33; 1-30-13; E-SW-S33; 3-7-20; of*, NW-SW-S33;
John French* SW-SW-S33; 5-13-37   9-4-35
Henry Hopkins E-SE-S33; 9-15-17
Cheney McCarty* SW-SE-S33; 4-18-36
Stephen Strickland NE-S34; 3-20-13; W-SE-S34; 1-30-16
Stephen Strickland, Sr.* E-NW-S34; 1-14-31
Samuel Wheeler* NW-NW-S34; 11-6-35; SW-NW-S34; 11-14-35
John Clement SW-S34; 11-16-09
James Perry Drake, Kn E-SE-S34; NE-SW, W-SW-S35; 2-17-37
James Skelton, Sr.* E-NE-S35; 3-23-37
Job H. Hall, Meigs Co., O. NW-NE, SE-SW-S35; 9-20-36
Jesse L. Williams, Mn E-NW-S35; 11-7-36
Johnson Wheeler* SE-SE-S35; 8-2-36

GIBSON COUNTY

James Dick W-SE-S35; 8-9-53
William Reavis, Jr.* NW-NE, SE-SW-S36; 11-18-50
Martin Reavis* NE-SE-S36; 6-13-36; SE-SE-S36; 5-9-36
Martin Reavis, Jr.* SW-SE-S36; 5-30-38

RELINQUISHMENTS

George Hartin W-NE-S2; 8-27-18; 9-24-21
David B. Brazelton NE-S3; 9-9-19; 3-28-25
John Whitsett E-NW-S3; 8-18-19; 9-17-21
Richard Daniel SW-S3; 9-7-19; 3-28-25
Joseph Whitesides W-NE-S4; 3-3-17; 3-28-25
George W.L. Jones SE-S4; 2-3-16; 11-6-28
David T. King NE-S9; 12-2-18; 3-28-25
Purnell Fisher E-NW-S9; 7-9-17; 6-20-29; E-NW-S10; 10-22-17; 6-20-
William Lathom SE-S9; 1-8-19; 6-20-29   29
Joshua Stapleton E-NE-S10; 2-10-19; 6-26-29
Stephen Fisher E-SW-S10; 8-19-17; 8-31-21
Randolph West NW-S12; 10-13-18; 6-29-29
Homer Chittendon NE-S13; 8-7-18; 9-13-21; E-SW-S13; 8-7-18; 7-2-
John Ewing SE-S14; 1-30-19; 3-28-25   27
William B. Dimick NE-S15; 8-7-18; 3-23-25; E-NW-S15; 8-7-18; 9-13-
   21; SE-S15; 8-7-18; 3-12-27; SE-S15; 8-17-18; 7-4-29
Erastus Townsend W-NE-S21; 9-12-18; 8-26-21
Vincent Woods E-NW-S21; 12-10-18; 7-30-21
Sylvester Maxum E-NE, W-NW, SE-S22; 8-7-18; 6-2-29;W-SW-S22;8-7-18;
Thomas Chapman W-NE-S23; 12-22-18; 3-25-25   7-4-29
John N. Trusdale W-SE-S24; 9-26-18; 3-30-25
William Reavis NE, W-NW-S25; 10-30-18; 3-25-25
Isham Reavis E-SE-S25; 2-3-16; 9-8-21
David Banta NW-S29; 12-7-18; 12-9-24
Alexander Abercrombie W-SW-S29; 8-6-19; 4-30-27
Malinda Goodwine NE-S30; 1-17-17; 8-30-21
George Ish NW-S34; 6-26-16; 9-9-29
Stephen Strickland E-SE-S34; 1-30-16; 8-1-21
William Hanks W-SE-S2; 1-29-18; 7-4-29
Stephen Fisher W-SW-S10; 8-19-17; 7-4-29
William Holman NW-S24; 10-15-18; 7-4-29
John J. Neely W-SE-S30; 11-15-15; 7-4-29
Joel Prewitt NE-S31; 6-27-18; 7-4-29
James Wheeler E-SW-S33; 3-7-20; 7-4-29

T 2 S, R 11 W
(Seminary Twp.)

William Archer NE-S1; n.d.; NE-S2; n.d.
Robert M. Evans NW-S1; n.d.
Alexander Dick E-SW-S1; 10-21-22
Walter Wilson & James Kell W-SW-S1; 9-3-27
Thomas Potter SE-S1; n.d.
William Barker E-NW-S2; 5-5-28; W-NW-S2; 8-5-28
Silas Edrington E-SW-S2; 9-3-27
John Alexander W-SW-S2; 5-5-28

Calvin Minnis E-SE-S2; 10-21-22
John W. Woods W-SE-S2; 9-3-27
Alexander Devin E-NE-S3; 6-26-30
Robert Stormont W-NE-S3; 4-4-31
James Skedmore NW-S3; 5-5-28
Alex Wilson & Robert Sloan W-SW-S3; E-SE-S4; 5-5-28
Charles Harrington & Samuel Robinson E-SE-S3; 1-25-29
Thomas Manning E-NE-S4; 5-5-28
Daniel Catlin W-NE-S4; 3-4-33
Cooper Harris E-SW-S5; E-SE-S7; W-SW-S10; 9-11-30
John Montgomery W-SE-S7; 9-7-32.   Omission--William Embree
Cornelius Clark E-NE-S9; 8-8-29.   W-SE-S4; 3-4-33
Thomas Montgomery W-NE-S9; 8-16-32.
William Barr E-SW-S9; 8-16-29
Thomas McMullen E-SE-S9; E-SW-S10; 6-13-29
Nehemiah Alcorn W-SE-S9; 6-30-29
Onetus D. Chaffee E-NE-S10; 10-6-28
Moses Morse W-NE-S10; 12-10-28
Hosea Ashmeed E-NW-S10; 8-5-28
Robert Sloan W-NW-S10; 8-5-28
John J. Neely E-SE-S10; 10-6-28; W-NE-S12; 10-21-22
Hugh McMullen W-SE-S10; 8-5-29
Walter Wilson & Willis Howe E-NE-S11; 9-7-27
Peter Hanks W-NE-S11; 5-5-28
James Minnis E-NW-S11; 9-9-27
Elisha Embree W-NW-S11; 4-11-31
Polly Strain E-SW-S11; 9-4-27; W-SW-S11; 2-6-29
William Harrington SE-S11; n.d.; SW-S12; n.d.; NE-S14; n.d.
Thomas Embree E-NE-S12; 10-21-22
Samuel Lessley E-NW-S12; 10-22-22
John Lessley W-NW-S12; 9-4-27
Toissant Dubois SE-S12; n.d.
Isaac Montgomery NE, NW-S13; n.d.
John N. Truesdell SW-S13; 9-5-27
John C. Warrick E-SE-S13; 9-6-27; W-SE-S13; 9-5-27
William Wills E-NW-S14; 9-5-27
Aaron LaGrange W-NW-S14; 9-7-27; E-SE-S16; 10-14-30; E-SW-S21;
Henry Ayres W-SW-S14; E-SE-S15; 9-5-27   10-7-28
Elijah Knowles E-SW, W-SE-S14; 9-5-27
Robert Williams E-SE-S14; 9-5-27
Johnson Fitzgerald E-NE-S15; 5-5-28; E-NE-S16; 6-27-29
Richard Land W-NE-S15; 5-22-30
Azariah Ayres NW-S15; n.d.
William Embree E-SW, W-SE-S15; 5-5-28
John Stewart W-SW-S15; 5-5-28
James McNeely W-NE-S16; 12-15-28
Ephraim Dickey E-NW-S16; 12-15-28
William Embree & James McAllister E-SW-S16; 8-29-29
Isaac Woods, Sr. W-SW-S16; 3-4-33; W-SE-S16; 1-5-29; W-NE-S21;
Isaac Reed E-SW-S17; 1-23-33.   9-6-27; SE-S21; n.d.
James Purkins & John Purkins W-SW-S17; 9-6-31; E-SE-S18; 9-16-31
John Mauk E-SE-S17; 12-31-32
Samuel Dougan W-SE-S17; 12-5-32
Thomas Roberts E-NE-S19; 5-6-28

Solomon Byrn W-NW-S19; 6-14-30
G.B. Duncan & T. Gambril E-SW-S19; 12-10-28
Elijah Melton W-SW-S19; 9-6-27
Jacob Spore E-SE-S19; W-SW-S20; 12-1-32
William Keitly W-SE-S19; 12-1-32
Fielding Lucas E-NE-S20; 12-1-32
Samuel Hall W-NE-S20; 8-5-28; E-NW-S20; 5-6-28
Joseph & Abraham Mauk W-NW-S20; 1-3-30
George Dougan E-SW-S20; 7-15-30
Isaac Woods, Jr. E-SE-S20; 5-5-28
Isaac Reed W-SE-S20; 8-24-30
John Embree E-NE-S21; 5-6-28
Joseph L. Woods E-NW-S21; 5-6-28; W-NW-S21; 8-1-29
Thomas Williams W-SW-S21; 2-7-29
Thomas Emison S22; n.d.
William P. Woods E-NE-S23; 9-6-27
Samuel H. Woods W-NE-S23; 9-6-27
John N. Truesdell NW-S23; 9-6-27
Joseph Woods SW-S23; n.d.
Samuel L. Hogue E-SE-S23; 5-6-28
John C. Warrick W-SE-S23; 5-6-28
Samuel L. Boicourt E-NE-S24; 9-6-27
James Scantlin W-NE-S24; 9-6-27
Samuel Hogue NW-S24; 9-6-27
William Embree & John N. Truesdell SW-S24; 9-6-27
William Lynn E-SE-S24; 5-6-28
B. Brown & William Daniel W-SE-S24; 5-6-28
Samuel Hall NE, NW-S25; 9-7-27; E-SW-S25; Nov.-29; E-NE-S26; 11-
    28-28; W-NE-S26; 9-7-27; E-NW-S26; 9-8-28; W-NW-S26; 5-5-28
Martin Tenison W-SW-S25; 9-14-30
John King E-SE-S25; 8-5-28
William Embree W-SE-S25; 10-6-28
John Hudelson E-SW-S26; 12-29-28
Samuel Hudelson W-SW-S26; 5-6-28
William Embree & S.H. Woods E-SE-S26; 12-29-28
Simon Orr W-SE-S26; 11-9-31
Robert Anderson NE-S27; n.d.; NW-S28; n.d.
John Stewart E-NW-S27; 9-13-27
Thomas Vanlandingham W-NW-S27; 9-7-27
Matthias Mounts SW-S27; n.d.
Samuel Hogue & Hugh McCary SE-S27; n.d.
James Emison NE-S28; n.d.; SE-S28; n.d.
A. Blythe & Jesse Emmerson W-SW-S28; 9-15-27
Tolliver Hughes E-SW-S28; 9-13-27
Walter Bridges E-NE-S29; 6-24-29
Eli Garret W-NE-S29; 10-25-31
James S. Hill E-NW-S29; 8-20-30
Isaac Reynolds W-NW-S29; 6-27-31
Mahlon Stone E-SW-S29; 1-10-29
William Thornton W-SW-S29; 4-1-29
Elhanan W. Emmerson E-SE-S29; 9-7-27
William Emmerson W-SE-S29; 9-7-27
Presley Hurt E-NE-S30; 12-6-32
Samuel Mauk W-NE-S30; 9-21-31

Gillan Harris E-NW-S30; 5-26-30
Thomas Guinn W-NW-S30; 9-7-27
Henry Gambral E-SW-S30; 6-26-30; W-SW-S30; 8-5-28
John Aldridge E-SE-S30; 5-6-28
Joseph Mauk & Joseph Roberts W-SE-S30; 12-10-28
Wiley Marvel E-NE-S31; 5-6-28
Abraham Mauk W-NE-S31; 5-5-30
William W. Waters E-NW-S31; 5-6-28; W-NW-S31; 9-8-27
George Martin E-SW-S31; 9-13-27
Ithaba Knoles W-SW-S31; 10-23-31
Ivel Jones E-SE-S31; 5-6-28
Fielding Lucas W-SE-S31; 5-6-28
Thomas Emison NE-S32; n.d.
Joseph Thornton E-NW-S32; 5-6-28
Andrew Smith W-NW-S32; 9-8-27
John Malone E-SW-S32; 3-20-30; W-SW-S32; 12-10-28
James Smith E-SE-S32; 10-23-22; W-SE-S32; 5-25-30; E-NW-S33; 5-20-
   31; W-NW-S33; 9-8-27; SW-S33; n.d.; W-SE-S33; 5-6-28
Jacob Warrick NE-S33; n.d.
Joseph Fields E-SE-S33; 6-26-30
David L. Woods E-NE-S34; 5-6-28
James W. Hogue W-NE-S34; 6-1-31
James VanSandt E-NW-S34; 5-5-28; W-NW-S34; 9-8-27
James McAllister E-SW-S34; 12-15-28
John Montgomery W-SW-S34; 8-2-30
William P. Witherspoon E-SE-S34; 5-14-31; W-SW-S35; 12-27-28
James Witherspoon W-SE-S34; 12-15-28
Alexander Finney E-NE-S35; 3-10-33
John Wallace W-NE-S35; 3-2-31
Samuel Hudelson NW-S35; 12-29-28
William McIntyre E-SW-S35; 10-1-31
John Richie E-SE-S35; 8-29-32
Asaph Brown W-SE-S35; 3-2-31
John Arbuthnot E-NE-S36; 6-26-30
Macklin Spain W-NE-S36; 8-20-30
Franklin Wallace E-NW-S36; 3-15-32
David Taylor E-SE-S36; 10-14-30

Tracts in this book (township) marked sold by the quarter, were dis-
posed of by the Trustees of Seminary in Gibson, while it belonged
to Knox County, and date of sale or entry not known by the Commis-
sioner. The above tract book (township) I believe is correct.
                                    James Smith Comr. S.C.I.
                                    Oct. 14, 1833

                            T 2 S, R 12 W

Lewis A. Bradley, Hamilton Co., O. SE-S2; 10-25-54
James Sharp* W-NE-S3; 2-2-39
Harris Sharp* NE-NW-S3; 6-16-36; SW-NW-S3; 6-24-39
John Mock* NW-NW-S3; 8-5-34; NE-NE-S4; 1-18-36
Abner Landsdown* NE-SW-S3; 9-6-37
Joel Landsdown* SE-SW-S3; 9-8-37
George Waller Sharp* NW-SE-S3; 6-24-39

Roland Burbridge Richards* E-SE-S4; 8-26-36
Moses Montgomery* NE-NEfr-S5; 12-15-34
Jacob Johnson* SE-NEfr, Lot 2-W-NEfr-S5; 1-18-36; Lot 1-W-NEfr-
Thomas Montgomery* NWfr-S5; 10-19-35   S5; 10-19-35
John Hughes, Dn NE-SWfr-S5; 4-5-36; of*, Lot 4-W-SWfr-S5; 4-5-36
William Riley Strickland* Lot 3-W-SWfr-S5; 1-16-36; NE-NW-S7; 7-18-
Moses Bedell, Wabash Co., Ill. E-SEfr,SW-SEfr-S5;7-18-36.   36
Thomas Gwin* FrS6; 1-5-22; E-NW-S27; 1-29-20
Sarah Muse* NE-NE-S7; 5-16-36
Daniel Muse* SE-NE-S7; 7-18-36
George Black, Wabash Co., Ill. NW-NE-S7; 5-13-33
Samuel White* SW-NE, NE-SE-S7; 2-19-36
Thomas Muse* NW-NW-S7; 6-8-36
George Jackson* SE-SE-S7; 1-23-36
Aaron Strickland* SW-SW-S8; 7-20-36
Andrew Lynn* NE-NE-S9; 8-30-36
Parson Creek* SW-NW-S17; 12-5-56
James Ward* SE-SW-S17; 8-10-37
Ezra Forbis* NW-SW-S17; 1-16-36; SW-SE-S17; 9-5-36
Abraham Mauck* SW-SW-S17; 5-26-36; SE-SE-S17; 9-19-36;E-NE-S25;11-
James Muse NW-S18; 1-16-19   29-28
Joseph Roberts* SW-NE-S21; 9-4-39; W-SE-S23; 9-16-17
James Floyd Duncan* SE-NW, NW-NW-S21; 8-15-39
Jeremiah Vardimon Yager* NE-SW-S21; 9-7-39; NW-SE-S21; 8-19-39
Andrew Smith* SE-SW-S22; 7-26-41
Jacob Moury, Hr E-SW-S23; 1-5-22
John Downey E-SE-S23; 4-14-20
Robert Denbo, Hr NE-NE-S24; 9-11-35; SW-NE-S24; 3-5-35
Samuel Mauck, Hr SE-NE-S24; 6-18-32
Greenberry Duncan SW-S24; 8-14-18; W-NE-S26; 8-15-16
Robert Stormont SE-S24; 2-3-19
George M. Johnson W-NE-S25; 5-28-13
Joseph Mauk* NE-NW, NW-NW-S25; 9-17-35
Julius Mauck* SE-NW-S25; 10-13-36
John Rutter* SW-NW-S25; 12-31-36
James Stewart* NE-SW, SW-SW-S25; 3-18-37; SE-SW-S25; 4-13-37
Charles Hamilton Bellas+ NW-SW-S25; 6-29-36
Moses Hopper SE-S25; 1-25-08
Barns Reeves, Kn E-NE-S26; 12-29-29
James Montgomery NW-S26; 6-6-10
Samuel Cosey* SE-SW-S26; 8-3-36
Wiley Jenkins Bauldwin* SW-SW-S26; 4-13-35
Joshua Overton SE-S26; 1-2-16
John McFadin* NE-NE-S27; 5-22-33
Joseph Yager* SE-NE-S27; 2-13-49
James Sherman Haskins* SW-NE-S27; 3-29-37
Joseph John Williams* SW-NW-S27; 3-11-36
Ephraim Music* W-SW-S27; 12-28-29
Wiley Jenkins* SE-SE-S27; 10-10-35
William Forbis W-SE-S27; 9-23-18
Andrew Lewis W-SW-S30; 11-22-56
Lewis Harmon* SE-NE-S32; 12-26-36
Saxton Harmon* NE-SW-S32; 6-20-36
Thomas Waters E-SE-S32; 3-3-20

Lewis Harmon, Jr.* W-SE-S32; 7-20-29
William Carlton E-NE-S33; 3-7-17
James Rice Waters* SW-NE-S33; 3-11-33; SE-S33; 2-20-17
John James Frazer* SE-NW-S33; 5-6-36
Nathaniel Overton* W-NW-S33; 9-22-30
John Skelton SW-S33; 10-3-16
James Smith NE-S34; 11-24-07
William Gambril NW-S34; 9-30-15
James R. & William Waters SW-S34; 3-6-16
James Emison SE-S34; SW-S35; 5-20-07
John Montgomery NE-S35; 1-21-11
John Benson NW-S35; 1-25-08
Joseph Montgomery SE-S35; 7-28-07
Milley Selsor* NE-NE-S36; 4-1-36
William Henry Brown* SE-NE-S36; 11-29-32
Tandy Baily Montgomery* NW-NE-S36; 10-20-35
Thomas M. Johnson* SW-NE-S36; 10-1-32
Jacob Kern NW-S36; 9-4-16
Asa Music SW-S36; 5-7-14
Fielding Lucas* E-SE-S36; 1-18-36
James Stewart, Sr. W-SE-S36; 3-12-19

RELINQUISHMENTS

John Auldridge NE-S18; 6-16-19; 8-31-21
George M. Johnson E-NE-S25; 5-28-13; 9-18-21;W-NE-S25;5-28-13; 7-
Green B. Duncan E-NE-S26; 10-15-16; 9-13-21   4-29
Thomas Gwin W-NW-S27; 1-29-20; 6-25-27
Jonathan Wells E-SW-S27; 9-15-19; 9-15-21; W-SW-S27; 9-15-19;
William Forbis E-SE-S27; 9-23-18; 3-28-25.   11-22-24
Thomas Waters W-SE-S32; 3-3-20; 8-31-21
William Carlton W-NE-S33; 3-7-17; 3-28-25
James Stewart, Sr. E-SE-S36; 3-12-19; 9-4-21
John Emison NE-S36; 10-6-18; 7-4-29

T 2 S, R 13 W

John Auldridge* FrS1; 4-16-24
Ezra Baker, Wabash Co., Ill. Coffee Island-S12-S13-S14; 2-17-51
John Hughes, Dn N-Nfr-S12; 4-5-36
Milo Sawyer, Hamilton Co., O. Lots 1-2-S-Nfr-S12; 7-5-37
Ezra Baker, Jr., Wabash Co., Ill. SWfr-S12; 11-14-35; W-NEfr-S13;
    11-28-35; E-SW-S13; 7-9-36; Lot 1-Nfr-S14; 4-24-35; Sfr-S14; 11-
Joseph Mowrer* SE-NEfr-S13; 11-20-35   28-35
James Seaman, Daniel D. Walters, & Steven Walters NWfr-S13; 8-1-18
William Purcell* F-Nfr-S23; 4-11-36
Ephraim Wonzer, Wabash Co., Ill. Lot 2-N-Nfr-S23; 6-22-36
Abraham Breedlove* Lot 3-S-Nfr-S23; 7-13-39
William Tougan Lovellett Lot 4-S-Nfr-S23; 6-15-38
Elias White, Wabash Co., Ill. NE-SEfr-S23; 8-15-36
David Benson, Ps SE-SEfr-S23; 2-9-37
John Thompson, Wabash Co., Ill. W-SEfr-S23;Lot 2-N-Nfr-S26;3-12-36
George Black, Wabash Co., Ill. NE-NW-S24; 4-1-39

Sarah Black, Wabash Co., Ill. SW-NW-S24; 5-21-39
John Cash, Wabash Co., Ill. N-Nfr-S26; 1-30-37
Elijah Pauley, Vb S-Nfr-S26; 3-30-36
Abijah Davis, Ps N-Sfr-S26; 10-3-33
Jefferson Jordan* Lot 7-S-Sfr-S26; 11-21-34
Moses Bump* FrS31; 2-15-36
Martin Bump* Lot 1-N-Sfr-S32; 1-22-36
Daniel Crowley* Lot 2-N-Sfr-S32; 8-5-34; Lot 4-S-Nfr, N-Sfr-S33;
    2-8-36; S-Sfr-S33; 7-2-30
Thomas Ashley* S-Sfr-S32; 9-8-30
Joshua Jordan* Lot 1-N-Nfr, Lot 3-S-Nfr-S33; 3-29-37.   25-74
George W. McCurdy, Mn Lot 2-N-Nfr-S33; 2-8-73; Lot 5-N-Sfr-S35;7-
William Barker* Lot-2-N-Nfr-S35;8-5-35;Lot 7-S-Sfr-S35;3-1-36.
Eliba Jordan* Lot 3-S-Nfr-S35; 2-27-36
John Jordan* Lot 6-N-Sfr-S35; 3-11-35

RELINQUISHMENTS

Seaman Walters, D. Walters, & S. Walters SWfr, SEfr, NEfr-S13;
    8-1-18; 8-24-22
August Tongast Sfr-S14; 10-25-17; 8-14-22; Nfr-S14; 10-25-17;
Miles Armstrong FiS23; 2-15-20; 3-28-25   3-28-25

T 3 S, R 8 W

John McClelland, Green Co., O. NE-S5; 10-31-39; E-SE-S6; 11-10-37
Hugh Watt, Green Co., O. NE-NW, NW-NW-S5; 11-23-38; NW-SE-S6;
    3-12-39
Thomas Bell* E-SW-S5; 10-8-38; E-SE, SW-SE-S7; W-SW-S8; 1-15-39;
    SE-SW-S17; 11-2-36; SW-SE-S19; 1-10-39; E-NW-S20; 8-22-36;
    NW-NW-S29; 1-10-39
Robert McGreger* W-SW-S5; SE-NW-S8; 8-2-39; SW-SE-S6; 7-6-36;
    NE-SW-S18; 6-5-39
Sanford Howa* SW-SE-S5; 7-20-36
Farris Farmer* NE-NE-S6; 10-11-38
Robert McConnel* W-NE-S6; 6-20-36
Joseph Wilson, Alleghany Co., Pa. NW-S6; W-SW-S7; 5-13-37
Robert Patterson* SW-S6; 12-9-36
Matthew Kell* NE-NE-S7; 4-7-37
John McGreger* SE-SE-S7; 4-7-37; NW-NE-S7; SW-NW-S8; 7-18-33
Zacheus Wilson, Alleghany Co., Pa. NW-S7; 5-9-37
Henry Martin* E-SW-S7; 3-27-37; NE-SW-S17; 10-19-36; W-SW-S17;
    1-4-19; NW-NE-S19; 12-9-39
David Farris* NW-SE-S7; 6-8-36
Alexander Holcomb* SW-NE, NW-SE-S8; 9-28-36
Thomas Ewing, William Hummer, & Robert Coorlay, Sr. NE-NW-S8;
John Kell* NW-NW-S8; 10-19-38   9-28-36
Reuben Baldwin* E-SW-S8; 9-7-39
William Lynn* SW-SE-S8; NW-NE-S17; 8-9-36
Samuel Baldwin NW-S17; NE-S18; 6-10-19
Samuel McDill SE-S17; 1-4-19
Andrew McGreger* SE-SW-S18; 9-25-33
Calvin Minnis* SE-S18; 9-25-20

GIBSON COUNTY

David Wilson* W-SW-S19; 2-13-39;E-SW-S30;1-22-39;NW-NW-S31;7-12-39
John Killpatrick, Sr.* SE-SE-S19; 8-9-37
Henry Hopkins* E-NE-S20; 9-19-18; E-SE-S20; 1-4-19
James B. McGarrah* W-NE-S20; 3-4-19
Robert Spear* E-NE, NE-SE, W-SE-S29; 10-3-39; W-NE, E-NW-S29; 8-27-
Thomas Killpatrick* SW-NW-S29; 8-27-39   39
John Killpatrick* E-NE-S30; 8-24-31; W-NE-S30; 7-15-36
Josiah Killpatrick* E-NW-S30; 8-9-37
Silas Edrington* W-NW-S30; 4-16-23
Samuel McDill* W-SW-S30; 3-19-38
Solomon Simpson* NE-SE-S30; 11-12-40; SE-NW-S31; 3-31-49
William Simpson* SE-SE-S30; 3-19-38; W-SE-S30; W-NE-S31; 5-6-28./39
William Harbison* E-NE-S31; W-NE, W-SW-S32; 1-19-39; W-SE-S31;5-2-
William Rainey* NE-NW-S31;11-30-42;NE-NW-S32;10-6-38;W-NW-S32;
William S. Turner E-SW-S31; 8-3-53   1-22-39
Hugh Simpson* E-SE-S31; 10-31-34
Andrew Jackson Barker* SE-NW-S32; 11-9-35
James Kelly Killpatrick, Kn E-SE-S32; 1-23-39
Elizabeth Kirk* NW-SE-S32; 1-28-39
Agnes Black* SW-SE-S32; 4-22-39

RELINQUISHMENTS

Henry Martin E-SW-S17; 1-4-19; 8-20-21
David Banta SW-S19; 1-26-19; 7-1-29
John Killpatrick E-NE-S30; 4-17-19; 11-27-28
James B. McGarrah W-NE-S20; 3-4-19; 7-4-29

T 3 S, R 9 W

Elihu McCulloch* NW-NW-S1; 9-27-36
Robert Castbolt Murphy, Greene Co., O. SW-NW-S1; 6-27-39; SE-NE-
   S2; 6-27-39
David Martin* E-SW-S1; 1-9-39; W-SW-S1; 7-15-36; SE-SE-S1;12-2-35
Reuben Martin* SW-SE-S1; 12-26-38
Jane P. McCulloch* NE-NE-S2; 4-6-37
•Amos Burton, Greene Co., O. W-NE-S2; 3-20-39; SW-NE-S9; 3-20-39;
   SE-NW-S9; 10-19-39; W-SE-S9; 3-29-39
George Galloway, Greene Co., O. NW-S2; 1-9-39
Charles Clark Manahan* NE-SW-S2; 1-9-39; W-SE-S2; 10-8-36
Reason Mason, Greene Co., O. SE-SW-S2; 1-9-39; of*, SW-SW-S2; 10-
William McCleary NW-SW-S2; 6-10-51   19-39
Samuel McCullough* NE-SE-S2; 9-27-35; E-NW-S3; 10-3-36
Thomas McCreary Harbison* SE-SE-S2; 6-20-36
James Devin* SW-NE, E-SW, W-SE-S3; 10-15-36
Robert Steele* NW-NW-S3; 10-8-36
James Steel* SW-NW-S3; 2-23-36; W-SW-S3; 2-19-40; NE-NE-S4; 10-
   15-36; SE-SE-S4; 10-8-36
Willard Carpenter* NE-SE-S3; 6-20-53
Thomas Harbison* SE-NE-S4; 10-3-36
William Sterett, Greene Co., O. W-NE, NE-SE, W-SE-S4; 3-16-39
David Null, Greene Co., O. NW-S4; 1-9-39; E-SE-S9; 5-27-39; of*
   NE-NW, W-SW-S9; 5-12-46

Levi Burton, Greene Co., O. SW-S4; 1-9-39
John McClelland* E-NE-S5; 10-9-50
Aaron Wilson* W-NE, E-NW-S5; 8-1-36
John Wilson, Greene Co., O. W-NW-S5; SE-NE-S6; 6-18-36
Samuel Henderson* NE-SW-S5; 11-9-36
David Donley McGarrah* SE-SW-S5; 12-20-34
William Pearson W-SW-S5; 2-14-18
James Skelton, Sr.* NW-SE-S5; 10-17-36
Ralph Skelton* SW-SE-S5; 10-3-36   8-12-36
Francis Amory, Jr. & George W. Amory NE-NE-S6; 8-5-36; NE-SE-S6;/
William Reavis* NW-NE-S6; 4-8-37; NE-NW, NW-NW-S6; 9-6-36; W-SE-
Joseph Beasley* SW-NE-S6;4-8-37;E-SW-S6;6-6-36.   S6;6-6-36/
Grandison Vickers* SE-NW-S6; 6-25-36; SW-NW-S6; 6-13-36
Stacy Vickers* W-SW-S6; 9-7-36
Jonas Mayhall* SE-SE-S6; 6-1-36
Wilson McGrew* NE-S7; 3-25-36; NE-NW-S7; 12-13-15
William Skelton* SE-NW-S7; 12-28-36
John L. Woods* NE-SW-S7; 9-10-36; NW-SW-S7; 6-6-36
Elias Reavis* SE-SW-S7; 10-10-32
Joseph C. Compton* SW-SW-S7; 9-20-47
Allen Wilson* E-SE-S7; 10-14-37
Robert Skelton* NW-SE-S7; 1-21-36
Robert Skelton, Jr.* SW-SE-S7; 11-2-37
Littleton Bowen Mariner* NE-NE-S8; 6-6-49
John Skelton* SE-NE-S8; 9-26-38; W-NE-S8; 6-1-36; SW-NW-S9; 5-25-
John Miller E-NW-S8; 2-24-19   39
Jacob Skelton & Joshua Wing Stephens W-NW-S8; 9-1-36
Jacob Skelton E-SW-S8; 12-31-18
Jacob Skelton, Sr.* NW-SW-S8; 10-27-37
John Wire* SW-SW-S8; 6-14-44
James Willet French* NE-SE-S8; 7-14-41; NW-NW-S9; 8-18-49
William Jackson Mason* SE-SE-S8; 12-26-46
Andrew Mason, Clark Co., O. W-SE-S8; 7-14-41
Bassel Burton, Greene Co., O. E-SW-S9; 3-20-39
John Martin* E-NE-S10; 5-27-39; E-SE-S10; 12-20-38; NW-SE-S10;
   7-6-36; SW-SE-S10; 8-9-33
Benjamin Burton* NE-NW, NW-NW-S10; 3-12-47
Samuel McCullough, Jr., Wk NE-NE-S11; 6-20-36; SE-NE-S11; 8-16-33
William Booker* NW-NE-S11; 3-7-39
David Null, Greene Co., O. NW-S11; 3-20-39; of*, SW-NW-S13;1-25-48
George Galloway, Greene Co., O. E-SW, W-SE-S11; 5-28-39
George McGregor* W-SW-S11; 5-27-39; SW-NW-S12; 7-15-36; NE-NE-S15;
   8-9-33; NW-NE-S15; 7-15-36
Samuel Hamilton Wood* E-SE-S11; 12-3-38
Robert Castbolt Murphy, Greene Co., O. W-NE-S12; 6-27-39
David Martin* NW-NW-S12; 8-16-33; W-SE-S12; 6-12-38; E-NE-S13;
   6-16-38; SE-NE, SW-NE-S15; 1-19-39
John Kell* E-SW-S12; 6-7-38; E-SE-S12; 6-19-39.   9-9-50
Alexander Holcomb* W-NE-S13; 1-22-39; E-NW-S13; 10-16-39; E-SE-S14;
William Wotton Sweeney, Chester Co., Pa. NW-NW-S13; 10-12-48;
Henry Martin* SW-S13; 10-16-37   Swaney?
James McGarrah Killpatrick* E-SE-S13;2-9-39;W-SE-S13;11-2-38
John Steel* W-NE-S14; 11-27-30
Elias Skelton* NE-NW, NW-NW-S14; 1-7-51

Andrew Harper Steel* SE-NW-S14;11-16-37; NW-SE-S14; 4-7-37
David Elihu McCulloch* SW-NW-S15; 4-11-37; W-SW-S15; 5-19-46
William Jackson Mason* NE-NE-S17; 10-1-47
William McCleary* W-NE-S17;6-6-36; E-NW-S17;8-25-25; NW-NW-S17;
John Wire* SW-NW-S17; 8-9-49   11-29-36
William Shields, Clinton Co., O. W-SW-S17; 6-29-41
James Logan McCleary* SE-SE-S17; 10-2-43
Samuel Hall* NW-SE-S17; 9-22-47
Peter Penzwire* SW-SE-S17; 8-31-49. See Parywire below
Allen Wilson NE-NE-S18; 10-14-37
William McCleary* W-NE-S18; 11-29-36; SE-NE, SW-NE-S20; 6-10-51
Joshua Wing Stephens, Vb E-NW, E-SW-S18; 9-1-36;E-NW-S28;8-13-36
Francis Amory, Jr. & George W. Amory W-NW, SW-SW-S18; 8-5-36
William Taylor* NW-SW-S18; 4-27-36
Jonas Mayhall* SE-S18; 11-29-36; NW-S27; 11-29-36
Washington Rice* NE-NE-S19; 3-4-47
James Hamilton Woods* SE-NE-S19; 3-17-47; SW-NE-S19; 10-19-48
William Depriest* NW-NE-S19; 3-17-47
Patrick E. Woods* NE-SW-S19; 3-12-49
Stephen L. Taylor* NW-SW-S19; 1-25-51
Charles T. Shanner* SW-SW-S19; 12-13-50
William Reavis, Jr.* NE-NE-S20; 4-18-49; NE-SW-S22; 4-18-51
Peter Parywire* NW-NE-S20; 8-23-50. See Penzwire above
Samuel Meek* NE-SW-S20; 12-26-50; NW-SW-S20; 10-19-48
Landalin Hoesels* SE-SW-S20; 1-17-44
Jacob Washington Skelton* SW-SW-S20; 1-7-48
Samuel McDonald* NE-S21; 11-7-50
Aaron Wilson* SE-SW, SW-SE-S21; 2-7-38
Jesse Ingram* SE-SW-S22; 7-26-49
Riley Welcher West* SW-SW-S22; 1-14-50
Samuel Aneas Kinkade, Kn NE-SE-S23; 6-18-40
James Orin, York Co., Pa. SE-SE-S23; E-SE-S24; 3-5-40; SW-S24;
     2-25-40; W-SE-S24; 3-12-40; NW-NE-S25;3-5-40;NW, W-SE-S25;2-15-
John Bell Killpatrick* SW-SE-S23;7-15-36; E-NE-S26; 10-16-39; '40
     W-NE-S26; 1-9-39   ,
David McCullough Harbison* E-NE-S25; 6-14-39
Adam Harbison* SW-NE-S25; 9-10-39
John McMillen* W-SW-S25; 1-27-37; E-SE-S26; 11-17-37.
Elizabeth Jane McDill* E-SE-S25; 8-3-36
Robert Spear, Fl NW-S26; E-SE-S27; 10-13-38; E-SW-S26; 9-24-38;
William McGarrah* NW-SW-S26; 5-13-37.   W-SE-S26; 9-24-34
Ephraim Taylor* SW-SW-S26; 7-20-36
William McCullough* SE-NE, SW-NE-S27; 3-7-37
Henry Jackson Coffman, Fl E-SW, NW-SW-S27; 10-13-38;SW-SW-S29;10-
Josiah Killpatrick* NW-SE-S27; 8-9-37; W-NE-S28; 9-1-36.   13-38;
William Absalom Boyce, Wk SW-SE-S27; 1-30-37   of*
Howell Bass* NW-NW-S28; 5-22-39
Jordan Bass* SW-NW-S28; 9-25-48
Hugh & Thomas McMullin* SW-S28; 8-27-47
Philip Bouts NE-S29; 2-18-51
John Ingram* NE-SW-S29;/11-12-50
William A. McDowell* SE-SW-S29; 7-30-50; NE-S30; 3-15-50
Robert Brownlee* NW-SW-S29; 7-24-52
Rufus Breed* E-SW, NW-SW-S30; 6-6-49

Solomon Whitney, Vb SW-SW-S30; 1-9-39
William Neuman, Vb SE-NE-S31; E-SW-S32; 5-4-39
Jacob Linzich, Vb NW-NW-S31; 10-12-40
John Wheaton, Vb E-SW, W-SE-S31; 10-25-37
John Morris, Vb E-SE-S31; 10-25-37; SW-NW, W-SW-S32; 3-15-37
Hugh McMillin & Thomas McMillan* NE-NE-S32; 9-22-47; E-NW-S33;
John Peter Freuderberg, Vb SE-S32; 4-7-47. MLW   9-4-47
Samuel McCullough* NW-NW-S33; 7-7-47
Hugh McMullin* SW-NW-S33; 9-22-47
Thomas Allen Criswell* NE-SE-S33; 10-6-47
Stephen Van Price* SE-SE-S33; 9-15-47
Frederick Finger NW-S34; 10-31-50. MLW
William Absalom Boyce, Wk SW-SW-S34; 10-19-36
Conrad Macaber SE-S34; 10-31-50
Samuel McDill* NE-NE-S35; 11-2-38
Josiah Killpatrick* SE-NE-S35; 11-2-36;NW-NE-S36;10-16-39;NE-NW-S36
William Adams Simpson* NW-NE-S35; 10-5-40. /11-2-38;NE-SW-S36;
Robert Alexander Saxton* NE-NW-S35; 2-9-37   12-20-37
John E. Colman SW-S35; 10-31-50
William McGarrah* E-SE-S35; 5-13-37
David Wilson* NE-NE-S36; 7-12-39
James McMillen* SE-NE-S36; 1-22-39; SW-NE-S36; 12-1-37
John Millan* SE-NW-S36; n.d.; SW-NW-S36; 9-7-36
Robert Bradshaw* SE-SW-S36; 8-5-34
Maria Louisa McDill* W-SW-S36; 6-20-36
John Simpson, Chester Dist., S.C. SE-S36; 9-6-36

RELINQUISHMENTS

William Pearson W-SE-S6; 3-10-19; 9-18-21; E-SE-S8; 3-10-19; 11-
Elijah Knowes NE-S7; 1-6-19; 2-21-25   22-24
Elisha Strickland SW-S7; 1-26-19; 7-3-27
John Miller W-NW-S8; 2-24-19; 8-31-21
Jacob Skelton W-SW-S8; 12-31-18; 7-3-27
David Hart, Robert Stockwell, J.W. Jones SE-S28; 9-12-18;8-25-21

T 3 S, R 10 W

James Vickers* NE-NE-S1; 6-27-36; SE-NE-S1; 12-21-35
Francis Amory, Jr. & George W. Amory W-NE-S1; NE-NE, E-SW-S2;
William Hannah, Ps SE-NW-S1; 8-17-36   8-5-36
Samuel Wheeler* NW-NW-S1; 12-12-36
Elisha Strickland* SW-NW-S1; 3-25-36; SE-NE-S2; 6-17-36
Jonas Mayhall* E-SW, NW-SW-S1; 11-29-36
William Lathom SE-S1; 2-4-19
James Strickland* NW-NE-S2; 12-28-36
George Manning* SW-NE-S2; 9-20-36; NE-SE-S2; 12-12-36
Stephen Strickland* NE-NW-S2; 9-16-36
James Perry Drake, Kn SE-NW, NW-SW-S2; 2-27-37
Jonathan Young* W-NW-S2; 8-29-36
Elisha Embree* SW-SW-S2; 2-6-36
John Reed Hugh, Vb NW-SE-S2; 3-4-37
William Shaw, Vb SW-SE-S2; 3-21-37

Francis Amory, Jr., Vb   E-NE-S3; 3-10-37;E-SE-S10;W-SW-S11;3-10-37
William Depriest*   NW-NE-S3; 3-3-36; E-NW-S4; 3-3-36
John Depriest*   E-SW-S3; 3-14-36; NW-SW-S3; 6-25-36; SW-SW-S3;
Daniel Putman   NW-S3; 12-3-11   12-17-34
Hazael Putnam   SE-S3; SE-S4; 5-7-14
Elijah Putman   NE-S4; 12-19-16
Zachariah Hall*   NW-NW-S4; 6-23-36
James C. Woods*   SW-NW-S4; 1-12-37
Isaac McReynolds*   NE-SW-S4; 1-12-37
James Hamilton Woods*   SE-SW-S4; 3-7-36;NE-NE-S9;3-11-36;NW-NE &
William P. Wood*   W-SW-S4; 5-6-37   NE-NW-S9;10-13-36
John Wheeler*   NE-NE-S5; 10-28-33
Ellenor Estes*   SE-NE-S5; 11-3-35
Hugh Woods*   NW-NE-S5; 11-3-35
Bartlett Bennet Estes*   SW-NE-S5; 6-2-36
James Hollis Speer*   NE-NW-S5; 2-8-36
Jacob Speer*   SE-NW, NE-SW-S5; 10-31-35
John J. Neely*   W-NW-S5; 9-24-27
David Ayers*   SE-SW-S5; 9-9-36
Alexander Conner*   W-SW-S5; 5-27-35; E-SE-S6; 3-5-30;NW-NW-S8;2-20-
William Embree*   SE-S5; 5-14-36   47
Abraham Brokaw*   E-NE-S6; 4-19-36; W-NE-S6; 9-7-18
Johnson Fitzgarrald   NW-S6; 1-29-16
James Fitzgerrald   SW-S6; 1-29-16
Daniel Reavis   W-SE-S6; 8-19-17; NW-S7; 5-3-16
Amassa D. Foster*   E-NE-S7; 5-27-35; W-NE-S7; 4-21-19
Richard Ingram   SW-S7; 12-4-16
Daniel Brown Tucker, New York City   E-SE-S7; 10-12-33
Robert M. Evans   W-SE-S7; 6-27-17
Philip Sumner*   E-NE-S8; 8-10-20
Dickson Woods*   W-NE-S8; 5-20-36
Hamilton Woods*   NE-NW-S8; 11-9-35
George Barnhard Weber*   SE-NW-S8; 5-23-38
Hume Falls*   SW-NW-S8; 2-12-47
George Siddle*   NE-SW-S8; 2-16-36
James Pierce*   SE-SW-S8; 2-16-36
John Kent, Vb   NW-SW-S8;/1-18-39
Thomas Nickels*   SW-SW-S8; 12-9-36
George Cidels*   E-SE-S8; 10-30-32; SW-SW-S9; 1-12-37
Isaac Hudspeth*   W-SE-S8; 3-5-30
George Michael Burrucker*   SE-NW-S9; 7-24-38
William Embree*   NW-NW-S9; 7-25-36
James Wood*   SW-NW-S9; 6-13-36
John Richey*   NE-SW, NW-SE-S9; 6-13-36
Willis Howe*   SE-SW-S9; 11-11-36; SW-SE-S9; 8-5-36
Barbara Yierling*   NW-SW-S9; 6-22-36
Elisha Embree*   E-SE-S9; 4-6-36; E-NE-S10; 8-1-36; W-NE-S10; 9-9-
   36; W-SE-S10; 3-11-36; NW-NW-S11; 8-1-36
John Wolfkill   NW-S10; 11-27-17
Lewis Neepert*   SE-SW-S10; 6-6-49
Elisha Embree & Samuel Hall*   W-SW-S10; 2-6-36
William Shaw, Vb   E-NW-S11; 2-25-37
James H. Davis*   SW-NW-S11; 11-13-49
William Neavis, Jr.   NE-SW-S11; 9-3-49

William A. McDowell SE-SW-S11; 7-3-50; SE-NW-S12; 12-15-50; E-SW, SW-SE-S12; 3-15-50
Reuben Manning* NE-NE-S12; 11-9-36
James Strickland* NW-NE-S12; 12-28-36; SE-SW-S13; 5-1-50
Benjamin Hayhurst, Miami Co., O. SW-NE, SW-NW, NW-SW, NW-SE-S12;
Isaac Strickland* NE-NW-S12; 3-25-36   5-29-39
Stephen Strickland* NW-NW-S12; 12-7-36
Kenneth Compton* SW-SW-S12; 4-18-49
Joshua Wing Stephens, Vb E-NE, E-SE-S13; 8-13-36
James Myers & William Hannah NW-NE-S13; 2-14-37
William Skelton* SW-NE-S13; 1-19-37
William Hannah* NE-NW-S13; 3-10-37
Isaac Kennerly, Jr., Vb W-NW-S13; 9-8-36
Isaac Taylor* NE-SW-S13; 1-2-39
Daniel Strickland* SW-SW-S13; 9-20-50; NW-SE-S14; 4-12-48
James Kneremer, Vb NW-SW-S13; 3-25-40
William Taylor* NW-SE-S13; 4-17-37
George Adam Mayer* NE-NE, NW-NE-S14; 11-2-36
David Taylor, Butler Co., O. SE-NE, SW-NE-S14; 8-14-37
John T. Walker NW-S14; 4-21-48
George Sidler* SE-SE-S14; 6-8-49
Robert Skelton, Sr. SW-SE-S14; 6-4-50
Francis Amory, Jr., Vb E-NE-S15; 3-10-37
Elisha Embree* W-NE, E-NW-S15; 3-30-36
Robert Shannon* E-SW-S15; 8-25-36
John Woods, Jr.* SW-SW-S15; 12-14-36
Hosea Holcombe* W-SE-S15; 3-1-37
John Stewart NE-S17; 11-14-17
John Henry Schonk* NE-NW-S17; 6-17-35
Peter Brokaw* SE-NW-S17; 7-20-36; SW-NW-S17; 11-9-35
Alexander Conner* NW-NW-S17; NE-NE-S18; 8-5-34; E-SW-S17; NW-NE-
Thomas Browning W-SW-S17; 4-15-19   S20; 12-5-36
Richard Ingrum* NE-SE-S17; 8-5-34; SE-NE-S18; 3-31-37; NE-SE-S18;
Thomas Williams* SE-SE-S17; 9-15-35   11-12-35
Othniel Hollis* W-SE-S17; 7-27-36
Thomas Gedney* W-NE-S18; 6-16-31
John McGough E-NW-S18; 8-24-16
Frederick Davidson+ W-NW-S18; 8-15-31
Thomas H. Martin E-SW-S18; 11-14-17
William Holbrooks* NW-SW-S18; 8-5-34; W-SE-S18; 3-12-31
John Shannon Adams, Vb SW-SW-S18; 8-21-34
Enoch Knox+ SE-SE-S18; 5-26-36
James, Seman, Daniel D., & Stephen Walters E-NE-S19; 8-16-18
Reuben Walters* W-NE-S19; 7-19-31; E-NW-S19; 1-1-31; SW-NW-S19;
    1-30-34; E-SW-S19; 1-5-31; NE-SW-S20; 2-15-36
Stephen U. Lockwood, Vb NW-NW-S19; 7-15-36
Edward Burr Lockwood+ W-SW-S19; 9-1-35
Josiah Dean SE-S19; 11-26-17
Solomon Reavis* NE-NE-S20; 9-30-36
Samuel Williams* SE-NE, SW-NE-S20; 9-30-36
John Alexander McCullough* NE-NW-S20; 8-15-39
Joseph McGarrah* SE-NW-S20; 8-16-39; W-NW-S20; 8-15-39
Patrick W. King* SE-SW-S20; 5-25-39; SW-SW-S20; 1-16-39
Isaac Walters* NW-SW-S20; 7-18-36

Thomas Wallis* NE-SE-S20; 5-26-37; SE-NW-S21; 10-15-35
David Hossick* SE-SE-S20; 5-14-36
Robert Ervin* NE-S21; 5-31-36; NE-NW-S21; 12-24-36; NW-SE-S21;
Solomon Reavis* NW-NW-S21; 9-30-36   2-13-36
John Alexander McCullough* SW-NW-S21; 6-8-36
David Ayers* E-SW-S21; 2-16-33; SW-SW-S21; 12-2-33
Thomas Williams* NW-SW-S21; 11-9-38
Nicholas Wallis* SE-SE-S21; 2-16-36; SW-SE-S21; 2-13-36
Hosea Holcombe & Willis Howe* W-NE-S22; 9-5-36
John Gray Freeman* NE-NW-S22; 720-37; of Butler Co., O., NW-SW-
James Wallace* SE-SW-S22; 1-9-51   S22; 1-9-37
Hosea Holcombe* SW-SW-S22; 2-15-37
Frederick Albertz NE-S23; 6-6-49
John T. Walker SW-S23; SW-S24; 4-21-48
Daniel A. McKee* NE-NE, NW-NE-S24; 3-9-47; SW-NE-S24; 3-17-48
John Wire* SE-NE-S24; 3-8-48
Daniel Strickland* NE-NE-S25; 4-9-47
Jacob Skelton, Jr. & Samuel Mills* NW-NE, NE-NW-S25; 12-31-36
Francis Amory, Jr., Vb SW-NE-S25; 3-10-37
Willard Carpenter SW-S25; 6-21-53
John T. Walker NE-S26; 4-21-48
John Armstrong Graham, Wk W-NW-S26; 7-20-36
Thomas Smith* NE-SW-S26; 4-25-49
Samuel Hall* SE-SW-S26; 5-3-48
Henry Holcombe* SW-SW-S26; 7-27-39
Elisha Embree* W-NW-S27; 5-11-36
William Murfitt* SE-SW-S27; 10-25-48
Lewis Atville McDonald* SW-SW-S27; 3-16-46
Hosea Holcombe* E-NE-S28; 9-8-32; W-NE-S28; 2-10-36
William Moffatt, Chester Dist., S.C. NW, E-SW-S28; 9-5-36
William Reed, Vb W-SW-S28; 8-2-36
Samuel Myers* SE-SE-S28; 1-18-39
Robert Coorley* NE-NE-S29; 2-13-36
David Hossack* SE-NE-S29; 3-31-37; SE-SE-S30; 4-11-36. Hosick
William A. McDowell NW-NE-S29; SE-NW, W-NW-S30; 7-3-50
Charles Keys* SW-NE-S29; 7-10-39
Benjamin J. Day* NE-NW, W-NW-S29; 6-26-55
Vendelin Grunder* SE-NW-S29; 9-13-42
John Lininger, Huntington Co., Pa. E-SW-S29; 6-22-39
Peter Goodsell E-SE-S29; 2-19-19
Macklin Spain* W-SE-S29; 5-1-39
Hiram A. Hopkins* NE-NE-S30; 4-10-39
Reuben Walters W-NE-S30; 12-3-19
Martha Ralston* NE-NW-S30; 8-27-32
John Shannon Adams* NE-SW-S30; 10-3-36
William Reavis, Jr.* SE-SW-S30; 3-15-50
Samuel Adams* W-SW-S30; 6-3-35
James Madison White* NW-SE-S30; 9-1-35
Samuel Cory* SW-SE-S30; 8-18-36
Joseph McGarrah* NE-NE-S31; 6-27-36
David Donnelly McGarrah* SE-NE-S31; 5-19-37
James Scantlin, Vb W-NE-S31; 3-18-37
Thomas Tribble* NW-NW-S31; 3-6-37
George Williams, Ps E-SW, W-SE-S31; 1-25-39; W-SW-S31; 1-5-39

John Saiburt, Vb   E-SE-S31; 3-29-39
Joseph McGarrah*   NE-NE-S32; 8-17-36
William A. McDowell   SE-NE, SW-NE-S32; 7-3-50; SE-NW, SW-NW-S33;
George Kester*   NW-NE-S32;11-24-47; NW-NW-S33;5-27-44.   / 7-3-50
Samuel Corry*   SE-NW-S32; 12-3-36
David Donley McGarrah*   NW-NW-S32; 6-27-36; E-NE, NW-SE-S33;5-13-36
Ezekiel White*   SW-NW-S32; 9-18-33
Daniel Smith*   E-SW-S32; 8-31-33
William Reed*   NW-SW-S32; 12-6-36
Abraham Spain*   SE-SE-S32; 4-18-36
Daniel Taylor*   NW-SE-S32; 12-3-36
Macklin Spain*   SW-SE-S32; 6-27-36
Frederick Grasser*   NW-NE-S33; 1-27-51
Elihu Holcombe*   SW-NE-S33; 5-26-36; NE-SE-S33; 2-10-36
Hosea Holcombe*   SE-SE-S33; 5-26-36
Robert Skelton*   SW-SE-S33; 9-6-51
Samuel McDonald, Vb   NE-NE-S34; 3-16-46
Reuben Stallings*   SE-NE-S34; 11-2-36
William Kurtz*   NW-NE-S34; 3-17-54
William Stunkel*   SW-NE-S34; 1-15-51
James Hannah King*   SE-NW-S34; 6-7-36
John Witherow   E-SW-S34; 8-9-19
Elihu Holcombe*   W-SW-S34; 1-22-30; SE-SE-S35; 5-26-36
Hosea Holcombe*   NE-SE-S34; 5-26-36; W-SW-S34; 6-6-18; E-NE-S35;
   2-15-37; NE-SE-S35; 10-9-32; W-SW-S36; 1-19-36
Silas Messer Holcombe*   SE-SE-S34; 7-27-39; SE-NW-S35; 5-9-49;
   SW-NW-S35; 5-2-44.   Mercer
George Sidle*   W-NE-S35; 8-3-47
Henry Arburn*   NE-NW-S35; 8-16-48
Moses Stallings*   NW-NW-S35; 7-27-39
William Rahm   NE-S36; 3-28-49
Jonas Skelton*   NE-SW-S36; 3-10-48
John Sherry*   SE-SW-S36; 8-28-39

RELINQUISHMENTS

William Depriest   E-SW-S3; 2-20-19; 8-7-21; W-SW-S3; 2-20-19;
David L. Woods   E-NE-S5; 8-25-18; 10-22-24.   12-9-24
William Embree & Jos. (Jas.?) Woods   W-NE-S5; 1-22-19; 10-22-24
William Sharry   NW-S5; 10-26-16; 3-28-25
Abraham Brokaw   E-NE-S6; 9-7-18; 3-28-25
Daniel Reavis   E-SE-S6; 8-19-17; 7-2-29
Amassa D. Foster   E-NE-S7; 4-21-19; 5-11-29
Robert M. Evans   E-SE-S7; 6-27-17; 6-27-29; SW-S8; 1-5-19; 8-30-21;
   NE-S18; 6-27-17; 6-29-27
Thomas Gedney   E-SE-S8;12-3-19;8-29-21; W-SE-S8;12-3-19;3-28-25
Nathaniel H. Caldwell   SW-S10; 11-6-18; 1-8-25
Christian Graeter   NW-S17; 3-2-18; 8-30-21
Thomas Browning   E-SW-S17; 4-15-19; 9-30-23
John McGough   W-NW-S18; 8-24-16; 6-30-29
Thomas H. Martin   W-SW-S18; 11-4-17; 3-6-27
James Monroe   SE-S18; 11-18-17; 6-6-27
Ruth Walters   NW, SW-S19; 8-6-18; 3-6-27
Seaman Walters, D.Walters, & S. Walters   NW-S20;8-6-18; 8-24-22

GIBSON COUNTY

A.S. Morrow & J. Prewitt SW-S20; 6-27-18; 9-28-21
John S. Baker SW-S21; 1-18-19; 8-30-21
Peter Goodsell NE-S29; 2-19-19; 9-8-21
James Ralston W-SW-S30; 8-30-19; 12-21-24
John Witherow W-SW-S34; 8-9-19; 3-29-25
Hosea Holcomb E-SE-S34; 6-6-18; 9-18-21
William Putman E-SE-S5; 6-29-18; 7-4-29
Richard Tomkins NW-S12; 9-19-18; 7-4-29
Seaman Watters, D.Watters, & S.Watters W-NE-S19;8-6-18; 7-4-29
Peter Goodsell W-SE-S29; 2-19-19; 7-4-29

T 3 S, R 11 W

John Ayers* E-NE-S1; 6-2-35
Washington Wallace* W-NE-S1; 10-26-36
John Wright, Jr.* E-NW-S1; 8-4-36
James Thomas* W-NW-S1; 3-27-49
James R. Brothers* NE-SW-S1; 11-15-41
David Robinson* SE-SW, SW-SE-S1; 2-16-36
Hugh McMullin* NW-SW-S1; 9-15-48
Dausey Hallbrooks* SW-SW-S1; 2-8-36
Ezekiel Hopkins* NE-SE-S1; 8-5-36
William McIntire* SE-SE-S1; 12-24-35; NW-SE-S1; 1-7-37
Simon Orr* NE-NE-S2; 11-22-47
Silas Smith Stone* SE-NE-S2; 9-18-34; NE-SE-S2; 9-18-34
Warerum Day & Levi Day* NW-NE-S2; 8-5-36
Thomas McMullen* SW-NE, SE-SE, NW-SE, SW-SE-S2; 4-10-47; NE-SW-S2;
David L. Woods* NE-NW-S2;10-16-35;SE-NW-S2;10-27-35.   12-13-50
Moses Carson Witherspoon* NW-NW-S2; 12-24-32
William Henry Harrison Hill* SW-NW-S2; 3-28-42
John Barker* SE-SW-S2; 8-4-35
Andrew Sillavan* NW-SW-S2; 5-2-36; NE-SE-S3; 6-26-35
Elias Barker* SW-SW-S2; 8-4-35
Samuel Sillaven* NE-NE-S3; 6-4-32; W-NE-S3; 10-28-28
William Patterson Witherspoon* SE-NE-S3; 3-28-36
Isaac Woods, Sr.* NE-NW-S3; 11-6-32
Henry Johnson* SE-NW-S3; 10-31-38
Joseph Field W-NW-S3; 3-28-31
Harrison Smith* NE-SW-S3; 7-12-39
John Montgomery* SE-SW-S3; 4-6-33; SW-SE-S3; 11-21-35
John Depriest* W-SW-S3; 6-15-33
John Smith* NW-SE-S3; 5-5-35
John Byrn* E-NE-S4; 3-7-31
Adam Miller* W-NE-S4; 7-22-26
John Hamilton NW, SW-S4; 5-19-07
Willis Alsop* NE-SE-S4; 9-28-35; NW-SE-S4; 11-18-33
Robert McGary* SE-SE-S4; 4-3-37
Isan Lewis* SW-SE-S4; 4-16-35
George T. Boring* NE-S5; 3-6-15; SE-S5; 3-15-15
Thomas L. Ash* NW-S5; 2-10-14
Nicholas Yager* E-SW-S5;11-22-33; E-NE-S6;10-26-19; W-NE-S6;2-16-
Clement Estes W-SW-S5; 8-22-16   36
Robert McCrary* E-NW, W-NW-S6; 2-16-36

Samuel Hirons SW-S6; 2-1-14
Ellinder Warrick SE-S6; 1-2-08
Harrison McGary NE-S7; 10-22-16
Logan McCrary* NE-NW-S7; 2-20-39
William Carloss Wilson* SE-NW-S7; 5-15-32
Jonathan Jaques* W-NW-S7; 1-23-17
Walter C. Montgomery" SW-S7; 11-22-16
Burkett Hughes† SE-S7; 10-11-14
William R. McGary NE-S8; 10-30-16
Francis Hopkins NW-S8; 10-11-11
John Hull* NE-SW, NW-SW-S8; 8-5-34
Edmund Fields* SE-SW, SW-SW-S8; 9-21-35
Robert Ash* SE-S8; 2-3-17
John Martin Witherspoon* NE-NE-S9; 8-13-36; NW-NW-S10; 11-6-33
Willis Smith Montgomery* SE-NE-S9; 11-21-35; SW-NE-S9; 8-20-35
Wright Pritchett* NW-NE-S9; 11-19-35; SE-SE-S9; 1-16-36
Robert McGary NW-S9; 10-31-07
Azariah Ayres SW-S9; 7-15-19
Greenup Thompson* NE-SE-S9; SW-NW-S10; 3-12-39; NE-SW-S10; 6-11-38
William Gudgel* NW-SE-S9; 8-6-35; SW-SE-S9; 1-27-35
Durham C. Redmen* SE-NE-S10; 1-16-51
Nathan Montgomery* NW-NE-S10; 9-7-36
Montgomery Mounts* SW-NE, SE-NW-S10; 12-15-35
John Simpson* NE-NW-S10; 4-7-35
Andrew Jackson Thomas* SE-SW-S10; 4-28-37
James Belont* NW-SW-S10; 12-26-50; SW-SW-S10; 12-13-50
Ephraim Thomas* SE-SE-S10; 12-13-50
Luke Edwards Hardy* NW-SE-S10; 12-24-35
John Wright* SW-SE-S10; 3-23-44
Benjamin Lemasters, Pi NE-NE-S11; 6-21-36
Reuben Walters* SE-NE, NE-SE-S11; 1-13-51; W-NW-S13; 2-8-37
William Legrange* NW-NE-S11; 11-15-36
John Woods* SW-NE, NW-SE-S11; 9-13-36
John Barker* NE-NW-S11; 7-22-35
James Furgason, Ps SE-NW-S11; 10-17-36
Elias Barker* NW-NW-S11; 11-7-32
Martin Smith* SW-NW-S11; 10-21-36
Jesse Barker, Jr.* NE-SW-S11; 11-15-36
John Jefferson Douglas* SE-SW-S11; 11-17-35; SW-SE-S11; 3-26-33
Jonathan Wright* NW-SW-S11; 4-23-39
Patsey McGary* SW-SW-S11; 4-28-37
Isaac Pennington Douglas* SE-SE-S11; 10-9-32
Alexander Conner* E-NE-S12; 3-12-31; E-SE-S13; 6-25-36
George Pearce, Jr.* NW-NE-S12; 8-8-35; NE-NW-S12; 12-28-36
George Pierce* SW-NE-S12; 12-30-34
Dausy Hallbrooks* NW-NW-S12; 2-8-36
George Halbrook* E-SW-S12; 8-4-35
John Ames & John Barlow† W-SW-S12; 2-10-45
William Mangrum* SE-S12; 12-27-11
Allen Ingram* NE-S13; 1-2-10
William Halbrooks, Sr.* E-NW-S13; 7-16-36
Enoch Walters* E-SW-S13; 7-16-36
William Low, Ps W-SW-S13; 10-12-32
Marcus Sherwood* W-SE-S13; 12-3-33

Alexander Rosborough* E-NE-S14; 2-14-34
Zenas Martin Weed* NE-NW, NW-NW-S14; 4-23-39
David Robb* SE-NW-S14; E-SW-S14; SE-NE-S15; 8-25-32; SW-SE-S22;
John Simpson* SW-NW-S14; 7-25-32   9-17-36
Isaac Dougless* W-SW-S14; 1-4-31
Hudson Berry Brothers* NE-SE-S14; 3-8-36
Charles Whiting* SE-SE-S14; 7-13-33
Jesse Knoles* NW-SE-S14; 2-8-34
Davinport Hughes* NE-NE, NW-NE-S15; 1-25-37
James Sides* SW-NE-S15; 11-23-42;NE-SE-S22;11-28-35;SE-SE-S22;
Franklin Hawkins* NE-NW-S15; 12-6-34   9-24-36
Robert McGary, Jr.* NW-NW-S15; 4-8-37
Thomas Hawkins* SW-NW-S15; 12-6-34
Andrew Jackson Thomas* SE-SW-S15; 1-18-36
Greenup Poe* NW-SW-S15; 11-25-35
William Minton* SW-SW-S15; 12-4-35
Ezekiel Rutledge* NE-SE-S15; 10-5-35; SE-SE-S15; 2-4-37
John Hill Brothers* W-SE-S15; 1-7-36
Johnson Rutledge* NE-NE-S17; 9-1-32
James McKiddy* SE-NE-S17; 8-24-32
Edmund Fields* W-NE-S17; 2-27-34
Stephen McKiddy NW-S17; 10-21-16
Joseph Montgomery SW-S17; 10-17-16
Joseph Scott* E-SE-S17; 7-13-31; SW-NE-S20; 1-15-36
Samuel Hawkins* NW-SE-S17; 2-25-34
Albert Warren Douglas* SW-SE-S17; 1-6-36
Braxton Clark NE-S18; 9-11-15
Solomon Davis NW-S18; 5-17-17
Walter C. Montgomery SW-S18; 11-22-16
John Wilson SE-S18; NE-S19; 11-1-17; NW-S19; 5-12-08
Smith Mounts SW-S19; 8-18-17
Jesse Knoles SE-S19; 11-13-16
Henry Thurman E-NE-S20; 3-10-19
William Montgomery* NW-NE, SW-NW-S20; 8-2-36
Franklin Hawkins* NE-NW-S20; 6-25-36
Robert Redmen* SE-NW-S20; 7-29-36
William Smith* NW-NW-S20; 10-5-32
Joseph Montgomery SW-S20; 11-22-16
John D. Boren E-SE-S20; 9-1-18
James West W-SE-S20; 9-26-18
Jesse Douglas* E-NE-S21; 5-9-31
John Pritchett W-NE-S21; 9-4-19
Abraham Robinson NW-S21; 2-3-17
Nicholas Boren SW-S21; 12-9-16
David Thomas* NE-SE-S21; 6-3-33; NE-SW-S22; 1-13-36; W-SW-S22;
Stephen Mead* SE-SE-S21; 9-24-36   7-5-31
Isham Robinson* W-SE-S21; 9-26-21
James Berry Brothers* E-NE-S22; 7-18-31
Isaac Pennington Douglas* W-NE-S22; 12-8-31
Hugh Sportsman* NW-S22; 10-28-19
Henry Hawkins* SE-SW, NW-SE-S22; 12-5-35
Charles Whiting, Jr.* NE-NE-S23; 12-13-34
David Miller* NW-NE, NE-NW-S23; 6-12-37
Henry Sides* SW-NE-S23; 8-13-34

John White Stewart* SE-NW-S23; 10-30-32
Alexander R. Downing* W-NW-S23; 12-21-30
William Brothers SW-S23; 8-22-18; NW-SE-S26; 7-25-36;E-NE-S33;
James Fitzgerald SE-S23; 5-1-18   9-24-18
Aaron Legrange NE-S24; 1-21-17
David Brothers* E-NW-S24; 12-11-34; W-NE-S33; 10-23-35
James Rosborough* W-NW-S24; 2-14-34
Joseph M. Woods* NE-SW, NW-SW-S24; 7-8-39
Henry Reel* SE-SW, SW-SW-S24; 5-13-35; NW-SW-S36; 2-15-37
Edward Durr Lockwood* NE-SE-S24; 3-3-34
Isaac Walters* NW-SE-S24; 7-18-36
Joseph Neely Reel* SW-SE-S24; 8-27-36
Thomas Whitten Marvel* NE-NE-S25; 1-31-37; W-NE-S25; 12-17-35
Samuel Adams* SE-NE-S25; 6-3-35; SE-S25; 9-17-18
Teekle T. Taylor NW-S25; 9-30-16
George Marvel* SW-S25; 12-17-35
Alexander Johnson NE, SW-S26; 7-22-17
William Miller NW-S26; 6-5-17
David Robb* E-SE-S26; 9-6-36
James Scott* SW-SE-S26; 1-16-36
Johnson Rutledge* NE-NE-S27; 6-21-39
Isaac Pennington Douglas* SE-NE-S27; 2-15-37; E-SE-S27; 2-13-36
William Rutledge* NW-NE-S27; 3-16-37
John Gilland McGregor, Ps SW-NE-S27; 2-28-37
George Washington Beloat* E-NW-S27; 4-22-35
John White Stewart* W-NW-S27; 4-4-33
James Noles SW-S27; 8-21-18
David Miller* NW-SE-S27; 8-9-36; SW-SE-S27; 8-12-36
Isaac Smith* E-NE-S32; 1-24-32
James Montgomery W-NE-S32; 4-17-17
Elisha Marvel NW-S32; 10-1-16; of*, NW-NE-S35; 12-14-35; NE-NW-S35;
Reuben Emmerson SW-S32; 5-24-14   7-29-36
Daniel McDowell SE-S32; 8-28-18
Edwin Chaffin* E-NW-S33; 1-12-36; W-SE-S33; 12-14-35
Archibald Simpson W-NW-S33; 3-16-19
James Curry SW-S33; 3-13-16
John Miller E-SE-S33; 2-13-19; of*, SE-NW-S35; 1-25-37; SW-NW-S35;
Jacob Privett* NE-NE-S34; 2-9-37   2-24-36
James Kitchen, Sr.* SE-NE-S34; 11-2-36
Joshua Duncan* W-NE-S34; 4-18-36
John J. Neely NW-S34; 1-26-16   10-31-38
James Kitchen* NE-SW-S34; 4-14-36; SW-NE-S35; 12-8-35;SW-SW-S35;/
William Ford Robinson* W-SW-S34; 4-13-29. Of Vb, SE-SW-S34;2-22-
Isaac Kennerly* NE-SE-S34;9-17-36; W-SE-S34;7-5-31.   33
Evans Boren* SE-SE-S34; 3-16-37
John Johnson E-NE-S35; 3-22-16   John Trible*
William Miller* NW-NW-S35; 2-24-36   W-NW-S36;7-7-29
Joshua Kitchen* NE-SW-S35; 12-30-36   *Thomas Marshall Gooch
James Lawrence McDowell* SE-SW-S35; 10-9-38.   E-SW,SW-SW-S36;4-25-
John Miller* NW-SW-S35; 1-25-37   37
Joshua Duncan* NE-SE, NW-SE-S35; 3-6-39   /Joseph Clark*
Benjamin Holcom, Vb SE-SE, SW-SE-S35; 1-18-37./SE-S36;2-16-37
George Trible* E-NE-S36; 3-20-34;NW-NE-S36;1-1-36; SW-NE-S36;9-30-
James Brumfield, Vb E-NW-S36; 1-18-37   36

RELINQUISHMENTS

Joseph Stapleton NE-S1; 11-7-16; 8-3-21
Clement Estes E-SW-S5; 8-22-15; 6-20-29
Nicholas Yager W-NE-S6; 10-26-19; 6-20-29
Robert McCrary NW-S6; 9-22-18; 4-30-27
Jonathan Jaques E-NW-S7; 1-23-17; 6-25-27
Daniel Reavis NE-S12; 12-4-16; 3-28-25
Azariah Ayres NW, SW-S14; 9-21-19; 3-20-25;SW-S9;7-15-19;7-4-29
David Dick, Jr. E-SE-S14;9-25-19;9-25-21; W-SE-S14;9-25-19;3-28-25
Benjamin Holcom NE-S17; 2-25-19; 9-29-28
John Pritchett E-NE-S21; 9-4-19; 6-10-29
H. Hawkins & John Sides E-NE-S22; 1-29-19; 9-8-21; W-NE-S22;1-29-
Robert McGary SW-S22;10-28-19;12-27-24.   19; 3-28-25
William Brothers W-NE-S28; 9-24-18; 3-28-25
Ephraim Knoles SW-S28; 2-3-19; 7-3-29
John Smith W-SW-S29; 10-4-17; 7-3-29
James Smith SE-S29; 10-4-17; 7-3-27
John Scott E-NE-S30; 8-30-16; 6-12-29
James Malone E-SW-S30; 12-6-17; 4-30-27
Harris Hunter E-NW-S31; 11-10-18; 3-28-25
Vachel Clark SW-S31; 10-22-16; 3-28-25
James Montgomery E-NE-S32; 4-17-17; 7-1-29
John D. Boren W-SE-S33; 10-4-17; 10-4-17 (sic)
David Miller SW-S34; 7-23-18; 3-29-25
Thomas F. Johnson SE-S34; 10-9-18; 3-6-27
John Johnson W-NE-S35; 3-22-16; 9-27-22
Thomas H. Martin NW-S35; 1-1-19; 3-28-25
John Ewing SE-S35; 11-9-19; 4-6-25
Robert Ash SE-S8; 2-5-17; 7-4-29
James Ferguson SE-S13; 1-21-17; 7-4-29
Braxter Clark NE-S18; 9-11-15; 7-4-29
Hugh Sportsman NW-S22; 10-28-19; 7-4-29
James Moles SW-S27; 8-21-18; 7-4-29
Archibald Simpson W-NW-S33; 3-16-19; 7-4-29

T 3 S, R 12 W

Oliver Lucas* NE-NE-S1; 10-6-52
Robert McCrary* SE-NE-S1; 1-18-36
Fielding Lucas* W-NE-S1; 3-30-22
Thomas Montgomery NW-S1; 8-27-07
James Stewart SW-S1; 4-5-13
Joseph Montgomery SE-S1; 1-31-17
Edward Stapleton NE-S2; 5-20-08
John, Jesse, & James McGary NW, SW-S2; 9-21-07
John Hamilton SE-S2; 5-20-07
James Emison NE, SE-S3; 5-20-07
Jacob Kern NW-S3; 9-4-16
Montgomery Warrick SW-S3; 11-22-16
Thomas Waters NE-S4; 4-18-10
Samuel Anderson & William Carlton NW-S4; 10-27-09
James Martin SW-S4; 4-18-14

Robert Anderson SE-S4; 3-11-09; NE-S5; 10-24-07
Thomas Gwin E-NW-S5; 11-18-18
Thomas Johnson* W-NW-S5; 9-9-30
Richard Simpson* E-SW-S5; 5-26-23
William Steel* W-SW-S5; 6-5-33
Lewis Jordan* E-SE-S5; 9-4-17
Lewis Harmon* W-SE-S5; 7-20-31
James Simpson* SE-NE-S6; 1-1-36
John Orr SW-S7; 1-2-54
John McFadden* E-SE-S7; 7-20-36
James Skelton* SW-SE-S7; 7-22-36; NW-NE-S18; 7-22-36
Eli Garret* NE-NE-S8; 6-14-36
Syrack Harmon* SE-NE-S8; 5-18-36
James Garrett* NW-NE-S8; 6-22-36
John Robinson* SW-NE-S8; 7-4-36
Featherton Cross* E-NW-S8; 12-6-30
Henry Garret* SW-NW-S8; 7-11-32; E-SW-S8; 8-17-18; NW-SW-S8; 10-
    22-32; W-SE-S8; 5-16-31
Bennett Harmon* NE-SE-S8; 7-13-36
Tabitha Baldwin* SE-SE-S8; 11-21-36
Shubal Garret* NE-NE-S9; 5-24-35; SE-NE-S9; 6-14-36; W-NE-S9;
Bailey W. Gwin* NE-NW-S9; 5-15-39   8-22-28
Greenberry Baldwin* SE-NW-S9; 10-1-32; NE-SW-S9; 8-12-33
John Simpson, Sr.* NW-NW-S9; 2-15-37
Lewis Harmon* SW-NW, NW-SW-S9; 6-6-36
John James Frazer* SE-SW-S9; 5-6-36
Hiram Jordan Frazer* SW-SW-S9; 5-6-36
James Jordan* E-SE-S9; 8-23-31;NW-SE-S9;12-14-33;SW-SE-S9;5-28-33
John A. Miller NE-S10; 5-20-07
Thomas Sharp NW-S10; 10-30-16; SW-S14; 3-5-16
Joseph Griffin E-SW-S10; 10-26-16; E-NW-S15; 5-6-16
James Elliott Sharp* W-SW-S10; 5-13-33
Jacob Warrick's heirs SE-S10; 1-2-13; SE-S11; 4-8-12
John Hunter NE-S11; 4-14-13
Jacob Warrick NW-S11; 5-20-07
John W. Maddox SW-S11; 10-12-13
Thomas Stone NE-S13; 1-20-10; NW-S13; 10-22-16
James Montgomery SW-S13; 12-11-13
Walter C. Montgomery SE-S13; 5-20-07
George Sharp NE, SE-S14; 12-13-13
James Patton NW-S14; NE-S15; 5-20-07
Jeremiah Cash* NW-NW-S15; 8-5-34
David Wheeler* SW-NW-S15; 5-6-33
David Gemble SW-S15; 4-14-15
Robert Anderson SE-S15; 12-25-11
Edward Wells NE-S17; 5-29-09
Jesse York Welborn, Ps NE-NW-S17; 11-19-32
John Awldridge* SW-NW-S17; 10-26-36
Benjamin Forrest* W-SW-S17; 3-26-38
Anthony Griffin* SE-S17; 11-28-15
Henry Robbison* NE-NE-S18; 3-7-39
William Chalmers* NE-SW-S18; 9-1-36
Thomas Robinson* SE-SW-S18; 1-25-39
John Floner SW-SW-S18; 12-4-51

William Garrett* SE-S18; 6-24-36
Abraham Wells NE-S19; 5-11-15
William Simpson* NE-NW-S19; 9-20-36; E-SW-S19; 1-1-36
Ephraim Simpson* SE-NW-S19;9-16-35;NW-NW-S19;3-11-51;SW-NW-S19;
Washington Creek* NW-SW-S19; 2-10-37   8-31-37
Isom Creek* SW-SW-S19; 4-6-36; NE-NE-S30; 7-29-36
Jacob Creek E-SE-S19; 6-8-19; NW-SE-S19; 11-9-33;NW-SW-S20;4-27-
Pearson Creek* SW-SE-S19; 9-25-37   36
John Endecott NE-NE, W-NE-S20; 7-19-51
Samuel H. Wheeler SE-NE, E-SE, NW-SE-S20; 2-1-51
William S. Moolry* NE-NW-S20; 3-15-51
Thomas Redden Auldridge* SE-NW-S20; 8-27-36
Thomas Garett NW-NW-S20; 3-21-51
Amos Garret* SW-NW-S20; 2-21-37
James Auldridge* NE-SW-S20; 9-11-37
Samuel Wheeler* SE-SW-S20; 10-28-50; SW-SE-S20; 7-26-51
James Garret, Sr.* SW-SW-S20; 7-22-36; NW-NW-S29; 7-22-36
Charles Grier E-NE-S21; 8-15-15; of*, NW-NE-S21; 4-5-36; SW-NE-
Hiram Westfall* NE-NW-S21;4-5-36.   S21; 10-21-35
James Ash* SE-NW, W-NW-S21; 2-5-45
Jacob Paden* E-SW-S21; 9-26-28
Charles S. Wiggins* NW-SW-S21; 9-18-51; SW-SW-S21; 8-27-51
James Walrond SE-S21; 3-6-16
William McCormick NE-S22; 8-25-13
Joseph Wasson* E-NW-S22; 5-21-29; SW-S22; 5-3-14
Matthew Thompson W-NW-S22; 4-5-15
James Patton SE-S22; 5-20-07
Micajah W. Sharp NE-S23; 7-13-15
Jacob Warrick's heirs NW-S23; 5-17-13
Joshua Nichols SW-S23; 8-5-11; SE-S23; 12-27-11
Thomas Alcorn NE-S25; 7-6-12
Jesse Emonerson SE-S25; 11-21-10. Emmerson?
Eddy Knoles NW-S25; 9-5-14; SW-S27;/10-19-14;SE-SE-S29;1-3-34
Samuel Montgomery SW-S25; 7-3-15
John Caldwell NE-S26; 9-24-10
William Officer SE-S26; 3-14-10
Daniel Fisher NW-S26; 10-24-10
Prettyman Knoles SW-S26; 12-30-11
James Patton NE-S27; 5-20-07
James Ash SE-S27; 4-29-16
William Redman NW-S27; 9-18-15
William Stillwell E-NE-S28; 12-3-16
John Redman* NW-NE-S28; 12-31-33; NE-NW-S28; 12-22-35
William Knoles* SW-NE-S28; 12-30-33; E-SW-S28; 1-1-31
Morgan Harris* SE-NW-S28; 12-14-35
Lawson E. Hobbs* NW-NW-S28; 12-19-50
William Hunter* SW-NW-S28; 12-6-36; E-SE-S28; 12-3-16; W-SE-S28;
James McClure W-SW-S28; 3-19-18   1-1-31
Andrew Baird* NE-NE-S29; 2-16-50
Calvin Westfall* SE-NE-S29; 2-26-50
Noah Murphy* W-NE, E-NW-S29; 3-11-51
William R. Davis* SW-NW-S29; 5-26-51
James Price* NE-SW-S29; 1-24-37; of Lw, SW-SW-S29; 8-31-36
Benjamin Williams, Ps SE-SW-S29;1-24-37; of*, NW-NW-S30;9-30-35

Samuel Church* NW-SW-S29; 7-28-51
Morgan Harriss* NE-SE-S29; 9-30-35
Solomon Knoles* NW-SE-S29; 7-22-39; SW-SE-S29; 9-24-35
Joseph Garton* SE-NE-S30; 7-5-37
David Gamble W-NE-S30; 8-11-18; W-SE-S30; 10-30-17
Harry Hunter E-NW-S30; 1-29-19
William Williams* SW-NW-S30; 6-10-36
Hiram Harrelson & John Johnson SW-S30; 5-21-15
Clement Willy* NE-SE-S30; 1-27-37
Elijah Saulmon, Jr.* SE-SE-S30; 3-2-37; NW-SE-S31; 2-9-36
Robert C. Davis* E-NE-S31; 1-14-31
George Williams* NW-NE-S31; 5-30-36; of Ps, SW-NE-S31; 8-16-33
James Eaton, Barren Co., Ky. NW-S31; 9-11-21
Pearson Newsum SW-S31; 5-26-15
David Smith E-SE-S31; 12-8-18
George Johnson & William Ross Davis SW-SE-S31; 3-14-36
Jesse Davis E-NE-S32; 8-28-18; of*, SW-NE-S32; 3-30-36; SW-NW-
John Price, Ps NW-NE-S32;4-27-37.   S33; 1-11-34
Benjamin Williams, Ps NE-NW-S32; 1-24-37
Moses Goodwin, Ps SE-NW-S32; 12-20-36
Joel Davis & William Ross Davis NW-NW-S32; 3-7-36
Joel Davis* SW-NW-S32; 9-30-35
Robert C. Davis E-SW-S32; 11-14-18
Robert Clark Davis* NW-SW-S32; 3-21-36
Adam Smith* SW-SW-S32; 3-21-36
William Ross Davis* NE-SE-S32; 12-12-34
Hontage Saulman* SE-SE-S32; 8-26-33
Wiley Marvel* W-SE-S32; 11-17-31
Philip W. Martin NE-S33; 10-7-16
David Stillwell E-NW-S33; 9-30-17
Eli Knoles* NW-NW-S33; 3-23-33
John Garton* NE-SW-S33; 11-30-33; SE-SW-S33; 10-11-32
William Johnson* NW-SW-S33; 10-1-32
George Johnson* SW-SW-S33; 12-8-34
Edward McReynolds* E-SE-S33; 11-17-31
John Johnson* NW-SE-S33; 10-1-32; SW-SE-S33; 12-19-33
John Barr NE-S34; 3-6-16
Joseph Johnson NW-S34; 10-24-10
Benjamin Montgomery SW-S34; 6-11-16
Jesse Kimball SE-S34; 8-17-13
Joshua Wilson NE-S35; 5-19-13; NW-S35; 8-14-16
John Marvel SW-S35; 10-31-16
Nathan Knoles SE-S35; 5-28-17
Randolph Clark NE-S36; 7-22-14
Benniah Gragg NW-S36; 12-11-13; SW-S36; 8-9-13
Thomas Igo SE-S36; 12-20-11

RELINQUISHMENTS

Henry Garret W-SW-S8; 8-17-18; 8-27-21   6-30-27
William McCormick W-SE-S9; 6-23-18; 9-26-21; E-SE-S9; 6-23-18;/
Joseph Griffin W-SW-S10; 10-26-16; 6-29-29; W-NW-S15; 5-6-16;
Jacob Creek W-SE-S19; 6-8-19; 6-25-29   9-20-21
Charles Crier W-NE-S21; 8-15-15; 3-28-25

Matthew Thompson E-NW-S22; 4-5-15; 3-24-25
William Stillwell W-NE-S28; 12-3-16; 8-24-21
James McClure E-SW-S28; 3-19-18; 4-4-29
William Hunter W-SE-S28; 12-3-16; 3-6-25; W-NW-S33; 1-21-18; 6-27-
Jesse Howchin W-NW-S30; 12-9-19; 11-12-28   27
Robert C. Davis NE-S31;11-14-18;3-6-27; W-SW-S32;11-14-18;9-8-21
David Smith W-SE-S31; 12-8-18; 6-25-27
Jesse Davis W-NE-S32; 8-28-18; 9-11-21
John & George Johnson E-SW-S33; 11-20-17; 6-25-27
William Wells E-SE-S33; 11-28-17; 6-25-27
John Williams W-SE-S33; 11-17-19; 6-25-27
Lewis Harmon W-SE-S5; 7-13-19; 7-4-29
David Burton E-NE-S30; 7-23-18; 7-4-29
James Montray SE-S32; 2-9-18; 7-4-29

T 3 S, R 13 W

John Jordon* W-FrS2; 1-12-35
Jacob Pruett Jordon* FrS4; 7-7-32; N-Nfr-S9; 2-12-36
Isaac Stroud Casselberry* FrS5; 6-20-36
William Hopkins Kinchloe, Ps FrS6; 2-10-37
Henry Hill Denby, Jr.* Lot 3-Efr-S7;6-14-36;Lots 1,3-NWfr-S8;
River Jordon* Lot 4-Efr-S7; 5-20-36; W-NW-S17; 10-14-25 5-20-36
Young Lemar* Wfr-S7; 2-7-37
William L. Bishop, Ps Lot 2-NWfr-S8; 11-9-54
Joshua Jordan* S-Nfr-S9; 1-22-36; E-SWfr-S9; 5-27-30; Lot 2-SEfr-
Jordan Hunt* Lot 1-SEfr-S9; 11-13-36   S9; 8-5-34
Jesse Barker* Lot 1-FrS10; 8-5-34
Peter Smith* Lot 2-FrS10; 11-2-37; Lot 3-FrS10; 10-4-34
Asa Watts* Lot 4-FrS10; 2-23-36
Eliba Jordan* N-NWfrOS11; 11-15-37
Jesse Barker* S-NWfr-S11; 11-6-36; NW-SWfr-S11; 12-18-34
Joseph Waldon, Kn SE-S12; 10-11-54
Jacob Asbury Paden* SE-SW-S14; 10-31-39; SW-SE-S14; 9-25-39
Absalom Jordan* NE-NW-S15; 6-20-36
Asa Watts & Joel Davis* NW-NW-S15; 10-4-34
Henry Hunt" NW-SW-S15; 7-25-36
Alfred Jordan* NW-NE-S17; 1-22-36; E-NW-S17; 11-16-29
Pressley.Cartwright, Ps NE-NEfr-S18;6-28-36;W-NEfr-S18;6-25-36
Stephen Herring, Ps E-NWfr-S18; 8-5-34
James Crowley* W-NWfr-S18; 5-22-33; W-SWfr-S18; 3-26-29
Thomas Barnett* NE-SWfr-S18; 5-9-37
James Tweedle* NE-NW-S19; 4-3-37;W-NE-S21;9-29-31;SW-SE-S21;10-7-
John Davis* SE-NW-S19; 7-31-36; NE-SW-S19; 5-13-33   36
John Wilkins* W-NW-S19; 5-15-29
William Armstrong Waters* SE-SW, SW-SW-S19; 11-15-36
James Moutray* NW-SW-S19; 5-13-33
Thomas Ashley" NE-SE-S19; 6-27-39; NW-SW-S20; 7-25-36
Peter Guthrie* SE-SE-S19; 11-16-32; SW-SW-S20; 8-16-33
John H. Hepner, Su NW-SE, SW-SE-S19; 10-26-54
Elijah Rook E-NE-S20; 1-20-18
Mary Jordan* SW-NE-S20; 7-1-36
John Fifer* E-SW-S20; 7-25-36

David Smith* NE-SE-S20; 3-23-33; W-SW-S21; 10-29-31
George Overton* SW-NW-S21; 11-2-38
Over R. Jordon E-SW-S21; 1-27-18. River Jordan?
Chauncey Pierce* E-SE-S21; 2-2-37
Peter Smith* NW-SE-S21; 12-30-33
William Garner Summers* E-NE-S23; 3-19-38
Washington Creek* SE-SW-S24; 2-10-37
Rumzy Bary Creek* SE-SE-S24; 8-18-36
Henry Harrison Conner* SW-SE-S24; 9-16-36
Redwine Davis* NE-NE-S25; 6-25-50
Greenberry Simpson* NE-SW-S25; 10-15-38
Stephen Garrett* SE-SW-S25; 4-1-39
Joseph Garnon* NE-SE-S25; 4-28-37
Gillison Creek* SE-SE-S25; 6-17-37
Jacob Oglesby, Ps NW-SE-S25; 6-21-37
Joseph Newsum, Ps SW-SE-S25; 12-2-39
John Fifer* NE-NW, NW-NW-S29; 8-8-36
John Thomas* SE-SW-S29; 4-17-39
Thomas Ashley* SW-SW-S29; SE-SE-S30; 7-25-36
George L. Clark, Ri NE, NE-SW, NE-SE, NW-SE-S30; 10-11-54
Isaac Williams* NE-NW-S30; 7-16-36; of Ps, SE-SW-S30; 6-24-54
Joseph Williams* SE-NW-S30; 7-16-36
Daniel Williams* NW-NW-S30; 7-13-36; SW-NW-S30; 10-4-32
William Daugherty* NW-SW-S30; 10-26-54
Joshua Reeder, Ps SW-SW-S30; 1-5-38
William Davis, Ps SW-SE-S30; 7-17-39

RELINQUISHMENTS

Iver R. Gordain W-SW-S21; 1-27-18; 3-18-25. River Jordan?

T 3 S, R 14 W

James Tweedle* SW-NEfr-S12; 3-1-37; Lots 3,6-N-SEfr-S12; 8-13-36;
    W-NE-S13; 8-18-36; NW-S13; 4-29-37
A. I. (J.?) Cooper, Ps N-NWfr-S12; 6-12-39
James Crowley* Lot 4-S-SEfr-S12; 7-1-36
Thomas Barnett* Lot 5-S-SEfr-S12; 2-8-36; NE-NE-S13; 1-25-36
Napoleon Grayson Lots 1-2-Nfr-S11; 4-28-37
Andrew Clark* SE-NE-S13; 9-23-35
Jacob Carbaugh* E-SW-S13; 5-23-29
George Flower, Edwards Co. Ill. W-SW-S13; 8-21-20; SE-S13; 7-5-20
Thomas Scott, Ck Lot 1-NTr-S14; 10-24-54
William S. Ward, Ck Lot 2-Nfr-S14; 10-24-54
John Carbaugh* Lot 3-Nfr-S14; 1-22-36; Sfr-S14; 5-20-33
George Webb, White Co., Ill. FrS21; 10-6-32
Robert Harmon, Ps Lot 2-S-NEfr; NWfr-S23; 7-25-36
Alvin Bacon Carpenter, Vb SWfr-S23; W-SE-S23; 3-16-37
James R. Barnett NE-S24; 10-24-16
John Wilkins* E-NW-S24; 6-11-29
William Wilkins* NW-NW-S24; 4-19-37
Caleb Huet Griffin* NE-SE-S24; 12-16-38
John White* E-NE-S25; 6-30-36; NE-SE-S25; 5-13-33

John Waller, Ps W-NE-S25; 7-9-36
Uriah Emmerson Boren, Ps NE-SW-S25; 12-30-35
John Bazel Rachels, Ps SE-SW, SW-SE-S25; 7-9-38
William Lewis Burton, Ps NW-SW-S25; 12-30-35
Isaac Thomas NW-SE-S25; 3-12-33
John Carbaugh* NE-NWfr-S26; 4-19-37
James Cray & Robert Didlake Walden SE-NWfr-S26; .5-1-37; W-SW-S26;
    NEfr, E-SE-S27; 6-27-36. Is James' surname Walden & Gray a mid-
Isaac Williams, Ps W-NWfr-S26; 12-11-34   dle name?
John Dennis Stephens SW-SE-S26; 9-30-39
William Hudson, Sr. Lot 3-NWfr-S27; 6-1-36
John Harman Lot 4-NWfr-S27; 11-5-35
William Hudson NE-SW-S27; 6-1-36
Abel Vaughn NW-SE-S27; 6-27-36
Robert D. Waldon SW-SE-S27; 8-31-36

T 4 S, R 10 W

Frederick Cruse* W-N-E, W-S-E-S1; 12-2-44
Frederick Bising* E-N-E, E-S-E-S1; 9-15-47; NE-NE-S12; 12-29-49;
William Hampton, Vb W-S1; E-E-S2; 6-21-39   Besing
Henry Stunkel* W-E-S2; 10-21-40
Lewis Luhring* W-S2; 10-23-40
Frederick Stunkel* E-E-S3; 10-23-40
Daving Luhring* W-E-S3; 10-23-40   11-16-39
Michael Baechel, Stark Co., O. W-S3; SE-NE-S9; E-SE-S10; SE-S11;
David Donley McGarrah* W-W-S4; 5-16-39; E-S5; 8-31-35; E-W-S5; 5-16-39
George Sollman* E-E-S6; 3-29-47
Anton Center* W-E-S6; 8-29-44; W-S6; 6-21-43
Henry Rolfsmeyer, Butler Co., O. E-NE, E-SE-S7; 12-13-38
Christian Sandall, Butler Co., O. W-NE, E-SW, W-SE-S7; 12-13-38
Charles Graeter, Kn NW-NW-S7; 3-16-43
Pierre Wittman* SW-NW-S7; 3-8-42
Adam Widener, Vb NW-SW-S7; 9-10-40
Andrew Dash, Vb SW-SW-S7; 9-27-39
Solomon Mail* NE-NE-S8; 9-8-35
John Withrow* SE-NE-S8; 12-3-38; NE-NE-S9; 7-25-36; W-NE, E-NW-
    S9; 12-19-38; NW-NW-S9; 12-3-38; E-SW-S9; 3-12-19; W-SW-S9;
    7-25-36; E-SE-S9; 5-3-39; W-SE-S9; 10-14-29
Henry Runge* W-NE, E-NW-S8; 6-26-38
Henry Myer* SW-NW-S8; 4-2-47
Christian Cruse, Vb SW, W-SE-S8; 4-12-38
Adam Smidt, Vb E-SE-S8; 11-17-38
George Byers* SW-NW-S9; 9-10-36
William Stallings* NE-NE-S10; 7-27-39; NW-NE-S10; 6-7-36
William Kyrtz* NW-NW-S10; 3-17-54
Arnold Dickmire* SW-NW-S10; 5-1-50; NE-SW-S10; 12-2-44
Henry Dickmeir* W-SW-S10; 6-26-38
Levin Ireland* E-NE-S11; W-NW-S12; 5-3-39; SW-NW-S13; 3-8-36
Henry Busing* W-NE-S11; 10-30-40; NW-NE-S12; 12-6-43; SW-NE-S12; 1-9-
David Sharnst* E-NW-S11; 10-12-40   50
Henry Fisher* W-NW-S11; 10-12-40; E-NW-S12; 9-12-42
Frederick Strictmoerder* SW-S11; 10-5-39

John Thomas Wilkison* SE-NE-S12; 12-2-47
Thomas Ballard* NE-SW, NW-SE-S12; 10-31-37
John Carter, Vb SE-SW-S12; 11-27-37
Abraham Dillbeck* SE-SE-S12; 2-15-37
John Holcombe* E-NE-S13; 10-7-36; W-NE, SE-NW-S13; 2-15-37
John Arburn, Vb NE-NW-S13; 12-13-47
John Morris, Vb NW-NW-S13; 3-4-37   36
William Covey⁺ NE-SW-S13;3-8-36;SE-SE-S13;12-10-33;NE-NE-S14;7-12-
John A. Rockwell, Norwich Co., Conn. W-SW-S13; W-SW-S14; 8-13-36;
William Embree* NE-SE-S13; 6-25-36   SE-SW-S13; 8-17-36/
Aaron Were Hill, Vb W-SE-S13; 6-28-36
Levin Ireland* SE-NE-S14; 12-10-33
William Ireland* NW-NE-S14; 12-8-36; NE-NW-S14; 12-25-40
William Kurtz* SE-NW-S14; 3-17-54
Joseph Duff* E-SW-S14; 11-22-32   9-12-33
William Jefferson Withrow* NE-SE-S14;3-8-36; of Vb, SW-SE-S14;
William Trumble Thomas Jones SE-SE-S14;9-10-36. (2 men?)
Richson Withrow* NW-SE-S14; 5-3-39
Elijah Duff* E-NE-S15; 10-3-39; NW-SE-S15; 7-25-36
Jackson Duff* NW-NE-S15; 9-11-39; SW-NE-S15; 10-12-38
Jacob Winkelmann* E-NW-S15; 3-8-48
John Withrow* W-NW, NE-SW, W-SW-S15; 8-7-38; SE-SE-S15; 7-25-36;
    SE-NE-S17; 8-7-38
Isaac Anderson, Wk SE-SW, SW-SE-S15; 3-7-37; NE-SE-S15; 3-14-37
Michael Wehner, Vb NE-NE-S17; 4-12-38
Henry Cruse, Vb W-NE, NW-S17; 4-12-38; E-SE-S17;5-26-38;W-SE-S17;
Mary Brose, Vb SW-S17; 4-12-38   5-1-39
Benjamin Franklin McGehee, Vb NE-NE-S18; 1-30-39
Benjamin McGehee & Jesse Rose SE-NE-S18; 6-18-36
Frederick Staser, Vb W-NE, NE-NW-S18; 1-30-39
Abel Loyd* SE-NW-S18; 1-27-38; NE-NW-S18; 10-9-37
Albert Warren Douglass* NW-NW-S18; 9-24-38
Randolph Owens* SW-NW-S18; 6-17-36
John Christopher Stasir, Vb SE-SW-S18; 8-15-38
William Lewis S. Loyd, Vb NW-SW-S18; 11-27-37. (2 men?)
Sebastian Neabarger, Vb SW-SW-S18; 7-13-38
Joseph Rietzel, Vb NE-SE-S18; 10-5-48; NW-SE-S18; 2-15-47
Anthony Obert* SE-SE-S18; 3-29-47; of Vb, SW-SE-S18; 9-21-40

RELINQUISHMENTS

Joseph R. Brown W/Ø (mark not clear) -S4; 12-17-18; 8-30-21;
    NE-S9; 12-14-18; 3-29-25
Hasael Putman & Reddin Putman NW-S9; 8-8-17; 9-13-21
Joseph Duff SW-S13; 6-24-20; 3-29-25
Elias Barker W-NW-S18;8-13-17;9-13-21; E-NW-S18;8-13-17;7-3-27
John Withrow W-SW-S9; 3-12-19; 7-4-29

T 4 S, R 11 W

Elizabeth Shafer, George Grep (Grop?), & Charles V. Shafer, Vb
    E-S1; 9-11-40
Alexander Mitchell* E-W-S1; 7-8-44
Luther Wilson Stewart, Vb W-W-S1; 3-3-37

Elijah Yeager, Mercer Co., Ky. E-S2; 10-7-36; E-W-S2; 10-16-37
Edwin Chaffin* W-W-S2; 3-9-37; NW-NW-S11; 3-9-37
Ezekiel Boren* E-E-S3; 3-16-37; W-S4; 1-26-16
Abraham Land* W-E-S3; 3-6-37; E-W-S3; 11-3-36
George Washington Jordan* W-W-S3; 10-15-36; SW-NE-S9; 1-31-34
Francis Jourdan E-S4; 12-25-15
Elijah Turner E-S5; 12-20-15; W-SW-S7; 12-25-29
Isham Robinson W-S5; 2-3-17
Jesse Emmerson* E-S6; 12-27-33
James Kitchens W-S6; 8-10-17
Stephen Harris* NE-NE-S7; 1-11-37; NE-NW-S7; 3-1-33
Jehiel McConnell, Ps SE-NE, SW-NE-S7; 12-29-35
John Boren* NW-NE-S7; 3-12-34; E-NW-S8; 1-5-25; SW-NW-S8; 7-14-
    32; W-SW-S8; 12-23-33
Robert Montgomery* SE-NW-S7; 1-4-36
Samuel Montgomery W-NW-S7; 10-31-16
William Wilkinson* NE-SW-S7; 8-5-34
Samuel Miller* SE-SW-S7; 9-6-32
Isiah Wilkinson* NE-SE, NW-SE-S7; 12-29-35
Samuel Hampson Boren* SE-SE-S7; 4-2-35
James Wilson* SW-SE-S7; 2-21-34; E-SW, W-SE-S8; 1-20-32; SE-SW-
Joseph Rosborough* E-NE-S8; 12-19-28   S9; 1-14-37
Reuben Emmerson W-NE-S8; 1-6-17
Stephen Harris* NW-NW-S8; 3-1-33
Aaron Murphy, Ps E-SE-S8; 6-16-32; NW-SW-S9; 8-5-39
John Miller E-NE-S9; 2-2-16
James Boren Blythe* NW-NE-S9; 1-16-34; SW-SW-S9; 3-12-34
Ezekiel Boren* NE-NW-S9; 10-6-32; SE-NW-S9; 12-29-35; NE-SW-S9;
George Marvel* W-NW-S9; 12-16-28   1-16-39
James Cawson E-SE-S9; 5-21-19
Nicholas Robinson* NW-SE-S9; 2-24-35; SW-S10; 5-8-16; W-SE-S10;
John Mitchell, Vb SW-SE-S9; 11-2-48   7-21-18
Martin Luther Robinson* E-NE-S10; 5-8-37
William Mangrum* W-NE-S10; 1-24-34; NW-S10; 2-2-16
Michael Dean Robinson* E-SE-S10; 4-20-36
Joseph Summers* E-NE-S11; 12-12-36
Elijah Yeager, Mercer Co., Ky. W-NE-S11; 10-7-36
William Rutledge* E-NW-S11; 3-16-37
Edward Chaffin* SW-NW-S11; 3-28-38
George Yeager, Ps NE-SW-S11; 11-19-38; NW-SW-S11; 10-16-38; SW-SW-
Daniel McDowell* SE-SW-S11; 8-10-38   S11; 9-19-38
Joel Yeager, Ps NE-SE, NW-SE-S11;1-18-37
Moses Yeager, Ps SE-SE-S11; 11-19-38; SW-SE-S11; 4-15-37
John Hardman* NE-NE, SW-NE-S12; 11-15-44
Adam Luts* SE-NE-S12; 8-14-43
Anthony Shafer* NW-NE-S12; 5-24-42
John Stewart* NE-NW-S12; 3-3-37; W-NW-S12; 2-26-19
John Brothers, Jr. SE-NW-S12; 12-19-38
Michael Dean Robinson* SE-NE-S14; 9-24-38; of Vb, E-SW-S12;
    SE-SE, SW-SE-S14; 8-23-38
Allen Brils, Ps W-SW-S12; 2-27-37
John Trible* SE-S12; 9-4-23
John Wright* NE-NE-S13; 5-17-38
John Christopher Staser, Vb SE-NE-S13; 1-30-39

James Briles, Ps W-NE-S13; 1-18-39
George Low, Ps E-NW-S13; 2-27-37
Thornton Williams, Ps W-NW-S13; 2-27-37; NE-NE-S14; 8-17-38
James Powell, Ps E-SW-S13; 2-3-37
Conrad Staser, Vb W-SW-S13; 8-20-38
John Hanft, Vb E-SE-S13; 3-19-38; SW-SE-S13; 8-20-38.
George Davis, Vb NW-SE-S13; 2-8-38
James Williams, Ps W-NE-S14;9-6-38;NE-NW-S14;11-19-38;SE-NW,SW-NW-
Protuimon Montgomery* NW-NW-S14; NE-NE-S15; 6-10-38. S14;8-17-38
Nelson Martin, Vb NE-SW-S14;7-8-39;NE-SE,NW-SE-S14; 6-4-38
John Geisler, Vb SE-SW-S14; 5-4-39
George Davis, Vb NW-SW-S14; 11-26-40
John Nigley Powell* SW-SW-S14; 3-5-44
Daniel McDowell* SE-NE, SW-NE-S15; 12-16-36
Berry Martin* NW-NE-S15; 9-7-37
Martin Luther Robinson* NE-NW-S15; 1-30-34
Daniel McDowell, Sr.* SE-NW-S15; 1-18-39
Thomas Martin, Vb NW-NW-S15; 6-7-38
William Wilkinson* SW-NW-S15; 5-22-39
Alexander Powell, Vb E-SW-S15; 3-22-37 E-SE-S15; 7-8-39
William Watkins* NW-SW-S15; 3-14-37; SW-SW-S15; 5-18-36
Charles Martin, Vb W-SE-S15; 12-31-38
Aaron Murphy* SE-NE-S17; 1-4-36
Wesley Redman* NW-NE-S17; 1-21-36; NE-NW-S17; 1-19-35
George Alexander Moore* SW-NE-S17; 2-8-36; SE-NW-S17; 4-2-35
Daniel Fisher* NW-NW-S17; 10-12-32
Samuel Hampson Boren* SW-NW-S17; 12-29-35
John Bixler, Vb E-SE, SW-SE-S17; 9-17-39
John Doss Boren, Jr.* NW-SE-S17; 2-8-36
Patrick Calvert, Vb NE-NE-S18; 4-6-36
John McNary Boren* SE-NE, NW-NE-S18; 12-14-35
John Milton Forrest* SW-NE-S18; 3-26-33
Rene Carter, Ps NE-NW-S18; 12-14-35
Winchester Johnson* SE-NW-S18; 2-20-36
Abner N. Long* W-NW-S18; 1-20-30
Joseph Cater* E-SW-S18; 6-6-31
William Finch, Vb SW-SW-S18; 8-1-36
Stephen Harris* NE-SE-S18; 2-25-39
Simon Williams, Ps SE-SE, SW-SE-S18; 1-1-35

RELINQUISHMENTS

Samuel Montgomery E-NW-S7; 10-31-16; 12-27-24
Robert B. McConnell SW-S7; 10-29-17; 4-3-27
Reuben Emerson E-NE-S8; 1-6-17; 4-20-21
John Miller W-NE-S9;2-2-16;2-2-16(sic);NW-S9;3-26-19;3-28-25
James Cawson W-SE-S9; 5-21-19; 9-26-21
Nicholas Robinson E-SE-S10; 7-21-18; 9-24-21
John Stewart E-NW-S12; 2-26-19; 8-31-21
S. Hornbrook & E. Maidlow SW-S15; 12-16-18; 3-28-25
Thomas Rosborough NE-S18; 11-18-19; 12-27-24
William Davis NW-S18; 11-12-18; 6-25-27

T 1 N, R 7 W

John Wise* Wfr-Nfr-S6; 4-1-37

T 1 N. R 8 W

Elijah Palmer* Lot 6-W-E-Nfr-S1; 4-22-37
John Stork* Lot 7-W-E-Nfr-S1; 7-9-36; Lot 1-SEfr-S2; 9-15-57
James Wyant* Lots 2,5-E-W-Nfr-S1; 12-29-35
Jacob Reel* Lot 3-E-W-Nfr-S1; 3-28-36
Joseph Hogue* W-NE-S2; 3-21-24
Joseph McGarraugh* E-NW-S2; 7-17-37
Ashley C. Elder NW-NW-S2; 12-7-52. MLW 68643
Alexander McCray SW-NW-S2; 8-18-52. MLW 53431
Henry Reel* NE-SW-S2; 1-23-37
Thomas Porter Marcy* SE-SW, SW-SW-S2; SE-SE-S3; 10-3-37
Jacob Summel* NW-SW-S2; 6-2-36
William Risley* Lot 2-SEfr-S2; 7-29-36; Lot 3-SEfr-S2; 7-27-37
Abraham Reel* E-NE-S3; 5-22-31; SW-NE-S3; 6-29-36
David Reel, Jr.* NE-NW-S3; 11-12-38
William Hewell* NW-NW-S3; 2-7-51. Horrell?
Catherine Shaner* SW-NW-S3; 5-16-36
Jacob Warner* E-SW-S3; 4-21-37; W-SE-S3; 4-21-37; NW-NE-S10; 5-7-37
Lazarus Noland, Greene Co., O. W-SW-S3; 5-6-39
David Reel* NE-SE-S3; 1-5-37
Andrew C. Adams E-NE, W-NE-S4; 3-21-49. MLW 38446
Solomon Tevenbaugh* E-NW, W-NW, W-SW-S4; 8-13-21
Absalom Collins* E-SW-S4; 8-14-28
John Ralph Snyder* NE-NE, W-SE-S5; 8-27-39
Samuel Ralph Snyder* SE-NE-S5; 3-18-37
Jacob Bonewits* SW-NW-S5; 5-18-39; SE-NE-S6; 6-19-40
Jesse Sampson* Efr pt-NW-S6; 3-22-36
Preston Wease* Nfr-Lot 3-S7; 3-14-36; Lot 4-SWfr-Nfr-S8; 3-7-36
George W. Stillwell, Mn SEfr-S7; 2-3-70
Alexander Leslie, Pi Lot 2-W-SEfr-Nfr-S8; 5-10-54
Samuel M. Hitt, Joseph J. Merrick, William Price, & Benjamin Price
    E-NE, W-NE, W-SE-S9; W-NW, E-SW, SW-SW-S10; 3-23-36; E-SE-S9;
Philip Commarle* SE-NW-S9; 1-2-38; E-SW-S9; 10-9-37.   2-22-36
Philip Warner* NE-NE-S10; 2-21-39
Joseph Adams* SE-NE-S10; 11-4-37
Aaron Grider, Pi SW-NE-S10; 2-10-37
Aaron Reel* NW-SW-S10; 2-20-36
John Knox* NE-SE-S10; 5-5-38; SW-SW-S11; 4-7-36; Lot 2-W-E-Nfr-
Jacob Summit* NW-SE-S10; 2-18-37   S15; 1-11-36
Albion McCray* NE-NE-S11; 10-2-54
Jacob Miller, Pe Lots 3-4-Wfr-S12; SE-NE-S11; 9-25-37; Lot 2-W-
    SE-SEfr, SE-SW-S11; 9-29-37
Joseph Gamble* W-NE-S11; 6-11-22
William Cummins, Pi E-NW-S11; 10-11-26; Lot 7-Wfr-S12; 3-14-37
John Stork, Jr.* W-NW-S11; 4-23-27; NW-SW-S11; 5-29-33; E-SEfr-
    S11; 6-4-36; of Pi, Nfr-S14; 5-18-26
David Junkin* NE-SW-S11; 9-24-25; Lot 1-W-SE-SEfr-S11; 6-20-36
Alexander McCray* E-E-Nfr-S15; 11-18-25; Nfr-S17; 10-7-34
John Sturk* E-SWfr-Nfr-S15; 3-4-37

David A. Leonard   Sfr-S17; 8-29-15
Hiram Wright, Pi NEfr-Fr Lot 1-S18; 2-15-36
William Wright, Pi NEfr-Fr Lot 2-S18; 1-23-36
John Crist, Pe NEfr-Fr Lots 3-4-S18; 5-23-36
Elijah Link, Pe W-NWfr-S18; 5-23-36

RELINQUISHMENTS

Daniel O. Blenies NEfr-Sfr, SWfr, SE-Sfr-S14; 9-24-18

T 1 N, R 9 W

Nimrod Tevenbaugh* E-NE-S1; 6-11-32; E-NW-Nfr-S1; 8-16-23; SWfr-
   Nfr-S1; 8-10-35; Lots 7-8-Wfr-S12; 1-5-36
James Evans Thomas* SW-NW-Nfr-S1; 2-29-36
George W. Tevenbaugh* E-NEfr-S2; 8-21-26
John Reel* W-NWfr-S2; 5-2-37; SE-NE-Nfr, SW-NE-Nfr-S3; 3-7-36
Robert Reel* NE-SW-S2; 4-11-36; NE-NE-Nfr-S3; 3-26-36
Charles Pressey* NW-SW-S2; 4-3-38
John Wease* SW-SW-S2; 4-9-36
Jacob Tevenbaugh* E-SE-S2; 1-13-24
Riley Tevenbaugh* SW-SE-S2; 2-23-36; S-N-Efr-S11; 4-1-36; Lot 6-
   N-S-Efr-S11; 2-25-36
Nimrod Ray* SE-NW-Nfr# E-SWfr-Nfr-S3; 8-18-35. # 3-11-36
Jackson Sampson* Lot 1-E-SEfr-Nfr-S3; 4-8-36
James Thorne* Lot 2-E-SEfr-Nfr, W-SEfr-Nfr-S3; 3-7-36
John Knox* W-SWfr-Nfr-S3; 12-16-34
John Reynolds, Baltimore Co., Md. SW-SW-S4; 5-10-36
David Snider* SE-SE-S4; 3-26-36
Frederick J. Myers* SW-SE-S4; 9-26-42
Willis Washington Hitt* NE-S5; 1-8-36; NWpt-Nfr-S9; 4-11-36
Thomas Small* W-NWfr-S5; Lot 1-E-Efr-S6; 4-7-36; SE-NWfr, E-SWfr-
Aquilla H. Sampson* W-SWfr-S5; 10-30-54   S5; 8-19-39
Willis Washington Hitt (Hill?) E-SEfr-S5; 1-1-36
Samuel M. Hitt, William Price, Joseph J. Merrick, Benjamin Price
   (names bracketed and Maryland written at the end) Lots 1,6-Nfr-
   S8; 2-18-36; E-SEfr-S5; 1-1-36; W-SEfr-S5; 2-18-36; Lot 1-SEfr-
Isaac Mahl* Lot 6-W-Wfr-S6; 4-27-37   S5; 4-1-36
John Ray* Lot 1-Ept-Nfr-S9; 4-5-36
Jesse Morris* Lot 2-Ept-Nfr-S9; 3-26-39
William Crow* W-N-N-Efr-S11; 1-19-35
James Wesley Sampson* E-N-N-Efr-S11; 1-5-36
James Thorn & Robert Crow* NWfr-S11; 4-29-37
Henry Kollmann* Lot 7-S-S-Efr-S11; 8-9-53
Samuel Robinson* Lot 8-S-S-Efr-S11; 7-3-55
Solomon Tevebaugh* Lot 1-Wfr-S13; 2-25-36; Lot 2-Wfr-S13; 9-2-39;
   Lot 1-N-N-Efr-S14; 2-25-36
Henry Holdman* Lot 3-Wfr-S13; 1-14-70
James H. Holt* Lot 3-S-N-Efr-S14; 10-11-54

Peter Kimmons* Wfr-S1; 8-8-36
Henry Martin* Lot 1-NEfr-S3; 6-13-36; SE-NW-S3; 2-6-37
Abram Frederick* Lot 2-NEfr-S3; 3-6-37
Charles Chaney, Db NE-NW-S3; 9-17-35
Arthur Patterson, Vincennes* W-NW-S3; 6-19-24
Harvey Westfall* E-SW-S3; 2-7-45; NW-NW, NE-NW-S8; 1-19-48
Payton Johnson⁴ NW-SW-S3; 10-31-35; SE-NE-S4; 9-9-36; SW-NE-S15;
    10-21-33. See Payton Johnson Roderick
Thomas Westfall* SW-SW-S3; 9-9-33; NE-NE-S4;5-18-35;E-SE-S4;9-9-33
James Stewart Mayes* Lot 3-SEfr-S3; 2-22-37; Lot 5-SEfr-S3;5-18-35
Jacob Harper, Samuel Judah, Thomas Westfall, Edward Smith, & George
    W. Harper E-NW, E-SW, W-SE-S9; 5-19-35; W-NW-S9; 5-22-35;
    same names plus Edward Judah, W-S4; 5-19-35
Dominick Gettings* NW-NE-S6; 5-11-36
Jane Crock* SE-NE-S7; 12-17-47
Prestly Decker* SW-NE-S7; 8-24-39
Michael Catt* SW-SW-S7; 9-28-35
Nicholas Johnson* E-SE-S7; 7-9-29
Joseph Williams* NW-SE-S7; 8-13-33
Jesse McMillan* SW-SE-S7; 2-8-36
George Canada* SW-NW-S8; 2-23-48
John Decker* SEfr-S8; 3-22-33; Efr-S17; 10-11-32
Joseph Vaudry* E-NE-S9; 4-23-28
Andrew Purcell, Sr.* W-NE-S9; 2-6-36
Joseph Kimmons, Gi NE-SE-S9; 10-11-32; of*, SE-SE-S9; 12-30-34
Anna Roderick* Nfr-S11; 7-14-55
John Cannon* N-S-Wfr-S11; 12-25-37; E-SWfr-S14; 8-29-48
Danford Lane, Lw Lots 2-3-Efr-S11; 10-3-35
John Maxwell* Lot 4-Efr-S11; 3-15-36
John Baker* E-E-Nfr-S12; 7-3-28
Thomas Johnson* Lot 7-SWfr-S12; 1-14-36; Lot 6-SWfr-S12; 1-13-36
John L. Key, Stuart C. Key, & William Key, Jr., Gi Efr-S12; 7-14-
    52; same names minus William Key, Jr., Lot 9-Efr-S13; 6-28-48
Alexander Maxwell* Lot 1-N-N-Wfr-S13; 12-16-36
John Roderick* Sfr-S11; 1-23-30; NEfr-S14; 5-28-28; Lot 4-W-SWfr-
    S14; 2-20-39; Lot 1-E-SEfr-S14; 9-7-50; Lot 1-E-E-Nfr-S22; 2-20-
Henry Kimmons* S-N-Wfr-S13; 3-10-37   39
Sebastian Conger, Pi Lot 5-S-Wfr-S13; 8-31-37
John Davidson Conger, Pi Lot 6-S-Wfr-S13; 9-28-38
Peyton Johnson Roderick* Lot 2-W-SWfr-S14; 9-4-39; Lot 3-W-Sfr-
    S14; 12-18-49; MLW 49920; Lot 2-N-N-Wfr-S23; 12-18-49; Lot 5-
    S-N-S23; 11-18-49. See Payton Johnson
Ebenezer Sutton, Wk E-SEfr-S14; 2-15-36
James McGowan* NE-NE, Lot 3-W-SWfrOS15; 8-22-37; NW-NE-S15; 8-25-
Samuel Bedell* SE-NE-S15; 7-16-36   37
George Firman* NE-NW-S15; 8-6-36
Gilbert Howell, Wayne Co., N.Y. SE-NW, SW-NW-S15; 8-3-37
William McGowan* NW-NW-S15; 10-3-36
Robert Thompson* Lot 2-SEfr-S15; 8-26-43
James Spoywood Edward* Lot 1-SEfr-S15; 7-11-39
Nicholas Johnson* Wfr-S17; 7-8-29
John Crock* NEfr-S18; 7-10-29

Henry Crow* Lot 1-E-NW-S18; 9-10-50
John Johnson* Lot 4-E-NW-S18; 8-5-34
Sarah Catt* Lot 3-E-NW-S18; 1-18-50
William Hays* Lot 5-SWfr-S18; 9-30-47
Harrison Warth* Lot 6-SWfr-S18; 2-10-57
Thomas Pick & Andrew Purcell, Sr.* NEfr-S19; 11-29-36; N-Wfr-S20;
John Mikesell* SWfr-Nfr-S19; 4-1-35   12-5-36
Jacob Smith Youngman* Lot 5-N-S-Wfr-S20; 6-17-35
Garrot Wells Mikesell* Lot 6-N-S-Wfr-S20; 9-1-35
James Dirk, Jr. (Dick?) Wpt (SW-SW)-S-S-Nfr-S20; 11-3-52
Morgan Jones* Wpt (SE-SW)-S-S-Nfr-S20; 5-24-36
David Crock* Ept-S-S-Wfr-S20; 3-14-36
Peter Chalmers* Npt-Efr-S21; 4-17-37
David Robb, Gi Spt-Efr-S21; 9-14-25
Peter Day* Lot 2-E-E-Nfr, W-E-Nfr-S22; 2-20-39
Charles Sechman* W-Nfr-S22; 4-10-37
James Spottswood Edwards* Lot 3-N-N-Wfr-S23; 11-3-41
James Sutphen Lot 4-S-N-Wfr-S23; 11-1-52. MLW 13054

T 1 N, R 11 W

Anthony Massalt* NW-SE-S1; 4-24-51
Josiah Lawrence, William Oliver, & Lucius Barber NW, W-SW-S3;
    W-NE, W-NW-S4; NEfr, Lot 1-NWfr-S5; 5-11-36; E-NE, E-SE-S4;
    4-27-36; NW, SW, SE-S10; NW, SW-S11; NE, NW, SW-S15; 5-14-36;
    Lots 1,2,3-E-E; Lots 4,5-W-E; Wfr-FrS19; Lot 4-W-Wfr-S20; 5-
    12-36; W-Efr-S20; N-NW, Lot 1-S-NW-S20 or S21; 5-13-36; NE-S21;
    5-17-36; SW, SE-S21; 5-17-36; W-NEFr¼, NW, NE-SW, W-SW-S22;
    5-17-36
James Perry Drake & John Wise* Lot 4-NWfr, SWfr, W-SE-S5; NW-S9;
    10-17-35; N-NWfr-S8; 10-30-35
Francis Heiney & Thomas H. Fanning, Cayuga Co., N.Y. E-SE-S5; 5-5-
William Randolph Haddon, Su NE, NWfr-S8; 3-23-36.   36
Lucinda Tousey, Dn NE, SE-S9; 3-22-36
Omer Tousey, Dn SW-S9; 3-22-36
William P. Catt NE-NW-S12; 9-7-50
George Anthis, Wb S-SE-S13; 12-19-32
Abraham Barekman* Lots 2-3-E-FrS19; 8-18-35
Abraham Barekman, Jr.* Lot 1-E-Efr-S20; Lot 2-S-NW-S21; 1-20-35
Isaac Barekman* Lot 2-E-E-FrS20; 8-11-41; Lot 3-W-Wfr-S20; 12-26-35
Peter Jacobus* E-Wfr-S20; 1-19-36
John Warth* E-NE-Fr¼-S22; 7-21-29
Henry Hulbert* SE-SW-S22; 12-8-35
George Kuykendall* SEfr-S22; 5-2-29
Philip C. Pellenz* Lot 2-Nfr-S23; 11-17-54
John Warth* Lot 3-Nfr-S23; 8-5-34; Lot 4-N-S-Wfr-S25; 2-22-39
Harrison Warth* Efr-NE-S23; 4-22-57; Sfr-S24; 9-20-36
Vincent Barnett, Gi Lots 8-9-N-Efr-S25; 2-13-49; Lot 7-N-Efr-S25;
    5-27-57; Lot 10-S-Efr-S25; 11-11-51
Jacob Jacobus* N-N-Wfr-S25; 5-9-38; Sfr-S23; Nfr-S26; 11-19-35
Peter Jacobus* Lot 2-S-N-Wfr-S25; 10-15-36; Lot 1-S-N-Wfr-S25;
    6-4-36; Sfr-S27; 6-30-29
Jacob Miller* Lot 6-S-S-Wfr-S25; 3-8-36

Willis Wilks* Lot 3-N-S-Wfr-S25; 1-11-36; Lot 5-S-S-Wfr-S25; 6-4-
Nathaniel Kuykendall* Wfr-S23; NWfr-S26; 7-6-29   36
Jacob Miller, Gi SWfr-S26; 8-2-25; W-SEfr-S26; 3-3-30
Thomas Step* Efr-S27; 10-24-35
Henry Hulbert* Lot 1-Wfr-S27; 12-8-35
Asa Kuykendall* Lots 2-3-Wfr-S27; 9-20-36
Josiah Lawrence, William Oliver, & Lucius Barber NE, NW-S28; 5-17-
36; NE, NW-S29; 5-13-36; NE-S30; 5-12-36
William Sisco* SE-SEfr-S28; 8-19-39
Alfred Bellwood* Lot 1-E-NW-S30; 9-18-35
Nathan Finch* Lot 2-E-NW, NE-SW-S30; 6-15-36
Thomas Trulock* W-NW-S30; 7-6-35
John Lindsey, Wn Lots 3-4-W-SW-S30; 12-13-36
Harvey Vanderhoof* NE-NE-S31; NW-NW-S32; 6-6-39; NE-SE-S33; 5-25-
37; N-N-Wfr-S34; 4-27-29; Lots 3-4-S-S-Wfr-S34; 1-23-36; Lot 4-
E-NEfr-S35; 10-30-34; Lot 2-N-Wfr-S36; 8-5-34; S-Wfr-S36; 1-26-35
William Slusher SE-NE-S31; 2-24-38
St. Clair Miner W-NE, E-NW-S31; 12-21-54
Henry A. Hayden W-NW-S31; 12-26-54
George Washington Claypoole* SE-S31; 8-3-36
Joseph Dart, Lawrence Co., Ill. E-NW-S32; 2-3-57
Eli Slusher* SW-NW-S32; 1-29-38; SE-SE-S33; 3-29-37; SW-SE-S33;
John Miller, Fo SE-SW-S32; 8-4-37   1-2-38
Martin Miller* NW-SW-S32; 10-10-37
Andrew Miller, Fo E-SE-S32; NW-SW-S33; 4-27-37
Jonathan Davis* NW-SE-S32; 2-23-57
David Fansher* SW-SE-S32; 3-28-37
Peter Sisco & Henry Rollis* E-NE-S33; 3-19-38
Jacob Kuykendall* SE-NW-S33; 6-5-37
James Slott, Wabash Co., Ill. NE-SW-S33; 8-26-36
Charles Gregory* NW-SE-S33; 6-4-36
Henry Rawlis* Nfr-S34; 4-2-36
Thomas Jacobus* Sfr-S34; 7-5-30; W-SWfr-S35; 8-9-25
Jonathan Purcell* Lot 1-S-N-Wfr-S34; 12-1-34
Daniel Beadle* Lot 2-S-N-Wfr-S34; 7-5-30
Joseph G. Crow, Gi N-S-Wfr-S34; 8-17-29
David Jennings+ Lot 1-E-NEfr-S35; 9-26-36; Lot 2-W-NEfr-S35; 8-29-35
Peter Barrekman* Lot 3-W-NEfr-S35; 5-29-35
Martin Anthis, Wabash Co., Ill. NWfr-S35; 6-10-30
Henry Barekman* E-SWfr-S35; 3-28-36
Joshua Barekman* Lots 5-6-SEfr-S35; 1-7-36
Jacob Miller* Lot 1-N-Wfr-S36; 8-29-36

T 1 N, R 12 W

Alfred Bellwood Lot 1-E-Efr-S25; 6-2-35; Wfr-S25; 7-30-33
John Hyde Lot 3-E-Efr-S25; 7-1-35
Daniel Thompson Taylor Lot 4-W-Efr-S25; 7-1-35
John Taylor Lot 2-W-Efr-S25; 5-14-35
Joseph Brown Andrew Correll (2 men?) FrS26; 7-17-29
Alexis LeRoy FrS33; E-FrS34; E-Wfr, W-Wfr-S34; 3-9-36
John Ramsey Lot 1 fr-S35; 5-18-35; Lot 2 fr-S35; 8-14-35
Daniel Thompson Taylor, 1st NW-NE-S36; 5-27-37; NE-NW-S36; 6-14-36

Abraham Hurd SE-NW-S36; 5-22-37
George Baryear NW-NW-S36; 7-1-55 (35?)
George Rogers SW-NW-S36; 5-25-36

T 2 N, R 8 W

Andrew Buroy* Lot 5-N-S1; 7-18-36
Abraham Bugher* Lot 6-N-S1; 5-20-36
Andrew Wile* Lot 7-Nfr-S1; 6-8-36
Elmina Mabel Walls* Lot 3-Wfr-S1; 3-16-40
Andrew Lillie Lot 1-Efr-S2; 10-15-35
Hiram Albert, Da Lot 2-Efr-S2; 6-28-36
Meshack Porter* Lot 3-Wfr-S2; 7-14-41; Lot 5-Wfr-S2; Lot 3-FrS3;
     6-28-41; NEfr-S10; 7-14-41
John Steen* Lot 4-Wfr-S2; 11-2-36; Lot 1-FrS3; 12-17-39
Shadrack Porter* Lot 2-FrS3; 11-27-39
John Franklin* NE-NEfr-S8; 10-23-52
William Batchelor, Da NE-NEfr-S11; 9-25-35
Jonathan Ward, Da SE-NEfr-S11; 3-19-36
Joshua Gilbert* NW-NEfr-S11; 9-29-35
Samuel Bogan Steen* SW-NEfr-S11; 5-25-36; Lot 3-W-NWfr-S11;5-30-36
Richard Merrell* Lot 1-E-NWfr-S11; 3-19-39
Levi Albert* Lot 4-E-NWfr-S11; 4-10-39
James Bloxsom* Lot 2-W-NWfr-S11; 5-23-36
Alfred Robinson* E-SW-S11; 5-6-36
Peter Stephenson, Hamilton Co., O. W-SW-S11; 1-16-39
Andrew Ward, Da SE-SE-S11; 12-19-35   6-6-36
William Miller, Hamilton Co., O. NE-SE, W-SE-S11;5-27-36; E-SW-S14;
Josiah Lawrence, William Oliver, & Lucius Barber E-Wfr-S12; S-SWfr-
     S12; NEfr-Wfr, E-SWfr, SE-SWfr, SEfr-S13; N-NW, Lots 2-3-S-N-
     Wfr, Lots 4-5-N-S-Wfr, Lots 6-7-S-S-Wfr-S24; 5-11-36
Jacob Fuller* N-NWfr-Wfr-S12;4-2-36; Lot 3-S-NWfr-Wfr-S12;7-17-37
William Walls, Da Lot 2-S-NWfr-Wfr-S12; 6-25-38
Peter Stephenson* N-SWfr-S12; 4-17-39
William Rogers* E-NWfr-S13; 1-5-36; NW-NWfr-S13; 10-1-35
Jacob Huffman* SW-NWfr, NE-SWfr-S13; 12-4-35
Benjamin Vincennes Becker* E-NE-S14;8-24-35; W-NE-S14; 12-4-35
Clayton Rogers* E-NW-S14; 1-6-36; NE-SE-S14; 8-5-34; E-SW-S23;
     W-NE-S26; 1-6-36
Joseph Markle, Westmoreland Co., Pa. W-NW-S14; 5-17-38
John Smith, Da NW-SW-S14; 6-9-40
Jesse Crabs, Da SE-SE-S14; 10-16-38
Lemuel Edwards, Da NW-SE-S14; 8-23-36
A. C. Keylman, Washington, D.C. Lots 1,2,3,4,9-S16; 9-26-76
Andrew Cooper Conn* Nfr-S17; 6-10-39
Ellen Dafren (Dufren)* Sfr-S17;7-18-39; Lot 2-W-NEfr-S20;7-18-32
David Light* Lots 2-3-FrS18; 7-27-36
Elias Like* NE-SW-S19; 10-31-40; SE-SW-S19; 7-2-42
Martin Thacker* SW-SW-S19; 8-30-39
Allen Rodarmel* Lot 6-E-SEfr, SW-SEfr-S19; 7-12-39
Francis Teague* Lot 1-E-NEfr-S20; 4-18-51
Isaac Smith* Lot 3-W-NEfr-S20; 7-30-42
George Thorn* NWfr-S20; 7-5-36
Charles Antler* E-SWfr-S20; 10-5-39; W-SWfr-S20; 3-7-36

James Edwards, Da NE-NE-S23; 1-4-37
Absalom Reel* W-NE-S23; 1-11-36; SW-SE-S23; 5-19-37
Sarah Rogers, Da E-NW-S23; 5-20-36
William Jordin* SW-SW-S23; 10-9-39
David Wining Rodarmel, Da NW-SE-S23; 5-9-37
Milton Crabb, Da Lot 1-N-N-Wfr-S24; 3-14-36
Gabriel Willson* N-NE-Wfr-S25; 5-14-36
Stephen Bolding* Lots 1-2-S-NE-Wfr-S25; 6-9-36
James Douglass Williams* NE-NW-Wfr-S25; 11-14-50; NW-NW-S27; 9-16-
    39; NW-SW-S27; 7-31-39; E-NE-S28; 9-19-36; W-NE, E-NW-S28; 6-22-
    49; W-NW-S28; 7-11-49. MLW 32432. SE-S29; 8-26-50; NE-NE -
    S33; NW-NW-S34; 10-28-52. MLW 34283
William Stibbins, Bullitt Co., Ky. SW-Wfr, SEfr-S25; 8-6-35; NE-
    Wfr, NE-NW-Wfr, NW-NW-Wfr-S36; 9-2-39
George Washington Williams* SE-NW, NE-SW-S26; 4-22-39
Hiram Collins, Da NW-NW-S26; 1-18-36; E-NE, SW-NW-S27; 10-17-36
John Rizley* W-SW-S26; 5-24-22
David Collins* E-SE-S26; 7-7-32
Charles Willey, Da W-SE-S26; 11-30-39
Israel Mead* W-NE-S27; 10-11-24
John Jordan* E-NW-S27; 10-11-24
Jacob Small* NE-SW-S27; 4-12-50; SE-SW-S27; 2-9-50
John Spillman Collins* SW-SE-S27; 10-24-39
William Perry, Da W-SW-S28; 3-9-40
Jacob & Nimrod Tevebaugh* NE-SE-S28; 4-4-36
Asa Thorn* W-NW-S29; SE-NE-S30; 3-7-36
Peter Schorsch* E-SW-S29; 10-20-40
Jacob Thorn* NW-SW-S29; 5-11-39
John W. Bartlow* NE-NE-S30; 9-3-52;NW-NE-S30;3-18-52;SW-NE-S30;
Joshua Thorn* N-NWfr-S30;9-11-25.   11-20-50. MLW 25790
Solomon Tevebaugh* Lots 1-2-SWfr-S30; 9-2-37
James Richards* NE-SE-S30; 3-10-51; SE-SE-S30; 3-8-51
Charles Thorn, Jr.* NW-SE-S30; 7-9-39
Harvey Clenden Baldwin* SW-SE-S30; 11-3-46
Solomon Tevebaugh, Jr.* NEfr-S31; 2-9-39
Benjamin V. Beckes* SWfr-S31; 10-15-24
Job Wease, Pi E-SE, NW-SE-S31; 8-20-39
Jessey Sampson* SW-SE-S31; 8-1-39
John Adam Like* SE-NE-S32; 8-6-38
John Wilson* W-NE-S32; 7-29-39
Jackson Sampson* SW-NW-S32; 9-17-39
John Anderson, Gi E-SW, W-SW-S32; 11-8-37
John Taylor* E-SE-S32; 10-29-25
John A. Culbertson* NW-SE-S32; 3-23-54
William Kinchen Campbell* SW-SE-S32; 2-7-37
Philip Jones* SE-NE-S33; 9-14-39
Alexander Leslie, Pi NE-NW-S33; 7-10-54
Abel Secmore Collins* SE-NW, W-NW-S33; 9-2-39
Polly Jones* NE-SE-S33; 6-28-36
Samuel Adams SW-SE-S33; 1-12-54
Preston Wease* E-NE-S34; 4-15-25
Alexander McCray* W-NE-S34; 7-1-31; E-NW-S34; 10-12-29
James Shrader Stafford* SW-NW-S34; 1-7-39
James N. Stafford* E-SW-S34; 1-24-51

Philip B. Stafford* W-SW-S34; 7-31-30
Solomon Collins* NE-NE-S35; 1-18-36
Benjamin V. Beckes & Joseph Collins E-NW-S35; 8-16-22
Joseph Collins* W-NW-S35; 7-31-21
Absalom Reel* E-SW-S35; 10-5-37
John Gibson Phillips* NW-SW-S35; 5-9-37
Jacob Reel SW-SE-S35; 1-16-37
Thomas Binkley SE-NW-Wfr-S36; 11-6-54; SW-NW-Wfr-S36; 11-7-54

T 2 N, R 9 W

Benjamin V. Beckes* FrS3; FrS8; FrS18; 6-23-21
Lorenzo Gamble* Lot 2-FrS13; 12-23-37; Lot 3-FrS13; 4-4-37
Isaac Coon* FrS19; 1-18-36
William Kirk* E-Efr-S20; 4-27-35
George Leach* Nfr, Lots 1-2-N-Sfr-S21; 1-9-36
George Leach & Albert Gallatin How Lot 3-N-Sfr-S21; 6-28-36
John Stermer, Jefferson Co., Ky. Lot 4-S-Sfr-S21; E-Efr-S27 & 28;
David Like* Efr-S24; 5-11-37   6-19-39
James Thorn* Efr-S25; 5-16-33
Alexander McCray* Sfr-S25; 8-1-23
Philemon Clonenger* Lot 1-W-Efr-S28; 10-4-36
Jacob Tevebaugh* Lot 5-W-Efr-S28; 7-29-36
William Kirk* Lots 2-3-N-Wfr-S28; 1-11-36; Efr-S29; 1-29-52
Michael O. Herron* Lot 6-Spt-Wfr-S28; 3-29-37
Willis W. & Caleb Hitt* Sfr-S29; 2-13-40
Ephraim Jordan* FrS31; Lots 1-2-Wfr-S32; 11-28-35
Willis Washington Hitt* Sfr-S32; 1-11-36
Willis W. Hitt, Benjamin V. Beckes, & John C. Holland NEfr-S33;
John Craft Holland Lots 3-4-SWfr-S33; 1-11-36.   1-8-36
Charles Pressey* NEfr-S35; 4-3-38
David Wilson* SE-SWfr-S36; 3-11-36
David Ralph Snyder* Lot 3-SEfr-S36; 4-4-36
Samuel Ralph Snyder* Lot 6-SEfr-S36; 9-9-35

T 2 N, R 10 W

John Barekman, Jr.* FrS1; 5-31-36
Henry Wyant* Nfr-S2; 1-28-39
James McGowen* E-Sfr-S2; 10-13-42
Patrick Carroll* Lot 2-FrS3; 10-4-47
John H. Holscher* Lot 3-FrS3; 10-27-51
Henry Sote* FrS5; 8-1-39
Amable Busha* FrS6; 6-16-36
John Marie Gonard (Gouard?)* Wfr-S7; 10-28-34
Ferdinand Eberwine* Efr-S7; 7-25-37; NE-SW-S8; 7-31-37; SE-SW-
   S8; 11-11-37; SW-SW-S8; 7-25-37
Francis Bavellet* Lot 1-NWfr-S8; 2-5-38; Lot 2-NWfr-S8; 7-30-35
Pierre Calasier (Cabasier?)* NW-SW-S8; 9-8-35
John William Gifford* NE-Wfr, NW-Wfr-S9; 8-18-43
Isaac Mail* NWfr-S10; 5-23-35; Lots 2-3-E-SWfr-S10; 2-21-40; Lot 1-
   E-SEfr-S10; 2-29-36; W-SEfr-S10; 2-17-40; N-Sfr-S15; 2-15-40
ERROR: This township continued at top of page 105

Thomas T. Smith* NE-NW-Fr-S27; 9-11-41. (Continued from page 105)
William Youtt* Lot 2-W-NW-FrS27; 11-18-43
Basil Miner, G1 SW-SWfr-S27; 8-4-36
Isaac Joseph* Lot 4-NWfr-S28; 4-21-54
Samuel H. Miller* Lot 5-NWfr-S28; 9-21-39
Rebeccah Catt* SE-SE-S28; 10-24-38
Thomas Canady* NE-NE-S29; 6-22-36
Jacob Poorman* SE-NE-S29; 10-15-39
Henry Sote* NW-NE-S29; 10-22-39
Anthoni Mugensturm⁴ SW-NE-S29; 2-11-43
Lewis Robins* Npt-W-NW-S29; 8-20-38; SE-NE-S30; 8-11-38
Francis White* Spt-W-NW-S29; 4-2-38
William Shepherd* W-SW-S29; 7-21-21
Morgan Jones* W-NE-S30; 5-12-36; SEfr-S30; 5-5-36
Anthony Cary* SE-NW-S30; 8-1-37
Jerome Bonapart Myers* NW-NW-S30; 12-31-40
James White NE-SW-S30; 8-12-37
Joseph Cardinal* SE-SW-S30; 10-24-37
Neal William White* W-SW-S30; 12-12-54
Francis Mahorney* Lots 1-2-NEfr-S31; 2-18-36; NW-SEfr-S31;10-15-35
Emanuel Tongas(?), Lv NE-NW-S31; 1-23-39
Philip Shepard Board(?)* NE-SEfr-S31; 12-28-35
Isaac Catt* SE-SEfr-S31; 11-29-36; SW-SEfr-S31; 2-8-36
John Devore* NW-NW-S32; 11-29-36; SW-NW-S32; 2-10-36
Daniel Stilwell* NE-NE-S33; 6-6-36
Niely Devinney Stilwell* SE-NE-S33; 5-31-36
Jacob Harper, Samuel Judah, Thomas Westfall, Edward Smith, George
   W. Harper, & Edward Judah E-NW, SW-S33; 5-19-35
George Duffield Hay* E-SE-S33; 9-1-36; W-SE-S33; 9-27-36
James B. Wheeler* N-Nfr-S34; 7-25-22
Henry Martin* Lot 2-S-Nfr-S34; 7-19-36
John Bilderback* NE-SW-S34; 1-26-37
Jacob Case* SE-SW-S34; 3-22-36
William Miner* W-SW-S54; 3-10-30
Thomas Glass* Lot 3-SEfr-S34;3-8-38;Lot 4-SEfr-S34;5-30-36;Sfr-S35;
John Wolf* Nfr-S35; 3-7-38   3-4-33

                          T 2 N, R 11 W

Charles Delisle* Lot 1-Efr-S1; 6-15-36; Lot 4-NEfr-S2; 5-16-36
John Busha* Lot 3-Efr-S1; 5-16-51
Joseph Streiby* Lot 4-Efr-S1; 7-26-53
John L. & Lawrence Busha, Jr.* Lot 2-Efr-S1; n.d.
Pierre Andr, Sr.* Lot 1-NEfr-S2; 12-14-36
Pierre Gumlin* Lot 2-E-NW-S2; 5-23-36
Vital Busha, Jr.* S-E-NW-S2; 5-20-36
Pierre Cornoyer & William Page* Lot 3-W-NW-S2; 5-20-36
Ambrose Cornoyer* S-W-NW-S2; 5-19-36
John Baptiste Richardville, Sr.* SW, SW-SEfr-S2; 5-16-36
John Richardville, Jr. NW-SE-S2; 5-19-36
Lawrence Busha* E-SE-S2; 5-30-36
Hiram Decker & Joseph Brown* Lot 1-FrS3; 5-20-36
Vital Busha, Sr.* Lot 2-FrS3; 5-2-36
(continued on page 106)

John Mail* Lot 4-NEfr-S10; 2-21-40
Hirjate Medearis, Su Lot 4-E-Efr-S11; 5-24-36
Henry Barkman* S-Efr-S11; 12-10-36
John Brooks Dunning* Lot 1-FrS12; 4-4-42; Lot 3-FrS12; 5-4-36
Michael Jost* Lot 2-FrS12; 3-1-42
Barbara Harbin* Lot 4-FrS12; 9-7-40
John Thorn* FrS13; 4-27-24
John McCormick* Lot 1-N-Nfr-S14; 11-14-38
Nathaniel Merrill Lot 2-N-Nfr-S14; 6-8-52. U.S.W. 39865
Lee Milam* S-Nfr-S14; 7-8-39; N-Sfr-S14; 2-2-40
Francoise Dubois NEfr-S15; 2-7-52. MLW 8525
Addison A. Hosmer, Washington, D.C. FrS16; 9-26-76. Rev.B.L.W.
Lewis Kiar* NE-NE-S17; 9-15-37; NE-SW-S17; 1-8-36
Margaret Uont (Yount?)* SE-NE-S17; 8-14-37
Simon Gabriel Brute* NW-NE-S17; 3-21-38; E-SE-S17; 3-21-38
Alfred Decker* SW-NE-S17; 6-15-37; NW-SE-S17; 6-15-37
Anthony Cartier* SE-NW-S17; 9-19-37
Robert Ball Shreve* SE-SW-S17; 1-26-36
Samuel Judah & Jacob Harper W-SW-S17; NE-NW, NW-NW-S19; 12-26-35
John Herm Mosz, Hamilton Co., O. SW-SE-S17; 6-24-48
Ferdinand Eberwine* Lots 1-2-Ept-NEfr-S18; 7-25-37
John Marie Gonard* NEfr, W-NWfr-S18; 10-28-34
Lambert Barrois, Jr.* NE-SW-S18; 7-31-37
John William Gifford* SE-SW-S18; 11-6-37
Ambrose Laderoote* Lot 5-W-SW-S18; 5-23-36
Samuel Judah* NE-SEfr-S18; 12-26-35; NW-NW-S20; 1-8-36
Lewis Dupre, Jr.* SE-SEfr-S18; 2-19-33
Jacob Harper* Lot 4-W-SEfr-S18; NE-SE-S19; 12-26-35
Anthony Cary* E-NE-S19; 3-15-30
Henry Kimmons* NW-NE-S19; 8-8-33
Francis Marooney* SW-NE-S19; 7-12-33
Joseph Cardinal* SE-NW-S19; 9-15-34
Henry Racine* SW-NW-S19; 12-23-35; NW-SW-S19; 10-31-35
Joseph Cary* SE-SW-S19; 7-3-39
Celestine Guinevere de la Hailandiere* SE-SE-S19; 8-30-44.
John Cary* NW-SE-S19; 10-30-35
Michael Cary* SW-SE-S19; 7-26-36   John Pea* Lot 1-FrS26
James White* Lot 1-N-NEfr-S20; 4-18-37   5-20-36
Herman Wierling* Lot 2-N-NEfr-S20; 7-17-41. John Mason McCord*
Elias White* S-NEfr-S20; 10-6-30   Lot 2-FrS26; 6-1-44
James Cardinal* SW-NW-S20; 10-13-42
Francis William Gravel* N-SEfr, Lot 3-S-SEfr-S20; 10-22-39
Sylvester Heirmond Almy* Lot 4-S-SEfr-S20; 5-3-37.
Alfred Almy* Nfr-S21; 4-20-37   *Frederick Claycomb
Robert Black, Gi Sfr-S21; 8-3-29   Lots 1,4-E-NEfr-
Jacob Pea* Nfr, S-Sfr-S22; 10-26-39   S27; 4-11-36
William T. Scott E-Efr-S22; 2-17-53. MLW 23199. *Lucretia Claycomb
John Devore* W-Efr-S22; 2-26-39; Wfr-S22; 9-30-36.   W-NEfr-S27;
William Hayes* Efr, Lot 1-N-Wfr-S23; 2-16-36.   4-13-36
Catherine Claycomb* Lot 2-N-Wfr-S23; 11-24-36.
Homer Edson* Lot 3-S-Sfr-S23; 7-2-39; Lot 4-S-Sfr-S23; 7-8-39

(continued on page 104)

T 2 N, R 11 W
(continued from page 104)

Robert North Carnan* Lot 3-FrS3; 5-20-36
Amable Busha & Henry Richardville Lots 3,4,5-Nfr-S10; 5-18-36
Josiah Lawrence, William Oliver, & Lucius Barber Lots 1-2-Sfr-S10;
   NW, SW-S11; 5-17-36
John Baptiste Bonhomme* NE-S11; 5-18-36
James Theriac* SE-S11; 5-18-36
Joseph Stralby Lot 1-Nfr-S12; 8-26-52. NLW 16155
John Busha* Lot 2-Nfr-S12; 5-20-36
Amable Andre* Lot 3-Nfr-S12; 3-13-37
Joseph Doloner (Dolorier?)* Lot 4-SWfr-S12; 6-3-36
John Lewis Delorier & Andrew Delorier* Lot 5-SWfr-S12; 5-17-36
John Marie Gourd (Gonard?)* Efr-S12 & 13; 12-5-36
Nicholas Smith* E-NEfr-S13; 2-15-39
Henry Bultman* W-NEfr-S13; 5-14-39
Patrick Carroll* NWfr-S13;1-11-38;S-NEfr-S14;4-18-37;E-NW-S14-
Troussaint Barrois* NE-SWfr-S13; 12-15-38.   4-25-37
Mitchell Bonhome* SE-SWfr, NW-SE-S13; 12-13-38
Francis Ravellet* Lot 1-W-SWfr-S13; 10-9-37
John Peter Maltell* Lot 2-W-SWfr-S13; 10-29-34
Jacob Poorman* NE-SE-S13; 12-17-38
Lewis Turpin* SE-SE-S13; 12-13-39
Peter Cahasier* SW-SE-S13; 12-10-38
Augustus Mominee & Anthony Mominee* Lot 1-N-NEfr-S14; 5-21-36
Augustus Mominee* Lot 2-N-NEfr-S14; 6-10-36
Josiah Lawrence, William Oliver, & Lucius Barber W-NW-S14; 5-17-36;
   Nfr, Sfr-S15; 5-14-36
Thomas Heeney & Thomas H. Fanning, Cayuga Co., N.Y. SWfr, W-SEfr-
William Mieure* E-SEfr-S14; 5-24-36   S14; 5-3-37
Ambrose Maltell* FrS21; 7-17-21
Pierre Campaynotte* Nfr-S22; 6-28-21
H. A. Foulds* NEfr-S22; 1-19-70
John Edeline* Efr-S22;2-25-36; NE-SW-S23;7-30-26;NW-SW-S23;5-28-36
Gabriel Boyer* NEfr-S23; 5-24-36
Francis Buchey (Busha?)* NWfr-S23; 7-2-21
Joseph Mette* SE-SW-S23; 4-25-37
·Louis Uno* SW-SW-S23; 7-24-37
Pierre Mette* NW-SEfr-S23; 7-17-37
Francis Busha* SW-SEfr-S23; 8-16-37
Pierre Denno* NE-NE-S24; 10-16-37
Robert Ball Shrive (Shreve?)* SE-NE-S24; 4-29-37
Lambert Flatter* Npt-W-NE-S24;.12-16-39
Lewis Boyer* N-NWfr-S24; 5-24-36
John Baptiste Richard* NE-SW-S24; 10-6-37; W-SE-S24; 10-3-37;
Robert Ball Shreve* NE-SE-S24; 4-29-37   Richardville?
Martiale Grenier* SE-SE-S24; 12-15-37
John Didri* NW-NE-S25; 5-23-39   # 269
Sarah Turney & Harriet Caldwell E-NE, E-SE-S26; 3-31-38; C Warrant/
John Caldwell & Mary Ann Caldwell W-NE, W-SE-S26; 3-31-38; CW 269
Lucinda Tousey, Dn NW-S26; 7-12-36
Patrick Carroll* E-NE, SW-NE, NE-SE, NW-SE-S27; 5-1-37
John Marie Barrois* Lot 1-W-NE-S27; 6-2-36

Josiah Lawrence, William Oliver, & Lucius Barber NW-S27; 5-14-36
Thomas H. Fanning & Francis Heeney, Cayuga Co., N.Y. SW, S-SE-S27;
Louis Ravalet* N-Nfr-S28;7-20-21;S-Nfr-S28;9-5-35.   5-5-37
Omer Tousey, Dn Lots 3-4-SWfr, S-SEfr-S28; W-NEfr, NWfr, SWfr,
   W-SE-S33; FrS32; 3-22-36
John#Laplante* Lot 1-N-SEfr-S28; 5-23-36; E-NEfr-S33; 9-6-21;#error
James Stewart* Lot 2-N-SEfr-S28; 8-31 35, SW-NW-S34; 2-27-38.   for
Hyacinth Laplante* NW-SW-S34; 3-2-39   Joseph.
Isaac Cooper* SW-SW-S34; 12-26-54
John Turney* E-NE-S35; 6-27-38
Charles Dawes* SE-S35; 12-22-39

                        T 3 N, R 8 W

Josiah Lawrence, William Oliver, & Lucius Barber Lot 1-N-Wfr-S2;5-
Alexander Melton* Lot 2-N-Wfr-S2;12-10-35;S-Wfr-S2;3-14-25.   17-26
John Parker Harrel, Dn Nfr-S11; 7-16-39
Philip Barton, Barton Peck, & John Thompson, Da Sfr-S25; 9-21-35;
   N-Wfr-S36; 9-15-35
Sion Smith Harbin* Wfr-S25; 6-2-35
Charner Hawkin, Da Lots 1-2-FrS26; 9-3-36
Abram Harbin Westfall* E-NE-S35; 1-12-36; Lots 1-2-E-NWfr-S35;
Allen Cartwright Harbin* NW-NE-S35; 1-18-36   2-6-36
William Scott* SW-NE-S35; 8-5-39
Otis Wilcox, Coshocton Co., O. W-NWfr-S35; 11-29-32
Andrew Wilas, Da SWfr-S35; 8-15-21
William & Richard Wood SEfr-S35; 9-20-22
Hiram Albert, Da Lots 4-5-S-Wfr-S36; 12-8-35
John Jackson Davis* Sfr-S36; 10-27-32
    The following entry may be in either Knox or Daviess County:

Frederick Ernst Goodsell NEfr-S36; 4-13-46

                        T 3 N, R 9 W

Donation Lands. No land entries made in this region.

                        T 3 N, R 10 W

Elias Bedell* FrS10; 3-9-29
Samuel Emison* Lot 1-FrS26 & 27;3-10-36; Lot 2-FrS26; 6-27-35
George Wyant* Lot 1-FrS35; 12-9-35
Patrick Carroll* Sfr-S34; 11-4-30
John B. Bonhomme* FrS31 & 32; 8-29-29

                        T 3 N, R 11 W

All books say contents not known. Has only 56 acres in FrS11.

                        T 4 N, R 7 W

Nicholas Hoover, Franklin Co., O. Nfr-S5; 10-26-37
Hiram Hulen, Da Lot 3-Wfr-S5; 3-15-39

William Harrison Walls, Da   Lot 4-Wfr-S5;1-3-40;Lot 5-Wfr-S5;2-23-4
John Chambers, Joseph Chambers, Nathan Robertson, Samuel Chambers,&
   Alexander Chambers   Lot 3-W-Nfr-S6; 12-31-35

T 4 N, R 8 W

James Chambers*   E-NE, E-SE-S2; 12-18-35;NE-NE-S11; 3-14-37
Wilson Fairhurst*   NW-NE-S3; 8-18-36
Daniel Pace*   NE-SW, NW-SW-S3; 11-30-44
Henry Viche   SE-SW, SW-SW, SE-SE, W-SE-S3; 2-15-49. MLW 40554
Horatio Q. Wheeler & Charles Schaffer   SW-S4; 3-21-49.   MLW 31065
Simon Stelting*   NE-SE-S4; 3-16-49
Rufus Breed   E-NE-S5; 6-19-49.   MLW 33513
George Crooks*   E-NWfr-S5; 3-7-32
Benjamin Franklin Cox*   W-SWfr-S5; 12-16-34; E-NW-S8; 1-20-36; SW-
   NW-S8; 11-10-36; of Shelby Co., Ky., NW-NW-S8; 8-5-34
Charles Jarrald, Sr.*   E-SE-S5; 3-14-29
John Fairhurst*   SW-SE-S5; 5-27-36; SE-NE-S8; 4-26-37
Samuel Farris*   W-NE-S8; 2-26-22
John Lemen Cox*   SE-SWfr-S8; 12-12-38; SW-NW-S9; 11-12-38
James Piety Cox*   SE-SE-S8; SW-SW-S9; 1-14-36
Andrew Dunn*   SW-SE-S8; 1-16-36
Jacob Rollar*   NE-NW-S9; 8-26-44
William Stroud, Gn   E-SE-S9; 4-13-30
Isaac Ransom   SE-NE-S10; 10-4-53.   MLW 1138
Daniel Roster*   SE-NW-S10; 1-3-52
Rufus Breed   SW, SE-S10; 6-19-49.   MLW 32658; MLW 21315
John Herrington*   SE-NE-S11; 7-27-38
Joseph McGee   NW-NE, NE-NW, NW-NW-S11; 6-14-52.   MLW 7610
Alfred B. Robinson   SW-NE,SE-NW,SW-NW,NW-SW-S11;3-20-49.MLW 25182
James T. Cox*   NE-SW-S11; 9-24-53
Emri Neal*   SE-SW-S11; 1-14-39
James L. Prather*   SW-SW-S11; 4-18-51
Charles Hooper*   E-SE-S11; 11-18-37
Nathan Ashby*   W-SE-S11; 6-17-29
Manasseh Reeves*   NEfr-Wfr-S12; 6-23-23
Wilson Neal*   E-NW-Wfr-S12; 12-22-35
Robert Buckels*   W-NW-Wfr-S12; 2-13-30
William Simison*   NE-SW-Wfr-S12; 6-1-39
Obadiah FitzPatrick*   SE-SW-Wfr-S12; 2-1-39; of Da, E-NWfr-Nfr-S13;
   12-19-35; SW-NWfr-Nfr-S13;10-1-32; of Kn, E-SE-S14; 2-13-30
James Goodman*   W-SW-Wfr-S12; 11-8-38
Alexander R. Hinds, Da   SEfr-S12; 8-23-28
John Skain*   NEfr-Nfr-S13; 7-19-39
James L. Goodwin*   NW-NWfr-S13; 7-14-51
James Ashby*   SWfr-Nfr-S13; 8-6-28
John Hayes, Da   N-E-NE, NW-NE-S14; 1-16-38
Jonathan P. Cox*   NW-NE-S17; 7-21-36
David Morris*   SW-NE-S17; 1-26-39; NE-SWfr-S17; 3-26-36; NW-SE-S17;
   4-12-36; NWfr-S20; 4-26-36
Rachel Cox*   NE-NW-S17; 6-20-36
John L. Cox*   SE-NW-S17; 10-10-54
John Mensch*   W-NW-S17; Lots 1-2-FrS18; 4-25-42
Philip Cook*   W-SWfr-S17; 12-31-34

KNOX COUNTY

Andrew Cook* Lot 3-FrS18; 4-29-36
Rufus Breed NEfr-S20; 6-19-49. MLW 26120
Stacy English, Gn W-NE-S21; 5-8-39
John Morris* W-NW-S21; 6-16-36
Bennet Mason & William Davenport* NE-SWfr-S21; 5-2-39
Samuel Bunting* SE-SWfr-S21; 5-21-39
William Hobert* Lot 6-W-SWfr-S21; 12-13-53
Benjamin V. Beckes* SE-S21; 6-21-21
Samuel Alfred Bunting* W-NW-S22; 6-5-40; Lots 2-3-FrS27; 5-25-40
James Harlin* E-SW-S22; 9-14-30
William Burwell Willis* W-SW-S22; 5-8-39;Lot 2-W-SEfr-S22;7-26-39
Wilson Brown Drullinger, Fo E-SWfr-S23; 2-5-39
John McVey Frakes* SE-SWfr-S23; 8-29-36
John Goodman* NE-SE-S23; 12-14-35;Lot 5-W-W-Wfr-S24; 6-27-36
James Ashby* SE-SE-S23; Lot 6-W-W-Wfr-S24; 5-30-36
John Hayes, Da W-SE-S23; 1-16-38
Frederick B. Parker* N-N-Wfr-S25; 2-9-37
John Bicknell, Jr.* S-N-Wfr-S25; 4-30-36
Nathan Ashby* Lot 3-S-N-Wfr-S25; 12-22-35
Samuel Bicknell* Lot 4-N-S-Wfr-S25; 10-19-35
Wilson Hunnicut* Lot 5-S-S-Wfr-S25; 3-18-36
William Shafer* Lot 6-S-S-Wfr-S25; 11-12-53
John FitzPatrick* NE-NEfr-S26;12-14-35;Lot 1-W-NEfr-S26;10-23-35;
    NWfr-S26; 1-30-39
Joseph Ashby* SE-NEfr-S26; 10-19-35; Lot 3-SEfr-S26; 11-17-35
Jacob Hyser* Lot 2-W-NEfr-S26; 3-4-36
Eleazer Godfrey* Lot 4-SEfr-S26; 11-15-36
Abraham Hooper* Lot 1-FrS27; 2-1-39
Mumfred Bicknell* SW-NE-S28; 12-20-38; Lot 3-SEfr-S28; 3-26-36
Joel Wampler* Lot 1-NWfr-S28; 12-28-40
James Bicknell* Lot 2-NWfr-S28; 5-22-39
Abner Melton* Lot 2-NEfr-Nfr-S35; 10-31-35
Caleb Beckes* Lot 3-NEfr-Nfr-S35; 8-5-34
William Hunnicutt* Wfr-Nfr-S35; 2-11-39
Parmenas Webb Beekes* SEfr-Nfr-S35; 11-9-39
Martin Luntenberger, Da Sfr-S35; Sfr-S36; 4-19-43
Bennet Mason* Lot 2-N-N-Wfr-S36;2-9-39;S-N-Wfr-S36; 2-7-39

T 4 N, R 9 W

Hiram A. Foulks* Npt-NW-S1; 1-19-70
William Howard* Spt-NWfr-S1; 8-16-34; SW-SE-S2; 3-15-36
William Cox* E-SWfr-S1; 2-5-34
Samuel Lindsey* W-SWfr-S1; SE-SW-S2; 1-14-36
James Pace* SEfr-S1; 3-4-30
Levi McCord* Lots 1-2-E-NEfr-S2;1-15-36; SE-NW-S2; 3-26-36
James Parker Martin* NW-NEfr-S2; 4-11-39; NE-NW-S2; 8-5-34
Jackson Hollingsworth* SW-NEfr-S2;4-22-36;NE-SW-S2; 12-2-33
Ferdinand Hollingsworth* W-NW-S2; 9-25-37; W-SW-S2; 1-7-36; Lot 3-
    E-NEfr-S3; 5-23-35; Lot 1-E-NEfr-S3; 10-24-27; Lots 2-3-W-NEfr-
    S3; 10-14-37; Wpt-SEfr-S3; 1-11-42; Ept-SEfr-S3; 1-7-36; SW-
    NWfr-S10; 11-27-51. MLW 16331
Abraham Hollingsworth* NW-SE-S2; 2-25-36

George Washington Sartor* E-SWfr-S3; 4-29-37
James Sartor* Lot 6-W-SWfr-S3; 8-8-39
James Madison Emison* FrS4; FrS8; NWfr-S9; 2-12-39
John Hollingsworth* Lot 1-NEfr-S9; 12-15-38; NW-NWfr-S10;5-27-47
John Underwood* Lot 2-NEfr-S9; 1-19-36; Lot 3-E-SWfr-S10; 3-13-34
Thomas Hollingsworth* Efr-S10; W-NW-S11; 1-19-36; NE-NW-S12;
    4-6-33; SE-NW-S12; 8-5-34
Clark Hill* E-NWfr-S10; 6-3-39
Hugh Barr* Lot 2-E-SWfr-S10; 8-8-43; SE-NEfr-S15; 5-6-52
Daniel T. Hollingsworth* W-SWfr-S10; 1-31-29
William Duncan Piety* E-SEfr-S10; 12-5-35; Lot 4-W-SEfr-S10; 4-6-
    52; W-SWfr-S11; 1-15-36. MLW 27325
Isaac Dale* NE-NE-S11; 4-13-36; SE-NE-S11; 7-20-35
Levin Clark* W-NE, NE-NW-S11; 12-18-38; SE-SWfr-S11; FrS13;4-21-
    37; W-NEfr-S14; 12-12-33; NE-NW-S14; 8-2-33; SE-NW-S14; 1-18-36;
    W-NW-S14; 12-18-37; SEfr, E-SWfr-S14; 6-9-28; W-SWfr-S14; 2-11-
    36; W-NEfr-S15; 1-4-40; SEfr-S15; 2-22-35
John Robinson* SE-NW-S11; 1-12-36
Levin Larkin Clark* NE-SWfr-S11; 12-12-36
Spier Spencer Ruby* NE-SE-S11; 1-19-36; SEfr-S12; 10-1-35
David Laymon Clark* NW-SE-S11; 12-13-36
Charles Bartley* W-NEfr-S12; 12-12-36
John Sartor* NW-NW-S12; 2-4-37
John Scott* NE-NEfr-S15; 8-12-39
Daniel Tramel Hollingsworth* NWfr-S15; 3-14-34
Barnes Reeves* FrS19; 10-17-21
Daniel Hollingsworth* FrS20 & 29; 10-15-21
John A. Barr* FrS21; 12-19-54
John Crosby FrS30 & 29; 11-12-21

T 4 N, R 10 W

Ellis Greenfield, Su Nfr-S1; 4-12-36
Andrew Fullerton* Sfr-S1; Nfr-S12; Fr 7-T4N, R9W (description
    not clear); 8-4-53
Isaac Snow* W-NEfr-S3; 9-22-37
Andrew Purcell, Jr. & Ferguson Redman NE-NWfr-S3; 8-9-36
James Graham* SE-NWfr-S3; 10-16-36
John Sproatt* W-NWfr-S3; 7-14-36
Samuel Harris, Lw Lots 1-2-N-SWfr-S3; 2-16-36; Lot 2-FrS4;10-26-36
Charles Brewer* S-SWfr-S3; 1-3-37
William Stuart & Emanuel Meisenhelter* SE-SEfr-S3; 2-13-38
Samuel Meisenhelter, Ad NW-SEfr-S3; 12-5-53
John Welch Allen* SW-SEfr-S3; 4-15-37
Joshua Vance, Lw Lot 1-FrS4; 1-20-36
Joseph Shaw, Lw Lots 1,2,3-N-Nfr-S10; 2-10-36; Lots 4-5-S-Nfr-
    S10; 1-12-36; Lots 6-7-Sfr-S10; 1-9-36
Samuel Meisenhelter, Ad & Emanuel Meisenhalter* SE-NE-S11;12-5-53
John Daugherty Gardiner* SW-NW-S11; 5-16-37; Lot 2-E-SEfr-S11;
    12-30-36; Lot 3-FrS12; 12-31-36
Daniel Horrell Phillips* SE-SW-S11; 6-28-36; Nfr-S13; 12-10-36;
    Lot 1-E-NEfr-S14;7-8-36;NW-NEfr-S14;8-15-36. Howell?
Stephen Burnet* Lot 1-E-SEfr-S11; 4-1-54

Samuel & William Jacob Wise W-SW-S11; 6-18-36; SW-NEfr-S14; 7-4-
    36; N-NWfr-S14; 6-18-36; S-NWfr-S14; 6-25-36
Ceasar Embry* N-Sfr-S13; 10-4-32
Henry Price* Lot 1-S-Sfr-S13; 8-3-35
Forgeson Redman* Lot 2-S-Sfr-S13; 3-14-36;W-NWfr-S24; 3-14-36
James Madison Emison* Lot 2-E-NEfr-S14;11-7-36;Lot 3-N-Sfr-S14;
William Burtch* Lot 4-N-Sfr-S14; 7-6-36   11-7-36
William Fuller* S-Sfr-S14; 10-17-54
John Crockwell Clark* Lot 5-S-Sfr-S14; 7-1-36; Lots 1-2-FrS22;
    7-8-36; S-NWfr-S23; 7-1-36
William Welton* Lot 3-FrS22; 6-22-36
Anthony Williams* E-NE-S23; 12-31-56
John R. Andrews & Daniel Pettyjohn, Lw NW-NE-S23; 2-23-37
Caleb Hitt, LaSalle Co., Ind. (no such Co.; so prob. Ill.) SW-NE-
James Perry Drake* N-NWfr-S23; 6-21-36.   S23; 11-9-36
Simon Gabriel Brute* SWfr, W-SE-S23; 6-8-36
Luther Cooper Cochran, Lw NE-SE-S23; 5-1-37
John Collins* SE-SE-S23; 2-8-36
Henry Dogan Wheeler* NEfr, Lot 4-N-SWfr-S24; 1-2-37
Henry Price* E-NWfr-S24; 8-3-35; Lot 3-N-SWfr-S24; 8-1-35; S-SWfr-
John Young* SEfr-S24;3-17-34;Efr-S25;2-18-34.   S24;1-5-36
Henry Young* Wfr-S25; 8-1-35
Peter Hoke, Louisville, Ky. Sfr-S25; 11-7-33
John Collins & Henry Price* E-NE-S26; 12-29-35
Willis Washington Hitt* NW-S26; 7-1-36; NWfr-S26; 7-5-36; Lot 3-
    N-SWfr, SE-SWfr-S26; 1-11-36; SW-SWfr-S26; 12-2-35; Lot 4-N-SWfr-
    S26; 12-2-35; Lots 1-2-N-SEfr, Lot 7-S-SEfr-S26; 2-9-36; FrS27;
    5-9-54; Fr334; FrS35; 12-2-35
James Tupper Caughran, Lw SW-NE-S26; 1-19-36
Andrew Frederick & David Getty FrS36; 6-12-30 (38?)

T 5 N, R 6 W

Winthrop Foot, Lw E-Nfr, E-W-Nfr, Lot 2-W-W-Nfr-S5; E-E-Wfr-S6;
Henry Dixon, Gn Lot 1-W-W-Nfr-S5; 2-19-36.   4-16-36
William Dillon, Da W-W-Sfr-S5; 7-3-35
Isaiah Johnston, Lw Lot 3-E-W-Sfr, Lots 4,7-W-E-Sfr-S5; Lots 3,6-
    S-Wfr-S6; 2-15-36
George Dixson, Gn Lot 8-E-W-Sfr-S5; W-E-Wfr-S6; 2-8-36
Jacob Wesner, Da Lot 5-E-E-Sfr-S5; 2-18-39
Thomas Elsmore, Da Lot 6-E-E-Sfr-S5; 3-25-35
George Hoke, Jefferson Co., Ky. E-NW-Wfr, W-NW-Wfr-S6; 10-18-22
James Sweeney*Lot 4-S-Wfr-S6; 8-5-34
Aaron Williamson, Gn Lot 5-S-Wfr-S6; 2-9-36
John Langdon Allard, Fl Lot 1-Efr-S6; N-E-NE-Efr, Wfr-S7;11-4-36
Joseph Dixson, Gn Lot 2-Efr-S6; 2-15-36
Mary Hannah, Da W-NE-Efr-S7; 2-13-33
John Murphy, Da NWfr-Efr-S7; 5-9-32
Jonathan Johnston Lots 3-4-Sfr-S7; 2-15-36
Isaac Skomp* Nfr-S18; 2-6-36

Stephen Dixson, Gn E-NE-Nfr-S1; 3-8-31
Daniel Slinkard, Da S-W-NE-Nfr-S1; 10-18-38; S-E-NW-Nfr-S1;9-24-36
John Slinkard* N-E-NW-Nfr-S1;4-13-37; S-W-NW-Nfr-S1; 6-18-36
Isaiah Johnston, Da N-E-SW-Nfr-S1; 4-19-36; Lots 1-2-SEfr-Nfr-S1;
    2-15-35; of*, SW-SW-S2; 3-22-51; of Da, Lot 3-SEfr-Wfr-S12;4-20-
Garrison Evans, Gn S-E-SW-Nfr-S1; 5-9-35   36
Isaac Skomp* W-SW-Nfr-S1; 2-6-36;E-NW-S11;2-6-36;SW-NW-S11;8-5-34
John Houggland, Gn N-E-NE-S2; 2-20-36
Thomas Anderson, Jr.* N-E-NW-S2;10-8-32; N-W-NW-S3; 2-22-36
John Musser, Mr NE-SW-S2; 5-9-37
Jonathan Golden* SE-SW-S2; 6-10-40
Winthrop Foot, Lw E-SE-S2; 4-16-36;Lots 1-2-NEfr-Wfr-S12;4-16-36
Levi Anderson* NW-SE-S2; 7-27-44
Henry John Slinkard, Gn SW-SE-S2; 3-21-36;E-NE-S11; 4-28-30
Rufus Breed E-NW, S-W-NW, NE-SW-S3; 6-19-49
Samuel Skomp* SE-SW-S3; 4-2-39; E-SE-S3; 9-13-28
Henry S. Scomp* W-SE-S3; 5-28-31
Rufus Breed W-NE, SW, NE-SE, NW-SE-S4; 6-19-49
Pressley Anderson* SE-SE-S4; 1-9-55
Peter Carroll* SE-SE-S5; 12-10-39
Matthew Stafford SW-SE-S5; 8-19-48; NE-Nfr-S8; 8-19-48
John Wells, Su E-NW-S6; 1-3-54
James Jarrel, Gn W-NW-S6; 2-22-49
Herman Begeman E-SW-S6; Lots 1,3-W-Nfr, SEfr-Nfr, E-E-Sfr, Lot 5-
    E-E-Sfr, E-W-Sfr-S7; 2-27-49; of*, Lot 6-Sfr-S8; 12-9-53
Charles Butler, New York City NE, NE-SE, W-SE-S9; 7-4-36
John McCombs* SE-SE-S9; 9-25-35
Samuel Skomp NE-S10; 9-5-20; of*, W-NW-S10; 12-23-29; SE-SW-S10;
    4-2-39; SE-S11; 9-5-20
Thomas Anderson E-NW-S10; 4-8-18; of*, SE-SW-S11; 5-4-35
John Skomp* NE-SW-S10; 6-18-40
Allen Reaves SE-S10; W-NE-S11; 5-12-19
Samuel Switser Skomp* NW-NW-S11; 7-2-39
Moses Slinkard* NE-SW-S11; 1-11-40; W-NW-Wfr-S11; 2-6-36
William Journee W-SW-S11; 8-20-19
William Duncan, Lw E-NW-Wfr-S12; 2-15-36
Samuel Reggan* E-SW-Wfr-S12; 3-3-34; S-W-SW-Wfr-S12; 3-6-34
Moses Slinkard* NW-SW-Wfr-S12; 2-6-36
Jonathan Johnston, Da SE-SE-Wfr-S12; 2-15-36
Winthrop Foot, Lw N-NE-Wfr, S-NE-Wfr, E-NW-Wfr, N-SW-Wfr, S-SW-
    Wfr, SEfr-Wfr-S13;4-19-36;Lots 1-2-E-SE-Nfr-S14; 11-22-36;
    Sfr-S14; 4-19-36
Samuel Skomp* N-W-NW-Wfr-S13; 2-6-36; E-NE-Nfr-S14; 2-20-34
Thomas Anderson* SW-NW-Wfr-S13; 1-7-34; NW-NE-Nfr-S14; 2-27-39
Henry Swittzer Skomp* SW-NE-Nfr-S14;4-16-36;W-SE-Nfr-S14;1-9-36
John Johnson* NE-NW-Nfr-S14; 3-8-37; SE-NW-Nfr-S14; 7-18-36; E-SW-
    Nfr-S14; 2-14-36; W-SW-Nfr-S14; 7-18-36
Matthew Smock, Shelby Co., Ky. W-NW-Nfr-S14; 1-15-23
John Skomp* Lot 1-E-E-Nfr-S15; 3-21-34
Job McMurry* Lot 3-E-W-Nfr-S15;12-5-54; Lot 4-E-W-Nfr-S15;11-4-37
Albert McMurry* Lot 9-E-W-Sfr-S15;9-23-37;Lot 10-W-W-Sfr-S15;8-10-
William Wallace McClure Lot 11-W-W-Sfr-S15; 4-25-44.   36

Lewis L. Watson* Nfr-S17; 2-16-39
Robison C. Anderson* E-NEfr-S17; 5-9-30
Conrad Begemann E-SW-S17; 7-26-52
Frederick Pohlmeier & Henry Nagle NW-SW-S17; 1-13-53
James Gano* SW-SW-S17; 3-25-33
James Jarrel, Gn E-SE-S17; 6-6-31; NE-NW-S21; 11-14-35
William Polmeier & Henry Pohlmeier NE-S18; 2-22-49
William Polmier* N-E-NW-S18; 1-9-54
William Begeman SE-NW, E-SW, W-SE-S18; 2-22-49
Jonathan P. Cox* E-NE-S19; 5-31-30; W-NE-S19; 10-23-28
Austin & Marcus Medley E-NW-S19; 6-5-30
Marcus Medley* NE-SW-S19; 6-18-36
Henry N. Meier* NW-SW-S19; 5-11-49
Austin Medley* NW-SE-S19; 1-9-36; SE-SW-S21; 1-28-36.
Philip Slaughter* SE-NE-S20; 5-23-37
Frederick Slaughter* SE-NW-S20; 6-11-44
John F. Burden* W-NW-S20; 6-5-30
George Washington Ballew, Da NE-SE-S20; 5-15-37;NW-SW-S21;5-15-37
John Jackson, Mercer Co., Ky. E-NE-S21; 9-16-36; NE-SW-S21; 9-19-
   36; W-SE-S21; 9-19-36; W-NW, E-SW, W-SW-S22; 9-16-36
James Burras* SW-NE-S21; 3-26-38; of Fl, W-NE-S28; 6-12-37
Thomas Anderson* W-NW-S21; 5-28-31
John Williamson* SE-NW-S21; 11-5-36; Nfr, Wfr-S24; 1-12-38
John F. Spears, Jessamine Co., Ky. SW-SW-S21;E-NE,E-SE,Lot 1-W-SE-
James Killion, Da E-SE-S21; 6-9-36; E-NE-S28;1-11-36./S22;9-27-37
David Killion* Lot 4-W-SE-S22; 9-6-33
Winthrop Foot, Lw E-NE, E-SW, W-SW, Lot 3-SEfr-Wfr-S23; 4-19-36
Henry Switzer Skomp W-NE-S23; 1-25-36; NE-NW-S23; 2-3-34
James Burnes (Barnes), Da SE-NW-S23;1-13-36;W-NW,Lots 4-5-SEfr-Wfr-
Winthrop Foot Lots 4,9-Wfr & Sfr-S24;11-22-36.   S23; 1-11-36
Alexander Killion Lot 2-Nfr-S26; 1-22-53
David Killion, Jr., Da N-N-Wfr,Lot 4-S-N-Wfr,-S27; 1-11-36; Lot 5-
   S-Wfr-S27; 5-7-36
William Alfred Killion Lot 3-S-N-Wfr-S27; 2-11-43
Moses Cawood Lot 9-S-Wfr-S27; 7-4-36
Enos Grimsley, Da Lot 8-S-Efr-S27; 5-18-36
Josiah Wallace* E-NW-S28; 3-23-43
Moses Cawood* NE-SW-S28; 7-4-36; SE-SW-S28; 9-14-38; W-SW-S28;
   6-30-36; of Da, SW-SE-S29; 10-15-38
David Alexander McClesky E-SE-S28; 1-11-36
William Sparks, Da NW-SE-S28; 1-21-36
George Smyth, Da SW-SE-S28; 1-20-36
John Chambers & Jos. (Jas.?) Chambers* E-SW-S29; 11-10-28
Michael Robertson* SW-SW-S29; 10-23-33
Nathan Green Robertson* E-SE-S29; 8-14-34
William Jarrel* NW-SE-S29; 3-18-34
John Chambers* E-NW-S30; 4-4-37; N-E-SW-S30; 2-24-37; NE-SW-S31;
   12-28-35; NW-SW-S31; 12-31-35
Andrew Burnside* W-NW, E-SE-S30; 7-7-21   1-29-29
Levi Chambers* SE-SW-S30;1-30-37; W-SW-S30;8-7-29; of Su, E-NW-S31;
William Comstock* W-SE-S30; 6-24-30; W-NE-S31; 3-9-30
Jackson Azbell* NE-NE-S31; 11-19-33
James Goodman, Da W-NW-S31;3-22-30;SE-SW-S31;12-28-35;SW-SE-S31;
William Ferguson* SE-NE-S31; 12-31-35   12-29-35

Jos. (Jas.?) Chambers, John Chambers, Nathan G. Robertson, Samuel
  F. Chambers, & Alexander Chambers W-SW-S31; 1-5-36
James G. Bynum* E-SE-S31; 12-11-37
Edward White Robertson* NE-NE-S32; 1-8-?; NW-NWfr-Wfr-S33;1-5-36
Jarit Keith* SE-NE-S32; 7-27-48
William James NW-NE-S32; 11-5-38
Michael Robinson, Da E-NW-S32; 3-5-30
William Tigert* NW-NW-S32; 3-12-44
Luke Cassiday* SW-NW-S32; 6-6-36
John R. Haddon* Lot 4-SWfr-Nfr-S32; 6-5-54
Isaac Demoss* Lot 3-SWfr-Nfr-S32; 11-20-54
John Cawood, Da Lot 5-SWfr-Nfr-S32; 3-19-36
Andrew McCormick, Da Lots 1,6-SEfr-Nfr-S32; 6-15-43
John Robertson, Da Lot 1-NEfr-Wfr-S33; 4-28-36
George Smith, Da Lot 2-NEfr-Wfr-S33; 1-9-36
Moses Cawood, Da E-NWfr-Wfr-S33; 1-5-36
Moses Cawood Robertson SW-NWfr-Wfr, Lot 8-SWfr-Wfr-S33; 4-5-36;
  Lot 5-Efr-S33; 1-1-52; (might be in Da.; near border line)
Michael Robison McCormick Lot 7-SWfr-Wfr-S33; 1-21-36; Lot 6-SWfr-
  Wfr-S33; 6-10-36
John Simpson Pringle Lot 3-SEfr-Wfr-S33; 12-28-44; Lot 4-Efr-
  S33; 2-22-44; (might be in Da.; near border line)
Elisha Hyatt, Da Nfr, Wfr-S34; 6-1-50

RELINQUISHMENTS

Thomas Anderson W-NW-S10; 4-8-18
Allen Reaves E-NE-S11; 5-12-19
William Journee E-SW-S11; 8-20-19

T 5 N, R 8 W

Eli Jarrel* NW-NE-S1; 7-12-39
John Nelson, Su SW-NE-S1; 9-8-37
William Ricketts, Ru SE-NW, N-SE-Nfr-S1; 11-21-39
Franklin Jarrel* NW-Nfr-S2; 10-14-50
Union Brower SW-Nfr-S2; 1-11-53
William Leach E-W-Sfr-S2; 9-15-51. MLW (8608?)
William Jarrel, Jr.* Lot 1-Nfr-S3; 11-12-38
William Jarrel* E-E-Sfr-S3; 11-12-38
John Smith* NW-Sfr-S3; 12-29-36; of Su, E-NE-Sfr-S4; 12-24-38
John Brant Hayward, Su E-SW-Sfr-S3; 10-7-31
Henry Faught* S-SW-Sfr-S3; 4-30-36
Daniel Reesinger* W-NW-S5; 10-13-34; E-NE-S6; 11-13-30; NE-NW-S6;
  12-4-37; of Jefferson Co., Ky., W-NW-S6; 9-14-30
Isaac Robbins* NE-SW-S5; 8-16-36
John Robbins* W-SW-S5; 4-23-31; SE-NW-S6; 4-1-47; E-SE-S6; 3-6-
  22; SW-SE-S6; 11-26-38
James Blevins* Lot 2-N-SWfr-S6; 6-9-36
Daniel McArthur* E-NE-S7; 5-21-30
George Hager, Su NW-NE-S7; 3-20-38
William McArthur* SW-NE-S7; 4-20-37
Jacob Davis, Su Lot 6-S-SWfr-S7; 8-31-35

Moses Robbins* NE-SE-S7; 11-15-36; SE-SE-S7; 12-30-35;W-SE-S22;
James McArthur* W-SE-S7; 9-9-30   2-5-39
Jonathan Brentlinger, Su SW-NE, NW-SE-S9; 5-23-37
Philip Rench* NE-SE-S9; 8-23-50
Ernst Kampmeir NE-NE, W-NE-S10; 7-20-49. MLW
William Jarrell* SE-NE-S10; 10-18-32
John Jarrell* NE-SE-S10; 12-24-39
James Jarrel Lots 1-2-E-NWfr-Sfr-S12; 9-8-37
Rufus Breed NE-SW-Sfr, NW-SW-Sfr, W-E-SE-Sfr, W-W-SE-Sfr-S12;5-19-
Frederick Schwarsze* SW-NW-S13; 1-27-48   49. MLW
Frederick Schwarze, Henry Nierste, & Louis Unwerfahrt SE-SW, W-SW-
    S13; NE-SE-S14; 3-19-49. MLW 38665
Frederick Kneger* NE-NE-S14; 11-15-50
James Ganoe* SE-NE-S14; 2-10-37
Joseph Medley* W-NE-S14; 12-30-24
Stephen Tyner* SE-NW-S14; 3-21-40
Luke Cassidy* NW-NW-S14; 11-20-38
James Piety Cox* SW-NW-S14; 5-21-39
Conrad Mesch* NW-SW-S14; 1-27-48
Christian Decker, Vb SW-SW-S14; 10-19-47
Henry Nierste SE-SE-S14; 6-22-50
Anthony Deppe* NW-SE-S14; 1-27-48
John Schwarze* SW-SE-S14; 4-10-49
John Robbins NW-NW-S15; 3-16-52. MLW. NE-NE-S18; 8-27-35, of *
Henry Selger* SW-NW-S15; 8-20-49
Angeline Homelman* SW-SW-S15; 2-25-45
John Keith* SE-SE-S15; 4-6-37; E-SW-S17; 6-21-21; SE-SE-S17; 4-9-
    36; W-SE-S17; 6-21-21; SW-SE-S18; 12-22-35; Lot 1-W-NEfr-S20;
John Bower* NW-NW-S17;1-4-37; NW-SW-S17;3-16-38.   8-5-34
Henry Keith* SW-SW-S17; 12-22-35
Martin Miller* SE-NE-S18; 3-1-37
Nicholas Davis* W-NE-S18; 9-13-21; Lot 1-NWfr-S18; 8-31-35
James Polke* S-SWfr-S18; 9-7-35
Warren Cash Keith* NE-SE-S18; 5-24-37; SE-SE-S18; 8-5-34
Ernest Woltingmire* NW-SE-S18; 8-2-53
William Patterson* E-Efr, Lots 1-2-W-Efr-S19; Lots 5,7-E-Wfr,
    Lots 3-4-W-Wfr-S20; 6-5-34
Robert Lemen Lot 5-SWfr-S19; 8-4-35
Jesse Beem Keith Lot 6-W-NEfr-S20; 4-9-36; E-SE-S22;4-8-37; Bean
Jacob Schrieth* NW-NE-S21; 2-22-45   of *
John Christian Boberyer NE-SWfr-S21; 8-13-49
Thomas F. Chambers SE-SWfr-S21; 2-19-47
John Swartz NE-SE-S21; 4-6-48
Charles Franklin Hooper SE-SE-S21; 8-14-47
Wesley Gordon Hooper W-SE-S21; 6-28-47
George Smith, Campbell Co., Ky. NE-S22; 5-4-37
Henry Viche* E-NW-S22; 2-17-45
John Smith* NW-NE-S23; 6-1-50; NE-NW-S23; 2-13-49
Frederick Waggoner* SW-NE-S23; 2-21-49; SE-SW-S23; 2-13-49
George Cain, Harvey Co., Ky. NW-NW-S23; 3-15-38
Tavner Bowin* E-SW-S23;1-31-39; of Su, W-SE-S23; 11-29-38
Isaac Robbins* NW-SW-S23; 1-31-39
William Wesley Robbins SW-SW-S23; 3-7-39
Martin Robbins NE-SE-S23; 1-31-39

Rufus Breed W-NE, NW-NW-S24; 5-19-49. MW
Horatio G. Wheeler & Charles Scaffer SE-NW, NE-SW, W-SE-S24; 3-20-
   49. MW 40968. Shaffer
Gert Heines SW-NW, SE-SW-S24; 3-2-49. MW. Hines
John Ferguson E-SF-S24; 6-15-36
Thomas Hollingsworth E-NE-S25;7-2-21;W-NE-S25;6-21-21;SE-SW-S25;
Frederick Waggoner NW-NW-S25; 6-1-50   12-14-35
Abner Lemon, Grayson Co., Ky. SW-NW-S25; 9-13-36
Henry Highmeyer NE-SW-S25; 2-21-50
Joseph Medley* NW-SW-S25; 2-15-36
Benjamin Keith* SW-SW-S25; 4-9-36
Ambrose Asbell* NE-SE-S25; 1-2-39
Samuel Irvin Chambey SE-SE-S25; 6-4-39
Jeremiah Davis NW-SE-S25; 1-4-36
Henry Highmeyer & Louis Lutkeymayer SW-SE-S25; 2-11-51
Abner Lemon, Graceland Co., Ky. NE-NE-S26; 9-13-36
Abraham Hollingsworth* SE-SW-S27; 11-5-40; SW-SE-S27; 5-20-42;
   NE-SW-S33; 10-20-47; SW-SW-S33; 9-20-47
Aquilla Jones, Lw SE-NE-S26; 2-13-37; W-NE, E-SE-S26;.2-11-37;
   of*, NW-SE-S26; 11-27-38
Isaac Robbins* E-NW-S26; 2-12-39; SW-NW-S26; 2-13-49
Jesse Bean Keith* NW-NW-S26; 4-9-36;SE-NE,NE-SE-S35; 4-9-36
McElway Goodman* NE-SW-S26; 12-19-42
Charles Hooper* NE-NE-S27; 9-24-39
Henry M. Gilham* SE-NE, W-NE, SE-NW-S27; 2-22-49
Susan McCord* NE-NW-S27; 12-15-38
William Hooper* SW-NW-S27; 12-9-44
William Cox* NE-SW-S27;1-11-37; NW-SE-S27;1-5-36; FrS30; 8-5-34
Johnston Woods* E-SE-S27; E-NE-S34; 9-7-46. MW
Henry Kansler Wise* Nfr, Sfr-S29; 2-9-39
Alexander Chambers* NWfr-S32; 12-11-37
Joseph Crook* NW-SW-S32; 3-12-39; NW-NW-S33; 11-26-51. Crooks
Ethan A. Allen* E-SW-S32; SW-SW-S33; 11-20-37
David Ruble* E-NE-S33; 8-5-39
Samuel E. Hollingsworth SW-NW-S33; 3-27-51
Levi Chambers SE-SW-S33; 4-3-52
Thomas Hollingsworth* W-NE-S34; 4-26-37
Sarah McCord* SE-NW-S34; 12-17-38
Alexander Rankin Hinds* NE-SW, SW-SW-S34; 2-1-37
Andrew Barton Hinds* NW-SW-S34; 9-29-38
Murdock McRay* NE-SE-S34; 12-27-48
Thomas Bourne* NW-SE-S34; 7-27-36
Wilson Fairhurst* SW-SE-S34; 12-12-36   49. MW
Henry Faelke & Simon Meier NE-NE-S35;2-15-49;W-NE,NE-NW-S35;2-13-
William Howard W-NW-S35;11-6-?; W-SW-S35; 11-6-? MW
Henry Faelke* NE-SW-S35; 6-25-50
Sarah Ann Purdy* SE-SE-S35; 1-1-36
Greenberry Batman* SW-SE-S35; 2-6-36

                    T 5 N , R 9 W

Joseph Howard, Oldham Co., Ky. E-NE, E-SEfr-S1; 5-20-30
Warren Pearce* Lot 1-W-NEfr-S1; 6-8-35
Washington Allen Pearce Lot 2-NWfr-S1; 2-26-39

Richard Pierce, Su Lot 3-NWfr-S1; 10-16-37
Elonzo Cotton, Su Lot 4-NWfr-S1;1-26-35;NE-NE-S5;6-6-36;NW-NE-S5;
Harrison Smith, Su Lot 5-E-SW, Spt-SEfr-S1;6-26-37.   4-14-36
William Brown, Su Lot 6-E-SW, Spt-SEfr-S1; 1-29-35
Daniel Kimberlin, Su NW-SWfr-S1; 4-20-38
Moses Bourn, Mg SW-SWfr-S1; 3-4-36
James Blevins* Npt-W-SEfr-S1; 5-30-37
Milton P. Gee SW-NW-S4; 8-5-53
James Routledge* SE-NE-S5; 5-31-36; W-NW-S10; 2-4-39
Augustus Latture (Lattour)* SW-NE-S5;5-17-36; SE-NW-S5; 2-18-34
Jacob Wolfe* NE-NW-S5; 8-5-34
John Conner* W-NW-S5; 3-25-23
Joseph Latshaw, Su Lot 1-SWfr-S5; 2-11-34
William Dickey Martin, Su Lot 2-SWfr-S5; 8-27-35
William Clark* NE-SE-S5; 7-8-36
Solomon Conrad, Gn SE-SE-S5; 11-11-39
Joseph Latshaw, Sr.* NW-SE-S5; 5-9-36
Robert Blakely Martin, Su SW-SE-S5; 6-22-36; N-Wfr-S6; 5-18-25
John Sproate, Su Sfr-S5; 5-30-22; NEfr-S7; E-NW-S8; 5-24-22
Samuel Martin, Su Efr-S6; 8-31-22
Frederick Moeler & Jared P. Hedden S-Wfr-S6; 12-10-27.   37
John Sproate, Sr.* Lot 4-Wfr, Lot 3-W-E-Sfr-S7; 8-5-34;NW-S15;5-27-
William Harper* Lot 5-Wfr-S7; 8-22-35   39
Jacob Rudolph Snapp* NE-SE-S7; SW-NW-S8; 11-21-36;NE-SE-S10;1-24-/
Samuel Neely & Dunn Harper* SE-SE-S7;1-3-37. May be all one name
John Whitfield Ewing* Lot 6-W-E-Sfr-S7; 12-29-36
Benjamin Ridgeway* E-NE-S8; 2-4-37; NE-SW-S10; 2-4-39
Jared Pick Hedden* NW-NE-S8; 2-2-38
William Tichernor (Tichenor)* SW-NE-S8;6-4-36;NW-SE-S8; 2-6-37
William Dickey Martin, Su NW-NW-S8; 8-27-35
Benjamin Sproate* NE-SW-S8; 2-1-38
Preston Norman* SE-SWfr-S8; 1-23-37
Elijah Snapp* W-SWfr-S8; 4-5-37
John Wolfe* NE-SE-S8; NW-SW-S9; 2-6-37
William F. Snapp* NE-NW-S9; 2-28-54
John Sproate, Jr.* SW-SW-S9; 5-15-37; NW-NE-S15; 6-22-36
John Bailey SE-SE-S9; 5-27-37
Jesse Cox SE-SW-S10; 4-11-36
Robert Duckworth* SE-SE-S10; 2-2-44; NE-NE-S15; 12-24-39
Nicholas Harper* W-SE-S10; 6-18-36
James Miller* SE-NE-S11; 1-12-36; Lot 2-Nfr-S12; 1-12-36
Richard Robinson+ SW-NE-S11; 2-18-53
George Tevebaugh* SEfr-S11; 1-8-36; Lot 4-S-Wfr-S14; 1-30-35
H.A. Foulk* SW-S12; 1-19-70
William Bourn, Su Lot 1-Nfr-S12; 1-29-35
Thomas Jefferson Kyle* Lot 2-Nfr-S13; 1-5-36
Charles Bartley* N-SWfr Lot 4-S-SWfr-S13; 2-10-37
Prince Allen* Lot 3-S-SWfr-S13; 8-5-34
James Polke* E-SEfr-S13; 10-1-35
Eli Embers* W-SEfr-S13; 6-13-40
Samuel Miller* Lot 1-N-Wfr-S14; 7-2-36
Abraham Miller, Jr.* Lot 2-N-Wfr-S14; 3-20-34; S-Wfr-S14;1-8-39;
William Fairhurst* Sfr-S14; 3-12-51.   SE-NE-S15; 1-1-36
John Miller, Su NE-SE-S15; 4-20-37

Elijah Duckworth* SE-SE-S15; 10-23-38
Harrison G. Miller* NW-SE-S15; 11-24-53
John Scandling* SW-SE-S15; 10-6-53
Caleb Clark* Wfr-S17; 2-9-37; E-NEfr-S18; 12-29-36
John Baxter Harper, Cf NW-NEfr-S18; 12-16-35
Horace Buckner Shepard* SW-NEfr-S18; 4-7-35; Sfr-S18; 8-5-34
Lemuel Harper* NWfr-S18; 8-17-31
Samuel McClure* FrS19; 3-24-36; Lot 1-Wfr-S29; 3-14-36
Abraham Hollingsworth+ NE-NE-S22;2-19-39; SW-NE-S22; 6-21-36
Russell Sight* SE-NE-S22; 2-8-36; SW-NWfr-S23; 11-21-33
Sanders Light+ NE-NW-S22; 5-19-52
William Harper* SE-SW-S22; 7-7-36
Samuel McClure, Sr.* W-SW-S22; 3-2-39
James Blevins+ NE-NEfr-S23; 10-4-43
John Mills* SW-NEfr-S23; 9-20-36
George Clark+ Lot 4-SW-NEfr-S23; 5-5-41
Blewford Light* Lots 2-3-E-NWfr-S23; 11-28-36
George Tevebaugh* NW-NWfr-S23; 1-30-35
Charles Polk* Lot 5-E-SWfr-S23; 2-24-35; SEfr-S23; 2-13-37; Lots
   2-3-E-NWfr-S24; 1-16-36; NW-NWfr-S24; 1-7-36
John Liles* NW-SWfr-S23; 9-15-36
John Patterson* E-Efr-S24; 6-27-35
Zebedee Causey* W-Efr-S24; 8-5-34
John Blevins* SW-NWfr-S24; 9-11-38
William VanMeter Polke* SWfr-S24; 10-5-39   S35;1-21-37
James Risley* FrS25; 6-12-54; Lot 6-S-SEfr-S26; 12-7-35;S-NEfr-/
Samuel Lindsey* NE-SWfr-S26; 1-12-36   5-4-36
Thomas Piety* SW-SWfr-S26; 9-6-36;N-NEfr-S35;6-23-21;NE-NW-S35;/
B.V. Beckes & Samuel Lindsey* Pt-W-SWfr-S26; 6-23-21
William Bell* N-SEfr-S26; 12-12-36
James Duncan Piety* SE-NE-S27; 12-27-37; Nfr-S36; 6-1-22
Jesse Harper* SW-NE-S27; 3-19-39
Robert Beneficl* NWfr, Lot 1-S-SWfr-S27; 6-25-36
Mark Dennis* N-SWfr-S27; 8-20-39
George W. Hill* Efr-S28; 6-12-54
Pardon Sheldon* Lot 2-Wfr-S29; 2-12-36
John Alexander McClure* E-NEfr-S30;1-9-37; W-W-NEfr-S30; 12-3-38
Thomas Wilson McClure* SW-NEfr, NWfr-S30; 12-3-38
William Harrison McClure* SWfr-S30; 6-16-36
George Madison Ockletree* Lot 1-E-SEfr-S30;6-20-36; Lot 4-E-SEfr-
Henry Stripe+ Lot 3-W-SEfr-S30; 8-29-36.   S30; 4-16-36
Amos Wooden* FrS31; 7-2-21
Moses Threlkeld* E-NE-S34; 1-6-36
James Phillips* Lot 1-W-NE-S34; 1-20-53
David Phillips* Lot 4-SEfr-S34; 8-20-36
Samuel Duncan Piety* NW-NW-S35; 2-11-36
Russell Adkins* SW-NW, Lot 2-W-SW-S35; 2-19-39
James Parker Martin* E-SW-S35; 10-16-33
Mary Hollingsworth* SEfr-S35; 10-26-33
Bernard Hollingsworth* SEpt-SEfr-S35; 2-6-38
Jesse Hollingsworth Sfr-S36; 1-15-36

Benjamin Wolf, Su Nfr-S1; 5-24-30; E-NEfr-S2; 9-22-31; W-NEfr-S2;
    3-22-33; E-NWfr, W-NWfr-S2; E-NEfr, W-NEfr, NWfr-S3; Nfr-S4;3-
Jacob Wolf, Su W-Sfr-S1;7-2-31;W-E-Sfr-S1;3-13-32.   21-36
Roberts Latshaw, Su E-E-Sfr-S1; 3-22-32
Vance Wolfe* SWfr-S2; Lots 5-6-SEfr-S3; 7-26-36
Henry Sprinkle, Wythe Co., Va. SEfr-S2; 11-15-32; NEfr-S10;7-16-36
John Jenkins* Lots 7-8-SWfr-S3; Lots 1,4-E-Sfr-S4; Lots 1-2-N-
    Nfr-S9; 12-22-35
Josiah Lawrence, William Oliver, & Lucius Barber Lots 2-3-W-Sfr-
    S4; N-SWfr, S-SWfr-S9; 5-17-36
William Hayes* FrS8; 1-11-37; W-NWfr-S10; 3-7-37;E-NW-S21;12-23-36
Elijah Clark* Lots 3-4-S-N-S9; 1-1-36; Lot 5-S-Nfr-S9; 10-1-35;
    NW-SEfr-S9; 8-3-33
Patty Hill* E-SEfr-S9; 7-12-36; SW-SEfr-S9; 10-10-36
Coonrod Winemiller, Ps SE-NWfr-S10; 3-7-37
James Winemiller* NE-SW-S10; 3-25-37
Thomas Winemiller* SE-SW-S10; 4-13-39
Jonathan Douglass* NW-SW-S10; 9-3-36; E-NW-S14; 8-1-31
Asa Allen Robertson, Sr.* SW-SW-S10; 12-29-36
John Conner & Edward Ray Watson Lots 5-6-SEfr-S10; 2-5-35
John Elsea* Lot 4-SEfr-S10; 7-14-36
John Jenkins* and Su, NE-FrS11; 4-6-35; Wfr-S11; 3-10-32; W-SW-
    S12; 9-18-32; NE-NE-S14; 12-22-35
William Jenkins, Su SE-FrS11; 1-28-37
John Tichenor & David Hedden Tichenor E-NE-S12; 3-5-32
Jacob Wolfe, Su W-NE, NW-S12; 3-6-32
John Sinclear, Su E-SW-S12; 9-8-32
James Routledge, Su SE-S12; 11-9-32; NE-NW-S13; 5-22-35
David Hedden Tichenor* NEfr-S13; 11-10-32
James Madison Emison* SE-NW-S13; 8-11-35; Lot 3-SWfr-S13; 8-3-35
Rufus Norman* NW-NW-S13; 12-21-35
Solomon Wolfe* SW-NW, Lots 4-5-SWfr-S13; 10-8-36; SE-NE-S14;
George Harper, Jr.* Lot 1-SEfr-S13; 3-24-34.   5-21-33
William Harper* Lot 6-SEfr-S13; 8-22-35; Lot 2-SEfr-S13; 4-14-35
Thomas Newman & Jonathan Douglass* W-NE-S14; 5-19-28
Alvin Hampton Forqueran* NW-NW-S14; 9-27-33
Harrison Nance* SW-NW-S14; 10-7-34
Asa Allen Robertson, Vb E-SW-S14;8-14-33; NW-SW-S14; 9-8-34
Henry Fowler* SW-SW-S14; 12-29-36; SE-SE-S14; 8-14-33; of Crawford
    Co., Ill., SW-SE-S14; 8-14-33; Lots 2-3-FrS17; 12-21-35; NE-NE-
Solomon Wolfe* NE-SE-S14; 5-21-35.   S21; 12-29-36
Asa Allen Robertson, Jr. NW-SE-S14; 5-11-35
Hampton Forqueran* NE-NE-S15; 2-11-36
Isaac L. Ray* SE-NE-S15; 2-28-39
John Edwards* NW-NE-S15; 7-9-39; SW-NE-S15; 6-2-37
Josiah Lawrence, William Oliver, & Lucius Barber NW-S15; 5-17-36;
    SW, SE-S15; 5-14-36; W-NEfr, E-NW, NW-NW-S22; 5-17-36
James Routledge* Lot 1-FrS17; 6-3-36
Albert Badollet* N-Nfr, S-Nfr, Sfr-S20; W-NW, W-SWfr-S21;4-7-36
Rufus Austin* SE-NE-S21; 9-12-36
John Phillips* NW-NE-S21; 1-2-37
Samuel G. Minard* SW-NE-S21; 2-13-37

John Sproatt* E-SWfr-S21; 5-13-33
Horace Buckner Shepard E-SEfr-S21; 5-9-36
Peter McDonald & Henry D. Wheeler Lots 1-2-W-SEfr-S21; 7-22-37
Benjamin Wolf E-NEfr-S22; 1-24-35; of Su, Ept-SEfr-S22; 1-24-35
Bluford Hall* SW-NW-S22; 5-14-36; NW-NW-S23; 1-16-39
Harriet Sanford* Lot 6-N-SWfr, NWpt-SEfr-S22; 5-13-36
Walter Liles* Lot 7-S-SWfr, SWpt-SEfr-S22; 12-9-36
William Hayes* Lot 8-S-SWfr, SWpt-SEfr-S22; 7-26-37; SE-SW-S23; 12-
Richard J. Morris+ NE-NE-S23; 5-28-36   23-36
Preston Norman" SE-NE-S23; 1-25-36; SW-SW-S24; 8-14-37
Asa Allen Robertson* NW-NE-S23; 5-9-35
Samuel Wise* SW-NE, SE-NW-S23; 7-5-37
Asa Allen Robertson, Jr.* NE-NW-S23; 12-22-35
Elijah James, Crawford Co., Ill. SW-NW-S23; 10-6-35
Henry Winemiller* NE-SW-S23; 10-3-36; of Ps, W-SE-S23; 8-11-35
Samuel Gunsellus Minard* NW-SW-S23; 1-27-35; SW-SW-S23; 12-21-33
Abraham Nelson W. Sellars* NE-SE-S23; NW-SW-S24; 6-26-37
John Edwards* SE-SE-S23; 9-5-43
Lemuel Harper* NEfr-S24; 7-8-33
Asa Olney & Joseph Buck Fordice Lot 1-NWfr-S24; 8-17-41
Vance Wolfe Lot 2-NWfr-S24; 6-24-37
Samuel McClure Lot 3-SWfr-S24; 3-28-36; NEfr-S25; 2-24-31
John Alexander McClure Lot 4-SWfr-S24; 3-19-34; SEfr-S24; 8-5-34
Sterett McClellan E-NW, W-NW-S25; 9-11-32; NE-SW-S36; 1-24-37
Miles Curry SWfr-S25; 4-16-35
Nathaniel Hall McClure SEfr-S25; 6-8-35
James Madison Emison* E-NE-Nfr-S26; 12-10-47
Robert Benefiel* W-NE-Nfr-S26; 9-3-36
Henry Hill* NW-NW-S26; 10-30-35; Lot 3-Sfr-S28; 4-21-36
Amos Hogg* NE-NW-S26; 10-30-35; E-NWfr-S35; 7-6-36
John Sproatt+ Lot 2-S-NWfr-Nfr-S26; 9-2-35; FrS33; 9-3-35
George Washington Boatman Lot 1-S-NWfr-Nfr-S26; 9-19-35
Irvin Steward Wilkins* SWfr-Nfr-S26; 10-26-36
John Wesley Allen* Lot 3-SEfr-Nfr-S26; 9-5-36
James Norman" Lot 4-SEfr-Nfr-S26; 4-22-37
Samuel Farmer* Sfr-S26; 8-13-36
Peter McDonald* Lot 1-N-Nfr-S27; 7-17-37
Henry Winemiller* Lot,2-N-Nfr-S27; 12-15-36
Leonard Harrison Minard Lot 3-S-Nfr-S27; 9-3-36
Joseph Pinkard* NE-SW-S27; 7-14-36
Benjamin J. White* SE-SW-S27; 1-11-51
John Sproatt, Sr.* W-SW-S27; 5-16-36
John Law* Lot 5-SEfr-S27; 6-29-36
Josiah Lawrence, William Oliver, & Lucius Barber Lots 1-2-Nfr-S28;
Andrew Wilkins+ Lot 4-Sfr-S28; 4-21-36   5-14-36
George Price* NE-NE-S34; 7-20-33; NW-NWfr-S35; 7-20-33
Henry Kansler Wise* SE-NW-S34; 7-4-36
Nathan Broogue* NW-NW-S34; 7-5-36
Rachel James* SW-NW-S34; 6-11-36
John Garret* E-SW, NW-SW-S34; 6-11-36
Thomas Blizzard* SW-SW-S34; 8-24-37
Simon Herder* E-NE-S35; 9-11-32
Samuel Farmer+ Lot 1-W-NE-S35; 10-31-35; Lot 2-W-NE-S35; 3-23-36
James Herder Lot 4-E-SEfr-S35; 2-28-38; Lot 2-NEfr-S36; 1-26-36

James Madison Emison* E-SW-S35; 8-16-36; Lot 3-E-SEfr-S35; 6-24-
   39; W-SEfr-S35; 10-24-37
William Henry Harrison McClure NE-NE-S35;12-3-38;SE-NE-S35;9-5-36
Andrew Wayne McClure SW-NE-S36; 1-11-37
John Curry NWfr-S36; 7-27-35
James Franklin McClure Lot 5-SEfr-S36; 1-11-37
Samuel McClure Lot 6-SEfr-S36; 6-16-36
Hiram S. Hunchett, Su Lot 7-SEfr-S36; 11-30-54

T 1 S, R 11 W

John Wise* Wfr-S1; E-NE-Wfr-S2; 5-10-36
Harvey Vanderhoof* W-NE-Wfr-S2; 9-19-36; NE-NW-Wfr-S2; 7-22-36;
   W-NW-Wfr-S2; 8-9-28
Thomas Jacobus* SE-NW-Wfr-S2; 6-2-36   17-35
Joseph Humphreys, Gi Lots 2-3-E-SW-Wfr-S2; 12-28-35;SW-SE-S3;10-
Silas Humphreys, Gi SW-SW-Wfr-S2; 4-29-36;SE-SE-S3; 10-28-35.
Dycy Brittonham* Lot 1-SE-Wfr-S2; 5-9-36
George Humphreys, Gi Lot 4-SE-Wfr-S2; 4-29-36
Daily Jacobus* NE-NEfr-S3; 3-29-36; SE-NW-S3; 2-13-37
Jacob Jacobus, Jr.* W-NEfr-S3; 7-15-29
John Jones, Hamilton Co., O. W-NW-S3; 10-19-54
Adam Purcell* E-SW-S3; 11-12-36; NW-SW-S3; 3-15-37; NW-SE-S3;
   8-19-36; SE-NW-S4; 3-15-37
William Winston Pritchett, Gi SW-SW-S3; 6-1-37
William Slusher* SE-NE-S4; 6-9-37; SW-NE-S4; 3-31-37
Jackson Harness* NW-NE, NE-NW-S4;6-2-36;NE-NE-Nfr-S5; 8-16-36
Elisha Hurd, Gi W-NW-S4; 2-25-23; see following entry
Elijah Hurd* W-SWfr-S4; 5-21-29. Possibly also Nfr-S9; descrip-
   tion not clear. SE-Wfr-S5; 5-21-29. Error for Elisha above?
Henry Pilgrim, Gi E-SEfr-S4; 6-1-37
Thomas Jacobus* W-SEfr-S4; 11-3-31; SE-NE-Nfr-S5; 6-2-36
Adam Decker* NW-NE-Nfr-S5; 8-1-36
Martha J. Hershey* SW-NE-Nfr-S5; 2-9-70
Ezra Chapman* SW-NW-Nfr-S5; 6-7-37; Lot 5-W-SE-Wfr-S7; 7-6-36
William Woodhouse* W-SW-Nfr-S5; 4-14-37
Daniel Green Putnam, Wabash Co., Ill. Lot 6-pt of SW-Nfr, E-SE-
   Wfr-S6; 3-8-36
Samuel Putnam, Wabash Co., Ill. Lot 1-N-W-Wfr-S7; 7-11-36; Lot 4-
   S-N-Wfr-S7; 7-15-36; E-SE-Wfr-S7;7-11-36; Wfr-S8; 2-20-37
Daniel Curtis* Lot 2-W-W-Wfr-S7; 5-3-36
Henry Shadle, Wabash Co., Ill. Lot 3-S-N-Wfr, Lot 6-W-SE-Wfr-S7;
William Chenoweth Fullerton* SWfr-Wfr-S7; 6-20-36.   8-23-36
Jeremiah Pritchett, Hr Nfr-S9; 10-25-37
Joseph Humphreys, Gi Lot 1-Nfr-S10; 10-17-35
Adam Purcell* Lot 2-Nfr-S10; 8-19-36
William Reavis, Jr. W-SE-Sfr-S10; 11-22-53
Silas Humphreys, Gi Wfr-S11; 10-28-35
William French, Gi Lot 4-E-SWfr-Sfr-S11; 7-22-43
Richard M. Parrett, Gi SW-SWfr-Sfr-S11; 8-14-54
James Breading E-NEfr-S12; 10-5-18
Thomas Field, Gi NW-NEfr-S12; 1-17-37
William Martin, Gi SW-NEfr-S12;1-6-38; E-SEfr-S12; 3-27-30

Owen Turner, Gi E-NWfr-S12; 8-4-41
Azza Harrison, Mason Co., Ky. E-SWfr-S12; 10-15-24; of Gi, SW-SEfr-
  S12; 2-16-33; NW-SEfr-S12; 8-24-36
John Gordon, Gi W-SWfr-S12; 10-22-31
George Humphreys NE-S13; 1-12-08; NW-S13; 10-9-13; of Gi, W-NW-
  S15; 11-3-25; E-SW-S15; 10-23-30
William Beading (Breading) SW, SE-S13; 10-8-07
Uriah Humphreys, Gi W-NW-S14; 12-9-31
Abraham Spain, Gi W NW-S14; 1-28-31
Michael Kammack NW-S14; 3-2-10
John Adams SW-S14; 1-21-08
Joseph Adams SE-S14; 0-12-11
James Adams, Gi E-NE-S15; 12-1-34
James Adams, Sr., Gi NW-NE, NE-NW-S15; 12-14-36
James Adams, Jr., Gi SW-NE-S15; 12-1-34; SE-NW-S15; 3-2-36
Hugh McFarland Griggs, Gi NW-SW-S15; 6-5-33
Joseph Milburn SE-S15; 3-23-11
Andrew Culbertson, Gi SE-NE-Efr, SW-NE-Efr-S17; 12-21-35
Thomas Payne, Gi NW-NE-Efr-S17; 2-23-36
Felix Milburn, Gi NWfr-Efr-S17; 8-12-36
Abraham Bruner, Gi E-SW-Efr-S17; 8-8-31
William Madison* Wfr-S17; Lots 1-2-Nfr-S18; 11-1-54
John T. Buckner, Wabash Co., Ill. Lot 4-Nfr-S18; 11-21-57
William Chenoweth Fullerton* Lot 3-Nfr-S18; 5-7-36

T 1 S, R 12 W

George Baryear* NE-NEfr-S1; NW-NE-S11; 4-29-37
William Woodhouse* SE-NEfr-S1; 4-12-38; SW-NEfr-S1; 8-29-36
Abraham Decker* NW-NEfr-S1; 8-23-37
Henry Woodhouse & Thomas Kelly SEfr-S1; 9-29-28
Samuel Baryer* SWfr-S2; 8-20-36
William Hazleton Ramsey* Lot 1-SEfr-S2;8-9-36;Lot 2-SEfr-S2;7-7-35.
Alexis Leroy* Efr, Wfr-S3; FrS4; 3-9-36.   George Humphreys,Sr.
James Townsend* FrS10; 8-11-34.   FrS23;3-9-19;NE-
Joseph Shields* NE-NE-S11; 3-4-48.   S26;11-6-19.
Thomas A. Smith, Jr.* SW-SW-S11; 11-24-49.
Ezra B. Carey, Wabash Co., Ill. SE-S11; 11-18-56.
William Chenoweth Fullerton Lots 1-2-NE, N-SEfr-S12; 4-10-37.
William Caudle Lot 3-NWfr-S12; 5-16-58   Joseph C.
John H. Ano, Wabash Co., Ill. Lot 4-NWfr-S12; 12-9-56.   Hard(Heard?
Richard Stillwell, Wabash Co., Ill. S-Nfr-S13; 8-3-36.   NW-SE-S15;
William Ramsey* E-Sfr½-S13; 4-18-26   9-13-53
John Stillwell, Wabash Co., Ill. W-Sfr½-S13; 5-2-33.
Abraham Russell, Wabash Co., Ill. NE-NW-S14; 5-19-37.
Charles Newell Gould, Wabash Co., Ill. SE-NW-S14; 4-21-37
Archibald Roberts, Wabash Co., Ill. SW-NW-S14; 4-7-37
William Greathouse, Vb SW, SE-S14; Lot 6-E-Nfr-S22; 6-16-36;Nfr-
William R. Sprague* NE-NEfr-S15; 4-14-36.   S23; 6-16-36
Caroline Putnam* W-NEfr-S15; 4-14-36
James Townsend, Wabash Co., Ill. NWfr-S15; 12-30-28; N-SWfr-S15;
  6-8-29; W-Nfr-S22; 6-6-29; of*,S-SWfr-S15; 3-10-34
John Lewis Mayes* E-SE, SW-SE-S15; 10-24-54
Walter Terrell, Wabash Co., Ill. Lot 7-E-Nfr-S22; 8-11-36

T 3 N, R 1 W

William Martin* E-NE-S1;12-4-33;E-NW-S1;8-15-27;NE-SE-S1;8-5-34
Allen Toliver* W-NE-S1; 6-25-29; NW-SE-S1; 3-1-35
John Maxwell W-NW-S1; 11-25-19
William Terrel SW-S1; SW-S4; 10-10-16
William Burton* SE-SE-S1; 2-22-39
Timothy Murry* SW-SE-S1; 12-1-33
William Toliver E-NE-S2; 12-31-18
Philip Warron* W-NE-S2; 5-7-25
Robert McLean NW, SW-S2; 5-6-17
William McLean SE-S2; 10-1-16
Zechariah Sparling NE-S3; 2-17-18
Samuel Spurling* E-NW-S3; 12-30-36
Enoch Davis* W-NW-S3; 11-5-27
William Kither* E-SW-S3; 8-21-21
Richard Burton* SW-SW-S3; 1-13-37; SE-SE-S4; 1-7-34
John Workman SE-S3; 8-7-17
William Baldwin E-NE-S4;6-21-17;E-NW-S5;4-20-19;W-NW-S5;2-2-19
Washington Cox* NW-NE-S4; 6-14-39; NE-SE-S4; 10-19-35
Robert Burton* SW-NE-S4; 5-20-36; SE-NW-S4; 12-22-35
Theophilus Baldwin W-NW-S4; 2-2-19
Jesse Hill W-SE-S4; 12-4-17
Martin Hardin E-NE-S5; 9-13-16
Louis Sturgen* W-NE-S5; 9-11-33
Charles Toliver SW-S5; 6-21-17
William Connelly SE-S5; 1-2-17
William Maxwell NE-S6; 2-2-19
Simon Gilbert NW-S6; 9-28-16
Jesse Toliver* NE-SW-S6; 11-1-35
Peter Eller* SE-SW-S6; 1-13-35
Joshua Childress* NW-SW-S6; 11-14-35; SW-SW-S6; 12-2-35
Jarrett L. Erwin* E-SE-S6; 5-19-29
David May* NW-SE-S6; 12-9-35
Jacob Toliver* SW-SE-S6; 12-9-35; NW-NE-S7; 11-14-35
Richard Hall* NE-NE-S7; 10-29-35; NE-NE-S8; 2-11-35
George Isom* SE-NE-S7; SE-NE-S8; 11-14-35
John Toliver* SW-NE-S7; 11-5-35
David Cox* NE-NW-S7; 10-29-33
Wells Landreth* SE-NW-S7; 7-9-39
James Tincher* NW-NW-S7; 12-2-35
Thomas Landreth* SW-NW-S7; 6-13-36
Davidson Carter* NE-SW-S7; 12-5-36
Robert Skaggs* W-SW-S7; 8-7-23
David Toliver* NE-SE-S7; 6-17-36; SE-SE-S7; 11-14-36
George Isom & Stephen Isom* W-NE-S8; 5-14-30
Young Edwards, Ash Co., N.C. E-NW-S8; 7-22-22
John Isom, Grayson Co., Va. W-NW-S8; 9-9-22
Anthony Isom* NE-SW-S8;11-3-34;SE-SE-S8;6-17-39;SW-SE-S8;12-17-36
Eli Way* SE-SW-S8; 11-14-35
Jeremiah Workman* W-SW-S8; 11-28-31
Dennis Isom* NE-SE, NW-SE-S8; 12-9-35
Matthew Fielder* E-NE-S9; 12-6-31; W-NE-S9; 1-24-28
Young Burton* NE-NW-S9; 11-1-32

Troy Cox* SE-NW-S9; 11-10-35
Washington Cox* NW-NW-S9; 10-19-35
William Edwards* SW-NW-S9; 4-12-36
Elijah Corder* SE-SW-S9; 6-19-43
George Isom* NW-SW-S9; 7-2-36
Jesse Tolliver* SW-SW-S9; 11-12-38
John Cox* NW-SE-S9; 5-14-39
William Denney E-NE-S10; 3-12-18; of*, SW-SW-S13; 10-21-33
Alfred Burton* NW-NE-S10; 1-18-37
David Burton* NE-NW-S10; 8-29-36
William J. Burton* NW-NW-S10; 10-9-35; SW-NW-S10; 2-5-45
Allen Landreth* NE-SW-S10; 1-13-37
Zachariah Burton* E-SE-S10; W-SW-S11; 4-23-28;E end-Sfr-S15;10-26-
William Burton* W-SE-S10; 4-23-28. /35;of Or;SE-SW-S13;1-29-40
Alfred Meaden & John Hayes NE-S11; 7-31-18
William McNeal NW-S11; 10-1-16
Robert McLean, Or E-SW-S11; 5-22-27
David Mounts* NE-SE-S11; 2-11-39
Henry Miller* SE-SE-S11; 1-18-36
John McLean* W-SE-S11; 11-11-23; E-SE-S13; 4-17-17
John Ford* NE-NE-S12; 1-31-37
Lewis Ford* SE-NE-S12; 10-4-32
Robert Hall, Jr.* W-NE-S12; 12-6-34; NW-NE-S13; 6-15-33
Alfred Meaden NW-S12; 2-19-19
Bluford G. Davis* E-SW-S12; 4-17-26
Jesse Hill* W-SW-S12; 12-1-28
John Toliver E-SE-S12; 8-20-21; of *, NE-NE-S18; 2-3-37
Isom Hall W-SE-S12; 9-25-26
John Lowry E-NE-S13; 5-6-17
William Toliver* SW-NE-S13; 6-13-33; NE-SW-S13; 1-18-36
Winston Krows* E-NW-S13; 6-2-29
William M. Blair W-NW-S13; 5-6-17
John Jay Barnett* W-SE-S13; 10-21-31
James Fulton NE-Nfr,NW-Nfr,SW-Nfr,W-SE-S14; 12-27-16
Hugh Fulton* E-SE-Nfr-S14; 1-9-36
William Duncan, Or Sfr-S14; 2-11-36
Richard Barton* E-NE-Nfr-S15; 2-8-26
Redden Riggs* W-NE-Nfr-S15; 4-23-28
John Barton* E-W-Nfr-S15; 12-10-23
John M. Burton* W-W-Nfr-S15; 1-16-32
William Holmes* SE-Nfr-S15; 2-8-26
Reuben Benedict, Or NE-NE-S17; 4-4-39
Marvin Cleveland* SE-NE-S17;12-25-44;NW-SE-S17;12-1-36; see below
Marion (Marvin?) Cleveland, Or W-NE-S17; 12-12-31; see above
Anthony Way, Or E-NW-S17; 5-28-31
Anderson Way, Or NW-NW-S17; 10-28-36
Eli Way* SW-NW-S17; 2-23-36; NE-SW-S17; 12-1-36
George Bolivar Hall* SE-SW, SW-SW-S17; 2-5-45
William Landreth* E-NW-S18; 2-18-37
James Ard* NW-NW-S18; 1-1-33
John Nellams Bond* SW-NW-S18; 7-27-39
Aaron Riggs, Or W-SW-S18; 2-5-45
John Bond* SE-SE-S18; 2-13-37; SW-SE-S18; 6-6-36

RELINQUISHMENTS

John Maxwell E-NW-S1; 11-25-19
William Toliver W-NE-S2; 12-31-18
William Baldwin W-NE-S4; 6-21-17
William Torrel E-SE-S4; 12-4-17
William Denny W-NE-S10; 3-12-18
William M. Blair E-NW-S13; 5-0-17
Lewis Byram Sfr-S14; E end-Sfr-S15; 4-23-17
Theophilus Baldwin E-NW-S4; 2-2-19
James Fulton E-SE-Nfr-S14; 12-27-16
John McLean W-SE-S13; 4-17-17
John Bell SW-S9; 12-4-16
May Lowrey & John Lowrey W-NE-S13; 5-6-17

T 3 N, R 2 W

Thomas Landreth* SW-NE-S1;11-11-35;NE-SW-S1;1-28-37;NE-NE-S13;
William Edwards* NW-NW-S1; 9-9-52   12-16-35
Jackson Burton* SW-NW-S1; 2-7-53; SE-NE-S2; 4-24-52; MLW 27909;
   SW-SE-S2; 4-24-52; MLW 27910; SE-NW-S3; NE-SE, NW-SE-S10; 1-27-
   53; SE-SW, W-SW, E-SE, SW-SE-S11; 10-3-54
James Blevins* NE-SE-S1; 11-1-38; SE-SE-S1; 1-9-51
Andrew J. Toliver* NW-SE-S1; 1-3-52; SW-SE-S1; 11-7-51
Dennis Isom* NE-NE-S2; 2-7-53
Alexander A. Hunster NE-NW, NW-NW-S2; 2-19-53; SE-NE, NW-NE, SW-NE,
   NE-NW-S3; 2-1-53; MLW 22740, 43061; W-NW-S3;2-1-53. Hunter
John Burton SE-NW, SW-NW-S2; 1-19-53
John Edwards, Or E-SW-S2; 12-31-22
James Blair* NW-SE-S2; 12-27-32
Earl Douglass, Mt SE-NE-S3; 5-22-37; NE-SW-S3; 1-13-40
Joseph Denny, Mt W-NE-S3; 8-25-25
Samuel Batchelor, Mt E-NW-S3; 8-17-27
A. G. Hogeman, Washington, D.C. W-NW-S3; 9-26-76
Charles Morrison, Mt SE-SW-S3; 1-13-40
Samuel Hopper, Mt NE-SE-S3; 11-10-37
Michael Marley* NE-NE-S3; 7-19-36
John Ray* E-SW-S3; 10-1-23; W-SW-S3; E-NE-S5; 6-24-22
George Hord* NW-SE-S3; 2-21-37; NE-NW-S6; 2-4-53
Jehu Johnston (Johnson)* NE-NE-S4; 4-3-47; NE-NW-S5; 5-31-52;
   MLW 34919; NW-NW-S5; 8-22-53; MLW 14212; NE-NE-S6; 4-22-51. 53
Miles H. Carter SE-NE, SW-NE-S4; 6-11-52; MLW 33442; NW-NE-S4;12-10
George Jones* NE-NW-S4;12-5-53;NW-NE-S5;2-3-53;NW-SE-S5;6-4-52;MLW
George Packer, Mt SE-NW-S4;11-28-53;SW-NW-S5;8-22-53.   55112
Thomas Jones* NW-NW-S4;12-12-36;SW-NE-S5;3-12-39;E-SE-S5;10-1-23
William Hayes SW-NW-S4;1-27-53;NW-SW-S4;9-27-53. MLW 43768
William Connerly* SE-SW-S4; 2-23-37; NE-SE-S9; 5-30-52
Daniel Le Butler NE-SW-S4; 1-17-53
Davidson Coleman SW-SW-S4; 6-5-52. MLW 19309
John Saunders, Or SE-S4; 7-1-20
Nelson A. Gurney SE-NW-S5; 2-4-53
George W. Cochran E-SW,SW-SE-S5;SE-NW,W-NW-S10;10-20-52. MLW 28748
Alexander Coleman W-SW-S5; 6-5-52. MLW 27162
Isaiah Stewart Myers* SE-NW-S6; 12-25-38

Thomas Banks* W-NW-S6; 6-4-28
Nicholas Koons SW-S6; 3-19-18; SE-S6; 3-7-18
Cyrus M. Allen NE-S7;4-9-57; NW-NE,NE-NW,NW-NW-S8; 1-19-53
John Terrell* NE-NW, SW-NW-S7; 10-5-48; NE-SW, NW-SW-S7; 3-8-36;
   SE-SW-S7; 1-27-53; E-SE, NW-SE-S7;2-3-53;SW-SW-S8;2-15-53. MLW
Henry Terrill, Mt SE-NW-S7;7-5-36;SW-SE-S7;3-8-36.   21215
George P. Baldwin NW-NW-S7; 1-6-52; E-NW-S9; NE, NE-NW-S10;W-NW-
William R. McCord NE-NE,SE-NE,SW-NE,SE-NW,SW-NW-S8;2-19-53,/ S11;
John Purser, Hamilton Co., O. NE-SW, NW-SW-S8; 1-4-55. /1-6-53.
Daniel Pettay SE-SW-S8; 6-22-54. MLW 4312
John Quinn W-NE-S9; 9-22-18
William Hoard* W-SE-S9; 7-27-20
Casper Heimen (Hinnen) SE-SE-S9; W-SW-S10; 1-4-55 ; Hamilton Co.,O.
William McNab E-SW-S10; 5-16-53; NW-NE-S15; 7-22-53. MLW 84967
Jacob Crosnore* SE-SE-S10; 12-7-36
Robert Wadsworth* SW-NE-S11; 9-30-33
William May NE-SW-S11; 4-17-52. MLW 21261
William Scott Mayrs, Kn SE-SW-S11; 10-9-57
John Landreth* NE-SE-S11; 1-23-37; NW-SW-S12; 2-1-37
Nathaniel Landreth* SE-SE-S11; 10-11-38
John Vest Coulter* NW-SE-S11; 4-22-52; MLW 49448; SW-SE-S11; SE-
   SW-S12; 1-31-52; SW-SW-S12; 1-28-52; NE-SE-S14;9-6-47;NW-SE-S15;
James Tincher* NE-NE-S12; 5-20-39   2-7-53
Coalby Lanham, Or SE-NE-S12; 6-24-36
Thomas Tate, Or W-NW-S12;10-14-22;E-SE-S12;9-27-22;SW-SE-S12;12-
Franklin Toliver* NE-NW-S12; 10-16-36   15-38
Sterling Williams* NE-SW-S12; 9-19-39
Nelson Tate* NW-SE-S12; 7-1-36
Rhoda Ard* SE-NE-S13; 1-11-37
Marine Davis* SE-NW-S13; 12-24-38
Lemuel S. Coulter* SW-NW-S13; 5-6-37; SE-NE-S14; 1-24-37
Jonathan Repp W-SW-S13; 9-1-16
Joel Hughs* NW-SE-S13; 2-6-45
Richard Beasley* W-NE, E-NW-S14; 10-18-25
Nathaniel Anderson Coulter* NE-SW, W-SE-S14; 9-6-47
Robert Skaggs* SE-SE-S14; 4-18-36
Charles B. Coulter* SW-NE-S15; 10-10-54
David Bruner SW-S15; 3-7-18
Daniel Pettay, Noble Co., O. NE-NE-S17; 6-22-52; NE-NW-S17;
   6-22-54. MLW 32110
William G. Hyndman, Hamilton Co., O. SE-NE,SW-NE,SE-NW,SW-NW-S17;
Francis Asbury Pettay, Noble Co.,O. NW-NE-S17;6-22-54. /12-20-54
John Dickinson* NW-NW-S17; 1-7-52
David Barnett, Ws SW-S17; 11-3-54
Henson Tolbert NE-SE,NW-SE-S17;10-1-52; of Or, SE-SE-S17;2-25-54
Seldon Chapman Fish, Or SW-SE-S17; 3-22-39
John Terrell* NE-NE, NE-NW, NW-NW-S18; 8-2-55
Henry Dickinson SE-NE-S18; 12-18-52; SW-NE-S18; 11-21-53
Hezekiah Jones* NW-NE-S18; 3-18-35
Josiah Sutton SE-NW, SW-NW-S18; 2-3-53
David Jones, Or E-SW-S18; 2-22-37; SW-SE-S18; 10-16-32
George Pinkney* NE-SE-S18; 6-6-36
Merrit Trowbridge, Or SE-SE-S18; 11-26-52
Jacob N. Elliott, Mt NW-SE-S18; 8-5-53

RELINQUISHMENTS

John Quinn E-NE-S9; 9-22-18; W-NE-S9; 9-22-18; 7-4-29
Michael Bruner W-NE, E-NE-S18; 11-29-19
Levi S. Stewart SE-S18; 4-17-19

T 4 N, R 1 W

Henry Speed Nfr-S1 & 12 (2?); Nfr-S6 & 7; Sfr-S6; Wfr-S7; 9-25-16
Elias Copelin* Lot 1-NE-Nfr-S2; 7-2-35
Isaac Holman Scoggan* Lot 2-NE-Nfr-S2; 2-15-36
Ezekiel Blackwell W-Nfr, SEfr-Nfr-S2; 9-25-16
William Trueblood Sfr-S2; 9-25-16
Jonathan Lindley Nfr-S3; 9-25-16
Joshua Taylor W-E-Sfr;E-NW-Sfr;E-SW-Sfr-S3; 8-29-17
Auron Davis* Lots 1-2-W-NW-Sfr-S3; E-NE-S4; 10-17-34
Jacob Fisher Myers* W-SW-Sfr-S3; 4-10-33
Jeffery Russell* NE-NW-S4; 1-24-37
Jonathan Derry* SE-NW-S4; 6-29-48
Robert Woods* W-NW-S4; 1-3-37; N-N-Wfr-S5;12-13-27;S-N-Wfr-S5;
Gray Bird* SE-SW-S4; 5-11-44   6-22-35
Frederick Rice (Ross) Nugent* SW-SW-S4;5-10-38;E-NE-Sfr-S8;3-24-38
David Nugent* NE-SE-S4; 5-4-33
Gabriel Nugent* SE-SE-S4; 10-31-36
William Connelly* W-SE-S4; 11-18-37; Lots 1-2-NWfr-Sfr-S8; 2-18-
   36; W-SE-Sfr-S8; 1-28-36; NW-NE-S9; 11-27-38; SE-SW-S9; 1-13-37;
   NE, NW-S10; 1-3-18; NE-NE-S17; 1-28-36; SE-S17; 12-4-17; W-NW-
Robert Fields Efr-S5; 8-30-17   S21; 1-1-22
Oliver Cox* S-Wfr-S5; 1-8-36
Ezer Cleveland, Or W-NE-Sfr-S8; 2-1-39
John Jackson Collins* E-SW-Sfr-S8; 1-18-36
Josiah Franklin Collins* W-SW-Sfr-S8; 1-18-36
John Bass* E-SE-Sfr-S8; 1-31-32
Peter Leech* NE-NE-S9; NE-SW-S14; 2-20-36; NW-SW-S14; 12-18-37;
   W-SE-S14; 3-20-39
George Cockinghour* SE-NE-S9;10-15-32;NE-NW-S9;8-5-34;NE-SW-S15;
William Melvin* SW-NE-S9; 3-9-37   2-1-39
Comadore Collins* SE-NW-S9; 10-13-36
Frederick Rice Nugent* NW-NW-S9; 1-28-39
Thomas Henry Biggs* SW-NW-S9; 1-28-39
John Rector* NE-SW-S9; 1-30-39
Alexander Neal* NW-SW-S9; 3-22-37
Thomas Melvin* SW-SW-S9; 12-3-33
Charles W. Smith* NE-SE-S9; 1-14-37 (31?)
Moses Bass* SE-SE-S9; 2-18-36
Josiah Connely* W-SE-S9; 11-7-20; NE-S19; 6-4-17; E-SE-S19;
   8-13-22; E-NE-S21; 11-7-26
George Hinton, Jr. E-SW-S10; 9-4-19
Alexander Coleman* W-SW-S10; 1-25-31; SW-SE-S19; 3-20-39
William Irwin SE-S10; 1-21-18
Willis Richardson Roads* Lot 1-NE-NE-S11; 11-5-38
David Mitchell* Lot 2-SE-NE-S11; 1-7-39
Isaac Collins E-SW-S11; 2-2-31
Mahlon Collins* W-SW-S11; 3-17-32

Levi Orton* NE-SE, NW-SE-S11; 8-5-34
Joseph Pless* SE-SE-S11; 5-15-39
John Pless* SW-SE-S11; NW-NE-S14; 8-22-33; NE-NE-S14; 1-11-37
Arthur Henrie & Benjamin Drake W-NE, NWfr-S11; 7-30-18
Ezekiel Blackwell NEfr-Sfr, E-SE-Sfr-S12;3-9-18; SW-S18; 9-25-16
Samuel Blackwell Lot 1-Wfr-Sfr-S12; n.d. (unless 11-27-37 below)
Abraham Jones* Lot ? (see Lot 1 above) -Wfr-S12; 11-27-37 (date
   is bracketed with Samuel Blackwell above)
Jordon Orton* E-SW-Sfr, NW-Sfr-S12; 8-5-34
John Lowery, Wm SW-SW-Sfr-S12; 9-16-36
John Garrison* W-SE-Sfr-S12; 8-5-34
Oliver Cox* Nfr-S8; 1-8-38
John Finger NE-S13; 1-10-17; of*, NE-SE-S13; 1-13-37
Joseph Culberson NW-S13; 10-14-18
Revel Horsey* SE-SE-S13; SW-NE-S14; 1-11-37
Charles Blasley* NW-SE-S13; 2-13-50
Comfort Hansley* SW-SE-S13; 1-21-39
Reuben Dodson* SE-NE, NE-SE-S14; 4-13-35
William White* E-NW-S14; 9-12-32
Peter Stattes & Albert Stattes* W-NW-S14; 1-31-32
Daniel Hansley* SE-SW-S14; 8-11-36
Jesse Hodges* E-NE-S15; 2-1-31
William Erwin W-NE-S15; 1-21-18
Thomas Melvin* E-NW-S15; 9-11-29
Nancy Thomason* W-NW-S15; 3-20-39
Elizabeth Johnston* SE-SW-S15; 5-26-38
Samuel Hardin Shumall* W-SW-S15; 1-29-39
Ishom Meadors SE-S15; 11-28-16
Samuel Spurlen* SE-NE-S17; 12-2-33
Joel Connelly NW-S17; 11-17-17; NW-S30; 11-17-17
Josiah Trueblood SW-S17; 4-11-18
William Carmichael W-NE-S17; 3-23-18
William Lindley NE, SE-S18; 10-3-16
C. Bullitt & T. Bullitt NW-S18; 9-25-16
Jonathan Lindley NW-S19; 9-25-16
Jacob Taylor* NE-SW-S19; 2-17-36; NE-NE-S22; 2-17-36
Benjamin Connolly* SE-SW-S19; 11-9-38
Elijah Connelly* W-SW-S19; 6-18-24
Rachel Johnson* NW-SE-S19; 12-28-33; NW-NW-S20; 2-24-36
Alexander Thompson Connelly* E-NE-S20; 1-28-36
Aaron Davis W-NE-S20; 11-1-19; of*, E-SE-S20; 7-9-24
John Pace* E-NW, SW-NW-S20; 1-1-34
Joseph Connely* E-SW-S20;6-22-25;NW-SW-S20;1-1-34;W-SE-S20;12-24-30
John Weaver* SW-SW-S20; 4-1-36
Moses Bass* NW-NE-S21; 2-18-36; NE-SW-S23; 1-14-37
Daniel Davis* E-SW-S21; 12-18-23; NW-SW-S21; 12-3-35
Andrew Davis* E-SE-S21; 4-10-37
Winthrop Foot* W-SE-S21; 10-10-36
Peter Phillips* SE-NE-S22; 2-11-36; NW-SE-S22; 9-12-32
John Ross Nugent* NW-NE-S22; 3-12-34; SW-NW-S23; 1-14-37
Stephen White* SW-NE, SE-NW-S22; 10-10-32
John Garges* NE-NW-S22; 3-5-36
Lewis Phillips W-NW-S22; 9-15-17; E-NW-S24; 1-12-39
Hannah Phillips* NW-SW-S22; 11-9-32

William Toliver E-SW-S22; 2-4-18
Jonathan Alexander* E-SE-S22; 6-18-31;SW-NE-S27;9-28-36;SE-NW-S27;
John Phillips* SW-SE-S22; 10-28-33   12-10-36
Harling Pope* W-NE-S23; 4-27-44
Isaac Morris* NW-NW-S23; 3-5-36; NE-NE-S24; 3-30-37
Lambeth Dodson* SE-SW-S23; 12-4-33
John Bass* NW-SW-S23; 9-28-36
Charles Joy Simpson* SW-SW-S23; 8-22-32
Zebedee Wood SE-S23;1-26-20;NE-NW, NW-NW-S25;E-NE-S26; 6-28-36
Asa Irwin* SE-NE-S24; 11-2-38; SW-S24; 11-13-48; MLW 6045;
    E-SE-S24; 2-2-39
Jonathan Bass* W-NE-S24; 8-9-37
James Beazely* W-NW-S24; 9-20-49
Arthur Neal* NW-SE-S24; 6-14-49
Benjamin Sutton* SW-SE-S24; 2-22-36
Joseph Tirey* SE-NE-S25; 1-5-37
Thomas Tirey* SW-NE-S25; 10-3-36
Willis Harrell* SE-NW-S25; 8-25-34
Arta Garrison* SW-NW-S25; 11-13-32
William Wedster* NE-SW-S25; 1-20-36
Eli Walker* SE-SW-S25; 4-11-37
Benjamin Alexander* NW-SW-S25; 9-1-36
William Asbury McKnight, Or E-SE-S25;8-9-24;SW-SE-S25; 9-28-33
Peter Leatherman* NW-SE-S25; 9-19-33
Daniel Phillips* NW-NE-S26; 1-4-36
John Wood* SW-NE-S26; 8-19-36
Michael Donahoo NW-S26; 11-29-17
David Faris E-SW-S26; 12-15-17
Samuel Griffin Hoskins* W-SW-S26; 10-2-29; NW-SE-S26; 1-11-37;
    NE-NW-S27; 3-9-37; NE-SE-S27; 7-20-33
Anselm Wood* NE-SE-S26; 5-9-37
Peter Phillips* E-NE-S27; 5-8-29
Philip Hillebrand, Ws NW-NE-S27; 10-12-35
Commodore Perry Hillebrand* NW-NW-S27; 3-24-37
Thomas McKnelly* SE-SW-S27; 1-14-36
Enoch Davis* W-SW-S27;11-3-35;E-SE-S28;9-7-33;SW-SE-S28;9-27-33
Timothy Roark* SE-SE-S27; 1-2-32
John McNalla* NW-SE-S27; 10-22-32
John Pluess* SW-SE-S27; 3-9-37
Jacob Whoover* NE-NE-S28; 10-7-35; NW-SE-S28; 1-25-36
Isaac Whoover* SE-NE-S28;4-20-39;SW-NE-S28;8-4-36;SE-NW-S28;
Bledsoe Harden* NW-NE-S28; 7-24-37   1-26-36
James Cambern* NE-NW-S28; 7-27-36
William Tirey* SW-NW-S28; 1-12-39; see William Frey below
John Tirey* NE-SW-S28;10-6-35;SE-SW-S28;12-26-35;W-SW-S28;10-16-33
Joseph Connelly* NE-NE, NW-NE-S29; 1-12-39
William Frey (Tirey?) SE-NE-S29; 1-12-39; see William Tirey above
Wiley Weaver* SW-NE-S29; 11-2-35
John Weaver* E-SW-S29; 12-10-23; SW-SW-S29; 4-1-36
John Miller* NW-SW-S29; 2-27-39
Theophilus Baldwin* E-SE-S29; 6-11-27; W-SE-S29; 11-17-23
Thomas Davis* NE-NE-S30; 8-17-36
Jesse Beasley W-SW-S30; 9-3-18
John Burton* SE-SE-S30; 9-4-47

John Miller* NE-SE-S30; 10-10-50; E-NE-S31; 1-12-39; SE-NW-S32;
   2-27-37; W-NW-S32; 6-20-35; NE-SW-S32; 1-9-37
Anderson Burton* W-SE-S30;9-15-51;NW-SE-S31;2-22-39;SW-SE-S31;
Allen Burton* NW-NE-S31; 5-14-39   5-31-36
Anderson Beasley* NE-NW, W-NW-S31; 3-1-52
George Tincher* SE-NW-S31; 6-3-36
Eli Burton* SE-SW-S31; 3-5-36
Francis Fincher (Tincher?) W-SW-S31; 12-17-19
Aquilla Gilbert E-SE-S31; 12-21-16
John Maxwell* E-NE-S32; 6-29-27; W-NW-S33; 10-19-26
John Weaver* NW-NE-S32; 12-26-33
Wesley Weaver* NE-NW-S32; 12-31-36
William Maxwell W-SW-S32; 2-2-19
Troy Cox* NE-SE-S32; 10-22-36; NW-SW-S33; 6-8-36
Young Burton* SE-SE-S32; 6-3-37; NW-SE-S32; 8-24-35
John Mathews Higginsbotham* SW-SE-S32; 1-9-37
Enoch Davis* NE-NE-S33; 9-7-33
William Billings* SE-NE-S33; 12-28-36
Theodore Pridmore* W-NE-S33; 12-12-31
Edward Edwards* E-NW-S33;10-26-27;SE-SE-S33;11-12-32;W-SE-S33;
Constantine Conelly* E-SW-S33; 11-23-26   5-31-36
Henderson Edwards* NE-SE-S33; 8-17-36
William Webster* NE-NE-S34; 1-4-36
John Edwards* SE-NE-S34; 5-14-39; NE-NW, NW-SW-S34; 1-14-36
Bledsoe Hardin* NW-NE-S34; 10-3-32
Catherine Bedwell* SW-NE-S34; 9-5-36
William Edwards* SE-NW-S34; 11-12-32; SW-NW-S34; 11-11-33
Enoch Davis* NW-NW-S34; 8-13-36; NW-SE-S34; 12-28-36
David Edwards* SE-SW-S34; 2-6-45
Washington Cox* SW-SW-S34; 5-20-36   9-7-33
William Billings* E-SE-S34;2-2-31;SW-SE-S34;11-3-35;SW-SW-S35;
Zebedee Wood* NE-NE-S35; 3-16-33; SE-NE-S35; 3-30-36
Eli Williams* W-NE-S35; 2-26-22
John Sutton E-NW-S35; 2-19-17
Harvey McFall* W-NW-S35; 7-15-36
Abraham Miller E-SW-S35; 5-30-31
Silas Sutton* NW-SW-S35; 1-25-36
Philip Warren E-SE-S35; 11-11-33
David Faries* W-SE-S35; 5-14-23
Jeremiah Lewis (Laws?)* N-NE-S36; 11-5-36
Andrew Fander* SE-NE-S36; 8-5-34
Jeffrey Clark* SW-NE, NE-NW-S36; 1-17-39
John Sheeks* E-SW, W-SE-S36; 8-15-36; E-SE-S36; 3-10-34
Jonas Finger* NW-SW-S36; 3-30-36
John Wood* SW-SW-S36; 8-19-36

RELINQUISHMENTS

Joshua Taylor W-NW-Sfr, W-SW-Sfr-S3; 8-29-17
Adam Siler Nfr-S8; 3-11-19
Arthur Henrie & Ben. Drake Efr-S8; E-NEfr, SW, SE-S11; 7-30-18
George Hinton, Jr. W-SW-S10; 9-4-19
Ezekiel Blackwell NWfr-Sfr, E-SW-Sfr, W-SW-Sfr, W-SE-Sfr-S12;3-9-
   18; NW-S14; 1-21-18; NEfr-NFr-S2; 9-25-16

William Erwin E-NE-S15; 1-21-18
William Carmichael E-NE-S17; 3-23-18
David Raymond SW-S19; 9-25-16
Joseph Pless NE-S21; 3-23-18
Lewis Philips E-NW-S22; 9-15-17
David Faris W-SW-S26; 12-15-17
William Maxwell E-SW-S32; 2-2-19
Francis Tincher E-SW-S31; 12-17-19
Aquilla Gilbert W SE-S31; 12-21-16
William Toliver W-SW-S22; 2-4-18
John Sutton W-NW-S35; 2-19-17
George Hinton, Jr. E-SW-S10; 9-4-19; 7-4-29
Joseph Culberson NW-S13; 10-14-18; 7-4-29
William Baldwin E-SE-S23; 11-30-18; 7-4-29

T 4 N, R 2 W

Henry Speed Nfr, Efr-S1; 9-25-16
John Towell Wfrs-S1 & 12; 10-29-16
Abraham Kern* NW-S2; 1-5-32
Andrew Jackson Williams & James Dickson Williams* E-SW-S2;9-2-44
William Williamson Adamson* NW-SW-S2; 11-2-35
Simon Smith* SW-SW-S2; 8-5-34
Benjamin Beeson NE, SE-S2; 9-29-17
Silas Dixon NE-S3; 10-8-16
Simon Ruebottom NW-S3; NW-Nfr, SW-Nfr, SE-Nfr-S4; Nfr-S9; S-Nfr,
    E-E-Nfr, W-E-Nfr, E-W-Nfr, W-W-Nfr-S10; 10-8-16
Jonathan Lindley SW, SE-S3; 9-21-16
Isaiah Lamb* NE-NE-Nfr-S4; 8-29-33
Prior Lewis Williams SE-NE-Nfr-S4; 2-25-39; NW-NE-Nfr-S4; 2-21-
    39; SW-NE-Nfr-S4; 8-5-34
James Mulloy NE-S5; 6-12-18
Garret G. Williams* N-NW-S5; 9-9-54; S-NW-S5; 10-27-47
Eleand Williams* S-SW-S5; 5-6-37
Bartemius Williams NW-SW-S5; 6-29-52; W-SW-S6; 9-9-54; of*, Lot 2-
    NWfr-Nfr-S7; 3-9-57
Ephraim Lee SE-S5; 9-21-16
John Gregory Hall* NE-NE-S6; 4-12-37
George Kinder* NE-NW-S6; 7-30-51
Henry Woody, Mt SE-NW-S6; 2-7-37; SW-NW-S6; 2-1-37
Asa Veatch, Or NW-NW-S6; 2-3-37
Richard Williams* NE-SW-S6; 8-16-32; SE-SW-S6; 9-2-44
Isaac Williams* Efr-Nfr-S7; 8-8-22; Nfr-S8; 9-21-16; Ept-N-Sfr,
    Wpt-N-Sfr-S9; 7-18-31; Lot 2-Nfr, Lot 5-Nfr-S11; 5-4-36
Peter Fuherer, Gn SW-Nfr-S7; 4-21-56
Joseph Hastings Sfr-S7; 9-28-16
Killis Box* Lot 1-E-E-Sfr-S8; 4-14-36
Arthur Hastings* W-E-Sfr-S8;8-5-31;E-W-Sfr, W-W-Sfr-S8;7-18-31
Absalom Fields* E-SE-Sfr-S9; 8-5-31; NW-SE-Sfr-S9; 4-25-36;
    SW-SE-Sfr-S9; 4-14-36; Sfr-S10; 10-9-16
Samuel Etchason* NE-SW-Sfr-S9; 5-2-36
Walker White* SW-SW-Sfr-S9; 8-16-44
Miles West* Lot 3-Nfr-S11; 2-18-36; Lot 4-Nfr-S11; 4-1-36
Thomas Lindley Efr-S12; 9-21-16

Joseph Richardson NE, SE-S13; 9-17-16
Ezekiel Blackwell E-NW-S13; 9-21-16; E-SW-S13; 3-9-18;E-NW-S24;
James Beasley* W-NW-S13; 12-11-28   9-21-16
John Maxwell* W-SW-S13; 9-10-35
Jonathan Lindley Sfr-S14; 9-21-16; NE-S24; 9-21-16
Abram Holladay Nfr-S14; Efr-S15; 10-8-18
William Cochron Wfr-S15; 1-14-18
Ephraim Beasley' E-NE-S17; 7-8-28
John Chapman+ NW-NE-S17;1-25-36;SW-NE-S17;11-7-32;SE-S17;10-8-17
Thomas Coulter NW-S17; 9-28-16
Robert Fields* SW-S17; 9-17-17; W-NE-S28; 8-27-31
John Luttrell N-N-Efr-S18; 11-4-18
Walker White* S-N-Efr-S18; 7-18-31
Samuel White* S-Efr-S18; 7-2-31
John & Gideon Coulter S-N-Wfr,E-SW-Wfr,SE-Wfr-S18; 8-25-17
Thomas Barnes, Mt W-SW-S18; 11-13-28
Henry Speed Lot 1-Efr-S19; Efr-S24; 4-28-18
Robert Bryant* Lot 2-Efr-S19; 2-13-49; S-NE-S23; 2-19-39
John Bluelbertson (Culbertson?)* Lot 3-Efr-S19; 11-15-50
John Johnson* Lot 4-Efr-S19; 2-17-36
Roger McKnight Wfr-S19; 3-25-18; Nfr-S30; 3-25-18
Jehu Barnes, Pk NE-NE-S20; 10-22-32
Jehu Doan* SE-NE-S20; 12-5-38
William Beavers* NW-NE-S20; 1-12-38; SW-NW-S28; 6-18-36
Benjamin Marley* W-SE-S20; 8-25-31
William Bowden* NE-NE-S21; 3-21-69
John Blevins* SE-NE,W-NE,SE-SE,W-SE-S21;SW-NW,NW-SW-S22;10-6-54
Joshua Barnes* NE-NW-S21; 6-20-36; W-NW-S21; 4-28-30
Mary Chapman SE-NW, NE-SW-S21; 8-2-53
Thomson Burton* SE-SW, W-SW-S21; 10-7-54
James Atcheson NE-SE-S21; 12-14-52; of*, SE-SW-S29; 6-7-51
Josiah Trueblood E-NE-S22; 10-21-16
Henry William Connelly* W-NE-S22; 3-12-36;W-NW-S23; 3-12-36
Milton Beaver* NE-NW-S22; 4-15-48
Stewart Daniel* SE-NW-S22; 6-20-36
John Atchason* NW-NW-S22; 1-10-57
James McGinnis* E-SW-S22; 3-12-36
William Hail* SW-SW-S22; 7-6-53; SE-SW-S23; 4-15-48;NE-NW-S27;
Henry Cosner SE-S22; 9-17-17   7-6-53
George Washington Beasley* NE-NE-S23; 3-18-33
Jesse Beasley* NW-NE-S23;NW-NW-S24;10-11-32;W-NE-S25;1-31-32
Samuel Dever* E-NW-S23; 4-25-36
John Whitton* NE-SW-S23; 6-18-36
William Davis, Mr W-SW-S23; 10-1-31
Tucker Williamson* E-SE-S23; 2-19-39
Nathan Dever* NW-SE-S23; 12-21-47
Anderson Beasley* SW-SE-S23; 2-24-52; SW-SW-S29; 9-23-52
William Connelly* SW-NW-S24; 11-27-38
John Conneley SW-S24; 1-2-17; NW-S25; 1-3-18;SE-NE,SW-NW,NE-SE-S3
Joel Connly SE-S24; 12-23-16   SE-NE-S30; 12-13-52
Josiah Connely E-NE-S25; 6-4-17
Francis M. Edwards* E-SW, NW-SW-S25; 10-6-54
Lewis Blackwell* SW-SW-S25; 8-15-57
Joel Y. Hunter* E-NW-S26; 10-5-54

Myron H. Lincoln, Mt NE-SW, SE-SE, W-SE-S26; 9-27-54; SE-SW-S28;
   SW-NW-S33; 9-25-54; NE, E-SW-S35; 9-27-54
James Taincher, Mt SE-SW-S26; 8-8-53
George Tincher* NW-SW-S26; 4-16-57
Stephen Tincher* SW-SW-S26; 9-13-50
Henry Burton, Or NE-SE-S26; 8-10-53
John M. McNab, Gn SE-NW-S27; 5-30-56
Amrila Forbes, Jefferson Co., Ky. W-NW, SW-S27;E-SE-S28;9-25-54
Lewis West* NE-SE, W-SE-S27; 10-6-54
George W. Barnes* SE-SE-S27; 10-29-51
Samuel White* E-NE-S28; 10-30-54
Thomas Whiteon* NE-NW-S28; 11-9-37
Thomas Burton* NW-NW-S28; 10-7-54
Isaac Beavers* SE-NW-S28; 7-10-39; NW-SW-S28; 11-11-37
Eli Barnes* NE-SW-S28; 3-9-52
Jehu Johnson SW-SW-S28; E-NW, NW-NW-S33; 2-16-53; W-SE-S33; 1-27-
   53; of*, NW-NE-S34; 3-28-54; E-NW, SW-NW-S34; 10-2-54
John Ray, Sr. NE-NE-S29; 12-11-52
Wiley Dawson* W-NE-S29; 10-26-54; NE-NW-S29; 10-21-54
Joseph Ray SE-NW,NW-SE-S29;2-1-53; of*, SE-NW-S32; 10-29-53
John Bright Culbertson (see Bluelbertson on preceding page)*
   NW-NW-S29; NE-NE-S30; 3-13-47
Allen Higgenbotham* N-SW-S29;3-13-55;SW-NE-S30;3-13-47;SE-S30;
George Chapman* SE-SE-S29;11-8-54;SW-SE-S29;4-5-54.   10-7-54
Robert Bryant* NW-NE-S30; 3-13-47
Alexander King Lot 2-NW-Sfr-S30;2-15-53; of Mt, SE-NW-Sfr-S30;
James E. Bryant* Lot 1-NW-Sfr-S30; 12-24-56.   2-27-39
James Johnson* NW-NE-S31; 6-15-40
Willis Jones SW-NE, SE-NW-S31; 10-4-52
John Johnson NE-NW-S31;9-27-52; of*, NW-SW-S34;6-20-36;SW-SW-S34;
John Munday NW-NW-S31; 6-4-52. MLW 35710.   12-25-38
William Munday* SW-NW-S31; 3-14-54; NW-SW-S31; 9-23-?
Thomas Jones* NE-SW-S31;2-24-52;SE-SW-S31;10-4-52;NE-SW-S32;4-14-
George Jones SW-SW-S31;9-27-53;S-SW,SW-SE-S32;2-3-53.   47
Thomas Johnson, Mt NE-SE-S31; 12-25-38
Manley Marley* SW-NW-S32; 6-13-36
Joseph Ray, Jr.* NW-SW-S32; 11-12-53; NE-SE-S32; 11-3-53
William Blair* SE-SE-S32; 2-21-37
Alexander Coleman* NW-SE-S32; 10-29-53
William West* NE-NE-S33; 2-18-57
James Beavers, Or SE-NE-S33; 6-18-36
John Swain W-NE-S33; 12-4-18
Sarah Johnson* NE-SE-S33; 10-9-44
John M. Johnson* SE-SE-S33; 8-1-55
Isom Burton* S-NE-S34; 10-8-38
John Hopper* NW-NW-S34; 3-4-57
Ransom Tinsley* NW-SE-S34;SE-NW-S35;2-26-51; NE-NW-S35; 10-5-54
Mary Sloan* SW-SE-S34; 11-28-56
John Rennels* E-SE-S35; 3-21-25
Milton Tinsley* NW-SE-S35; 9-21-50
George Culbertson SW-SE-S35; 11-4-52
Elizabeth Brewer* E-NE-S36; 10-3-54
Eli Burton* NE-SW, SW-SE-S36; 10-4-54; SE-SE-S36; 12-13-51
Isaac Edwards SE-SW-S36; 5-4-53

Granville Crump* NW-SW-S36; 1-25-38
James Blevins* SW-SW-S36; 1-8-38
William T. Spicely N-SE-S36; 7-23-52

RELINQUISHMENTS

Peter Quackenbush NW-S6; 5-5-17
Simon Ruebottom Lots 2,3,4-Nfr-S11; 10-8-16
John & Gideon Coulter N-N-Wfr, W-SW-Wfr-S18; 8-25-17
Gideon Coulter Lots 2-3-Efr-S19; 4-28-18
Ezekiel Blackwell W-NW-S13;W-NW-S24;9-21-16; W-SW-S13; 3-9-18
Josiah Trueblood W-NE-S22; 10-1-16
Josiah Connely W-NE-S25; 6-4-17
John Banks W-NE-S33; 7-1-19
Thomas Tague E-NW-S23; 8-17-18
David Marley E-NE-S20; 6-19-18
Henry Cosner W-SW-S23; 7-27-18
Silas Luttrell S-N-Efr, S-Efr-S18; 11-4-17
David Evans Sfr-S9; 2-15-19
Henry Speer Sfr-S8; 5-8-18; 7-4-29
Daniel Westfall W-NE-S23; 2-18-19; 7-4-29

T 5 N, R 1 W

James Pace E-NE-S1; 4-4-20
William Fish* W-NE-S1; 9-30-31
Hiram Kilgore NW-S1; 12-9-16; E-NW-S2; 6-29-18
Charles Kilgore SW-S1; 12-9-16
Preston Beck SE-S1; 12-9-16
William Bristoe* NE-S2; 12-9-16
Dixon Brown W-NW-S2; 10-28-17
Andrew Owens E-SW-S2; 1-23-18
James Denson W-SW-S2; 1-16-19; SE-S3; 12-12-18
John Owens* E-SE-S2; 5-29-29
James Riggins NE-S3; 12-26-18
Mark Tully NW-S3; 2-20-18
Thomas Hill* E-SW-S3; 9-16-20
Robert Whitely & William Kelsey W-SW-S3; 3-16-30
Robert Whitely* E-NE-S4; 5-29-29
Alfred Allison* SW-NE-S4; 8-5-34
Stephen Shipman NW-S4; 3-18-08
Absalom Hart SW-S4; 6-15-18
Samuel Blevins* E-SE-S4; 12-23-29
Hezekiah Blevins* W-SE-S4; 4-2-31
William George* NE-NE-S5; 11-21-32
Silas Mallett* SE-NE-S5; 12-19-32; SW-NE, W-NW-S5; 9-16-37;
   NE-NW-S5; 1-5-36
Elizabeth Lamb* NW-NE-S5; 9-5-36
Moses Fell* E-SW-S5; 9-22-35
John H. Tylor* W-SW-S5; 8-28-20
Preston Beck, Hiram Kilgore, Reuben Kilgore, & Moses Woodruff
   E-SE-S5; 6-13-25
Washington Reynolds* NW-SE-S5; 6-13-36
Abraham Reynolds* SW-SE-S5; 3-5-36

David Fidler* N-NE-S6; 11-8-44
James Chestnut* SE-NE-S6; 1-14-37; NW-SE-S6; 1-3-37
James Baels* SW-NE-S6; 4-6-37
Henry Williams* NE-NW-S6; 12-7-44
Gideon Potter* SE-NW-S6; 2-21-39; W-NW-S6; 9-5-36
Peter Gabert* E-SE-S6; 6-23-36
Isaac Boyd* SW-SE-S6; 11-8-37
Sanders Howard NE-S7; 1-5-19
Starling Sims NW-S7; 1-5-19
John Sims* NE-SW-S7; 10-2-33; W-NE-S8; 8-4-35
George Grundy Dunn* SE-SW, NW-SW-S7; 7-26-36
Aaron Hodges* SW-SW-S7; 1-18-36
John Boyd, Jr.* E-SE-S7; 11-22-26
Elbert Howard* W-SE-S7; 11-21-26
Preston Beck, Moses Fell, Reuben Kilgore, Hiram Kilgore, Moses
    Woodruff, & Payton Bristow E-NE-S8; 11-18-24
John Hackler* NE-NW-S8; 2-8-36
Joseph Gillis Laughlin* SE-NW-S8; 1-19-36; NE-SW-S8; 2-19-36
Elias Patterson Kenady* NW-NW-S8; 3-1-36
Lewis Potter* SW-NW-S8; 2-22-36
Nathan Jackson* SE-SW-S8; 8-28-35
Reuben Rany* W-SW-S8; 12-23-26
Jacob Clark, Jr.* SE-S8; 7-1-20
Hiram Kilgore & Moses Woodruff NE-S9; 11-29-23
Moses Woodruff, Preston Beck, Hirem Kilgore, & Reuveb Kilgore
    E-NW-S9; 6-13-25
Samuel Tomlinson & Christian Graeter W-NW-S9; 12-10-24
Isaac Mitchell* E-SW-S9; 10-8-30; SW-SW-S10; 8-5-34
Abraham Mitchell* W-SW-S9;8-5-34;E-SE-S9;9-19-18;SE-S11;3-16-18
Joel Greer* W-SE-S9; 7-30-33
Matthew Borland* E-NE-S10; 6-22-30; E-SE-S10; 6-29-31
Thomas Hill* W-NE-S10; 10-6-20
Absalom Hart NW-S10; 6-15-19
John Owens* NE-SW-S10; 12-16-35; NW-NW-S11; 8-17-35
Sally Laughlin* SE-SW-S10; 2-26-35
John Greger* NW-SW-S10; 3-23-36
Moses McBride* W-SE-S10; 8-13-31; E-NE-S15; 9-25-22
Robert Whitely NE-S11; 2-19-17; E-SW-S12; 9-19-18
Charles Mitchell* E-NW-S11; 6-29-31
Diver Williams* SW-NW-S11; 10-26-35
Henry Fry* E-SW-S11; 9-14-25
William Gooldy* W-SW-S11; 5-15-30
Vinson Williams NE-S12; 6-9-17
Reuben Kilgore & Simpson Kilgore NW-S12; 12-9-16
Reuben Kilgore* W-SW-S12; 8-14-27; SE-S12; 9-19-18
John Spears NE-S13; 10-12-18
Richard Bivens* E-NW-S13; 7-28-28
Reuben Kilgore & William Cook W-NW-S13; 12-8-26
Winthrop Foot* E-SW, W-SE-S13; 12-14-27; W-SW-S13; 11-16-25;
    E-NW-S20; E-NW-S29; 4-4-36; W-SW-S21; 3-23-36; W-SE-S21;
    NE-NW-S35; 2-24-36; SE-SW-S26; 2-15-36
Marquis D. Knight* E-SE-S13; 4-17-29
Preston Beck NE-S14; 4-14-18
Simpson Kilgore NW-S14; 12-19-17

William Carmichael SW-S14; 3-23-18
Isaac Stewart & Samuel F. Irwin E-SE-S14; 2-15-25
Moses Woodruff* W-SE-S14; 7-12-24
Robert Mitchell* W-NE-S15; 5-13-30
Peter Gabbert NW-S15; 10-10-17; of*, E-SW-S15;3-16-30;W-SW-S15;
Moses McBride & Jesse Rector E-SE-S15; 5-14-30. 1-3-31
Joseph Rector* W-SE-S15; 2-16-24
William Carten NE-S17; 7-25-18
Henry Pairsel NW-S17; SE-S18; 6-12-18
John Donaldson SW-S17; 4-19-20
John Hackler* E-SE-S17; 10-13-30
James Tanner Dougherty* NW-SE-S17; 1-28-36
Alexander Southerland* SW-SE-S17; 2-22-36
John Boyd* N-NE-S18; 2-9-36
William Chestnut* SE-NE-S18; 2-22-36
George Washington Parris* SW-NE-S18; 2-6-36
Holland Pitman NW-S18; 8-28-18
Michael Tanner* NE-SW-S18; 1-19-36
Thomas Hill* SE-SW-S18; 4-10-37
Charles Kilgore, Da NW-SW-S18; 11-12-32
Michael Farmer* SW-SW-S18; 1-19-36
Martin Ribelin NE-S19; 12-9-17
David Ribelin NW-S19; 12-9-17
Abraham Kern* SW-S19; 3-23-36
Joseph James SE-S19; 2-5-19
William Daugherty E-NE-S20; 12-8-18; NW-S21; 10-6-17; NW-S23;
    11-18-17; of*, W-NE-S21; 11-28-33
Isom Hodges* W-NE-S20; 12-6-31
David Wilson V-NW-S20; 4-14-18
Joseph Rector* E-SW-S20;11-18-26;SE-SE-S20;4-8-36;SW-SE-S20;
Timothy Ward W-SW-S20; 5-1-18 11-30-32
John D. Laughlin* E-NE-S21; 3-5-25
Andrew Campbell* NE-SW-S21; 4-4-36; SE-SW-S21; 8-18-32
Aaron Beesley* NE-SE-S21; 2-24-36; E-NW-S22; 11-5-30
John Gyger* SE-SE-S21; 2-24-36
Joseph Reaney* E-NE-S22; 3-10-29
Joseph Culbortson* W-NE-S22; 11-16-25
Stephen Potter* W-NW-S22; 11-30-32
John Hawkins SW-S22; 3-31-20; SE-S22; 10-23-17
Reuben Kilgore* E-NE-S23; 11-16-22
Arta Garrison W-NE-S23; 1-24-18
Isaac Stewart & Samuel F. Irwin E-SW-S23; 2-25-25
George Rainy* W-SW-S23; 1-25-26
Thomas McMannus SE-S23; 4-9-17
Marquis Knight NE-S24; 10-30-16
John F. Ross & Ebenezer McDonald NW-S24; 8-5-17
Joseph Glover SW-S24; 10-16-16
James Gregory SE-S24; 9-25-16
Ezekiel Blackwell NE-S25; 3-9-18
John Hays NW-S25; 9-25-16
James Maxwell SW-S25; 7-30-17
Hillary Toon* E-SE, SW-SE-S25; 4-22-36
Thomas Fisher* NW-SE-S25; 3-14-34
William Thornton NE-S26; 9-25-16; NW-S26; 10-2-16

Richard Evans* NE-SW-S26; 1-2-33
Ebenezer McDonald SE-S26; 2-17-18
Levi Reed* E-NE-S27; 7-26-28
Samuel Daugherty W-NE-S27; 9-15-16
Levi Rector* E-NW-S27; 7-5-28
John Cups* W-NW-S27; 4-25-29;SW-NE-S35;8-17-35;SE-NW-S35;11-29-33
Robert Daugherty E-SW-S27; 9-15-17
John & Henry Lowry* W-SW-S27; 9-8-31
Alexander Butler SE-S27; 9-15-17
George Pomeroy Lynd* NE-NE-Nfr-S28; 18-9-35
Lemuel Butler, Jessamine Co., Ind. (Due to a change in the Ohio
    River bed, Jessamine Co. is now in Ky. M.R.W.) SE-NE-Sfr-S28;
John Warwick Lynn* W-NE-Nfr-S28; 12-5-35.   8-14-32 .
Lewis Beck* E-W-Nfr-S28; 5-30-29; W-W-Nfr-S28; 11-14-33; E-NEfr-
    Nfr-S29; 5-28-36
Milton Thompson Dougherty* SE-Nfr-S28; 5-2-36
Joseph Rector* W-NEfr-Nfr-S29; 3-23-37
James McCracken* NW-NW-Nfr-S29; 4-21-36
Joseph Rudyard* SW-NW-Nfr-S29; 8-9-36
William McLane* Lots 1-2-N-SWfr-Nfr-S29; 8-11-36; S-SWfr-Nfr-S29;
Robert Hollowell Sfrs-S28 & 29; 9-25-16   4-10-33
Isaiah Budyard (Rudyard?)* SE-NE-S30;9-11-33;SW-NE-S30;10-18-33
John Budyard (Rudyard?)* NW-NE-S30; 2-2-38
David Fisher* NE-NW-S30; 12-15-34
John Rains* SE-NW-S30; 4-13-36
John Duncan W-NW-S30; 9-23-16; W-SW-S30; 11-18-17
Adam Siler E-SW-S30;SW-S31;1-16-18;SE-S30;12-17-17;NE,NW-S31;
Jonathan Lindley SE-S31;Wfr-S32;Efr-S34;9-25-16.   8-7-17
Robert Fields Efr-S32; 9-25-16
Robert Wood* NE-SW-Sfr-S33;3-16-33; W-SW-Sfr-S33; 8-5-34
Robert Wood, Jr.* SE-SW-Sfr-S33; 5-1-38
James Davis* NW-SE-Sfr-S33; 10-10-36
Daniel Pursel* SW-SE-Sfr-S33; 1-29-39
Jacob Piles & Jonathan Williams NE, NW, E-SE-S33; Nfr-S34;12-1-17
William Foot (Winthrop Foot?) E-NE-S35; 12-7-16
William McFall* NW-NE, NW-SE-S35; 6-25-35
Joseph Glover* W-NW-S35; 1-2-33
Thompson H. Biggs* E-SW-S35; 8-17-35
John Gardner W-SW-S35; 9-25-16
James McCune, Jr.* NE-SE-S35; 6-17-35
James McCune, Sr.* SE-SE-S35; 7-2-35
Enos Nugent* SW-SE-S35; 12-31-34
Fetter & Hughes NE, SE-S36; 1-28-18
John F. Ross & Ebenezer McDonald E-NW-S36; 8-5-17
Joseph Rawlins* W-NW-S36; 2-19-29
Dixon Brown SW-S36; 10-28-17

RELINQUISHMENTS

John Chesnut NW-S6; 8-19-18
Abraham Mitchel W-SE-S9; 9-19-18
Robert Whitely W-SW-S12; 9-19-18
Fetter & Hughes SE-S14; 8-6-18
William Daugherty SW-S15; NE-S21; 11-18-17;E-NE-S20;12-8-18;7-4-29

Samuel Pearson SW-S18; 8-9-17
Timothy Ward E-SW-S20; 5-1-19
Samuel Daugherty SW-S23;E-NE-S27; 9-15-17; E-SW-S29; 2-25-18
Jacob Plos & Jonathan Williams SW-Sfr, W-SE-Sfr-S33; 12-1-17
William Foot W-NE-S35; 10-7-16
Ebenezer McDonald SE-S25; 2-7-18;SE-S26;2-17-18;7-4-29
Marquis Knight NW-S27; 1-26-18
John F. Ross & Ebenezer McDonald W-NW-S36; 8-5-17
Robert Daugherty W-SW-S27; 9-15-17
Ezekiel Blackwell NW-S35; 1-21-18; SE-S35; 9-25-16;NE-S25;3-9-18;
John Gardner E-SW-S35; 9-25-16   7-4-29
James Pace W-NE-S1; 4-4-20
Abraham Fox NE-S18; 2-25-19; 3-3-30
John Marsall E-NE-S30; 5-22-19; 3-3-30
Dixon Brown W-NW-S2; 10-28-17; 7-4-29
Reuben Kilgore SE-S12; 9-19-18; 7-4-29
James Denson W-SW-S2; 1-16-19; 7-4-29

T 5 N, R 2 W

David Sears* NW-NE-S1; E-SE-S3; 4-1-36; NE-SW-S10; 4-13-36; SE-
    NW-S12; 1-28-37; NW-SE-S22; 1-21-36; NW-S26; 12-9-16
Jesse Hodges* SW-NE-S1; 2-11-36
Elijah Gartin E-NW-S1; 10-30-18
Uriah Moore* NW-NW-S1; 2-27-36; SE-NE-S2; 3-20-46
William Farris* SW-NW-S1; 6-18-36; W-SW-S1; 2-6-36
Abraham Kern* E-SW-S1; 9-3-29; W-SE-S1; 6-7-24
William Kethers* E-SE-S1; 9-20-20
Thomas Fauntleroy Lee* NE-NE-S2; 12-19-32
James Dunch* NW-NE-S2; 10-26-32
Charles Beevers* SW-NE-S2; 3-29-36; NW-SE-S2; 4-4-36
Isaac Grindstaff* NE-NW-S2; 2-7-45
Harris Walker, Gn SE-NW-S2; 4-3-37
Josiah Pierce* NW-NW-S2;2-20-45;SE-NW-S3;6-17-36;SW-NW-S3;7-18-38
John McWilliams* NE-SW-S2; 4-27-36
Rhodes Nuckolls* SE-SW-S2; 3-9-36; SW-NW-S10; 5-19-35
James Nuckolls* SW-SW-S2; 2-11-36
James Pierce* NW-SW-S3; 2-11-36
William Riley Parker* SW-NE, NW-SE-S3; 10-16-37
Henry Pierce* NE-NW-S3; 10-24-37
John Hurt* NW-NW-S3; 8-9-38
Newton Pierce* NE-SW-S3;10-31-36;SE-SW-S3;3-24-34;SW-SW-S3;
William Kern* E-NE-S4; 1-20-32   11-2-38
John Short, Sr. W-NE-S4; 1-5-19
John Monren Fields* NE-NW-S4; 12-30-44
Henry Muller* SE-NW-S4; 10-4-33
Thomas Armstrong* NW-NW-S4; 2-11-36
John Short* SW-NW-S4; 12-7-44; NE-SW-S5; 7-31-35; SW-SW-S5;
    1-7-37; SE-S5; 12-29-17
Thomas Hurt* NE-SE-S4; 8-9-38
James Armstrong* SE-SE-S4; NE-NE-S5; 12-31-44
Thomas Short* W-SE-S4; 9-5-22
Thomas Luckey* SE-NE-S5; 1-7-37
John Roberts W-NE-S5; 12-29-17

Reuben Short E-NW-S5; 12-29-17
Charles Washington Short* NW-NW-S5
John, Samuel, & Wesley Short* SW-NW-S5; 3-29-39
Samuel, Wesley, & Martin Short SE-SW, NW-SW-S5; 11-19-38
Wesley & Samuel Short* E-NE-S6; 3-15-39
Isaac Waggoner W-NE, NW-S6; 4-14-18
Zachariah Loveall, Sr., Mt NE-SW-S6; 10-10-36
James Manas Lovell, Mt SE-SW-S6; 7-11-37
Iredill Fields* NW-SW-S6; 1-11-34
Noah Boone* SW-SW, NE-SE-S6; NW-NE-S7; 10-31-36; W-SE-S6; 12-30-
    44; E-NE-S7; 10-35-38; SW-NE-S7; 2-3-34; SE-SE-S7; 6-21-44
Joel Woodall* SE-SE-S6; 2-17-36
Noah Waggoner* NE-SE-S7; 7-20-36
Elijah Boon W-SE-S7; 8-16-17
Jeremiah Boone NW, SW-S7; 6-3-17
William Cochran E-NE-S8; 7-9-18
Hansford Short* NW-NE-S8; 12-8-36; NE-NW-S8; 11-3-38
Reuben Mayfield* SW-NE-S8;6-5-37; SW-NW-S8;10-8-51. MLW 12626
Ellington Talley* SE-NW-S8; 10-25-38; NW-NW-S8; 12-8-36
John Rochester SW-S8; 6-18-17
Wesley Short SE-S8; 12-29-17
James Armstrong* NE-NE-S9; 12-31-44
Deddridge & Owens Short* S-NE-S9; 2-5-45
Thomas Hurt* NW-NE-S9; 10-31-33
Thomas Short* E-SW-S9; 10-31-28
Doddridge Short* W-SW-S9; 3-6-38
John Heddrick* E-SE-S9; 8-30-25
John Crooke NE-S10; 11-4-17
Josiah Price* NW-NW-S10; 2-15-45
Henry Skeen* SE-SW-S10; 11-29-33
William Fields* W-SW-S10; 2-11-36
Daniel Todd SE-S10; 11-4-17 .
William Riley Parker* E-NE-S11; 12-1-36
Henry Grindstaff* W-NE-S11; 8-8-44; SE-NW-S11; 6-7-41; NW-NE-S15;
    10-18-38; NE-NE, SE-NW-S18; 2-6-45; E-NE-S24; 8-14-35
James Nuckolls* NE-NW-S11; 9-1-37
Archibald Wood W-NW-S11; 9-21-16
Abraham Kern* E-SW-S11;1-28-37;SE-SE-S11;1-21-36;W-SE-S11;11-27-26
Ezra Nuckolls* W-SW-S11; 12-28-36
William Cather* NE-SE-S11; 7-16-38; SW-SW-S12; E-NE-S15; 12-6-36;
    SW-SE-S13; 2-6-36
John Parks Darnall* N-NE-S12; 2-9-36
Ezra Sears* NE-NW-S12; 9-25-35; W-NW-S12; 12-16-34
Fetter & Hughes E-SW-S12; 9-21-16
Sims Cather* NW-SW-S12; 1-10-37
Job Ward* E-SE-S12; 6-6-36
George Grundy Dunn* NW-SE-S12; 7-26-36
James Crane SW-SE-S12; 6-6-36
Michael Farmer* E-NE-S13; 11-22-26; W-NE-S13; 9-9-23
Adam Karn NW-S13; 12-9-17
Simon Karn SW-S13; 12-9-17
Dobson Stephenson* E-SE-S13; 7-29-25
Alexander Julius Kern* NW-SE-S13; 10-30-33
Robert Gartan & Richard Browning NE-S14; 9-16-17

Isaac Martin* E-NW-S14; 2-6-27
Ambrose Kern* NW-NW-S14; 1-28-37; SW-NW-S14; 3-19-34
Henry Speed SW-S14; 9-21-16; NW-S23; 9-21-16.
Elijah Garton SE-S14; 9-23-17
Julius Chestnut* SW-NE-S15; 1-23-37
Jacob Hackler* NW-SW-S15; 4-13-36; SW-SW-S15; 11-8-33
Elbert Howard E-SE-S15; 1-5-19
John Chestnut, Jr.* NW-SE-S15; 12-31-36; SW-SE-S15; 11-2-35
Reuben Mayfield* NE-NE-S17; 12-30-44
John Craig* NW-NE-S17; 8-26-36
Elijah Goff* SW-NE-S17; 3-7-36
William Dillard NW-S17; 11-27-17
Jacob Waggoner SW-S17; 10-21-17; of Mt, W-NW-S18; 3-11-36
Michael Waggoner SE-S17; 4-24-17
David Mounts* NW-SW-S18; 9-1-46
Elnathan Burk* SW-SW-S18; 2-27-50
Joseph Sergeant E-NW-S19; 4-4-17
Joel Hubbard* NW-NW-S19; 6-9-36
Henry Wagoner, Mt NE-SW-S19; 6-16-37
George S. Monson* SE-SW-S19; 6-6-54
Alexander Waggoner* NW-SW-S19; 1-8-52
Trulove Brown, Mt SW-SW-S19; 4-28-37
James Corbin, Mt SE-SE-S19; 1-12-37
Robert Campbell* NW-SE-S19; 2-26-45
Michael Waggoner NE-S20; 4-24-17; NW-S31; 4-24-17
Henry Wagoner NW-S20; 4-4-17
Thomas McAfee* NE-SW-S20; 8-5-34
Dabney Harris* NW-SW-S20; 3-26-36
Daniel Baker* NW-SE-S20; 1-10-37
Harrison Speers* SW-SE-S20; 1-18-36
Washington Speer* NE-NW, SW-NW-S21; 6-17-36
Richard Reynolds* NW-NW-S21; 3-23-39
Richard Speer+ NE-SW-S21; 6-17-36; SE-SE-S29; 10-18-36
Esaw Burgest Nimrod Melton (2 men?), Speer Co., Ind. (no such Co.)
    NW-SW-S21; 4-6-39
Benjamin H. Chestnut* SE-SE-S21; 11-13-38
Henry Woody* SW-SE-S21; 11-2-35
Elbert Howard NE-S22; 10-11-17
Daniel Baker* NE-NW-S22; 10-5-35
William Inman* SE-NW-S22; 2-22-36
Abraham Chestnut* NW-NW-S22; 1-25-38
Benjamin Chestnut E-SE-S22; 1-5-19
John Inman* SW-SE-S22; 9-25-35;NE-NE-S27;2-10-36;NW-NE-S30;4-3-55
James Gratan (Garten?) NE-S23; 9-28-16
Joseph Sullivan & John L. Dunkin SW-S23; 9-23-17
Fetter & Hughes SE-S23;NW, SW-S24;NW, SW-S25; 9-21-16
William Cathers* W-NE-S24; 8-14-35
David Fisher* E-SE-S24; 11-23-27
Abraham Kern* W-SE-S24; 7-5-25;E-SE-S35;6-17-31;W-SW-S36;3-21-31
Archibald Wood NE, SE-S25; 9-21-16; NE-S36; 9-28-16
John Dunkin NE-S26; 9-23-17
Eli Kern* NE-SW-S26; 1-3-37
William Sears* SE-SW-S26; 1-21-36; SW-SW-S26; 1-2-36
William Rains* NW-SW-S26; 12-11-32

Abraham Kern Adamson* N-SE-S26; 5-15-37
John Williams Adamson* SE-SE-S26; 12-16-34; SW-SE-S26; 12-4-32
George Inman* NE-NE-S27; 2-10-36
Garret Williams* SE-NE, NE-SE-S27; 10-29-32;NW-SW-S32; 3-29-52
Ezra Sears+ SW-NE-S27; 10-26-38
Edward Sears* SE-NW-S27; 4-1-36
Edward Sellers* W-NW-S27; 12-9-31; NW-SW-S27; 10-26-38; NE-SW-
    S28; 3-2-48; NE-SW-S32; 7-26-50
Albert Kern* SE-SW-S27; 5-10-38
John W. Smith* SE-SE-S27; 2-22-36
Simon Smith* NW-SE-S27; 1-23-37; SE-NE-S28; 2-21-33
Isaac Boyd* SW-SE-S27; 10-6-36
Sarah Smith* NE-NE-S28; 6-25-37
Zachariah Smith* NW-NE-S28; 1-28-37; NW-SW-S34; 1-20-36
George Washington Morris+ N-NW-S28; 4-13-36
Benjamin Smith* SE-NW-S28; 3-21-46
Elijah Powell* SW-NW-S28; 10-14-47
Alexander Julius Kern* SE-SW-S28; 1-10-37
John G. Hall* NW-SW-S28; 10-31-54;SW-SW-S32;9-5-36; Gregory
Benjamin Sears*. SW-SW-S28; 10-23-48; NE-NW-S33; 5-16-44
Permenius Lamb* S-SE-S28; 10-29-44
Henry Inman* SW-NE, NW-SE-S29; 1-28-39; SE-NE-S30; 5-20-53
Dennis Call* NE-NW-S29; 1-19-44
William Woodrum E-SW-S29; 7-15-19
Robert Mitchell* NW-SW-S29; 10-27-36
George Pulse* SW-SW-S29; NE-NW-S32; 10-10-36
Joel Bridges, Mt NE-SE-S29; 2-16-37
Jacob Grindstaff* NE-NE-S30; 9-6-47
John Inman, Sr.* SW-NE-S30; 6-2-54
Jesse Towell E-SW-S30; 10-29-16
John Mitchell* SW-SW-S30; 8-27-35; SW-NE-S31; 2-6-37
Robert Mitchell W-SE-S30; 3-16-18; NW-NE-S31; 12-26-34
William C. Powell* E-NE-S31; SW-NW-S32; 5-13-51
George Kinder* SE-SW-S31; 7-30-51
Henry Sears+ W-SW-S31; 11-8-54
Sarah Woody+ SE-SE-S31; 10-18-38
Thomas Dowels* NW-SE-S31; 2-20-33
Charles McAfee* SE-NW-S32; 6-2-54
William Brown* NW-NW-S32; 5-13-51
William Moore* SE-SW-S32; 7-25-50
Barton Sears* E-SE-S32; 10-25-43
John Simeon Kern* W-SE-S32; 9-29-47
Elbert Evans+ SE-NE-S33; 11-8-33; SW-SE-S34; 2-16-36
Isaac Williams E-SW-S33;2-18-17; of*, SW-SW-S33;8-16-32;NW-SW-S33;
Jonathan Lindley SE-S33; 10-8-16   5-4-35
David Sears* E-NE-S34; 1-5-32
Andrew Sears+ NW-NE-S34; 1-27-36; SW-NE-S34; 3-19-34
Peyton Wilson NW-S34; 10-29-16
Alexander Cox* NE-SW-S34; 2-11-47
Isaiah Lamb* SE-SW-S34; 11-1-33
Ivy Adamson* SW-SW-S34; 6-24-33; NE-SE-S34; 11-2-35
David Fisher* SE-SE-S34; 10-28-33
Joshua Evans* NW-SE-S34; 1-21-36
Martin Ribelin NW-S35; 10-20-18

Eli Kern* E-NE-S35; 6-25-37; E-NW, NW-NW-S36; 2-20-45; SW-NW-S36;
   1-3-37; NE-SW-S36; 9-6-44; SE-SW-S36; 12-16-34;NW-SE-S36;9-6-44
Ambrose Kern* NW-SE-S35;5-15-37;SW-SE-S35;1-26-36;E-SE-S36;1-3-37
John Williams Adamson* W-NE-S35; 12-16-34
Thomas Braxton SW-S35; 10-25-16
Samuel Massey, Or SW-SE-S36; 1-3-37

RELINQUISHMENTS

Samuel Boyd NW-S10; 11-18-17
Fetter & Hughes NE, SE-S11; W-SW-S12; 9-21-16
Elbert Howard W-SE-S15; 1-5-19
Absalom Sergeant W-SE-S18; 5-25-18; E-SE-S18; 5-25-18; 7-4-29
Adam Kern SE-S24; 11-18-18
Jesse Towell W-SW-S30; 10-29-16
Robert Holaday NE-S31; 10-25-16
William Woodrum NW-S32; 11-23-19; W-SW-S29; 7-15-19; 7-4-29
Martin Ribelin NE-S35; 9-26-18
John Short, Sr. E-NE-S4; 1-5-19
William Cochran W-NE-S8; 7-9-18
John & Wesley Short SW-S9; 12-29-17
Archibald Wood E-NW, SW-S11; 9-21-16
Joseph Sergeant W-NW-S19; 4-4-17
Benjamin Chestnut W-SE-S22; 1-5-19
Isaac Williams W-SW-S33; 2-18-17
Elijah Gartin W-NW-S1; 10-20-18
Isaac Waggoner E-NE-S6; 4-14-18
Elijah Boon E-SE-S7; 8-16-17
John Rochester SW-S8; 6-18-17
Elbert Howard E-SE-S15; 1-5-19; 7-4-29

T 6 N, R 1 W

Elias Kinser* NE-NE-S1; 9-6-47; W-NE-S1; 8-10-47
Colin W. Yale, Cook Co., Ill. E-NE, W-SE-S1; 3-4-56
Joshua Sowder, Mr NE-NW-S1; 11-15-34; Lowder of*, NW-SE-S11;1-18-
Gentry Haggard, Mr SE-NW-S1; 2-26-38   36
John Deckard* W-NW-S1; 12-1-31
William A. Meadows* SE-SW-S1; 2-25-45;NE-SW,SE-SE-S2; 2-12-45
James D. Galloway* NW-SW-S1; 6-2-47
George Johnson Covey* SW-SW-S1; 4-3-37
David Stuart* SE-SE-S1; 5-1-50
John Meadows* NE-NE-S2; 9-10-35; SW-NE-S13; 9-17-32
Isham Edds* SE-NE-S2; 5-23-36; NE-SE-S2; 1-12-37
Nathaniel Vert* NW-NE-S2; 9-29-34
William Stuart, Mr SW-NE-S2; 12-31-36
Clayborne Hollaway, Mr SE-NW-S2; 7-27-37
John Hanson* W-NW-S2; 10-11-37; S-SW-S2; 2-5-45; SW-NE-S3;7-2-49;
   NW-NW-S3; 4-5-36; E-NE-S4; 8-14-24; W-NE, E-NW-S4; 6-18-24;E-NE,
   NW-NE-S10;NE-NW, SW-NW-S11; 2-5-45; NE-SW-S11; 11-9-50
David Miller, Mr NW-SW-S2; 11-15-34; SE-NW-S11; 3-12-39.
Elisha Farris, Mr NW-SE-S2; 10-27-40;of*,SW-NE-S11;6-14-36;NW-NW-
Joel Watson* SW-SE-S2; 8-11-36;of Mr,SE-SE-S5;2-25-36. / S12;
William Edds* SE-NE-S3; 9-19-39.   /8-12-39

Edward Humston* NW-NE-S3; 8-2-39
Daniel Hanson* SW-NW-S3; 8-7-37
Adam Dirting SW-S3; 12-9-16
Matthew S. Taylor* W-NW-S4; 6-18-24
Jacob Hattabaugh E-SW-S4; 10-24-16
Jacob Vert* W-SW-S4; 8-24-24
William Curl SE-S4; 9-25-16
Hamilton Redick NE-S5; 6-3-17
William Lemon* E-NW-S5; 2-23-36; NW-SE-S5; 5-28-32
John McCrea* W-NW-S5; 6-18-36; NE, SE-S6; 6-17-36; E-NW, E-SW,
    NW-SW-S6; 4-12-37
Milford Haddon Vert* E-SW-S5; 2-11-36;NW-SW-S5;2-15-37;SW-SW-S5;2-
Garrett Beverly Blackwell* NE-SE-S5;4-5-36;NE-NW-S8;3-18-37.   19-36
James Buchanan, Mr W-NW-S6; 10-5-35
John Fairley, Jr.* SW-SW-S6; NW-NW-S7; 12-28-35
Andrew McFadden* NE-NE-S7; 4-12-37
Robert Anderson* NE-SE-S7; 8-6-55; SE-SE-S7;NW-NW-S8; 4-12-36
John Anderson* SE-NE-S7;SW-NW-S8; 8-6-35; W-NE-S7; 3-11-36
John Fairley E-NW-S7; 12-27-19; of*, SW-NW-S7; 4-29-33; NW-SW-S7;
John Goodwin E-SW-S7; 3-30-18   8-5-34
Elephalet Pearson* SW-SW-S7; 7-23-35
Robert Anderson, Jr. W-SE-S7; 10-2-19
Lazarus Barkley, Bath Co., Ky. SW-S8; 3-17-23; of*, W-SE-S8;
    1-12-27; SE-NW-S8; 2-15-37
John Hargis NE-S8; 10-29-16
Martin R. Judah* E-SE-S8; 2-17-36
William Leakey NE-S9; 1-14-17
Jesse Brown NW-S9; 9-25-16
James Culley SW-S9; 12-24-16
Michael Hattabaugh SE-S9; 12-31-16
James Hayes* SW-NE-S10; 4-9-44
Jacob Bruner W-NW-S10; 10-28-18
John Lowe* N-SW-S10; 12-8-38
John Lewis Moore* SE-SW-S10; 12-4-38
Elisha Kinser* SW-SW-S10; 2-6-36
Patrick Williams* E-SE-S10; 4-9-44
Richard Buckner* W-SE-S10; 2-4-26
Adam Walls* NE-NE-S11; 10-20-33
John Prince* SE-NE-S11;7-8-37;NE-SE-S11;5-9-36;NE-SW-S12;7-14-44
William Smith Faris* NW-NE-S11; 3-25-39
Milton Stewart, Mr NW-NW-S11; 6-28-43
Washington Roger McKnight* SE-SE-S11; NW-NE-S14; 1-25-50
Isaac Anderson, Jr E-NE-S12; 3-12-56
George Johnson Covey* NW-NE-S12; 6-8-36; NW-SW-S12; 4-3-37
James Meadowes* SW-NE-S12; 11-30-46
George Faris* SE-NW-S12; 7-8-37; SW-NW-S12; 5-9-36
Jacob Deckard* SE-SW-S12; 7-18-38
William Deckard, Mr SW-SW-S12; 7-24-35; SW-NW-S13; 6-14-36
John Bailey* E-SE-S12; 2-2-22
John Hood Meadows* SW-SE-S12; 7-14-36
Jacob Meadows* NE-NE-S13; 10-14-37; NW-NE-S13; 5-21-44
William Johnson* SE-NE-S13; 5-15-44
Caswell Donica S-SW-S14;N-NW-S23;9-22-49;MLW 338;NW-NE-S23;5-16-55;
    of*,SW-NE-S23;NW-SW-S27;10-13-53;NE-NW-S25;3-5-44

Pinkney Moore* NE-NE-S15; 8-2-44
Samuel Daniel Judah* SE-NE-S15; 9-3-44
Samuel W. Brown* W-NE-S15; 2-13-26
Samuel Kinser* NE-SW-S15; 8-5-34
Winepark Judah* S-SW-S15; 2-17-36
George McKnight* E-NW-S13; NE-NE, NE-SE-S14; 12-18-43; NW-NW-S13;
    11-25-44; E-SW-S13; 6-14-36; NE-SE-S24; 12-18-43; W-SE-S24;
    9-30-31; SE-NW-S25; 6-15-35
Henry Johnson* NW-SW-S13; 3-5-36; SE-NE-S14; 3-2-37
David Carter* SW-SW-S13; 5-20-39
James Garrison NE-SE-S13; 6-15-53
Alfred Ramsey* SE-SE-S13;3-18-44;NW-NE-S24;11-2-37;SE-NW-S24;9-19-3
Elijah McKnight* NW-SE-S13; 10-6-37
George Stultz* SW-SE-S13; SW-NE-S24; 11-13-34
William McKnight* SW-NE-S14; 1-25-50;SE-SE, NW-SE-S14; 10-6-37
Jeremiah Anderson* NW-SW-S15; 3-17-34; W-SE-S19; 1-26-36
James Cully NW-S15; 7-14-17
George Washington Reed* E-SE-S15; 7-30-40
John Reed, Jr., Jk W-SE-S15; 2-22-36
Eli & John W. Judah* E-NE-S17; 2-17-36
Benjamin Brinegar, Bath Co., Ky. NW-S22;3-26-22; of*,W-NE-S17;
Edward Barkley, Bath Co., Ky. NW-S17; 3-17-23   2-20-36
Henry Brown SW-S17; 10-8-18
John Zumwalt SE-S17; 10-12-18
Henry Leonard NE-S18; 10-23-18
John Sanklin, Bath Co., Ind. (no such Co.; prob. Ky.) E-SW-S18;
Nicholas Bruner* NW-SW-S18; 10-13-36   9-3-24
Samuel Blackburn* SW-SW-S18; 4-12-37
Patrick Tylor NW-S18; 5-31-17
William Quillen SE-S18; 12-8-18
Thomas Anderson* E-NE, SW-NE-S19; 3-4-36; NW-NE-S19; 8-5-34
William Lemon* NE-NW-S19; 8-5-34
Cyrus Blackburn* SE-NW-S19; 3-5-36; NE-SW-S19; 4-12-37
Samuel Bennett* W-NW-S19; 3-5-36
Milton Blackburn* W-SW-S19; 4-12-37
John Anderson* NE-SE-S19; 6-3-36
John Dryden NE-S20; 2-17-17
George Tyler* NE-NW-S20; 7-27-35
Robert Love Donaldson* SE-NW-S20; 7-27-35; NE-SW-S20; 3-4-36
David Anderson* NW-NW-S20; 3-4-36
James Anderson* SW-NW-S20; 3-17-31
James Chestnut* S-SW-S20; 8-11-36
John Etter* NW-SW-S20; 3-5-36
Joshua Gullett SE-S20; 1-15-18; NW-S21; 11-2-16
John Quillen NE-S21; 8-10-18
Adam Housh (Kouse?) SW-S21; 8-27-17; SE-S21; 11-2-16
Benjamin Grayson* E-NE, SW-NE-S22; SW-NW-S23; 8-31-35; E-SE-S22;
John Reed* NW-NE-S22; 8-2-44   6-24-36
William Chambers* NE-SW-S22; 11-4-40; NW-SE-S22; 8-7-40
John Stipp* SE-SW-S22; 10-4-32; E-NW, NW-NW-S27; 8-5-34
William Perkins* W-SW-S22; 3-9-21
Michael Stipp* SW-SE-S22; 2-20-36
John Grayson* SE-NW-S23; 1-9-36
George Silver SW-S23; 8-14-17

Peter Harmonson E-SE-S23; 1-29-18
James Erwin W-SE-S23; 10-16-18
Eli Hendricks* E-NE-S24; 11-2-37
David Carter* NE-NW-S24; 5-20-39
Thomas Elrod SW-S24; 10-13-17
William McDaniel* SE-SE-S24; 7-13-32
William Stults* W-NW-S25; 3-4-36
Roger McKnight NE-S25; 5-1-17
Jacob Castleman E-SW-S25; 5-1-17
Henry Long* W-SW-S25; 3-9-31
John Williams SE-S25; 12-3-16
John C. & William Humston E-NE-S26; 6-2-31
Reuben, Hiram, & Simpson Kilgore W-NE-S26; 8-12-18
Peter Harmonson, Josiah Lee, & George McKnight E-NW-S26; 5-18-25
Winthrop Foot W-NW-S26; 5-20-36
Thomas Mitchell* E-SW-S26; 9-11-29; SE-SW-S29; 6-4-44
Levi Mitchell* W-SW-S26; 6-2-31; SE-SW-S27; 3-12-39
John Owens* E-SE-S26; 2-5-28
Logan Fish* W-SE-S26; 9-21-29
William Perkins* E-NE-S27; 4-18-29; W-NW-S28; SE-NE-S29; 6-19-37;
Richard Ryan, Jr.* W-NE-S27; 6-15-35.   /NE-NE-S29; 3-11-36
Jacob Mitchell* NE-SW-S27; 8-27-39
James Owens* SW-SW-S27; 1-13-37
Simpson Kilgore SE-S27; 4-4-20
Thomas Reynolds NE-S28; 1-2-17
Jameson Hamilton* E-NW-S28; 7-15-26
Isaac Trogdon* E-SW-S28; 1-10-38
John Hoon* NW-SW-S28; 6-13-36
Owen Owens* SW-SW-S28; 7-12-37
Abraham Reynolds* NE-SE-S28; 9-29-35
Jesse Etter* SE-SE-S28; 3-11-36; SW-SE-S30; 6-13-36
John Shryer* W-SE-S28; 12-27-24
Nelson Lemonds* NW-NE-S29; 12-12-36; NE-NW-S29; 12-29-35
James Hopkins* SW-NE, NW-SE-S29; 4-9-44
Westard Aimsted Trogdon* NW-NW-S29; 11-26-46
John Owen Lemon* SW-NW-S29; 8-11-36
Joseph Lemmonds* SW-SW-S29; 4-30-39
Joseph Owens* NE-SE-S29; 12-29-43
William Purkins Owens* SE-SE-S29; 6-12-44
Lewis Sillars* SW-NW-S30; 8-24-44
Charles Burton* NE-SW-S30; 6-13-36
Thomas Roy* SE-SW-S30; 3-23-37
David Burton* NW-SW-S30; 2-27-36
William Roy* SW-SW-S30; NW-NW-S31; 3-23-37
William Lemonds* E-SE-S30; 12-12-36
Joseph Hamer* NE-NE-S31; SE-NW-S32; 2-20-37
Isaac Tumey* NW-NE-S31; 6-19-37
William Columbus Potter* SW-SW-S31; 2-21-39
Andrew McClelland* NE-NE, SW-NE-S32; 4-9-44
Owen Owen, Jr.* SE-NE-S32; 5-17-39
Thomas Mitchell* NE-NW-S32; 5-23-44
John Henry McClelland* NW-NW-S32; 5-20-44
Absalom Hart* SW-NW-S32; 12-12-32
Absalom Sergeant SW-S32; 4-7-17

Silas Mallett* NE-SE-S32; 9-16-37; W-SE-S32;W-SE-S33; 1-15-36
Elizabeth Lamb* SE-SE-S32; 7-28-36
William Perkins* NE-NE-S33; 6-19-37
Owen Owens, Wayne Co., Ky. E-SW-S34; 9-11-29; of*, SE-NE, SE-NW-
    S33; 12-7-35; W-NW, W-SW-S34; 2-9-30
Jeremiah Lewis* NW-NW-S33; 11-12-32; SW-NW-S33; 8-11-36
James George E-SW-S33; 3-24-26; of*, W-SW-S33; 3-11-36
Joshua Hopkins, Wy E-SE-S33; 8-19-29
Isaac Mitchel* E-NE-S34; 7-30-30
Roger Whiteley* W-NE, E-NW-S34; 9-5-21
Samuel Mason* E-SE-S34; 11-8-32
Moses Hodges* W-SE-S34; 12-18-32
Ephraim Trabue* N-NE-S35; 7-13-32
William Edwards* S-NE-S35; 9-23-33
Henry McGee NW-S35; 8-18-18
Reuben & Hiram Kilgore SW-S35; 6-29-18
Hiram Kilgore SE-S35; 1-23-18
Thomas Allen NE-S36; 4-23-17
Jacob Castleman NW-S36; 5-1-17
Reuben Kilgore SW-S36; 12-19-17
William Fish SE-S36; 12-30-16

RELINQUISHMENTS

Jacob Hatterbaugh W-SW-S4; 10-24-16
Robert Anderson, Jr. E-SE-S7; 10-2-19
Jacob Bruner E-NW-S10; 10-28-18
Samuel Crain & William Hoggatt NE-S14; 3-10-17; SE-S14; 4-30-17
Jacob Castleman SE-S24;NE-S35;W-SW-S25;SW, SE-S26; 5-1-17
Stephen Shipman SE-S32; 3-18-18
John Hanson NW-S1; 3-21-18
Henry Wice SE-S5; 11-25-16
John Goodwine W-SW-S7; 3-20-18
Reuben, Hiram, & Simpson Kilgore E-NE-S26; 8-12-18
John Fairley W-NW-S7; 12-27-19
Adam Davis NW-S32; 6-11-17
James Sweaney SW-S15; 6-28-17; 3-3-30. Jacob Castleman NW-S36;
George Sheeks SE-S34; 7-17-18; 7-4-29.   5-1-17; 7-4-29
Henry McGee NW-S35; 8-18-18; 7-4-29. Thomas Reynolds W-SE-S33;
James Owens SE-S35; 1-23-18; 7-4-29.   1-15-20; 7-4-29

T 6 N, R 2 W

Jacob Zike* NE-NE-S1; 8-3-36
James Buchanan, Mr SE-NE-S1; 10-5-35
Andrew McFaddin* W-NE, S-NW-S1; 4-25-37
James Fairley* NE-NW-S1; 12-28-35
Samuel Baugh* NW-NW-S1; 8-8-36
Matthias Sears* E-SE-S1; 9-7-31
Elizabeth Rogers* NW-SE-S1; 7-19-36
John Low* SW-SE-S1; 10-17-32
Abraham Hartman SW-S1; 8-19-17
James Sare, Mr N-NE, E-NW-S2; 9-30-36
Martin Brown, Mr SE-NE-S2; 7-16-40

Rouben Sare, Mr SW-NE-S2; 3-30-37
Lewis Jones, Mr W-NW, W-SW-S2; 10-29-31
Jonathan Tatum* NE-SE-S2; 8-21-39
Elijah Linthicum, Mr SE-SE-S2; 12-28-35; NW-SE-S2; 1-20-37
Adelia Heberd, Kn NE-NE-S3; 7-24-55
Thomas Jones, Mr SE-NE-S3; 3-13-43
John Nance, Mr W-NE-S3; 10-29-51
Alfred Jones* E-NW, SE-SE-S3; 10-27-36
John Pedigo* W-NW-S3; 4-1-37
Henry Wade* E-SW-S3; 8-9-37; NW-NW-S19; 10-21-33
Eli Powell NE-S4; 3-14-17
John Pedigo, Sr.* S-NW-S4; 3-13-39
Joseph East, Mr NW-NW-S4; 1-1-36
Reuben Davis* SE-SW-S4; 8-5-34
Ralph Lowder* W-SW-S4; 2-2-31;NW-S9;2-19-17;NW-SE-S9; 5-14-39
Alexander Clark SE-S4; 7-14-17
Richard Nance, Mr NW-NE-S5; 11-26-38
William Graves, Mr NW-NW-S5; 11-26-36; of*, NE-NW-S5; 2-11-45
Jesse Rainbolt, Gn SE-SW-S5; 9-7-35
James Madison Hodges* NW-SW-S5; 6-21-49
William McGill* SE-SE-S5; 10-18-33
Alfred Storme* SW-SE-S5; 2-19-45
Joseph Fennington, Mr E-NE-S6; 10-29-31
William Harvey Rider* NW-NE-S6; 1-10-39
Adam Rainbolt* SW-NE-S6; 6-14-39; SE-NW-S6; 8-9-38; SW-NW-S6;
    5-12-36; E-SW-S6; NW-NW-S7; 9-7-35; W-SE-S6;NE-NW-S7; 2-22-36
Jesse East, Mr NE-NW-S6; 2-28-40
Samuel Fox* W-SW-S6; 7-23-21
John Holmes* SE-NE-S7; 10-2-43
Henry Wade* NW-NE-S7; 1-14-39
Dillard Wilson* SW-NE-S7; 12-21-44
Robert Abercrombie* SE-NW-S7; 2-22-36
William McGill* E-SW-S7; 5-16-36; SW-SW-S7; 11-18-35
Dillard Wilson* SE-SE-S7; 1-7-39
Jordan Willson* NW-SE-S7; 12-9-44; SW-SE-S7; 5-18-37
Jesse Davis NE-S8; 9-24-16
Warner Davis NW-S8; 9-24-16
Robert Halladay SW-S8; n.d.
John Smith* SW-SE-S8; 10-5-43
Benjamin Holder* NE-NE-S9;12-10-40;SE-NW-S10;10-17-35;SW-NW-S10;
John Holder* SE-NE-S9; 4-2-40; NW-NW-S10; 4-25-37.   7-19-33
Nehemiah Melton* SE-SW-S9; 11-25-35
Zachariah McGill* SW-SW-S9; 1-7-39
Lynden Lowder* NE-SE, SW-SE-S9; 11-25-35
Lewis Jones* NE-S10; 7-4-31
John Giles* SE-SW-S10; 9-22-36; NW-NE-S15; 9-22-36
Benjamin Phipps E-SE-S10; 1-29-18
Reuben Holderman* W-SE-S10; 11-2-31.   S12; 4-22-26
Robert Anderson* E-NE-S11;NE-SE-S13;1-19-37;E-NW-S11;7-5-37;W-NE-/
Matthias Sears* SW-NE,E-SE-S11;2-23-37;E-SW,W-SE-S11;11-26-25;
    SW-SW-S11; 7-10-43; SW-S12; 7-5-17
Jubel Meadows* E-NE-S12; 4-29-22
Michael Sears NW-S12; 7-5-17
William Newcomb E-SE-S12; 7-9-17

Eliphalet Pearson* W-SE-S12;SE-SW-S15;7-23-35;SW-NW,NW-SW-S15;
William Kern* NE-S13; 5-3-22; NE-S14; 9-10-17.   11-21-44
Jesse Gray* E-SW-S13; 1-27-34; SW-SW-S25; 1-8-36
Joseph Rainbolt* NW-SW-S13; 7-30-32; SW-SE-S13; 1-8-36
James Milton Gray* SW-SW-S13; 3-7-37; NW-NW-S24; 3-7-37
William Humphreys Anderson* SE-SE, NW-SE-S13; 2-19-36
William Leakey NW-S13; 1-15-17
Mark Trueblood* E-NW-S14; 7-14-27
William Trueblood* NW-NW-S14; 1-26-37
Alexander Lamb* SW-NW-S14; 1-19-36
Thomas Hopper SW-S14; 6-25-17
Henry Scott, Ck E-SE-S14; 10-5-26
William Hopper W-SE-S14; 9-12-17
Phreborn Garrison Paugh* E-NE-S15; 12-14-38; SW-NE-S15; 1-5-37;
   N-NW-S15; 9-22-36; NW-SE-S15; 1-14-37
George Musser* SE-NW-S15; 4-12-37
John Peters* NE-SW-S15; 8-26-35
Mercer Owens* SW-SW-S15; 1-18-36
Abner Davis, Jeffersonville, Ind. E-SE-S15; 12-21-31
Elijah Scarbrough* SW-SE-S15; 9-26-35
Nathan Melton* SE-NE-S17; 11-25-35
Jacob Holmes* SW-NE-S17; 12-9-44
William Lambert Crooks* NE-SW-S17; 11-30-38; NW-SE-S17; 6-20-36
Michael (Melchert?) & Jeremiah Helmer* SE-SW-S17; 3-6-40
George McDaniel* W-SW-S17; 10-21-35
Isaac Odell* NE-NE-S17; 1-11-36; SE-SE-S17; 8-20-35
Jonathan Osborn NE-S18; 12-26-16
Charity Stone, Gn E-NW-S18; 2-15-45
Broker Wilson, Gn W-NW-S18; 12-27-33
Hiram Stone* NE-SE-S18; 6-2-46
Clark Rush* SW-SE-S18; 1-11-39
Azel Rush SW-S18; 4-10-18
Ralph Lowder* E-NE-S19; 5-14-39; NE-NW-S19; 8-10-35
William Myers* NW-NE-S19; 2-15-39; NE-SW-S19; 2-22-45
James Beaty* SE-SW-S19; 3-16-46;E-NE-S30;2-8-27;SW-NE-S30;10-13-
Daniel Mires* NW-SW-S19; 9-12-46.   / 35; SW-SE-S19;8-14-35
James Slown, Gn SW-SW-S19; 10-19-35; E-NW-S30; 10-19-35.
Ely Dye* E-SE-S19; 3-12-22
William McDowell* E-NE-S20; 2-13-30; NW-NE-S20; 12-23-44
Levi White* SW-NE-S20; 1-20-36
Sephrona Lyons* NW-NW-S20; 2-4-37
George Washington McReynolds* SE-SW-S20; 11-6-35.
Kenneth Dye* W-SW-S20; 9-4-40
John Brand Hayward* W-SE-S20; 2-9-39
Melchert (Michael?) & Jeremiah Helmer* E-NE-S21; 10-17-35;NW-NW-
Jeremiah Melton* NW-NE-S21; 3-18-34   S34; 3-22-41
John McDowell* SW-NE, NE-NW-S21; 3-18-34
Alexander Herron* SE-NW, SW-SW-S21; 12-1-35
Franklin Perry Stark* NW-NW-S21; 12-28-38
Isaac V. Buskirk E-SW-S21; 7-20-18
John Herron* NW-SW-S21; 2-6-36
Samuel Owens* E-SE-S21; 3-12-22
Joshua McDowell* W-SE-S21; 1-8-36
Fetter & Hughes NE-S22; 9-23-16

William Kerr E-NW-S22; 1-9-17; SE-S23; 9-10-17
John Pedigo* W-NW-S22; 2-16-30
Joseph Taylor SW, SE-S22; 9-23-16
Thomas Cobb* NE-NE-S23; SE-SE-S24; NE-NE-S25; 3-19-39
Doctor Bridwell* SE-NE-S23; 1-18-36; SW-NW-S24; 1-19-36
Benjamin Dawson W-NE-S23; 3-19-19
Archibald Wood NW-S23; 9-23-16
John Gey SW-S23; 2-26-17
Samuel Bennett* NE-NE-S24;8-5-34;SE-NE-S24;9-30-44;NW-SE-S24;3-5-
James Cartin* NW-NE, NE-NW-S24; 2-8-36   36
Vachiel Cravins* SW-NE-S24; 3-10-36
George Bridwell* SE-NW-S24; 2-7-34
Elisha Burton* NE-SW-S24; 2-7-34
John Harrison Smith, Ck SE-SW, SW-SE-S24; 10-15-36
Cuthbert Bridwell* W-SW-S24; 12-21-27
Robert Bennett, Mt NE-SE-S24; 5-19-37
Levi Sellars* SE-NE-S25; 2-7-37
Daniel Jefferson Walker, Ck W-NE, E-NW-S25; 9-14-36
Simpson Coats* W-NW-S25; 6-2-23
James Chestnut* E-SW-S25; 12-3-21
Robert Graham* NW-SW-S25; 12-14-38
Leonard Roy* E-SE-S25; 3-21-36; NE-NE-S36; 3-21-36
Benjamin Potter* NW-SE-S25; 2-19-36
John Chestnut* SW-SE-S25; 10-7-35
Nehemiah Odell* E-NE-S26; 1-11-36
Samuel Tincher* W-NE-S26; 4-23-28
Abraham Kern* E-NW-S26; 7-5-25
William Tincher W-NW-S26;12-17-17;NW-SW-S26;9-7-37;NW-SE-S26;1-25-
William Preston* NE-SW, SW-SW-S26; 1-9-36   36
Shelton Wood Preston* SE-SW-S26; 8-12-37
Jacob Sears* E-SE-S26; 9-16-31
William Cuppy* SW-SE-S26; 3-29-36
Joseph Odell* E-NE-S27; 10-17-31
John Vestal* W-NE, E-NW, W-NW-S27; 6-7-24
Ensle Odell* E-SW-S27; 2-13-30; NE-SW-S34; 1-11-36
Josias Athon* NW-SW-S27; 1-15-36
Ezekiel Short* SW-SW-S27; 3-29-36
John Short* E-SE-S27; 9-4-35
John Roberts* W-SE-S27; 7-13-25; W-NE-S34; 9-5-30
Reuben Davis NE-S28; 10-3-16
Harrison Beasley* NE-NW, E-SE-S28; NE-NW-S33; 12-1-35
Isaac Herron* SE-NW-S28; 4-10-33
Cornelius D. Weld & Ashor Fowler Scranton NW-NW-S28; 1-11-36
Silas Beasley* SW-NW-S28;11-13-33;SE-SW-S30;6-27-38;W-NE-S33;2-6-36
Martin Smith* W-SE-S28; 12-29-29
Lawson Oliphant* NE-NE-S29; 2-15-45
Orange Dye* SE-NE-S29; 2-5-45; SW-SE-S29; 7-13-40
Kenneth Dye* NW-NE-S29;2-11-45;SW-NE-S29;3-9-36;E-SW-S29;1-7-39;
John Armstrong* NW-S29; 9-15-17;NW-NW-S33;8-5-35. /NW-SW-S29;8-4-35
Abraham Waggoner* SW-SW-S29; 10-2-35
Levi Butcher* NE-SE-S29; 5-21-44
John Luther Short* SE-SE-S29; 8-14-35; SW-NW-S33; 3-16-46
Thomas Ferguson, Gn NW-NE-S30;7-22-35; of*, NW-SE-S29; 4-1-37
Alfred Short* NE-SW-S30; 3-16-46

Ralston Ferguson* W-NW-S30;3-23-46;E-SE-S30;8-27-31;NW-SE-S30;8-5-
Andrew Selsor, Gn NW-SW-S30; 8-5-34   34
Abraham Waggoner, Gn SW-SW-S30; 11-11-36; SW-SE-S30; 12-13-36;
   NE-NE, NW-NW-S31; 1-14-39
Ari Armstrong* SE-NE-S31;12-17-44;NE-NE-S32;1-7-37;SE-NE-S32;1-11-
Jonathan Bridges* NW-NE-S31; 6-12-33   34
Jonathan Waggoner, Gn SW-NE-S31; 1-14-39
Samuel Steel E-NW-S31; 11-18-17
Isaac Titsworth Bridges, Gn SW-NW-S31;8-5-34; NW-SW-S31; 12-11-34
John Dunkin E-SW-S31; 9-23-17
John Roberts Stone, Gn SW-SW-S31; 8-5-34
Sampson Coats & Samuel Simon SE-S31; 6-24-17
Robert Ferguson* NW-NE-S32; 10-5-35
Semer Cobb SW-S32; 9-23-16
John Dishman SE-S32; 9-10-18
Thomas Hurt (Hunt?)* E-NE-S33;1-28-39;NW-SW-S33;2-11-45;NW-SW-S34;
Thomas Hunt (Hurt?)* SE-NW-S33; 7-3-48   12-6-36
John Hurt* E-SW-S33;2-11-45;SE-SE-S33;7-23-33;SW-SW-S34;2-11-36.
Thomas Armstrong* SW-SW-S33; 2-11-36.
Samuel Taylor* NE-SE-S33; 9-16-37. James Bunch* SE-SE-S35;2-6-36
Elijah Crews* NW-SE-S33;11-19-36.   Samuel L. Sayre* NW-SE-S35;
Zachariah Loveall* SW-SE-S33;11-2-38.   12-26-44
Josias Fletcher Athon* NE-NE-S34;11-6-37.   John Witcher Phipps*
Sophronia Crooke* SE-NE-S34;2-5-45.   SE-NE-S36;11-29-36
Caleb Odell* NE-NW-S34;8-20-35.   William Burton* W-NE-S36;11-
Isaac Odell* SE-NW-S34;1-5-37.   2-26
Sarah Gray* SW-NW-S34;2-4-39.   Adam Hostedler NW-S36;7-9-17
Josiah Pierce* SE-SW-S34;7-29-44.   Jackson Leroy Moore* NE-SW-
Jesse Hodges* NE-SE-S34;2-7-38.   S36; 12-28-44
Abram Knott* NW-SE-S34;3-2-36.
William Riley Parker* SW-SE-S34;6-28-38. John William Adamson*
John Cuppy* E-NE-S35;3-25-24.   W-SE-S36;1-26-36
Alexander Sutherland* W-NE-S35;12-4-44.   Uriah Moore* SE-SW-S36;
John Pierce* NE-NW-S55;1-28-39.   8-14-37;SW-SW-S36;
Joseph Athon* NW-NW-S35;3-31-37.   8-14-44
Ralph Graves Norvell* SW-NW-S35;12-5-44.
Samuel Sayre* E-SW-S35;12-26-44.
Milton Short* NW-SW-S35;Feb.1845;SW-SW-S35;3-16-46.
John Bunch* NE-SE-S35;10-23-37;SW-SE-S35;4-4-36.

RELINQUISHMENTS

John Goodwine NE-S10;3-30-18   William Kerr W-NW-S22;1-9-17
William Newcomb W-SE-S12;7-9-17   Henry Speed NW-S28;NE-S29;
Thomas Buskirk SW-S13;4-10-16   9-28-16
William Hopper E-SE-S14;9-12-17   John Dunkin W-SW-S31;9-23-17;
Isaac V. Buskirk W-SW-S21;7-20-18   7-4-29
William Tincher E-NW-S26;12-17-17 Lewis Sentenay W-NW-S33;9-15-
Marquis Knight NE-S27;9-23-16   18; 7-4-29
Joseph Taylor NW-S27;9-23-16
John Dotton SE-S15;12-12-17
Samuel Steel W-NW-S31;11-18-17
Warner Davis SW-S4;10-3-16
Benjamin Phipps W-SE-S10;1-29-18

T 1 N, R 3 W

Archibald Elkins* SW-NE, E-NW,NE-SW-S1; 10-12-39;W-SW-S1;6-13-40
Jonathan Lindley, Sr., Or NE-NE-S2;6-11-33;W-NE,E-NW-S2;6-11-38
Thomas Burnett, Or NW-NW-S2; 6-21-39
John Freeman, Or SW-NW-S2;1-30-37; of*, E-NE-S3; 10-3-54
Samuel Newton Lindley, Or NE-SW, NW-SE-S2; 7-22-39
Stanford Freeman* NW-SW-S2; 3-12-38
Anton Crabhorn, Ln W-NE-S3; 9-22-57
Albert Quackinbush* E-NW-S3; 8-20-55
George Stanfield* SE-NE-S4; 2-6-38
Harrison Lindley, Or NE-SE-S4; 10-25-40
James Hawkins* SW-NE-S5; 6-7-36
Daniel Edwards* NE-NW-S7; 8-23-37; NW-NW-S7; 6-21-54
Nancy A. Brewer, Lv SW-NW, SE-SW-S7; 10-19-54
John Simmons* N-SE-S7;8-7-39;NE-SW-S7;8-18-57; latter adds Jr.
Daniel Pace, Db SW-NE-S12; 3-12-39; NE-SW-S12; 5-3-39

RELINQUISHMENTS

Moses Simmons NE-S5; 9-11-19
William & Michael Deniston SE-S7; 10-18-19
Johnston Farriss NW-S8; 12-17-19
Enos Morland NE-S2; 2-8-19
William Robison NE-S3; 11-17-17; 7-4-29

T 1 N, R 4 W

William Bennett Connell, Or NE-NE-S1; 1-7-37
James Hawkins* SE-NE-S1; 3-8-39
Harrison Connell, Db NW-NE, NE-NW-S1; 1-7-37
Robert McNutt W-NW-S1; 1-26-19
William Bisben Pine, Ps SE-SW-S1; 11-12-40
Samuel Wininger* NW-NE-Efr-S1; 12-11-56
John Wininger, Or SW-NE-Efr-S1; 8-15-36
Caleb Reinhart* NWfr-NE-Efr-S1; 2-10-30
Frederick Shotts* S-Efr-S1; 5-21-19; E-NW-S12; 10-20-20
William Ballow Wfr-S1; Nfr-S11; 9-23-14
Samuel Fitzgerald & Abraham Wise NEfr-Efr-S3; 8-22-18
Elisha Kilburn NE-NWfr-S3; 12-9-33
John Waggoner SE-NWfr-S3; 10-30-39
Henry Kilbourn* W-NWfr-S3; 3-29-52; MLW 73496
John Kilburn* NE-SW-S3; 5-26-49; SE-SW-S3; 12-7-36; SW-SW-S3;
    10-7-54; NW-SE-S3; 10-8-53; MLW 55699
Thomas M. Gibson NW-SW-S3; 2-4-53; MLW 3163
William Harbison* SW-SE-S3; 12-9-33
John Meads SE-NE, NE-SE-S4; 1-29-53; MLW 19962
Seperate Hendrickson SW-NE,SE-NW,NE-SW,NW-SE-S4;7-7-52. MLW 8709
John W. Nance* SE-SE-S4; 10-6-54
James Rankin Steel* SE-NE-S5;3-16-48;NE-NE-S5;8-23-52. MLW 55808
James Street* NE-NW-S5; 10-11-51
William R. Inman* NW-NW-S5; 10-9-54
Heddy Bradbury* SW-SW-S5; 9-10-50; SW-NW-S5; 4-22-51
Richard Gilson SE-S6; 8-14-49; MLW 32825

Abednigo White Inman* W-SE-S7; 8-14-49; NE-NE-S7; 4-1-50; E-NW-
   S8; 8-31-52; MLW 36831; NE-NW-Nfr-S19; 4-4-50; SE-NW-Nfr-S19;
   10-6-54; SW-NW-Nfr-S19; 11-24-53
Walter W. Pangburn NE-SE,W-NE,SE-NE-S7;11-8-50; MLW 7628
Nathaniel Ledgerwood* NW-NE-S8; 10-6-54; NW-NE, NE-NW-S9; 9-22-
   52; MLW 12487
John Dillon* SW-NE-S8; 6-6-51
Anthony Hendrixon W-NW-S8; W-SW-S8; 3-24-52; MLW 7943
Jacob Fishor NE-SW, NE-SE, W-SE-S8; 2-7-52; MLW 6980
Andrew J. Allen SE-SW-S8; 1-25-53; MLW 42392
Drewry Hembree* SE-SE-S8; 10-9-54; NW-SW-S9; 2-16-53; MLW 172
Abel T. Morgan, Da E-NE,SW-NE,SE-NW,S-SW,W-SE-S9; 10-2-54
John Hembree* NE-SW-S9; 1-17-51
Anthony Stroot NE-SE-S9; 4-23-52; MLW 21431
John Lemmon* SE-SE-S9;4-18-37; Lot 5-S-N-Wfr-S15; 1-12-39
Willis Hubbs, Db Efr-S10; 3-10-32
Marshall Key Wfr-S10; 9-23-18
William Jones & Frederick Shotts Lot 1-Sfr-S11; 4-30-18
Ezekiel Rutherford* Lot 2-Sfr-S11; 10-14-35
Ephraim Sutton* SE-SW-FrS11; 2-4-37
Mark Rutherford* Lot 2-N-N-Wfr-S15; 10-14-35
George Bates, Fl S-Wfr-S15; 12-9-33
James McElwain N-NE-Nfr-S19; 9-18-51; MLW 10751
Phebe Farr, Pi SE-NE-Nfr-S19;E-NW,SW-NW-Wfr-S20; 10-3-54
Robert Harris (Farris?) SW-NE-Nfr-S19; 9-19-54
John Kyle NW-NW-Nfr-S19; 12-11-51; MLW 16464
John T. Throop, Or SWfr-Nfr-S19; 6-13-57
William Hays* E-SE-Nfr-S19; Nfr-S30; 3-11-30
John Gwin, Hr W-SE-Nfr-S19;3-14-31;SE-Wfr-S20;5-12-32;Nfr-S29;
Edmund Gwin Sfr-S19; 9-29-17   6-20-31
John Mead N-NE-Wfr-S20; 1-29-53; MLW 11023
George Holmes Gwin* S-NE-Wfr-S20; 6-9-36
John Chattin NW-NW-Wfr-S20; 2-15-53; MLW 24324
John Porter SW-Wfr-S20; 5-23-18
Edwin Ulysses Blagrave, Da Wfr-Wfr-S20; 6-17-36

RELINQUISHMENTS

Samuel Fitzgerald & Abraham Wise SW-Wfr, SE-Wfr-S3; 8-22-18
William Jones & Frederick Shotts Efr-S10; Lot 2-Sfr, SW-Sfr,
   SE-Sfr-S11; 4-30-18
Frederick Shotts SW-S1;6-3-19;NWfr-Efr, Efr-S3; 5-21-19
Robert McNutt E-NW-S1; 6-26-19

T 1 N, R 5 W

William Edgar McIntosh, Oh W-NE-S1; 2-24-45
John Collins, Da SW-SW-S1; 6-17-39
Thomas Steel, Kn NE-SE-S1; 4-16-38
Joshua McIntosh, Oh W-SE-S1; 2-24-45
Michael Abel, Da SE-NW-S1; 4-28-38
Robert Foster W-NW-S1; 3-5-19
Joseph Baker Abel, Da SW-SW-S1; 10-17-37
John McIntosh E-SE-S1; 2-24-45 ; of Oh

Joel Bradbury* NW-NE-S12; 10-3-42
Emanuel Davis NE-NW-S12; 4-4-51
Israel R. Waters SE-NW-S12; 5-9-70
Margaret McCord NW-NW-S12; 1-14-40
William Oneal SW-NW, NW-SW-S12; 9-19-51; MIW 6020
Abednigo White Inman* NE-NE-Nfr-S24;8-14-49;SE-NE-Nfr-S24;10-6-54
Hillary Mattingly, Da NW-NE-Nfr-S24; 10-4-54
John Davison, Pi SW-NE-Nfr-S24; 11-29-59; MIW 40714
Elias Thrasher, Po Lots 1-2; W-NWfr-Nfr-S24; 3-23-37
Isaac Harris SWfr-Nfr, SEfr-Nfr-S24; 4-21-17

RELINQUISHMENTS

Wesley Wallis NE-S13; 5-7-16
John Davis SW-S13; 5-7-16
Joseph Hays SE-S13; 2-2-18
Isaac Harris NE-Nfr, NW-Nfr-S24; 4-21-17
William Jones NE-S12; 11-10-18

T 2 N, R 3 W

George H. French, Or NE-NE-S1; 9-29-38
Earl Douglass* SE-NE-S3; 5-22-37; NE-SW-S3; 1-13-40
Joseph Denny* W-NE-S3; 8-25-25
Samuel Batchelor* E-NW-S3; 8-17-27
A. G. Hegoman, Washington, D.C. W-NW-S3; 9-26-76
Charles Morrison* SE-SW-S3; 1-13-40
Samuel Hopper* NE-SE-S3; 11-10-37
Thomas Robbins, Kn E-NE-S4; 9-13-31
Moses Norman* W-NE-S4; 9-8-31
Lewis Gammon* NE-NW-S4;3-13-37;SE-SE-S5;10-19-38;SW-NW-S10;10-31-38
Nancy Gammon* SE-NW-S4; 9-25-33
Drury Gammon, Lw E-SW-S4; 10-28-23
Joseph Campbell, Mr W-SE-S4; 10-23-37
William Nash* E-SE-S4; 9-8-31
Lyman C. Austin* W-SE-S4; 10-19-24
Nathan Fisher E-NE-S5; 5-8-20
John B. Winstandley, Fd W-NE-S5; 5-2-55; NE-S6; 5-9-55
John Wesley Albright* SE-NW, NE-SW-S5; 6-2-36
James Nichols Mullican* SE-SW-S5; 2-11-39
Hiram Pepper, Kn NW-SW-S5; 2-13-37
James Southern, Or SW-SW-S5; NE-NE-S14; 10-19-38
Hiram Kirk, Or NE-SE-S5; 10-22-38
Jesse Martin* W-SE-S5; 9-19-31
Enos Morclan* NE-NW-S6; 12-26-36
David Burrett Summers* E-SW-S6; 11-26-38; W-SE-S6; 2-11-39
Charles Forse* NW-SW-S6; 9-2-39
Harden Gammon* SW-SW-S6; 11-10-36
Daniel Southern, Or NE-SE-S6; 10-19-38
Thomas Smith* NW-NW-S7; 11-24-38
Terrence McManus* SW-NW-S7; 8-1-40
William Martin* NE-NE-S8; 3-2-39
Elihu Stout, Kn NE-NE-S9; 10-1-39
Lyman Godfrey Austin* SE-NE-S9; NE-SE-S10; 10-12-38

William Way* W-NE, NE-SW-S9; 12-18-38; E-NW-S9; 12-19-36; NW-NW,
   SW-SE-S9; 3-10-36
Hannah Way* SE-SW-S9; 1-19-38
William Spencer* NE-NE, SW-NE-S10; 5-27-39
Reuben Day* SE-NE-S10; SW-NW-S11; 7-10-37
Charles Morrison* NE-NW-S10; 1-13-40; NW-SE-S10; 9-11-38
Charles Mortimer Hamner, Fd E-SW-S10; 11-6-37
John, Samuel, & William Jacob Wise, Kn W-SW-S10;10-12-38; W-SW-
Miles Shepard* S-SE-S10; 5-13-39   S11; 10-19-38
Jacob Moulder, Or E-NW-S11; 7-10-37; of*, E-SW-S11; 1-25-39
John P. Davis* NW-SE-S11; 8-21-39
William Davis* SW-SE-S11; 10-19-38
Wesley Norman* SW-NW-S12; 2-25-39
Daniel W. Southern* NW-SW-S12; 10-13-54
William Danny* SW-SW-S12; 3-12-39
John Shaw, Or NE-SE-S12; 2-19-38; E-NE-S13; 8-10-37
John McCracken, Or SE-SE-S12; 10-29-38
James Clark, Or SW-NE-S13; 1-15-39; NE-SE, W-SE-S13; 9-12-37
William Kirby, Or W-NW-S13; 10-5-38
James Wilson* SE-SE-S13; 10-25-38
Anna Goldsmith* SE-NE-S14; 2-21-37
James Corson Gill* NW-NE-S14; 10-20-38
John Gill, Or SW-NE, SW-NW-S14; 9-13-38; NE-NW-S14; 10-24-38
James Morrison* SE-NW-S14; 4-9-36; NW-NW-S14; 10-19-38
John Kenley, Or W-SW-S14; 9-5-28
William Day* SW-NE, NE-SW-S15; 2-25-39
Ira Harding & Thomas Billings* SW-NW-S15; 9-27-41
Joseph Spencer* NE-SE-S15; 4-9-36; NW-SE-S15; 5-21-36
William Frazier Bessie, Or SE-SE-S15; 5-7-36
Wyatt Boen* NE-SW-S17; 11-11-39
Elizabeth Cooper, Or SW-SW-S17; 3-29-38
Henry Tomlinson* SE-SW-S18; NW-NW-S19; 12-11-38
John Robert Tomlinson* NE-SE, W-SE-S19; SW-NW-S20; 11-28-38
John A. Smith, Or SE-NE, NE-SE-S20; 8-5-34
George Shirley, Or S-SE-S20; 8-5-34
Henry Shirley, Or NW-SE-S20; 10-12-36; NE-SW-S22; 10-1-32
Charles Bruner* SW-NW-S21; 2-27-34
Henry Miller, Or E-SW-S21; 7-12-36
Thomas Butler* NW-SW-S21; 6-7-36
John Waldrip, Or SE-SE-S21; NW-NW-S27; 5-29-37
Martin Neel* SW-SE-S21; 10-20-37
James Kenley* NE-NE-S22; 4-9-36
William Frazer Bressie, Or SE-NE-S22; 5-7-36
Alfred Kellums, Or SE-NW, W-NW-S22; 8-23-37
Andrew Abel, Or W-SW-S22; 4-17-37
Lewis Jones, Mr SE-S22; SE-SE, W-SE-S23; 5-4-37
Jacob Rice, Hr W-NE-S23; 5-22-38
Garrett Shirley, Or NW-NW-S23; 3-11-36; SW-NW-S23; 5-18-36
Alexander Clark, Or S-SW-S23; 2-21-37; NE-NE-S26; 5-20-39
Jacob Brown Lindley, Or NE-SE-S23; NE-NW-S25; 10-1-36
Charles Mortimer Hamner, Fd NE-NE-S24;E-NE,SW-NE-S25; 11-6-37
James Wilson, Or SE-NE-S24; 6-29-36; of*, NW-NE-S24; 10-25-38
Zachariah Lindley, Or SW-SE-S24; NW-NE-S25; 6-16-35; of*, SW-NE-
   S24; 7-30-41; SE-SW-S24; 11-16-37

William Harrison Lindley, Or SE-NW,NE-SW-S24;6-16-35;SE-NW-S25;2-9-
Jonathan Lindley, Or SW-NW,NW-SW-S24;8-19-35;NW-SE-S24;1-15-39. 39
George Winsor, Ws SW-S25; 8-22-37
William Berry & Washington Trumble, Or SE-SE-S25; 11-21-37
William Clark, Or S-NE-S26; 6-11-38
Jonathan Clark, Or NW-NE, NE-NW-S26; 2-21-37
Margaret E. Powell* E-SW-S26; 10-18-54
William Stanfield, Or NW-SW-S26; 10-31-37; SW-SW-S26; 6-29-37
Samuel Clark, Or NE-SE-S26; 5-20-39
Isaac Joseph E-SW-S27; 7-10-57; MLW 33416
Abner Baker NE-S28; 3-24-18; of*, NW-SE-S28; 3-14-39
Thomas Martin E-NW-S28; 10-14-16
Lyman Godfrey Austin* W-NW-S28; 9-25-33; SW-S28; 9-30-16
Alfred Freeman* E-NE-S29; 10-31-37
Thomas Roby* W-NW-S29; 5-21-57
Washington Watson E-SW-S29; 3-25-16
Jackson Noakes* SE-NW-S30; 12-11-38
Henry Loyd* NW-NW-S30; 10-20-37
John Croan* SW-NW-S30; 6-12-38; NW-SW-S30; 1-7-39
Bedford Shelmire, Adams Co., Miss. E-SW-S30; 6-13-37
Jeremiah P. Hinton* NE-NW-S32; 3-18-39
Joseph Neff NE-SW-S32; 11-21-54; MLW 61109
Jesse F. Neff, Coshocton Co., O. SE-SW-S32; 11-21-54
Joel G. Jones* NW-SW-S33; 6-3-57
James Jones SW-SW-S33; 3-6-52;#of*, NE-SE-S33; 1-26-37; #MLW48212
Alfred Freeman* E-NE-S34;8-21-37;SE-NW-S34;3-3-37;SW-NW-S34;
Allen Clinton* NE-NW-S35; 5-6-58   12-24-38
Harrison Connel, Or SE-NW-S35; 4-28-52
John Freeman, Or NW-NW-S35; 8-10-36
Florian Bartl* SW-NW, NW-SW-S35; 7-14-37
Harrison Lindly* SW-SW-S35; 6-11-38
McKinsy Wolfington, Or SE-NE-S36; 7-20-39; SW-NE-S36; 2-16-37;
   E-SE-S36; 12-29-35

RELINQUISHMENTS

Frederick Shotes E-NW-S5; 10-9-17
Washington Watson NE-S29; 6-29-16; W-SW-S29; 3-25-16
Stephen R. Yelchehers (?) W-SE-S29; 10-26-16; see Gilcrease below
Michael Pippin E-NW-S3; 10-10-17.
Thomas Martin W-NW-S28; 10-14-16.   James Jones E-SE-S33;4-18-18
Hurbrit Marshall NW-S35;2-24-15.
John Watson NW-S29;8-17-14;3-3-30.   Johnson Raney SE-S20;9-30-15
Clement Horsey NE-S4;2-17-17;7-4-29.
Stephen R. Gilcrease E-SE-S29; 10-26-16; 7-4-29
John Peck NE,W-S20;6-25-16;7-4-29; N,S-S24; S25; 6-25-16;7-4-29;
   SW, SE-S23; 7-5-16; 7-4-29
Jeremiah Jones NE-S34; 6-29-16

T 2 N, R 4 W

Matthias Shotts NE-S1; 5-10-19
Charles C. Root, Jefferson Co., Ky. NW-S1; 12-23-31
John Crockwell Clark, Kn E-SW-S1; 7-9-39

William Burtch, Kn W-SW-S1; 10-12-38
Enos Morelan* NE-SE-S1; 10-16-38
Terrence McManus* SE-SE-S1; 4-3-40
John Riley* W-SE-S1; 3-9-40
Charles F. Downing E-NE-S2; 8-3-31
Walter Franklin* NE-NW-S2; 3-18-41
John Dennis Woolverton, Vincennes, Ind. W-NW-S2; 11-22-32
John, Samuel, & William Jacob Wise, Kn SE-S2; 6-28-39
Franklin Mears & William Lewis E-NE-S3; 4-19-30
Thomas Owens, Fd E-NW-S3; 2-23-38
John M. Prentiss W-NW-S3; 10-2-19
Samuel Terry SW-S3; 5-15-16
Robert Smith* NE-SE-S3; 9-2-37
Abraham Mericle* SW-SE-S3; 7-6-39
Whitfield Force* NE-NW-S4; 1-29-35
Asa Martin* SE-NW-S4; 10-4-38; NE-SW-S4; 10-26-37
James Lonsdale, Ck W-NW-S4; 7-25-37
Charles Brewster, Kn SE-SW-S4; 6-27-39
George Washington Rathbone & Henry Faunt Le Roy, Kn W-SW-S4; 6-27-39
Robert Kennedy & Elisha Kilburn NE-S4; 9-6-14
George C. Hunter, Jefferson Co., Ky. SE-NE-Nfr-S8; 7-20-53
John Kelley, Lawrence Co., Ill. NW-NE-Nfr-S8; 1-25-36
George Lonsdale* SW-NE-Nfr-S8;4-29-39;SEfr-Nfr-S8; 7-25-37
Joseph Teverbaugh* N-NW-Nfr-S8; 12-12-33
Abraham Teverbaugh* Lots 3-4-S-NW-Nfr-S8;12-5-34;SWfr-Nfr-S8; 1-25-36
Frederick Shotts Nfr-S9; 11-17-15; Efr-S10; 10-20-14.
John F. Mansfield Sfr-S9; Wfr-S10; Wfr-S15; 12-10-07
George Harris, Or NE-NE-S11; 6-28-39
Thomas Smith* NE-NE-S12; 8-24-38
John Riley* SE-NE, W-NE-S12; 10-10-39
James Waldrip, Or SE-NW-S12; 8-9-39
Joseph Abel* SW-NW-S12; 8-9-39
Alvan Cushman Efr-S15; Efr-S27; Efr-S28; 5-17-17
John Collins NE-NE-S17; 8-15-53; MLW 57162.   S17;10-19-53
John Downey, Da SE-NW-S17;9-13-53; of*,SE-NE,W-NE-S17;10-3-54;NE-N
Jabez Reaves Art, Jefferson Co., Ky. W-NW-S17; 3-3-43
William White Jackman* SE-SW-S17; 4-3-49
James Beatty NW-SW-S17; 12-15-53; MLW 41900
Sylvanus C. Sutton* SE-SE-S17; 9-30-54; NE-NE-S20; 12-23-53
David A. Kelly* NW-SE-S17; 4-28-57
Mason J. Sherman NE-NE-S18;7-25-53;MLW 36143; NW-NW-S18;11-17-53;
Daniel Harris S-NE-S18; 10-25-52; MLW 4443.   MLW 27055
Lemuel Kelley* NW-NE-S18; 3-13-49; SE-NW-S18; 9-11-50
David Cardin Burris* NE-NW-S18; 8-19-50
Felix Holland & John Mullin, Armstrong Co., Pa. SW-NW-S18;8-9-48
Joseph A. Chandler SE-SW, SW-SE-S18; 12-21-53; MLW 12858
Thomas J. Brooks SW-SW-S18; 2-19-53; MLW 81668
Nathaniel R. Hunt* SE-NE-S19; 5-12-54
Josiah Hunt* SE-NW, NW-SE-S19; 2-4-37
Benjamin Creny* SW-NW, NE-SW-S19; 1-3-44
Mary A. Hatch SE-SW-S19; 4-1-52; MLW 42437
Teague Dickerson, Bullet Co., Ky. SW-SW-S19; 3-23-39
John Bousman* SW-SE-S19; 12-25-37; Wfr-S22; 2-8-37
Nathaniel Jennings NW-NE-S20; 1-17-53; MLW 27724

William W. Jackman NW-S20; 11-28-48; MLW 33967
John Mushrush* SW-S20; 6-2-43
Harvey McMilling SW-SE-S20; NW-NE-S29; 1-17-53; MLW 19140
William Terrel* W-NE-S21; 10-7-54
William Armstrong, Jefferson Co., O. NE-NW-S21; 11-30-48
William Ritter* SE-NW-S21; 9-10-50
John C. Walker W-NW-S21; 10-14-53; MLW 21079
George W. Boner* NE-SW-S21; 1-10-53; MLW 72620; NW-SW-S21; 2-16-49
Mary Hunt* SW-SW-S21; 6-6-49
Samuel Baugh E-SE-S21; 10-2-52; MLW 22424
William Jane* NW-SE-S21; 10-9-54
John F. Bayard, Jr. SW-SE-S21; 9-24-52; MLW 58337
Isaac Haller* SE-NE-S25; 12-17-38; SE-SE-S25; 6-12-38
Jacob Leedes, Wb SW-NE-S25; 11-7-37
Thomas Daily* NE-SW-S25; 1-18-48
Richard Hendrickson* SE-SW-S25; 3-3-49; SW-SW-S25; 6-19-37
William Jacob Wise, Kn NE-SE-S25; 12-24-38
Art Lord, Wabash Co., Ill. NW-SE-S25; 6-8-37
David Watson* NE-NE-S26; 2-5-38
John Irvin, Kn NE-SE-S26; 9-6-37; of*, SE-NE-S26; 7-25-39
Manoah Sullivan, Or N-NE-Wfr, S-NE-Wfr-S28; 9-12-36
John F. Redman E-NW-Wfr-S28; 8-14-54; MLW 51316
Lewis Moore* SE-SW-Wfr-S28; 9-5-36
Jeremiah Brown* NE-NE-S29; 12-21-53
Samuel Sutton* SE-NE-S29; 2-21-50
Jesse Wilkerson Cummings SW-NE-S29; 10-9-52; MLW 47829; NW-SE-
    S29; 10-9-52; MLW 71642
Robert Gilkerson* NE-NW-S29; 2-5-51; SE-NW-S29; 4-16-49
Joseph Allen McCord, Da SE-SW-S29; 5-5-47
William Warder Gillock* NE-SE-S29;3-26-50; SW-SE-S29; 1-21-48
John Gilkison, Jefferson Co., O. NE-S30; 3-15-39
William Truelove NW, SW-S30; 10-31-18
William B. Gilkison, Jefferson Co., O. SE-S30; 3-15-39
Burr Morris* NE-NE-S31; 10-7-54
William Cochran* NW-NW-S31; 2-15-44
Thomas Elmore* SW-NW-S31; 3-13-48
Sarah Tewell (Terrell?) NW-NE-S32; 1-13-53; MLW 75858; SW-NE-S32;
    1-13-53; MLW 72790. See below   above
Sarah Ann Duell (Terrell? Tewell?) E-NW-S32;3-5-52;MLW 25546; see/
John Brown SW-NW-S32;SW-NW-S32;9-9-53;MLW 89342; NW-SW-S32;12-23-
William Hardy* NE-SW-S32; 10-2-54   52; MLW 64247
John T. Markman* NE-SE-S32; 10-7-54
Asa White* SE-SE-S32; 7-26-52; SE-NWfr-Sfr-S33; 11-29-36; NE-SW-
    Sfr-S33; 9-2-52; MLW 1287; NW-SW-Sfr-S33; 12-26-49
Richard Weaver Nfr-S33; Nfr-S34; 7-22-18
Lewis Moore N-NEfr-Sfr-S33; 10-2-51; MLW 14904
Anthony Loyd* S-NEfr-Sfr-S33; 10-17-54
John Moore* NE-NWfr-Sfr-S33; 5-17-36
Alexander Robertson* SE-SW-Sfr, SW-SW-Sfr-S33; 10-10-54
Lloyd Rutherford E-SE-Sfr-S33;2-7-53;MLW 11039;SW-SE-Sfr-S33;3-8-
Eliphalet Haskins* NW-SE-Sfr-S33;4-24-57;S-Sfr-S34;4-17-47.   54
Seth White* E-Sfr-S34; 7-15-51
John Waggoner* NWpt-Sfr-S34; 4-8-47
George Waggoner, Db NW-NE-S35; 7-17-37

Grandison Farris* SW-NE-S35; 8-29-36
Elisha Hoskins* NE-NW-S35; 8-29-36
Nelson Watson* SE-NW-S35; 11-23-37
William Golding Green* NW-NW-S35; 4-3-39
James Green* SW-NW-S35; 1-12-39
Thomas James Conell* SE-SE-S35; 8-10-39
Gilbert Griswold SW-S35; 8-28-16
Simeon Hendrixson* NE-NW-S36; 8-22-37
Susannah Connell, Or S-SW-S36; 2-3-37
Thomas Tillory Treadway, Db NW-SE-S36; 11-1-37

RELINQUISHMENTS

Thomas Moorehead & Robert Taylor, Jr. Wfr-S7; Wfr-S34; 9-23-18
Nathaniel F. Ruggles SW-S11; 5-10-19
John M. Prentiss E-NW-S3; 10-2-19
Levi James SE-S3; 11-7-17
William Harris NW-S4; 1-3-18
Robert Gardner NWfr,.SWfr-S5; 9-18-17
Samuel Fitzgerald & M. Day SW-Wfr, SEfr-Wfr-S6; 8-22-18
John C. Wenzel Wfr-S15; Wfr-S22; 6-4-19; Sfr-S33; 5-24-19
Frederick Shotts SW-S4; 3-12-19; SE-S4; 3-12-19
David Doan & Ransom Davis NE-S25; 7-8-17
John Smith NE-S35; 7-19-19
Lyman G. Austin NW-S35; 8-28-16
William Mattox W-SE-S30; 12-4-19
Doyer Fitch W-NW-S2; 8-26-19; 3-3-30
Mathias Shotts NE-S1; 5-10-19; 7-4-29
Frederick Shotts NW-S1; 10-10-17; 7-4-29; E-NE-S2; 9-16-17; 7-4-
    29; Efr-S7; Nfr-S8; 9-3-16; 7-4-29
Jesse Shelmire SE-S35; 11-22-19; 7-4-29

T 2 N, R 5 W

Abraham Tevenbaugh NE-S1; 10-10-15
Cornelius Ridge NW-S1; 3-25-18
Jonathan Raney* NE-SW-S1; 3-15-39
Thomas Hodge* SE-SW-S1; 11-6-50
James Raney* NW-SW-S1; 3-15-51; E-NW-S12; 3-27-39
John Cold E-SE-S1; 2-29-16
Patrick McMahan* NW-SE-S1; 11-24-37; SW-SE-S1; 11-5-40
John Hosmer & Ezekiel Porter NE, SE-S12; 12-16-17
Michael Downey* NW-NW-S12; 6-25-51; SW-NW-S12; 3-27-50
Philip McGovran* E-SW, NW-SW-S12; NW-S13; 4-11-39
Lucy Collins, Da SW-SW-S12; 8-17-38
Andrew Ward* NE-NE-S13; 2-13-49
Samuel Hatch* SE-NE-S13; 8-21-40
John McGovran* W-NE-S13; 4-23-39
Mary Shircliff NE-SW, NW-SE-S13; 11-11-51; MLW 12137
William Dunn* SE-SW, W-SW-S13; 4-29-41
Michael Truelove* NE-SE-S13; 1-30-37
Patrick McCrisikin, Alleghany Co., Pa. SE-SE-S13; 5-24-41;NE-NE-
William Truelove* SW-SE-S13; 12-11-32.   S24; 5-24-41
Edward McCresaken* SE-NE-S24; 1-14-42

Thomas Gillock* E-SE-S24; 4-29-41
George Hartford, Jefferson Co., O. W-SE-S24;NW-NE-S25; 6-3-44
James Cannon, Jr.* SW-NE-S25; 3-7-50; NW-SE-S25; 7-5-48
William Cannon* E-NW, SW-NW-S25; 2-6-45
Henry Peachee, Da NW-NW-S25; 10-31-40
Jabez Reaves Art, Fleming Co., Ky. SW-S25; 9-21-40
John Cannon* NE-SE-S25; 12-6-40
Fielder Gillock* SE-SE-S25; 3-17-51
Elias Arvin SW-SE-S25; 2-14-52; MLW 34722
James Cochran* NE-NE-S36; 8-9-39
Robert Workman E-NW-S36; 7-19-52; MLW 38379
George W. Alford, Da SW-NW-S36; 5-27-39
James Barr Gilley E-SW-S36; 7-10-52

RELINQUISHMENTS

Thomas Moorhead & John Moorhead SE-S13; 9-23-18
Whitfield Force SW-S1; 2-5-20
John Gold W-SE-S1; 2-29-16
J. Hosmer & E. Porter SW-S12;12-16-17;7-4-29;NW-S12;9-12-18;7-4-29

T 3 N, R 3 W

Hickman Bruner* SW-NE-S2; 2-7-37
Josiah Blair* NE-SW-S2; 3-16-36
John Johnston, Lw SW-SW-S2; 1-29-39
Thomas Dorsett* NE-SE-S2; 2-13-37
Hiram P. Lucas* SE-SE-S2; 5-6-58
Nathan Hendricks N-Efr, SE-Efr-S3; 2-10-19
Joel Norman* SWfr-Efr-S3; 10-14-54
William Norman* N-Wfr-S3; 11-8-31; SE-NEfr-Nfr-S4; 6-28-36
Nelson Tate, Lw S-Wfr-S3; 10-19-31
Thomas Edmondson NW-NE-Wfr-S3; 6-5-52; MLW 30893; Lot 1-E-W-Nfr-
    S4; 6-5-52; MLW 47144
James Norman NE-NEfr-Nfr-S4; 6-13-53
Willoby Blake* SW-NEfr-Nfr-S4;6-28-36; SEfr-Nfr-S4; 7-6-29
Darwin Alexander Clark, Lw Lot 4-E-W-Nfr,Lot 3-W-W-Nfr-S4;2-15-36
Asher Wilcox Clark* Lot 2-W-W-Nfr-S4; 3-7-39
Nelson A. Guerney Lot 5-W-Sfr-S4; SW-SW-Efr, SW-SE-Efr-S17; Lot 4-
    SWfr-Nfr-S18; NE-SE-S20; 9-21-52; SW-NW-S22; SW-NE, SE-NW-S26;
    10-8-52
William S. Turner Lot 6-W-Sfr-S4; NE-SWfr-Efr, NW-SE-Efr-S17; 9-9-
    52;Lot 1-E-E-Sfr-S18;9-21-52;NE-S22;10-5-52;W-NW-S23; 9-9-52
Samuel & Emanuel Masonhelter, Adams Co., Pa. E-Sfr-S4; NWfr-Efr-
    S17; SW-NE, SE-NW-S24; 12-5-53
Samuel Perry Sfr-S5; 9-29-16
John Nye, South Carolina Nfr-S5; 7-25-20; S-Efr-S8; 9-11-19
Jonas Wildman, Columbiana Co., O. E-NW-Wfr-S6; 11-30-38
Gainer Ellis* NW-NW-Wfr-S6; 12-12-44
Harvey Marley* SW-NW-Wfr-S6; 12-3-38
George Chapman, Lw SE-SW-Wfr-S6; 4-24-39
Benjamin Marley, Lw NW-SW-Wfr-S6; 11-11-37
Henry Marley* SW-SW-Wfr-S6; 3-14-39. Harvey? see below
Harvy Marley* NE-NW-S7; 12-3-38

Thomas Walker* SW-SW-S7; 7-6-54
Thomas James* N-NE-Efr-S8; 2-25-36
James Asbel* SE-NE-Efr-S8; 10-14-54
James Bryant* SW-NE-Efr-S8;5-8-39; NWfr-Efr-S8; 3-1-32
Samuel Perry Wfr-S8; 5-13-16
Joel Slopper* NE-SE-S10; 1-11-39
Ezer Cleaveland, Lw SW-SE-S10; 2-24-51
John Terrell* NE-NE, SW-NE-S11; 4-3-52; SE-NE-S11; 1-27-53;
    NW-NE, SE-SW-S11; 3-18-52
James Johnson* NE-NW-S11; 3-8-52
John Roberts* SE-NW-S11; 10-5-48; NW-SW-S11; 10-19-48
Susan Kirk, Or W-NW-S11; 4-3-26
James Roberts* NE-SW-S11; 2-28-52
Thomas Dorsett SW-SW-S11; 10-16-52
Stephen Green SE-S11; 7-17-52
James Howard* NE-NW-S12; 1-9-39
William Terrell* NW-NW-S12; NW-NE-S13; 12-14-38; W-SE-S12; 7-5-
    36; of Lw, E-SW-S12; 7-31-24
William Long E-SW-S13; 10-17-18
DeWitt Langford W-SW-S13; 1-5-52
Isaac Edwards, Or SE-SE-S13; 8-5-34
John T. Howard NE-Efr-S17; 5-20-52; MLW 11180
John Whittington, Or NE-SE-Efr-S17; 1-16-51
William Holt* SE-SE-Efr-S17; 8-20-57
Susan Davis* E-E-Nfr-S18; 9-8-35
Willis Daugherty* W-E-Nfr-S18; 7-30-27
Nancy, Elizabeth, & Ichabod Vanderveere* E-NW-Nfr-S18; 12-7-36
Madison Vandeveer* NW-NW-Nfr-S18; 9-16-39
Thomas Walker SW-NW-Nfr-S18; 7-6-54
Nancy & Elizabeth Vandeveere SWfr-Nfr-S18; 5-4-38
John Shields* W-Sfr-S18;7-18-31; of Da, W-E-Sfr-S18; 12-26-46
Henry Daugherty & Enos Holbert Wfr-S19; 7-30-27
Joel Halbert Efr-S19; 5-27-15; of*, NW-SW-S20; 3-6-39
William Hays NE-S20; 6-17-52; MLW 35781, 36765
Benjamin M. Thomas E-NW-S20;6-17-52;MLW 19045;NW-NW-S20;6-17-52;
Mason J. Sherman SW-NW-S20;6-4-52; MLW 38316.   MLW 29682
Harvey Manning E-SW-S20; 1-15-19
James Horsey* SW-SW-S20; 5-30-36; W-SE-S20; 3-6-39
John Sewell* SE-SE-S20; 3-22-37
Joshua York* E-NE-S21; 6-20-23
William Blake* SE-SW-S21; 1-11-37
Jacob N. Elliott NE-NW-S22; 5-15-52; MLW 39925
John Holt SE-NW-S22;5-15-52;MLW 42955;NE-SW-S22;5-11-52; MLW 29180
Alexander Annon SE-SW-S22; 8-16-52
James Scarlett* NW-SW-S22; 4-27-52
Martin W. Brett SW-SW-S22; 8-17-52; SE-S22; 8-2-52
Ezer Cleveland* NE-NE-S23; 4-1-52
Dewitt Langford SE-NE-S23; 11-23-52; NW-NE-S23; 11-17-52; NE-NW-
    S23; 11-13-52; NE-SE, S-SE-S23; 11-22-53
James Stewart Bond, Lw SE-NW-S23; 11-20-49
James Fletcher E-SW-S23; 7-1-52; MLW 13393
Otho W. Dowden, Dn SW-SW-S23;NE-SW, SE-S24;W-NW-S26; 2-24-54
Arthur J. Simpson E-NE-S24; 1-12-53
Harrison H. Smith NW-NE-S24; 1-8-53

James Smith NE-NW-S24; 12-23-52
James Dickens* NW-NW-S24; 9-27-53   58667
William H. & James L. Smith SW-NW,SE-SW,W-SW-S24;10-26-49; MLW /
Jeremiah C. Elliott* NE-NE-S25; 12-10-53; SE-NE-S25; 2-14-52
John Tindale W-NE-S25; 5-22-18
Christian Bruner SE-S25; 5-29-17; NE-S36; 11-29-17
Miles White E-NE, NW-NE, NE-NW-S26; 11-30-52
Hiram Spencer* N-NE-S27; 9-6-37
Miles Shepard* SW-NW,N-SW-S28;5-13-39; of Ws, E-SE-S34;W-NW-S35;
James Cole Wood* SE-SW-S28;SW-SE-S33;1-21-39.   8-17-31
John Trantor* SW-SE-S28; 3-23-37
Joel Halbert NW-S29; Efr-S30; 5-27-15
George Newton E-SW-S29; 6-10-19
Enos Halbert & Isaac Montgomery* W-SW-S29; 5-7-32
William Daugherty & James Stephens Wfr-S30; 7-13-14
Allison Henderson* W-SW-S32; 7-1-35
John Greenstreet* NE-NE-S33; 1-11-39
Michael Pipher, Or E-NW-S33; 12-21-38; W-SE-S34; 9-23-17
Franklin Baxter* N-SW-S33; 10-3-49
Joseph Acre* S-SW-S33; 10-31-54
Lemuel Horsey E-SE-S33; 3-18-18
William McKinney NW-SE-S33; 10-4-54; MLW 7532
Moses Norman E-NE-S34; 11-30-19
Daniel G. Green* E-SW-S34; 5-29-55
John, Samuel, & William Jacob Wise W-NE-S35; 5-15-38; of Kn,
    NE-SE, W-SE-S55; 10-16-54
Fanny Douglass* E-NW-S35; 11-9-31
William Douglass* NW-SW-S35; 5-26-55; SW-SW-S35; 6-11-55
Zilpha Robinson, Kn SE-SE-S35; 10-11-53
William M. Blair NW-S36; 12-1-19
George Winsor, Ws E-SE, NW-SE-S36; 8-22-37
Jonathan French* SW-SE-S36; 5-30-40

RELINQUISHMENTS

William Hunter W-SW-S2;E-SW-S23;9-20-19;NW-S35;8-30-17;3-3-30
George Addis SW-S33;11-15-17;W-SW-S32;1-16-18;7-4-29
Eli Hawkins & Samuel Peery NW-S7; 5-9-16
William Long W-SW-S13; 10-17-18
Leonard Trover (?) E-SE-S15; 10-9-18
John Tindale E-NE-S25; 5-22-18
George Newton E-SE-S29; 12-28-19
David Logan W-SW-S34; 5-31-19
Nathan Hindricks SW-Efr-S3; 2-10-19
Henry Cruse Nfr-S18; 10-25-17
Stephen P. Stringham SE-S22; 10-9-18
Henry Gardner NW-S23; 12-10-18
George Newton W-SW-S29; 6-10-19; W-SE-S29; 12-28-19
Moses Norman W-NE-S34; 11-30-19
Michael Pipher E-SE-S34; 9-23-17
David Evans Sfr-S18; 2-22-19; 3-3-30
John Cole Wfr-S3; 12-27-16; 7-4-29
John Nye Nfr-Efr-S8; 9-11-19; 7-4-29
William M. Blair NW-S36; 12-1-19; 7-4-29

T 3 N, R 4 W

Gainer Ellis* NE-NE-S1; 5-1-41
George Hamersly* W-NE, E-NW-S1; 4-23-39
Rufus Brown* NE-SW-S1; 2-21-44
John Murphy* SE-SW-S1; NE-NW-S12; 7-25-38
George Chapman, Lw SW-SW-S1; 4-27-39
Benjamin Marley, Lw SW-SE-S1; 11-11-37
Zachariah Sims NW-S2; 3-11-51; MLW 72329
John S. S. Hunter, Dn NW-SW-S2; SE-SW-S9; SE-SE-S10; 6-21-55
Moses McBride SW-SW-S2; 5-15-52; MLW 25931
Leonard Marlow NE-NE-S3; 2-16-53; MLW 13475; NW-NE-S3; 2-16-53
John W. Sims SE-NE-S3; 8-7-52; MLW 10356; SW-NE-S3; 8-7-52
Josiah Jackson, Stark Co., O. NE-NW-S3; 6-12-39
John W. Baker* SE-NW-S3; 10-23-54
Samuel Porter W-SW-S3; E-SE-S4; 10-30-52
George W. Crook NE-SE-S3; 2-19-53; NW-SE-S9; 1-3-55
John Barker SE-SE-S3; 10-17-53
Reuben Schooley* W-SE-S3; 1-22-39
Vincent Scott* NW-NW-S4; 3-29-48
William Reid* W-SW-S4; 11-23-40
Joseph Cannon* NE-NE-S5; 9-20-49; SE-NE-S5; 3-29-48; NE-SE-S5;
    10-20-36; NW-SE-S5; 2-8-45
Marion J. Sherman W-NE-S5; 11-25-52
William Houghton NE-NW-S5; 10-7-51; MLW 15175
Benjamin Daughty Ellis* SE-NW-S5; 3-15-49; SW-NW-S5; 6-8-52
Wilson Salmon* NW-NW-S5; 2-27-54
John C. Smith NE-SW-S5; 10-29-51; MLW 12980; NW-SW-S5; 10-29-51
Thomas Elsey* SE-SW-S5; 9-1-49; SW-SW-S5; 3-17-51
William Lamar* SE-SE-S5; 4-29-39; SW-SE-S5; 11-30-36
William McCameron* NE-NE-S6; 12-16-53; N-NE-S9; 11-22-52
John Newton Love* SE-NE-S6; 9-30-54
Rachel Adkins and others W-NE-S6; 10-2-51; MLW 8786
Richard Allen Crane E-NW-S6; 9-17-52
Milton Douglass Love* NW-NW-S6; 5-21-53; SW-NW-S17; 6-11-38
Hubbard Love* SW-NW, NW-SW-S6; 11-11-52; NW-NW-S8; 5-8-50
Upton Stucky* NE-SW-S6; 11-24-48; SE-SW-S6; 4-13-46; SW-SW-S6;
    5-6-50; NW-SE-S6; 9-26-54
Thomas M. Gibson NE-SE-S6; 11-23-52
John Ellis, Jr.* SE-SE-S6; 11-22-52; SE-SE-S7; 2-18-39
John Ellis, Jr. & William Ellis* SW-SE-S6; 11-29-49
John Johnson Reinhart NE-NE-S7; 5-19-53; SW-SW-S9; 11-30-52
John Ellis* SE-NE-S7; 8-19-35; W-NE-S7; 10-23-19
Martin Stucky* SE-NW-S7; 12-6-32; NW-NW-S7; 6-17-36
John Reily* E-SW-S7; 9-19-28
Henry Walker* W-SW-S7; 7-25-39
James Madison Love* NE-SE-S7; 2-19-36
Robert Elsey W-SE-S7; 7-30-19
John Smith E-NE-S8; 10-7-19
Wesley Reynolds Love* NE-NW-S8; 10-27-37
James Cannon* SE-NW-S8; 12-2-44
James Lawell, Hamilton Co., O. SW-NW-S8; 2-17-51
David Emmons* NE-SW-S8; 1-15-48; SW-SE-S8; 3-20-50
John Lamar* SE-SW-S8; 7-18-39

Harvey Allen Love* NW-SW-S8; 2-14-39; SE-NW-S17; 2-19-39
William Ellis* SW-SW-S8; 2-8-39
Richard Lamar* NE-SE-S8; 3-5-33; NW-SE-S8; 8-22-36
Nathaniel Reynolds* SE-SE-S8; NW-SW-S9;4-29-39;SW-NW-S9; 2-6-45
Elizabeth McCameron SE-NE-39; 12-21-52; SW-NE-S9; 11-22-52
John Seals SE-NW, NE-SW-S9; 3-13-52; MLW 2123
Jonathan Calvin NE-SE-S9; 6-11-52; MLW 51105
Hiram Davis* SE-SE-S9; 3-4-39
Thomas J., Mary E., Emily C., & James C. Lamar SW-SE-S9; 8-26-33
Mason J. Sherman E-SW-S10; 12-14-52; NE-SW-S11; 5-22-52; MLW 44042;
    E-SW, W-SE-S12; MLW 6375#NW-NE-S13; 12-2-52.   #5-22-52.
Henry Schooley* W-SW-S10; 3-12-39; SE-S11; NE-S14; 10-17-37
Abraham Mitchell, Jr NE-SE-S10; 2-19-39
Benjamin Thomas Mitchell, Jr W-SE-S10; 1-17-39
Amos Salmon* E-NE-S11; 11-10-47
Thomas J. Brooks W-NW-S11; 5-11-52; MLW 25395
Richard R. Matthews, Carroll Co., O. SE-SW-S11; 7-23-39
William Mitchell, Columbiana Co., O. W-SW-S11; 5-16-39
Benjamin M. Thomas E-NE-S12; 5-22-52; MLW 30152
Jonathan Milburn* W-NW-S12; 4-11-39
John Schooley* W-SW-S12; 6-12-39
Leonard T, Manning* E-SE-S12; 10-25-54
Elisha J. Canada* NE-NE-S13; 3-10-51
Thomas W. Stephens SE-NE-S13; 10-4-51; MLW 12330
Thomas Peck* NE-SW-S13; 5-15-52
James M. Sharum* SE-SW, W-SW-S13; 10-13-54
John Norman NE-SE-S13; 2-3-53
William Henry, Sr. SE-SE-S13; 4-24-52; MLW 43819
Reuben Schooley* E-SW-S14; 12-25-37
Abraham McBride* SE-S14; 12-25-37
Augustus J. Wise & Thomas J. Brooks NE-S15; 2-5-53
John Boyd NW-S15; 11-20-48; MLW 9589
Cyrus M. Allen & William S. Turner N-SW, W-SE-S15; 2-7-53
James Stephens* SE-SW-S15; 10-1-38; W-NW-Wfr-S29; 4-6-18
James Walker* SW-SW-S15; 8-3-36
Thomas Walker NE-SE-S15; 1-29-53
Benjamin Clements* SE-SE-S15; 3-18-47
John J. O'Bryan* E-NW-S17; 8-20-36; W-E-Nfr-S21; 12-11-52
Arnold Potter NE-S17; 9-25-17
George Fraim* E-SW-S17; 8-5-36
Joseph Raney, Jr.* SW-SW-S17; 8-29-37
George Mitchelbree SE-S17; 10-5-15
John Taylor* W-NE-S18; 5-31-23
Henry Walker* NE-NW-S18; 9-21-38
William Mitchell* SE-NW-S18; 4-13-50
Joseph Hays* NW-NW-S18; 10-9-38; SW-NW-S18; 7-11-51
Joseph Nicholas* NE-SW-S18;5-15-52;MLW42347;SE-SW,NW-SW-S18;12-18-51
Henry James Hymon* SW-SW-S18; 2-19-51
William Nicholas* NE-SE-S18; 2-5-38
Daniel Nicholas* SE-SE-S18; 7-23-39; NW-SE-S18; 1-31-38
James E. Nicholas* SW-SE-S18; 4-14-51
Joseph Raney* NE-NE-S19; 1-3-50
Thomas Cootee* S-NE-S19; 3-14-51; NW-SW-S19; 1-18-50
Hugh McMahan* NW-NE-S19; 5-22-52; MLW 28706;SW-SW-Sfr-S27;3-28-54

William A. Brown* NE-NW-S19; 4-1-51
William Gates S-NW-S19; 3-8-51; MLW 1586
Nelson A. Gurney NW-NW-S19; 9-21-52
Valentin Raney* NE-SW-S19; 6-5-37; NW-SE-S19; 10-20-36
James Marion Lemar* SE-SW-S19; 1-19-48
John Reiley* SW-SW-S19; 8-23-36
Thomas Cissell* NE-SE-S19; 3-22-52; MLW 12362; NW-SW-Wfr-S20;
   3-22-52; SE-NE-S30; 12-13-36; SW-NE-S30; 8-25-36
Thomas Walker* SE-SE-S19; Apr. 1840
William Hickman* SW-SE-S19; 1-22-39
George Peery* E-NE-Wfr-S20; 2-9-36
Peter O'Bryan* W-NE-Wfr-S20;10-27-27; SE-NW-Wfr-S20;8-18-36; SE-SW
   Wfr-S20;4-13-37; Lots 1-2-E-SE-Wfr-S20;2-16-36;NW-SE-Wfr-S20;
Charles Summers, Jr., Da NE-NW-Wfr-S20;1-24-43.   3-9-36
Thomas Queen* NE-SW-Wfr-S20;3-9-36;SW-SW-Wfr-S20;11-9-39
Charles Tewell* SW-SE-Wfr-S20; 10-20-38
James T. Cox, Kn Efr-S20; 2-18-53
James Walker* E-E-Nfr-S21;12-1-37;SE-NE-Nfr,NE-SE-Nfr-S22;12-1-36;
   SE-NW-Nfr-S23;1-12-39;W-NW-Nfr-S23;12-18-38;E-SW-Nfr-S23;
   2-16-39; NW-SW-Nfr-S23; 12-1-36
James S. Wood & John Drake W-Nfr-S21; 9-19-18
William Cook* Lot 1-E-E-Sfr, W-Sfr-S21; 9-22-35;Lot 2-W-E-Sfr-S21;
   2-6-36;E-Sfr-S22;3-15-39;W-Sfr-S22; 2-26-39
George Cook* Lot 4-W-E-Sfr-S21; 2-26-36
Amos Reily* NE-NE-Nfr-S22; 5-27-39
Cager Peek* SE-SE-Nfr-S22; 12-29-35; W-SE-Nfr-S22; 1-22-39; SW-SW-
   Nfr-S23; 2-12-36; Mfr-S27; 6-8-35
John Hitt* E-E-Nfr-S23; 6-8-47
Joseph Walker* NE-NW-Nfr-S23; 9-8-38
William S. Turner E-NE-Efr, E-NW-Efr-S24; 10-5-52
Russell Davis* Lots 3-4-W-NW-Efr-S24; 7-6-39
William Lee, Lw SWfr-Efr-S24; 7-14-35
Absolem Fields NE-SE-Efr-S24; 5-29-52; MLW 12332
James Stephens* S-SE-Efr-S24; 9-8-35
Isom Daugherty* NW-SE-Efr-S24; 9-3-52
Joseph Warner Wfr-S24; 4-23-18
Eunice Hale, Salem Co., Mass. N-Sfr-S25;12-30-36;Lot 1-W-Sfr-S25;
Silas Halbert* Lots 3-4-E-Sfr-S25; 2-17-36   12-24-36
William Daugherty & James Stephens Nfr-S25; 7-13-14
Wiley Orrinder* E-NE-Efr-S26; 8-22-34
Charles Hitt* SW-SW-Efr-S26; 9-23-37; NW-NE-S28; 2-13-49
Welter Franklin* NE-SE-Efr-S26; 10-31-37
John Nye, South Carolina Wfr-S26; 7-25-20
Art Lord* Lot 1-NEfr-Sfr-S27; 9-14-37
William Riley Davis* NW-SW-Sfr-S27;SE-SE-S28;10-12-54;NE-SE-S28;
William Bledsoe* E-SE-Sfr-S27; 11-15-54   12-7-47
John S. S. Hunter, Dn SW-NE, NW-SW-S28; 6-21-55
James Peery* NE-NW-S28;12-21-37;E-SW-S28;4-24-37;NEfr-Wfr-S29;
Charles Forse* SE-NW-S28;9-25-37;SW-NW-S28-1-6-37.   2-12-36
Charles Yeats* NW-NW-S28; 10-28-54
Whitfield Forse* SW-SW-S28; 4-11-39
William Hays Efr-S29; 7-30-17
Henry Clifton, Jr.* NE-NW-Wfr-S29; 4-24-37
Peter Carmickel* SE-NW-Wfr-S29; 5-20-36

MARTIN COUNTY

Silas L. Halbert* N-S-Wfr-S29; 2-17-36
Silas L. Halbert & Thomas Nisbit* S-S-Wfr-S29; 1-27-36
Andrew Carmichael* NE-NE-S30; 12-11-38
Marshall Hatton* NW-NE-S30; 4-20-46
George Shepard, Jr. NW-S30; 10-5-18
Benjamin Ridge SW-S30; 3-25-18
Philip Davis SE-S30; 9-17-17; Wfr-S31; 10-2-15
Isaac Dunn Efr-S31; Efr-S32; 8-17-13
General Washington Johnson Wfr-S32; 6-2-07
Owen McManus* E-NE-S33; 1-31-38; W-NE-S33; 8-3-37
John C. Wenzel NW, SW-S33; 5-24-19
Asa Martin* E-SE-S33; 11-17-31
John Green W-SE-S33; 10-9-18
Thomas Owens, Fd S-SW-S34; 2-23-38
John Hanley* NW-SW-S34; 2-13-40
James Mosyer* NE-NE-S35; 8-28-38
James McBride* NW-NE-S35; 3-18-41
William Hitt* NW-NW-S35; 7-11-39
Allison Henderson* NW-NE-S36; 1-11-39
Abner Decker, Kn NE-NW-S36; 5-11-38
Coalman Harper* NW-NW-S36; 12-26-36
George Booth, Baltimore, Md. SW-NW-S36; 3-18-41

RELINQUISHMENTS

James S. Wood & John Drake Efr½-Nfr-S21; 9-19-18
Joseph Warner NWfr-Efr, SW-Efr, SE-Efr-S26; 4-23-18
John Smith SW-S4; 10-12-19; NW-S7; 6-10-19
Morgan Day & Samuel Fitzgerald Wfr-S20; 8-25-18
James Stephens Sfr-Wfr, NEfr-Wfr-S29; 4-6-18
John M. Prentiss NW-S28; 7-8-19
Robert Elsey E-SE-S7; 7-30-19
Henry Speed E-SE-Efr, W-SE-Efr, Efr-S27; 5-14-16
Elisha Kilburn E-SE-S53; 1-3-18
John Ellis E-NE-S7; 10-23-19
Edmund Darrell Sfr-S21; Efr-S20; 4-14-18; 7-4-29
David Turman E-NE-S33; 7-8-19; 7-4-29
John J. Turman W-NE-S33; 4-5-20; 7-4-29

T 3 N, R 5 W

Hubbard Love* SE-NE-S1; 5-11-39
Thomas Seal* NE-NW-S1; 1-9-39
Benedict Padget* SE-NW-S1; 1-24-39
John Drake* W-NW-S1; 10-1-23; NW-S12; 2-6-19
John F. Henry (Harper?) & Thomas M. McClung SW-S1; 9-23-18
John Newton Love* SE-SE-S1; 3-13-39
John Reily* W-NE-S12; 10-23-19; W-SE-S12; 9-28-22
James S. Wood & Baldwin Berry* NE-SW-S12; 6-19-37
John Fitzgerald* SE-SW-S12; 5-12-48; SW-NW-S13; 6-14-40
James S. Wood* NW-SW-S12; 11-20-44
John Fitzgerald, Jr.* SW-SW-S12; 12-24-39
Jasper Sanders Hindman* W-NE-S13; 12-31-39
Bernard Mattingly* NE-NW-S13; 6-17-36; SE-NW-S13; 5-27-39

James Stewart Cissell, Da NW-NW-S13; 10-24-37
John Dickson Wood* SE-SW-S13; 8-10-37
Thomas Clark Williams* NW-SW-S13; 6-17-36
Patrick Kent, Hamilton Co., O. SW-SE-S13; NE-NW-S24; 11-7-40;
    of Da, SW-SW-S13; 11-7-40
Edward Reeves* E-SE-S13; 12-31-39
Thomas Gootee* NW-NE-S24;2-12-39;SW-NE-S24;8-23-36;SE-S24;2-3-18
Joshua Horner* SE-NW-S24; 2-3-40
Joseph Somers* NW-NW-S24; 12-11-38
Solomon Stuart E-SW-S24; 11-9-18
Emanuel Gates* NW-SW-S24; 11-22-49
William Lawson Crays* SW-SW-S24; 11-18-39
William Snyder NE-S25; 3-15-18
Clement Riney, Sr. E-NW-S25; 10-7-17
Alva Clark* NW-NW-S25; 8-23-37
Michael Hall* SW-NW-S25; 8-24-37
Jacob Christ SW-S25; 9-6-17
Joseph Riney SE-S25; 10-7-17
Jacob Myers NE-S36; 3-25-18
Cornelius Ridge E-NW-S36; 5-5-18
Jonathan Raney* NW-NW-S36; 12-6-39
Russel Davis* SW-NW-S36; 10-4-36
Philip Davis SW-S36; 4-20-18
Cager Peep SE-S36; 11-21-14

RELINQUISHMENTS

John Reiley E-NE-S12; 10-23-19
Solomon Stewart NW-S24; 11-9-18;W-SW-S24; 11-9-18; 7-4-29
Clement Riney, Sr. W-NW-S25; 10-7-17

T 4 N, R 3 W

Jefferson Veatch* SE-NE-S1; 8-23-37
Isaac Cox, Da W-NE-S1; 7-28-23
Charles McDermed* NW-NW-S1; 1-11-53; SW-NW-S1; 3-14-37; NE-NE-S2;
    12-26-54;SE-NE-S2;11-8-51;NE-SE-S2;12-15-36;SE-SE-S2;8-9-49
Bartemius Williams, Lw NE-SE-S1; 9-9-54
Solomon Osborn SW-S1; 10-15-18
Miles Cox* NW-NE-S2; 6-9-51; NE-NW-S2; 4-24-57
Isaac Smith* SW-NE-S2; 1-5-55; NW-SE-S2; 9-21-47
Jacob Kinder, Jr. SE-NW-S2; 12-31-52
Jeremiah Waggoner* NW-NW-S2; 2-24-45
John McHenry* SW-NW-S2; 3-9-47
Samuel Smith* SW-SE-S2; 5-21-36
Henry Waggoner* NE-NE-S3; 1-19-52; NW-NE-S3; 10-17-54
John Cox* SE-NE-S3; 1-31-53
Fleming Chastain* SW-NE-S3; 2-11-47
Wallace Craig, Lw NE-NW-S3; 3-8-52
Willoughby Luttrell* SE-NW-S3; 5-18-49; E-SE-S3; 11-5-40
Pleasant Stark* NW-NW-S3;1-20-51;E-NE-S4;10-17-44;SW-NE-S4;10-28-51
Hiram W. Peek SW-NW-S3; 10-15-52
Christian Pfeffer, Columbiana Co., O. SW-S3; 4-4-39
William Eaton* W-SE-S3; 8-27-27

Paul Farris NW-NE-S4; 12-4-51; MLW 14434
Henry Schooley* E-NW-S4; 6-12-39
Isaac Chastain, Lw NW-NW-S4; 2-13-45
Jackson Beasley, Lw NE-SW-S4; 11-3-52; W-SW-S4; 11-3-54
Abner Johnson, Da SE-SW-S4; 10-3-53
William Elkins* SW-SW-S4; 5-26-57; note says SW-SW- Re-entered
Peter Figley, Columbiana Co., O. E-SE-S4; E-NE-S9; 4-4-39
James Taylor E-NE-S5; 1-22-53
Joseph Cannon NW-NE-S5; 8-9-52; SW-NE-S5; 7-24-52
John F. Bayard, Jr. NE-NW-S5; 9-10-52
Lucy Ann Bennet* SE-NW-S5; 10-23-54
Sarah Bennett* NW-NW-S5; 10-23-54
Robert Bennett* SW-NW-S5; 10-23-54
Edward Ritchison* NE-SW-S5; 2-27-57
Absalom West* SE-SW-S5; 7-11-51; NE-NW-S8; 7-22-44
Alvin Gaither* NW-SW-S5;7-16-51;SW-SW-S5;7-18-55;NE-NW-S9;8-9-49
Richard Conquest SE-S5; 3-14-49; MLW 37882
Samuel R. Brown, Ws NE, E-SE-S6; 10-13-54
Charles H. Rose, Hamilton Co., O. N-NW-S6; 10-26-53; MLW 44101
Robert William Dowthitt* SW-NW-S6; 3-23-49
Elbert Howard Peyton* SW-NW-S6;9-6-47;NE-SW-S6;9-8-52;SE-SW,SW-SE-
Gabriel Reynolds, Lw NW-SE-S6; 12-20-44.   S6; 10-2-54
George Dickinson* N-NE-S7; 10-30-54
Riley Payne* SE-NE-S7; 10-26-47; NE-SE-S7; 7-5-52
Barnabas Payne* SW-NE-S7; 2-12-51; NW-NW-S8; 8-23-48
Henry Mouder* NE-NW-S7;4-15-57;SE-NW-S7;11-4-52;NE-SW-S7;11-3-52
Leonard Marlow W-NW-S7; 1-12-53
Robert Dinning* SE-SW, SW-SE-S7; 11-4-52; SE-SE-S7; 1-7-57
Joseph Phipps, Lw W-SW-S7; 5-9-49
Andrew Henson* NW-SE-S7; 1-25-50
Elizabeth Downs NE-S8; 10-6-48; MW 13289
John Hurrah Butler, Ow SE-NW, SW-SE-S8; 9-2-47
Thomas Payne* SW-NW-S8; 9-25-47
Jesse Henson E-SW-S8; n.d. MLW 5750
By Riley Payne's attorney W-SW-S8; 1-17-48
Eli Ranard, Ow N-SE-S8; 9-10-47
John Guthridge* SE-SE-S8; 7-7-51
Joab Cox* NW-NE-S9; 1-7-50
Charles Hyde Marshall* SW-NE-S9; 9-23-47
John Sims* SE-NW, N-SW-S9; 9-17-47
John Suttle Guthridge* SE-SW-S9; 9-25-47
George Washington Bond, Lw SW-SW-S9; 10-24-37
Abner Johnson, Da NE-SE-S9;9-14-53;SE-NE-S10;1-31-52; MLW 13624
Samuel Jimpy (Timpy?), Lw W-SE-S9;10-21-37; of*, SE-SE-S9;11-7-54
George Adams* NE-NE-S10; 11-17-54
Andrew Denton W-NE-S10; 6-7-19
Samuel Taylor* NE-NW-S10; 6-4-51
Spencer Griffin* SE-NW-S10; 10-11-44
David Hendrickson, Sh GW-NW, NW-SW-S10; 3-18-40
Job D. Anderson* SW-SW-S10; 9-6-51
Sylvester Kenedy* SE-NE-S11; 4-30-37
James Bowden* SW-NE-S11; 8-21-36
John Shields E-NW-S11; 4-19-19
Joseph D. Hammersly* E-SW-S11; 7-28-48

John Hammersly* NE-SE-S11; 1-23-37
Arthur D. Hastings, Lw SW-SE-S11; 7-29-47; SE-NE-S12; 4-11-55;
   MLW 14018; of*, SW-SW-S12; 2-13-49; NW-SE-S12;6-10-52;MLW 10699
Daniel W. Daniels* NE-NE-S12; 4-11-55
Michael Hammersly NW-S12; 10-15-50; MLW 45602
Wiley G. Hastings NE-SE-S12; 10-29-52
John Hinshaw* SE-SE-S12; NW-NE-Nfr-S13; 8-10-47
Baisel Gaither* NE-NE-Nfr-S13; 5-11-57
Asahel Chamberlain, Lw SE-NE-Nfr-S13; 4-17-39
Garret G. Williamson, Lw SW-NE-Nfr-S13; 3-9-57
Alvin Gaither* SE-NW-Nfr-S13; 8-21-37
Ralph Delamater* Lot 2-SWfr-Nfr-S13; 1-15-57
Adam Wible, Ws E-SE-Nfr-S13; 8-25-29
John Sellers* W-SE-Nfr-S13; 12-2-47
Robert Wood Sfr-S13; 1-16-18
Henry Sellers Lot 2-W-E-Nfr-S14;10-27-52; of Lw, NE-NW-Nfr,
   NW-NW-Nfr-S14; 7-24-47
Robert Fields Sfr-S14; 1-16-18
Job D. Anderson* NW-NW-S15; 10-31-54
Lorenzo Dow Adamson* SW-NW-S15; 1-20-55
Elizabeth Johnson, Lw SE-SW-S15; 5-26-38
Daniel R. Dunihue & Isaac Rector, Lw E-NE-S17; 8-26-44; W-NE-S17;
   8-31-44; NE-NW-S17; 2-20-45
Daniel R. Dunihue, Lw SE-NW-S17; 11-9-44; NW-NW-S17; 12-13-44; of*
   SW-NW-S17;8-13-53; S-NE, E-NW, NW-SE-S18; 9-28-54
Isaac Rector, Lw NE-SW-S17; 11-9-44
Obed Mercer, Lw SE-SW-S17;2-7-45; of*, SW-SE-S17; 5-19-41
William Henson* NW-SW-S17; 7-30-52; NW-NE-S18; 1-20-51
John Henson* SW-SW-S17; 11-1-52; SW-SE-S20; 3-13-48
Aaron Painter, Lw E-SE-S17; 11-10-38
George Washington Crooke, Lw NW-SE-S17; 7-27-44
Jacob Henry* NE-NE-S18; 8-22-53
James J. Dinning W-NW-S18; 8-14-52
John Dungy* NE-SW-S18; 10-19-50
William Noblitt* SE-SW-S18; 8-12-39; NE-NW-S20; 10-4-36
Seth Webster* NW-SW-S18; 1-25-51
David Porter" SW-SW-S18; 6-16-54
John Downs NE-SE-S18; 3-16-52; MLW 30319
Benoni Denney, Mr SE-SE-S18; 2-27-38
Samuel Marlow SW-SE-S18; n.d.
William Standley* NE-NE-S19; 6-28-36
Daniel Lundy, Mr SE-NE-S19; 10-21-37
James Saunders W-NE-S19; 5-11-52; MLW 21241
Elizabeth Noblitt* NE-NW-S19; 8-29-39
David Vigus* SE-NW-S19; 11-28-48
Thomas Miller* NW-NW-S19; 5-3-36
William Neel, Mr SW-NW-S19; 3-4-39
Samuel W. Piper* NE-SW, NW-SE-S19; 4-1-50
John L. Johnson S-SW-S19; 1-31-52; MLW 16406
Thomas Christian NW-SW-S19; 5-7-52; MLW 35495
John D. Tate* NE-SE-S19;3-30-52; of Da, SE-SE-S19;1-2-50;SW-SE-S19;
William Mercer* W-NE,SE-NW,SW-SW-S20; 4-30-39.   3-25-50
Samuel Mercer* NW-NW-S20; 11-15-51
Jesse Henson* E-SW-S20; 5-21-49

James Woodson Cawson* SW-SW-S20; 3-1-37
William Mitchell, Columbiana Co., O. NW-SW-S20; 9-3-44
Job Clark, Lw NW-SE-S20; 1-24-51
Williamson D. Dunn* NE-NE-S21; 6-3-57; NW-SW-S21; 8-29-55
Samuel Baugh S-NE-S21; 8-25-52
Jacob Long* NE-NW-S21; 12-16-52; SW-NW-S21; 5-21-50
Abraham Long SE-NW-S21; 10-8-44
William Erwin NW-NW-S21; 12-9-52
James Brown Huston* SE-SW-S21; 2-21-39; NE-NW-S28; 2-21-39
William Wolf Jones* SW-SW-S21; 2-20-39
William K. Johnson SE-S21; 6-23-53; MLW 5068; E-Nfr-S22; 1-15-51;
    MLW 70383; SW-Nfr-S22; 11-21-51; MLW 72869; E-NE-S27; 4-7-51;
    MLW 3854; E-NW-S27; 6-23-53; MLW 46577; W-NW-S27; 11-21-51;
    MLW 72762; E-NE-S28; 11-21-51
Lewis L. Watson NE-NW-Nfr-S22; 10-11-52
Margaret Crisham SE-NW-Nfr-S22; 12-11-52
William Eaton* Wfr-S23; 12-25-35   6-13-36
Robert Fields NE-Efr, N-NW-Efr-S23; 1-16-18; of Lw, S-NW-Efr-S23;/
Thomas Baley Eaton* SWfr-Efr-S23; 1-1-31; NW-SE-Efr-S23; 6-23-36;
    SW-SE-Efr-S23; 10-30-35; Wfr-S24; n.d.
Andrew Jackson Williams, Lw; Guardian for the minor heirs of Prior
    L. Williams, decd. E-SE-Efr-S23; NW-NW-Sfr-S25; Lot 4-S-N-Efr,
    NE-SEfr-Efr-S26; 9-2-47
Asahel Chamberlain, Lw Lot 1-N-N-Efr-S24; 4-17-39
Alvin Gaither* Lot 3-N-N-Efr-S24; 5-13-36
John W. Sellars* Lot 2-N-N-Efr-S24; 1-4-51
John Hinshaw* S-N-Efr-S24; 2-13-35; of Lw, N-S-Efr-S24; 8-13-31
James Denton* S-S-Efr-S24; 3-19-32
Roger McKnight Nfr-S25; 3-25-18
James H. McCindley* E-NW-Sfr-S25; 5-4-57
Absalom Bowden* NW-SW-Sfr-S25; 2-29-48
John Bowden* NE-SE-S25; 2-29-48
John Munday SE-SE-Sfr-S25; 6-4-52; MLW 17500
Thomas Edmondson* Lot 2-N-N-Efr-S26; 6-8-49
Myron H. Lincoln* E-SWfr-Efr, Lot 5-W-SWfr-Efr-S26; 8-9-54; W-NE-S27;
James Dilley* W-SWfr-Efr-S26; 2-15-45   8-23-54
John Blake, Sr.* Wfr-S26; 6-9-30
James Currant E-SW, W-SEfr-S27; 12-23-51; MLW 5111
Owen Lindly, Sr., Or NW-SW-S27; 5-9-53
Henry Lindley* SW-SW-S27; 8-19-44
James Lindley, Or Lot 1-E-SEfr-S27; 5-19-35
William S. Turner NW-NE-S28; 8-28-52; MLW 12283
John B. Hannah, Vb SW-NE-S28; 7-25-49; SE-NW-S28; 8-27-49
John Hamersly, Lw NW-NW-S28; E-SE-S29; E-SE-S30; 6-8-33; of*, SE-NE-S30;
Isaac Chauncey Bowden, Lw SW-NW-S28; 8-22-38   8-31-36
Aaron Stephen Bacon* E-SW-S28; 3-29-48; S-SW-S30; 3-16-43
Alonzo Sanford Wilcox, Lw W-SW-S28; 8-31-37
John B. Williams SE-S28; 4-1-50; MLW 23515
Jacob Hammersly* NE-NE, SW-NE-S29; 8-27-32
William Herron Huston, Lw SE-NE-S29; 6-27-57
David Huston, Lw NW-NE-S29; 7-13-37
Joseph Hastings* NE-NW-S29; 8-31-32
Edward Edwards* SE-NW-S29; 1-17-50; SW-NW-S29; 3-11-50
William Hastings* NW-NW-S29; 3-11-36

James Doke SW-S29; 7-31-19; E-SE-S31; 2-15-19
Samuel Huston, Lw W-SE-S29; 7-13-37
Harrison Gaither, Da NE-NE-S30; 4-10-49; of*, NE-NW-S30; 6-24-51
James Peek* NW-NE-S30; 2-20-50
Joseph Hughey* SW-NE-S30; 11-22-47
James Snodgrass* SE-NW-S30; 3-25-48
Richard Webster* NW-NW-S30; 2-28-49
John Batchelor SW-NW-S30; 2-6-52; MLW 19532
Nimrod Wildman, Columbiana Co., O. NE-SW-S30; 11-30-47
Henry Henson* NW-SW-S30; 10-20-53
Ganar Ellis, Columbiana Co., O. NE-NE, W-NE, SW-S31; 2-19-39
William Henry, Jr.* SE-NE-S31; 1048-36
Mccum Henry* NE-NW-S31; 7-15-36
Charles Crosser, Columbiana Co., O. SE-NW-S31; 7-1-39
James Bradley* W-NW-S31; 2-23-52
William T. Mitcheltree* W-SE-S31; 10-27-27
John Nye & Lewis R. Rogers NE-Nfr-S32; 9-11-19
John Magee, Gurnsey Co., O. E-NW-Nfr-S32; 11-30-36
William Henry* W-NW-Nfr-S32; 6-12-40
Felix Brundy Rawlings, Lw SW-Nfr-S32; 8-13-38
A. G. Heylman, Washington, D.C. Sfr-S32; 9-26-76
Lewis R. Rogers E-NE-S33; 2-23-52; MLW 27616
Gabriel Richards, Jk W-NE-S33; 10-19-37
Abner R. Brown W-NW-S33; 10-30-52
Thomas Edmondson NE-SW-S33;6-19-52;MLW 47589;W-SW-S33;7-3-52; MLW
William Wait Boyden, Ws SE-SW-S33; 1-14-37   12378
Nelson Tate, Lw NE-SE-S33; 5-28-32
David Boyden* SE-SE-S33; 3-21-37; of Ws, W-SE-S33; 1-14-37
David Matkin Efr-S34; 7-10-16
Edward Millis Wfr-S34; 10-3-16
Robert Dunlap* NE-NE-S35; 10-6-54; SW-SW-S35; 11-8-52
Israel W. Hendrickson, Lw SE-NE-S35; 10-7-54
James Harvey Farriss* NW-NE-S35;8-16-51; of Lw, SW-NE,SE-NW-S35;
Darwin A. Clark NE-NW, NW-SW-S35; 12-16-52   10-7-54
James Dilley* NW-NW-S35; 2-15-45
Joseph & William Fields* SW-NW-S35; 3-15-51
John Dorset NE-SW-S35; 1-20-53; SE-SW-S35; 11-9-52
William Melvin* NE-SE-S35; 2-4-54; SE-SE-S35; 5-1-54
Austin Blake* SW-SE-S36; 1-29-39

RELINQUISHMENTS

John Shields W-NW-S11; 4-19-19
Robert Fields S-NWEfr, SWfr-Efr, SE-Efr-S23; 1-16-18; Efr-S24;
James Doke SE-S29; 12-19-16; W-SE-S31; 2-15-19   3-31-18
John Nye & Lewis R. Rogers NW-Nfr, SW-Nfr, SE-Nfr-S32; 9-11-19
William Gray W-SE-S2; 9-2-18
Ezekiel Porter SW-S21; 6-30-18
Adam Shirley SE-S33; 8-12-19
Andrew Denton E-NE-S10; 6-7-19
Richard Speers E-SE-S30; 3-22-19; 7-4-29

Robert Williamson Douthitt NE-S1; 2-17-49; MLW 37367
Isaac K. Ridge, Pi NW-S1; 10-4-54
Logan Fish, Lw E-SW-S1; SE-SW, E-SE-S2; 12-30-44;NE-NW-S11;12-30-
Samuel Fairley, Lw W-SW-S1; 1-5-39   44
Nancy Fields, Da NE-NE, W-NE, SE-NW-S2; 10-11-54
John Smith Douthitt* SE-NE-S2; 6-6-49
Trulove Brown NW-NW-S2; 7-5-53; MLW 63558
Wesley H. Nichols SW-NW-S2;3-17-49;MLW 47359;N-SW,NW-SE-S2;3-17-49
Henry J. Bridges* SW-SW-S2; E-SE-S3; 9-29-54
David Nale* SW-SE-S2; 3-23-55
Michael Bowman* NW-NW-S3; 9-28-54; SW-NW-S3; 8-17-52
Pleasant Bowman N-SE-S3; 12-14-52
William Bowman* NE-NE-S4;9-6-54;W-NE-S4;3-7-48;NW-SE-S4;E-NE-S5;
James Holt* SE-NE-S4; 1-4-39   9-26-54
James Andes NW-S4; 5-3-49; MW
Patrick Clements* NE-SW-S4;11-1-54;NE-NE-S8;2-17-52;NE-NW-S8;1-1-39
Jonathan D. Calvin SE-SW-S4; 1-3-53;SW-SE-S9;2-13-54;SW-SE-S10;
Christian Keck* NW-NE-S5; 3-25-51; SW-NE-S6; 9-6-47   1-31-53
Richard Williams* SW-NE-S5; 5-30-53; SE-NW-S5; 12-18-38; NE-SW-
    S5; 11-7-34; NE-SE-S5; 1-25-51; NW-SE-S5; 2-1-37
Vincent Williams, Lw NE-NW-S5; 5-1-39
Richard Queen* NW-NW-S5; 3-1-36
John Williams, Lw SW-NW-S5;10-16-32;W-SW-S5;5-16-32; of*,SE-NE-S6;
George Redney, Da SE-SW-S5; 1-7-33   5-23-36
Thomas Mitchell, Da SE-SE-S5; 12-5-38
Patrick Clemmens* SW-SE-S5; 3-1-36
William Francis Sciscoe, Mr NE-NE-S6; 11-8-42
John Phipps, Lw NW-NE-S6; 2-3-48; NE-NW-S6; 3-22-49
Christian Poindexter* SE-NW-S6; 10-25-54; SW-SW-S6; 3-13-54
John Kutch, Mr W-NW-S6; 1-7-40
McHowell Keck & Christian Poindexter* NE-SW-S6; 2-18-52
Bazil Clemans, Jr.* SE-SW, NW-SE-S6; 12-14-38
Alexander Herron* NW-SW-S6; 4-15-46
Bazil Clemmons, Sr.* E-SE-S6; 1-20-36
James Ellis* NE-NE-S7; 10-23-52;NE-NW-S7;1-2-53;NW-NW-S7;10-7-54
Aaron Hendrickson SE-NE-S7; 9-9-52; SW-NE-S7; 9-19-52
William Clements* NW-NE-S7; 8-4-36
Mason J. Sherman S-NW,N-SW-S7;1-24-53;NE-SE-S8;SW-NW-S9;10-18-52;
    NE-SW-S17; 1-14-53
Isaac Jones* SE-SW-S7;2-18-50;NW-SE-S7;12-23-52;SW-SE-S7;10-18-53
William A. Strange* SW-SW-S7; 10-7-54
Jacob Jones* NE-SE-S7; 2-11-52
Thomas Mitchell* SE-SE-S7; 1-24-54; of Da, NW-NE-S8; 12-5-38
John Stout* SE-NE-S8; 1-17-55
Basil Clements* SW-NE-S8;6-15-53;SW-SW-S8;12-14-52;SE-SE-S8;10-17-
    54;SW-SE-S8;5-26-53;NE-NE-S17;5-26-53;MLW 82749;SE-NW-S17;6-13-
    53;SW-SW-S17;10-7-52;SE-NW-S18;6-15-53;MLW 4332
Joseph Queen* SE-NW-S8;2-13-49;SW-NW-S8;8-4-36;NW-SW-S8;12-21-52
Henry Williams* NW-NW-S8; 11-7-34
Joseph O'Brian* NW-SE-S8; 2-17-52
John L. Bridges* SE-NE, W-NE, E-NW-S9; 10-2-54
Mary Holland, Da NW-NW-S9; 10-19-54

William Martin Gilbreath* NE-SW-S9; 2-21-45
Sylvester O'Brien* SE-SW-S9; 10-27-54
James Sanders, Jr.* NW-SW-S9; 8-27-52
George W. Dickinson SW-SW-S9; n.d.
James A. Sharam, Da E-SE-S9; 10-12-54
Dorcas Gilbreath* NW-SE-S9; 9-3-53   9-14-53
Daniel Scervitus Snodgrass* NE-NE, W-NE-S10;9-28-54;SE-SE-S10;/
William Bowman SE-NE-S10;3-6-54;MLW 53072;SE-NW-S10;1-25-53;SW-NW-
William O. Welch* NE-NW-S10; 3-30-54   S11;3-6-54
John England, Lw SW-NW-S10; 9-8-38
Henderson Harris* NE-SE-S10; 9-1-49; NW-SE-S10; NW-NE-S15; 9-28-
   54; NE-NW-S15; 10-26-53; MLW 89910; NW-SW-S15; 2-26-49
John Bough* E-NE, NW-NE-S11; 10-3-54
George Washington McReynolds* SW-NE-S11; 7-15-52; SE-NW, NW-SW-
   S12; 4-25-48; SE-SW-S12; 8-31-52; NE-NW-S13; 8-31-53
Noah Boone, Lw SE-NW-S11; 10-24-50
Henry J. Bridges* NW-NW-S11; 9-29-54
Thomas Sargent NE-SW-S11; 9-27-54; MLW 17901
Christopher Brawand, Gn S-SW-S11; 12-2-56
Andrew J. Harris NW-SW-S11; 2-27-54; MLW 7632
Elias N. Woody* NE-SE, W-SE-S11; 11-9-54
Isaac Hill, Mr SE-SE-S11;10-6-47;SW-SW-S12;3-22-49;NW-NW-S13;10-6-
William M. Miller NE-S12; 9-21-48; MLW 17745   47
William Spalding, Da NE-NW, W-NW-S12; 10-10-54
James N. Dobson* NE-SW-S12; 10-30-54
Joseph Phipps, Lw NE-SE-S12; 1-15-50
John Payne* SE-SE-S12; 12-15-52; SW-SE-S12; 10-30-54
John W. Dobson NW-SE-S12; 4-14-50; MLW 4021
Thomas Hitchcock E-NE, NW-NE, SE-NW-S13; 6-30-52; MLW 14627,10445;
   SW-NW-S13; 6-16-54; MLW 97920
John Hitchcock* SW-NE-S13; 6-16-54
Samuel Buffington* E-E-SW, W-W-SW, SW-SE-S13; 4-19-52
Allen Pate* N-SE-S13; 3-22-52; MLW 16399
James Donahey SE-SE-S13; 12-9-52
John Raney NE-S14; 3-2-49; MLW 40892
William Bough NW-S14; 7-22-48; MLW 7002
James Glen, Kn E-SW,NW-SE-S14;11-18-54; NE-SE-S14; Nov. 1854
William Sinclair W-SW-S14; 10-28-53; MLW 45972
Samuel Drake* SE-SE-S14; 7-10-50;SE-NE,NE-SE-S17;1-8-53;NW-NE-S23;
Peter Flumerfelt* SW-SE-S14; 11-23-53   11-29-49
Alfred Girdley* NE-NE-S15; 11-15-51
George W. Brown* S-NE-S15; 10-24-54
John & Alphas Swayze* SE-NW-S15; 11-11-53
Morris Huston* SW-NW-S15; 2-13-49
George Best Brown* NE-SW-S15; 2-11-39
John Drake Sweazey SW-SW-S15; 12-27-52; NW-SE-S22; 8-14-52
Samuel Monroe Neel, Lw NE-SE-S15; 1-7-54
Elijah Bradshaw, Ow S-SE-S15; 10-24-54
John Swayze* NW-SE-S15; 10-2-54
James Miles NE-NW-S17; 11-1-52
John Baptist Miles* SE-SW-S17; 9-20-52; NE-SW-S19; 8-29-39
Thomas Mitchell NW-SW-S17; 9-23-52
James M. Queen* SE-SE-S17; 1-18-53; SE-SE-S20; 2-5-51
John H. Kidwell N-NE-S18; 1-8-53

Sylvester Kidwell, Jr.* SE-NE-S18; 4-20-49; SW-NE-S18; 1-10-53
William Ambrose Strange* NE-NW-S18;6-20-53;NW-NW-S18;2-21-49;SW-NW-
William Clemens* SE-SW-S18; 9-26-37   S18; 2-6-51
Sylvester Kidwell* NE-SE-S18; 4-13-46
Patrick Clements SE-SE-S18; 12-21-52; NW-SW-S20; 7-25-53
William Fish, Lw SE-SW, SW-SE-S19; 12-30-44;NE-NW-S30; 12-30-44
Corrhon Vliet, Mg W-SW-S19; 7-25-42
Basel Clements* N-SE-S19; 8-29-39
Ellender Miles & John H. Kidwell E-NE-S20;1-15-52; MLW 14118
Felix Miles, Sr.* NE-NW-S20; 8-23-48
Felix Miles* SE-NW-S20; 7-14-51; NW-NE-S32; 2-13-49
John A. Carrico* NW-NW-S20; 7-14-51
Joseph Miles* SW-NW-S20; 10-16-54
Thomas Faith E-SW-S20; 6-9-51; MLW 5506
George Runnier* SW-SW-S20; 2-17-52
Thomas M. Gibson* NE-SE-S20; 1-18-53
William Corbet* NE-NE-S21; 1-18-55. Corbey? see below
Miles White SE-NE, NE-SE-S21; 11-8-52; N-NE-S22; 10-28-52;
     W-NW, NE-SE, SW-SE-S22; 11-8-52
John P. Myers W-NE-S21; 9-6-52
William McFaith, Pk NE-NW-S21; 11-3-54
William Corbey SE-NW-S21; 1-13-53. Corbet? see above
Wilford Miles NW-NW-S21; 11-17-52
John Ellis* SW-NW, E-SW, NW-SE-S21; 10-5-54;NE-NW-S28; 10-5-54
James Ellis* NW-SW-S21; 9-30-50
Sylvester O'Brien* SW-SW-S21; 2-5-45; NW-SE-S27; 7-18-51
Thomas Christian* SE-SE-S21; 6-6-49
Thomas Christian, Jr.* SW-SE-S21; 4-24-52
William Bough S-NE, E-NW-S22; 9-3-49; MLW 7793
James Bradley E-SW-S22; 10-28-52; N-SE-S23; 11-6-52
Richard Burrows SE-SE-S22;SE-SE-S23;NW-NW-S26;E-NE-S27;10-18-52
James Clawson NE-NE-S23; 2-5-52;MLW 35672; S-NE-S23; 11-20-52
Jonathan D. Calvin SE-NW-S23;1-14-53;SW-NW-S23;6-15-53;SE-NE-S25;
     11-25-52;NW-SE-S25;9-9-52;E-SW-S27;2-13-54;NE-NE-S28;2-1-53;
     SW-NE, NW-SE-S28; 6-15-53
James A. Flummerfelt* NE-SW-S23;9-17-50;SE-SW-S23;9-29-52;SW-SE-S23;
Joseph Brown* NW-SW-S23; 2-5-45   11-14-54
Trulove Brown* SW-SW-S23; 6-21-47
James Donahey NE-NE-S24; 12-9-52
Seth Webster* SE-NE-S24; 9-28-52; SW-NE-S24; 2-5-39; SE-NW-S24;
     9-4-52; NE-SE-S24; 12-26-53; NW-SE-S24; 1-23-37
James A. Mason NW-NE, NE-NW-S24; 9-28-52
Jonathan Webster* NW-NW-S24; 1-16-52; SW-NW-S24; 8-12-52
Jacob Hammersley* NE-NW-S24; 10-21-51; SW-SE-S24; 2-5-39
George Dickinson SE-SW, NW-SW-S24; 10-18-52
John H. Lundy* SW-SW-S24; 12-8-54
George Lundy* SE-SE-S24; 12-8-54; SE-NW-S30; 6-4-53
Andrew Hamersley* NE-NE-S25; 7-20-44
Thomas J. Brooks NW-NE-S25; 5-19-52; MLW 1568
Richard Webster* SW-NE-S25; 11-5-51; NE-SE-S25; 2-5-39
James Snodgrass* E-NW-S25; 2-5-39
Isaac Calahan W-NW, W-SW-S25; 4-12-51; MLW 984
Thomas J. Jerome E-SW-S25; 5-15-52; MLW 8399
Louis Sanders SE-SE-S25;6-15-53;SW-SE-S25;8-14-52;S-SW-S26;8-12-52

Moses McBride   W-NE-S26; 5-15-52; MLW 32965
James Blades*   SW-NW-S26; 10-9-54
George Adams*   NE-SW-S26; 11-17-54
Zachariah Simes*   NW-SW-S26; 3-30-54
William Nixon   W-NE-S27; 10-8-52
John Newton Love   NE-NW-S27; 9-10-52
Hiram Lamb*   SE-NW-S27; 5-1-52
Eliza Lory   E-SE-S27; 12-4-52
Alexander Powell*   SW-SE-S27; 10-26-54
Bazil Clements   NW-NE-S28; 1-19-53; SE-NW-S29; 12-26-49; NE-SW,
   NW-SE-S29; 12-14-52; W-NE-S29; 9-19-44
Andrew J. Turney   SE-NW-S28; 10-27-52; NW-SW-S28; 2-1-53
Sarah Clements*   NW-NW-S28; SW-SE-S29; 2-13-49
Felix Miles, Jr.*   SW-NW-S28;12-21-49;NE-NE-S29;2-17-52;SE-NE-S29;
Thomas Faith   NE-SW-S28; 1-8-53   7-8-51
George Alexius Sharund   SE-SW-S28; 10-26-52
Thomas M. Gibson   SW-SW-S28; 2-19-53
John S. Standley   SW-SE-S28; 1-28-52
Richard Crane*   SE-SW, SE-SE-S29; 12-14-49; MLW 38827; E-NE, SW-NE-
   S32; 12-14-49; NE-NW-S32; 2-11-50
Isaac Elsbury Crane*   NE-SE-S29; 3-2-52
Henry Ash*   SE-NE-S30; 3-8-52
Ann Stites*   W-NW-S30; 7-10-44
Charles Paget*   SW-SW-S30;NW-NW-S31;2-20-36; NW-NE-S31; 6-5-51
Charles Strange, Sr.*   NE-SE-S30; 1-16-50
Ignatius Strange, Jr.*   SE-SE-S30; 7-24-48
Nancy Strange   NW-SE-S30; 7-18-51; MLW 2530
Ignatius Strange*   SW-SE-S30; 3-8-49
Samuel Gardner*   NE-NE-S31; 5-3-49; SE-NE-S31; 2-15-51
George T. Sparks*   SW-NE-S31;8-12-53;NE-SW-S31;5-8-54;SE-SW-S31;
John Ambrose Padget*   NE-NW-S31; 2-8-45   5-11-54
Benedict Simpson Padget*   SE-NW-S31; 2-13-49
William Padget*   SW-NW-S31; 8-16-36
John Lane*   SW-SW-S31; 6-28-38
Richard Allen Crane   E-SE-S31;W-SW-S32;8-19-48; MLW 12452.
Rachel Adkins and others   W-SE-S31; 10-2-51; MLW 8786.
William Cannon*   SE-NW-S32; 12-2-44.
William L. Crane   SE-S32; n.d.   / John Goldsberry*
Charles Fields*   NW-NW-S33; 5-19-52.   / SW-SE-S36; 2-19-38
John Cannon*   SW-NW, NW-SW-S33; 2-6-45.   /
Amos Salmon*   NE-SE-S33; 7-1-44.   / Mason J. Sherman
William Killian, Jr.*   SE-SE-S33; 3-18-50. / SW-NW-S36; 12-27-52
James D. Robinson   E-NE-S34; 10-7-52.
James Dominick Sharum*   SW-NE-S34;9-30-54;SE-NW-S34;4-20-46;SW-SE-
James Gallagher, Da   NW-NW-S34; 7-28-41   S34; 7-11-44
Josiah Jackson, Stark Co., O.   SW, NW-SE-S34; 6-12-39
Ozias Cooke, Da   E-SE-S34; 3-22-48   MLW 28698
Moses McBride, Carroll Co.,O.   W-SW-S36;3-30-39;NW-SE-S35;5-15-52;/
Felix Grundy Rawlings, Lw   SW-SE-S35;8-21-37
Phenies Iry, Columbiana Co.,O.   E-SE,NW-SE-S36;2-19-39
Peter Rumph, Columbiana Co.,O.   E-NE-S35;E-SW-S36;4-18-39.
Samuel Buffington   NW-NW-S36;5-11-52;MLW 14610.   / Lemuel Tague*
Jacob Purkey, Columbiana Co.,O.   SE-NW-S36;4-16-41./ NE-NE-S36;
Gideon McBride, Carroll Co.,O.   W-NE-S36;3-30-39. / 4-25-39

T 4 N, R 5 W

Philip Keck, Da N-NE, W-S-NE-S1; 9-6-47; E-S-NE-S1; 10-22-53
Alexander Maryfield, Da NW-S1; 10-26-44
Absalom Cooper, Da NE-SW-S1; 12-7-44
Robert McReynolds* NE-SE-S1; 2-5-48; SE-SE-S1; 2-21-52; SW-SE-S1;
   10-20-51; SE-NW-S12; 6-15-54
Robert Herron, Da NW-SE-S1; 12-7-44
Elzear Mattingly, Da NE-NW-S12; 10-26-54
Charles Kilgore, Jr.* NW-NW-S12; 9-28-47
John Woodruff* SW-NW-S12; 12-31-51
Moses Woodruff, Da W-SW-S12; 8-3-39
Henry Williams* W-SE-S12; 5-1-39
William A. Strange* NE-NE-S13; 9-9-37; SE-NE-S13; 12-17-38
James S. Wood N-NW-S13; 12-23-51; MLW 20107
John Scott* SE-NW-S13; 3-20-49
James Hendrixson* SW-NW-S13; 4-3-52
Ann Stites* E-SW, W-SE-S13; 7-10-44
Benjamin Allen Pate* NW-SW-S13; 5-9-49
George & Samuel Lundy* SW-SW-S13; 3-20-49
James Scott* NW-NE-S24; 8-22-37; SE-NW-S24; 7-8-44
Corshon Vliet, Mg SW-NE, E-SE-S24; 7-25-42
Jonathan Dilly Calvin* SW-NW-S24; 8-2-44
Jacob Standley, Muskingum Co.,O. W-SW-S24; 10-6-38
Joseph Strange* NW-SE-S24; 2-13-37; SW-SE-S24; 10-1-38
John S. Strange* NE-NE-S25; 2-13-49
Thomas Faith* SE-NE-S25; 8-18-46; of Da, SE-SW-S25; 12-3-42;
   NE-SW-S25; 9-28-40
Harrison Faith, Hr W-NE-S25; 3-18-39
Basil Clemonds* E-NW-S25; 11-14-44
William Sharum* SW-NW, NW-SW-S25; 9-26-39
Ricard Richardson Mathews* SW-SW-S25; 4-8-46
Charles Padget* NE-SE-S25;12-21-37;NW-SE-S25;12-11-38;E-NW-S36;
James B. Pagett* SE-SE-S25;12-21-37;SW-SE-S25;12-2-37.   11-15-37
William Kenser, Lw N-NE-S36; 11-14-37
William V. Love* SW-NE-S36; 9-23-37
William Mitchell, Columbiana Co.,O. W-NW-S36; 6-15-39
Leonard Gates* NE-SW-S36; 6-9-36
Benedict Padgett* SE-SW-S36; 12-26-36
Philip Fields, Da W-SW-S36; 6-24-37
John Lane* SE-SE-S36; 6-28-38
Johana Ryan, Hamilton Co.,O. W-SE-S36; 3-18-41

T 5 N, R 3 W

Henry Melton* NE-NE-S1; 3-5-44
Frederick Davis, Lw SE-NE-S1; 8-16-37
James W. Clawson* NW-NE-S1;10-14-37;SE-NW-S1;8-31-35;SW-NW-S1;
Isaiah Fields* SW-NE-S1; 2-11-36   8-24-36
Jeremiah Stone, Gn NE-NW-S1; 6-23-37
Robert Kipee, Gn NW-NW-S1; 7-15-36
John Moser* NE-SW-S1; 3-5-44; of Lw, NW-SE-S1; 9-8-35
Noah Boon, Lw NW-SW-S1;1-4-39;NE-SE-S2;12-3-36;SE-NE-S12;2-11-47;
Nicholas Sims, Da SW-SW-S1; 7-15-36.   NE-SE-S34;2-17-48

George Moser* NE-SE-S1; 2-14-35
Anthony Moser* SW-SE-S1; 3-5-44; SE-NW-S4; 2-9-52
William Copling Wilson, Gn NE-NE-S2; 11-3-35
John Chestnut, Sr., Lw SE-NE-S2; 10-4-38
William Thompson Chestnut, Gn NW-NE-S2; 12-17-38
William Chestnut, Gn SW-NE-S2; 2-2-37
Benjamin Franklin Hill* E-NW-S2; 11-26-38
Thomas Jefferson Hill, Lw W-NW-S2; NW-NE-S3; 8-4-37
Levi Rector, Lw E-SW-S2; 8-19-36; of*, W-NE-S3; 10-10-39
Thomas Hill, Lw NW-SW-S2; 3-20-37; of*, E-NE-S3; 11-26-38
Henry A. Hill* SW-SW-S2; 10-4-54
Henry Waggoner, Lw SE-SE-S2; 7-14-36
Elijah J. Miller* SW-NE-S3; 10-3-54
Samuel Cobb, Gn NE-NW-S3; 11-27-36
James M. Roberts* SE-NW-S3; 10-14-54
Samuel Blevins* NW-NW-S3; 11-15-37; SE-NE-S4; 10-22-38
William Mitchell, Lw SW-NW,NW-SW-S3;E-SE,SW-SE-S4; 10-7-39
Owen McBride* SW-SW-S3; 2-13-49
Elijah Miller, Lw N-SE-S3; 11-14-38
George Washington Carr* SE-SE-S3;7-31-48;SW-SE-S3;8-27-47;NE-NE-S10;
Joseph Hamilton Smith* NE-NE-S4;11-15-39;NW-NW-S4;3-3-49.   9-8-54
Moses Roberts* NE-NW-S4; 10-9-54
Jonas Smith* SW-NW-S4; 10-7-54
Thomas Banks E-SW, NW-SW, NW-SE-S4; 2-13-49; MLW 43819
Samuel Smith* SW-SW-S4; 10-30-54
William Vest, Boone Co., Ky. E-NE-S5;1-5-39; E-NW-S7; 10-10-39
Abraham Waggoner* NW-NE-S5; 1-25-51; NE-SE-S8; 12-24-38
Zachariah Roberts, Lw SW-NE-S5; 4-22-39; E-NW-S5; 9-6-39
Zachariah Cattron, Gn NE-SW-S5; 11-1-54
Elias Rawlins* SE-SW-S5;3-9-49;SW-SE-S5;7-25-36;of Da, W-SW-S10;
James Madison Rawlins* NW-SE-S5; 12-17-38   5-21-27
William Hatfield, Lw NW-NE-S6; 2-1-54
Wesley Fields* SW-NE-S6; 1-25-51
Albert Corbin* NE-NW-S6; 7-5-53; SE-NW-S6; 2-1-50
James Corbin* NW-NW-S6; 4-13-49
John E. George, Gn SW-NW-S6; 11-4-50
John P. Harryman* E-SW, N-SE-S6; 10-16-54
Absalom Cooper* W-SW-S6; 9-28-54
William Harryman* SE-SE-S6;5-11-49;NW-NE-S7;10-15-52;NW-NW-S8;
Seaborn Mayfield* SW-SE-S6;NE-NE-S7#NE-SW-S13;8-20-39.   9-26-53
Edmund Bridges* SE-NE-S7;9-11-54;SW-NW-S8;1-25-51;SE-SW-S8;10-13-54
Zachariah Smith* SW-NE-S7; 8-29-53; NE-SW, NW-SE-S7; 9-29-54
Valentine J. Shryock, Gn W-NW-S7; 6-17-39
Michael Ozee SE-SW-S7; 1-24-53
Jesse Pennington* NW-SW-S7; 3-26-51.   # 8-17-36
James Webster* SW-SW-S7; 9-28-54
Dancy Simpson NE-SE-S7; 1-24-53
George McReynolds* SE-SE-S7; 1-12-37
Levi Simpson, Boone Co., Ky. SW-SE-S7; NW-NE-S17; 9-19-40
Isaac Titsworth Bridges* E-NE-S8;10-12-38;W-SE-S8;12-13-36;SW-NE-
Joseph Johnson Badger W-NE,E-NW-S8;3-30-49;MLW 43318. /S15;3-16-45
John J. Jackson Bridges, Lw NE-SW-S8; 3-4-36
Jonathan Bridges, Lw NW-SW-S8; 3-4-36
John Alexander, Boone Co., Ky. SW-SW-S8; 10-10-39

John N. Brooks SE-SE-S8; 1-14-53
John Mitchell, Lw N-NE-S9; 10-7-39
Hezekiah Collier* SE-NE-S9; 11-16-48
Michael Elliott* SW-NE-S9; 2-13-54; NE-SE-S9; 3-29-51.   Omission:
Joseph Hamilton Smith* NE-NW-S9; 4-4-55.   /Isaac
James Owens S-NW, N-SW-S9; 11-20-48; MW 34183.   /Sizemore
Stephen Whitley* NW-NW-S9; 5-2-49.   /SE-SE-S9;
John C. Meeks* SE-SW-S9; 8-9-49; SW-SW-S9; 12-12-51.   /4-27-40.
David Lewis† NW-SE-S9; 11-8-54; SW-SE-S9; 3-9-49.
Thomas Hill, Lw SE-NE-S10; 4-10-37.
John Saunders* NW-NE, NE-NW-S10; 9-29-51; SW-NE-S10; 9-28-54.
George W. Baker* SE-NW-S10; 12-30-51
Hezekiah Collier, Ws NW-NW-S10; 7-23-38
Zachariah Loveall, Sr.* SW-NW-S10; 11-9-36
James Denson* E-SE-S10; W-SW-S11; 7-11-44
Starling Sims, Da SW-SE-S10; NE-NE-S15; 8-9-36
Levi Rector* NE-NE-S11;5-26-47; NW-NE, NE-NW-S11; 8-19-36
William Sims, Lw SE-NE-S11; 9-19-33
John Sims* SW-NE-S11;12-8-38;SE-NW-S11;4-7-46;SE-SW-S11;5-6-54;
    NW-SE-S11;6-15-49; of Lw, SE-SE-S11; 2-19-36
Henry Allen Hill, Lw NW-NW-S11; 12-8-38
Reuben McCormack* SW-NW-S11; 10-2-54
Amsted Baker* NE-SW-S11; 1-26-37
Emily Redmon* NE-SE-S11; 9-30-33
Reuben Raney* SW-SE-S11; 5-6-54; NE-NW-S14; 3-31-46
John Wallace* NE-NE-S12;9-8-48; W-NE,NE-SW,NW-SE-S12;10-10-48;MLW
James Harshfield, Jr., Bullet Co., Ky. E-NW-S12;4-13-40.   18338
William McCormick* NW-NW-S12; 12-10-33; SW-NW-S12; 11-13-35
Lacy McCormick* SE-SW-S12; 12-24-46
John Dishman NE-SE-S12; 1-19-52; MLW 20370
Thomas Deweis* SE-SE-S12; 2-11-39
John McCormick* SW-SE-S12; 12-24-46; NE-NE-S14; 1-11-51
Yelverton Lewis* NE-NE-S13; 9-1-36; SE-SW, SE-SE-S13; 3-26-36
Jacob Waggoner* SE-NE-S13; 9-1-36
Sally Wagoner* NW-NE-S13; 3-26-36
Levi Brock* SW-NE-S13; 11-20-48
James Sims* NE-NW-S13; 3-21-44; SE-NW-S13; 1-28-48
Allen Brock* NW-NW-S13; 10-8-40; SW-SW-S13; 2-13-49; SW-SE-S13;
    10-27-54; NW-NE-S14; 3-1-36
Joseph Rudyard* SW-NW-S13; 2-11-45; NW-SW-S13; 11-25-48
John, Adam, & Harrison Gore* NE-SE-S13; 10-18-54
Robert Baker* NW-SE-S13; 9-14-36
Iredell Fields* SE-NE-S14; 10-24-54
George F. Raney* SW-NE, SE-NW-S14; 10-12-54
Milton Short, Lw NW-NW-S14; 8-10-68
Hamilton C. Baker* SW-NW-S14; 4-26-49; W-SW-S14; 10-3-54
David Fisher* NE-SW-S14; 7-31-48; SE-SW, SE-SE-S14; 9-26-54;
    NE-SE-S14; 2-13-49; of Lw, W-SE-S14; 6-29-39
Zachariah Sims* NW-NE-S15; 1-26-37
Robert Owens* E-NW-S15; 10-9-50
Benjamin Cooper* NW-NW-S15; 9-29-36; SW-NW-S15; 11-3-36
Anderson J. Pool NE-SW-S15; 1-7-54; MLW 49887
William Landers* SE-SW-S15; 1-30-50; SW-SW-S15; 10-10-46
Jonas Smith* NW-SW-S15; 11-20-37; SE-NE-S20; 4-12-37

Hiram Roberts* NW-NE-S17;10-18-54;NE-NW-S17;11-3-53;SE-NW-S17;
Thomas Carter* SW-NE-S17; 4-20-54   2-28-52
John Alexander, Boone Co., Ky. W-NW-S17;E-NE,E-SE-S18; 10-10-39
Thomas Roberts* NE-SW-S17; 12-19-53
William Preston SE-SW-S17;NE-NW-S20; 8-13-53; MLW 21894
Joseph McCormick* NW-SW-S17;12-19-68;SW-SW-S17;2-16-48;NW-NW-S20;
Jesse Elliott* NE-SE-S17;11-26-56;SE-SE-S17;10-21-54.   1-14-54
Doncy Simpson* SW-NE-S18; 10-27-54
James Webster* NW-NW-S18; 9-28-54
Adam Cimbel SW-NW-S18; 11-6-57
William H. Harryman* NE-SW-S18; 10-4-51
Joseph Hert* SE-SW-S18; 10-13-54; SW-NW-S20; 9-17-51
Anthony Hurt* NW-NE-S19; 2-18-51; SE-NW-S20; 9-29-54
Columbus C. Parker SW-NE,SE-NW,W-SE-S19; 3-28-49; MLW 47362
Thomas Hert* NE-NW-S19; 12-12-54; NW-NW-S19; 10-27-54; of Lw,
   NW-NE-S20; 3-28-49; SW-NE, NE-SE-S20; 3-17-49
John Edmondson, Lw SW-NW-S19; 8-17-39
Elias P. Kenady* NW-SW-S19; 10-9-54
John Price* SW-SW-S19; 10-13-54
Thomas Donica, Edgar Co., Ill. NE-SE-S19; 2-4-39
Elbert Evans, Lw SE-SE-S19; 2-28-39
Elisha Baker* NE-NE-S20; 10-3-54.
George Sipes* SE-SE-S20; W-SW-S21; 9-25-54; SE-NW-S21; 4-26-51;
   NE-SW-S21; 1-30-37; SW-SE-S21; 3-21-36
Josephus Payton* NE-NE-S21; 2-16-49; SE-NE-S21; 11-9-48
Ephraim Centry Cox* NW-NE-S21; 4-14-48; NE-NW-S21; 6-18-53
Absalom B. Cox* SW-NE-S21; 4-17-50
John D. Thomasson, Lw NW-NW-S21; 5-25-57
Robert Baker* SW-NW-S21; 10-30-50
Christian Keck* NW-SE-S21; 2-9-37
Isaac Hutton* NE-NE-S22; NW-NW-S23; 10-26-46
Michael Rayleigh Hall* SW-NE-S22; 9-16-36
Peter Payton* NE-NW-S22; 9-30-54
Elbert Howard Payton* SE-NW-S22; 2-18-46
James H. Meek* W-SW-S22; 10-12-54
Francis M. Landers* NE-SE-S22;1-9-51;SE-NE-S23;NW-NW-S24;11-19-49
Francis White SE-SE-S22; 12-9-52
Albert McCormick* NE-NE-S23; SW-NW-S24; 10-10-54
Abraham Fisher, Lw NW-NE-S23; 2-18-53; NE-NW-S23; 2-25-52
Joseph C. Cooner* SW-NE-S23; 1-23-37
Absalom Cox SE-NW, NE-SW-S23; 4-14-52; MLW 29941
John Brock* SE-SW-S23; NE-NW-S26; 10-2-54; SW-SE-S23; 1-8-52
Jacob Hedrick* NW-SW-S23; 9-29-36; SW-SW-S23; 8-26-36
Thomas White* NE-SE-S23; 10-31-54; NW-SE-S23; 11-30-49
Jane Little, Beaver Co., Pa. SW-S24; 2-26-47; MLW 33421, 26602
Russell Waggoner, Lw N-SE-S24; 9-24-46
Truelove Brown* SE-SE-S24; 4-28-37
Jesse K. Baker* SW-SE-S24;E-NE-S25;10-9-54; SE-SW-S25; 1-16-55
John Asbury Baker* NW-NE-S25;8-10-53;SW-NE,SE-NW-S25;10-3-54;NE-NW-
Curtis C. Cox, Cn W-NW-S25; 9-30-54   S25; 12-19-56
Noah Keller* NE-SW-S25;9-26-53;NW-SW-S25;NE-SE-S26; 10-16-54
Jackson Inman, Lw SW-SW-S25; 7-30-51; NE-SE-S25; 6-20-53
Christopher Keller, Lw SE-SE-S25; 10-17-54
George Kinder* NW-SE-S25; 2-7-37

Isaac Kinder, Lw SW-SE-S25; 7-30-51
Rufus Mitchell* E-NE-S26; 10-4-54
Benjamin Cooper, Sr., Da W-NE-S26; 9-1-24
Samuel H. Mitchell SE-NW-S26; 5-10-53
Elijah Dotson* NW-NW-S26; 11-30-36; NW-NE-S27; 6-9-36
Richard Dotson* SW-NW-S26; 8-26-36
Levi Brock, Da E-SW, NW-SE-S26; 10-5-54
Elisha Fisher* NW-SW-S26; NE-SE-S27; 1-9-51; NE-SW-S34; 12-2-56;
    NW-SE-S34; 12-27-52
Elijah Craig* SW-SW-S26;NE-NW-S35; 9-18-54; NW-SE-S27; 3-8-52;
    SW-SE-S27; 8-19-53; NE-NE, W-NE-S34; 3-31-46.   7-30-57
Joseph Keller* SE-SE-S26;11-20-54;SW-SE-S26;11-23-54;NE-NE-S35;
Henry Grindstaff, Lw NE-NE-S27;11-3-48;SW-NE,NE-NW-S27;9-19-48.
Daniel Baker, Lw SE-NE-S27; 11-7-48
Isaac Mitchell, Lw SE-NW-S27; 9-9-48
Newton H. Williams, Dn E-SW-S27; 10-24-54
William B. Engleton* NW-SW-S27; 11-21-56   10-5-54
Stephen M. Isom, Lw SW-SW-S27;SE-SE-S28;E-NE,NW-NE-S33;NW-NW-S34;
Fleaming Chastine* SE-SE-S27;12-24-50;NE-SE-S32;6-15-49;SW-NE,
    NW-SE-S33;5-16-53;SE-NW-S33;12-23-50;SW-NW-S33;4-8-54
Isham Eddington NW-NE, NE-NW-S28; 8-5-54
Andrew L. Shaller SW-NE,SE-NW,NE-SW,NW-SE-S28;9-4-48;MLW 7577
William Sipes* W-NW-S28; SE-NE-S29; 8-1-49
Thomas Luttrell* SE-SW-S28; 11-23-53;NE-NW-S33;9-21-52;NW-NW-S35;
William B. Angleton* NE-SE-S28; 11-21-56   10-9-48
John Webb* SW-SE-S28; 9-22-54
William McCormick* N-NE-S29; 10-12-54
Enoch Smallwood, Mr SW-NE-S29; 11-7-38
George Flory, Mr NE-NW-S29; 11-2-38
Septima Bowman* NW-NW-S29; 1-30-37; SE-SE-S30; 5-24-36
William Webb* NE-SW-S29; 5-5-57
Nicholas Sims* SE-SW-S29; 8-23-47
James R. Toliver, Lw SE-S29; 10-5-54
Ambrose Carmichael, Gn W-NE-S30; 10-18-54
William Westley Stultz, Mr NE-NW-S30; 2-20-43
John W. Smith* W-NW, NW-SW-S30; 9-26-54
James Sims* E-SW-S30; 10-11-54
James Taylor, Lw SW-SW-S30; 9-3-46
Pleasant Bowman* NE-SE-S30; 10-3-38
James Snodgrass, Mr W-NE-S31; 9-20-37; NE-NW-S31; 10-10-37
John W. May, Lw N-SW, SE-S31; 10-4-54
Charles H. Rose, Harrison Co.,O. S-SW-S31; 10-26-53
William Allen* NE-NE-S32; 4-3-54
William McCord SE-NE-S32; 6-26-57; MLW 93487
Emsley Burton, Gn NW-S32; 10-5-54
John Fairley, Jr. Lw E-SW-S32; 10-16-38
Samuel Fairley, Lw NW-SW-S32; 1-5-39
Thomas Gee* SW-SW-S32; 4-8-50
George B. Hall, Lw SE-SE,W-SE-S32; W-SW-S33; 10-9-54
Robert Walker NW-NW-S33; 7-18-57
John Brant Hayward, Fulton Co., Ill. E-SW-S33; 4-3-37
Fleming Chastine & John Davis E-SE-S33;W-SW-S34;6-15-49; MLW 54433
Samuel Brown* SW-SE-S33; 9-24-53
John Craig* NE-NW-S34; 3-15-48

William Baker* SE-NE-S34;3-18-54;NE-SW-S35;10-16-54;NE-SE-S35;
John W. Baker, Lw SE-NW-S34; 9-17-46   12-15-36
William Craig* SW-NW-S34; 4-5-54
Peter Baker, Lw SE-SW-S34; 6-10-54; of*, SW-SE-S34; 10-9-54
Henry Waggoner* SE-SE-S34; 10-17-54
William Elliott* SE-NE, W-NE-S35; 10-21-54
William Baker, Jr.* SE-NW-S35; 10-16-54
Jacob Hammersley SW-NW-S35; 8-21-52; MLW 18874
Uriah Luttrell* SE-SE-S35; 8-6-35
Boone Cox* NW-SE-S35;1-25-57;NE-SW-S36;3-21-44;NW-SW-S36;1-26-52;
Christopher Keller, Lw NE-NE-S36;10-17-54.   /SW-SW-S36;5-17-51 /
Asa Veatch, Or SE-NE-S36; 2-3-37
James N. White, Lw NW-NE-S36; 1-25-55
Isaac Cox* SW-NE, SE-SW-S36; 3-14-37
George Brown, Lw E-SE-S36; 10-23-33
George Reaney W-SE-S36; 3-9-19; Relinquished E-SE-S36; 3-9-19

T 5 N, R 4 W

Malcom Davis* NE-NE-S1; 10-4-54
Zachariah Smith* SE-NE-S1; 12-23-50
Elijah Bobbitt, Boone Co., Ky. E-NW, NW-NW-S1; 1-5-39
John Inman, Lw SW-NW-S1; 2-8-38; of*, NW-SW-S1; 1-25-38
John E. George, Gn E-SW-S1; 10-14-54
Mary Records* SW-SW-S1; 11-29-50
Archibald Lanter NE-SE-S1; 6-12-52; MLW 27526
Absalom Cooper* SE-SE-S1; 9-28-54
Elijah M. Bobbitt* NE-NE-S2; 2-14-51
William Wilson Hume* SE-NE-S2; 4-13-49; SW-SE-S2; 2-14-51
William E. Browne NW-NE-S2; 5-16-53
Armstead Eavs* SW-NE, SE-NW-S2; 11-29-50
Isaac E. Pownall* N-NW-S2; 12-21-53
Elisha Inman* SW-NW-S2; 3-26-51; of Lw, N-SE-S2; 9-28-37
Solomon Inman* NW-SW-S2; 1-11-39
George Inman, Lw SW-SW-S2;SE-SE-S3;6-7-37; of*, NE-SE,SW-SE-S3;
    10-19-54;NE-NE-S10;1-8-50;NW-NE-S10;10-17-53;NW-NW-S11;4-26-51
David Duncan* SE-SE-S2; 1-4-39
Samuel G. Pownall, Columbiana Co., Ind. (no such Co.; so prob. Ohio
    NW-NE-S3; N-NE-S3; 6-20-53
George Stultz* SE-NE-S3; 6-7-53; W-NW, W-SW-S3; 1-2-38
Malissa Stulce* SW-NE-S3; 10-18-39
Frederick Hensley E-NW, E-SW-S3; 6-14-50; MLW 51155
Daniel Myers NW-SE-S3; 9-18-52
Redman Mise, Lw NE-NE-S4; 7-3-39
Hugh Bodel SE-NE, SW-NE, E-SE-S4;11-30-49; MLW 49836; of Licking
    Co.,O. SW-SE-S4; 12-1-49
William Whitaker, Coshocton Co.,O. NW-NE-S4; 2-13-49
Thomas Sharpless* S-SW-S4; 6-20-44
John W. Pierrin, Gn NW-SE-S4; 10-21-54
Samuel Wilson Howard, Boone Co., Ky. NE-NE, W-NE-S5; 6-17-39
John Haig Summerville, Gn N-NW-S5; 1-17-39
George Ledgerwood* SW-SW-S5; 1-6-36; SE-SE-S6; 11-15-38
Charles Gordon, Gn E-SE-S5; 11-12-51
David Wallace* NW-NE-S6; 6-6-36; of Gn, NW-SW-S6; 3-7-40

Nathaniel Ledgerwood* SE-NE-S6;11-27-37;NE-SE-S6;9-6-47;NW-SE-S6;
   1-17-39; SW-SE-S6; 12-29-35
Fielding Lewis Odonald, Gn SW-NE-S6; 11-30-48
Obadiah Truax Barker, Gn NW-NW-S6; 4-2-38
John George, Boone Co., Ky. SW-NW-S6; 3-22-39
James Haig* E-SW-S6; 3-7-40; of Mr, SW-SW-S6; 2-23-37; NE-NW-S7;
   SW-NE-S9; 1-10-53
David Ledgerwood* NE-NE-S7; 9-10-32
John Haig Summerville & William Summerville SE-NE-S7; 1-17-39
Jacob Ledgerwood* NW-NE-S7; 9-25-49
William Summerville SW-NE-S7; 2-7-53; of Gn, E-SE-S7; 10-19-43
James Richardson, Da SE-NW-S7; 8-16-48
Reuben Mullis* W-NW, W-SW-S7; 2-17-52
John H. Dillon* NE-NE-S8; NW-NW-S9; 3-2-52
William Sharpless* SE-NE-S8; 8-2-50
Thomas Elrod, Lw NW-NE-S8; 8-18-36; of*, W-SE-S8; 2-4-39
Silas Chambers & Charles Ledgerwood E-NW-S8; 3-4-31
Alvin Philips W-NW, W-SW-S8; 9-28-49; MLW 55683
Thomas Corbin* NE-NE-S9; 11-20-48
Thomas Sharpless* S-NE,S-NW-S9;3-16-52;MLW 16781;NW-SW-S9;11-17-54
William F. Donaldson, Gn NW-NE-S9; 4-10-52
James W. Phipps NE-NW-S9; 12-13-52
James Richardson, Jo E-SW, SW-SW-S9; 8-17-41
Silas Penz Waggoner* NE-SE-S9;3-28-54;SW-SE-S9;3-7-54;of Gn, NW-SE-
Hiram Fish* SE-SE-S9; 8-30-47   S9;3-26-51
James Vanmeter NW-S10; 9-6-49; MLW 61703
Anderson H. Smith E-SW-S10;1-7-53;MLW 27865; NW-SE-S10;1-22-53
William Philips NW-SW-S10; 10-21-52; NW-NW-S21; 10-21-52
Samuel Moore* SW-SW-S10; 2-17-51; SW-NW-S15; 2-1-39
Wiley G. Burton, Lw S-SE-S10;SW-SW-S11;SW-SE-S11;NW-NE,NE-NW,W-NW-
Daniel Dulen E-SE-S11;S-NW-S12;2-9-52;MLW 6877.   S14;10-5-54
Cyrus Kirkendall* N-NE-S11; 10-9-54
Philip Baker* SW-NE-S11; 8-19-39; NW-NE-S15; 3-31-37
Abraham Achor* N-SW-S11; 2-6-54
Drury Holt* SE-SW-S11; 8-10-44
James H. Waggoner* SE-SE-S11;W-SW-S12;10-9-54; NE-NW-S13;4-4-57
John Russell Baker* NW-SE-S11; 2-6-54
Absalom Cooper* NE-NE-S12; 9-28-54
James Penninger* SE-NE-S12; Mar. 7, n.d.
Josiah Hayworth NW-NE-S12; 11-21-53
Richard Browne* SW-NE-S12; 9-12-54; NW-SE-S19; 4-30-49
Isaac W. Roach* NW-NW-S12; 10-19-54
Thomas Webster* NE-SW-S12;NW-NE-S13;9-27-54; SE-SW-S12; 3-22-51
Jesse Penninger* NE-SE-S12; 3-18-48
James Webster* SE-SE-S12; 9-28-54
William Duncan* SW-NE-S13; 10-10-54
John W. Eaton* S-NW-S13; 4-4-57
James Waggoner NW-NW-S13; 1-5-52; of*, NE-NE-S14; 3-17-69
Elisha Sargeant* E-SW,W-SE-S13;9-4-55;SW-SE-S14;1-10-37;SW-SE-S23;
   1-28-n.d.;NW-NE-S24;3-25-54;NE-NE-S25;9-4-55
Robert Mitchell* E-SE-S13; 10-4-54
Alexander Waggoner* SE-NE-S14; 8-19-39
William S. Turner SW-NE-S14; 8-28-52
Joseph Sargeant SE-NW-S14; 10-29-51

William Cannon* NE-SW-S14; 10-31-36
John Waggoner* NW-SE-S14;1-14-39;SW-SE-S15;NW-NE-S22; 1-10-37
Thomas Sargeant* SE-NE, NE-SE-S15; -12-1-38
Thomas B. Eaton* SE-NW-S15; 12-31-47
Charles Gordon NW-SE-S15; S-SE-S17; 2-1-53
Silas Chambers, Da NE-NE-S17; 2-26-38
George N. Haig* SE-NE-S17; 10-6-54
Riley Stone, Gn W-NE-S17; 9-29-54
William Stultes, Lw NE-NW,SW-NW-S17;2-5-45;SE-NW-S17;2-4-45; of*,
    NW-NW-S17; 12-26-68
George Gordon, Coshocton Co.,O. E-SW-S17;3-10-54; MLW 29309, 7884
William O'Donal, Gn NW-SW-S17; 10-3-54
Cornelius Boman Roberts, Gn SW-SW-S17;SE-SE-S18;NE-NW,S-SE-S19;
Pleasant Philips* NE-NE-S18; 6-8-51   3-24-52
Frederick Robertson S-NE, N-SE-S18; 8-29-48; MLW 15550
Isaac Saint Clair* NW-NE-S18; 1-10-48; NE-NW-S18; 11-7-51
William Haywood, Gn SE-NW, NE-SW-S18; 9-16-51
John R. Gibson W-NW, NW-SW-S18; 10-27-49; MLW 55207
Anderson H. Smith, Gn SE-SW, SW-SE-S18; 9-16-51
Daniel Pruett* SW-SW-S18; 10-13-54
Thomas Lay* NE-S19; 11-19-49
Roland Allison Childs, Da SE-NW-S19; 5-15-49
Charles Ledgerwood, Gn NW-NW-S19; 12-9-53
Daniel Ketcham, Da SW-NW-S19; 9-9-47; NW-SW-S19; 12-7-53
Joseph G. Laughlin* NE-SW-S19; 12-20-51; of Da, SE-SW-S19;3-11-52
Levi Butcher, Mr SW-SW-S19; 10-15-38
John Holt* NE-SE-S19; 4-21-51; NE-NW-S33; 3-3-51
Eli Stultes* E-NE-S20; 3-12-50
David Wright, Mr NW-NE-S20; 1-2-50
John R. Laughlin, Da SW-NE-S20; 10-14-54
Alfred Philips NW-S20; 9-21-49; MLW 8182
Doswell Holt* E-SW-S20;1-28-39;SW-SW-S20;8-4-51;SE-SE-S20;4-2-49;
    SW-NW-S28;NE-SE-S29;9-21-37;NE-NE-S29;12-8-37;NW-NE-S29;7-1-51;
Moses McCarter, Da NW-SW-S20; 9-9-47   NE-NW-S29;5-24-54
Henry Holt* NE-SE-S20; SW-NW-S21; 10-3-54; SW-NE-S28; 11-1-44;
    NW-NW-S28; 6-10-37; NE-SE-S28; 5-8-54; SE-NE-S29; 9-27-36
Joseph Conder, Mr N-NE-S21; 4-27-50. Middle initial A.
Michael Fartney (Fortney, Fortner)* SE-NE-S21; n.d.; SW-NW-S22;
    12-30-50; NW-SW-S22; 1-14-39; NW-SE-S22; 10-9-54
Isaac Minnich SW-NE,SE-NW,NE-SW,NW-SE-S21; 4-18-49; MLW 45231;
    SW-NE, NW-SW, NW-SE-S25; 10-2-54
John Philips, Jr.* NE-NW-S21; 2-22-50
William McCormick SE-SW,E-SE,SW-SE-S21; 2-27-52; MLW 13156
John F. Bayard, Jr. NW-SW-S21; 9-24-52
Henry Holt, Jr.* SW-SW-S21; 6-24-50
John Cochran, Jr.* NW-NW-S22; 4-10-52
Jacob F. Osborn* E-SE-S22; 10-7-54
Drury Holt* SW-SE-S22; NW-NE-S27; NE-NE-S28; 10-3-54; NE-NW-S27;
    3-13-51; NW-NW-S27; 3-15-49; SW-NW-S27; 3-13-54
James R. Hainds, Mr E-NE-S23; 10-16-54
Absalom Sargent, Gn NW-NE-S23; 1-28-39
Solomon Inman* E-NW-S23; 1-11-39; NE-SE-S23; 11-6-54; NW-SE-S23; /
    3-8-52; of Lw, E-SW-S23; 10-30-37   /47
Willaby Inman* SE-SE-S23;10-17-54;SW-SW-S24;2-22-49;SE-SW-S26;9-11-/

Elias P. Kenady* E-NE, SW-NE-S24; 10-9-54
Solomon Edmondson, Lw NE-NW-S24; 9-30-39
Alfred Girdley* SE-NW-S24; 10-27-54
Elbert Evans, Lw NE-SW-S24; 2-28-39
Isaac Webster* SE-SW-S24; 9-28-36
Squire Wilson* NW-SW-S24; 3-23-37
John Edmondson, Lw NE-SE-S24; 8-17-39
Reuben Kilgore SE-SE-S24; 1-17-53
Zachous Carpenter Wilson, Cn NW-SE-S24; 3-23-37
David Borland, Lw SW-SE-S24; 10-14-37
John W. Smith* SE-NE, SE-SE-S25; 9-26-54
Sanford Webster* NW-NE-S25; 4-26-37
George Alexander Wilson, Cn NE-NW-S25; 3-23-37
Payton Bristow* SE-NW-S25; 3-12-36
John Grayson Edmondson* SW-NW-S25; 9-11-39
James D. Huff* NE-SW-S25; 11-20-56
Jacob Minnick* SE-SW-S25; 10-2-54; SW-SW-S25; 4-12-55;NE-NW-S36;
James Taylor* NE-SE-S25; 9-8-47   10-2-54
William H. Burton, Lw SW-SE-S25; 10-5-54
Myron H. Lincoln* NE-NE-S26; 9-25-54
Samuel Minnick* SE-NE-S26; 8-22-39
Jesse Barnes* N-NW-S26; 4-8-36; E-NE-S27; 1-21-54
Elisha Barnes* SE-NW-S26; 1-7-50; NE-SW-S26; 1-14-53
Henry Minnick* NW-SW-S26; 10-2-54
Trulove Brown, Jr.* SW-SW-S26; 10-24-54; NW-NW-S35; 10-24-54
Jacob Shutter, Ws E-SE-S26; 10-3-38
Andrew Selsor* NW-SE-S26; 5-28-51
Abraham F. McReynolds* SW-SE-S26; 6-2-53
David Duncan* SW-NE-S27; 12-21-40
William Toon* SE-NW-S27;2-23-52;NW-SW-S27;11-8-54;SE-SE-S28;E-NE,
    NW-NE-S33;9-30-54;SW-NW-S34;1-25-51; of Lw, SW-SW-S27;8-28-39
Lucian Toon* NE-SW-S27; 8-19-44
Willis Wilson* SE-SW-S27; 9-29-54
Garret Voris* E-SE-S27;1-28-39; of Or, E-SE-S34; 11-17-38
Garret Voris* NW-SE-S27;2-22-49; Thomas Inman* SW-SE-S27;10-26-49;
    These two entries bracketed & note says: Canceled May 17, 1844;
    See Commissioners letter on file.
James Holt* SE-NW-S28; 8-24-37
Henry Boman* NW-SW-S28; 12-26-37
Emberson Holt* SW-NE-S29; 3-22-49; SE-NW-S29; 10-10-53
Calvin Holt* W-SW-S29; 1-3-39
Pleasant Bowman* SE-SE-S29; 1-30-37; NE-NE-S32; 3-12-36
Aron Williams* SW-SE-S29; 2-18-45
John Osmyn Monroe Laughlin* (two men?) NE-NE-S30;3-27-46;SE-NE-S30;
Levi Butcher, Mr W-NE, E-NW-S30; W-NW-S31; 9-21-38   9-6-47
Martin Williams, Lw SE-NE-S31; 10-6-37; E-SE-S31; 3-1-36
James Hastin (Kastin?)* SW-NE-S31; 2-1-37; SE-NW-S31; 9-30-39
Christian Keck* NE-SW-S31;2-9-37;NW-SW-S31;3-31-38;W-NW-S32;8-29-39
Philip Keck* SE-SW-S31; 3-25-37; of Da, SW-SW-S31; 7-27-38
John Ketcham, Mr SW-SE-S31; 6-17-39
John Hastings, Lw NW-SE-S31; 11-20-33; W-SW-S32; 11-7-34, of*
Septima Boman* SE-NE-S32; 10-14-37
John Edwards, Lw W-NE-S32; 1-23-37
William Boman* NE-SW, NW-SE-S32; 1-2-39

Vincent Williams, Lw SE-SW-S32; 5-23-36; of *, SW-SE-S32;
   10-28-54. Vinson
Simon Clever E-SE-S32; SW, W-SE-S33; 11-28-48; MLW 30579, 30593
Thomas J. Sharam, Da SW-NE-S33; 12-12-54; SE-NW-S33; 10-12-54
James Boman* NW-NW-S33; 8-20-39
John A. Hamilton E-SE-S33; W-SW-S34; 11-28-48; MLW 30588
Willis Wilson* NW-NE, N-NW-S34; 9-29-54
Jacob Hamersly* SW-NE, NW-SE-S34; 9-29-54
Gainer Bough* SE-NW-S34; 9-27-53
Jacob Shutter, Ws NE-NE-S35; NW-NW-S36; 10-3-38
William H. Burton, Lw SE-NE-S35; W-NE, S-NW, NE-SW-S36; 10-5-54
John Miller W-NE, E-NW-S35; 3-26-49; MLW 34171
Robert Cartwright* SW-NW, NW-SE-S35; 10-5-54
William Brown* NE-SW-S35; 1-14-50; NW-SW-S35; 2-5-45
James R. Bridges E-SE, S-SW-S35; 3-22-49; MLW 33100
Simon Smith* NE-NE-S36; 3-10-51
George Washington Gee* SE-NE-S35; 11-21-53; NW-SW-S35; 3-8-49;
   NW-SE-S35; 3-10-51
Charles H. Rose, Hamilton Co., O. NE-SE-S36; 10-26-53
John Nicholas* SW-SE-S36; 9-26-54

RELINQUISHMENTS

Henry Griffin E-SE-S30; 4-25-20
James McCammon NW-S25; 12-16-19

John C. Bennington* NE-NW-S1; 1-7-57
John S. Bennett* SE-NW-S1; 4-16-52
Rachel Lucus* NW-NW-S1; 12-30-44
William Lucus* (Lucust) SW-NW-S1;5-30-44;NW-SW-S1; 2-11-47;NE-NW-
Willis Lamb' SW-SW-S1; 6-6-36   S4; 11-10-35
John Bunch, Ws SE-S1; NE-NE-S12; 11-3-54
James Leo' NE-NE-S2; 5-10-50
Joseph Lee* SW-NE-S2; 6-20-36
John Henderson Anderson* NW-NE-S2;10-26-32;E-SE-S4;9-17-27;W-SE-S4;
Solomon Lucas+ SW-NE-S2;6-27-36;W-NW-S2;12-31-17.   8-24-24
Zadock Long* E-SW-S2; 3-4-46
Amos Lock* NW-SW-S2; 7-26-37
Thomas Grimes* SW-SW-S2;9-21-33;NW-S3;SW-S15;9-25-16;SW-S10;12-9-16
Michael Myers* E-SE-S2; 12-9-25
Adam Wampler* NW-SE-S2; 12-5-36
Henry Burkart NE-S3; 9-25-16
William Anderson SW-S3; 9-25-16
Bartlett Woodward SE-S3; NE, SE-S10; 9-25-16
Adam Darting NE-S4; 9-25-16
Richard Randolph Richardson* SE-NW-S4;2-4-34;SW-NW-S4;9-17-34;NE-SW-
Richard Helms* NW-NW-S4; 8-5-34   S34;8-30-32
John Lucus* SE-NW-S4; 11-20-35
Robert Holmes* NW-SW-S4; 11-28-35
Solomon Wagaman* SW-SW-S4; SW-SE-S5; 12-13-33
Thomas Hancock E-NE-S5; 9-23-17
James Cully W-NE-S5; 9-1-17
Robert Fields NW-S5; 9-25-16
James Mitchell* E-SW-S5; 1-28-18; W-SW-S5; 7-2-31
John Wagaman* E-SE-S5; 12-13-33; E-NW-S9; 2-25-36
Joshua Wagaman* NW-SE-S5; 12-16-35; NW-SW-S9; 2-25-36
John Routt & Adam Brenton NE, W-SW-S6; 9-25-16
William Bigger NW-S6; 9-19-16
John Ketcham* NE-SW-S6; 8-5-34; E-SE, NW-SE-S6; 2-10-35
Joseph Ketcham* SE-SW-S6; 7-24-35
Allen Parham* SW-SE-S6; 4-21-36
Potter & Hughes NE, NW-S7; SW-S19; SW-S31; 9-25-16
John Storm SW-S7; 10-14-16; E-NE-S8; 1-28-18
John Baly King* NE-SE-S7; 11-13-35; SE-SE-S7; 1-15-36
John Kutch* W-SE-S7; 10-31-31; NW-NE-S18; 10-27-34
David Scott* W-NE-S8; 10-20-28; W-SE-S9; 12-30-17
Joseph Hobson* E-NW-S8; 12-28-55
James Haig* NW-NW-S8; 12-29-35
William Chandler* SW, W-SE-S8; 11-17-35; E-SE-S8; 8-11-36
John Scott* NE-S9; 1-8-17; SE-SW-S23; 6-4-36
John Tucker* W-NW-S9; 3-22-30
John Switzer* NE-SW-S9; 12-16-35
John Shipman* SE-SW-S9; 2-22-36
Solomon Wooden* SW-SW-S9; 8-29-36
George Kimberlin* NE-SE-S9;3-10-36;SE-SE-S9;11-3-36;W-NW-S14;
George Burkirk (Buskirk?) (Burkart?) NW-S10; 12-9-16   1-31-28
Samuel Pennington* NE-NE-S11; 6-27-36
Joseph Pennington* SE-NE-S11; 9-14-52

Andrew Deckard* NW-NE-S11; 9-15-52
John Selvy Bennett* SW-NE-S11; 3-31-46
Hezekiah Deckard* NE-NW-S11; 2-8-36
Jacob Deckard* SE-NW-S11; 11-12-46; W-NW-S11; 6-7-24; NW-NW-S12;
    10-26-32; NE-SW-S12; 1-29-38; NE-SW-S14; 1-31-28
Silas Woodward* SE-SW-S11; 12-23-33; W-SW-S11; 9-2-17
Patrick Garin, Jr S-NE, NE-SE-S12; 3-12-56
Frederick Wisely NW-NE, NE-NW-S12; 6-21-52; MLW 25339; of*, SW-SW-
    S12; 11-10-32; SE-NW-S12; 2-9-38; SW-NW-S12; 2-11-36
John Musser* SE-SW-S12; 6-27-39; NW-SW-S12; 6-29-35; SW-SW-S14;
    7-27-46; SE-SE-S15; 11-10-34; W-SE-S15; 12-19-16
Robert Clark* SE-SE-S12; 6-30-54
David Deckard* SW-SE-S12; 1-26-54
George Thresher* NW-SE-S12; 1-14-54
David Chambers, Sr.* SE-NE-S13; 2-11-45; SW-NE-S24; 2-7-54
John Deckard* NE-NW-S13; 10-26-50
Ephraim Baugh* SE-NW-S13; NE-NE-S14; 1-14-54
John Hellenbrugt* NW-NW-S13; 10-10-44
Joseph Baugh* SW-NW-S13; NW-NE-S14; 6-15-36; E-NW-S14; 12-1-31
David Chambers* NE-SE-S13; 7-17-39; W-SE-S13; 4-19-38
Isham Prince* SE-SE-S13; 6-14-36
Andrew Helton* SE-NE-S14; 10-21-52
Henry Deckard* SW-NE-S14;8-12-37;S-SE-S14;2-17-36;E-NE-S15;3-10-36
Jesse Wright* SE-SW-S14; 9-24-32
Henry Musser* NW-SW-S14; 1-26-37; NE-SE-S15; 3-6-37
Adonijah Isander Jennings* NE-SE-S14; 10-7-44
Abraham Floyd* NW-SE-S14; 2-19-52
Michael Deckard* NW-NE-S15; 3-5-36; SW-NE-S15; 5-11-35; NE-NE-S22;
    1-23-37; W-NE-S22; 3-20-24
George Paul NW-S15; SE-S29; 9-25-16; NE, SE-S21; 9-25-16
William Wismore NE-S17; 1-8-18
William Chandler* NE-NW-S17; 11-17-35; SW-SE-S18; 3-7-36
Solomon Wooden* SE-NW-S17; 7-24-35
William Smith* SW-NW-S17; 12-14-35
Andrew Johnson* NE-SW-S17; 10-5-32
William Henderson* SE-SW-S17; 8-29-36
James Storm W-SW-S17; 1-8-18
Michael Buskirk & Seth Goodwin SE-S17; 10-10-16
Nicholas Goodwin, Jr.* NE-NE-S18; 8-15-39
Matthew Flory* SW-NE-S18; 11-19-35; NW-SE-S18; 3-7-36
George Flory* NE-NW-S18; C-5-34
Zedekiah Adamson* SE-NW-S18; 11-18-35
Edmund Phillips* W-NW-S18; 6-7-24
Jacob Beals SW-S18; 1-10-17
Thomas Duffield E-SE-S18; 4-20-18
Samuel Smith NE-S19; 4-10-18
John Vandervoot NW-S19; 9-6-16
Michael Harvey SE-S19; 9-25-16
Jacob Muma NE-S20; 9-5-16
Joseph Strean NW, SW-S20; 1-15-17
Jonathan Lindley SE-S20; NW, SW-S29; NE-S31; 9-25-16
William Chambers* NW-S21;6-9-17;W-SW-S21;7-2-29;SW-NW-S35;7-15-36
Anthony Chambers* E-SW-S21; 7-2-29; SE-NE-S22; 10-5-32; E-SE-S22;
    11-11-31; W-SE-S22; 3-4-37; SW-SW-S23; 3-20-47

Andrew McKean NW-S22; 6-14-19
David Chambers* NE-SW-S22; 3-4-37; SW-SW-S22; 6-14-33; W-SE-S24;
   7-17-39; SE-NE-S25; 8-2-39
Anderson Chambers* SE-SW-S22; 4-19-38
Wesley Chambers* NW-SW-S22; 3-4-37; NW-NE-S24; 2-7-54
Bazil Hill* E-NE-S23; 8-27-38; SE-SW-S24; 12-22-38; W-SW-S24;
   12-4-38; NE-NW, W-NW-S25; 8-24-39
Alex. Johnson* NW-NE-S23; 8-19-36; SW-NE-S23; 7-6-35; SW-NE-S26; 12-14-
John Whisenand, Jr.* NE-NW-S23; 2-27-36   38
John Whisenand* SE-NW-S23; 6-13-35; NW-SE-S25; 12-17-38; SE-NE-
   S35; 8-24-39; NW-NW-S35; 1-12-38
George Whisenand* NE-SW-S23; 6-13-35; E-SE-S23; 1-12-38; NW-SE-S23;
Thomas Lloyd Lucas* NW-SW-S23; 12-13-38   8-13-36
John Johnston* SW-SE-S23; 10-15-35; W-NW-S31; 9-19-35
Catharine Alton NE-NW-S24; 9-19-54; MLW 99729
William Scott Mayer, Kn SE-NW-S24; 8-18-57
Alexander Skinner NW-NW-S24; 5-18-54
Berry Lucas* SW-NW-S24; 1-10-54; NE-SW-S24; 10-21-52
William Chambers, Jr.* NE-SE-S24; 8-12-36
John G. Chambers* SE-SE-S24; 6-29-46; W-NE-S25; 8-22-53
John Chambers, Jr.* NE-NE-S25; 8-12-36
James Clondenin* SE-NW-S25; 1-3-54
Perry Allen Meadows* NE-SW-S25; 12-18-43
Riley Wilson* SE-SW-S25; 8-16-37; W-SW-S25; 6-24-36
William Oliver Welch* NE-SE-S25; 5-5-36
Jacob Burns Meadows* SE-SE-S25; 1-30-39
Andrew Whisenand* SW-SE-S25; 6-4-36; NW-SE-S36; 6-4-36
Nicholas Whisenand* NE-NE-S26; 1-23-37; NE-NE-S35; NW-NW-S36; 8-5-34
John Whisenand, Sr.* SE-NE-S26; 2-27-36
James Service* NW-NE-S26; 5-24-38
Thomas Lucas, Sr.* E-NW-S26; 1-2-40
John Chambers, Sr.* NW-NW-S26; 11-15-48; SW-NW-S27; 3-10-36; E-SW-
   S27; 10-11-38; W-SW-S27; NE-SE-S28; 8-12-36
Joseph Benjamin Chambers* SW-NW-S26; 10-10-44
Zadock Long, Lw SE-SW, W-SE-S26; 6-24-36
John Scott E-SE-S26; 4-8-19
Anthony Chambers* E-NE-S27; 6-14-33; NE-SE-S27; 3-4-37
Anthony Wane Chambers* NW-NE-S27; 12-18-44
Squire Ray* SW-NE, N-NW-S27; 3-27-52
Henry Baugh S-SE-S27; 3-11-52; MLW 3317
John Chambers* NW-SE-S27; 8-3-47
John Durham NE-S28; 12-9-16
William Chambers NW-S28; 12-31-16; SW-S28; 6-9-17
Robert Taylor* SE-SE-S28; E-NE-S33; 2-23-36; SW-NE-S33; 7-7-36
George Redick* W-SE-S28; 12-25-21
Samuel Caldwell NE-S29; 9-25-16
John White S30; 9-26-16
George Sipeso, Lw E-NW-S31; 11-28-31
John Andrew Miller Lemon* (two men?) E-SE-S31; 2-23-36
William Wilson Lemon, Lw W-SE-S31; 7-11-36; NE-SW-S36; 9-2-36
John Smith NE-S32; 5-27-18
Samuel Allen NW-S32; 6-9-17
John Fairley SW-S32; 6-9-17
William Curl E-SE-S32; 12-9-16

Elijah Elliott* W-SE-S32; 7-23-27
Henry Taylor, Lw NW-NE-S33; 12-31-36
William Craig NW-S33; 12-19-16
William Lemon, Lw E-SW-S33; 12-21-29
William Shields W-SW-S33; 3-21-18
John Hanson, Lw NE-SE-S33;10-9-33;E-SE-S34;8-7-37;NW-SE-S34;9-24-
William Moore Humpston, Lw SE-SE-S33; 8-10-35   46
Conrad Hanson W-SE-S33; 9-1-17
William Green Phillips* NE-NE-S34; 6-18-36; SE-NW-S35; 12-16-33
William Phenster Chambers* SE-NE-S34; NE-NW-S35; 4-19-38
Daniel Hanson* W-NE-S34; 4-23-51
Elias Bruner* E-NW-S34; 3-4-37; NW-NW-S34; 3-10-34; SW-NW-S34;
    4-18-36; W-SW-S34; 10-28-18
Edward Humston, Lw SW-SE-S34; 8-2-39
William Whisenand* NW-NE-S35; 5-31-36
Lucian Q. Hogatt SW-NE, N-SW, NW-SE-S35; 7-14-48; MLW 7923
John Stuart* SE-SW-S35; 11-9-37; SW-SW-S35; 1-18-36
William A. Maddows, Lw SE-SE-S35; 2-6-45
Francis Ramsey, Lw SW-SE-S35; 2-5-45
Adela Trobridge, Cook Co., Ill. E-NE-S36; 3-4-56
Felix Miller* NW-NE-S36; 3-24-36
William R. Miller* SW-NE-S36; 1-27-54
Matthias Lemen, Or NE-NW-S36; 9-11-32
Andrew Helton, Lw SE-NW, SW-NW-S36; 3-18-48
Jesse Deckart* SE-SW-S36; 7-30-36; of Lw, SW-SW-S36; 1-18-36
George W. Walker, Gl NW-SW-S36; 4-29-56
Jacob Burns Meadows* E-SE-S36; 1-30-39
Henry Souder* SW-SE-S36; 7-14-36

                        RELINQUISHMENTS

Wheeler Mallet (?) SE-S4; 9-25-16
John Briscoe SE-S5; 12-9-16
John Routt & Adam Brenton E-SW-S6; 9-25-16
David Sears SE-S8; 1-3-18
David Scott E-SE-S9; 12-30-17
Cornelius Newkirk NW-S11; 9-2-17
Silas Woodward E-SW-S11; 9-2-17
John Musser E-SE-S15; 12-19-16; NE-S27; 12-3-18
Jacob Beals NW-S18; 1-10-17
John Lake W-SE-S22; 7-7-18; E-SE-S22; 7-7-18
John Scott W-SE-S26; 4-8-19
John Storm W-NE-S8; 1-28-18
Amos Lock NW-S9; 1-6-19
Andrew Chambers SW-S21; 10-16-17
William Curl W-SE-S32; 12-9-16; NW-S27; 1-1-18
James Storm E-SW-S17; 1-8-18
Elias Bruner E-SW-S34; 10-28-18
James Mitchell W-SW-S5; 1-28-18
Thomas Duffield W-SE-S18; 4-20-18
Richard Breaden E-SW-S33; 10-16-17
James Sweaney SW-S4; 6-27-17; 3-3-30
Thomas Hancock E-NE-S5; 9-23-17; 7-4-29
William Crawford SE-S6; 9-25-16; 7-4-29

Moses Olds NE-S1; 7-12-17
William Bigger NW-S1; 9-19-10
Richard Beem SW-S1; 9-24-16
William Dowden* NE-NE-S2; 10-8-34
Jacob Myars* SE-NE-S2; 4-21-36
John Crum W-NE-S2; 7-5-17
James Wright* NW-S2; 5-5-17; E-SE-S2; 12-31-35; W-SE-S2; 12-13-17
William Leakey SW-S2; 1-14-17
Isaac Withers NE-S3; 10-14-16
Thomas Paley Shipman* NE-NW-S3; 10-3-35; SE-NW-S3; 2-6-37
Jackson Crockett* SE-SW-S3; 12-31-44
John Stewart* NW-SW-S3; 11-24-47
Abraham May* SW-SW-S3; 0-2-36; NW-NW-S10; 12-23-35.   7-3-43
William May, Edgar Co., Ill. NE-SE-S3;10-25-33; of*, NE-SW-S25;/
Solomon May* SE-SE-S3;2-6-37;NE-NW-S21;12-29-34;W-NW-S21;5-2-51
William Coons* NW-SE-S3; 12-21-44
William Smith* NE-NE-S4; 12-19-44
William Sparks* SE-NE-S4; 5-15-47
John Griffiths* NW-NE-S4; 3-18-35; NE-NW-S4; 10-12-38
Alfred Griffiths* SW-NE-S4; 12-31-44
Henry Burch* SE-NW, NE-SW-S4; 10-31-38; SW-NW-S4; 12-23-35;
     NE-NW-S9; 1-3-53
James Gentry* NW-NW-S4; 11-30-39; NW-SW-S7; 2-4-34
John May* SE-SW-S4;4-5-37;SW-SE-S4;10-18-38; SW-SE-S15; 1-7-36
Pope Tarkington* SE-SE-S4; 10-27-38
David Carpenter* NE-NW-S5; 2-11-36
John Burch* SE-NW, W-SW-S5; 5-15-35;E-SW,W-SE-S5;11-11-19;E-SE-S5;
Silvanus Tarkington* NW-NW-S5; 8-5-34   11-25-36
Joel Burch* SW-NW-S5; 11-25-36
Benjamin Freeland NE-S5;NE-S7;6-28-17;NW-S7;5-2-17;SE-S7;1-17-18
John Sadler* E-NE-S6; 7-24-27; W-NE, NW-S6; 9-23-16; NE-SW-S6;
     9-18-32; W-SW-S6; 12-27-31
John Staley Sadler* SE-SW-S6; 12-10-38
Archibald Wood SE-S6; 9-23-16
James Crane* E-SW-S7; 3-11-39; SE-NE-S18; 4-16-35
John Workman, Gn SW-SW-S7; 10-16-38
William Patton* SE-NE-S8; 3-9-44
Randolph Ross* W-NE,SE-NW,SW-SW-S8;NW-NE,NW-NW-S18;6-5-39;NW-NW-S8;
John Southern Burch* NE-NW-S8; 10-31-38   5-8-39
Levi Henson Burch* SW-NW-S8; 9-10-38
Achilles Burch* NE-SW-S8;5-18-36;NW-SE-S8;6-1-48;SW-SE-S8;10-28-35
Absalom Baker* SE-SW-S8; 1-28-39
Elijah Burch* NW-SW-S8; 1-21-36; SW-NE-S17; 10-28-35
Spencer Griffin* NE-SE-S8; 12-5-35; SW-NW-S9; 10-28-35
Charles Burch* SE-SE-S8; 11-25-34; NW-NW-S9; 1-3-53; SE-SW-S9;
     1-16-39; W-SW-S9; 11-25-34
Eli Pope Tarkington* NW-NE-S9; 10-27-38
Ellsberry Washington Tarkington* SW-NE-S9; 2-5-45; SE-NW-S9;
     10-6-38; SW-SE-S9; 10-27-36
John Arthur* NE-SW-S9; 6-9-36
Preminter Morgan* NE-SE-S9; 10-30-50; SE-SE-S9; 5-6-37; SE-SW-S10;
     12-23-35; SW-SE-S10; 2-28-45

Elijah Morgan* SE-NE-S10; 12-13-39
Elijah James Morgan* SW-NE-S10;8-26-47;NE-SE-S10;9-22-36;NW-SE-S10;
John Koons* NE-NW-S10; 7-12-50   5-6-37
Nathaniel Crane* SE-NW-S10; 8-25-47; SW-NW-S10; 6-11-40
Absalom Morgan* W-SW-S10; 9-22-36
John White NE-S11; 1-14-17
Isiah White NW-S11; 8-21-17
Hugh Hill* NE-SW-S11; 8-17-36; W-SW-S11; 12-17-38
James Wright SE-S11;1-31-17;NW-S12;1-14-17; W-SE-S26; 7-31-17
John Storm NE-S12; 0-23-16
James Mitchell SW-S12; 1-14-17
Jacob Beals E-SE-S12; 1-10-17; NE-S13; 8-8-17
David Wright* NW-SE-S12; 7-29-36
Nicholas Shipman* SW-SE-S12; 8-5-34; NE-NW-S13; 7-4-36
Elmore Walker* S-NW-S13;4-2-36;SE-SW-S15;9-17-39;NW-SE-S15;3-24-37
Amanda King and the other heirs of William King E-SE-S13;6-23-31
William King & Robert McCain W-SE-S13; 12-16-16
Allen Parham* E-NW-S14; 4-21-36; NW-NW-S14; 9-22-36
Joseph Smith Walker* SW-NW-S14;SW-NW-S15;10-27-38;SW-SW-S15;1-18-39
John Henry Crum* NE-SW, NW-SE-S14; 12-18-37
Elizabeth Phillips* SE-SW-S14; 7-4-36
Martin Snow* SW-SW-S14; 9-7-36
Peter May* NE-SE-S14; 12-24-35; SE-SE-S14; 6-4-32
James &David Kirk* NE-NE-S15; 4-5-36
Peter Minks* NW-NE-S15;6-25-39;NE-NW-S15;11-26-36;SE-NW-S15;3-18-35
David Kirk* SW-NE-S15; 4-24-37
Joseph Arthur* NW-NW-S15; 8-24-32; NE-S21; 3-10-18
George Washington Walker* NE-SW-S18; 11-21-38; NW-SW-S18;3-20-36
Benjamin Sanders* SE-SE-S15; 12-7-35; E-NE-S22; 1-24-36
Alvis Martin King, Gn E-NE-S17; 2-5-45
David Carpenter* NW-NE-S17; 10-12-38; NE-NW-S17; 6-3-37
Charles Combs* SE-NW-S17;2-28-45;NE-SW-S17;2-6-45;SE-SW-S17;8-17-38
William Minks* NW-NW-S17; 1-19-39
John Crane* SW-NW-S17; NE-NE-S18; 4-16-35
Thomas Carter* W-SW-S17; 11-19-31; NE-SE-S18; 6-1-36
Alexander Lamb* E-SE-S17; 11-21-38; NE-SE-S20; 12-12-36
William Ragains* NW-SE-S17; 6-2-36; NE-NE-S31; 10-28-44
Bird Combs* SW-SE-S17; W-NW-S20; 12-16-35
George Washington Collins* SW-NE-S18; 7-30-33
Jackson Young McGee* NE-NW-S18; 2-12-36
John Carter, Gn SE-NW, NW-SW-S18; 12-20-32
James King, Gn SW-NW-S18; 1-12-39
Peter Lunsford* E-SW-S18; 12-11-23
Abraham Young* SW-SW-S18; 7-30-32
Sterling Hudson, Gn SE-SE-S18; 2-18-40
Starling Carmichael* NW-SE-S18; 4-12-37
Henry Arthur, Gn SW-SE-S18; 9-25-37
John Toddrill* N-NE-S19; 11-16-38
Martin Combs* SE-NE-S19; 4-8-35
Joseph Carmicol* SW-NE-S19; 12-12-36; E-NW-S19; 12-18-30
Joel Sexson* W-NW-S19; 9-4-27
Alexander Carmichael* E-SW-S19; 12-26-38
Archibald Carmichael, Gn W-SW-S19; 11-12-29
Henry Speed SE-S19; 9-24-16

John Storm NE-S20; 10-26-16
Elzey Woodard E-NW-S20; 6-24-18
John Sare* E-SW-S20; 12-9-35; SE-SE-S21; 12-25-38
Lemuel Sexson* W-SW-S20; 11-17-28
Hughes East* SE-SE-S20; 1-2-37; NW-SE-S20; 12-9-36
William East+ SW-SE-S20; 10-22-30
William Carr+ SE-NW-S21; 3-24-30
Drury Gilham* W-SW-S21; 10-28-29; W-SW-S21; 0-22-30; NW-SE-S21;
  NE-NW-S20; 0-10-32
Thomas Pinoney East* NE-SE-S21;12-16-35;SE-NW,NW-SW-S22;5-26-36
James Carmichael* NW-NE-S22; 5-27-36
James Gilham* SW-NE-S22;11-30-35;NE-NE-S26;2-9-39;SE-NW-S28;12-1-37
Henry Minks* NE-NW-S22; 12-15-38
Thomas Carr* NW-NW-S22; 3-24-38
Thomas Peter Graves* NE-SW-S22; 10-24-35
Jesse East* SE-SW-S22; 11-14-35; W-NW-S27; 1-21-36
David Kirk* SW-SW-S22; 10-19-35
John Kirk* E-SE-S22; 2-23-36
Michael Teague* W-SE-S22;E-NE-S27;2-23-36;NW-NW-S26;1-2-37
Thomas Sanders* NE-NE-S23; 4-5-37; NW-NE-S23; 4-16-36
Silas Inyart* NE-NW-S23; 3-12-38
David Conder* SE-NW-S23; 3-24-38; SW-NW-S23; SE-SE-S27;9-28-35;
  NE-SW-S23; 5-23-39; SW-NW-S26; 2-22-40
Greenberry Condor* SE-SW-S23; 5-27-36; SW-SE-S23; 2-9-39
Solomon Morgan* NE-SE-S23; 12-24-35; W-NW, W-SW-S24; 12-23-29;
  NE-SW-S24; 6-4-32
Ashberry Sare* SE-SE-S23; 8-10-44; SW-NW-S25; 3-28-49
Jacob Beals NE-S24; 1-10-17
George Flory* NE-NW-S24; 4-1-36
Caleb Hazel* SE-NW-S24; 1-8-33; NW-SE-S25; 3-7-36
Benjamin Barney* SE-SW-S24; 3-25-36
Richard Butcher* NE-SE-S24; 3-10-36
John White* SE-SE-S24;12-8-35;W-SE-S24;3-22-32;SE-NW-S25;3-31-36
William Wymore NE-S25; 7-31-17
Augustus Bowles* NE-NW-S25; 7-8-40
Alexander Smith* NW-NW-S25; 3-28-49
Hiram Hazel* SE-SW-S25; 4-4-48; SW-SE-S25; 1-30-44
Preston Wright* NW-SW-S25; 5-23-39
Elijah Wright* SW-SW-S25; 9-28-35; W-NW-S36; 4-6-36
Charles Johnston* NE-SE-S25; 12-23-34; SE-SE-S25; 3-31-36
Jacob Crum* SE-NE-S26; 9-28-35
John Crum* NW-NE-S26; 9-28-35
Jacob Gilham* SW-NE-S26; 12-1-36
William Hazel* NE-NW-S26; 8-5-36
Richard Hazel, Jr.* SE-NW-S26; 12-5-38
Jacob Hale* E-SW-S26; 8-5-31
William Stephenson* NW-SW-S26; 3-29-37
Zacharias Dicks* SW-SW-S26; 10-17-32; NE-S34; 6-21-17
Reuben Sears (Sare)* E-SE-S26; 11-26-31; NE-NE-S35; 12-24-35
Caleb Lowder W-NE-S27; 4-22-19
James Carmichael* E-NW-S27; 11-14-35; NE-SE-S27; 10-6-32
Richard Carmichael* NW-SE-S27; 12-26-38
Thomas Stephen Linthicum* SW-SE-S27;1-24-37; W-SE-S34; 10-25-31
George Farlow SW-S27; 11-25-17

Jonathan Howell E-NE-S28; 1-26-18
Joseph Arnold* W-NE-S28; 6-18-36
Peter Wright* E-NE-S29; 2-20-27
John Smith Fossett* NW-NE-S29; 12-29-34; NE-NW-S29; 8-5-34
Pleasant Fossett* SW-NE-S29; 12-12-36; SE-NW-S29; 6-16-36
Jonathan McBride* NW-NW-S29; 12-9-35
John Hall* SW-NW-S29; 1-12-38
Mary Brassfield* E-SW-S29; 11-28-37
David Burley Tilley* NW-SW-S29; 2-13-49; NE-SW-S31; 9-9-36;
   NW-SE-S31; 1-2-37; NW-SW-S32; 11-28-38
Alves Evans* SW-SW-S29; NW-NW-S32; 6-6-36
William Wright* NE-SE-S29; 11-9-35
James Eves Wooten* SE-SE-S29; 9-1-38
William H. Bennett* NW-SE-S29; 5-6-37
Joseph Pennington* SW-SE-S29; 1-12-38; NE-NW-S32; 2-8-34
Archibald Wood NE-S30; 9-24-16; NW-S30; 9-23-16
William Cilivan Graves* NE-SW-S30; 2-5-45
William Carter, Gn W-SW-S30; 2-18-30
Amanda Ferguson* NE-SE-S30; 7-8-48
Abel Edwards* S-SE-S30;6-6-36;NW-NE-S31;11-7-44;NE-SW-S32;12-15-38
William Smith* NW-SE-S30; 2-18-40
Nancy Edwards* SW-NE-S31; 9-25-39
William Hardin* SE-NW-S31; 10-1-38; SW-NW-S31; 3-21-36
William Carter, Sr., Gn NW-NW-S31; 10-30-43
Thomas Perkins East* SE-SW-S31; 1-2-37
John Phillips* NW-SW-S31; 11-24-36
Thomas Carmichael* NE-SE-S31; 11-14-38
James McLahlan, Lw SE-SE-S31; 7-9-36; of*, SW-SW-S32; 3-21-36
Thomas East* NE-NE-S32; 4-16-36
John Walker Evans* S-NE-S32;11-21-38;NE-NW-S33;8-3-32;W-NW-S34;
Joseph Pennington, Jr.* NW-NE-S32; 6-6-36   5-27-36
Andrew Jackson Wall* SE-NW-S32; 11-26-38; SW-NW-S32; 5-24-38
Peter Graves* SE-SW-S32; 11-20-38; SW-SE-S32; 5-2-36
Bartholomew Wall* NE-SE-S32; 1-16-39; NW-SE-S32; 9-22-36
Richard Nance* SE-SE-S32; 11-26-36
Thomas Wilson NE-S33; 3-14-17
Thomas Walker* SE-NW-S33; 4-16-36; W-NW-S33; 12-16-36
George William Zeigler, Ba E-SW-S33; 9-29-37
Joseph East, Lw NW-SW-S33; 4-4-38
Alexander Clark SE-S33; 6-11-17; SW-S34; 5-26-18
Thomas Linthicum* E-NW-S34; 9-16-33
William Jones* E-SE-S34; 9-26-25; SW-NW-S35; 8-10-32; E-SW-S35;
   2-2-31; W-SW-S35; 5-12-18; W-SE-S35; 10-27-36
John Low* SE-NE-S35; 5-4-37; of Lw, SW-NE-S35; 10-27-36
Dugan Rush* NW-NE-S35; 12-30-33; NW-NW-S35; 10-6-32
William Wright E-NW-S35; 7-31-17
John Miller* NE-SE-S35; 2-23-36   Joseph Inis Lemon, Lw
Lucean Sare* SE-SE-S35; 3-30-37   SE-SE,NW-SE-S36;6-25-36
James Smith* E-NE-S36; 1-5-24
John Johnson* SW-NE-S36; 5-23-39
William Sipes* NE-SW-S36; 1-15-36; SE-SW-S36; 11-4-33
Clabourne Sipes* NW-SW-S36; 8-6-36
Samuel Fairley, Lw SW-SW-S36;8-9-44   Henry Sipes*
John Roberts* NE-SE-S36; 3-15-34   SW-SE-S36; 1-16-36

MONROE COUNTY

RELINQUISHMENTS

John Briscoe NW-S5; 9-23-16
Robert Holaday SW-S7; 9-24-16
Gibson Garrot SE-S14; 10-13-19
Daniel Rawlings NE-S18;2-21-18
James Bennot NW-S21; 10-31-16
Joseph Mitchol NW-S24;5-27-17
Isaac Seabow NW-S25; 1-28-18
Caleb Sowder E-NE-S27;4-22-19
Jonathan Howell W-NE-S28;1-26-18
Joseph Sowder W-SE-S28;10-27-18
Joseph (James?) T. James E-SE-S2; 10-23-17
William & James James NE-S22; 2-24-19
Jesse & Richard Wright SW-S24; 7-31-17
William King & Robert McClain E-SE-S13; 12-16-16

William Wright W-NW-S35;7-31-17
William Jones E-SW-S35;11-12-18
John Sadler E-NE-S6; 9-23-16
Henry Speed SW-S20; 9-24-16
Jacob Sears W-NW-S23; 2-6-19
Richard Wright E-SW-S23;11-7-18
Jacob Beals W-SE-S12; 1-10-17
John White SE-S24; 9-8-17
John Crum E-NE-S2; 7-5-17
James Wright E-SE-S26; 7-31-17

T 8 N, R 1 W
(Seminary Township)

Thomas Slone E-NE-S1; 6-1-29; E-NW-S11; 10-6-28
Alexander Kelly W-NE-S1; 10-1-27
Joseph Piercy NW-S1; 10-1-27
John Armstrong E-SE-S1; 10-8-27
John Griffeth W-SE-S1; E-NW-S11; 10-8-27
Martha Goodwin E-SW-S1; 10-8-27
Robert Ewing W-SW-S1; 1-5-30
James G. Fleenor NE-S2; 10-27-27
Grandville Ward NW-S2; 10-1-27
Milton McPhetrige E-SE-S2; 10-1-27
William Curry SE-S2; 5-5-28; W-NE-S11; 10-10-28
Isaac Rogers W-SW-S2; 10-1-27
Aquila Rogers E-NE-S3; 10-1-27
Samuel Dunn W-NE-S3; 10-1-27
Thomas Smith SE-S3; 10-1-27
George Henry & James Borland E-NW-S6; 10-4-27
Ellis Stone W-NW, W-SW-S6; 10-1-27
Hiram Paugh E-SW-S6; 10-1-27
Abraham Pauley W-NW-S7; 10-1-27
Andrew Todd E-NW-S7; 10-8-27
Emsly Wilson W-NE-S7; 10-1-27
Samuel Dodds E-NE-S7; 5-10-28; NW-S8; 10-1-27; NE, E-SE-S8;
    5-3-30; W-SW-S18; 5-7-28
Alexander Murphy W-SW-S7; 10-1-27
Richard Hunter E-SW-S7; 10-1-27
George Isiminger W-SE-S7; 5-6-28; E-SE-S7;.10-2-27
William Dunning W-SW-S8;8-1-28;NE-S16;NE-S17;10-2-27;E-NW-S17;
Benjamin Freeland & Jesse Wright E-SW-S8;5-5-28.   10-4-27
James W. Clark N-NW-S9; 5-3-30
John Hight W-NE-S9; 10-2-27
Richard Shipp E-NE-S9; 10-2-27
William Bilbo SE-S9; 10-2-27
Zachariah Williams NW-S10 10-11-27
David Batherton W-NE-S10; 10-4-27

Benjamin Rogers   E-NE-S10; W-SW-S14; 10-2-27
John Goodnight SW-S10; 5-6-28
Tarlton Bell SE-S10; 9-17-29
Paris C. Dunning W-NW-S11; 10-4-27
Jacob Isiminger W-SW-S11; 10-4-27; E-NW-S14; 5-5-28
Jonathan Rogers E-SW-S11; 10-2-27
William Mize SE-S11; W-NE-S12; 5-5-28
John Hindman W-NW-S12; 10-9-28
James Gorden E-NW-S12; 1-4-30
Andrew Parkes E-NE-S12; 9-24-30
Moses Williams W-SW-S12; 10-2-27
Stephen Parkes E-SW-S12; 10-24-31
John A. Wilson W-SE-S12; 10-4-27
Garret Moore E-SE-S12; 10-2-27
Jacob House NE-S14; 5-5-28
Finney Coatney W-NW-S14; 5-5-28; W-SE-S22; 8-4-28
Samuel Kirtright W-SE-S14; 10-10-28
James O. Dillion(?) E-SW-S14; 4-1-30
Josias Baker E-NE-S15; 10-2-27; W-NE-S15; 10-8-27
Benjamin Tribble E-NW-S15; 8-4-28
Abednigo Walden W-NW-S15; 10-2-27
James Rogers SE-S15; 5-6-28
Lewis Harman E-SW-S15; 5-5-28
David Rogers W-SW-S15; 5-6-28
Thomas Shields E-NW-S16; 8-4-28
Henry D. Palmer W-NW-S16; 5-6-28
Levi Thatcher E-SE-S16; 10-11-27
John Nicholas W-SE-S16; 8-4-28
John P. Berry E-SW-S16; 5-7-28
William Knotts W-SW-S16; 10-13-27
Isaac Peuley W-NW-S17; E-NE-S18; 10-8-27
Daniel Travis E-SE-S17; 10-4-27
Thomas Carter W-SE-S17; 10-11-27; E-SW-S17; 4-1-30;E-SW-S18;
Absalom Keniday W-SW-S17; 10-4-27   10-11-31
Edward Borland W-NE, NW-S18; 10-2-27
Samuel Moore SE-S18; 10-2-27
George A. Ritter W-NW-S19; 8-4-28
Simon Adamson E-NW-S19; 10-3-27
Christopher Tislow W-NE-S19; 4-26-30
Evin Dollarhide E-NE-S19; 10-4-28; W-NW-S20; 10-2-27
Jesse Davar W-SW-S19; 8-4-28; SW-S26; SE-S27; 4-1-30; E-SW-S34;
    4-1-30; (last entry forfeited to the State, 6-30-32)
John Smith E-SW-S19;5-10-28;SE-S30;10-5-27;W-NW-S31;4-1-30;W-NE-
Christopher Rhorer W-SE-S19; 9-30-29   S31; 10-8-27
Samuel Patton E-SE-S19; 8-4-28; W-SW-S20; 5-5-28
Jacob Depue E-NW-S20; 10-3-27
John Allcorn W-NE-S20; 5-5-28
James Mathers E-NE-S20; 5-6-28
Jacob May E-SW-S20; 5-5-28
John Mathers W-SE-S20; 10-11-27
David Sears E-SE-S20; 10-3-27; E-NW-S29; 10-4-27
John M. Nicholson W-NW-S21; 10-13-27
William Davis E-NW-S21; 10-13-27
Robert D. Alexander NE-S21; 10-4-27

David Findly SW-S21; 10-3-27
Michael Keith· W-SE-S21; 10-3-27
William Taylor E-SE-S21; 10-3-27; W-SW-S22; 10-3-27;NE-S28;10-4-27
William Patrick W-NW-S22; 10-3-27; E-NW-S22; 10-8-27
James Hogan W-NE-S22; 5-6-28
John Bettenhouse & William Hagan E-NE-S22; 10-2-27
Jacob Pickle E-SW-S22; 5-6-28
Cornelius A. Demaroe E-SE-S22; 10-18-30
Francis Hall W-NW-S23; 4-1-30
James Burch E-NW-S23; 12-23-30
George See W-NE-S23; 4-1-30
Elijah Watts E-NE-S23; 4-1-30
Thomas Reynolds W-SW-S23; 8-4-28
James Brummitt E-NE-S25; 2-13-39; E-SW-S28; 10-4-27
Arthur McFarland E-SE-S25; 4-1-30
Bailey East W-NW-S26; 5-7-28
William Boriff W-SE-S26; 3-25-31
William Chandler E-NE-S27; 3-14-32; W-SW-S34; 10-8-27
Solloman Butcher W-NE-S27; 2-6-30; E-NW-S27; 10-3-27
Banner Brummit W-NW-S27; 10-3-27
Finly Acres E-SW-S27; 12-9-30
Berryman James W-SW-S27; 10-3-27; W-NW-S33; 5-5-28
James Alexander E-NW-S28; 10-5-27
William Alverson W-NW-S28; E-NE-S29; 10-4-27
John Messer E-SE-S28; 10-11-27
Robert Sanderson W-SE-S28; 10-11-27
Thomas Abbet W-SW-S29; 10-4-27
Cary James W-NE, W-NW-S29; 10-4-27
William Harvy SE-S29; 10-5-27
James Parsons E-SW-S29; 10-5-27
Charles Barkshire W-SW-S29; E-NE-S30; 10-8-27
Samuel Rhorer W-NE-S30; 10-5-27
Husleton Compton E-NW-S30; 10-5-27
Sollomon Green W-NW-S30; 10-5-27
Absalom Cooper E-SW-S30;.10-5-27

Fetter A. Shryer W-SW-S30; 10-5-27   John M. Tarr E-SE-S31;5-6-28
David May E-NW-S31; 5-5-28   Moses Grantham, Jr. E-SE-S33;
Mary Peter E-NE-S31; 5-6-28   10-11-27
John Ketcham SW,W-SE-S31;10-5-27   James Hetton W-NE-S34;5-5-28
William Peter W-NW-S32;5-6-28   David Wells W-SW-S33;5-5-28
Alexander Wheeler E-NW-S32;10-5-27   Samuel Boriff E-SW-S33;4-1-30;
Henry Flood E-NE-S32;8-4-28   W-SW-S33;4-16-30
Joseph Mitchell W-SW-S32;4-1-30   John Tate W-NW-S34;10-5-27;
Benjamin Willoughby W-SE-S32;3-30-30   E-NW-S34;4-1-30
William Fletcher E-NW-S33;5-6-28   Sollomon Lucas E-NE-S34;4-1-30
George Short NE-S33;10-13-27
William Ross W-NE, E-SE-S32; 10-5-27; E-SW-S32; 4-1-30

The above and foregoing is a true transcrip of the Tracts of Land.
The quantity of ground in each lot. The date of purchas and the pur-
chasers name, Taken from the Books in my office, of the Seminary
Township in Monroe County. Certified this 9th day of September 1833.
                                        James Borland Comr.

Arthur Patterson NE-S1; 9-30-16; SE-S24; 9-24-16; SW-S31; NE,SW-
Eli & David Matlock NW-S1; 12-23-17   S32;9-23-16
Vincent Lindsey* E-SW-S1; 6-18-24
Samuel Lyons* W-SW-S1; 12-13-25
Josiah Wright & Absalom Morgan SE-S1; 10-10-16
Jacob Cutler NE-S2; 10-14-16
William Wright NW-S2; 10-10-16
David Matlock SW-S2; 1-6-17; SE-S15; 11-2-16
George H. Johnson SE-S2; 7-24-27
David Sears NE-S3; 9-27-16
Eli P. Farmer* E-NW-S3; 11-17-24
Benjamin Asberry Allison* W-NW-S3; E-NE-S4; 5-23-36
James Parks SW-S3; 9-23-16
James Matlock SE-S3; 10-9-16; SW-S12; 1-6-17
Othias Carter* NW-NE-S4; 10-22-34
Joshua Owings Howe* SW-NE-S4; 8-11-41
Edward Archer* NE-NW-S4; 8-12-33
David Davis* NW-NW-S4; 11-1-32; NE-NE-S5; 10-2-32
James Davis* SW-NW-S4; 1-25-33
John Henry* E-SW-S4; 12-30-40
George Fritts* NW-SW-S4; 12-30-40; SE-NE-S5; 1-9-36
John Gwin* NW-NE-S5; 8-5-34; NE-NW-S5; 11-12-34
Thomas Edwards* SW-NE-S5; 8-5-35
Stanfield Wharton* SE-NW-S5; 12-21-35; SE-NE-S6; 7-25-35
William Nesbit* NW-NW-S5; 4-23-38; NE-NE-S6; 1-25-39
William Rice* SW-NW-S5; 12-5-33; NW-SW-S5; 12-17-38
James Ellis* NE-SW-S5; 10-12-38
Thomas Gwin* SE-SW-S5;3-22-36;SE-SE-S5;2-11-36;NW-NE-S8;9-6-39
Edmund Burks* SW-SW-S5; 2-12-36; E-NW-S8; 10-22-32
Thompson Edwards* NE-SE-S5; 1-25-36
George Moss* W-SE-S5; 5-20-29
Thomas Snoddy* W-NE-S6; 6-5-26; of Gn, N-SW-S6; 1-30-37
Booker Witt* E-NW-S6; 6-15-36
Thomas Raper, Gn W-NW-S6; 9-6-47
Lawson Ham, Gn SE-SW-S6; 10-6-36
Jacob Ham, Gn SW-SW-S6; 8-23-33
John Wharton* NE-SE-S6; 7-9-36
Samuel Edde* NW-SE-S6; 10-10-32
John Watson* E-NE-S7;9-1-35;W-SE-S7;4-10-48;MLW 4510;NW-SW-S8;4-3-
    37;NW-SW-S9;4-16-35;W-NE-S18;4-10-48;of Ck,E-SE-S8;4-23-28;W-NW-
Burton R. Ham, Gn NE-NW-S7; 10-13-51.   S18; 3-25-29
Wyatt Adkins* S-NW-S7; 7-12-44
William Burks* SW-NE-S8; 4-4-37
Stephen Coan* NE-SW-S8; 1-10-54; SE-SW-S8; 9-3-53
John Burks* SW-SW-S8; 11-7-33
Austin S. Reeves* E-NE-S9; 12-10-23
Robert Rice* NW-NE-S9;5-18-37;NE-NW-S9;5-25-35;NW-NW-S9;11-15-32;
John Reeves* SW-NE-S9; 5-25-35.   E-SE-S9;1-7-28
John Morris* SE-NW-S9; 6-6-36
Coonrod Kern* E-SW-S9; 4-13-35
Abraham Parrish* NW-SE-S9; 1-27-37
Eli H. Parish* SW-SE-S9; 7-6-38

Henry Sanders* E-NE-S10; 11-6-27
John Mahala* W-NE-S10; 11-2-24; NW-SE-S10; 5-28-32
Archibald Wood NW-S10;NE,NW-S15;SW-S25;9-23-16;SW-S10;9-24-16
William Deskins* E-SE-S10; 1-26-28
George Eller* SW-SE-S10; 2-27-35
Samuel Lee* E-NE-S11; 11-1-31
William Carrell* N7-NE-S11; 8-5-34
Reuben Ward' SW-NE, SE-NW-S11; 9-3-32
Elisha Sanders* NE-NW-S11; 8-5-34
Joseph Sanders* W-NW-S11; 6-11-32
John Allen SW-S11; NW-S14; 10-10-16
Francis Chartie SE-S11; 10-11-17
George Matlock NE, SE-S12; 10-11-16
Samuel Hardesty* E-NW-S12; 7-31-32
George Milam* W-NW-S12; 10-27-27
Jonathan Rains NE-S13; 10-11-16
George Daugherty* E-NW-S13; 9-18-31
Joseph Bunger* W-NW-S13; 10-19-31
John Carr SW-S13; 9-16-16; E-SE-S14; 9-23-16
John W. Lee SE-S13; 10-19-16
Eli Lee NE-S14; 1-6-17
James Borland SW-S14; 11-2-16
Moses Hall* NW-SE-S14; 9-15-32; W-NE, E-NW-S23; 1-25-30
Orion Crocker* SW-SE-S14; 9-15-32
William Newcomb SW-S15; 7-9-17; NW, SW-S22; 9-23-16
Joseph Hazlewood* SE-NE, W-NE, SE-NW-S17; 5-14-39
William Newton, Gn NE-NW-S17; 3-14-53   8-29-39
Enos Blair* NE-SW-S17;NE-NW-S18;5-20-39;NW-SW-S17;6-15-36;E-SW-S18;/
Fayette Blair* S-SW-S17; 6-8-39;NW-SE-S18;7-2-40; LaFayette
John Goodnight* SE-SE-S17; 11-1-32
Jacob Beall Lowe* SE-NW-S18; 10-3-36
Nicholas Sims* W-SW-S18; 10-30-28
Gabriel Abram* NE-SE-S18; 6-4-36
John Wilson W-NE-S19; 11-24-53; MIW 23961
Jackson Sims* NE-NW-S19; 6-30-36
Richard Crane, Gn SW-SW-S19;4-16-35;of*,SE-SE-S19;10-27-36;NE-SW-
Benjamin Dougherty Ellis* SE-SW-S19;3-22-38.   S19; 3-11-39
John Gardner, Gn NE-SE-S19; 10-30-35
Joseph Sanders* NW-SE-S19; 2-15-39
John Wharton* SW-SE-S19; 10-2-37
Burdel Dosson* N-NE-S20; 2-22-36
John House Bunger* SE-NE-S20;3-11-37;SW-NE-S20;8-26-37;NW-SE-S20;
William Porch* S-NW-S20; 12-10-35   3-10-37
Thomas Jefferson Scott* E-SW-S20; 2-8-39
Moses Hopwood* NW-SW-S20; 3-3-36
Jonathan Scott* SW-SW-S20; 10-12-38
James Givins* NE-SE-S20; 3-18-41
Robert Berry Givins* SE-SE-S20; 9-29-35
William Berry* SW-SE-S20; 11-30-39
Isaac Rogers* E-NE-S21; 10-3-25
Joseph Berry* W-NE-S21;12-25-26;SE-S21;W-NE-S28;W-SE-S32;9-23-16;
   W-NW-S33; 10-11-16; NE-S34; 9-6-17
Dudley C. Smith* E-NW-S21; 4-18-36
Littleberry West* W-NW-S21; 7-21-23

Thomas Jefferson Scott* E-SW-S21; 2-8-39
John A. Givens, Coonrod Kern, Jonathan Nichols, Committee of the
   Blue Spring Community W-SW-S21; 1-2-26
William Wilson NE-S22; 10-26-16
Pierre Chaewin(?) SE-S22; 10-11-17
Samuel Dodds* E-NE-S23; 1-28-30
Thomas Renshaw* W-NW-S23; 8-27-31
Solomon Philips* E-SW-S23; 1-13-36; SE-S23; 6-9-17
Henry Fritts* NW-SW-S23; 2-25-35
William Gay* SW-SW-S23; 2-18-36
John Harvey NE, NW-S24; 9-7-16
Jonathan Nicholas (Nichols? see above) SW-S24; 10-19-16
Solomon Green NE-S25; 9-23-16
Fetter & Hughes NW, SE-S25; NW, SW-S35; 9-23-16
Levin Lawrence NE-S26; 9-24-16
Joseph Garran & Als. Garrand NW-S26; 10-11-17
Gasper Koons* E-SW-S26;8-25-24;W-SW-S26;9-29-34;SE-SE-S27;S-SW-S34;
James Parsons SE-S26; 8-28-17   2-13-37
Adam Karn NE-S27; 12-9-17
Matthew Smith, Philadelphia E-NW-S27; 9-1-31
Isaac Rodgers W-NW-S27; 8-28-17
Adam Darting SW-S27; 9-23-16
Seth Goodwin* N-SE-S27; 4-10-37
William Gray* SW-SE-S27; 10-8-34
John A. Givens* E-NE-S28; 7-2-31; NW-NW-S34; 11-30-39
Adam Bower NW-S28; 9-23-16
John Briscoe SW-S28; 9-23-16
John Knisley Whisenand* E-SE, SW-SE-S28; 11-5-39
Hannah Nichols* NW-SE-S28; 9-18-39
William Berry* NE-S29; 9-28-35
Jacob Taylor, Lw NE-NW-S29; 1-4-39
Isaac Jones* SE-NW-S29; 7-7-38
William Weaver* W-NW-S29; 2-10-36
Abraham May* NE-SW-S29; 3-10-36
John Berry SE-SW-S29;NE-SW-S32;9-28-35;W-NW-S32;11-2-31;W-SW-S33;
Samuel Graybill* SW-SW-S29; 3-17-38   5-1-17
John M. Berry* E-SE-S29; 6-8-24
William Marrs* W-SE-S29; W-NE-S33; 1-3-29
John Wharton* E-NE-S30; 8-26-37
Henry Sanders* W-NE-S30; 10-12-38
John Watson* E-NW, NE-SW-S30; 4-16-35
Silvanus Tarkington* W-NW-S30;9-26-31;W-SE-S30;12-21-29;E-NW-S31;
Malden Baker* SE-SW-S30; 3-3-36   7-23-27
Alfred Coffey, Gn W-SW-S30; 10-3-31
Benjamin Ridge E-SE-S30; 1-6-20
Jesse Tarkington* NE-S31;9-23-16;W-NW-S31;11-11-31;SE-NW-S32;2-13-3
John Sadler* E-SE-S31; 9-23-16; W-SE-S31; 7-23-27
James Rogers* E-SE-S32; 7-10-29
James Shipman* E-NE-S33; 4-18-37
John H. Bunger* E-NW-S33; 7-10-29
Orion Crocker* E-SW-S33; 5-6-29
Absalom Baker* NE-SE-S33;12-19-35;SE-SE, W-SE-S33; 10-29-38
William Koons* NE-NW-S34; 2-13-37; SE-NW-S34; 10-5-35
Ammon Goodwin* SW-NW-S34; 1-9-38

William May* NE-SW-S34; 9-28-35
John Storm SE-S34; 9-23-16
Thomas McCrany NE-S35; 9-7-16; SE-S35; 9-23-16
Josiah Jackson NE, SE-S36; 9-7-16
John Johnson NW-S36; 9-23-16
Joseph Richardson SW-S36; 9-18-16

RELINQUISHMENTS

David Matlock NW-S3; 5-27-18
Samuel Caldwell NE, SE-S10; 9-24-16
David Matlock & Eli Lee NW-S12; 2-5-18
Robert Stafford & John Musser SW-S17; 8-14-19
Samuel Chambers & A. Petterson NE-S21; 12-3-16
John Collins W-SW-S21; 9-23-16
James Clark SW-S26; 12-12-17   Micah Newby NW-S13;6-5-17
John Briscoe SE-S20; 9-23-16   Henry Speed NE, NW-S23;9-23-16
Adam Bower NW-S32; 9-23-16   Isaac Rodgers E-NW-S27;8-28-17
John Dunn SE-S2;10-29-16   John Carr W-SE-S14;9-23-16
John Alexander NW-S31;2-2-19   Solomon Philips E-SW-S23;
John Smothers W-NE-S33;6-4-18   11-27-17
John Berry E-SW-S33;5-1-17
John Sadler W-SE-S31; 9-23-16; W-SE-S30; 11-11-18
Joseph Berry E-SE-S32;E-NE-S28;9-23-16; E-NW-S33; 10-11-16
Joseph Perisho NE-S5; 6-9-17; 7-4-29

T 9 N, R 1 W

Absalom Polley* Lot 1-E-Sfr-S1; 2-13-49
George H. Jackson* Lot 2-E-Sfr-S1; 11-2-53
William Burtch, Kn SW-SE-Sfr, SE-SW-Sfr, SW-SW-Sfr-S1;2-1-54;
    Lots 3-4-NWfr-Sfr-S1;1-18-54; SW-NE, SE-NW-S3; 2-17-54
George Matlock* NE-SW-Sfr, NW-SW-Sfr-S1; 2-17-36
Jacob Lentz* NW-NEfr-S2; 7-19-36
John Campbell* SW-NEfr-S2; 10-28-54
David Browning* E-NW-S2; 11-28-37
William Elliott* W-NW-S2;7-12-36; of Preble Co.,O.,E-NE-S3;8-18-41
John J. Owens* NE-SW-S2; 12-18-51
John Goodwine* SE-SW-S2; 8-17-36
John Noll* NW-SW-S2; 6-9-42
Jacob Yoder, Jr.* SW-SW-S2; 6-13-36
Isaac Taylor Griffith* NW-NE-S3; 2-13-49
Benjamin Marshall* NE-NW-S3; 3-16-52
Thomas Gilaspie* NE-SW-S3; 11-9-53; NE-SE-S3; 2-17-54
Alexander Gilaspie* SE-SW,SE-SE-S3; 11-2-53; MLW 4174
George Hinkle* NE-SE-S3; 8-26-39
John Noll* SE-SE-S3; 7-30-42
A. W. Leland, Richland Dist., S.C. E-NE, SW-NE, E-NW, SE-SW,SE-S4;
    W-NE, E-NW, E-SW, SE-S5; NE, N-NW-S9; 7-29-36
John Turner* NW-NE-S4; 4-7-34
Philip H. Smith* NW-NW-S4; 8-5-34
John Lewis Griffith* SW-NW-S4; 8-19-35; SE-NE-S5; 7-26-36
William McCoy* NE-SW-S4; 3-7-36
Emsley Wood* NE-NE-S5; 9-13-32

George Whisenand* NW-NW-S5;9-12-36;SE-NE-S6;10-1-35;W-NE-S6;9-20-20
Jonathan Owen Whisenand* NW-SW-S5; 4-2-46
John H. Dunning* SW-SW-S5; 1-7-35
Benjamin Ridge* NE-NE-S6; 1-4-36
John Ketcham NW-S6; 9-25-16
Henry Wampler SW-S6; 9-25-16
Adam Bowen SE-S6; 9-25-16
Albert Parkes* NE-NE-S7; 6-26-35; SW-NW-S0; 4-26-35
Rachel Dunning* SE-NE-S7; 7-7-36
Thomas Smith+ W-NE-S7; 9-26-16
James Matlock NW-S7; 9-25-16
William Julien SW-S7; 9-25-16
William J. Adair SE-S7; 9-25-16
John Stockton Barnes* NE-S8; 7-26-36
Samuel Riley Faris* E-NW-S8; 7-4-35
John Moore Dunning* NW-NW-S8; 8-27-22
George Parkes SW-S8;10-16-16;NW-SE-S8;6-26-35;SW-SE-S8; 2-8-36
William Tate* NE-SE-S8; 8-5-34
William Riddle* SE-SE-S8;.8-5-34   7-26-28
James Staton Rawlins* SE-NW-S9;8-15-34;SW-NW-S9;7-26-36;E-SE-S9;/
Roderick Rawlins* SW-S9;5-11-18;W-SE-S9;3-11-18;NW-S20;9-26-16
George Yoder* NE-NE-S10;8-5-34;SE-NE-S10;6-13-36;SW-NW-S11;12-21-50
Thomas Hill Blair* NW-NE-S10; 8-14-44
Zachariah Holler* SW-NE-S10; 10-14-33
James Blair* NE-NW-S10; 10-25-47
Daniel Gross* SE-NW-S10; 7-26-36; W-SW-S15; 9-27-31
Nathaniel Browning* E-SW-S10; 10-26-37
Aaron Goodwine* W-SW-S10; 12-15-28
George Hinkle* NE-SE-S10; 3-12-34
John Smith Hardisty* NW-SE-S1Q; NW-SW-S11; 7-19-36
William Martin* NE-NE-S11; 10-27-35
John Goodwine* NW-NE-S11; 8-17-36
James M/ McLane, Jr SW-NE, SE-NW-S11; 3-12-56
Anna Goodwine* NE-NW-S11; 7-10-43
John Jackson" NW-NW-S11; 7-12-43; SW-NW-S12; 10-12-36
Phebe Hardisty* SW-SW-S11; 9-27-36
William Paul* E-SE-S11;W-SW-S12;4-20-49; MLW 50019
James McLane, Jr NW-SE-S11; 3-12-56
Adam Gimble* SW-SE-S11; NW-NE-S14; 1-19-53; MLW 50090
Jonathan Dranam* SE-NW-S12; 10-27-35; E-SW-S12; 7-30-55
Francis B. Phelps, Wayne Co., Mich. SE-S12; 3-7-56
Rufus Ward, Jo NE-NE-S13; 4-3-49
Abner Goodwine, Gn SE-NE-S13; 2-1-38
Philip Henry* SW-NE-S13; 1-12-36; NW-SW-S13; 1-12-36
John Flener* NE-NW-S13; 12-8-51; SE-S27; 10-12-16
Jeremiah Holler* SE-NW-S13; 2-17-36
Robert E. Whitsell* NW-NW-S13;6-1-83(surely 53);SW-NW-S13;12-21-50
Paul Edmund* SE-SW-S13; 8-16-36
David Gray* SE-SW-S13; 1-26-36
William Goodwine SE-S13; W-NE-S27; 2-16-18
Cornelius Feeler* NE-NE-S14; 1-12-54
Sarah Haskett* SE-NE-S14; 1-31-48
William Bourke* SW-NE-S14; 12-5-53
Gilbert T. Paul* NE-NW-S14; 1-6-52

SE-NW-S14 is listed as Sold at Indianapolis, 4-19-56. The name of
George Walker, of G1, is inserted below in such a manner as not to
be clear whether he entered this location or was a co-purchaser
with Edmund Paul following:
Edmund Paul* NW-NW-S14; 2-10-54; (see above)
Abraham Everett* SW-NW-S14;NE-NE-S15;1-18-54;SE-NE-S15; 11-30-52;
Andrew Croucher, Jk E-SW-S14; 2-25-36   E-SE-S15;1-22-30
John Wood, Jk W-SW-S14; 6-5-22
William Goodwine, Jr.* NE-SE-S14; 12-3-33
Richard Snider* SE-SE-S14; 3-18-36; W-SE-S14; 8-22-31
Thomas Payne* NW-NE-S15; 1-13-54
John Walker Matlock* SW-NE-S15; 1-26-39
John Griffith* NW-S15; 9-4-17
Andrew Vannoy* NE-SW-S15; 10-7-35; SE-SW, W-SE-S15; 4-2-35
Jacob L. Payne* NE-NE-S17; 9-29-32
William Parks* SE-NE-S17; 7-9-35
George Ritter* NW-NE-S17; 11-14-35; SW-NE-S17; 7-11-33
John Hill* NW-S17; NW-S21; 10-11-16
James Parks* SW-S17; SE-S20; SE-S29; 9-26-16
C. Bullitt & T. Bullett SE-S17; NE-S20; 9-26-16
John Owens* NE,SE-S18;9-26-16;E-SW-S18;6-7-24;W-SW-S18;2-5-25
James Matlock* NW-S18; 6-2-17
Daniel Stout* NE-S19; 9-26-16
Thomas Barker* NW-S19; 1-3-18
James Caldwell* SE-S19; 9-26-16
Joseph Taylor* SW-S20; 9-26-16
James Day Robertson* NE-NE-S21; 1-12-39; NW-NW-S22; 5-20-36
Dabney Miller, Mg S-NE-S21; 2-10-34
John Miller* NW-NE-S21; 2-27-34
George Pall* SW-S21; 9-26-16
David Raymond* SE-S21; 9-26-16
James Invanall* NE-NE-S22; 3-7-34; NW-NE-S22; 10-7-35
Jonathan Hinkle* SE-NE, E-SW, SE-SE-S22; 1-27-35
Cravin P. Hester* SE-NW-S22; 2-17-36; W-SW-S22; 3-8-36
Archibald Campbell* SW-NW-S22; 1-22-36
John Walker Matlock* NE-SE-S22; 7-21-3_ (?)
Lawrence Wharton* W-SE-S22; NW-NW-S26; 3-26-36
Henry Yoder* NE-NE-S23;12-27-51;SE-NE-S23;8-5-34;SW-NW-S24;1-27-35
Nicholas Cook SW-NE-S23; 3-13-29; NW-SE-S23; 3-7-39, of*
William Burtch, Kn NE-NW-S23; 1-8-54
Peter Whitsell* SE-NW-S23; 8-11-47
James P. Rainey* NE-SW-S23; 7-25-36
George Hinkle* W-SW-S23; 7-19-36
Thomas Rader* NE-SE-S23; 2-10-36
Abraham Buskirk* NE-S24; 2-10-18
David Gray E-NW-S24; 8-11-31
Joseph Piercy* SW-S24; 10-28-35
Abraham Huff* E-SE-S24; 3-26-27
Thomas Heady* W-SE-S24; 9-20-21
John Buskirk* E-NE-S25; 12-8-17
Nicholas Fleenor* W-NE-S25; 2-6-36; NW-S35; 10-12-16
Thomas Buskirk, Shelby Co., Ky. NW-S25;4-10-18;of*,W-SE-S25;6-7-24
Jacob Budderback* SW-S25; 10-12-16
Michael VanBuskirk* E-SE-S25;2-20-36;W-SE-S26;5-31-36 (no Van)

John Rader* E-NE-S26; 3-30-32; W-NE-S26; 5-31-36
William Cook* NE-NW-S26; 1-21-37
James Dearmin* SE-NW-S26; 1-26-37
Joseph Davison, Sr.* SW-NW-S26; 1-12-36
Nicholas Fleenor, Sr. SE-SW-S26; 1-24-36
Stephen P. Scale W-SW-S26; 8-8-18
Thomas Wilson E-SE-S26; 8-23-24
James Jackson Alexander E-NE-S27; 3-10-36
Eleazer Dagget NW-S27; 9-5-16
James Borland SW-S27; 11-11-16
Gideon Frisee NE-S28; 9-5-16
Eli Lee NW-S28; 10-12-16
William Matlock SW-S28; 9-26-16
Samuel Humphreys SE-S28; 9-26-16
Thomas Graham NE-S29; 9-26-16
Lawrence Smoyer NW-S29; 8-23-17
Abraham Appler SW-S29; 9-27-16
Samuel Rogers NE-S30; 7-3-17
James Wood NW-S30; 8-20-17
Obadiah T. Barker E-SW-S30; 2-4-18
David Banta W-SW-S30; 8-5-34
Christian Eslinger SE-S30; 11-27-16
Obadiah T. & Thomas Barker NE-S31; 2-4-18
Isaac Whisenand NW-S31; 10-30-30
Titan Kemble SW-S31; 1-3-17   Joseph Taylor SE-S33;9-26-16
Simon Chawin SE-S31; 10-11-17   Henry Rodgers NE-S34;9-26-16
Henry Wampler NE-S32; 9-27-16   John Thompson NW-S34;9-26-16
Ebenezer Dickey NW-S32; 2-12-18   Wheeler Mallett SW-S34;9-26-16
Chesley D. Bailey SW-S32; 2-5-17   Samuel Scott SE-S34;9-26-16
Robertson Graham SE-S32; 5-26-17   Grandville Ward NE-S35;2-5-17
George Ritchey NE-S33;9-26-16   William Jackson SW-S35;10-7-16
George Headrick NW-S33;9-26-16   John Johnson SE-S35;10-7-16
David Rogers SW-S33;9-26-16
William McCrum NE-NE-S36; 9-24-51; MLW 12367
Sarah Cree SE-NE-S33; 6-3-52; MLW 7940
Elizabeth Gillaspie SW-NE-S36; 4-27-48
Thomas Heady NW, SW-S36; 10-8-16
David Smith E-SE-S36; 11-17-30
William Snider W-SE-S36; 3-15-27

RELINQUISHMENTS

Jesse Tarkington SW-S18; 7-17-17   David Kelly NW-S31; 6-30-18
James Pneuman SE-S22; 7-13-18   Michael Buskirk SE-S25;7-20-18
Abraham Buskirk NW-S24; 2-10-18
Roderick Rawlins E-SE-S9; 5-11-18
Stephen P. Scall E-SW-S26; 8-8-18
John Buskirk SE-S26; W-NE-S25; 12-8-17
William Goodwin E-NE-S27; 2-16-18
John Stokely E-SW-S5; NW-S8; 10-16-17
Thomas Smith E-NE-S7; 9-26-16
Samuel Haislet W-SW-S30; 10-28-17; 7-4-29
John R. Badger SE-S14; 5-7-19; 7-4-29
Titan Kimble SW-S31; 1-3-17; 7-4-29

Robert Delap* NE-NE-S1; 5-16-36; SE-NE-S1; 1-7-35
John Ketcham E-SE-S15;7-18-31;W-SE-S15;7-29-31;W-NE-S1; 10-14-16
Henry Kirkham NW-S1; 5-24-17
William Harrison Springgate* NE-SW-S1; 9-26-34
Elias Stine* SE-SW-S1; 8-6-35; NW-NE-S12; 6-1-35
John Armstrong W-SW-S1; 5-27-19
Henry Wampler* E-SE-S1;NW-S25;7-2-17;SW-NE-S12;1-11-36;NW-SE-S12;
James Dunning* W-SE-S1; 8-15-25   12-8-38
Fetter & Hughes NE,SE-S2;SW-S15;SW-S27;SW-S34; 9-24-16
Jonathan Lindley NW-S2;9-23-16; NW-S11;NE-S27;SE-S31; 9-24-16
John Isenhower* NE-SW-S2; 5-15-33
John Neese* SE-SW-S2; 10-15-34; SW-SW-S2; 10-11-34
John Elliott* NW-SW-S2; 4-29-33; W-SE-S5; 3-7-35
Joseph Evans NE-S3; 9-23-16
Roderick Rollins NW-S3; 9-23-16
Armstead W. Puett* E-SW-S3; 1-31-29
George Sharp* W-SW-S3; 6-8-24
Arah Osborn SE-S3; 9-11-16
Coleman Pewett NE-S4; 5-14-17; W-SW-S9; 6-10-17
William Sutherlin NW-S4; 9-18-17
Lewis Noel SW-S4; 10-4-16; SE-S4; 9-23-16
Nicholas Whisenand* NE-S5; 11-17-28
Robertson Farmer* E-NW-S5; 6-1-36; W-NW-S5; 4-14-36
Reuben Tomkins* NE-SW-S5; 1-23-37
John Everman* SE-SW-S5; 3-25-33
Jonathan Gilbert W-SW-S5; 2-12-18
Henry Hopewell* NE-SE-S5;6-18-32;W-NE-S8;12-23-31;NW-NW-S19;11-4-39
Archibald Kirby* SE-SE-S5; 6-28-32
John Hilemon* NW-NE, NE-NW-S6; 12-4-38   10-14-20
Thornton R. Hurley* SE-NW-S6;12-3-32; of Franklin Co., Ky.,SW-S6;/
Lewis Coffey* E-SE-S6;2-26-36;W-SE-S6;E-NE-S7;11-28-32;NW-NE-S7;
John H. Reeves* SW-NE-S7; 3-18-41   1-2-33
James Dowell* N-NW-S7; 1-12-39
Joel Anderson Dyer, Ow SE-NW-S7; 1-5-38
Jacob Rumple* SW-NW-S7; 1-2-32
Ellet Mounce* NE-SW-S7; 1-17-38; W-SW-S7; 10-29-31
Jonathan Gilbert* E-SE-S7;12-12-34;NW-S8;2-12-18;SW-S8;10-14-16
Samuel Hardesty W-SE-S7; 3-18-41
William Edmondson* NE-NE-S8; 8-29-34
Marraday Parks* SE-NE-S8; 5-8-33
Jacob Cutler* SE-S8; 11-14-16; NE, E-SE-S18; 10-14-16
George Sharp* NE-S9; 9-24-16; NW-S9; 10-1-16
Joel A. Kirby* E-SW-S9; 12-21-29
Joseph Reeves SE-S9; 5-28-17
Edward Elliott, Fleming Co., Ky. W-NE-S10;10-21-25; of*,E-NE-S10;
Samuel Parks* NW-S10; 9-24-16   2-26-27
James Wright* SW-S10; 9-24-16
James Parks* SE-S10; NW, SW-S14; 9-24-16
Archibald Wood* NE,SE-S11;NE,SE-S17;SW,SE-S21; 9-24-16
Alexander Owens* E-SW-S11; NE-S15; 4-5-25
James Goodwin* W-SW-S11; NW-S22; 9-24-16
Lewis W. Hays* E-NE-S12; 3-18-34

James Dunning* NE-NW-S12; 8-26-35
Loving Nighton* SE-NW-S12; 3-12-36
Jefferson Wampler* W-NW-S12;. 10-26-35; NW-NE-S25; 8-6-35
John McFetridge* E-SW, SW-SW-S12; 2-11-36
Martha Muckelroy* NW-SW-S12; 6-21-38
Lewis Hayes* NE-SE-S12; 1-11-36
Washington J. Houston, Bourbon Co., Ky. SE-SE-S12; 12-29-38
Cary A. Houston* SW-SE-S12; 3-12-36; SW-NW-S13; 10-2-32
John Stanger* NE-S13; 1-11-36
Noel Hall* NE-NW-S13; 2-11-36
Matthew McPhetridge* SE-NW-S13; 8-5-34
James Goodnight* NW-NW-S13; 2-11-36
Samuel Caldwell* SW-S13; NW, SW-S17; 9-24-16
Peter Houston* NE-SE-S13; 3-12-36
Harvey Houston* SE-SE-S13; 10-5-32
Francis Vanoy Hall* NW-SE-S13; 10-4-33; SW-SE-S13; 1-8-33
John Bigger NE-S14; 9-24-16
Samuel Elliott SE-S14; 9-24-16
Ambrose Carlton NW-S15; NE-S22; NW-S23; 9-24-16
Thomas Allen* E-NW-S18;11-25-25;NW-NW-S18;3-12-35;SW-NW-S18;2-7-34
William Bradford SW-S18; 10-19-16
Allen Wilson, Ow W-SE-S18; 9-22-31
John C. Corder* NE-NE-S19; NW-NW-S20; 6-18-32
Stephen Corder* SE-NE-S19; 12-4-38
Thomas Bonner* NW-NE-S19; 2-26-36
Abner Wilson* SW-NE-S19; 1-8-33
Henry James* NE-NW, NW-SE-S19; 3-12-39
Andrew W. Reeves, Ow SE-NW-S19; 2-17-36
William Freeman, Ow SW-NW-S19; 9-13-47
George A. Eisenhower* SW-S19; NE-NW, NW-NW-S30; 10-15-34
Macager Bray* NE-SE-S19; 5-14-44
Tilmon Mounts, Ow SE-SE-S19; 7-30-35
Archelaus Coffey* NE-NE-S20; NW-NW-S21; 2-11-36
John Hansford* SE-NE-S20;3-18-41;SW-NE-S20;12-17-35;SW-NW-S20;
    5-25-36; NE-SE-S20; 10-26-44
William Stogsdill, Ow NW-NE-S20;12-24-32;NW-SE-S20;8-12-33; of*
Emanuel F. Falkner* E-NW-S20;4-23-28.   NE-SW-S20;3-8-38
John Caldwell Smith* SE-SW-S20; 5-23-36
James Stogsdill, Ow NW-SW-S20; 11-5-35
John Stogsdill* SW-SE-S20; 3-21-36; SE-NE-S30; 5-25-36
Joseph Harris* NE-S21; 9-5-16
Mat Cley* NE-NW-S21; 2-5-38
James Starnes* S-NW-S21; 11-5-44
John Simons* SW-S22; NW-S27; 9-7-18
Benjamin Parks E-SE-S22; 12-21-29
John Brooks* W-SE-S22; 12-11-34
Williamson Dunn* NE-S23; 9-24-16
Asa Cottin* SW, SE-S23; 9-4-16
Christian Estinger* NE-S24; 1-10-18
John Gordon* NW, SW-S24; 9-24-16
John C. Harbison* NE-SE-S24; 4-6-36
David Whitesell* SE-SE-S24; 9-2-35; SW-NE-S25; 11-16-32
Pleasant York* W-SE-S24; 2-2-35
Jacob Whitesell, Ck E-NE-S25; 8-13-31

Hiram Worley* E-SW-S25; 2-8-27
John Garrison & James W. Alsup W-SW-S25; 2-8-25
Samuel Haislet* SE-S25; 10-28-17
John McCormick* NE, NW-S26; 9-24-16
William Mayfield* E-SW-S26; 9-14-27; W-SE-S26; 9-14-31
John Wier* W-SW-S26; 10-14-35;NW-NE, N-NW-S35; 10-14-35
Eli Lee* E-SE-S26; 2-5-17
C. & T. Bullitt* SE-S27; 9-24-16
Solomon Bower* NE-S28; 9-24-16
Joseph Kennedy* E-NW-S28; 11-22-24
Daniel Ranard* NW-NW-S28; 12-23-44; SW-NW-S28; 10-26-44
William Thornton* SW-S28; 9-24-16
Abel Bidgelow* SE-S28; 9-7-16; NE-S33; 9-7-16
James Adkins* NE-NE-S29; 5-25-36; SE-NE-S29; 2-22-36
Samuel Howe Smydth* NW-NE-S29; 2-24-36
Samuel Elmore* SW-NE-S29; 10-4-32
David Johnson NW-S29; 10-14-16
Littleberry Bray* NE-SW, NW-SE-S29; 3-18-41
William Vest* SE-SW-S29; 1-30-43
Jesse Benedu(?)* NW-SW-S29; 9-1-36
Nathan Bray* SW-SW-S29; 3-6-37; SW-SE-S29; 11-23-38
Leroy Senders* NE-SE-S29; 11-27-44
John Sanders* SE-SE-S29; 2-11-36
Tilmon Mounts* NE-NE-S30; 8-19-37
Nool Hall* NW-NE-S30; 9-5-44
Micajah Freeman, Ow SW-NW-S30; 9-4-44
John Fullen* SW-S30; 9-24-16; NW-NE-S31; 10-16-37; NW-S31; 1-28-17
William Baker SE-S30; 11-8-16
Elias Ranard* NE-NE-S31; 1-25-39
William Roseberry* S-NE-S31; 7-25-35
John Perisham SW-S31; 1-19-19
David Sears NE-S32; 9-24-16
Thomas Neisbet* E-NW-S32; 10-4-28
James Edds* NW-NW-S32; 6-5-35
William Nesbit* SW-NW-S32; 12-16-35
Daniel Zincks SW-S32; 9-24-16; W-SE-S32; 4-26-19
William Deskins* NE-SE-S32; NW-SW-S33; 10-22-34
John Gwin, Jr.* SE-SE-S32; 5-16-36
Willis Oliver NW-S33; 9-24-16
Edward Archer* E-SW-S33; 11-11-19; SW-SE-S33; 9-11-35
James Davis* SW-SW-S33; 1-16-39
Othias Carter* NE-SE-S33; 1-24-39; SE-SE-S33; 3-22-33
Edward Montgomery Archer* NW-SE-S33; 10-6-36
Thomas Hodges NE-S34; 9-24-16
Joseph Taylor NW-S34; 9-24-16
John Routt & Adam Brenton SE-S34; 9-24-16
Fielden Wood Poe* NE-NE-S35; 8-5-34
Samuel Wier* SE-NE-S35; 8-26-34
David Cherry* SW-NE-S35; 1-10-34; SE-NW-S35; 9-2-34
John Gamble* SW-NW-S35; 3-6-34
Samuel Rogers E-SW-S35; 1-6-17
David Thacker* W-SW-S35; 9-23-25
Benjamin Johnson SE-S35; 10-14-16
James Starnes* E-NE-S36; 3-21-31

John Garrison* W-NE-S36; 1-20-30
James W. Alsup* E-NW-S36; 1-20-30
William Poe* NW-NW-S36; 9-3-34
John Alexander* SW-NW-S36; 11-2-35
Frederick Smoyer SW-S36; 8-23-17
David S. Chambers SE-S36; 12-2-16

RELINQUISHMENTS

John Ketchem E-NE-S1; 10-14-16; SW-S2; 9-23-16
Henry Wampler W-SE-S1; 7-2-17; NE-S25; 1-19-18
John McCormick SW-S3; 9-23-16
Watson & Sayre E-NE-S5; 7-1-18
Jonathan Lindley NE-S10; SE-S24; 9-24-16
James Goodwine E-SW-S11; 9-24-16
Daniel Fetter, James Hughes, & S. Colman SE-S13; 7-1-18
David Raymond NE-S15; 9-24-16
Jacob Cutler NW, W-SE-S18; 10-14-16
Jacob Sears NW-S20; 7-5-17
Archibald Wood NW-S21; 10-14-16; NW-S28; 9-24-16
Eli Lee W-SE-S26; 2-5-17
Adam Darting NE-S30; 9-25-16
Elias Goodwine NW-S32; 9-24-16
Daniel Zinks E-SE-S32; 4-20-19
Thomas Hedges SE-S33; 9-24-16
Samuel Rogers W-SW-S35; 1-6-17
Ben Drake & Arthur Henrie NE-S36; 6-10-18
Gordon Phelps SE-S22; 9-24-16
Coleman Puvett(?) E-SW-S9; 6-10-17
John Shields NE-S7; 10-20-18
John Armstrong E-SW-S1; 5-27-19
Nathaniel Talbot NW-S36; 11-3-17
Frederick Smoyer NE-S12; 8-23-17
C. & T. Bullitt SE-S15; 9-24-16; 7-4-29
David S. Chambers SE-S36; 12-2-16; 7-4-29

T 10 N, R 1 W

Solomon Langwill* Lot 1-Sfr-S18; 8-14-37; Lot 2-Sfr-S18; 2-22-36;
   Lot 1-NEfr-Sfr-S19; NW-NE-S33; 3-17-36
Benoni Denny* Lot 2-NEfr-Sfr-S19; 2-9-36
William Carleton* Lot 3-NEfr-Sfr, E-SE-Sfr, NW-SE-Sfr-S19; 6-1-36;
   SE-SW-S29; SE-NW, W-NW-S32; 3-8-36
A. W. Leland, Richland Dist., S.C. NW-Sfr, SW-Sfr, SW-SE-Sfr-S19;
   E-Sfr, W-Sfr-S20; SW-NE, NW-NW, NE-SW, W-SW, SW-SE-S29; NE, NW, SE-S30;
   E-NE, NW-NE, NE-SW, W-SW-S32; SW-NW, SW-SW-S33; 7-29-36
Eli Chadwick, Kn Sfr-S21; 6-25-57
Nicholas, George W., & Philip Henry Smith Sfr-S27; 7-16-39
James Gaskins* E-E-Sfr-S28; 12-6-34; of Ws, W-SW-Sfr-S28; 9-21-27
Nicholas Smith* W-E-Sfr-S28; 3-20-29
Robert Walter, Ow NW-Sfr-S28; 11-8-31
Lee Brown* E-SW-Sfr-S28; 7-25-28; NE-NW-S32; 12-6-34
Stephen Gaskins* NE-NE-S29; 3-16-36
James Mulky, Cf SE-NE, NE-SE-S29; 10-6-32

William Gaskins* NW-NE-S29; 10-1-35
William McNeely* E-NW-S29; 1-14-36; of Kn, SW-NW-S29; 10-25-33
Daniel Ray* SE-SE-S29; NW-NW-S33; 9-17-35
William Scott* NW-SE-S29; 1-14-36
William & Jacob Millikan* E-SW-S30; 11-8-28
James Pennington* W-SW-S30; 9-12-17
William Burtch, Kn E-NE-S31; 4-13-57
Jacob Millikan* N-NW-S31; 8-25-36
Levi Ridge* SE-NW-S31; 5-14-44
Henry Putman* SW-NW-S31; 3-8-33
Emsley Wood* SE-SW-S31;4-1-35;E-SE-S31;9-12-36;SE-SE-S32;4-19-36
Benjamin Ridge* NW-SW-S31; 12-8-38
Allen Sims* SW-SW-S31; 4-1-35; NE-SE-S32; 10-5-32
John Patterson* W-SE-S31; 7-2-22
Angus McCoy Poe* SW-NE, SE-SW-S32; 6-28-36
Fielden Wood Poe* W-SE-S32; 6-28-36
Isaac Gillaspy* NE-NE-S33; 8-5-34; SE-NE-S33; 9-17-35; Lot 3-E-NWfr
    Sfr-S34; 5-12-38; W-NWfr-Sfr-S34; 2-24-30
John Turner* SW-NE-S33;10-13-32;NE-SE-S33;8-4-36;W-SE-S33;10-28-29
Washington Smith* NE-NW-S33; 11-15-37
Andrew Baker Anderson* SE-NW-S33; 5-3-36; NW-SW-S33; 9-13-32
William Sims* E-SW-S33; 4-19-36
Andrew Scott Tate* SE-SE-S33; 8-5-34
William Scott* Lot 4-E-NWfr-Sfr-S34; 3-15-38
Isaac Taylor Griffith* E-SWfr-Sfr-S34; 8-29-43
Benjamin Marshall* W-SW-Sfr-S34; 8-5-34
David Browning* E-SE-Sfr-S34;1-30-37; Lots 7-8-Sfr-S35; 8-24-36
Eleanor Griffith* SW-SE-Sfr-S34; 9-4-43
Jacob B. Lowe* Lot 9-Sfr-S35; 9-22-36

Remainder of this Township in the Crawfordsville District.

T 10 N, R 2 W

Peter Abel* E-Sfr, E-W-Sfr-S3; 3-20-23; NW-NE-S9; 3-30-46
John Davis* Lot 1-W-W-Sfr-S3; 5-19-36
John VanBuskirk, Ow Lot 2-W-W-Sfr-S3; 12-26-44
John Fullen Sfr-S4; 9-28-16
James Dowden, Ow Lots 1-2-E-SW-Efr-S5; 3-24-34
William Harrodd Dowden* W-SW-Efr-S5;3-23-35;NE-NW-S8; 8-25-36
Isaac V. Buskirk SE-Efr, N-Efr-S5; 7-29-18
Leeson Shirley, Ow Lot 1-E-Sfr-S6; 6-19-35; of*, Lot 4-E-W-Sfr-S6;
    NE-NE-S7; 6-13-39; SE-NE-S7; 5-29-44; NW-NE-S7; 12-14-44
Richard Shirley* Lot 2-E-Sfr-S6;10-17-34;Lot 3-E-W-Sfr-S6;9-25-34;
Emanuel Yoder* SW-NE-S7;3-22-36;NE-SE-S7;2-7-45./ W-W-Sfr-S6;12-4-29
Harrison McHenry, Ow E-NW-S7; 1-22-39; of*, NE-SW-S7; 12-25-44
John Haskett, Ow W-NW-S7; 12-26-34
John Barlow* SE-SW-S7; 1-22-39; W-SW-S7; 4-23-28; NW-SE-S7;1-29-39;
John Leason Shirley, Ow SE-SE-S7;8-29-35.   SW-SE-S7;12-14-44
James VanBuskirk* E-NE, NW-NE-S8; 2-10-36; NE-NE-S9; 12-21-44;
    E-NW-S9; 4-16-30; SW-NW-S9; 11-3-32; NW-SW-S9; 4-18-34
Christian Summit* SW-NE-S8; 12-15-32; SW-S27; 12-3-27
George Condief, Ow S-NW-S8; 11-21-44
Thomas Dittemore, Ow NW-NW-S8; 6-13-39

John Eli Farmer* N-SW-S8; 3-18-46
Matthias Berry, Kn SE-SW-S8; 8-12-44
William Brown* SW-SW-S8; 10-13-49; NW-NW-S17; 10-18-49
Isaac Buskirk* E-SE-S8; 3-31-39; W-NE-S10; 11-17-46
John Leeson Ashbaugh* W-SE-S8; 10-2-43; NW-NE-S17; 10-16-43
Hezekiah Wampler* SE-NE-S9; 5-24-39
John Bowland (Borland)* SW-NE-S9; 2-6-36; SW-SW-S9; 9-9-37
Thomas VanBuskirk* NW-NW-S9; 2-10-36
Henry Wallis* E-SW-S9; 8-26-29
John Burton* SE-S9;5-29-19;E-NE-S10;5-19-30;Lots 1-2-NWfr-Sfr-S11;
Sarah Abell* NE-NW-S10; 8-9-36   3-24-36
William Hite* NW-NW-S10; 3-6-37
Jeremiah York & Joseph Dagley SE-NW-S10; 1-29-50
Felix Grundy Hite* SW-NW, NW-SW-S10; 8-22-32
Lemuel Gentry, Mg NE-SW-S10; 9-4-34
William Rawlins* SE-SW-S10; 8-22-32
Andrew Wampler* SW-SW-S10; 3-24-36
Paschal Shelburn* NE-SE-S10; NE-NE-S15;5-19-36;NW-NW-S14;12-1-35
James Turner* SE-SE-S10; 5-16-36
Jeremiah Brisco* NW-SE-S10; 5-6-37
David Wampler* SW-SE-S10; 5-21-33
James Gentry* E-E-Sfr-S11;5-24-36; Lot 3-W-E-Sfr-S11; 10-22-39
Purnell Houston NE-SWfr-Sfr-S11;5-24-36; SW-NW-Sfr-S13; 9-15-35
Jefferson Wampler* SE-SWfr-Sfr-S11; 3-6-37
Henry Stine & Paschal Shelburne* W-SW-Sfr-S11; 2-12-36
Joseph Houston* Sfr-S12; 5-24-36; W-SW-S13; 6-6-31
Lemuel Gentry* NEfr-Sfr-S13; 5-4-46
James Houston* E-NW-Sfr-S13; 3-8-33
Henry Putman* E-SW-S13; 8-5-34
Benjamin Houston* E-SE-S13; 5-1-46
John Cooter* NW-SE-S13;2-12-53; MLW 52405; SW-SE-S13; 2-8-45
Levi McComber* E-NE-S14; 5-24-36
Henry Cosner* W-NE-S14; 5-24-36
Andrew Jackson Cosner* NE-NW-S14; 11-8-43; SE-NW-S14; 9-7-47
Isaac Litton, Ow SW-NW-S14; 5-19-47
David W. Ellett* NE-SW-S14; 2-18-53
Alfred Houston* SE-SW-S14; 6-8-46
Zenes K. Hoge* W-SW-S14; 2-25-45
William Hite* E-NW-S15; 3-21-39; W-NW-S15; 5-5-30
Jonathan Gilbert SW-S15; NW, SW-S22; 9-24-16
John Blane* NE-SE-S15; 8-5-34; SE-SE-S15; 6-17-36
Robert Blair W-SE-S15; 6-30-17
John F. (L.?) Ashbaugh* NE-NE-S17; 3-26-47
William H. Lindsey, Ow SE-NE-S17; 12-25-44
Elisha Labedew* SW-NE, E-NW-S17; 10-22-49
John Berry, Ow SW-NW-S17; 7-5-37
Francis O. Hall* E-SW-S17; 7-14-17
William Wilson* W-SW-S17; 5-26-31
Christopher DeVor* E-SE-S17; 1-15-23
Paul Stine* NW-SE-S17; SW-NE-S20; 2-16-36
Riley Wilson* SW-SE-S17; 9-18-34
John Absalom Ashbaugh, Ow NE-NE-S18; 12-14-44
Jacob Ashbaugh* SE-NE, NE-SE-S18; 1-24-37
Joseph Ashbaugh* NW-NE-S18; 1-24-39; W-NW-S18; 11-25-25

Augustin Shelburn* SW-NE-S18; 11-10-35
James Evans, Ow E-NW-S18; 10-2-35
John McCormick* SW-S18; E-SE-S21; 9-24-16;NW, SW-S29;9-24-16;NE-
Henry DeVor* SE-SE-S18; 9-2-43.   S30; 9-25-16
Anthony Reece, Ow W-SE-S18; 1-6-21
Henry Stine* NE-NE-S19;10-14-32;E-NE-S20;2-16-36;NW-NE-S20;11-3-34
Henry Grose* SE-NE-S19; 11-5-32
William Puett* W-NE-S19; 12-13-27;SE-NE-S25;5-9-36;NW-SW-S25;5-26-
Lewis L. Waldon* E-NW-S19; 11-24-25.   32;SE-S25;6-11-17
John Summet* W-NW-S19; 8-25-28;E-SE-S27; 3-25-31
Reuben Loving* E-SW-S19; 2-11-26
Amsted W. Puett* W-SW-S19; 9-6-24; W-NW-S30; 9-21-24
David Buzzard* E-SE-S19; 5-27-31
Zacheus Chambers, Ow W-SE-S19; 1-2-30; NW-SW-S30; 9-4-35
Hugh Burns* NW-S20; 9-25-16
Nicholas Whisenand* E-SW-S20; 3-23-27
Samuel Hartsock* W-SW-S20; 1-9-26
George Bowman* NE-SE-S20; 3-30-37
John Stine* SE-SE-S20; 11-3-34;W-NW-S28;8-5-34;E-NE-S29;8-5-34
Sarah Farmer* W-SE-S20; 4-23-28
Solomon Teague* NE-S21; 1-1-27
Jacob B. Lowe* NW-S21; 8-27-36
Abner Evans* SW-S21; 9-24-16
Henry Ritezel* W-SE-S21; 1-9-26
George W. Chambers* NE-NE-S22;5-9-37;SE-NE-S22;7-31-44; NW-NW-S23;
    11-10-48; SW-NW-S23; 11-17-46
Benjamin Botts* W-NE-S22; 5-24-25
Archibald Wood* SE-S22; NE-S27; 9-24-16
A. W. Leland, Richland Dist., S.C. NE-S23; S24; N-NE-S25;7-29-36
Paschal Shelburne, William Hite, & Parminter M. Parks E-NW-S23;
Eli Warren* NE-SW-S23;1-9-37;W-SW,W-SE-S23;11-8-43.   10-15-32
Hugh Warren* SE-SW-S23; 9-5-36
James Bailey* E-SE-S23; 10-15-17
Johnson Stiles* SW-NE-S25; 3-15-36; SW-SW-S25; 10-6-32
Tapley Taylor* E-NW-S25; 3-20-29
Robert Taylor* NW-NW-S25; 10-3-36
Willis B. Robinson* SW-NW-S25; 5-22-35
Moses Slaughter* E-SW-S25; 6-4-17
Chesley Bailey & James Matlock E-NE-S26; 10-25-17
Jacob Duncan* NW-NE-S26; 3-21-39
Chesley D. Bailey* SW-NE-S26; 2-13-33
Nathan Stansberry* NE-NW-S26; 10-9-34
William Putman* SE-NW-S26; 1-17-35; SW-NW-S26; 10-9-34
William R. Duncan* NW-NW-S26; 12-24-44
Nathaniel Clark* SW-S26; 5-29-17
William Ray* NE-SE-S26; 1-26-35; W-SE-S26; 10-27-18
William Ray, Jr. SE-SE-S26; 7-15-36
C. & T. Bullitt* NW-S27; 9-24-16
Alexander Wilson* W-SE-S27; 11-25-26
Fetter & Hughes* NE, SE-S28; 9-24-16
Gilbert Litten* E-NW-S28; 10-29-28; E-SW-S28; 11-13-30
William Brady* NW-SW-S28; 10-6-34; SE-SE-S30; 12-18-38
George Isenhower* SW-SW-S28; 10-15-33
Joshua White* W-NE-S29; 11-26-32

William Neese* E-SE-S29;11-23-31;NE-NE-S32;10-13-32;NW-NW-S33;10-12-
William O. Sansberry (Stansberry?) W-SE-S29;7-28-24.   32
George Sharp* E-NW-S30; 6-8-24
John Moore* E-SW-S30;1-6-21;SE-NE-S32;3-30-33;W-NE-S32;5-11-31
Joseph Wampler,Jr.* SW-SW-S30;12-18-38;NE-SE-S30;8-5-34;W-SE-S30;
John Allen* E-NE-S31;3-25-31;W-NE,W-SE-S31;11-4-30.   7-27-26
Joel Litten* E-NW-S31;11-23-31;NE-SW-S31;11-12-32;SE-SW-S31;1-12-39;
Lewis Logan Waldon* W-NW-S31;2-20-36.   W-SW-S31;2-26-36
Jesse C. Moore* E-SE-S31; 11-17-20
Julius Woodard* NW-S32; 11-15-16
David Bright* E-SW-S32; 12-21-29
John Burton* N-SW-S32; 9-6-19
George J. Sharp* E-SE-S32; 1-28-30
George Sharp* W-SE-S32; 4-14-25
Christian Summet* NE-NE-S33; 12-29-34
Enoch Stine* SE-NE-S33; 2-17-36
Henry James* NW-NE, NE-NW-S33; 2-16-36
William Steward* SW-NE-S33; 2-16-36
James Cross (Grose)* SE-NW-S33; 2-16-36; SW-NW-S33; 3-7-35
Henry Hopewell, White Co., Ill. E-SW-S33; 8-11-23
Peter Grose* W-SW-S33; 10-28-33
Willis Smith* E-SE-S33; 5-19-36
George Shuck* NW-SE-S33; 2-16-36; SW-SE-S33; 10-4-32
Archibald Wood NE-S34; 9-24-16
William Millikan NW, SE-S34; 12-16-16
William Kelso SW-S34; 9-24-16
John Bigger* NE, NW-S35; NW-S36; 9-24-16
Phineas Stephens SW-S35; 1-28-17. Jonathan Lindley E-SE-S35;9-24-16
Jefferson Wampler W-SE-S35;1-11-36.Samuel Jennings NE-S36;12-26-16
Johnson Stiles NW-SW-S36;1-28-39. Jacob Wampler SW-SW-S36;1-11-36
Thomas James NE-SE-S36;3-9-35.   John Kays W-SE-S36;6-6-17
Martin Wampler E-SW-S36; 12-25-26; SE-SE-S36; 1-11-36

Remainder of this Township in the Crawfordsville District.

RELINQUISHMENTS

Moses Slaughter W-SW-S25;6-4-17   Francis V. Hall W-SW-S17;7-14-17
John Hays E-SE-S36;6-6-17   Isaac V. Buskirk SW-Efr-S5;7-29-
William Ray E-SE-S26;10-27-18   Abner Evans NE-S21;9-25-16. /18
William Wilson NW-S23;10-14-16   James Bailey NW-S25;12-23-17
Peter Ham NE-S22;6-19-17
David Raymond SW, SE-S27; 9-24-16
John Burton E-SW-S32; 9-6-19; may be partly in Owen Co.
Robert Blair, alias Blain E-SE-S15; 6-30-17
Caleb White & David Cummings NE, SE-S19;8-27-18; Sfr-S6; 8-14-18
Daniel Fetter, James Hughes, & S. Colman NE, SE-S32; 7-1-18
Gwathmey & Bartholomew NW-S30; 9-24-16
John Ketcham E-NE-S20; NW-S21; 9-22-17
John McCormick NW-S18;NW-S19;SW-S19;W-SE-S21;9-24-16;SW-S20;9-25-16
Jacob Leabo W-SE-S14; 11-21-18; 7-4-29
James Bailey E-SE-S23; 10-15-17; 7-4-29
Chesly Bailey & James Matlock W-NE-S26; 10-25-17; 7-4-29
Jonathan Lindley W-SE-S35; 9-24-16; 7-4-29

T 1 N, R 6 W

Ebenezer Case* NW-Sfr-S8; 3-13-33; Sfr-S7; 9-22-14
Samuel Aikman E-Sfr; W-SW-Sfr-S8; 8-29-18
Charles Russell* NE-SW-Sfr-S8; 1-12-34
John Russell* SE-SW-Sfr-S8; 5-13-33
Peleg R. Allen Sfr-S17; 1-5-18
Thomas Pride NE-S18; 7-23-14
Woolsey Pride NW-S18; 6-7-14
John Case SW-S18; 9-22-14
Paul Tislow SE-S18; 8-1-15
Thomas J. Traylor* W-NE-S19; 6-28-31; E-NE-S19; 11-25-18
Jesse Trayler* W-NW-S19; 6-28-31; E-NW-S19; 8-1-17
William R. Campbell* NE-SW, SW-SE-S19; 2-11-37
Samuel Green, Db SE-SW-S19; 2-15-36
Matthew Trayler* NE-SE-S19; n.d.
Newton Lett* NW-SE-S19; 6-8-36
William Hicks DeBruler* NE-NE-S20; 2-6-36
Henry Pride* SE-NE-S20; 2-23-36
Joseph Hathaway W-NE-S20; 12-31-17
William Russell* NW-NW-S20; 7-21-36; W-SW-S29; 11-17-53
Solomon Rogerson* SW-SE-S20;10-8-49;SE-NW-S21;10-16-39;SW-NW-S21; 3-18-37
James Gray* NE-NE-S21; 10-12-35
William Gray* NW-NE-S21; 1-29-35; NE-NW-S21; 10-1-35
Lewis Trayler* NW-NW-S21; 4-18-45
Richard Abbet* NE-SW-S21; 9-6-34
Robert Foster* SE-SW-S21; 9-7-35
Elias Hayes* W-SW-S21; 7-6-31
Mary Aikman* SE-SE-S21; 4-29-50
Joseph Case Nfr-S22; 11-12-14
Nancy Miller NW-NE-S29; 1-3-52; MLW 20309
Richard Christian Dedrick* NE-SE-S29;3-22-51;SE-SE-S29;10-20-51
William Ellis Hargrave* NW-NE-S30; 3-14-44
Henry Stone* NE-NW-S30; 5-28-36
Thomas Hargrave* W-NW-S30; 2-18-36
Henry Scraper* SE-NE-S31; 1-12-36
James Brenton SE-S31; SW-S32; 12-16-16
Edward Teague* E-SE-S32; 1-21-30
John Teague* SW-SE-S32; 3-8-36
William Adams* E-SW-S33; 7-25-29; W-SW-S33; 6-8-29
John Scraper* NW-SE-S33; 3-7-36; SW-SE-S33; 3-14-36

RELINQUISHMENTS

Jonathan Postlethwait W-NW-S30; 3-21-18
Thomas J. Trayler W-NE-S19; 11-25-18
Richard Jones W-NW-S20; 10-20-17; 7-4-29
John Hickman E-NW-S30; 2-24-18; 7-4-29
Peleg R. Allen E-NE, E-NW, SW, SE-S20; 1-5-18
Samuel Aikman NWfr-Sfr, E-SW-Sfr-S8; 8-29-18
Samuel Hinman (Kinman?) SE-S19; 11-25-18
Jesse Trayler W-NW, E-SW-S19; 8-1-17
Alexander McCain SW-S21; 1-24-18
James Harris SE-S32; 2-16-18

Robert Owen, New Harmony, Ind. Sfr-S3; 4-4-26
Hiram Barber, Da E-E-Sfr, W-E-Sfr-S4; 6-6-31
William Kinman* NWfr-Sfr-S4; 12-15-35; N-Sfr-Lot 2-S5; 3-28-36;
   NE-SE-S17; 5-27-39
Wade Posey, Kn W-SW-Sfr-S4; 10-5-36
Jeromiah Arnold* NE-SW-Sfr-S4; 11-0-36; NEfr-Sfr-S7; 5-28-22;
   NE-S8; 8-28-18; SW-S9; 12-22-13
Isaac Coan* N-Sfr-Lot 1-S5; 3-31-35; SW-NW-S15; 6-11-36
Archibald Campbell* SWfr-Sfr-S5; 2-26-36; Sfr-Nfr-S6; 1-7-36
John Arnold* NE-SEfr-Sfr-S5; 3-7-36; NW-NW-S17; 2-6-37
Silas Saverns* SE-SEfr-Sfr-S5; 3-14-36
Elijah Chapman, Da Lot 1-E-W-Nfr, W-W-Nfr-S11; 1-25-36; Lot 2-
   E-W-Nfr-S11; 8-5-34
William Hinman, Jr.* (Kinman?) Lot 6-W-SE-Sfr-S5; 3-5-36
George Washington Savarns* Lot 7-W-SE-Sfr-S5; 12-14-35
William Rhoads* NWfr-Sfr-S7; 7-11-36
William Sullivan, George W. Pratt, & George M. Thacher SWfr-Sfr-S7;
John Arnold & John Wise Lot 1-SEfr-Sfr-S7;9-8-36.   7-21-36
Valentine Raney, Da Lot 2-SEfr-Sfr-S7; 3-31-36
Alexander Maclure, Ps E-SW, W-SW-S8; 4-25-36
George Rapp & Associates NW-S8; 12-5-15
Bryant D. Savarns SE-S8; 9-4-77(?)
Robert Todd NE-S9; NE-S17; 3-6-16
Alexander McCain NW-S9; E-NW-S15; 1-24-18; SW-S15; 2-3-16
George Coonrad SE-S9; 10-18-17
James Kinman Wfr-S10; 6-17-16
William Chapman NE-Nfr-S11; 9-1-18
Thomas McKain* Lot 4-N-SEfr-Nfr-S11; 12-15-34   7-27-36
Wesley Dabruler* Lot 3-N-SEfr-Nfr-S11;E-NW-S23;2-20-36;W-SW-S24;/
Levi Kinman* Sfr-S11; Sfr-S14; 12-2-13; NW-NW-S15; 5-30-37; SE-NE-
   S22; 1-7-37; W-NW-S23; 9-16-17
Joab Chappel, Db Sfr-S12; 5-4-26
Hiram Conn* N-NE-Sfr-S13;5-2-33; Lot 2-S-NE-Sfr-S13; 2-20-36
Isaac L. Horner* Lot 1-S-NE-Sfr-S13; 1-26-36
Randol Lott Wfr-Sfr, SEfr-Sfr-S13; 8-24-16
Robert Logan* E-NE-S15; 12-10-40
Joel Kinman W-NE-S15; 1-28-19
Hamilton McCain* SE-S15;4-22-18;NE-S23;2-19-18;NE-SE-S23;1-9-37
Joseph Arnold* E-NW-S17; 1-12-36 (30?)
Samuel Stuckey, Jr.* SE-SW-S18; SE-SW-S17; 4-21-35
Elizabeth Conrad, Kn NW-SW-S17; 8-22-34   39
John Henry Gilbert, Stark Co.,O. SW-SW-S17;E-NE-S19;W-NW-S20;5-17-/
Joseph Cross* NE-NE-S18; 11-1-36; SE-NE-S18; 6-18-36
Lewis Rhoads* NW-NE-S18; 8-25-36; SW-NE-S18; 4-4-36
James Milburn* NE-NW, SW-NW-S18; 10-3-36
George Frederick Hender, Ps SE-NW-S18; 11-30-39
James Nelson Coonrod* NW-NW-S18; 4-22-36
Charles Risley, Ps NE-SW-S18; 9-14-36
Aaron Wesley Sampson* NW-SW-S18; 3-31-35
John P. Williamson* SW-SW-S18; 12-2-50
Frederick Stuky* NE-SE-S18; 4-21-35; NW-SE-S18; 6-18-36
James William Bass* SE-SE-S18; 1-8-49

James Love Stuckey* SW-SE-S18; 10-17-36
John Franklin Coonrod* NW-NE-S19; 4-15-39
Susannah Moseley, late Susannah Malin, sole devisee of George Ryall,
    decd. E-NW, W-NW-S19; 8-31-47; MLW 27466
Samuel Alexander* SE-SW-S19; 11-15-41
Alexander Leslie* NE-SE-S19; 8-9-49
James Glezen* SE-SE-S19; 10-5-39
Marcus King* NW-SE-S19; 5-4-47
George Morrison* SW-SE-S19; 4-18-46
John Keith* SW-NE-S20; 4-4-36
Stephen Chappell* NE-NW-S20; 3-31-51
John Monroe Conrad* SE-NW-S20; 6-22-37
Elijah Hammond Glezen* SE-SW, SW-SW-S20; 2-10-42
John B. Tinn* NE-SW-S20; 5-1-50; NW-SW-S20; 3-1-50
John Miller, Kn SE-SE-S20; 3-21-39
Alexander George Green* SW-SE-S20; 6-7-44; NW-SW-S21; 12-27-39
Fleming Thomas* NE-NE-S21; 1-17-37
George H. Proffit* SE-NE-S21;4-1-45;W-NE, SE-S21; 4-1-46
Jasper Scraper* NE-SW-S21; 11-13-50
Whitfield Lett* SE-SW-S21; 8-22-36
Joseph Chew* NE-NE-S22; SW-SW-S23; 2-15-36
William McCain* NW-NE-S22; 1-17-37
Hugh McCain* SW-NE-S22; 7-11-36; NE-SW-S23; 8-4-36
James Ridgeway Chew* SE-NW, NE-SW-S22; 6-19-37
Jane Chew* SE-SW-S22; 8-20-38
Marcellus Chew* NE-SE-S22; 12-10-40; NW-SE-S22; 8-4-36
Robert Logan* SE-SE-S22; 3-18-41
Silas Keith* SW-SE-S22; 8-31-36
Andrew Hicks* SE-SW-S23; 1-13-37
Ashbury Alexander NW-SW-S23; 3-23-52; MLW 33989
Isaac McCain* NW-SE-S23; 4-9-36
George Scraper NE-S24; 10-20-17
Ezekiel G. Hays* E-SW-S24; 8-10-26
Hiram Kinman NW-S24; 1-25-15
Ezekiel Hase SE-S24; 2-8-17
James Richardson NE-S25; 8-1-17
William Hargrave NW-S25; 7-11-18
Greenfield DeBruler* NE-SW-S25; 7-27-36
Lemuel Hargrave* SE-SW-S25; 1-12-38
Matthew W. Foster W-SW-S25; 8-9-19
Henry Scraper* E-SE-S25; 6-29-29
Joseph Ainslay* NW-SE-S25; 3-1-36
Lemuel Barger Hargrave* SW-SE-S25; 5-5-38   12-30-33
Charles D. Bruler (DeBruler)* E-NE-S26;6-28-31;SW-NE,SE-SW-S26;/
Daniel, Mariah, & Mary Ogden NW-NE-S26; 6-11-53; MLW 45006
Jesse Carter* NW-NW-S26; 6-21-39
William Pride SW-NW-S26; 10-14-51; MLW 10108
William G. DeBruler* NE-SW-S26; 1-29-50
Richard Ainsley* W-SE-S26; 12-22-29; E-SE-S26; 10-30-18
Henry Battle E-NE-S27; 7-24-49; MLW 33037
Levi Beach* NW-NE-S27; 9-18-39
Andrew Cooper Conn* SW-NE-S27; 5-7-36
Stephen Chappel* SE-NW-S27; 8-19-33
George Tevenbaugh SW-S27; 1-30-16

Henry Battle E-SE-S27; 7-24-49
Benjamin Wallace* NW-SE-S27; 8-5-34
Elizabeth Chappel* SW-SE-S27; 10-27-35
James Evans* E-NE-S28; 11-27-40
Jesse H. Alexander* W-NE-S28; 8-27-38
John Kinman NW-S28; 12-8-18
John Asa Lett* SE-NE-S29; 5-22-37; E-SE-S29; 10-12-50; MLW 34475;
    NW-SW-S28; 6-4-36; NE-NE, NW-NE-S32; 10-12-50
Seburn Kinman* SW-SW-S28; 7-15-37.
Jesse Head Alexander* N-SE-S28; 3-7-36
Reuben Johnson, Oldham Co., Ky. SW-SE-S28; 5-13-40;W-NE-S33;5-13-40
John Miller, Kn NE-NE-S29; 3-30-39
Elijah Hammond Glezen* NE-NW-S29; 2-10-42
Lewis Thomas* SE-NW-S29; 6-4-36
Francis Davisson Allen* W-NW-S29; 7-2-39
Franklin F. Sawyer* E-SW-S29; 9-9-23
James Evans* W-SW-S29; 12-21-35
Levin Ward* NW-SE-S29; 1-11-37
David Frank* SW-SE-S29; 12-18-38
James Glezen NE-NE-S30; 1-20-38
Edwin Morrison* SE-NE-S30; 9-16-39
Samuel Kinman* NW-NE-S30; 7-8-36
Samuel Wesley Kinman* SW-NE-S30; 11-27-38
Strobridge Morrison, Astabula Co.,O. NE-NW-S30; 11-19-38
Mercus King* SE-NW-S30; 3-12-40
Azom Preston* W-NW-S30; 7-28-36
James Evans* SW-S30; 11-19-38
Henry Ofenlock* E-NE-S31; 1-29-40
Frederick Wagner* NW-NE-S31; 4-29-42
Martin Miley* SW-NE-S31; 5-18-36
Samuel Miley* E-NW-S31; 6-28-39
John Arnold* W-NW-S31; 8-19-36
Owen McCone* E-SW, NW-SW-S31; 8-12-39
Samuel Holler* SW-SW-S31; 3-26-36
Lewis Thomas* E-SE-S31; 10-16-39
John Fickling* W-SE-S31; 11-14-40
John H. Ficklin SW-NE, N-SE, NE-SW-S32; 7-13-49; MLW 33030
Wilson Evans Miley* SE-SW-S32; 4-6-46
Lewis Thomas* W-SW-S32; 10-16-39
George Washington Barnett* SE-SE-S32; 9-21-46
Joseph Chew* SW-SE-S32; 3-23-46
Conrad Gayspaugher, Tuscarawa Co.,O. NE-NE-S33; 5-31-41
John Jacob Knaht, Tuscarawa Co.,O. SE-NE-S33; 5-31-41;W-NW-S34;
Gabriel Johnson, Oldham Co., Ky. SW-S33; 11-19-38.   5-31-41
Henry Dedrick* E-SE-S33; 4-20-40
Michael Sorgus* W-SE-S33; 4-20-40
Richard Ainley (Ainsley?)* NW-NE-S34;10-15-38;NE-NW-S34;11-20-38
Whitfield Lett* SW-NE-S34; 8-1-36
Martha Thomas* SE-NW-S34; 6-13-36
Hugh McCain* NE-SW-S34; 2-15-37
Betsheba Whaley* NW-SW-S34; 6-13(?)-36
John Hayes* SW-SW-S34; 3-5-37
Josiah Chappell* NE-NE-S35; 2-25-36
William Walton, Jr.* SE-NE-S35; 7-11-39

PIKE COUNTY

John Stubblefield, Db NW-NE-S35; 5-8-39; NW-SW-S36; 8-8-39
Charles Luff* SW-NE-S35; 2-28-38; NW-SE-S36; 7-22-39
William Fowler* NE-NW-S35; 3-7-36
Jesse Childers Coleman, assee. of Andrew S. Bram(?) SE-S35;3-28-48;
Richard Lewis May* NE-NE-S36; 3-5-44   MLW 6980
Reason Chandley, Pe W-NE-S36; 12-2-39
James Harrison Barnett* NE-NW-S36; 8-12-36; SE-NW-S36; 9-12-36
Harbert Palmer DeBruler* NW-NW-S36; 3-11-36; SW-NW-S36; 8-29-36
Jacob Weedman, Db E-SW, SW-SW-S36; 9-18-39
Washington Green* NE-SE-S36; 1-8-39

RELINQUISHMENTS

Robert Todd SW-S8;3-6-18;NW,SE-S17;3-6-18;NE-SE-S18;3-6-18
Joel Kinman E-NE-S15; 1-26-19
Alexander McCain W-NW-S15; 1-24-18
Levi Kinman E-NW-S23; 9-16-17
Hamilton McCain W-SW-S23; 11-23-18; SE-S23; 2-19-18
Matthew W. Foster E-SW-S25; 8-9-19
Charles Debruler NE-S26; 1-26-19
Richard Ainley W-SE-S26; 10-30-18
James Harrell W-NE-S30; 10-4-19
William Chapman Nfr-S10;Wfr-Nfr, SEfr-Nfr-S11; 9-1-18; maybe Da Co.
Randle Lett Sfr-S12; NE-Sfr-S13; 8-24-16; maybe Da Co.

T 1 N, R 8 W

Archibald Campbell* Lots 8-9-Sfr-S1; NW-SE-Sfr-S14; 1-7-36; Lot 1-
   NEfr-Sfr-S14;3-7-34;SE-NW-S20;2-19-36; SW-S34; 1-6-17
David A. Leonard Sfr-S8; 8-29-15
William Rhoads* Lots 1-2-Nfr-Efr-S12; 1-12-36
William Sullivan, George W. Pratt, & George M. Thacher E-SE-Efr,
   W-SE-Efr,S-Nfr-Efr-S12;2-21-37;E-SW,W-SW,W-SE-S13;7-21-36; Lot 2-
   NEfr-Sfr,E-SW-Sfr,E-SE-Sfr,SW-SE-Sfr-S14;E-NE-S23;7-21-36;E-SE-
   S23;E-NE,NW-NE,NW,NE-SW,W-SW-S24;2-21-37;SE-SE-S34;8-1-36(5-21-36?
Jacob Stuckey* SWfr-Efr-S12; 8-2-36; SW-NE-S24; 7-30-36
Martin Warner & Martin W. Somers NE-S13; 7-8-18
John Cumins NW-S13; 2-20-15
Levin Sullivan E-SE-S13; 6-25-18
Charles Cummings* Lot 3-NEfr-Sfr-S14; 3-13-34
Daniel O. Blenies NW-Sfr-S14; Sfr-S15; 9-24-18
William Cummings* Lot 4-W-SW-Sfr-S14; 8-17-36
David Wease* E-SW,SE-SE-S18;5-21-36;NW-SW-S18;3-16-38;W-NE-S19;
   7-25-36;SW-S29;11-30-15;NW-S32;2-7-34
John Wease* SW-SW-S18; 1-23-37
Conrad Link, Pe NE-SE, NW-SE-S18; 5-23-36
Nathaniel & James Uriah Cummings SW-SE-S18; 2-19-39
George Washington Parker* SE-NE-S19; 2-16-36
Thomas Cummings, Pe NE-NW-S19; 5-23-39
David & Albert Gallatin Meriwether W-NE-S20; 5-18-35
David Meriwether, Jefferson Co., Ky. NE-NW-S20; 5-18-35
Jesse Richerson Kinman* SW-NW-S20; 5-26-36
Nathaniel Breadin, Jr. & George Ewing SW-S20; 7-7-15;NW-S29;6-7-15
Thomas J. Withers SE-S20; 6-7-15

James Campbell & Moses Harrell NE-S21; 11-30-15
Abraham Tourtellot NW-S21; 3-1-21
James Brenton SW-S21; 9-19-12; NW-S28; 5-30-07; E-SE-S35;12-29-35
Moses Harrel SE-S21; 9-20-15; SE-S27-9-18-13
John Conrad SE-S22;5-20-13;NE-S22;3-4-14;SW-S22;11-29-14;NW-S22;
Thomas Fowler* NW-NW-S19;12-23-35;SW-NE-S30;2-25-36.   1-12-15
Joshua Donson, Shelby Co., Ky. W-NE-S23; 6-30-26; of*, W-SE-S24;
    9-12-39; E-SE-S25; 2-25-30
Daniel Coonrod NW-S23; 11-24-13
Henry Miley, Jr. SW-S23; 12-31-14
William Timstall Wright* NW-SE-S23; 7-21-36
Hiram West Kinman* SW-SE-S23;SE-SW-S24;2-1-37;NE-NW-S25;5-22-37
David Miley* NE-NE-S25; 2-23-37; SE-NE-S25; 11-19-38
Henry Miley, Sr.* W-NE-S25; 3-13-34
Thomas Griffith* SE-NW-S25; 1-14-37
John Wesley Posey* NW-NW-S25; 1-30-37
Benjamin Williams* SW-NW-S25; 11-2-37
Albert Hammond* NE-SW-S25; 10-15-38
William Foster* SE-SW-S25; 8-29-37
Paul Tislow* W-SW-S25;SE-SE-S26;3-25-36;NE-SE-S26;4-29-36;NE-S29;
    5-29-07;NE-S34;1-7-14;NE-S35;5-30-16;NW-S35;1-7-14;E-SW-S35;
    6-30-31;W-NE-S36;10-6-38;SE-NW-S36;1-16-38;SW-NW-S36;1-16-38
John Davis Conrad* NW-SE-S25; 2-6-34
Tolbert Denson* SW-SE-S25; 4-11-37
Bryant D. Savarns NE-S26; 11-16-14
Henry Meily NW-S26; 1-17-13
James Campbell SW-S26; 3-6-16
Meredeth Howard* NW-SE-S26; 8-5-34
Malachi Marrick* SW-SE-S26; 2-6-36
Wolsey Pride NW-S27; 5-30-07; NE-S28; 8-8-08
Silas Rizley NE-S27; 1-30-08
George Wallace, Jr. SW-S27; 6-30-07
David Hornady* W-SW-S28; 1-16-36; E-SW-S28; 11-13-15
Hosea Smith SE-S28;6-22-12;NE-S33;3-28-14;SE-S33;2-8-14
Perry Campbell NE-SE-S29; 5-13-36; NW-SE-S29; 5-19-36.   8-24-16
Thomas Jennings Withers* SE-SE-S29;3-12-34;SW-SE-S29;9-6-32;NE-S32;
Henry Brenton* E-NE-S30;3-21-14;SW, SE-S30;4-7-17;NE-NW-S31;1-11-36
Joseph Williams* NW-NE-S30; 10-24-35
Jacob Pain E-NW-S30; 1-2-18
Susanna Lindsey W-NW-S30; 2-2-18
Thomas Williams NE-S31; 2-3-17
Henry White* NW-NW-S31; 8-20-36
John Shouls* SW-NW-S31; 3-23-36
Jeremiah Gladish* SE-NW-S31; 1-11-36
John Lester* E-SW-S31; 10-1-22
Henry B. Barders NW-SW-S31; 6-25-53; MLW 38738
Charles Slocum Fettinger* SW-SW-S31; 7-13-47
Joshua Selby SE-S31; 10-2-15
Tarleton Boren E-SW-S32; 6-20-16
Vincent Willis* W-SW-S32; 9-22-32
David Kinman SE-S32; 9-13-15
John Johnson E-NW-S33; 9-1-17
Thomas Crayton* W-NW-S33; 3-19-35
William Craton SW-S33; 4-19-15

PIKE COUNTY

Lemuel Baldwin NW-S34; 2-29-08
Philo Hays* NE-SE-S34; n.d. (or 5-21-36?)
Thomas Milburn* W-SE-S34; 1-20-24
John Butler, Jr.* NW-SW-S35; 8-5-34
William Smith* SW-SW-S35; 5-7-35
Eber(?) Osborn* W-SE-S35; 7-27-29
Samuel Niley* SE-NE-S36; 10-18-38
John Ward* NE-NW-S36; 12-12-37
Peter Tislow* NW-NW-S36; 2-9-36; (may be Paul)
Peter Brenton* SE-SE-S36; 9-20-39; SW-S36; 3-24-17
John Griffeth* NW-SE-S36; 2-9-36
Mary Washington Brenton* SW-SE-S36; 10-16-44

RELINQUISHMENTS

Levin Sullivan W-SE-S13; 6-25-18
James B. McCall NE-S23; 2-14-17; SE-S35; 2-17-17
Robert Todd SW-S24; 3-6-18
Thomas J. Withers NW-S25; 6-5-17; NW-S32; 4-9-17
Paul Tistone (Tislow?) SE-S26; 10-31-17; SW-S36; 5-30-16
David Hornady W-SW-S28; 11-13-15
Henry Brenton W-NE-S30; 3-21-14
Hamilton McCain NW-S31; 7-6-18
Tarleton Boren W-SW-S32; 6-10-16
Solomon Whitehead W-NW-S33; 11-27-17
Moses Harrell & J. Campbell NE-S21; 11-30-15; 7-4-29
T. Case & T. C. Stewart SE-S23; 5-19-17; 7-4-29

T 1 N, R 9 W

Nimrod Tevenbaugh, Kn Sfr-S1; 8-14-35
Edwin Phillips, Gi E-E-Sfr-S7; 5-2-39
John Crow* Lot 5-W-E-Sfr-S7; 5-22-39
Morgan Decker, Gi W-W-Sfr-S7; 12-6-37; Fr Lot 1-NWfr-S18; 5-22-39
Sebastian Conger* W-SEfr-Sfr-S8;6-14-36;E-W-Sfr-S8;1-8-36;NE-NE-S17;
James Gibson Crow* W-E-Sfr-S8; 5-22-39   12-1-34
Andrew Knight* E-SWfr-Sfr-S9; 7-21-37
Charles F. White & Elisha Colvin* NW-SWfr-Sfr-S9; 7-19-37
Walter Wilson* SW-SWfr-Sfr-S9; 7-24-54
James S. Crutchfield* E-Sfr-S9; 11-15-36   37
John Kirk, Kn E-NEfr-S10;5-22-37;Lot 1-W-NEfr-S10 & E-Sfr-S3;8-30-
Henry Catt* E-Sfr-S3; Lot 2-E-NEfr, N-NW-SE-S10; 4-8-35
Samuel Dunning* N-NWfr-S10; 8-18-44; S-S-Wfr-S11; 3-17-34; N-N-Wfr-
   S14; 5-30-35; S-N-Wfr-S14; 7-1-37
Daniel Catt* Lot 3-S-NWfr-S10; 3-7-37; Lot 6-E-SW-S10; 1-20-36
Zachariah Fowler Selby* S-E-SW-S10; 9-9-37
Thomas Campbell Stewart* Lot 5-W-SW-S10;5-11-37;Lot 3-Wfr-S26;5-18-
Michael Frederick* S-W-SW-S10;2-6-36;SE-NW-S21;7-29-39.   39
Philip Catt, Jr.* E-SE-S10; 3-19-34
Philip Catt* SW-SE-S10; 8-12-36
James Henry Enlow* N-Wfr-S11; 6-3-43
William Truxton Parker* Lot 3-N-S-Wfr-S11;3-10-34; Lot 4; 6-9-35
James Cummings, Pe Lot 1-E-NE-Efr, W-NE-Efr-S12; 8-19-37
David Brunk Shields* Lot 4-E-NE-Efr-S12; 8-9-36

Ovid Huff, Pe Lots 1-2-NWfr-Efr-S12; 7-15-37
David Wease* Lot 5-N-S-Efr-S12; 2-7-34; S-S-Efr-S12; 7-25-21;
    S-N-Efr-S13; 2-24-36;W-NEfr-S25;9-29-36;E-SE-S25;9-15-36
Samuel Huff, Pe Lot 6-N-S-Efr-S12; 6-7-36
James Gladish* N-N-Efr-S13; 3-13-32
Adam Snider* Lot 4-SWfr-Efr-S13; 4-13-37
Daniel Snider* Lot 5-SWfr-Efr-S13; 4-11-37
James Fowler* Lots 5-6-N-SWfr-Wfr-S14;2-19-36;SE-SW-S14;1-16-37
William Fouts* SW-SW-S14; 8-14-39
Leonard Burkheart* Lot 7-SEfr-Wfr-S14; 8-9-36;Lots 3,6-E-Efr-S24;
Daniel Spake* Lot 8-SEfr-Wfr-S14; 3-4-35   8-9-39
William Martin Tisdale, Da NE-NE-S15; 1-19-36
John Fouts SE-NE-S15; 3-8-36
George Catt W-NE-S15; 1-25-36
Bartley & George Catt E-NW-S15; 3-14-36
Sarah Jane Decker NW-NW-S15; 4-12-44
Charles Walter Stewart SW-NW-S15; 5-11-35
Elvis Spaw* SE-SE-S15; 8-2-39; Shaw:Lot 1-E-NEfr,NW-NEfr-S22;8-2-39
John Henry Gilbert, Stark Co.,O. W-SE-S15; 5-17-39
Jonathan Conger SE-NE-S17;11-16-35;SW-NW, NW-SW-S17; 6-5-39
Amos Catt* W-NE-S17; 3-18-39; NE-SE-S17; 7-1-44
William J. Conger* NE-NW-S17; 6-5-39; SW-NEfr-S18; 8-4-43
William Decker* NE-SW-S17; 6-5-39
Joseph Davidson* SE-SW-S17; 6-15-39
David Fouts* NE-SE-S15; 2-22-36; Lot 1-E-NEfr-S22; 3-24-36
Eirvin Catt* SE-SE-S17; 8-9-44; NE-NW-S21; 8-19-44
Morgan McDecker (M. Decker?), Gi S-NWfr-S18; 9-30-48
David M. Ennis* NW-NWfr-(of NEfr?)-S18; 12-11-54
Drury Hughes, Gi SW-NWfr-S18; 9-14-47
Josiah Davisson* SWfr-S18; 3-28-54
Joseph Davidson* Lots 3-4-SEfr-S18;6-15-39;Fr Lot 1-S19;3-28-36;
    Fr Lot 2-S19; 5-19-37
Levi Conger* Fr Lot 3-S19; 5-27-37; Lot 5-W-W-Sfr-S20; 2-4-40
Elisha Calvin* E-W-Sfr, SEfr-S20; 7-3-37
Elisha Macrury, Gi Lot 6-W-W-Sfr-S20; 12-14-35;Nfr-S29;10-31-35
Jacob Frederick* E-NE-S21; 4-6-36; SW-NW-S22; 4-30-33
Johnson Decker* NW-NW-S21; 5-22-39
Frederick Linda Frederick (?)* SW-NW-S21; 3-23-46
Alexander McKitterick, Belmont Co.,O. SEfr-S21;E-SWfr,W-SWfr,SEfr-
Edmund W. Fowler* E-Efr-S23; 5-25-29   S22; 6-25-22
Zepheniah Selby* Lot 1-W-Efr-S23; 2-25-36; Lot 4; 2-17-34
James Fowler* Lot 3-E-Wfr-S23;2-12-34;Lot 2-E-Efr-S24; 12-12-37
William Wright, Ws W-Wfr-S23; 4-18-33
Thomas Fowler* Lot 1-E-Efr-S24; 12-23-35
Alexander Leslie Lot 8-E-Efr-S24; 9-2-53; MLW 52828
Archibald Campbell* Lot 4-W-Wfr-S24; 2-19-36
Daniel Spake* Lot 5-W-Wfr-S24; 3-19-34
Franklin F. Sawyer* E-NEfr-S25; 11-3-21
Joseph Cheesman Morgan*NWfr-S25;2-16-36;SW-S25;6-22-21;Lot 1-E-Efr-
John Johnson* W-SE-S25;7-19-21.   S26;8-9-53;MLW 73667
John Borders* W-Efr-S26; 6-21-36
Thomas Lee* Lot 4-W-Efr-S27; 6-21-36
John Catt* Fr S27; 5-6-33
Leachman Heydon* Efr-S29; 10-27-35

John Hillman* Sfr-S29; 11-20-35; of Gi, W-NW-S32; 2-21-22
Thomas White, Jr.* Nfr-S30; 2-23-36
Azza Harrison, Mason Co., Ky. Nfr-S31; 11-12-25
James Hillman E-SWfr-S31;6-22-21;NW-SWfr-S31;5-28-39;SW-SWfr-S31;
William M. Wright E-SE-S31; 6-22-21   4-3-38
Daniel Hanes Roberts, Morgan Co.,O. NEfr, E-SW-S32;. 1-5-39
John J. Lownsdale, Gi E-NW-S32; 3-26-29
James Lownsdale, Mason Co., Ky. W-SW, SE-S32; Efr, Wfr-S33; NEfr,
    NWfr, SW, SE-S34; S35; NW, SW-S36; 6-22-21
Peter Robling* NE-NE-S36; 12-15-34; NW-NE-S36; 11-23-36
William Washington Robling* SE-NE-S36; 4-4-39
Wilson Robling* SW-NE-S36; 12-14-38
John Robling* NE-SE-S36; 6-4-36; SE-SE-S36; 1-25-37
Henry Hillman, Mason Co., Ky. W-SE-S36; 3-18-23

                    T 1 S, R 6 W

John Teague* NW-SW-S4; 3-4-3 ?
Edward Teague* NW-SE-S4; 6-17-44
Elijah Whaley* SW-SE-S4; 6-18-44; NW-NE-S9; 3-22-41
Andrew Abot, Ws E-SE-S5; 3-4-37
Solomon Regerson* E-NE-S6; 6-10-31
Twitty Hays* SE-NE, NE-SE-S7; 8-24-37
Alexander Black* SE-NE-S9; 5-13-44; NE-NW-S9; 12-27-39
Jonathan Weedman SW-NE-S9; 5-12-44
Robert Foster* NW-NW-S9; 2-29-44
Horace Plumer, Vb W-SW-S9; 12-23-51
Elijah Lindsey, Db SW-SE-S9; 8-23-36
Benjamin Oney Payne* E-SW-S17; 9-1-42
Thomas Gawthrop NE-NE-S19; 6-18-52; MLW 33872; NE-SE-S19; 4-11-55
William Jordon Hayes* NW-NE-S19;11-20-54;SW-NW-S19;10-10-49;NE-SW-
    S19;7-12-53;SE-SW-S19;7-10-53;NW-SW-S19;4-20-44;SW-SW-S19;10-10-
    49;NW-SE-S19;9-2-53;SW-SE-S19;11-20-54
Alexander Leslie N-NW-S19; 5-31-53; MLW 44164
John Scraper SE-SE-S19;5-31-53;MLW 5509;NW-S28;3-15-51;MLW 21237
Gamaliel Garretson, Fd E-NE-S20; 12-27-39; W-NW-S21; 12-14-39
William C. Davenport* N-SW, N-SE-S20; 10-2-54
Lawrence Demott NE-S21; 5-8-17
Arthur Chambers, Db NE-NW-S21; 6-24-39
Robert Brinton* E-SW-S21; 1-26-37
Andrew Anderson, Db NE-NE-S28;8-3-53;SE-NE-S28;3-18-41;NE-SW-S33;
William Anderson, Db E-NE-S29;E-NW-S33;10-5-39.   10-5-39
William Davisson, Dr E-NE-S33; 11-5-38
James Anderson, Db W-NE-S33;3-25-39; E-SE-S33; 1-30-40

                    T 1 S, R 7 W

John Smith* SE-NW-S1; 1-9-39
Jacob Chappel* SW-NW, NE-SW-S1; 2-28-37
William Hix DeBruler* NW-SW-S1; 9-7-37
Jonathan Risley* SE-NE-S2; 1-30-39
John Hays* NW-NW-S3; 8-4-36
Lewis Rhoads* SW-NW-S3; 11-18-39
James Cross* NW-SW-S3; 11-26-39

James Milton Abbet* NW-SE-S3;10-8-50;SW-SE-S3;10-17-50;NW-NW-S4;
William Abbet* E-NE-S4; 5-6-28   1-19-39
Christian Schell* NW-NE-S4; 9-2-47
Jesse Keith* SW-NE-S4; 3-23-37; NE-SW-S4; 8-31-36
George Sorgins* NE-NW, SW-NW-S4; 11-4-47; W-SE-S4; 10-30-57
Amos Keith* SE-NW-S4; 11-1-47
Jacob Sorgins* S-SW-S4; 11-4-47
Jeremiah Keith* NW-SW-S4; 9-13-37
James Cross* NE-SE-S4; 11-26-39
George W. Wyatt* SE-SE-S4; 1-15-51; NE-NE-S9; 9-24-50
Isaac Cox NE-NE-S5; 11-14-38; SW-NE-S5; 9-22-36
George Miley* SE-NE-S5; 8-4-36
Joseph Chew* NW-NE-S5; 3-23-46
Wilson Evans Miley* NE-NW-S5; 4-6-46
Daniel Hawkins* S-NW-S5; 5-27-52
Isaac Tarkington Thomas* NW-NW-S5; 2-13-49; SW-SE-S8; 11-26-36
Hezekiah Cox* NE-SE-S5; 10-21-37; SE-SE-S5; 9-11-37
William Cox* NW-SE-S5; 5-31-52
Philip Willis* SW-SE-S5; 3-12-69
John Thomas* NE-NE-S6; 3-7-36
Samuel Hollon* SE-NE-S6;1-2-39;NW-NW-S6;6-8-33;E-NW-S6;10-4-43
Paul Tislow* NW-NE-S6; 2-4-39
John Beadles Richardson* SW-NE-S6; 1-21-39; SE-NW-S6; 11-4-37
Wesley Brenton* NE-SW-S6; 9-5-37; SE-NE-S7;5-31-36; NE-SE-S7;
    11-9-35; NW-SW-S8; 5-11-37; W-NW-S18; 11-5-38
Henry Harden* SE-SW-S6; 4-1-33; NW-SW-S6; 11-9-38
John S. Beard* SE-S6; 12-20-48; MW h33882
Richard Selby* SE-SW-S7;4-8-33;W-SW-S7;4-17-32;W-SE-S7;2-3-35
Joshua Carter Thomas* SE-SE-S7;11-15-38;SW-SW-S8;3-16-33;NW-NW-S17;
Alexander Willis* NW-NE-S8; 12-10-44   11-26-36
Franklin F. Sawyer, Da NE-NW-S8; 12-5-53
Edmund Hollon* SE-NW-S8;2-28-37;SW-NW-S8;3-26-36; Holland
Lewis Thomas* SE-SW-S8; 9-5-36
David Abbet* NW-NE-S9; 10-8-50
William Cox NW-NW-S9; 2-15-51
Michael Thomas NE-SE-S9; 12-8-51; MLW 8202
William Henry Kinman* N-NE-S10; 5-30-43
Josiah Whitehead* S-NE-S10; 5-30-36
William H. Wyatt* NW-NW-S10; 9-25-50
Warren Smith NE-SE-S10; 10-3-33; of*, W-SW-S11; 5-15-37
Jesse Poe, Cf W-SE-S10; 2-20-54
Thomas Jarmon Trayler* N-NE-S11; 2-24-44; S-NE-S11; 6-13-36
Thomas Martin* SE-NW-S11; 6-6-42; SE-SE-S11; 8-16-51; E-NW-S14;
    2-24-44; SE-NE-S15; 1-13-51
Thomas Willis* NE-SW-S11; 5-8-39
David Trayler* SE-SW-S11; 2-26-44; SW-SE-S11; 3-1-45
James Edmondson NE-SE-S11; 2-5-52; MLW 19593
John Scraper* E-NE-S12; 12-10-50; NE-NW-S12; 6-17-44
Josiah Clayton, Vi W-NE-S12; 9-17-23
George Dean* SE-NW-S12; 6-16-49; SE-SW-S20; 5-14-49
Madison Trayler* NW-NW-S12; 2-28-44
Horace Palmer, Vb E-NW-S13; 12-23-51
Samuel McCutchen NW-NW-S13; 11-19-51
Willard Carpenter SW-NW-S13; 6-21-53

Samuel Lott* W-SW-S13; 5-14-39
Thomas Watson* NW-NE-S14; 10-23-38
John Hays* W-NW-S14; 11-16-39
John Koith* SE-SW-S14; 6-13-40
John Pruch* NW-SE-S14; 11-26-39
Joseph Kinman* SE-SW-S15; 3-12-33
William McCormaok, Washington Co., Ky. E-SE-S15; NE-S22; 2-9-39;
   of*, NE-NW-S22; 2-27-40
William Kinman* SW-SE-S15; 5-9-37
Lewis Thomas* NE-NW-S17;11-15-38; SE-SE, W-SE-S17; 5-5-37
Andrew Elder, Pe SE-NW-S17; 3-23-33; of*, NE-SW-S17; 3-27-37
Samuel Tally Thompson* SW-NW-S17; 1-24-39; NW-SW-S17; 2-12-39
Richard Selby* S-SW-S17; 11-9-47
James Madison Evans* NE-SE-S17; 11-8-36
Henry Gladish* E-NE-S18; 1-14-39; NE-SE-S18; 7-8-39
Esau Dearing, Marion Co., Ky. W-NE-S18; 12-31-38
Henry Nutt, Delaware Co.,O. E-NW, NE-SE-S18; 6-24-39
Charles Sebring* NW-SW-S18; 9-23-47
Jared Kinman* SW-SW-S18; 9-5-49
Augustus Hewins* SW-SE-S18; NE-S19; 11-3-38; NE-NW-S19; 11-9-47
David Upton* S-NW-S19; 2-18-48
John Kinman* NW-SW-S19; 9-9-47
Jacob Bright* SW-SW-S19; 8-6-37
Hugh Shaw, Sr.* NE-SE-S19; 10-18-37
Elvis Shaw* NW-SE-S19; 1-20-38
John P. Kinman* SW-SE-S19; 4-13-50; see 3rd entry below
Mat Brook Molton* NE-NE-S20; 1-5-50
Reuben Long* SE-NE-S20; 8-9-49
John S. (P?) Kinman* NW-NE-S20; 3-25-50; see 3rd entry above
James Holland* SW-NE-S20; 7-8-48
Henry Smith* NE-SW-S20; 2-9-50
Albert Bee* NW-SW-S20; 3-20-51
Ira Baldwin* SW-SW-S20; 7-17-37
Leonard Kinman* NE-NE-S21; 7-8-36
William Lewis Evans* SE-NE-S21; 9-14-36; SW-NW-S22; 6-2-37
Alvin Thomas Whight, Washington Co., Ky. NW-NE,NE-NW-S21;9-10-36
Fenley White* SW-NE,SE-NW-S21; 11-26-36; NW-NW-S21; 11-15-38;Fendley
Jesse Carter* SE-SE-S21; 3-1-44
Jeremiah Keith* NE-NW-S23; 11-18-39
James Brewster* NW-NW-S27; 11-5-38
Elijah Bruister* SW-SW-S27; 8-30-36
David Steele* SE-SW-S28; 10-29-39
John Rhorer, El NE-SE,W-SE-S28;5-25-39;E-NE-S32;E-NE,W-SW-S33;
   E-NE, W-NW, E-SE-S34; SW-NW-S35; 6-3-37
Moses Kenney* SE-SE-S28;. 6-3-37; of G1, NW-NW-S35; 10-31-36
Perry Brown* NE-S29;1-19-50;MLW 50049;NE-NE-S30;4-26-49;SW-NE-S30;
Coleman Smith* NE-NW-S29; 9-27-39   10-2-49
George Smith* SE-NW-S29; 10-23-38
Thomas Terril* NW-NW-S29; 4-13-37
George Dean* SW-NW-S29; 9-4-51; SE-SE-S30; 3-18-39
Isaac Fisher* NW-SW-S29; 11-7-39
Alexander Wiggs SW-SW-S29; 3-27-37
Henry Smith* NW-SE-S29; 2-21-44
Solomon Brewster* SE-NE-S30; 11-29-37

Jesse R. Kinman* NW-NE-S30; 6-12-51
Jacob Bright* NW-NW-S30; 2-2-37
Hugh Shaw, Sr.* SW-NW-S30; 7-8-37
Benjamin Ashby* N-SW-S30; 10-1-38
Alfrew Shaw* SE-SW-S30; 9-28-38
Edmund Chapman* NE-SE-S30; 6-24-39
Allen White Clifford* SW-SE-S30; 9-30-37
Daniel Craw* NE-NE-S31; 7-6-48
Newton Brenton* SE-NE-S31; 1-29-39
Hugh Shaw W-NE-S31; 10-2-17; W-NW-S33; 5-31-20
Joseph Davisson, Gi NE-NW-S31; 4-20-36
William Augustus Bronson* SE-NW-S31; 3-7-38
Samuel Leeper, Gi W-NE, E-NW, SW-NW, W-SE-S32; 6-3-37
William Black* NW-NW-S32; 6-29-35
Matthew W. Foster & John Hathaway E-SW-S32;6-15-33;W-SW-S32;2-13-3
Elvis Shaw* E-SE-S32; 5-20-25
Joseph Rohrer, Gi E-SW, W-SE-S33; 6-3-37
Margaret Nelson W-SW-S34; 12-22-51; MLW 8404
Miles Law Evans NE-NE, W-NE-S35; 5-26-53; MLW 15941, 34427
Charles F. White SE-NE-S35; 8-11-51; MLW 6488
Andrew Corn* SE-SW-S35; 1-19-37
Thomas Brewster* NW-SW-S35; 10-28-39; NW-SE-S35; 4-15-44
James Corn* NE-SE-S35; 4-15-44
Benjamin Corn* SE-SE-S35; 2-16-39

RELINQUISHMENTS

John Butler NE-S6; 2-3-18; 8-22-21
Samuel Kinman NE-S23; 6-6-15; 8-24-21
John Brenton W-NW-S30; 10-27-17; 6-29-29
Hugh Shaw E-NE-S31; 10-2-17; 3-9-25
Robert Brenton W-NW-S5; 5-1-17; 7-4-29

T 1 S, R 8 W

James Brenton* NE-NE-S1; 5-31-36
Robert Adams Black* SE-NE-S1; 12-11-37
John Overling Selby* NW-NE-S1; 12-18-35; SW-NE-S1; NE-SE-S12;
    2-3-37; NE-SE-S11; 6-2-44; SW-NE-S12; 9-5-49; W-SW-S13; 4-5-39
William Abbet* E-NW-S1; 11-30-18
Jacob Miley* NW-NW-S1; 3-26-36
John Tislow* SW-NW-S1; 3-30-36; NW-SW-S1; 3-25-36; SW-NE-S2;
    1-2-39; E-SE-S2; 7-17-20; NW-SE-S2; 1-17-37
John Miley* SE-SW-S1; 8-19-36
John Selby Kinman, Pe NE-SE-S1;4-5-39; of*; NE-NE-S12; 12-9-44
James Richardson Kinman* SE-SE-S1;11-8-32;NW-SE-S1;1-23-44;SW-SE-S1
Malichi Warrick* E-NE-S2; 12-2-17   12-18-3
David Miley* NW-NE-S2; 5-26-35; SE-NE-S11; 11-21-48
Michael Thomas* NE-NW-S2; 12-3-35; NW-NE-S12; 10-31-44
Caroline Miley, Rebecca Miley, & Amanda (Miley?)* SE-NW-S2;4-6-46
George Washington Wingate* W-NW-S2; 5-7-35
Andrew J. Hart, Da NE-SW-S2; 1-16-51
Franklin Meadows* SE-SW-S2; 12-5-38
Robert Johnson* W-SW-S2; 5-11-30

Isaac Dyer* SW-SE-S2;10-31-36;NW-SE-S4;2-6-36;SW-SW-S11;10-2-38
John Lock Nichols* NE-NE-S3; 8-5-34; NW-NE-S11; 8-10-39
William Sullivan, George W. Pratt, & George M. Thacher SE-NE,W-NE-
    S3; SW-NE-S3; W-NW-S10;8-1-36; SE-SW,NE-SE-S3;2-25-37; W-SE-S3;
    SW, SE-SE, W-SE-S10;E-NE,SE-S15;2-22-37;SW-NE-S15;2-27-37;NW, SW-
    S15; 7-21-36;NE, SW, SE-S20;10-14-36;NE, E-NW,NW-NW,E-SW,SE-S21;
    7-21-36;NE, SE-S22;2-22-37;E-NW,SW-NW,SW-S22;E-NE-S28;8-1-36;
    SW-S28;2-21-37;W-SE-S28;7-21-36;NE,NW,SE-S29;SE-NE,W-NE,NW-S31;
    10-14-36;E-NE,E-NW,SW-SW-S30;2-21-37;E-NE,SW-NE,E-NW,SW-NW-S32;
    2-25-37;S-NE,NW-S33;3-6-37;SW-S35;8-1-36
Thomas Jeffries* E-NW-S3; 10-9-18
William Fettner* NW-NW-S3; 12-9-33; SW-NW-S3; 10-25-36
James Upton* NE-SW-S3; 4-9-35; NW-SW-S3; 2-6-36
Matthew Watson Foster* SW-SW-S3; 8-1-36; SE-SE-S4; 8-9-36
Andrew Ralston Johnson* SE-SE-S3; 4-25-36
Hosea Smith* NE-S4; 1-17-17
Jesse Alexander* E-NW-S4; 9-23-31; NW-NW-S4; 8-12-36
Ephraim Dickey, Ci SW-NW,S-SW-S4; SE-NE-S5; 12-2-36
Franklin Fayette Sawyer* N-SW-S4; 1-18-36
Benjamin Franklin Wyatt* NE-SE-S4; 10-3-36
Franklin Wyatt* SW-SE-S4; 9-12-36
Elijah Malott* NE-NE-S5; 8-12-36; NW-NE-S5; 2-9-37
Oliver Hazzard Perry Malott* (2 men?) SW-NE-S5; 12-7-38
John Kinman* NE-NW-S5; 6-3-39
Vinson Willis* SE-NW-S5; 1-30-37
Philip Willis* NW-NW-S5; 12-6-36
James Green Amos* SW-NW-S5; 5-24-39; NE-SE-S6; 5-18-38
John Pew Kinman* NE-SW-S5; 7-9-39
Walter Hays, Jefferson Co., Ky. SE-SW-S5; NE-NW-S8; 12-21-38
John Selby W-SW-S5; 9-12-18
John Willis* SE-S5; 11-28-36
Otho Harrison* NE-NE-S6; 1-11-36; SE-NE-S6; 11-8-36
David Wease* W-NE-S6; 1-23-37
Jeremiah Claddish* NE-NW-S6; 6-7-37
John Miller* SW-NW-S6; 12-6-37
Joseph Hawkins SW-S6; 5-25-19
Jacob Young* SE-SE-S6; 6-21-38
Luke Loveless* NW-SE-S6; 8-15-36
Isaac Loveless, Sr.* SW-SE-S6; 1-9-39
Joseph Loveless* E-NE-S7; 7-17-26; NW-NW-S8; 12-30-37
Isaac Loveless* W-NE-S7; 5-2-36; NW-S7; 12-21-19
Samuel Rumble* E-SW-S7; 6-5-37
John Blaze* NW-SW-S7; 8-21-38
William Loveless* SW-SW-S7; 8-15-36; NE-NW-S18; 12-1-37
William Rumble* NE-SE-S7; 5-2-36
Alexander Rumble* SE-SE-S7; 2-21-37; SE-NW-S18; 1-9-39
Henry Loveless* NW-SE-S7; 5-2-36
Henry Beck* SW-SE-S7; 3-18-39; NW-SW-S8; 3-23-36; SW-SW-S8;4-10-38;
    NE-NE-S18;8-29-35; SE-NE-S18; 10-16-38
Abner Luce, Wk NE-NE-S8; 1-2-39
Andrew McGillem* SE-NE-S8; 9-23-37; W-SW-S18; 12-14-38
John Beck* W-NE-S6; 7-6-24
William Helsey* SE-NW-S8; 10-29-38
Jackson Willis SW-NW-S8; 11-1-52

Jacob Helsey (Helsly)* NE-SW-S8; 8-15-36
Valentine Heart Denning, Wayne Co.,O. SE-SW-S8;6-16-37;SE-S8;6-16-
James Madison Nants* NE-NE-S9; 7-30-36   38
Thomas Nants* SE-NE-S9; 10-16-35; NW-NE-S9; 7-30-36
Emanuel Wyatt* NE-NW-S9; 9-24-47
John Alexander Decker, Pe SE-NW-S9; 5-24-36
Jesse Alexander* W-NW-S9; 8-12-36
Benjamin Hardin, Pe N-SW, E-SE-S9; 5-24-36
Lemuel Davis, Cumberland Co., Pa. S-SW, NW-SE-S9; 5-10-37
Josiah Johnson* SW-SE-S9; 1-20-36
Joseph Defendall* NE-NE-S10; 1-23-37; SE-NW-S11; 10-29-40
Newitt Battle* S-NE, SE-NW-S10; 12-15-36
Thomas Smith* NW-NE-S10; 1-13-37
John Silvanus Johnson* NE-NW-S10; 1-15-36
Henry Battle* NE-SE-S10; 12-15-36
Jackson Steele* NE-NE-S11; 4-6-46
Robert Johnson* NW-NW-S11; 1-15-36
Rowene Hewins* SW-NW, E-SW, W-SE-S11; 11-3-38
William Miley* NW-SW-S11; 1-20-36
John Harrison Overlin* SE-SE-S11; 3-9-44
Richard Selby* SE-NE-S12;5-19-53;SE-SE-S12;4-8-33;W-SE-S24;2-18-48
Peter Brenton, Sr.* N-NW-S12; 7-26-37
John Whipps Davisson* SW-NW-S12; 12-31-38
John Defendall* E-SW-S12;5-22-37;NW-SE-S12;4-30-33;SW-SE-S12;10-1-
Jonathan Jacob Bowman* NW-SW-S12; 1-4-39   33
Samuel Bilderback* SW-SW-S12; 6-18-44
Elijah Lane* NE-NE-S13; 2-5-34; NW-NE-S13; 6-14-37
Jeremiah Stinman* SE-NE-S13; 2-9-37
John Hawkins Lane* SW-NE, NE-NW-S13; 8-14-47
John Palmer* SE-NW-S13; 11-23-48; NW-NW-S13; 9-11-48
Peter Brenton Selby* SW-NW-S13; SE-NE-S14; 6-12-44
Daniel Hillman* NE-SE-S13; 12-31-38
John Abell* SE-SE-S13; 7-3-39
Daniel Hawkins* NE-NE-S14; 8-25-47
Zilpha Hewins* W-NE-S14; E-NW-S23; NW-SW-S26; 11-3-38
Darwin Hewins* NW-S14;11-3-38;NW-SW-S14;4-20-39; Erwin? see below
Erwin Hewins* NE-SW-S14;W-NW,W-SW-S23;SW-NW-S26;11-3-38; see above
Hugh Shaw Ferrell (Terrell?)* SW-SW-S14; 4-12-37
John Jackson Lownsdale* NE-SE, W-SE-S14; 8-2-38
Maxwell Willis NW-NE-S15; 2-4-37
Thomas Martin, Monongalia Co., (W.) Va. NE,NW,SE-S17;NE-SE-S19;
Ford Dejarnatt, Ws NE-SW-S17;8-14-37;S-SW-S17;3-9-37.   5-6-37
William West* NW-SW-S17; 6-16-36
Lewis Beck* NW-NE-S18; 2-12-36; SW-NE-S18; 10-22-38
Thomas Traylor* W-NW-S18; 11-24-37; SW-SW-S21; 6-10-36
William Denning* E-SW, SW-SE-S18; 5-30-39; NW-SE-S18; 12-24-44
William Gullet* NE-SE-S18; 12-4-35
Valentine Hart* E-NW-S19; 10-18-39; see V. H. Denning
Hugh Harris, York Dist., S.C. W-NW, E-SW-S19; 9-7-36
Hiram Frederick* W-SW-S19; 8-29-36
William West* NE-NW-S20; 8-16-37
Alexander Hill* SE-NW-S20; 9-26-48
Richmon Barrett NW-NW-S20; 2-19-44
Michael Shoulee* SW-NW-S21; 12-23-35

George Miller* NW-SW-S21; 6-10-36
John Pue Hinman (Kinman?)* NW-NW-S22; 1-10-33
Heirs of John Dodson, alias Dotson, decd. NE-S23;8-31-47; MLW27222
Benjamin Williams* E-SW, W-SE-S23; 3-27-37
John Browing Mitchell* E-SE-S23; 4-22-37
Joseph Ward* E-NW-S24; 2-26-48
William Jefferson Hager* NW-NW-S24; 4-14-49
Benjamin Franklin Wyatt* SW-NW-S24; 11-11-44
David Upton* NE-SW-S24; 12-31-44
William Tisdale* NE-SE-S24; 3-5-50; SE-SE-S24; 6-12-39
Peter Hedges* NE-NE-S25; 7-10-37
George Dean* SE-NE-S25; 10-26-38
Benjamin Franklin Morss* NW-NE-S25; 10-26-38; NE-SE-S25; 3-7-40
Benjamin Brewster* SW-NE-S25; 6-6-37
John Crow* N-NW-S25; 3-23-37
John Hardin* SE-NW-S25; 6-30-36
Alfred Shaw* SW-NW-S25; 6-16-36
John Wease* SW-S25; 9-19-17
Jesse Bryant* NW-SE-S25; 4-27-37
Hugh Shaw, Jr.* SW-SE-S25; 6-6-37
Franklin Taylor Dedman* SE-NE-S26; 6-17-36
William Miller* NW-NE, NE-NW-S26; 3-27-37
James Hedges* SW-NE-S26; 6-16-36; SE-S26; 1-16-15
Jefferson Hedges* SE-NW-S26;1-26-38;NE-SW-S26;8-17-36;SE-SW-S26;
John Wright* NW-NW-S26; 12-15-36   8-24-47
Samuel Hedges* SW-SW-S26; 3-24-54
Christian Miller* N-NE-S27; 11-28-36
Daniel Crow* SE-NE-S27; 12-16-36; SW-NW-S27; 6-22-36
James Crow* SW-NE-S27;1-26-38;NE-SW-S27;1-13-36;NW-SE-S27;2-13-36
Mary Crow* E-NW-S27; 2-2-37; SE-SW-S27; 6-22-36
Enoch Noland* NW-NW-S27; 12-6-36
Robert Brenton* W-SW-S27; 9-23-14
Samuel Dedman W-NE-S28; 10-11-17; NW-S28; 4-8-17
John Brenton E-SE-S28; 12-28-16
James McAdams, Gi SW-S29; NW-NW-S32; 4-12-36
Michael Frederick W-NE-S30; 1-5-19
John Knight* NW-NW-S30; NE-NE-S31; 3-24-36; NW-SW-S30; 3-17-36
Bazil Simpson* SW-NW-S30; 9-17-35; SW-SE-S30; 9-21-32
Isaac Knight E-SW-S30; 2-2-18
John Bradberry, Gi E-SE-S30; 4-12-36
Benjamin McAtee & Daniel Frederick* NW-SE-S30; 3-24-36
James Atkinson* NW-NE-S32; 11-7-36
William Darwin Clark, Gi NE-SE-S32; 10-5-40
Thomas Bilderback* NE-NE-S33; 9-13-32
John Portress Traylor* NW-NE-S33; 11-2-36
Sally Jerrell NW-S34; 8-11-14
Willard Carpenter, assee. of William Gavit NE-S36;12-17-47;MLW6697
Joseph Bower, Wk SE-SW-S36;6-7-39./.Alfred Davis,Db SW-SE-S36;11-23-
Samuel Green & Henry Stone* SE-SE-S36; 2-15-36.   36

RELINQUISHMENTS

William Abbet W-NW-S1; 11-30-18; 6-25-29
Malachi Marrick W-NE-S2; 12-2-17; 3-9-25

John Asher E-NW-S2;10-20-18;9-25-21; W-NW-S2;10-20-18;4-6-25
Thomas Jeffries W-NW-S3; 10-9-18; 9-25-21
Elijah Malott NW-S4; 3-13-18; 12-25-24
William Dedman NW-S22; 12-16-17; 7-2-87
John Defendall NW-S25; 10-27-18; 6-22-27
Benjamin Koath (Koith? Hoath?) NE-S26; 10-13-18; 3-30-27
William Hart NW-S26; 3-6-30; 9-7-31
Robert Brenton E-SW-S27; 9-23-14; 0-27-31
Samuel Dedman E-NE-S20; 10-11-17; 9-18-31
John Brenton W-SE-S28; 12-20-16; 9-26-21
John Davisson E-NW-S30; 5-15-18; 8-7-21
Isaac Knight W-SW-S30; 2-2-18; 6-12-29
Samuel Deadman W-NE-S28;10-11-17;7-4-29;NW-S28;4-8-17;7-4-29
William Doughten E-NE-S33; 9-1-17; 7-4-29
Michael Frederick W-NE-S30; 1-5-19; 7-4-29
John B. Dobbins & John Glass SE-S30; 8-15-17; 7-4-29
John Glass W-NW-S30; n.d.; 7-4-29

T 1 S, R 9 W

Jacob Young, Vb NE-NE-S1; 1-25-37; of*, NW-NE-S1; 3-14-39
Daniel Young* SE-NE-S1; 8-16-37
George Shouls* SW-NE-S1; 9-30-36
Charles S. Fittinger* NE-NW-S1; 8-7-52
John Shouls* SE-NW-S1; 2-12-36; NE-SW-S1; 11-22-36
Alexander Counce, Ci NW-NW-S1; 2-11-37
Samuel Rumble* SW-NW, NW-SW-S1; 10-3-33
William Robling* SE-SW-S1; 1-28-35; NE-NE-S12; 5-17-38
Daniel Grubb* SW-SW-S1; SE-NW, W-NW-S12; 11-22-36
Thomas Fowler* SE-S1; 10-8-18
Henry Borders, Sr.* NE-NE-S2; 2-17-36
Henry Grubb* SE-NE-S2; 10-2-44; SW-NE-S2; 10-29-40
Henry Borders, Jr.* NW-NE-S2; 4-18-37; NE-NW-S2; 1-7-35
George Fettinger* NW-NW-S2; 11-1-44
George Grubb* SW-NW-S2; 1-15-39; NE-SW-S2; 11-25-36; NW-SW-S2;
    12-22-34; NE-NW-S12; 8-27-35
James Garwood* SE-SW-S2;9-12-35;SW-SE-S2;12-23-34;NW-SE-S4;2-13-38
Joseph Garwood* SW-SW-S2; 9-14-32; E-NE-S10; 3-13-37
William McAtee* E-SE-S2; 11-3-36
Samuel Fettinger* NW-SE-S2; 10-20-35; E-NW-S4; 12-7-37
Joshua Young* E-NE-S3;6-19-37;NW-NE-S3;7-18-37;SW-NE-S3;3-23-50
Tarleton Boren* NW-S3; 2-22-15
John Devendale & John Chambers SW-S3; 9-18-17
John Grubb* NE-SE-S3; 1-11-39
Valentine Grubb* SE-SE-S3; 6-16-36; SW-NW-S10; 10-8-38
Albert Logan Masters* NW-SE-S3; 10-30-49; SW-SE-S3; 10-15-49
Benjamine Reynolds* NE-S4; 2-22-15
James Lownsdale, Mason Co., Ky. W-NW-S4; 5-19-21
Thomas Martin* NE-SW-S4; 2-18-39; NW-SW-S4; 3-8-39
John Devendale* E-SE-S4; 10-29-17
Andrew B. Chambers* SW-SE-S4; 5-28-37
Philip Devendale NE, NW-S5; 12-28-14
Fielding Colvin, Ci NE-SW-S5; 5-28-39
Joseph Colvin, Ci NW-SW-S5; 7-8-37

Joseph Davisson* SW-SW-S5; 5-3-39
Matthew Raney, Gi NE-SE-S5; 9-11-38
John McClelland Jones* SW-NW-S8; 2-6-37
William Curtis* NE-NE-S9; 11-30-39
Valentine Crabb (Grubb?)* SE-NE-S9; 1-15-39
Lewis Grubb* NW-NW-S9; 8-22-43
Fielding White* SW-SW-S9; 2-10-45
John Pemberton* SE-S9; 10-26-18
Richard Hail* NW-NE-S10; 9-6-37
Jane M. Davisson* SW-NE-S10; 11-17-48
Isaiah McQueen* E-NW-S10; 10-24-18
Josiah Young* NW-NW-S10; 11-24-36
Thomas Jefferson Brittingham* NE-SW-S10; 2-15-49
Orville Hale* SE-SW-S10; 4-9-46
George Washington Brittingham* NW-SW-S10; 2-13-49
Wesley Minton Whitehead* SW-SW-S10; 4-6-46
Richard Masters* NE-S11; 10-8-18
Zachariah McAtee* E-NW-S11; 2-10-30; SE-SW-S11; 3-7-36
Thomas Pemberton W-NW-S11; 10-26-18
John Dent* NE-SW-S11; 10-14-33
Robert Cravens Johnson* NW-SW-S11; 3-26-39   3-7-36
Pleasant Hightower* E-SE-S11;9-24-33;NW-SW-S12;10-12-35;SW-SW-S12;/
Levi Shaver* NW-SE-S11;3-23-39;NE-NE-S23;4-17-39;NW-SW-S23;11-21-36.
Anderson Barrett* SW-SE-S11; 10-9-43
John Blaze* SE-NE, NE-SE-S12; 10-31-36
Andrew Grubb* W-NE-S12; 12-22-34
Louis Robling* NE-SW-S12; 4-13-36; NW-SE-S12; 10-5-37
Andrew West* SE-SW-S12; 10-22-32
Robert Barrett* SE-SE-S12;11-23-36;SW-SE-S12;2-24-34; NE-NE-S13;
    8-12-39; SW-NE-S13; 12-1-37
Adam Snider* SE-NE-S13; 11-12-32
John Beck* NW-NE-S13; 11-7-36
Michael Kime* NW-S13;10-30-19;NE-SW-S13;3-28-39; of*,E-NW-S24;6-30-
    22;NE-SW-S24;E-SE,NW-SE-S25;3-15-36; W-NW-S36; 3-28-36
James Duff Crow* SE-SW-S13; 3-28-39
Robert Johnson* W-SW-S13; 5-28-51
Wilson Barrett* SW-SE-S13; 8-12-39
Children & heirs of George Green, decd. NE-S14; 8-31-47
Felix Semore Falls* E-SW-S14; 9-2-53; N-NE-S15; 9-11-47
Squire Gates Barrett* NE-SE-S14; 9-10-47
Spencer Barrett* SE-SE-S14; 11-16-39
John Colvin* NW-SE-S14; 2-1-39
Alexander Harlley* SE-NE-S15; 5-22-46
James Mancey* SW-NE-S15; 2-11-47
William Moffatt, Chester Dist., S.C. NW-S15;6-21-37; SW-S15;12-24-
    42; SE-SW-S24; W-NE, NW-S25; 9-7-36
Jack Miller SE-SE-S15; 8-8-39
John Shoaf* NE-NE-S22; 9-14-47
Benjamin Shaver* SE-NE-S22; 11-16-35; SW-NW-S23; 1-25-37
Joseph Hannon, Cumberland Co., Pa. W-NE, NW-S22; 5-16-37
Edwin Robb* NE-SW-S22;9-27-47;of Gi,SE-SE-S22;2-29-36;of*,NW-SE-S22
Henry Cline* SE-SW-S22; 11-21-36   12-9-36
Maxwell Wilson, Mr W-SW-S22; 9-30-36
James Barnes* NE-SE-S22; 4-6-36

Josiah McAtee* SW-SE-S22; 2-22-36; E-NE-S27; 10-23-35
Henry Shaver* SE-NE-S23; 8-22-37; SW-NW-S24; 8-7-39
Andrew Atkinson* NW-NE-S23; 2-12-45
William Shaver* SW-NE-S23; 5-6-39
William Miller* NE-NW-S23; 7-25-39; NW-SW-S24; 4-10-39
Peter Young* NE-SW-S23; 5-20-39
Henry Woodry* S-SW-S23; 7-24-39
James Atkinson* NE-SE-S23; 8-13-47
Ramson Philips* SE-SE-S23; 8-14-50
Thomas Miller* NW-SE-S23; 7-25-39
Umprey Simpson* SW-SE-S23;9-3-38;NE-NE-S26;11-2-35;NW-NE-S26;9-22-
Matthew Harper* E-NE-S24; 8-6-39   36
Zacheus Spurling* NW-NE-S24; 2-18-39
Joseph Shigley, Greene Co.,O. SW-NE-S24; 6-13-39
Absalom Carr, Fayette Co.,O. SE-S24; 6-13-39; E-NE-S25; 5-30-39
Joseph Woodry* NE-SW-S25; 5-30-36; SW-NW-S26; 4-12-39
Lewis Cloin* SE-SW-S25; 10-30-54
Phillip Wallen* SW-SW-S25; 7-30-44
Isaac Knight* NE-SE-S25; 6-28-39
Jacob Decker* SE-SE-S25; 8-12-39
Edward McLaughlin* NW-SE-S25; 5-16-49
Basil Simpson* SE-NE-S26; 1-9-37
Isaac Woodrew* SW-NE-S26; 9-16-35; SE-NW-S26; 1-31-37
James Finney, Gi NE-NW-S26; 8-11-36
Peter Wodry* NW-NW-S26; 9-10-38
Isaac Simon & Samuel Plough SW-S26; 8-6-19
John Gardner, Gi W-NW-S27; 11-5-35
Samuel Barnes* SW-SE-S26; 1-31-37
James Bonner Miller, Gi E-SW, W-SE-S27; 9-30-36
John Decker & William Miln, Gi W-SW-S27; 3-16-36
William Miln W-SW-S27; 3-16-36
William Phillips NE-SE-S27; 1-20-53
Alexander Barnes* SE-SE-S27; 1-31-37
David Barnes, Gi NE-NE-S35; 1-31-37
Thomas Hart* SE-NE-S36; 12-4-72

RELINQUISHMENTS

Nathan Stephens SW-S2; 10-24-18; 9-27-21
John Devindall W-SE-S4; 10-29-17; 3-30-25
Thomas Pemberton E-NW-S11; 10-26-18; 6-11-27
Michael Kine SW-S13; 10-30-19; 8-28-21
James Brockman NE-S25; 11-24-18; 9-19-22
Anthony M. Leake NW-S25; 11-24-18; 9-19-22
Isaiah McQueen W-NW-S10; 10-24-18; 7-4-29

T 2 S, R 6 W

William Davisson, Dr E-NE-S4; 11-5-38; SW-NE-S4; 3-18-39
John Robert Pennor, Db NE-SE-S4; 5-1-39
John W. Lewis* SE-SE-S4; 6-5-39; of Db, E-NE-S9; 3-12-39
James Arnold* E-SW, NW-SW-S7; 10-10-54
David Abbott* SE-S7; 10-3-54
James Washington Cockrum, Gi W-NW-S8; 3-23-37

Abraham Davendall* W-SW-S8; 10-5-54; W-NW-S17; 10-4-54
Charles F. White E-NW-S9;8-19-53;MLW 40542;NW-NW-S9;12-30-53;MLW
Albert S. White* SW-NW-S9; 10-25-54   40223
John Rizley, Db NE-SE-S9; 7-23-39
James Hudelson & William J. Casey E-NW-S17; 8-22-53; MLW 28432
Daniel Hendricks* SW-SW-S17; 3-30-36; SE-SE-S18; 4-12-36
A. B. Lockhart & Robert Barnes SE-S17; 10-31-53; MLW 21488
Moses Hams* NE-NE-S18; 6-27-51
William Dodd SE-NE, NE-SE-S18; 11-11-51; MLW 14544
Calvin Bacon, Mt W-NE, NW, N-SW-S18; 9-25-54
Ransom Voyles, Sp S-SW-S18; 11-4-54
Elizabeth Robinson* NW-SE-S18; 11-2-57
James Hendricks* SW-SE-S18; SW-SW-S30; 2-13-37
Levi Voyles, Wk NE-NE-S19; 11-4-54
John Hendrix* SE-NE-S19; 1-23-39; SW-NW-S30; 7-10-38
John Miller* SW-NW-S19; 6-29-38; SW-SW-S19; 12-29-36.   25494
Benjamin Clark SE-SE-S19; 10-1-53; MLW 25494;NE-NE-S30;10-1-53;MLW/
George Dean* SE-NE-S20; 1-31-53; MLW 12468; SE-NW-S21; 1-31-53;
    MLW 53182; W-SE-S31; 10-29-52
Orval E. Judson* W-NE-S20; 10-16-54
Joseph Taylor* SW-NW-S21; 1-23-39
William Rust, Sp SW-SW-S21; 9-30-54; of*, E-NW-S28; 7-8-51
Samuel W. Postlethwait, Db N-SE-S21; 10-2-54
Isaac A. Postlethwait, Db E-SW, W-SE-S28; 9-27-54
William D. L. Postlethwait* E-SE-S28; 9-26-54
Cornelius Jaco, Wk SE-S30; W-NE-S31; 9-30-54
David Tate NW-SE-S32; 1-24-53; MLW 66888
Thomas L. Byrd, Gi SW-SE-S32; 10-26-54.   S33;7-17-54
Casper Henry Todrank, Db NE-NE-S33;10-19-54;SE-NE-S33;5-1-52;W-NE-/
William Landmehr* NE-NW-S33;4-4-54; of Db,SE-NW-S33;7-17-54.
Phebe Bolin, Db NE-SE-S33; 6-6-42

T 2 S, R 7 W

John Hathaway* SE-NW-S1; 6-27-38
Edward Corn* SE-SW-S1; 3-31-37; NE-NW-S12; 4-6-36
William Corn* SW-SW-S1; 2-16-39; SW-SE-S1; 4-10-37
Frederick Aust (Anst?) SW-S3; 1-29-51; MLW 26327
Henry Miley, Db, son of Henry Miley SE-NE-S4; 2-11-39
Robert Brenton* E-SW-S4; 10-4-21; W-NW-S5; 5-1-17
Benjamine Houchin* W-SE-S4; 1-16-39
Joseph Rohrer, Gi NE-S5; 6-3-37
Warren Smith* NE-NW-S5; 12-4-37
Benjamine Ashby* W-SW-S5; 6-3-39; SW-SE-S8; NW-NE-S17; 1-24-39;
    E-SW-S17; 9-17-51; E-NE-S18; 6-3-22; NW-NE-S18; 5-26-53
George Dean* SE-NE-S6; 2-12-39; W-SW-S6; 11-22-52
Henry Hunter* NW-NE-S6; 2-8-39
John Hathaway* SW-NE, NE-NW-S6; 2-16-39; NE-SW-S6; 6-20-50
Edward Vernatt Bowers, Ashtabula Co.,O. SE-SW-S6; 3-17-40
Stephen Bowers* SW-SW-S6; 8-11-49
Stephen Hamby, Wk SW-SE-S6; E-NE, NW-NE-S7; 12-31-38
Joseph Bower, Wk SW-NE, E-NW-S7; 6-7-39
Asahel Whitman* NE-SW-S7; 5-27-53
Alexander Wiggs* SW-SW-S7; 11-7-39
Willard Carpenter W-NE-S8; 12-29-53; MLW 299

James Ashley E-SW-S8; 1-5-19
Samuel Howe Johnson* NW-SW-S8; 10-1-38
Robert Thompson* SW-SW-S8; 9-20-38
John Harden* NW-NE-S9; 4-17-37
John Almon SW-NE-S9; 6-16-51; MLW 7802
Henry Harden* NE-NW-S9; 2-16-48
Charles P. Nash* SE-NW-S9; 6-2-55
Willard Carpenter S-SE-S11; 12-20-53; MLW 30833
James Washington Cockrum, Gi NE-S12;SE-NW,W-NW,NW-SW-S12;3-23-37
William Hathorn* NE-SW-S12; 7-26-38
David Corn* SW-SW-S12; SW-SW-S13; 2-1-37
William & Samuel Hathorn* W-SE-S12; 3-17-38
William Ashby* SE-NE-S17;6-3-39;SE-NW-S17;3-25-39;W-NW-S17;6-3-22
Peyton Ashby* SW-NE,NW-SE-S17;6-20-37;E-SE-S17;6-3-39;SW-SE-S17;
Jacob Pancake SW-NE-S18;6-14-53;MLW 70218.   6-5-49
Alexander Wiggs* NW-NW-S18; 11-7-39
Harrison Thompson* SW-NW-S18; 6-6-36;SW-NE-S30;10-13-51;MLW 9537
Robert McBay* NE-SE-S18; 6-14-53
Joseph Pancake* NW-SE-S18; 4-13-37
William Pancake* SW-NE-S19; 10-6-38; NW-NW-S19; 6-4-39
Samuel Bilderback* E-SW-S20; 3-5-49
William Price Woolsey* W-SE-S20; 2-20-39
Alexander Leslie NE-NE-S24;6-27-54;MLW 97747;NW-S24;1-30-57;SE-NE-
John Miller, Jr.* SE-NE-S24;2-4-39.   S25; 5-10-54
George Dean* NW-SE-S25; 1-26-53; SW-SE-S25; 1-20-53
Samuel D. Thompson, Gi SW-S26; 10-4-54
George Waller King* E-NE-S29;3-7-50;NW-NE-S29;9-28-46;SW-NE-S29;
Robert Bradshaw W-NW-S30;10-23-51;MLW 10678.   1-5-38
James Burdett* SE-SW-S30; 4-4-37; NE-SE-S30; 5-26-53; NW-SE-S30;
    10-13-51; of Wk, SW-SE-S30; 5-26-51
Ephram Reed Richardson* SW-SW-S31; 12-21-46
Samuel J. Wakeland, Wk E-SE-S35; 10-7-54
Peter Kinder E-NE-S36; 1-26-53

RELINQUISHMENTS

Robert Brenton E-NW-S5; 5-1-17; 8-25-182-?
James Ashley W-SW-S8; 1-5-19; 6-25-29

T 2 S, R 8 W

John Clinton NE-S1; 6-12-49; MLW 50165
Heirs of John Miller, decd. SW-S1; 8-31-47
William Jerauld, Gi NE-NE-S2; 3-1-38
Rufus Breed SW-S2;6-6-49;MLW 23779; W-SW-S3;6-6-49;MLW 40328;can-
    celed by letter of Com., 12-16-51; NE-S21;6-6-49;E-SW-S6;6-6-49;
    MLW 45664;NW-S27;6-6-49;MLW 36404;NE-S28;6-6-49;MLW 37111;NE-SW,
    W-SW-S28;6-6-49;MLW 51462
Horace Plummer, Vb SE-NE-S3;SE-NE,NW-SE-S4;NE-NW-S9;12-23-51
William E. Green SW-NE-S3; 3-10-52; MLW 29419
Isaac Street E-SW-S3; 8-4-52
Isaac Montgomery W-NE-S4; 9-25-26; of Gi, SW-NW-S21; 4-22-39
Joseph Rutledge Brown, Gi E-NW-S4;5-11-36;W-NW-S4;4-20-36;SW-S4;
Henry Beck* SW-SE-S4; 2-11-45   4-6-36

Thomas Martin, Monongalia Co., (W.) Va. NE,SW-S9;NE,NW,SE-S10;W-NW-
Jacob Warrick Hargrove, G1 SE-NW-S9; 12-5-53   S11; 6-28-39
George W. Massey NW-NW-S9; 8-18-53
Nicholas Jasper Hargrove, G1 SW-NW-S9; 4-15-36
Henry Coleman* E-SE-S9; 11-4-23
James H. Fleanor, G1 W-SE-S9; 4-15-39
Samuel Deadman Coleman* SW-SW-S10; 8-19-37
William Gilbert NE-S11; 8-31-47; MLW 23822
William Trentham SW-S11; 8-31-47
William B. Coalman NE-NE, W-NE-S12; 4-19-51; MLW 66725
John Wiggs* NE-SW-S12; 1-18-50
William Carroll Wiggs* SE-SW-S12; 10-20-48
John S. Johnson* NW-SW-S12; 1-11-51
James A. Steal* SW-SW-S12; 12-24-49
Asahel Whitman* NE-NE-S13; 11-3-49; NW-NE-S13; 11-10-49
Martin Burch* SE-NE-S13; 3-16-46; SW-NE-S13; 11-10-49
James Madison Brenton* SE-NW-S13; 3-18-39
Arthur Thompson* NE-SE-S13;6-20-37;SW-SE-S13;8-20-49;NW-SE-S24;5-30-
Peyton Pancake* SE-SE-S13; 2-20-50   36
Mary Thompson* NW-SE-S13; 4-27-40
William Morrison E-NE-S14; 6-10-52; MW 20109
David Dagget English* NW-NE-S14; 7-28-48; NE-SW-S14; 2-6-37
Jesse Gross Davis* SW-NE-S14; 9-21-50; SE-SW-S14; 7-14-49; W-SW-
     S14; 6-5-51; MLW 6271; NE-NW-S23;11-25-48; of G1, E-NE-S22;3-29-
Noah Fox NE-NE-S15; 12-12-51; MLW 18597   37
William Black* SE-NE-S15; 12-24-49
Philip Coleman* NW-NE-S15; 3-29-36
Newton Brenton* SW-NE-S15; 1-6-54
John Coleman* NE-NW-S15; 9-6-39; SE-NW-S15; 3-24-36
Leeright Houchins SW-S15; 11-26-49; MLW 42689
Harvey Montgomery, G1 NW-NW-S21; 4-18-36
Joseph H. Reynolds & I.(J?) Reynolds* NW-SW-S21; 8-24-46
Samuel Black* W-NE-S22; SE-NW-S23; 2-22-39
William W. Colman* NE-NW-S22; 10-7-48
John J. Davis SE-S22; 9-1-49; MLW 59588
John Crow* W-NW-S23; 1-31-20
Henry Black* E-SW-S23; 5-29-27
John Black* NE-SE-S23; 8-5-34
David Black* NW-SE-S23; 8-13-39; SW-SE-S23; 10-4-36
David Jackson Davis* SW-NW-S24; 9-10-38
Harrison Thompson* NE-SW-S24; 4-6-36; E-SE-S24; 8-10-49
David Johnson SW-SW-S24; 6-12-57; MLW 7237
William Coleman, Vb NW-SW-S25; 8-15-37
Willard Carpenter E-NE-S25;6-21-53;MW 42386;W-SE-S34;6-20-53;MLW
John Black, G1 SW-SW-S25; 11-17-38   321
Robert Ashby* SW-NW-S25; 8-9-39
Henry Black* NE-NW-S26; 2-6-37
William Lawson Black, G1 SE-SW-S25; 1-30-39
William S. Turner SW-NW-S26; 8-1-53
Milton Hinslow* SW-SW-S26; 5-18-36
James Mason* SW-SE-S27; 1-19-39; NE-SW-S27; 6-16-53; of G1, SE-SW-
     S27; 10-31-36; NE-NW-S34; 10-31-36
Simpson Ritchey* SE-SE-S27; 10-7-46
Harry O'Neal, G1 SE-SW-S28; W-NW-S34; 12-6-38

James McClure, G1 NE-NW, W-NW-S33; 10-22-36
George Woolsey* SE-NW-S33; 8-2-33; SE-NW-S34; 6-6-36
Jesse Houchin* SE-SE-S33; 8-3-33
Samuel Powers* NE-NE-S34; 1-11-38
Conrade Coleman* SE-NE-S34;10-17-36;NE-SE-S34;4-27-36;NW-SW-S35;
John Batten Hagoman* SW-NE-S34;11-15-36;SW-S34;4-27-36.   3-9-39
William Cutright* SE-SE-S34; 4-18-36; SW-SW-S35; 12-21-37
Samuel Powers* NW-NW-S35; 1-11-39
Martha Lewis* SW-NW-S35; 9-15-37
William Almon* SE-SW-S35; 4-28-37
Joshua Ashby* NE-NE-S36; 12-13-37; NW-NE-S36; 7-16-39

RELINQUISHMENTS

William Terry E-SW-S4;3-2-19;9-18-21; W-SW-S4;3-2-19;10-28-26
John Barker NW-S15; 9-26-17; 9-13-21
James Kell W-SE-S26;11-2-16;9-29-21; E-SE-S26;11-2-16;3-28-25
James B. McGarrah W-SE-S27; 11-7-17; 9-22-21
James Lessley NE-S33; 3-5-19; 9-8-21

T 3 S, R 6 W

Dudley Montgomery* E-SW-S5; 10-7-54
John D. Stevens* NE-NE-S6; 9-11-57
William M. Woolsey* SE-NE-S6; 2-28-57
Jane W. Posey, Wk W-NE, E-SE, NW-SE-S6; 9-29-54
Erastus D. Kinder* E-NW-S6; 11-5-57
John Adam Mayo SW-SE-S6;NW-NE-S7;9-15-53;MLW 43566; Adams
Eldredge Woolsey* NE-NE-S7; 1-29-50
Aaron F. Miller SE-NE-S7; 8-9-53; MLW 12667
Mark Marshall, Wk SW-NE-S7; 10-20-54
James Hendrix* NE-SW-S7; 3-28-51
William D. Turner, Da SE-SW-S7; 2-27-57
George Nicholson* SE-S7; W-NE, E-NW-S18; 9-27-54
Jonathan R. Tilman SW-S8; 12-9-52
Herman Henry Telljohann (Katterjohn? see below), Db SE-NE-S9;12-23-
Henry Katterjohn, Db E-SW-S9; 12-7-44; see above   44
Herman W. Katterjohn, Db E-SE-S9; 12-7-44; see above
John Bonner NW-S17; 7-2-52; MLW 56541
Ezekiel Powell NW-SW-S17; 7-2-52; MLW 53569
Henry F. Wiefking, Db SW-SW-S17; 2-7-54
Lawrence Kirby SE-S17; 7-16-51; MLW 2489
Henry Enlow E-NE-S18; 1-12-54; MLW 35948
John Jones, Wk E-SW, S-SE-S18; NW-S19; 9-28-54
Columbus W. Baulden, Wk W-SW-S18; 9-27-54
Robert M. Bolin N-SE-S18; 2-16-54; MLW 21981
George C. Maroum E-NE-S19; 7-16-51; MLW 1983
Jesse Bradley W-NE-S19; 7-16-51; MLW 2541
Hansel Ingram, Wk SW-SW-S20; 3-13-39
Barney Ingram, Wk SE-SE-S20; 3-13-39

T 3 S, R 7 W

Temple Woolsey* NE-NW-S3; 5-31-37

Jesse Houchin* SE-SE-S3; 1-16-39; W-SE-S3; 5-31-37
Allen White Clifford* NE-NW-S4; 7-30-39
William Grissum* SE-NW-S6; 1-11-50
Barnet Carlon* SW-S6; 5-6-50; MLW 61337
William Simpson E-NW-S7; 9-11-51; MLW 6472
Chesterfield Houchin E-NW, E-SW-S9; 1-18-51; MLW 55587
James Johnson W-SW-S11; 10-23-51; MLW 10315
William Wilson E-SE-S11; 10-23-51; MLW 11042
Henry C. Smith* E-SW-S12; 10-6-54
Columbus W. Boulden, Wk E-SW, SE-S13; 9-27-54
Samuel Scott* NE-SW-S14; 10-6-54; SE-SW-S14; 4-27-54
Robert Glenn SE-S14; 4-24-51; MLW 69
John Tubman* SE-NW-S15;4-20-40;SW-NW-S15;4-10-37;NW-SW-S15;1-13-53
James R. Smith* SW-SW-S15; 1-9-54
George Rice* SE-SE-S15; 8-14-39
Phineas Kellogg E-NE-S18; 9-5-51; MLW 3457
William Harper W-NE-S18; 9-5-51; MLW 8410
Joshua Stephens, Wk NE-SW-S18; 9-10-53; SE-SW-S18; 1-24-53
John Stuckey NW-SE-S18; 12-13-52; E-SE-S20; 12-22-51; MLW 4859
David Lockhart* SW-SE-S18; 5-11-52
Thomas W. Wilson NE-NW-S19; 7-19-52; MLW 31288
William B. Lambert SE-NW, NE-SW, N-SE-S19; 10-25-50; MLW 54732
John Cabbage SE-SW-S19; 2-3-53; MLW 12165
Joseph Huez S-SE-S19; 10-8-50; MLW 12368
William C. Richardson* NE-NE-S20; 7-15-51
Isaac E. McSwain SW-S20; 10-25-50; MLW 27506
Samuel Powers, Wk NW-SE-S20;2-10-51;of*,SE-SW-S21;3-14-37;SW-SE-S21;
Dolly Chissenhall SW-SE-S20; 1-15-52; MLW 2931.   1-18-36
Simeon Powers* NE-NW, SW-NW-S21; 10-21-48; NW-NW-S21; 12-16-48
Ebenezer Hutchinson, Wk SE-NW-S21; 10-26-54
James Black E-SE-S21; 10-23-51; MLW 10316
James Bryant* NE-NE-S22; 10-4-54
George C. Hart SE-NE-S22; 7-1-52; MLW 42654
John Scales* NE-NW-S22; 7-17-48
Jotham C. Hutchinson, Wk SE-NW-S22; 10-18-54
Calvin Lockhart* E-SE-S22; 7-8-51
Samuel Blackford* NW-NE-S23; 10-18-37
James Masterson Wittinghill, Wk SW-NE-S23; 8-17-39
David Wilson E-NW-S23; 10-23-51
Andrew L. Robinson E-SW, W-SE-S23; 5-23-51; MLW 2380
William Corn* NW-SW-S23; 8-12-51
Lurinda Wittinghill, Sp SW-SW-S23; 10-13-37
George B. Walker NE-S24; Dec. 1851; MLW 2692
Sarah Lane NW-S24; 5-28-51; MLW 2431
John L. Walker SW-S24; 5-23-51; MLW 2434
Catherine Walker SE-S24; 11-5-51; MLW 7840

T 3 S, R 8 W

Aaron Coker* NW-NE-S1; 9-23-39
William Tisdale* SE-NW-S1; 4-11-37; NW-NW-S1; 3-22-36
Thomas Almon* SW-NW-S1; 5-2-36
Elihu Campbell* NW-SW-S1; 4-26-51
John Lemasters* SW-SW-S1; 12-5-49

Simeon Lemasters* NW-SE-S1; 6-23-36; SW-SE-S1; 3-30-38
John Almon* N-NW-S2; 8-22-36
John James Davis, Gi SW-NW-S2; 10-12-36
Benjamin Lemasters* SE-SE-S2; 5-2-36; NE-NE-S11; 6-21-36
John Battan Hageman NE-NE-S3; 9-30-36
Benjamin Johnson* NW-NE-S3; 10-19-36
William Almon, Sr.* NW-NW-S3; 2-13-40
Martin Stewart* NE-SW-S3; 3-24-37
William Mason* SE-SW-S3;12-21-43;NE-NE-S10;2-13-37;NW-NE-S10;10-24-
Richard Elliott Stewart* NE-NE-S4;6-6-36;NE-NW-S4;11-20-39.   36
James McGarrah Killpatrick, Gi SE-SW-S4; 1-8-39
Benjamin Lance* NW-NE-S9; 6-27-49
Robert Speer* SW-NE-S9; 12-5-50
William Reavis, Gi SE-NE-S10; 9-3-49
Robert Simpson* SW-NE-S10;10-20-49;SE-SE-S10;8-5-34;NE-NE-S15;2-28-
Arnett Mason* NE-NW-S10; 2-20-37   37
John Byrn, Gi SE-NW, N-SW-S10; 11-27-39
Alex. Lovercool* NW-NW-S10; 8-22-36
Thomas Crow Ferguson* E-SE-S11; 1-27-37
David Grissom* NW-NE-S12; 2-23-37
William Turner SE-SE-S12; 8-3-53
Peter Furguson* NE-NW-S13; 6-23-36; NW-NW-S13; 2-28-37
David Bilderback* SE-NW-S13; 3-22-37; NE-SW-S13; 7-13-36
Lorenzo Dow Parker*. SW-NW-S13; 11-9-36; NW-SW-S13; 9-26-36
Abijah Humprez* SE-SW-S13; NE-SW-S24; 3-23-50; NE-NE-S23; 9-22-49;
   of Wk, NW-SW-S24; 2-19-48
Nathaniel Perry* NW-SE-S13; 2-27-52
Samuel Ringer* SW-SE-S13; 2-27-52
John Carmichael Ricketts* NW-NE-S14;7-28-49; SW-NE-S14; 2-15-45
Mary Simpson, Gi E-NW-S14; 7-28-36
William Greene* NE-SW-S14; 9-2-36
James Beaty* SE-NW-S15; 3-30-38
Samuel Shlater* W-NW-S15; 2-23-19
John Ferguson, Wk SE-SE-S22; 8-18-36
James L. Reed* SE-NE-S23; 10-28-51
Pleasant Eps Erskins SE-S23; 8-12-48; MLW 18362
James W. Stephens, Wk NE-NE-S24; 8-11-49
Joshua Stephens, Wk SE-NE-S24; 3-30-50
Thomas McCleary* NW-NE-S24; 12-20-47; SW-NE-S24; 1-5-50
Daniel Hutchinson, Wk NW-S24; 2-28-48
George Reed* SE-SW-S24; 2-12-48
Thomas Hooker, Jr., Vb SW-SW-S24; 9-15-41
Daniel Hutchinson, assee. of Jeremiah Wyatt SE-S24;1-6-48;MLW 6006

RELINQUISHMENTS

Henry Hopkins SW-S14; 7-13-19; 11-22-24; SW-S15; 7-13-19; 3-28-25;
   W-NW-S23; 7-13-19; 3-28-25
Samuel Shlater E-NW-S15; 2-23-19; 3-28-25
John N. Trusdale W-SE-S22; 6-16-19; 8-28-21; E-SE-S22; 6-16-19;
   3-30-25

ABBOTT Andrew-219;David-220-228;
  James-220;Richard-211;Thomas-
  195;William-220(2)-225
ABEL Andrew-154;John-224;Joseph-
  152-156;Michael-9-152;Peter-207;
  Sarah-208;Thomas-16-20-21
ABERCROMBIE Alexander-66-67;Rob-
  ert-147
ABRAM Gabriel-197
ACRE Abraham-181;Finly-195;Jos-
  eph-161
ADAIR William-200
ADAMS Andrew-96;Edmund-9;George-
  167-174;James-57-122(3);John-40;
  79-80-122;Joseph-96-122;Samuel-
  57-80-85-102;William-211
ADAMSON Abraham-141;Ivy-141;John-
  141-142-150;Lorenzo-168;Simon-
  194;William-131;Zedekiah-186
ADDIS George-161
ADKINS James-205;Rachel-162-174;
  Russell-118;Wyatt-196
ACLAND Robert-21
AIKMAN Adam-32;Hugh-19(2);James-
  24;John-15-22-31-33;Mary-211;
  Samuel-16-19-211(2);Thomas-21
AINSLEY Joseph-213;Richard-213-
  214-215
ALBERT Hiram-101-107;John-29;
  Levi-101
ALBERTZ Frederick-80
ALBRIGHT John-153
ALCORN John-194;Nehemiah-68;
  Thomas-88
ALDRIDGE James-88;John-70-72(2)-
  87;Thomas-88
ALEXANDER Abner-23;Asbury-23-24-
  213;Benjamin-129;James-195-202;
  Jesse-214(2)-223-224;John-18-67-
  176-178-199-206;Jonathan-129;
  Robert-194;Samuel-213
ALFORD Franklin-15;George-15;
  James-15(2);Wayne-15
ALLARD John-50-51-111
ALLEN Andrew-152;Calvin-45;Char-
  les-9-15;Cyrus-37-126-163;Elias-
  18;Elihu-59(2)-43;Ethan-116;
  Francis-214;Harrison-15;Hiram-
  25-38;James-9-10-11-21(2)-22-24-
  29-45;John-11-18-21-29-30(2)-31-
  33-34(2)-46-110-120-197-210;Jos-
  eph-9;Moses-22-32;Peleg-11-211
  (2);Prince-117;Rachel-32;Samuel-
  187;Susannah-9;Thomas-10-146-

204;William-9-29(2)-30-179
ALLENDER Joseph-33
ALLISON Alfred-134;Benjamin-196;
  Joseph-17-31;William-31-33
ALMON John-230-234;Thomas-233;
  William-232-234
AIMY Alfred-105;Sylvester-105
ALSOP James-205-206;Willis-82
ALTON Catharine-187;Joseph-29
ALVERSON William-195
ALVIS Thomas-57
AMES John-55-83
AMMERMAN Mary-30;Peter-16
AMORY Francis-75-76-77-78-79-80;
  George-75-76-77
AMOS James-283
ANDERSON Andrew-207-219;David-144;
  Isaac-93-143;James-144-219;Jere-
  miah-144;Job-167-168;John-39-40-
  41-102-143-144-185;Levi-112;
  Pressley-112;Robert-69-87(2)-143
  (2)-146-147;Robison-113;Samuel-
  10-34-86;Thomas-112(3)-113-114-
  144;William-148-185-219
ANDES James-171
ANDRE Amable-106;Pierre-104
ANDREWS John-111-187
ANGLETON William-179
ANNON Alexander-160
ANO John-122
ANST see Aust
ANTHIS George-99;Martin-100
ANTLER Charles-101
APPLEGATE Jonah-43
APPLER Abraham-202
ARB Peter-36-39
ARBURN Henry-81;John-93
ARBUTHEWS John-62
ARBUTHNOT John-66-70
ARCHDEACON Nicholas-15;Richard-15
ARCHER Edward-196-205(2);William-
  67
ARD James-124;Rhoda-126
ARMS Anderson-19(2);James-19
ARMSTRONG Ari-150;James-138-139;
  John-149-193-203-206;Miles-73;
  Thomas-138-150;William-157
ARNOLD Aaron-12;James-228;Jeremiah-
  212;John-212(2)-214;Joseph-192-
  212;Samuel-35
ARRELL James-22
ART Jabez 156-159
ARTHUR Henry-190;James-17-21;John-
  17-18-189;Joseph-190

ARVIN Elias-159;Joshua-13
ASBELL Ambrose-116;James-160;
  Jackson-113
ASH see Ish;Charles-37;Henry-174;
  James-68(2);Raphael-25;Robert-
  83-86;Thomas-82
ASHBAUGH Jacob-208;John-208(3);
  Joseph-208
ASHBY see Ashley;Benjamin-228-
  229;James-108-109;Joseph-109;
  Joshua-232;Nathan-42-108-109;
  Peyton-230;Robert-231;William-
ASHER John-226   230
ASHLEY see Ashby;James-230(2);
  Thomas-73-90-91
ASHMEAD Hosea-65-68
ATCHASON James-132;John-132;
  Samuel-131
ATCHLEY Solomon-48
ATHON Joseph-150;Josias-149-150
ATKINSON Andrew-228;James-225-228
*AUSTIN Lyman-153(2)-155-158;
  Rufus-119. *AUST Frederick-229
AUTREY James-49-50(2)
AYRES Azariah-68-83-86;David-78-
  80;Henry-68;John-82

B see P
BABCOCK Henry-59
BACON Aaron-169;Calvin-229
BADGER John-202;Joseph-176
BADOLLET Albert-119
BAECHEL Michael-92
BAILEY Chesley-202-209(2)-210;
  James-209-210(2);John-117-143;/
BAIRD Andrew-88.   see Balay/
BAKER Abner-155;Absalom-189-198;
  Amsted-177;Daniel-140(2)-179;El-
  isha-178;Ezra-72(2);George-177;
  Gideon-46-50;Hamilton-177;Jesse-
  178;John-82-98-162-178-180-181;
  Jonas-48;Josias-49-194;Little-
  ton-16;Malden-198;Peter-180;Phi-
  lip-181;Robert-46-177-178;Wil-
  liam-38(2)-47-180(2)-205
BALAY William-47
BALDRIDGE Samuel-53
BALDWIN Columbus-232-233;Daniel-
  10;Francis-10-11;George-126;
  Greenberry-87;Harvey-102;Ira-
  221;Jesse-10;John-10(2)-11;Lem-
  uel-217;Reuben-73;Samuel-73;Ta-
  bitha-87;Theophilus-123-125-129;
  Thomas-24;Wiley-71;William-10-
  20-123-125-131
BALENTINE Harvey-58(3)

BALES James-135
BALL James-51
BALLARD James-53;Thomas-93
BALLENGER William-54
BALLOW see Balay;Buck-34;George-
  10-11-113;William-9(2)-22-151
BANKS Elijah-24;John-134;Thomas-
  126-176;William-80
BANTA David-67-74-208
BARBER Allen-23-24;David-62;Hiram-
  12-212;Lucius-36-42-45-99-100-
  101-106(2)-107(2)-119(2)-120;
  Nancy-60;Sarah-64
BAREKMAN Abraham-99(2);Henry-100-
  105;Isaac-99;John-103;Joshua-
  100;Peter-100
BARKER Andrew-74;Elias-66-82-83-
  93;Jesse-83-90(2);John-65-82-83-
  162-232;Obadiah-181-202(2);Thom-
  as-46-201-202;William-67-73
BARKLEY Edward-144;Lazarus-143
BARLOW John-83-207
BARNES see Bourne,Byrne,Burnes;
  Alexander-228;David-59-228;Eli-
  133;Elisha-183;George-133;Hugh-
  209;James-42-51(3)-227;Jehu-132;
  Jesse-183;John-200;Joshua-132;
  Robert-229;Samuel-228;Thomas-132
BARNETT David-126;George-214;Ja-
  mes-91-215;John-124;Thomas-90-
  91;Vincent-99
BARNEY Benjamin-191
BARR Hugh-19-30(2)-31-34-110;Ja-
  mes-28;John-13-15-19-89-110;Rob-
  ert-19-31;William-68
BARRETT Anderson-227;Gates-227;
  John-62;Lucinda-62;Richard-59;
  Richmon-224;Robert-227;Samuel-
  62;Spencer-227;Squire-227;Wil-
  liam-62(2);Wilson-227
BARROIS John-106;Lambert-105;
  Toussaint-106
BARTHOLOMEW Mr.-210
BARTL Florian-155
BARTLEY Charles-110-117
BARTLOW John-102
BARTON see Burton;John-124;Phil-
  ip-35-107;Richard-124
BARYEAR George-101-122;Samuel-122
BASCOM Alfred-43
BASS Howell-76;James-212;John-127-
  129;Jonathan-129;Jordan-76;
  Moses-127-128
BATCHELOR James-24;John-170;Sam-
  uel-125-153;William-21-32-50-51-
  101

BATEMAN see Boatman;Greenberry-
BATES George-152   116
BATHERTON David-193
BATTHUS John-20.   224
BATTLE Henry-213-214/;Newit-224
BAUGH Ephraim-186;Frederick-46;
  Gainer-184;Henry-187;John-172;
  Joseph-186;Samuel-146-157-169;
  William-172-173
BAVELLET Francis-103
BAXTER Franklin-161
BAYARD John-157-167-182
BEACH Levi-213
BEAIS Jacob-186-188-190-191-193
BEARD John-220;Thomas-24
BEASLEY Aaron-136;Anderson-130-
  132;Ephraim-132;George-132;Har-
  dy-61-62;Harrison-149;Jackson-
  167;James-129-132;Jesse-129-132;
  Joseph-75;Richard-126;Silas-149;
  Thomas-62
BEATTY Edward-15;James-148-156-
  234
BEAVERS Charles-138;Isaac-133;Ja-
  mes-133;Milton-132;William-132
BECK Henry-223-230;John-223-227;
  Lewis-36-157-224;Preston-134(2)-
  135(3)
BECKES Benjamin-101-102-103(3)-
  109-118;Caleb-109;Parmenas-109
BECKETT John-13(2)-19;Samuel-
  13(2)-14;William-13-17-19
BEDELL Daniel-100;Elias-44-107;
  Moses-71;Samuel-98
BEDWELL Catherine-130
BEE Albert-221
BEEM Richard-189
BEESON Benjamin-131
BEGEMANN Conrad-113;Herman-112;
  William-113
BELDING Stephen 30-34-102
BELL Hiram-58;John-125;Tarlton-
  194;Thomas-60-73;William-118
BELLAS Charles-71
BELLWOOD Alfred-100(2)
BELOAT George-85;James-83
BEMOUNT Andrew-40
BENEDICT Reuben-124
BENEDU(?) Jesse-205
BENEFIEL John-39-40-41;Robert-
  118-120
BENHAM Anthony-33;William-50
BENJAMIN Ezekiel-16
BENNETT James-193;John-185-186;
  Lucy-167;Mathias-49;Robert-149-
  167;Samuel-144-149;Sarah-167;

William-192
BENNINGTON see Pennington;James-
  207;John-33-41-185;Moses-29;
  Reuben-41
BENSON David-72;John-72
BERKSHIRE Charles-195;Cornelius-
  28;John-21
BERLIN John-55
BERLITZ Philip-14
BERRY Baldwin-165;James-38;John-
  34-194-198(2)-199-208;Joseph-
  197-199;Matthias-208;William-18-
  25-155-197-198
BESING see Bising, Busing
BESSIE William-154(2)
BETTERHOUSE John-195
BICKNELL Alfred-42;James-109;
  John-109;Munfred-109;Samuel-109
BIGELOW Abel-205
BIGGER John-204-210;William-185-
  189
BIGGS Thomas-127;Thompson-137
BIGHAM Eli-61-65;James-65
BIIBO William-193
BILDERBACK David-234;John-104;Sam-
  uel-224-230;Thomas-225
BILLINGS Thomas-154;William-130(2
BINKLEY Thomas-103
BIONS Harrison-36
BISHOP William-90
BISING see Busing;Frederick-92
BITTROLFF John-65
BIVENS Richard-135
BIXLER John-95
BLACK Agnes-74;Alexander-219;Dav-
  id-231;George-71-72;Henry-231(2)
  James-233;John-58-231(2);Robert-
  105-222;Samuel-231;Sarah-73;Wil-
  liam-222-231(2)
BLACKBURN Cyrus-144;Mathew-40-42;
  Milton-144;Samuel-144
BLACKFORD Samuel-233
BLACKWELL Ezekiel-127-128-130-132
  134-136-138;Garrett-143;Lewis-
  132;Samuel-128
BLADES James-174
BLAGRAVE Edwin-152
BLAIR see Blane;Enos-197;James-9-
  125-200;Josiah-159;LaFayette-197
  Robert-208-210;Thomas-200;Wil-
  liam-124-125-133-161(2)
BLAKE Austin-170;John-169;William
  160;Willoby-159
BLANE see Blair;John-208
BLASLEY Charles-128

BLAZE John-223-227
BLEDSOE William-164
BLENIES Daniel-97-215
BLEVINS Hezekiah-134;James-114-
117-118-125-134;John-118-132;
Samuel-134-176
BLIZZARD Thomas-120
BLOXSOM James-101
BLYTHE A.-69;James-94
BOARD Philip-104
BOARDMAN James-24;William-23
BOATMAN see Bateman;George-120
BOBBITT Elijah-180(2)
BOBERYER John-115
BODEL Hugh-180
BOICOURT Samuel-64-69. Bowling
BOLIN Phebe-229;Robert-232;see/
BOMBERGER see Boberyer
BOND George-167;James-160;John-
124(2)
BONER see Bruner;George-157
BONEWITS Jacob-96
BONHOMME John-106-107;Mitchell-/
BONNER John-232;Thomas-204. 106/
BOOKER William-34-35-75
BOONE Elijah-139-142;Jeremiah-
139;Noah-139-172-175
BOOS Michael-35
BOOTH George-165
BORDERS Henry-216-226(2);John-218
BOREN see Boring;Evans-85;Ezek-
iel-94(2);John-84-86-94-95(2);
Nicholas-84;Samuel-94-95;Tarle-
ton-216-217-226;Uriah-92
BORIFF Samuel-195;William-195
BORING see Boren;George-82
BORLAND David-183;Edward-194;
Francis-61;George-193;James-193-
195-197-202;John-208;Matthew-37-
135
BOSWELL Craven-60;Henry-55;James-
55;Nancy-55;William-55
BOTTS Benjamin-209
BOURNE see Barnes,Byrne,Burnes;
Moses-117;Thomas-116;William-117
BOURY John-30
BOUSMAN John-156
BOUTS Philip-76
BOWDEN see Boyden;Absalom-169;Is-
aac-169;James-167;John-169;
William-132   154
BOWEN see Bower;Tavner-115;Wyatt-
BOWER see Bowen;Adam-198-199-200;
Edward-229;John-39-115;Joseph-
225;229;Solomon-205;Stephen-229
BOWLES Augustus-191

BOWLING see Bolin;William-26
BOWMAN Booker-24;George-53-209;
Henry-183;James-184;Jonathan-224
Michael-171;Pleasant-171-179-183
Shadrach-31;Septima-179-183;
William-171-172-183
BOX Killis-131
BOYCE William-76-77
BOYD Isaac-135-141;John-23-135-
136-163;Samuel-142
BOYDEN see Bowden;David-170;Wil-
liam-170
BOYER Gabriel-106;Lewis-106
BRACHER Meredith-57   225
BRADBURY Heddy-151;Joel-153;John-
BRADFORD George-34;John-35;Jos-
eph-34;William-34-35-204
BRADLEY see Brady;Francis-17-30;
James-25-170-173;Jesse-232;Lew-
is-70;Patrick-17-18-31
BRADSHAW Elijah-172;Robert-77-230
BRADY see Bradley;Patrick-26-
27(2);William-209
BRAM(?) Andrew-215
BRAMBLE Levin-26
BRANAM Jonathan-200
BRASSFIELD Mary-192
BRATTAIN Benjamin-30;James-28;
John-17;Robert-27-51;William-35
BRAWAND Christopher 172
BRAWDES James-25
BRAXTON Thomas-142
BRAY John-39-42-50-51;Littleberry
205;Macager-204;Nathan-205
BRAZELTON David-67;John-65;Wil-
liam-66
BREADING James-58-121;Nathaniel-
215;Richard-188;William-122
BREED Rufus-43-50-59-62-76-108(2)
109-112(2)-115-116-230
BREEDLOVE Abraham-72;Nathan-62
BRENTLINGER Jonathan-115
BRENTON Adam-185-188-205;Henry-
216-217;James-211-216-222-231;
John-222-225-226;Mary-217;Newton
222-231;Peter-217-224;Robert-219
222-225-226-229-230;Wesley-220
BRESSIE see Bessie
BRETT Martin-160;Patrick-35
BREWER Charles-110;Elizabeth-133;
George-13-17;Mark-18-19;Nancy-
151;Thomas-30(2)
BREWSTER Benjamin-225;Charles-156
Elijah-221;James-221;Solomon-221
Thomas-222

BRICKER Hiram-46
BRIDGES Edmund-176;Henry-171-172;
  Isaac-150-176;James-184;Joel-
  141;John-171-176;Jonathan-150-
  176;Walter-69
BRIDWELL Cuthbert-149;Doctor-149;.
  George-149
BRIGHAM see Bigham
BRIGHT David-210;Jacob-221-222
BRILES Allen-94;James-95
BRINEGAR Benjamin-144
BRINER John-48
BRISCOE Jeremiah-208;John-188-
  193-198-199   134
BRISTOW Payton-135-183;William-/
BRITTINGHAM Dycy-121;George-227;
  Lucy-56;Thomas-227
BROADS see Brawdes
BROCK Allen-177;Caleb-9-10-11;
  John-178;Levi-177-179
BROCKMAN James-228
BROKAW Abraham-78-81;Peter-79
BRONSON William-222
BROGUE Nathan-120
BROOKS John-177-204;Thomas-28-
  156-163(2)-173
BROSE Mary-93
BROTHERS David-85;Hudson-84;James-
  82-84;John-84-94;Thomas-21;
  William-85-86
BROWER Union-114
BROWN Abner-170;Asaph-70;B.-69;
  Bazil-64;Commodore-61-221;Char-
  les-21-24;Dixon-154-137-138;Geo-
  rge-172(2)-180;Henry-144;James-
  10-30;Jeremiah-157;Jesse-143;
  John-52(2)-56-157;Joseph-30-55-
  59-61-62-64-65-93-100-104-173-
  230;Lee-206;Martin-146;Perry-61-
  221;Richard-181(2);Rufus-162;
  Samuel-144-167-179;Trulove-140-
  171-173-178-183;William-52(2)-
  72-117-141-164-180-184-208
BROWNING David-199-207;Nathaniel-
  200;Richard-139;Thomas-41-79-81
BROWNLEE George-55;Robert-55-76
BRUCE Alexander-28-32;Isaac-44;
  Squire-44(2);Spier-44;William-
BRULER see DeBruler.   44(2)
BRUMFIELD James-85
BRUMMIT Bonner-195;James-195;
  Samuel-47;William-47
BRUNER see Boner;Abraham-57-122;
  Charles-154;Christian-35-161;Da-
  vid-126;Elias-188(2);Frederick-
  57-58;George-35;Hickman-159;

Jacob-143-146;John-57;Michael-
  127;Nicholas-144
BRUTE Simon-26-105-111
BRYANT James-133-160-233;Jesse-
  225;Robert-132-133
BUCHANAN James-143-146
BUCKELS Robert-108;William-42
BUCKNER James-24;Jesse-51(2);John-
  122;Richard-143
BUDDERBACK Jacob-201
BUDYARD see Rudyard
BUFFINGTON Samuel-172-174
BUGHER Abraham-101;Augustus-40-41
BULLITT C.&T.-128-201-205-206-209
BULTMAN Henry-106
BUMP Martin-73;Moses-73
BUNCH James-138-150;John-150-185
BUNGER John-197-198;Joseph-197
BUNNELL Abigail-32;Jacob-34-44
BUNTING Samuel-109(2)
BURCH Achilles-189;Charles-189;El-
  ijah-189;George-9;Henry-189;Ja-
  mes-195;Joel-189;John-29-32-40-
  41-189(2);Levi-189;Martin-231;
  William-12-57-111-156-199-201-207
BURCHFIELD Thomas-61(2)
BURDEN John-113
BURDETT James-230
BURGEN Isaac-25-27
BURGEST Esau-140
BURGET George-40
BURK Edmund-196;Elisha-11(2);Elna-
  than-140;Hulick-11(2);John-196;
  William-196-200
BURKART George-185;Henry-185;
  Leonard-218
BURKETT John-58
BURNES see Barnes,Bourne,Byrne;
  James-113
BURNETT Stephen-110;Thomas-151
BURNSIDE Andrew-113
BUROY(?) Andrew-101
BURRIS Charles-43;David-156;James-
  15-113;Jesse-19;John-13-14;Over-
  ton-15;Peter-13-27-28;Rice-15;
  Robert-30-32(2);Thomas-13-32
BURROWS Richard-173
BURTON see Barton;Alfred-124;Al-
  len-130;Amos-74;Anderson-130;Ba-
  zil-75;Benjamin-75;Charles-145;
  David-90-124-145;Eli-130-133;El-
  isha-149;Emsley-179;Henry-133;Is-
  om-133;Jackson-125;John-124-125-
  129-208-210(2);Levi-75;Richard-
  123;Robert-123;Thomas-133;Thom-
  son-132;Wiley-181;William-92-123-

124(2)-150-183-184;Young-123-
130;Zachariah-124
BURRUCKER George-78
BUSHA Amable-103-106;Francis-
106(2);John-104(2)-106;Lawrence-
104(2);Vital-104(2)
BUSING see Bising;Henry-92
BUSKIRK Abraham-201-202;Isaac-
148-150-208;James-207;John-201-
202-207;Michael-186-201-202;
Thomas-150-201-208
BUTCHER Levi-149-182-183;Richard-
191;Solomon-195
BUTLER Alexander-137;Calvin-31-
36;Charles-33-36-44-112;Daniel-
125;John-167-217-223;Lemuel-137;
Thomas-154
BUZZARD David-209
BYERS George-92;Gottlieb-37;John-
BYNUM James-114   66
BYRUM Lewis-125
BYRD Gray-127;Thomas-229
BYRNE see Barnes,Bourne,Burnes;
John-82-234;Solomon-69

C see K & G
CABASIER see Calasier
CABBAGE John-233
CAHAN John-14
CAHASIER see Calasier
CAHILL Thomas-30-31-32;William-13
CAIN George-115;Michael-19
CALASIER Peter-106;Pierre-103
CALDWELL Harriet-106;James-201;
John-10-88-106;Mary-106;Nathan-
iel-81 ;Samuel-187-199-204
CALFFLY William-43
CALL Dennis-141
CALLAHAN Isaac-173
CALVERT Patrick-95
CALVIN Elisha-218;Jonathan-37-
163-171-173-175
CAMBERN(?) James-129
CAMMACK Michael-122
CAMPAYNOTTE Pierre-106
CAMPBELL Andrew-136;Archibald-
201-212-215-218;Elihu-233;James-
18-31-216(2)-217;John-199;Jos-
eph-153;Perry-216;Robert-140;
William-102-211
CANADA Elisha-163
CANADAY see Kennedy
CANNON James-159-162;John-24-98-
159-174;Joseph-162-167;William-
159-174-182
CARBAUGH Jacob-91;John-91-92

CARDINAL James-105;Joseph-104-10
CAREY Anthony-104-105;Ezra-122;
John-105;Joseph-105;Michael-105
CARLISLE Joseph-46
CARLON Barnet-233
CARLTON Ambrose-204;William-72(2
86;208
CARMICHAEL Alexander-190;Ambrose
179;Andrew-165;Archibald-190;Ja
mes-191(2);Joseph-190;Peter-164
Richard-191;Starling-190;Thomas
192;William-128-131-136
CARNAHAN James-16-21-23-25-31;Ro
ert-16;Wilson-17(2)
CARNAN Robert-106
CARPENTER Alvin-59-91;David-189-
190;Willard-60-63-74-80-220-225
229-230-231;William-59
CARR Absalom-228;George-176;John
197-199;Thomas-191;William-191
CARRICO John-173;Joseph-27(2)
CARRITHERS Andrew-55
CARROLL Patrick-103-106(2)-107;
Peter-112;William-41-197
CARTER see McCarter;David-144-14
Davidson-123;Jesse-213-221;Joel
39;John-55-93-190;Miles-125;Mos
es-48;Othias-196-205;Rane-95;Th
mas-178-190-194;William-192(2)
CARTIER Anthony-105
CARTWRIGHT see Cutright;Pressley
90;Robert-184
CASBOLT Polly-64;Robert-64
CASE Abraham-44;Ebenezer-211;Jac
ob-104;John-11-24-211;Joseph-10
211;T.-217
CASEY William-229
CASH Jeremiah-87;John-73
CASSELBERRY Isaac-90
CASSIDY Francis-25-34-35-36-37;
John-19;Luke-114-115
CASTLEMAN Jacob-145-146(3)
CASTLES John-14
CASTO Jonathan-39;Noah-39
CATER Joseph-95
CATHER Sims-139;William-138-139-
CATLIN Daniel-56-68·   14
CATT Amos-218;Bartley-218;Daniel
217;Ervin-218;George-218(2);Hen
ry-217;Isaac-104;John-52-218;Le
is-52;Michael-98;Philip-217(2);
Rebecca-104;Sarah-99;William-99
CATTRON Zachariah-176
CAUDLE William-122
CAUGHRAN see Cochran

CAUSEY Zebedee-118
CAVANAUGH B.T.-58;Pierce-19
CAVENESS Sion-37
CAWOOD John-43-114;Moses-43-44(2)-
  113(2)-114;Smallwood-40-41;
  Smith-50
CAWSON see Clawson
CECIL see Cissell
CHADD Joseph-10;Samuel-9-10;
  William-32-35
CHADWICK Eli-206
CHAEWIN(?) Pierre-198;Simon-202
CHAFFEE Onetus-68
CHAFFIN Edward-94(2);Edwin-85
CHALMERS Peter-99;William-87
CHAMBERLAIN Asahel-168-169
CHAMBERS Alexander-114-116;Ander-
  son-187;Andrew-188-226;Anthony-
  186-187(2);Arthur-219;David-
  186(2)-187-206(2);George-209;Ja-
  mes-108-113-114;John-108-113(2)-
  114-187(4)-226;Joseph-66-113-
  114-187;Levi-113-116;Norman-66;
  Samuel-114-199;Silas-181-182;
  Thomas-115;Wesley-187;William-
  144-186-187(2)-188;Zacheus-209
CHAMBEY Samuel-116
CHAMNESS Joel-31;Samuel-31-35
CHANDLER Isaac-49;John-14;Joseph-
  156;Nathan-45;William-185-186-
  195
CHANEY Charles-98;Elijah-45;John-
  45;Mark-45;William-45
CHAPMAN Edmund-222;Elijah-12-22-
  23-24-25(2)-212;Ezra-121;George-
  133-159-162;James-23;John-132;
  Justus-10;Mary-132;Rezin-20;Tho-
  mas-65-67;William-10-11(2)-22-
  24-25(2)-212-215
CHAPPELL Elizabeth-214;Jacob-219;
  Joab-212;Josiah-214;Stephen-213/
CHANDLEY Rezin-215.   (2)/
CHARTIC Francis-197
CHASTAIN Fleming-166-179(2);
  Isaac-167
CHATTIN John-152
CHAWIN see Chaewin
CHERRY David-205
CHESTER Robert-12
CHESTNUT Abraham-140;Benjamin-
  140(2)-142;James-135-144-149;
  John-137-140-149-176;Julius-140;
  William-136-176(2)
CHEW James-213;Jane-213;Joseph-
  213-214-220;Marcellus-213
CHILDRESS Joshua-123;Thomas-62

CHILDS Roland-182
CHISSENHALL Dolly-233
CHITTENDON Homer-67;William-64
CHRIST Jacob-166; see Crist
CHRISTIAN Thomas-168-173(2)
CHRISTY John-55-63
CHURCH Samuel-89
CISSELL James-26-166;Thomas-164
CLARE John-27
CLARK Alexander-147-154-198;Alva-
  28-166;Andrew-91;Asher-159;Ben-
  jamin-229;Braxter-84-86;Caleb-
  118;Cornelius-66-68;Darwin-159-
  170;David-110;Dennis-30-33;Eli-
  jah-119;George-91-118;Gustavus-
  37;Jacob-135;James-26-154-193-
  199;Jeffrey-130-169;John-20-111-
  155;Jonathan-155;Joseph-85;Levin-
  110(2);Mathew-27-64;Nathaniel-
  209;Peter-18;Randolph-89;Robert-
  45-48-186;Samuel-155;Vachel-86;
  William-117-155-225
CLAWSON James-47-94-95-169-173-
CLAY Mat-204.   175/
CLAYCOMB Catherine-105;Frederick-
  105;Lucretia-105
CLAYPOOLE George-100
CLAYTON Josiah-220
CLEARY Michael-25;William-41
CLEMENTS Basil-171(3)-173-174-175;
  Benjamin-163;John-66;Patrick-
  171(2)-173;Sarah-174;William-37-
  171-173
CLENDENIN James-187
CLEVELAND Ezer-127-160(2);Marion-
  124;Marvin-124
CLEVER Simon-184
CLIFFORD Allen-222-233
CLIFFT Daniel-10-11;George-10
CLIFTON Henry-34-164;Nathan-35
CLINE Henry-227
CLINTON Allen-155;John-230
CLOIN Lewis-228
CLONENGER Philemon-103
CLUTTER Eneas-26
COAN see Conn;Andrew-11;Isaac-212;
  Stephen-196;William-11
COATNEY Finney-194
COATS Simpson-149-150
COBBS Henry-30;Jesse-49-50;Samuel-
  176;Semer-150;Thomas-39-49-50-51-
  149;William-42-50
COCHRAN see Cockrum;George-9-125;
  James-111-159;John-16-182;Luther-
  111;William-9-152-139-142-157
COCKINGHOUR George-127

COCKRUM see Cockran;Columbus-59;
  James-59-60(2)-61(2)-63-228-230;
  Jordan-62
COFFEY Alfred-198;Archelaus-204;
  Lewis-203
COHEN see Coan,Conn
COKER Aaron-233
COLBERT Daniel-32;Jesse-12;Levi-
  10;Tolever-11
COLE John-13-161
COLEMAN Alexander-125-127-133;
  Burrille-34;Christopher-24(2);
  Conrad-232;David-11-12-18;David-
  son-125;Henry-60-62-231;Jesse-
  215;John-18-24-77-231;Page-59;
  Philip-231;S.-206-210;Samuel-
  231;William-53-231(3)
COLLIER Hezekiah-177(2)
COLLINS Abel-102;Absalom-96;Com-
  adore-127;David-102;George-190;
  Hiram-102;Isaac-127;John-15-102-
  111-127-152-156-199;Joseph-
  103(2);Josiah-127;Lucy-158;Mah-
  lon-127;Solomon-103;Thomas-59
COLVIN Elisha-217;Fielding-53-
  226;John-227;Joseph-226;Richard-
  53
COMBS Bird-190;Charles-190;Mar-
  tin-190; see Coombs
COMER see Conner;Daniel-21;Sam-
  uel-16
COMMARLE Philip-96
COMPTON Husleton-195;Joseph-75;
  Kenneth-79
COMSTOCK William-113
CONDER David-191;Greenberry-191;
  Joseph-182
CONDIEF George-207
CONDRON Michael-19-20
CONGER John-98;Jonathan-218;Levi-
  218;Sebastian-98-217;William-218
CONLIN Thomas-13
CONN see Coan;Andrew-101-213;
  Hiram-212
CONNELL Harrison-151-155;Patrick-
  12;Susannah-158;Thomas-158;Wil-
  liam-151
CONNELLY Alexander-128;Benjamin-
  128;Constantine-130;Elijah-128;
  Henry-132;James-15-41(2);Joel-
  128-132;John-132;Joseph-128-129;
  Josiah-127-132-134;Michael-13;
  William-123-125-127-132
CONNER see Comer;Alexander-78-79-
  83;Henry-91;John-117-119;Mich-
  ael-31;Samuel-24

CONQUEST Richard-167
CONRAD Daniel-216;Elizabeth-212;
  George-212;James-212;John-43(2)-
  213(2)-216(2);Solomon-117
COOK see Crooks;Andrew-109;George-
  164;Henry-42;Nicholas-201;Philip-
  108;William-37-38-135-164-202;
  Willis-37-38
COOMBS see Combs;Benjamin-48
COOPER A.J.-91;Absalom-175-176-
  180-181-195;Benjamin-177-179;Eli-
  zabeth-154;Henry-27;Isaac-107;
  Joseph-178
COOTER John-208
COPELIN Elias-127
COPUS John-44-45
CORBETT William-173
CORBEY William-173
CORBIN Albert-176;James-140-176;
  Thomas-181
CORDER Elijah-124;John-204;Ste-
  phen-204
CORN Andrew-222;Benjamin-222;Da-
  vid-230;Edward-229;James-222;
  William-229-233
CORNOYER Ambrose-104;Pierre-104
CORNWELL George-56
CORRELL Andrew-100;Joseph-100
CORRY see Curry;Samuel-80-81
CORTRIGHT see Kirtright
COSBY see Cosey;Abner-18;Charles-
  20-22;Jacob-18;James-18;Overton-
  15-18-22(2);Samuel-71
COSLUIT James-44
COSNER Andrew-208;Henry-132-134-
  208/
COTTER Hugh-33.
COTTON Asa-204;Elonzo-117
COUGHLAN James-12-28
COULTER Charles-126;Elijah-63;Gid-
  eon-132-134(2);John-37-126-132-
  134;Lemuel-37-126;Nathaniel-126;
  Thomas-132
COURTNEY James-46-47;Robert-49
COUTCHMAN Andrew-44;Benjamin-44;
  George-44
COVEY George-142-143;William-93
COX Absalom-178(2);Alexander-141;
  Benjamin-108;Boone-180;Curtis-178
  David-123;Enoch-26;Ephraim-178;
  Hezekiah-220;Isaac-166-180-220;
  James-108(2)-115-164;Jesse-117;
  Joab-167;John-61-108(2)-124-166;
  Jonathan-109-113;Leonard-42;Mil-
  es-166;Oliver-127-128;Phineas-48
  50;Rachel-108;Troy-124-130;Wash-
  ington-123-124-130;William-109-
  116-220(2)

-242-

CRABB see Grubb
CRABS Ellen-24;Jacob-22;Jesse-23-
101;Milton-22-102
CRAIG Elijah-179;John-140-179;
Wallace-166;William-180-188
CRAMER Philip-19
CRANE Isaac-174;James-139-189;
John-190;Nathaniel-190;Richard-
162-174(2)-197;Samuel-146;Wil-
liam-174
CRAVENS Vachel-149;William-59
CRAWFORD Andrew-55;Holly-59;Sam-
uel-36;William-188
CRAYS William-166
CRAYTON Thomas-216;William-216
CREE Sarah-202
CREEK Gillison-91;Isom-88;Jacob-
88-89;Pearson-71-88;Rumzy-91;
Washington-88-91
CRENY Benjamin-156
CREWS see Cruse
CRIST John-97; see Christ
CRISWELL Thomas-77
CROAN John-155
CROCK see Crooks;David-99;Jane-
98;John-98
CROCKER Orion-197-198
CROCKETT Jackson-189
CROOK see Cook,Crock;George-108-
162-168;John-23-139;Joseph-116;
Ozias-36(2)-174;Sophronia-150;
William-148
CROSBY John-110
CROSNORE Jacob-126
CROSS Featherton-87;James-219-
220;Joseph-212;William-17
CROSSER Charles-170
CROUCHER Andrew-201
CROW Daniel-222-225;Henry-53-99;
James-217-225-227;Jason-53;John-
52-217-225-231;Joseph-66-100;
Mary-225;Robert-97;William-64-
97;Winston-124.
CROWLEY Daniel-73;James-90-91
CRUM Conrad-58;Jacob-191;John-
189-190-191-193
CRUMP Granville-134
CRUSE Christian-92;Elijah-150;
Frederick-92;Henry-93-161;Robert-
CRUTCHFIELD James-217.   19/
CULBERTSON Andrew-57-122;George-
133;John-102-132-133;Joseph-
21(2)-128-131-136;Josiah-34-44
CULLY James-143-144-185
CUMMINGS Charles-215;David-210;
James-215-217;Jesse-157;John-

215;Nathaniel-215;Thomas-215;
William-96-215
CUNNINGHAM Andrew-52;Green-52;Jon-
athan-48;Michael-25;Samuel-53;
Stewart-55;Thomas-47;William-47-
CUPPS John-137.   48/
CUPPY John-150;William-149
CURL William-143-187-188
CURRANT James-169
CURRY see Corry;James-85;John-121;
Jonathan-61-62;Miles-120;William-
CURTIS Daniel-121;William-227./193
CUSHMAN Alvan-156
CUTLER Jacob-196-203-206.   .232
CUTRIGHT see Cartwright;William-/

D see T
DAGGETT Eleazer-202
DAGLEY Joseph-208
DAILY Thomas-157
DALE Isaac-110
DAMRELL Edmund-165
DANIEL Daniel-168;Richard-55-67;
Stewart-132;William-56-69
DANT James-26-31;William-31
DARNALL John-139
DART Joseph-100
DARTING Adam-143-185-206
DASH Andrew-92
DAUGHERTY George-197;Henry-160;
Isom-164;James-136;Joel-51;John-
36-39;Joseph-29-41;Milton-137;
Robert-137-138;Samuel-137-138;
William-91-136-137-161-164;Willis
DAVENPORT William-109-219. /160
DAVIS Aaron-127-128;Abijah-73;Ab-
ner-12-148;Adam-146;Alfred-12-31-
225;Andrew-128;Benjamin-28;Blu-
ford-124;Daniel-128;David-193-
231;Elisha-28;Emanuel-153;Enoch-
17-123-129-130(2);Frederick-175;
George-95(2);Hiram-163;Jacob-114;
James-78-137-196-205;Jeremiah-
116;Jesse-89-90-147-231;Joel-
89(2)-90;John-62-90-107-153-154-
179-207-231-234;Jonathan-100;Lem-
uel-224;Lewis-12-28;Malcolm-180;
Marine-126;Nicholas-115;Philip-
28-165-166;Ransom-158;Redwine-91;
Reuben-147-149;Robert-12-16-89(3)
90;Russell-164-166;Samuel-66;Sol-
omon-84;Susan-160;Thomas-129;War-
ner-147-150;William-45-88-89(3)-
91-95-132-154-164-194
DAVISSON Elijah-53-54;Frederick-
79;Jane-227;John-11(2)-63-64-153-

224-226;Joseph-53-54-63-64-202-
218(2)-222-227;Josiah-218;Wil-
liam-219-228
DAWES Charles-107
DAWSON Benjamin-149;Burdel-197;
John-47-56;Shelton-56;Smith-56;
Wiley-133
DAY Benjamin-80;Levi-82;Mark-57;
Morgan-28-158-165;Peter-99;Pres-
ley-15-16;Reuben-154;Wareum-82;
Wiley-57;William-154
DEAN George-220-221-225-229(2)-
230;Josiah-79;Matthew-19
DEARING Esau-221;Thomas-10-20
DEARMIN James-202
DeBRULER Charles-213;Greenfield-
213;Harbert-215;Wesley-212;Wil-
liam-211-213-219
DECKARD Andrew-186;David-186;Hen-
ry-165;Hezekiah-186;Jacob-143-
186;Jesse-188;John-142-186;Mich-
ael-186;William-143
DECKER see McDecker;Abner-165;Ab-
raham-122;Adam-121;Alfred-105;
Christian-115;Elizabeth-52;Hir-
am-104;Jacob-228;John-57(2)-98-
224-228;Johnson-218;Morgan-217;
Prestly-98;Ransom-52;Sarah-218;
Thomas-52;William-218
DEDMAN Franklin-225;Samuel-225-
226(2);William-226
DEDRICK Christian-24-25;Henry-
214;Lucas-43(2);Parker-43;Rich-
ard-211
DEFENDALL Abraham-229;John-224-
226(3)-228;Joseph-224;Philip-
DEJARNATT Ford-224.   226/
De La HAILANDIERE Celestine-20-
DELAMATER Ralph-168   105/
DELANEY Patrick-20
DELAP Robert-203
DELINGER Joseph-46
DELISLE Charles-104
DELK James-20
DELORIER John-106;Andrew-106;Jos-
DEMAREE Cornelius-195.   eph-106
DEMOSS Isaac-114;William-15
DEMOTT Lawrence-219
DENBO Robert-71
DENBY Henry-90
DENISTON Michael-151;William-151
DENNING James-168;Job-40;Robert-
167;Valentine-224;William-224
DENNIS Beverly-49-50;Mark-118
DENNO Pierre-106
DENNY Benoni-168-206;Joseph-125-

153;William-124-125-154
DENSON James-134-138-177;Joshua-
216;Tolbert-216
DENT John-227
DENTON Andrew-167-170;James-169
DePAUW John-10-11
DEPPE Anthony-115
DEPRIEST John-78-82;William-76-78-
DEPUE Jacob-194   81/
DERRY Jonathan-127
DESER Anthony-18
DESKINS William-197-205   132
DEVER Jesse-194;Nathan-132;Samuel-
DEVIN Alexander-57-58-65-68;James-
62(2)-74;John-60-62-63;Joseph-
56-57-58
DeVORE Christopher-208;Henry-209;
John-104-105
DEWEES Thomas-141-177
DEWEY Charles-11
DICK see Dirk;Alexander-67;David-
86;James-52-67;Thomas-99
DICKENS James-161
DICKERSON Daniel-12;George-167-
172-173;Henry-126;Isaac-30;John-
126;Teague-156;William-30
DICKEY Ebenezer-202;Ephraim-68-223
DICKMIRE Arnold-92;Henry-92
DICKS Zacharias-191
DIDRI John-106
DILL see McDill;Alexander-61;Phil-
emon-60;Solomon-60-61;William-62
DILLARD William-140
DILLBECK Abraham-93
DILLEY James-169-170
DILLON Isaac-50;James-194;John-
152-181;Jonathan-53;William-49-
50-111
DIMICK William-60-63-64-67
DIRK see Dick;James-99
DISHMAN John-150-177
DITTEMORE Thomas-207
DIXON George-111;Henry-111;Joseph-
111;Silas-131;Solomon-49;Stephen-
DOANE David-158;Jehu-132.   112
DOBBINS John-226
DOBSON James-172;John-172
DODDS Samuel-193-198;William-229
DODDRILL see Toddrill
DODSON Elijah-179;John-225;Lam-
beth-129;Reuben-128;Richard-179
DOKE James-170(2)
DOLLARHIDE Evin-194
DONAHUE Charles-9;Daniel-168(2);
James-15-27(2)-172-173;Michael-
129;

Terry-15

DONALDSON John-28-136;Robert-144;
  Stephen-28;Thomas-21-22-24;Wil-
  liam-181
DONICA Caswell-143;Thomas-178
DONOVAN Timothy-20
DORRELL James-61
DORSETT John-170;Thomas-159-160
DOTTON John-150
DOUGHTEN William-226
DOUGLASS Albert-84-93;Earl-125-
  153;Fanny-161;Isaac-83-84(2)-85;
  Jesse-84;John-83;Jonathan-119(2);
  William-161
DOUTHITT John-171;Robert-167-171
DOWDEN James-207;Otho-160;William-
  109-207
DOWELL James-203
DOWNEY James-61;John-13-14-71-
  156;Michael-158;Thomas-14
DOWNING Alexander-85;Charles-156;
  James-18
DOWNS Elizabeth-167;John-168
DOYLE John-37-38
DRAKE Benjamin-128-130-206;Jacob-
  11(2);James-66(2)-77-99-111;
  John-164-165(2);Samuel-172
DRULLINGER Wilson-109
DRURY Washington-38
DRYDEN John-144
DUBOISE Francoise-105;Toissant-68
DUCKWORTH Elijah-118;Robert-117
DUELL see Terrell,Tewell;Sarah-
  157
DUFF Elijah-93;Jackson-93;Jos-
  eph-61-93(2)
DUFFIELD Thomas-186-188
DUFREN Ellen-101
DUFFY Patrick-19
DUGAN George-69;Samuel-68
DULEN Daniel-181
DUNCAN Andrew-61;David-180-183;
  Greenberry-69-71-72;Jacob-209;
  James-71;John-137-140(2)-150(2);
  Joshua-85(2);Shadrach-54;William-
  61-62-112-124-181-209
DUNGY John-168
DUNLAP Robert-170
DUNN Andrew-108;Bridget-37;George-
  139;Isaac-165;James-38-51;John-
  199;Samuel-193;Thomas-37;William-
  158;Williamson-169-204;Zephaniah-
  49;*George-135
DUNNING James-203-204;John-105-
  200(2);Paris-194;Rachel-200;Sam-
  uel-217;William-193

DUPRE Lewis-105
DURHAM John-187
DYE Ely-148;Hiram-35;Kenneth-148-
  149;Orange-149
DYER Isaac-223;Joel-203

EAGLE George-33;John-44
EANIS John-54; see Eaves
EARNEST Henry-47
EAST Bailey-195;Hughes-191;Jesse-
  147-191;Joseph-147-192;Thomas-
  191-192(2);William-191
EATON James-89;John-181;Thomas-
  169-182;William-166-169
EAVES see Eanis;Armstead-180
EBERWINE Ferdinand-103-105
ECKERT Moses-43
EDCLINE John-106
EDDINGTON Isham-179
EDDS Elijah-29-30;Isham-142;James-
  205;Samuel-196;William-142
EDMONDSON James-220;John-178-
  183(2);Solomon-183;Thomas-159-
  169-170;William-203
EDMUND Paul-200
EDRINGTON Silas-67-74
EDSON Homer-105
EDWARDS Abel-192;Daniel-151;David-
  130;Edward-130-169;Francis-132;
  Henderson-130;Henry-22-23(2);
  Hugh-19;Isaac-133-160;James-98-
  99-102;John-18-22-23-25-119-120-
  125-130-183;Joseph-21;Lemuel-101;
  Nancy-192;Thomas-37(2)-196;Thomp-
  son-196;William-124-125-130-146;
  Young-123
EGAN Michel-13;Patrick-29-30
EGGLESTON Seth-61
EISENHOWER George-204-209;John-
ELDER Andrew-221;Ashley-96. 203/
ELKINS Archibald-151;Wesley-50;
  William-167
ELLER George-197;Peter-123
ELLETT David-208
ELLIOTT Dawson-47;Edward-203;Eli-
  jah-188;Jacob-126-160;Jeremiah-
  161;Jesse-178;John-203;Joseph-59;
  Michael-177;Samuel-204;Shadrach-
  31-32-33;William-28-31-32-180-199
ELLIS Andrew-39;Benjamin-162-197;
  David-23-44;Goiner-159-162-170;
  Jacob-39(2);James-171-173-196;
  John-11-162(3)-165-173;William-
  162-163
ELMORE Isaac-49(2)-51;Rezin-49;

-245-

Samuel-205;Stephen-49;Thomas-157
ELROD Thomas-145-181
ELSEY John-119;Robert-29-162-165;
 Thomas-162
EISMORE Thomas-111
EISWICK Jacob-45
ELWYN Charles-61
EMBERS Eli-117
EMBREE Caesar-111;Elisha-59-61-
 66-68-77-78(2)-79-80;John-69;
 Thomas-68;William-60-68(3)-69(3)-
 78(2)-81-93
EMERSON see Emison;Daniel-33;El-
 hanan-69;Jesse-69-88-94;Reuben-
 85-94-95;William-69
EMISON see Emerson;James-69-72-
 86-110-111-119-120-121;John-72;
 Samuel-52-107;Thomas-69-70
EMMONS David-162
ENDECOTT John-88
ENGLAND John-172
ENGLETON William-179
ENGLISH Alexander-40-50-51(2);
 Andrew-51;David-231;John-50-51;
 Stacy-109
ENLOW Henry-232;James-217
ENNIS see Eanis;David-218
ENYART Silas-191
ERSKINS Pleasant-234
ESTES Bartlett-78;Clement-82-86;
 Ellenor-78
ESTINGER Christian-202-204
ETTER Jesse-145;John-144
EVANS Abner-209-210;Alves-192;
 Charles-57;Clement-24;David-134-
 161;Elbert-141-178-183;Garrison-
 112;James-209-214(3)-221;John-
 192;Joseph-203;Joshua-141;Mires-
 222;Richard-137;Robert-45-64-65-
 67-78-81;Thomas-57(2);William-
 221
EVERETT Abraham-201;John-44;
 Josiah-20
EVERMAN John-203
EWING George-215;John-12-64-67-
 86-117;Nathaniel-57;Robert-193;
 Thomas-73

F see P & V
FAELKE Henry-116(2)
FAGINS Henry-13(3)-14;Isaac-29-
 30;Joseph-30;Obadiah-29-32;Walt-
FAIRCHILD Henry-40.   / er-30
FAIRHURST John-108;William-117;
 Wilson-108-116
FAIRLEY James-146;John-143(2)-

146-179-187;Samuel-171-179-192
FAITH Harrison-175;Thomas-41-173-
 174-175
FALKNER Emanuel-204
FALLS Felix-227;Hume-78;Robert-54
FANNING Thomas-99-106-107
FANSHER David-100
FARRIS see Harris;Anderson-43;An-
 drew-43(2);David-59-73-129-130-
 131;Elisha-142;George-143;Grand-
 ison-158;Isaac-63-66(2);James-
 170;Johnston-151;Paul-167;Samuel
 108-200;William-48-138-143
FARLOW George-191
FARMER Eli-196;Farris-61-73;Flem-
 ing-60-61;Isaac-60;John-62-208;
 Jonathan-43;Michael-136-139;Rob-
 ertson-203;Samuel-120(2);Sarah-
 209;William-60
FARR George-16;John-17;Phebe-152;
 Robert-17-55;William-17
FARRELL Patrick-27
FARTNEY Michael-182
FAUGHT Henry-114
FAUNT Le ROY Henry-156
FEATHERSTONE Patrick-9
FEELER Cornelius-200
FELL Moses-134-135
FELINER Nicholas-46-49
FENDER Andrew-130
FERGUSON Amanda-192;James-66-83-
 86;John-116-234;Peter-234;Rals-
 ton-150;Robert-150;Thomas-149-
 234;William-113
FERRELL see Terrell;Hugh-224
FETTER Daniel-137(2)-139-140-142-
 148-185-198-203-206-209-210
FETTINGER Charles-216-226;George-
 226;Samuel-226
FETTNER William-223
FICKLIN John-214(2)
FIDLER David-135;Henry-39-41;
 Levi-39;William-39
FIELDER Matthew-123
FIELDS Abraham-56;Absalom-131-164
 Bruce-17;Charles-174;Edmund-83-
 84;Ezekiel-56;Iredell-139-177;
 Isaiah-175;John-138;Joseph-70-82
 170;Keen-56(2);Nancy-171;Philip-
 175;Reuben-54-56;Robert-48-127-
 130-157-168-169-170-185;Stephen-
 56;Thomas-17-121;Wesley-176;
 William-139-170
FIFER John-90-91
FIGLEY Peter-167
FINCH Nathan-100;William-95

FINDLY David-195
FINGER Frederick-77;Jonas-130;
  John-128
FINNEY Alexander-70;James-60-228;
  John-55;Samuel-21
FIRMAN George-98
FISH Hiram-181;Logan-145-171;
  Seldon-126;William-134-146-173
FISHER Abraham-178;Daniel-88-95;
  David-137-140-141-177;Elisha-
  179;Henry-46-92;Isaac-221;Jacob-
  152;John-36-58-66;Michael-48;Na-
  than-153;Paul-48;Purnell-64-67;
  Stephen-67(2);Thomas-136
FITCH Doyer-158
FITZGERALD Benjamin-22(2);James-
  78-85;John-165(2);Johnson-68-78;
  Samuel-13-25-151-152-158-165
FITZPATRICK John-109;Obadiah-108;
  Patrick-31
FITZSIMONS James-15
FLANIGAN James-14
FLANKLER Martin-28
FLANNER John-87
FLATTER Lambert-106
FLEENOR James-193-231;John-60-62-
  63-200;Nicholas-201-202
FLEISHER Martin-41
FLETCHER James-160;William-195
FLOOD Henry-195
FLORER David-36-38
FLORY George-179-186-191;Matthew-
FLOWER George-91   186
FLOYD Abraham-186
FLUMMERFELT James-173;Peter-172
FLYNN James-14;William-36
FOOT William-137-138;Winthrop-50-
  111-112(2)-113(2)-128-145
FORBIS Amrila-133;Ezra-71;Wil-
  liam-71-72
FORCE Charles-153-164;Whitfield-
  156-159-164
FORD John-124;Lewis-124
FORDICE Joseph-120
FORQUERAN Alvin-119;Hampton-119
FORREST Benjamin-87;John-95
FORTNER see Fartney
FOSSETT George-35;John-192;Plea-
  sant-192
FOSTER Amassa-78-81;Henry-16;Mat-
  thew-213-215-222-223;Robert-152-
  211-219;William-18-61-216
FOULKS Hiram-106-109-117;William-
  31-32
FOUTS David-218;John-218;William-
  218

FOWLER Edmund-218;Henry-119;James-
  218(2);Jesse-44;Thomas-216-218-
  226;William-215
FOX Abraham-138;John-19;Noah-231;
  Samuel-147
FOYLES Thomas-28
FRAIM George-9-28-163
FRAKES John-109
FRANCIS Lewis-51
FRANK David-214
FRANKLIN John-23(2)-101;Pleasant-
  36;Walter-156-164
FRAZER Hiram-87;John-72-87
FREDENBERG John-77
FREDERICK Abram-98;Andrew-111;Dan-
  iel-225;Frederick-218;Hiram-224;
  Jacob-218;Michael-217-225-226
FREEL Hugh-27
FREELAND Aaron-29;Benjamin-189-
  193;Jacob-35
FREEMAN Alfred-155(2);John-80-151-
  155;Micajah-205;Stanford-151;
  Stephen-52(2);William-204
FRENCH George-153;James-75;John-
  66;Jonathan-161;William-121
FRISEE Gideon-202
FRITTS Andrew-49;George-196;Henry-
FRY Henry-155   198
FUHERER Peter-131
FULKERSON Thomas-37
FULLEN John-205-207
FULLER Jacob-101;William-111
FULLERTON Andrew-110;William-121-
  122(2)
FULTON Hugh-124;James-124-125;
  John-16;Richard-49

G see C & K
GABBERT John-37;Peter-135-136
GADBERRY James-40-46;John-46-49;
  Wilson-45
GAFFNEY Michael-31
GAITHER Alvin-167-168-169;Basil-
  168;Harrison-170
GALLAGHER James-174
GALLOWAY George-74-75;James-142
GALVIN James-17-18-19
GAMBLE David-87-89;John-205;Jos-
  eph-96;Loranzo-103
GAMBRIL Henry-70;T.-69;William-72
GAMMON Drury-153;Harden-153;Lew-
  is-153;Nancy-153
GANO James-113-115
GARDNER Henry-161;Hugh-53;John-
  53-110-137-138-197-228;Robert-
                158;

Samuel-174;Thomas-27
GARGES John-128
GARIGAN Philip-20
GARIN Patrick-186
GARLAND John-41
GARNON-91-Joseph
GARRAND Als.-198;Joseph-198
GARRETSON Gamaliel-219
GARRETT Amos-88;Eli-69-87;Gibson-
193;Henry-87-89;James-87-88;
John-120;Marion-40;Shubal-87;
Stephen-91;Thomas-88;William-88
GARRISON Arta-129-136;James-144;
John-128-205-206
GARTEN Elijah-138-140-142;James-
48-140-149;John-89;Joseph-89;
Robert-139;William-48-136
GARWOOD James-226;Joseph-226
GASKINS James-206;Stephen-206;
William-207
GATES Emanuel-166;John-27;Leon-
ard-175;William-164
GATEWOOD Robert-47;William-47-48
GAVIT William-225
GAWTHROP Thomas-219
GAY John-10-149;William-198
GAYSPAUGHER Conrad-214
GEDNEY Thomas-79-81
GEE George-184;Milton-117;Thomas-179
GEIGER John-136
GEISE Sophia-66
GEISLER John-95
GENTER Anton-92
GENTRY James-189-208;Lemuel-
208(2)
GEORGE James-146;John-176-180-
181;William-16-134
GETTINGS Dominick-98
GETTY David-111
GIBBENS see McGibbens;Asahel-29
GIBNEY Michael-9
GIBSON John-37-46-182;Lewis-39(2);
Richard-9;Thomas-151-162-173-
174;William-27
GIFFORD John-103-105
GILBERT Aquilla-130-131;John-212-
218;Jonathan-203(2)-208;Joshua-
101;Simon-123;William-231
GILBREATH Dorcas-172;Willet-36;
William-172
GILCHRIST Stephen-155
GILES John-147
GILHAM Drury-191;Henry-116;Jacob-
191;James-191
GILKISON John-157;Robert-157;
William-157

GILL James-154;John-154
GILLEACE Thomas-27
GILLESPIE Alexander-199;Elizabeth-
202;Isaac-207;Thomas-199
GILLEY George-15;James-14-15(4)-
19-159;Robert-16
GILLIAN-38-Edward
GILLOCK Fielder-159;Thomas-159;
William-157
GILMORE William-36-48
GILSON Richard-151
GIMBEL Adam-178-200
GIRDLEY Alfred-172-183
GIVENS James-197;John-198(2);Mil-
ton-34;Robert-197
GLADISH Henry-221;James-218;Jere-
miah-216-223
GLASGOW Polly-25
GLASS John-226;Thomas-104
GLENN James-172;Robert-233
GIEZEN James-213-214;Elijah-213-
GLOVER Joseph-136-137.   214
GNAT Martin-59
GODFREY Eleazer-109
GOFF Elijah-140;Ignatius-27
GOLD James-14;John-16-158-159;
William-14
GOLDEN Jonathan-112;Thomas-17-
21(2)-25
GOLDMAN Catherine-40
GOLDSBERRY John-174
GOLDSMITH Anna-154
GONARD John-103-105-106
GOOCH Thomas-85
GOODMAN James-42-108-113;John-
109;McElway-116
GOODNIGHT James-204;John-194-197
GOODSELL Frederick-107;Peter-80-
82(2)
GOODWIN Aaron-200;Abner-200;Am-
mon-198;Anna-200;Elias-206;James-
108-203-206;John-143-146-150-199-
200;Malinda-67;Martha-193;Moses-
89;Nicholas-186;Seth-186-198;
William-200-201-202
GOOLDY William-135
GOORLAY Robert-73-80
GOOTEE Charles-38;Silas-26;Thom-
as-163-166
GORDON Charles-180-182;George-182;
James-194;John-122-204;Samuel-
56;William-56-58
GORE Adam-177;Harrison-177;John-
GOULD Charles-122.   177
GRABHORN Anton-151
GRAETER Charles-92;Christian-81-
135

-248-

GRAGG Benniah-89
GRAHAM James-41-110;John-22-42-
51-80;Robert-149;Robertson-202;
Samuel-36-37;Thomas-33-41-49-202
GRANNON Bernard-30;Michael-26
GRANTHAM Moses-195
GRASSER Frederick-81
GRAVEL Francis-105
GRAVES John-13;Peter-192;Thomas-
191;William-147-192
GRAY David-200-201;James-92-148-
211;Jesse-148;Sarah-150;William-
GRAYBILL Samuel-198./170-198-211/
GRAYSON Benjamin-144;John-144;
Napoleon-91
GREATHOUSE William-56-57-122
GREEN Alexander-213;Daniel-161;
George-227;James-158;John-17-
165;Samuel-211-225;Solomon-195-
198;Stephen-160;Washington-215;
William-158-230-234
GREENFIELD Ellis-110
GREENSTREET John-161
GREENWOOD Thomas-17-31
GREGER John-135
GREGORY Charles-100;Daniel-22;
George-9-11-20;Isaac-10-18-20-
23;James-11-136;Jeremiah-34;
John-10;Jonathan-20(2)-23;Robert
GRENIER Martiale-106.   18
GREPP George-93
GRIBBINS Michael-41
GRIDER Aaron-96
GRIER Charles-88-89;Joel-135
GRIFFIN Anthony-87;Caleb-91;Hen-
ry-51-184;Joseph-87-89;Spencer-
167-189
GRIFFITH Alfred-189;Eleanor-207;
Isaac-199-207;John-189-193-199-
201-217;Thomas-216;William-61
GRIGGS Hugh-54-56-122
GRIGSBY Demps-53-55;George-56
GRIMES Thomas-185
GRIMSLEY Enoch-42;Enos-113;Mar-
tin-51
GRINDSTAFF Henry-139-179;Isaac-
138;Jacob-141
GRINNON James-14;Patrick-14
GRISHAM Margaret-169
GRISSOM David-234;William-233
GRISWOLD Gilbert-158
GROOMS John-40;Zachariah-40
GROSE Daniel-200;Henry-209;James-
210;Peter-210
GROVE Charles-40;Jacob-51;John-
40;William-40

GRUBB Andrew-227;Daniel-226;
George-226;Henry-226;John-226;
Lewis-227;Valentine-226-227
GRUNDER Vendelin-80.
GUDGEL Andrew-62;William-83
GUIRCY William-64
GULLETT John-46;Joshua-144;Wil-
liam-224
GULLICK Henry-34;John-54;Jonathan-
GUMLIN Pierre-104.   54
GURNEY Nelson-125-159-164
GUTHRIDGE John-167(2)
GUTHRIE Peter-90
GWATHMEY Mr.-210
GWIN Bailey-87;Edmund-152;George-
152;John-152-196-205;Thomas-58-
70-71-72-87-196

HACKLER Jacob-140;John-135-136
HADDON see Heddon;John-114;Wil-
liam-99
HAGER George-114;William-225;Phil-
HAGGARD Gentry-142   /ip-27(2)
HAILANDIERE see De la Hailandiere
HAIG George-182;James-181-185;
John-181
HAISLET Samuel-202-205
HALBERT Enos-160-161;Joel-160-
161;Silas-164-165(2)
HALBROOKS Dausy-82-83;George-83;
William-79-83
HALE Eunice-164;Jacob-191;Or-
ville-227;Richard-227
HALEY Thomas-11
HALL Bluford-120;Francis-195-204-
208-210;George-124-179;Isom-124;
Job-66;John-131-141-192;Michael-
166-178;Moses-197;Noel-204-205;
Richard-123;Robert-124;Samuel-
56-63(2)-66-69(2)-76-80;Zachar-
HALLER Isaac-157.   iah-78
HAM see Hum;Burton-196;Jacob-196;
Lawson-196;Mathis-48;Moses-229;
Peter-21-210
HAMBY Stephen-229
HAMER Joseph-145
HAMILTON Jameson-145;John-82-86-
184;William-59-62
HAMMER see Hamner;Christopher-39
HAMMERSLEY Andrew-48-173;George-
162;Jacob-169-173-180-184;James-
45-46-48;John-168-169;Joseph-
167;Michael-168
HAMMOND Albert-216;Elijah-11;Job-
15(2)
HAMNER see Hammer;Charles-154(2)

HAMPTON William-92
HANCHETT Hirem-121
HANCOCK Thomas-185-188
HANFT John-95
H!NKS Peter-68;William-63-67
HANLEY John-165
HANNAH Alexander-50;Andrew-42-43-
50;John-169;Mary-50-111;Nathan-
50;William-50-77-79(2)
HANNON Joseph-227
HANSFORD John-204
HANSLEY Comfort-128;Daniel-128
HANSON Conrad-188;Daniel-143-
188;John-142-146-188
HARBIN see Harlin;Allen-107;Bar-
bara-105;Sion-107
HARBISON Adam-76;David-76;John-
204;Thomas-56-74(2);William-74-
151
HARD see Hurd,Heard;Joseph-122
HARDIN Benjamin-224;Bledsoe-129-
130;Henry-220-230;John-225-230;
Martin-123;William-23-192
HARDING Ira-154
HARDISTY John-200;Phebe-200;Sam-
uel-197-203
HARDMAN see Harman;John-94
HARDY Luke-83;William-157
HARGIS John-143;Thomas-43;Wil-
liam-42
HARGROVE Jacob-59-231;John-55-65;
Lemuel-213(2);Linzey-54-55;Mar-
tin-59;Nicholas-65-231;Thomas-
211;William-58-59-63-211-213
HARKLET William-48
HARLIN see Harbin;James-109
HARLLEY Alexander-227
HARMAN see Hardman;John-92;Ben-
nett-87;Daniel-46-49;Lewis-71-
72-87(2)-90-194;Robert-91;Sax-
ton-71;Syrack-87;Thomas-15
HARMONSON Peter-145(2)
HARNESS Jackson-121
HARPER Adam-63
HARPER Coleman-165;Dunn-117;Eli-
jah-63;George-98-104-119;Jacob-
98-104-105(2);Jesse-118;John-61-
118-165;Lemuel-118-120;Matthew-
228;Nicholas-117;Robert-62;Sam-
uel-117;Thomas-61;William-62-63-
117-118-119-233
HARRELL see Horrell,Hewell;Isaac-
36;James-215;John-107;Moses-
216(2)-217;Willis-129
HARREISON Hiram-89
HARRINGTON Charles-57-68;Edmund-
43;

George-43;John-43-108;William-
61-64-65-68
HARRIS see Ferris;Andrew-172;Coop
er-68;Dabney-140;Daniel-17-32-
156;George-156;Gillan-70;Hender-
son-172;Hugh-53-224;Isaac-153(2)
James-211;Jesse-16;Joseph-204-
211;Morgan-88-89;Nathan-28;Rob-
ert-152;Samuel-28-110;Stephen-
94(2)-95;William-158
HARRISON Azza-54-122-219;Jeremiah
58;Joseph-50;Otho-223
HARRYMAN John-176;William-176-178
HARSHA Daniel-42;John-29
HARSHFIELD James-177
HART Aaron-29-41;Absalom-134-135-
145;Anderson-33(2);Andrew-222;
David-77;Elam-34;George-233;Ja-
mes-33;Patrick-13;Ralph-33-34
Thomas-228;Valentine-224;William
HARTFORD George-159.   226
HARTIN George-63-64-67;Jacob-63;
James-65;John-64;Margaret-63
HARTMAN Abraham-146
HARTSOCK Samuel-209
HARVEY Alexander-53;Andrew-53;
John-198;Michael-186;William-195
HASKETT John-207;Sarah-200
HASKINS see Hoskins;Eliphalet-157
James-71
HASSELBRINK Frederick-66
HASTIN James-183
HASTINGS Arthur-131-168;Isaiah-48
John-50-183;Joseph-48-131-169;
Wiley-168;William-50-169
HATCH Mary-156;Samuel-158
HATFIELD William-176
HATHAWAY John-222-229(2)
HATHORN Samuel-230;William-230(2)
HATTABAUGH Jacob-143-146;Michael-
HATTON Marshall-165;Robt-58./143/
HAWKINS Amos-34;Benjamin-9-16;
Caly-17;Catherine-21;Charner-
31(2)-107;Daniel-220-224;Eli-22-
35-36-161;Franklin-84(2);Henry-
84-86;Jacob-34-35-107;James-
151(2);John-24-34-136;Jonathan-
33(2);Joseph-223;Moses-34;Sam-
uel-84;Thomas-84;William-34-35
HAYDEN Henry-100
HAYHURST Benjamin-79
HAYNES William-51
HAYS Alexander-24;Benjamin-31-52;
Elias-211;Ezekiel-213(2);George-
14-31(2)-33-104;James-52-143;
John-65-108-109-124-136-210-214-

219-221;Joseph-9-31-153-163;Lew-
is-203-204;Philo-217;Robert-10-
24;Twitty-219;Walter-223;William-
17(2)-99-105-119-120-125-152-
160-164-219
HAYWARD John-114-148-179
HAYWOOD William-182
HAYWORTH Josiah-181
HAZEL Caleb-191;Hiram-191;Rich-
ard-191;William-191
HAZLEWOOD Joseph-197
HAZZARD Oliver-223;
HEACOX Alfred-47
HEAD John-39;William-39
HEADY Thomas-201-202
HEALY Samuel-32
HEARD see Hard,Hurd
HEBERD Adelia-147
HEDDON see Haddon;Isaac-42;Jared-
117(2)
HEDGES Elizabeth-54;James-225;
Jefferson-225;Peter-225;Samuel-
225;Thomas-206
HEDRICK George-9-202;Jacob-9-15-
178;John-139;Peter-33-35(2)
HEENEY Francis-99-106-107
HEFREN David-27;Lawrence-27
HEGEMAN A.G.-11-125-153-170;John-
232-234
HEIBLER see Hiebler
HEIMAN Casper-126
HEINES Gert-116
HELLENBRUGHT John-186
HELMER Jeremiah-148(2);Melchert-
148;Michael-148
HELMS Richard-185;Robert-185
HELPHASINE William-11
HELPHINSTINE Asa-46
HELSEY Jacob-224;William-223
HELTON Andrew-186-188
HEMBREE Drewry-152;John-152
HENDER George-212
HENDERSON Allison-161-165;Samuel-
75;William-186
HENDRICKS Daniel-229;Eli-145;Ja-
mes-229-232;John-229;Nathan-159-
161
HENDRICKSON Aaron-37-171;Anthony-
152;Austin-37;David-167;Israel-
170;James-175;John-37;Richard-
157;Separate-151;Simeon-158
HENKEL see Hinkle
HENRY Arthur-128-130-206;George-
193;Jacob-168;James-17;John-25-
28-45-165-196;Macum-170;Philip-
200;William-163-170(2);

HENSLEY Frederick-180
HENSON Andrew-167;Henry-170;Jesse-
167-168;John-168;William-168
HEPNER John-90
HERBERD William-12
HERDER James-120;Simon-120
HERRING Stephen-90
HERRON Alexander-148-171;Isaac-
149;John-148;Michael-103;Robert-
175;William-36
HERSHEY Martha-121
HESTER Cravin-201
HETTON James-195
HEWELL William-96; see Horrall
HEWINS see Hughen;Augustus-221;
Darwin-224;Erwin-224;Rowene-224;
Zilpha-224
HEYDON Leachman-218
HEYLMAN see Hegeman,Hilemon
HICKMAN John-211;William-164
HICKS Andrew-213
HIEBLER Bernhart-18
HIGGENBOTHAM Allen-133;John-130
HIGHMEYER Henry-116(2)
HIGHT John-193
HIGHTOWER Pleasant-227.   203
HILEMON see Heylman,Hillman;John-/
HILL see Hitt;Aaron-93;Alexander-
224;Bazil-187;Benjamin-176;Clark-
110;George-118;Henderson-18;Hen-
ry-12-32-120-176-177;Hugh-190;
Isaac-172;James-69;Jesse-123;
John-201;Patty-119;Robert-32;Tho-
mas-134-135-136-176(2);William-82
HILLEBRAND Commodore-129;Philip-
129
HILLMAN see Hilemon,Heylman;Dan-
iel-224;Henry-219;James-219;
John-219
HINDE Thomas-58(2)-59
HINDMAN Jasper-165;John-194
HINDS Alexander-42-44-108-116;An-
drew-116;James-182
HINKLE Anthony-43(2)-44;David-40-
43;George-199-200-201;Jonathan-
201;Milton-44;Philip-43
HINMAN see Kinham
HINNEN see Heimen
HINSHAW John-168-169
HINSLOW Milton-231
HINSON see Henson
HINTON George-127-130-131;Jere-
miah-155
HIRONS Samuel-83
HISER Jacob-109
HITCHCOCK John-172;Thomas-172

HITE Felix-208;William-208(2)-209
HITT see Hill;Caleb-103-111;Char-
  les-164;John-164;Samuel-96-97;
  William-165;Willis-97(2)-103(3)-
HIXSON David-35   111
HOARD George-125;William-126
HOBBS Joseph-21;Lawson-88
HOBERD William-109
HOBSON Joseph-185
HODGE see Hogue
HODGES Aaron-135;Isom-136;James-
  147;Jesse-128-138-150;Moses-
  146;Thomas-158-205
HOGE see Hogue
HOESEIS Landalin-76
HOGAN James-195;William-195
HOGATT Lucian-188;William-146
HOGG Amos-120
HOGSHEAD David-22
HOGUE James-65-70;John-36-61;Jo-
  seph-36-96;Samuel-63-69(3);Wil-
  liam-65;Zebulon-36;Zenas-208
HOLCOMB Alexander-73-75;Benjamin-
  85-86;Elihu-81(2);Henry-80;Hos-
  ea-79-80(3)-81(2)-82;John-93;
  Silas-81
HOLDER Benjamin-147;John-147
HOLDERMAN Reuben-147
HOLDMAN see Holman;Henry-97(2)
HOLLADAY Abram-132;Robert-142-
  147-193
HOLLAND Edmund-220;Felix-156;Ja-
  mes-221;John-11-103(2);Mary-
  171;Samuel-220
HOLLAWAY Clayborne-142
HOLLER Jeremiah-200;Samuel-214;
  Zachariah-200
HOLLINGSWORTH Abraham-109-116-118;
  Bernard-118;Daniel-110(3);Ferdi-
  nand-109;Isaac-9-16-34;Jackson-
  109;Jesse-118;John-110;Joseph-
  20-42;Mary-118;Samuel-33-116;
  Thomas-110-116(2)
HOLLOWELL Robert-137. ⌐44-
HOLMES Jacob-148;John⌐147⌐William
HOKE George-111;Peter-111.   124
HOLLIS Othniel-79
HOLMAN see Holdman;William-67
HOLSCHER John-103
HOLT Calvin-183;Doswell-182;Dru-
  ry-181-182;Emberson-183;Henry-
  182(2);James-97-171-183;John-
  160-182;William-160
HOMAN J.B.-51
HOMELMAN Angeline-115
HONEY James-30

HOOD William-56
HOOKER Thomas-234
HOOPER Abraham-109;Charles-108-
  115-116;Wesley-115;William-116
HOOVER Abraham-42-43-51;John-
  43(2)-44;Nicholas-42-43-44-107;
  Peter-43;William-43
HOPEWELL Henry-203-210
HOPKINS Edward-25;Essick-16-17;
  Ezekiel-82;Francis-83;Henry-63-
  64-66-74-234;Hiram-80;James-145
  Joshua-146;Patrick-26;Zelek-18
HOPPER John-133;Moses-71;Samuel-
  125-153;Thomas-148;William-148-
HOPWOOD Moses-197   150
HOREN James-14;John-19
HORNADY David-216-217
HORNBROOK S.-95
HORNER Isaac-212;Joshua-166
HORRELL see Hewell,Harrell;James
  11;Jason-12-22;John-12-22;Thom-
  as-11-22-23-25;William-12(2)-22
HORSEY Clement-155;James-160;Lem-
  uel-161;Revel-128
HOSACK David-80(2);Thomas-55
HOSKINS see Haskins;Elisha-158;
  Samuel-129
HOSMER Addison-105;John-158-159
HOSTETTER Adam-150
HOUCHIN Benjamin-229;Chesterfiel-
  233;Jesse-90-232-233;Leeright-2
HOUGHTON William-12-162
HOUGLAND John-112
HOUSE Jacob-194
HOUSH Adam-144
HOUSTON Alfred-208;Benjamin-208;
  Cary-204;Harvey-204;James-34-
  208;Joseph-208;Peter-204;Purnel
  208;Washington-204
HOUTS George-23(2)-24-25
HOWARD Baldwin-47(2)-48;Elbert-
  135-140(2)-142(2);James-160;John
  160;Joseph-116;Meredith-216;Sam-
  uel-180;Sanders-135;William-109-
  116
HOWE Albert-103;Joshua-196;San-
  ford-73;William-56;Willis-59-63-
  68-78-80
HOWELL Gilbert-98;Jonathan-192-
  193
HUBBARD Joel-140;Wesley-48;Willi
HUBBS Willis-152.   48
HUDDLESON James-55-229;David-60;
  John-69;Samuel-69-70
HUDGEN see Hughen
HUDSON John-31;Sterling-190;Will-
                            iam-92(2)

-252-

HUDSPETH Isaac-66-78
HUEY see Hughey
HUEZ Joseph-233
HUFF Abraham-201;James-183;Ovid-218;Samuel-218
HUFFMAN Jacob-101.   45
HUGHEN see Hughey,Hewins;Samuel-/
HUGHES Arthur-18;Burkett-83;Davinport-84;Drury-218;Edward-14;James-20-28-137(2)-139-140-142-148-185-198-203-206-209-210;Joel-126;John-14-26-71-72;Tolliver-69
HUGHEY see Hughen;Joseph-62-170;Samuel-23
HUGO John-77
HULBERT Henry-99-100
HULEN Edmund-42;Hiram-43-107;Thomas-43
HULL John-83
HUM see Ham,Hume;David-47
HUME William-180
HUMMER William-73
HUMPHREYS Abijah-234;Elijah-54;George-54-56-57(2)-58(2)-60-63(2)-121-122(2);John-40;Joseph-54-58-121(2);Samuel-202;Silas-121(2);Uriah-56-122
HUMSTON Edward-143-188;John-145;William-145-188
HUNNICUTT William-109;Wilson-109
HUNSTER see Hunter;Alexander-125
HUNT see Hurt;Henry-90;Jordan-90;Josiah-156;Mary-157;Nathaniel-156;Thomas-150;William-15
HUNTER see Hunster;George-156;Harris-86;Harry-89;Henry-229;Joel-132;John-13(2)-16-87-162-164;Richard-193;William-88-90-161
HURD see Heard,Hard;Elijah-121;Elisha-121;Abraham-101
HURLEY Thornton-203;Timothy-28
HURT see Hunt;Anthony-178;John-138-150;Presley-69;Thomas-138-139-150-178;Joseph-178
HUSSEY James-53;Richard-64;Zachariah-64
HUSTON David-169;James-169;Morris-172;Samuel-170;William-169
HUTCHINSON Daniel-234(2);Ebenezer-233;Jotham-233
HUTHER Adam-66;Frederick-65
HUTTON Isaac-178
HYATT Elisha-11-114
HYDE John-100
HYMON Henry-163
HYNDMAN William-126

IGO Thomas-89
INGRAM see Mangrum;Allen-83;Barney-232;Hansel-232;Jesse-76;John-76;Richard-78-79
INMAN Abednigo-152-153;Elisha-180;George-141-180;Henry-141;Jackson-178;John-140-141-180;Solomon-180-182;Thomas-183;Willaby-182;William-140-151
INVANALL James-201
IRELAND Levin-92-93;William-93
IRWIN Asa-129;James-145;Jarrett-123;John-157;Robert-80;Samuel-39-136(2);William-127-128-131-169
IRY Phenics-174
ISH see Ash;George-58-67
ISIMINGER George-193;Jacob-194
ISOM Anthony-123;Dennis-123-125;George-123(2);John-123;Stephen-123-179

J see Y
JACKMAN William-156-157
JACKSON Arm-23;George-71-199;Hezekiah-12;James-12;John-113-200;Josiah-174-199;Littleton-48;Nathan-135;Ulysses-10;William-202
JACO Cornelius-229
JACOBUS Daily-121;Jacob-99-121;Peter-99(2);Thomas-100-121(2)
JAMES Berryman-195;Cary-195;Elijah-120;Henry-204-210;James-193(2);Joseph-136-193;Levi-158;Rachel-120;Thomas-160-210;William-114-193
JAMISON Alexander-37
JANE William-157
JAQUES Jonathan-83-86
JARRELL Eli-114;Franklin-114;James-112-113-115;John-115;Sally-225;William-61-113-114(2)-115
JARVIS Amos-21-25-35
JEFFRIES Thomas-223-226
JENKINS John-119(2);Wiley-71;William-119;Zebulon-45-49
JENNINGS Adonijah-186;David-100;Nathaniel-156;Samuel-210
JERAULD Charles-108;Sylvester-57;William-230
JEROME Thomas-173
JETER Horatio-38
JETT William-19
JIMPY Samuel-167
JOHNSON Abner-167(2);Alexander-40-85-187;Andrew-19-186-223;Benjamin-205-234;Charles-191;

Christopher-50(2);David-60-205-
231;Edward-17-50-51;Elijah-22-23;
Elizabeth-128-168;Gabriel-214;
General-165;George-71-72-89(2)-
90-196;Henry-82-144;Hiram-18(2);
Isaac-15-19-20;Isaiah-48-49-50-
111-112;Jacob-58-71;James-133-
160-233;Jehu-125-133;John-218-
224-231;Jonathan-24-48-50-111-
112;Joseph-89;Josiah-224;Laban-
23;Lewis-60;Morgan-15-20;Nicho-
las-98(2);Payton-98;Rachel-128;
Robert-16-222-224-227(2);Reuben-
214;Samuel-230;Sarah-133;Stephen-
18-20-24;Thomas-23-64-65-72-86-
87-98-133;Washington-165;William-
42-57-89-143-169;Winchester-95
JONES Abraham-128;Alfred-147;Aq-
uilla-116;Coleman-20;David-126;
Ebenezer-21;George-64-67-125-133;
Harvey-26;Hezekiah-126;Isaac-171-
198;Jacob-171;James-64-77-155(2);
Jeremiah-155;Joel-155;John-12-14-
53(2)-121-227-232;Joseph-10;Levi-
70;Lewis-35-147(2)-154;Morgan-
99-104;Moses-51;Parmenas-20;Phi-
lip-102;Polly-102;Richard-211;
Thomas-10-20-21-53-93-125-133-
147;Vance-22;Venson-44;Wesley-57;
Wiley-41-53;William-11(3)-12-24-*
93-152(2)-153-169-192-193;Wil-
lis-133; *William-25
JORDAN Absalom-90;Alfred-90;Eli-
ba-73-90;Ephraim-103;Francis-94;
George-94;Jacob-90;James-87;Jef-
ferson-73;John-73-90-102;Joshua-
73-90;Lewis-87;Mary-90;Over-90-
91(2);William-102
JOSEPH Isaac-104-155
JOST Michael-105
JOURNEE William-112-114
JUDAH Edward-98-104;Eli-144;John-
144;Martin-143;Samuel-98-104-
105(2)-144;Winepark-144
JUDSON Orval-229
JULIEN William-200
JUNKIN David-96

K see C, G, N
KALLETT Michael-19(2)
KAMPMEIR Ernst-115
KARN see Kern;James-33-35;Philip-
33
KATTALL see Kallett
KATTERJOHN see Telljohann;Henry-
232;Herman-232
KAUFFMAN George-20;Henry-76(2)
KASTIN see Hastin

KAYS John-210
KEAL Philip-20
KEATLEY see Keitly
KECK Christian-49-171-178-183;
McHewell-171;Philip-47-49-175-183
KEFFE Dennis-27
KEITH Amos-220;Benjamin-116-226;
George-30-32-34;Henry-115;Jarit-
114;Jeremiah-220-221;Josse-116-
220;John-115-213-221;Michael-195;
Silas-213;Warren-115
KEITLY William-69
KELL Alexander-63;Archibald-59;Ja-
mes-59-63-67-232;John-73-75;
Matthew-59-73
KELLER Christopher-178-180;Joseph-
179;Noah-178
KELLOGG Phineas-233
KELLUMS Alfred-154
KELLY see Ketty;Alexander-193;Dav-
id-156-202;John-14-156;Lemuel-
156;Nicholas-13;Thomas-122
KEISEY William-134
KEISO Joseph-9;Samuel-35;William-
9-210
KEMBLE Titan-202(2).
KENDALL John-30
KENLEY James-154;John-154
KENNEDY see Kennerly;Absalom-194;
Elias-135-178-183;George-98;Jam-
es-27-31;John-21-14;Joseph-205;
Robert-156;Sylvester-167;Thomas-
104
KENNERLY Isaac-79-85
KENNEY Moses-221
KENT John-78;Patrick-166
KERNER see Hepner
KERN Abraham-131-136-138-139-140-
149;Adam-139-198;Albert-141;Alex-
ander-139-141;Ambrose-140-142;
Coonrod-196-198;Eli-140-142;Jac-
ob-72-86;John-141;Simon-139;Wil-
liam-138-148-149-150
KERR see Kern
KESTER George-81;Robert-15-17
KETCHAM Daniel-48-182;Jacob-47-50;
John-47-49-183-185-195-200-203-
206-210;Joseph-185;Marshall-50;
Silas-49;Solomon-49
KETTY see Kelly;Cornelius-27;
James-30
KEY Charles-80;John-98;Marshall-
152;Stuart-98;Thomas-58;William-
54-98
KEYIMAN A.G.-101.
KIAR Lewis-105
KIDWELL James-27;John-172-173;
Nicholas-31;Sylvester-173(2)
KILBURN Elisha-151-156-165;Henry-
151;John-151

KILGORE Charles-37(2)-134-136-
175;Hiram-37-134(2)-135(3)-145-
146(3);Reuben-36-37-134-135(5)-
136-138-145-146(3)-183;Simpson-
36-50-135(2)-145(2)-146;Stephen-
37
KILLION see Millian;Adam-39-41;
Alexander-42-113;Daniel-50;Dav-
id-41-113(2);Frederick-33-39;Ja-
cob-39;James-42-44;Jonas-39;Ma-
thias-39-44-51;Wiley-41-44-45;
William-37-40-41-44-51-113-174
KILLPATRICK James-74-75-234;John-
74(3)-76;Josiah-74-76-77;Thomas-
KIMBALL Jesse-89.   74
KIMBERLIN Daniel-117;George-185
KIME Michael-227-228
KIMMONS Henry-98-105;Joseph-98;
Peter-98
KINCAID Samuel-76
KINCHLOE William-90
KINDER Erastus-232;George-131-
141-178;Isaac-179;Jacob-166;
Peter-230
KING Alexander-57(2)-133;Alvis-
190;Amanda-190;David-67;George-
230;James-37(2)-81-190;John-69-
185;Marcus-213-214;Patrick-79;
Robert-37;Solomon-64;William-
190(2)-193
KINGSBURY Robert-66
KINMAN David-216;Hiram-213-216;
James-212-222;Jared-221;Jesse-
215-222;Joel-212-215;John-214-
221(3)-222-223(2)-225;Joseph-
221;Leonard-221;Levi-212-215;Sa-
muel-211-214(2)-222;Soburn-214;
William-12-212(2)-220-221
KINNAR Rodom-58
KINSER Elias-142;Elisha-143;Sam-
uel-144;Tyre-37;William-175
KIPEE Robert-175
KIRBY Archibald-203;Joel-203;Law-
rence-232;William-154
KIRK Daniel-53-54-55;David-190(2)-
191;Dickson-54;Edmund-53;Edward-
10;Elizabeth-74;Hiram-153;James-
53-190;John-191-217;Richard-53;
Robert-54;Susan-160;William-
103(2)
KIRKENDALL see Kuykendall;Cyrus-
KIRKHAM Henry-203.   181
KIRKMAN Joseph-63
KIRTRIGHT Samuel-194
KITCHEN James-85(2)-94;Joshua-85
KITHER William-123

KLUSMAN Henry-66
KNABLE Francis-28
KNAHT John-214
KNEGER Frederick-115
KNEIPP Charles-58
KNEREMER James-79
KNIGHT Andrew-217;Isaac-225-226-
228;John-225;Joseph-46;Marquis-
135-136-138-150;Moses-31-36
KNIGHTON Loving-204
KNOLES Eddy-88;Eli-89;Elijah-68-
77;Ephraim-86;James-85-86;Jesse-
84(2);Nathan-89;Prettyman-88;
Rhesa-70;Solomon-89;William-88
KNOTT Abram-150;William-194
KNOX Enoch-79;John-96-97
KOLB Lewis-65
KOONS Alexander-226;Gasper-198;
Isaac-103;John-190;Nicholas-126;
William-189-198
KOUSE see Housh
KROWS see Crow
KRUSE see Cruse
KURTZ William-53-59-60-81-92-93
KUTCH John-49-171-185
KUYKENDALL see Kirkendall;Asa-
100;George-99;Jacob-100;John-
42;Nathaniel-100
KYLE John-28-152;Matthew-12-28;
Nicholas-21;Thomas-117

LABEDEW Elisha-208
LADEROOTE Ambrose-105
LAGRANGE Aaron-68-85;William-83
LAFFERTY Joseph-48
LAGOW John-57-63
LAKE John-188
LALUMIERE Simon-29
LAMAR Emily-163;James-163-164;
John-162;Mary-163;Richard-163;
Thomas-163;William-162;Young-90
LAMB Alexander-50-148-190;Edward-
18;Elizabeth-134-146;Hiram-174;
Isaiah-131-141;Permenius-141;
Willis-185
LAMBERT Richard-34;William-233
LANCE Benjamin-234;John-54-56
LAND Abraham-94;Richard-68
LANDERS see Sanders;Francis-178;
William-177
LANDMEHR William-229
LANDRETH Allen-124;John-126;Nath-
aniel-126;Thomas-123-125;Wells-
123;William-124
LANDSDOWN Abner-57-70;Joel-70
LANE Danford-98;Elijah-224;John-

174-175-224;Sarah-233
LANGFORD DeWitt-160(2)
LANGWILL Solomon-206
LANHAM Coalby-126
LANTER Archibald-160
LAPLANTE Hyacinth-107;Joseph-107
LASHLY Delilah-18;George-35
LATHOM Harrison-59;Jonathan-64;
  William-55-57-60-67-77
LATOUR Augustus-117
LATSHAW Joseph-117(2);Roberts-119
LATTE Samuel-13
LAUGHLIN John-136-182-183;Joseph-
  48-135-182;Monroe-183;Sally-135;
  Thomas-18
LAW Jeremiah-130;John-120
LAWELL James-162
LAWRENCE Josiah-36-42-45-99-100-
  101-106(2)-107-119(2)-120;Levin-
  198;Samuel-63-65;William-60-63-
LAY Thomas-182.   64
LEABO Jacob-210
LEACH George-103(2);John-56;Peter-
  127;William-114
LEAKE Anthony-223
LEAKEY see Luckey;William-143-148-
LEAP Jacob-43.   189
LEATHERMAN Peter-129
LEATHERS William-55
LEDGERWOOD Charles-46-181-182;Da-
  vid-45(2)-181;Elswick-46;George-
  46-180;Jacob-181;Nathaniel-45-
  152-181;William-45-46
LEE see See;Andrew-49;Eli-196-
  197-199-202-205-206;Ephraim-131;
  James-185;John-36-197;Joseph-
  185;Josiah-145;Samuel-197;Thom-
  as-138-218;William-164
LEEDES Jacob-157
LEEPER Samuel-222
LEHEARTY Richard-41
LELAND A.W.-199-206-209
LEMASTERS Benjamin-83-234;John-
  233;Simeon-56-60-234
LEMON Abner-116(2);John-145-152-
  187;Joseph-145-192;Matthias-188;
  Miller-187;Nelson-145;Robert-115;
  William-143-144-145-187-188
LENNON John-26;Patrick-26-27-29
LENTS Jacob-38-199;John-38;Nel-
  son-38;Nicholas-38;Vincent-38;
  William-37
LEONARD David-97-215;Henry-144
LeROY see Faunt LeRoy;Alexis-100-
  122
LESLIE Alexander-12-96-102-213-

218-219-230;James-53-60-63-64-
  65-232;John-68;Samuel-68
LESTER Abraham-40-41-43;Ebenezer-
  43;John-51(2)-216;Joseph-42-43;
  Robert-42-43;William-42-51
LETT James-20-23;John-214;Newton-
  211;Randel-212-215;Thomas-33(2);
  Whitfield-213-214
LEVY Matthew-20
LEWIS Andrew-55-71;David-177;Isam
  82;Jeremiah-130-146;John-228;Mar
  tha-232;Stephen-53;William-93-
  156;Yelverton-177
LIGHT see Like,Sight;Blewford-118
  David-101;Sanders-118
LIKE see Light,Sight;David-103;
  Elias-101;John-102;Robert-41
LILES John-118;Walter-120
LILLIE Andrew-25-101;James-41;
  Robert-40
LINCOLN Myron-133-169-183
LINDLEY Harrison-151-155;Henry-
  169;Jacob-154;James-169;Jonathan-
  *127-128-131-132-137-141-151*186-
  203-206-210(2);Owen-169;Samuel-
  151;Thomas-131;William-128-155;
  Zachariah-154;   *Jonathan-155
LINDSEY Elijah-219;John-100;Sam-
  uel-109-118(2);Susanna-216;Vin-
  cent-196;William-208
LININGER John-80
LINK Conrad-215;Elijah-97
LINTHICUM Elijah-147;Thomas-191-
LINZICH Jacob-77.   192
LITTEN Gilbert-209;Isaac-208;Joel-
  210;William-40
LITTLE Jane-178
LIVERMAN John-10
LLOYD Mr.-23;Abel-93;Anthony-157;
  Henry-155;S.-93;William-93
LOCK Amos-185-188
LOCKHART A.B.-229;Calvin-233;
  David-233
LOCKWOOD Edward-79-85;Stephen-79
LOGAN David-17-161;John-26;Rob-
  ert-16-212-213
LONERGAN David-14
LONG Abner-95;Abraham-169;Henry-
  145;Jacob-169;James-47;John-
  50(2);Reuben-221;William-160-161;
  Zadock-185-187
LOOMIS Albert-59
LORD Art-157-164
LORRY Eliza-174
LOSE William-65
LOTT Samuel-221

LOVE Harvey-163;Hubbard-162-165;
  James-162;John-162-165-174;Mil-
  ton-162;Wesley-162;William-26-
  175
LOVELESS Henry-223;Isaac-223(2);
  Joseph-223;Luke-223;William-223
LOVELL James-139;Zachariah-139-
  150-177
LOVELLETT William-72
LOVERCOOL Alex.-234
LOVING Reuben-209
LOWDER Caleb-191;Joshua-142(2);
  Lynden-147;Ralph-147-148
LOWE George-95;Jacob-197-207-209;
  John-143-146-192;William-83
LOWELL see Lavell
LOWERY Henry-137;John-124-125-
  120-137;May-125
LOWNSDALE George-156;James-156-
  219-226;John-219-224
LUCAS Berry-187;Fielding-69-70-
  72-86;Hiram-159;Jeremiah-21;Jes-
  se-34-36;John-43-56-185;Martin-
  42;Oliver-86;Rachel-185;Robert-
  56;Solomon-185-195;Thomas-187(2);
  William-185
LUCE Abner-223
LUCKEY see Leakey;Thomas-138
LUFF Charles-215
LUHRING Daving-92;Lewis-92
LUNDY Daniel-168;George-173-175;
  John-173;Samuel-38-175
LUNSFORD Peter-190
LUNTENBERGER Martin-109
LUTKEYMAYER Louis-116
LUTTRELL John-132;Silas-134;Thom-
  as-179;Uriah-180;Willoughby-166
LUTZ Adam-94
LYND George-137
LYNN Absalom-58;Andrew-71;Daniel-
  15;Isom-57;James-55-57;John-137;
  William-69-73
LYONS Jeremiah-14;Patrick-14;
  Samuel-196;Sophronia-148

Mc see names without the Mc
McADAMS James-225;John-9
McADOW John-17
McAFEE Charles-141;Thomas-140
McALLISTER James-68-70
McARTHUR Daniel-114;James-115;
  William-114
McATEE Benjamin-225;Daniel-26;
  George-26;Josiah-228;William-
  226;Zachariah-227
McAVOZ Luke-9

McBAY Robert-17-31-230
McBRIDE Abraham-163;Gideon-174;
  James-165;John-13-48;Jonathan-
  192;Joshua-38;Moses-135-136-162-
  174(2);Owen-176;Samuel-37-38;
  William-37-48
McCABE Bryan-16
McCAFFERTY Green-12-18
McCAFFRY Thomas-19
McCAIN see McClain,McLean,McCone;
  Alexander-211-212-215;Andrew-187;
  Hamilton-212-215-217;Hugh-12-213-
  214;Isaac-213;Robert-190;Thomas-
  212;William-213.
McCALL Alexander-26-29;James-26-
  63-217;Michael-29
McCAMMON James-184
McCAMERON Elizabeth-163;William-
McCARDLE Philander-9.   162
McCARTER see Carter;Moses-49-182
McCARTNEY Henry-55(2)
McCARTY Cheney-66;James-20. 193
McCLAIN see McLean,McCain;Robert-/
McCLEARY James-76;Thomas-234;
  William-74-76(2)
McCLELLAND Alexander-44;Andrew-
  36-145;James-31-60-61;John-73-
  75-145;Joseph-60-61;Sterett-120;
  Wesley-18
McCLESKY David-113;John-42;Joseph-
  9-42
McCLUNG Thomas-25-28-165
McCLURE Alexander-212;Andrew-121;
  James-65(2)-88-90-121-232;John-
  118-120;Nathaniel-120;Samuel-
  118(3)-120-121;Thomas-118;Wil-
  liam-112-118-121
McCOMBER Levi-208
McCOMBS John-112
McCONE Owen-214
McCONNELL James-62;Jehiel-94;John-
  61;Robert-63-73-95
McCORD David-9;James-15;John-105;
  Joseph-157;Levi-109;Margaret-
  153;Sarah-116;Susan-116;William-
  126-179
McCORMICK Adam-42;Albert-178;An-
  drew-42-114;John-42-105-177-205-
  206-209(2)-210;Joseph-178;Laca-
  177;Michael-114;Reuben-177;Thom-
  as-43;William-29-32-33-88-89-
  177-179-182-221
McCOY Duncan-18;William-199
McCRACKEN Andrew-27(2);James-27-
  137;John-16-31-154;Richard-16;
  Thomas-32;William-16

McCRANY Thomas-199
McCRARY see McGary;Elisha-218;
　Logan-83;Robert-82-86(2)
McCRAY Albion-96;Alexander-96(2)-
　102-103;John-65-143
McCRISIKEN Edward-158;Patrick-158
McCRUM William-202
McCULLOM Cornelius-57
McCULLOCH David-76;Elihu-63-74;
　Jane-63-74;John-79-80;Margaret-
　63;Samuel-49-74-75-77;William-76
McCUNE Alexander-14;James-137(2)
McCURDY George-73
McCUTCHEN Samuel-220
McDANIEL George-148;Thomas-57;
　William-145
McDECKER see Decker;Morgan-218
McDERMED Charles-166
McDILL see Dill;Elizabeth-76;Mar-
　ia-77;Samuel-62-73-74-77
McDONALD Arthur-19;Cephas-29;Eb-
　enezer-136-137(2)-138(2);Fran-
　ois-29;James-29(2)-32-35;John-
　21;Lewis-80;Patrick-19;Peter-
　120(2);Samuel-76-81;Thomas-14
McDOWELL Daniel-85-94-95(2);Jam-
　es-85;John-148;Joshua-148;Wil-
　liam-58-59-60-76-79-80-81-148
McELEARNY John-30
McELWAIN James-152
McEVOY James-32
McFADDEN Andrew-15-143-146;John-
　71-87
McFAITH William-173
McFALL Harvey-130;William-137
McFARLAND Arthur-195
McGARRAH David-75-80-81-92;James-
　62-63-74(2)-232;Joseph-79-80-81-
　96;William-76-77
McGARY see McCRARY;Harrison-83;
　Hugh-69;James-86;Jesse-86;John-
　86;Patsey-83;Robert-82-83-84-86;
　William-83
McGEE Henry-146(2);Jackson-190
McGEHEE see Magee;Benjamin-93(2);
　Jesse-16;John-32;Joseph-108
McGHAN William-39
McGIBBENS see Gibbens;Levi-29
McGILL William-147(2);Zachariah-
McGILLEM Andrew-223.　　　　147
McGINDLEY James-169
McGINNIS James-132
McGOUGH John-79-81
McGOVRAN John-158;Michael-17;
　Philip-158
McGOWAN James-98-103;John-52;
　William-98

McGREGOR Andrew-73;George-75;
　John-73-85;Robert-73
McGREW Wilson-75
McGUIRE John-18-19-39;William-39
McHENRY Harrison-207;John-166
McHUGH Bernard-14
McINNERNY Matthew-27-29
McINTOSH John-152;Joshua-152;
　William-152
McINTYRE William-70-82
McKANNA Peter-14-15
McKEE Daniel-80
McKIDDY James-84;Stephen-84
McKINLEY see McGindley;Edward-22
　George-32(2);James-31;John-30
McKINNEY William-161
McKISSICK Martin-64
McKITTERICK Alexander-218
McKNIGHT Elijah-144;George-144-
　145;James-29;Roger-132-145-169;
　Washington-143;William-129-144
McLAUGHLIN Edward-228;James-192;
　Thomas-20
McLEAN see McClain;James-200(2);
　John-124;Robert-123-124;William
McLEAR Charles-32(2).　　　123-137
McLIN George-29
McMAHAN Hugh-163;James-15;Pat-
　rick-158
McMANUS Owen-165;Patrick-16;Ter-
　ence-153-156;Thomas-136
McMILLAN see Millan;Harvey-157;
　James-77;Jesse-98;John-76
McMULLIN Enis-14;Hugh-55-68-76-
　77(2)-82;Thomas-57-68-76-77-82
McMURRY Albert-112;Job-112
McNAB John-133;William-126
McNALLY Catherine-27;Franois-31;
　John-129;Thomas-129;William-27-
McNEAL William-124　　　　　　31
McNEELY James-68;William-207
McNUTT Robert-151-152
McPHETRIDGE John-204;Matthew-204
　Milton-193
McQUEEN Isaiah-227-228
McRAY Murdock-116
McREYNOLDS Abraham-183;Edward-89
　George-148-172-176;Isaac-78;Jos
　eph-48;Robert-175
McSWAIN Isaac-233
McWILLIAMS see Williams;Alexande
　64;David-64;John-64-138

MACABER Conrad-77
MADDEN Levi-29
MADDOWS see Meadows

MADDOX John-87
MADE Patrick-20
MADIGAN Patrick-13
MADISON William-122
MAGEE see McGehee;John-170
MAHALA John-197
MAHEE see Mehew;Thomas-29
MAHEW see Mahee;John-29(2)
MAHONEY see Marooney
MAIDLOW E.-95
MAIL Isaac-97-103;John-105;Solomon-92
MAJOR George-20;Robert-30-34-35;William-34
MALLETT Ambrose-106;John-106;Silas-134-146;Wheeler-188-202
MALOTT Elijah-223-226;Oliver-223;Perry-223
MALIN Susannah-213
MALONE James-86;John-70
MANGRUM see Ingram;William-83-94
MANIFIELD Joseph-52-53
MANNING David-45;Francis-61;George-77;Harvey-160;Joseph-61;Joshua-46;Leonard-163;Reuben-79;Thomas-57-68;William-61
MANSFIELD John-156
MARCUM George-232
MARCY Thomas-96
MARINER Littleton-75
MARKLE Joseph-54-101
MARKMAN John-157
MARLATT Joseph-51
MARLEY Benjamin-132-159-162;David-134;Harvey-159(2);Henry-159;Manley-133;Michael-125
MARLOW Leonard-162-167;Samuel-168
MARMADUKE Jesse-18
MAROONEY Francis-104-105
MARRS William-198
MARSHALL Benjamin-199-207;Charles-167;Hurbrit-155;John-55-138;Mark-232
MARTIN Asa-156-165;Berry-95;Charles-27-95;David-74-75;George-70;Henry-73-74-75-98-104;Isaac-140;James-86-109-118;Jesse-153;John-75;Michael-19-27;Nelson-95;Philip-89;Reuben-74;Robert-117;Samuel-117;Thomas-57-79-81-86-95-*155(2)-220*226-231;William-56-64-117(2)-121-123-153-200
MARVEL Elisha-85;George-85-94;John-89;Thomas-85;Wiley-70-89
MARYFIELD see Mayfield
MASON Andrew-75;Arnett-234;Bennet-*224 (Thomas Martin above)

109(2);David-59;James-59-173-231;Reason-74;Samuel-146;William-75-76-234
MASSALT Anthony-90
MASSEY George-231;Samuel-142
MASTEN Stephen-33-35-44(2)
MASTERS Albert-226;Richard-227
MATHERS James-194;John-194
MATHIS see Matthews
MATKIN David-170
MATLOCK David-196(2)-199(2);George-197-199;James-196-200-201-209-210;John-201(2);William-202
MATTHEWS Michael-26;Reuben-9;Richard-163-175
MATTHEWSON Daniel-40
MATTINGLY Augustin-27-30;Bernard-165;Eleazer-175;Henry-26;Hillary-31-153;James-13-19;Richard-34;Sylvester-19
MATTOX William-158
MAUK see Mock;Abraham-69-70-71;John-68-70;Joseph-69-70-71;Julius-71;Samuel-69-71
MAUZY John-30;Thomas-30
MAXAM John-65;Sylvester-65-67
MAXWELL Alexander-98;James-136;John-98-123-125-130-132;William-123-130-131
MAY Abraham-189-198;David-123-195;Jacob-194;John-179-189;Peter-190;Richard-215;Solomon-189;William-126-189-199
MAYER see Mahee,Mahew,Meyers
MAYES James-98;John-122
MAYFIELD Alexander-175;Reuben-139-140;Seaborn-176;William-205
MAYHALL Jonas-75-76-77;Timothy-60
MAYO John-232
MEADEN Alfred-124(2)
MEADORS Isham-128
MEADOWS Franklin-222;Jacob-143-187-188;James-143;John-142-143;Jubel-147;Perry-187;William-142-188
MEADS see Made;Israel-102;John-151-152;Stephen-84;Thomas-16-31;William-16-17-31(2)-32-33
MEARS Franklin-156
MEDEARIS Hirjate-105
MEDLEY Austin-113(2);Joseph-115-116;Marcus-113(2)
MEEHAN Thomas-27
MEEK James-178;John-177;Samuel-76
MEISENHELTER Emanuel-56-110(2)-159;Samuel-56-110-159

MEKERSOM James-55;Joseph-55
MELION John-17
MELTON Abner-109;Alexander-107;
   Calistus-26;Elijah-59-69;Esau-
   140;Henry-175;Jeremiah-148;Mich-
   ael-60-61-63;Nathan-148;Nehemi-
   ah-147;Nimrod-140;Stephen-38;
   Thomas-25
MELVIN Thomas-127-128;William-
MENSCH John-108.   127-170
MERCER Obed-168;Samuel-168;Wil-
   liam-168
MEREDITH Thomas-34
MERICLE Abraham-156
MERIWETHER Albert-215;David-
   215(2).   101
MERRELL Nathaniel-105;Richard-35;
MERRICK Joseph-96-97;Malachi-216-
MESCH Conrad-115.   225
MESSER see Musser;John-195
MEST William-133
METTE Joseph-106;Pierre-106
MEYERS Daniel-39-40-41-42-148-
   180;Elias*44(2);Fanny-44;Fred-
   erick-40-41-42-97;George-79;Hen-
   ry-92-113;Isaiah-125;Jacob-127-
   166-189;James-79;Jerome-104;
   John-39-40(2)-173;Joseph-40(2);
   Michael-185;Samuel-80;Simon-116;
   William-126-148-187; *Elias-
   40(2)-41(2)
MIEURE William-106
MIKESELL Garret-99;John-99
MILAM George-197;Lee-105
MILBURN Cary-56;David-54;Felix-
   122;James-212;John-56;Jonathan-
   163;Joseph-122;Robert-64-66;
   Thomas-217
MILES Ellender-173;Felix-173(2)-
   174;James-172;John-172;Joseph-
   173;Wilford-173
MILEY Amanda-222;Caroline-222;Da-
   vid-216-222;George-220¢Henry-
   216(3)-229;Jacob-222;John-222;
   Martin-214;Rebecca-222;Samuel-
   214-217;William-224;Wilson-214-
MILLAN seeMcMillan;John-77. /220/
MILLER Aaron-232;Abraham-117(2)-
   130;Adam-52-82;Alexander-10-11;
   Andrew-45-100;Christian-225;Dab-
   ney-201;Daniel-51;David-84-85-
   86-142;Elijah-176(2);Ezekiel-38;
   Felix-188;George-225;Harrison-
   118;Henry-124-154;Hiram-38;Jack-
   227;Jacob-96-99-100(2);James-
   117-228;John-45-46-57(2)-64-75-

77-85(2)-87-94-95-100-117-129-
   130-177-184-192-201-213-214-223-
   229-230(2);Joseph-31-32(2)-33;
   Martin-100-115;Nancy-211;Peter-
   56;Philip-45;Samuel-94-104-117;
   Smith-54;Thomas-168-228;William-
   53-85(2)-101-172-188-225-228
MILLIAN Benson-51
MILLIKAN Jacob-207(2);William-
   207-210
MILLIS Edward-170
MILLS Daniel-61;James-55-64(2);
   John-118;Samuel-80
MILN William-57-228(2)
MINARD Leonard-120;Samuel-119-120
MINER Basil-104;St.Clair-100;
   William-104   190
MINGS Henry-191;Peter-190;William
MINNICK Henry-183;Isaac-182;Jacob
   183;Samuel-183
MINNIS Calvin-57-61-62-68-73;Ja-
   mes-60-62-68;Thomas-62
MINTON William-84
MITCHELL Abraham-135-137-163;Alex
   ander-93;Benjamin-163;Benniah-
   54;Charles-135;David-127;Isaac-
   135-146-179;Jacob-145;James-185-
   188-190;John-94-141-225;Joseph-
   193-195;Levi-145;Lucy-59;Robert-
   49-136-141(2)-181;Rufus-179;Sam-
   uel-66-179;Stacey-66;Thomas-
   145(2)-171-172;William-163(2)-
   169-175-176
MITCHELTREE George-163;William-
MIZE Redman-180;William-194. /170
MOALER Frederick-117
MOCK see Mauk;John-58
MOFFATT William-53-80(2)-227
MOLLOY James-131;Michael-20;Peter-
   19;William-19(2)
MOLTON Mat-221
MOMINEE Anthony-106;Augustus-106
MONAHAN Charles-74.   (2)/
MONROE James-81
MONSON George-140
MONTGOMERY Benjamin-89;Dudley-232
   Elijah-36;Harvey-231;Isaac-59-60-
   64-68-161-230;James-30-32-71-85-
   86-87;John-27-68-70-72-82;Joseph-
   59-72-84(2)-86;Moses-71;Nathan-
   83;Pretuimon-95;Robert-94;Samuel-
   88-94-95;Tandy-72;Thomas-68-71-
   86;Valentine-14;Walter-83-84-87;
   William-84;Willis-83
MONTRAY see Moutray
MOOLRY William-88

MOONEY see Mumey
MOORE Edward-55;Garrett-194;
  George-95;Jackson-150;James-30-
  47-50;Jesse-210;John-54-143-157-
  210;Joshua-39(2);Lewis-157(2);
  Pinkney-144;Samuel-60-81-194;
  Thomas-32;Uriah-138-150;William-
  18-49-58-141
MOORHEAD James-31-32;John-11(2)-
  159;Robert-16;Thomas-9-11(2)-
  16-158-159
MORGAN Abel-152;Absalom-190;Char-
  les-28(2);Elijah-190(2);James-
  27;Jesse-28(2)-47;Jonathan-12-
  24-25;Joseph-218;Josiah-10-12;
  Moses-11-23;Preminter-189;Solo-
  mon-191;William-11-46
MORLAND Enos-151-153-156
MORRIS Burr-157;David-108;George-
  141;Isaac-129;Jesse-97;John-57-
  77-93-109-196;Richard-120;Wil-
  liam-43
MORRISON Charles-125-153-154;Ed-
  win-214;George-213;James-154;
  Strobridge-214;William-231
MORROW A.S.-82
MORSE Benjamin-225;John-60(2)-
  63;Moses-68
MOSELY Robert-57-58;Susannah-213
MOSER see Musser;Anthony-176;
  George-176;James-165;John-175
MOSS George-196
MOSZ John-105
MOUDER Henry-167
MOULDER Jacob-154
MOUNTS David-124-140;Ellet-203;
  Matthias-69;Montgomery-83;Smith-
  84;Tilmon-204-205
MOURY Jacob-71
MOUTRAY James-90(2)
MOWRER Joseph-72
MUCKELROY Martha-204
MUGENSTURM Anthony-104
MULHERON Anthony-19
MULKY James-206
MULLER Henry-138
MULLICAN James-153
MULLIN James-12;John-156
MULLIS Reuben-46-181
MUMEY Jacob-186;Patrick-57
MUNDAY John-133-169;William-133
MUNFORD John-55
MURET Julius-29
MURPHY Aaron-94-95;Alexander-193;
  Hugh-64;John-18(2)-49-50-111-
  162;Michael-36-107;Noah-88;Pat-

rick-14;Robert-74-75;Samuel-64;
  Thomas-29
MURRAY Christopher-14;Samuel-17;
  Timothy-123
MUSE Daniel-71;James-71;Sarah-
  71;Thomas-71
MUSHRUSH John-157
MUSIC Asa-72;Ephraim-71
MUSSER see Messer,Moser;George-
  148;Henry-186;John-112-186-188-
  199

N see K
NACLE Henry-113
NAIL William-132
NANCE Harrison-119;James-224;
  John-147-151;Richard-147-192;
  Thomas-224
NANCEY James-227
NASH Charles-230;William-153
NAYLON Dennis-14;Michael-14;
  Patrick-14
NEABARGER Sebastian-93
NEAL Alexander-127;Arthur-129;Da-
  vid-171;Emri-108;Martin-154;Sam-
  uel-172;William-168;Wilson-108
NEELY John-66-67-68-78-85;Samuel-
NEEPERT Lewis-78   117
NEESE John-203;William-210
NEFF Jesse-155;Joseph-155
NELSON John-114;Margaret-222
NESBIT Thomas-165-205;William-
  196-205
NEWBY Micah-199
NEWCOMB William-147-150-197
NEWKIRK Cornelius-188
NEWMAN James-202;Thomas-119;
  William-77
NEWSUM Joseph-91;Pearson-89
NEWTON George-161(3);William-197
NICHOLAS see Nichols;Daniel-163;
  James-163;John-184;Jonathan-198;
  Joseph-163;William-163
NICHOLS see Nicholas;Hannah-198;
  John-49-59-194-223;Jonathan-198;
  Joshua-88;Thomas-48-78;Wesley-171
NICHOLSON George-232;John-194;
  Simon-22
NIEBARGER see Neabarger
NIERSTE Henry-115(2)
NIXON Abraham-54;Andrew-57;Rob-
  ert-54;William-174
NOAKES Jackson-155
NOBLE John-50
NOBLITT Elizabeth-168;William-168
NOEL Lewis-203

NOLAND Edward-14;Enoch-225;Law-
rence-13-14;Lazarus-96;Robert-13
NOLL John-199(2)
NOON John-145
NORMAN James-120-159;Joel-159;
John-163;Moses-153-161(2);Pres-
ton-117-,120;Rufus-119;Wesley-
154;William-159
NORRIS Bernard-25-26;Charles-13-
40;John-25-26;Richard-26;William
NORTH Peter-14.   54/
NORVELL Ralph-150
NOSSETT William-59
NUCKOLLS Ezra-139;James-138-139;
Rhodes-138
NUGENT David-127;Enos-137;Fred-
erick-127(2);Gabriel-127;John-
NULL David-74-75   128
NUNNALLY Hosea-39;Levi-40
NUTT Henry-221
NYE John-159-161-164-170(2)

OBERT Anthony-93
O'BRIEN Cornelius-15;John-26-37-
163;Joseph-171;Peter-164;Syl-
vester-172-173
OCHLER Dennis-19
O'CONNOR Michael-19-51
ODELL Caleb-150;Emsley-47-149;Is-
aac-148-150;Joseph-149;Nehemiah-
149
O'DONALD Fielding-45-181;William-
45-182
OFENLOCK Henry-214
OFFICER William-88
OGDEN Daniel-213;Maria-213;Mary-
OGLESBY Jacob-91   213
OGLETREE George-118
OLDS Moses-189
OLIPHANT James-52;Lawson-149
OLIVER William-36-42-45-99-100-
101-106(2)-107(2)-119(2)-120;
Willis-205
OLNEY Asa-120
O'NEIL Calvin-53;Harry-231;Harvey-
65;Henry-45-52;Hugh-45;James-45;
John-53;Samuel-45;Timothy-18;
William-153
ORIN James-76
ORR Adam-56;John-59-64-65-66-87;
Simon-69-82
ORRINDER Wiley-164
ORTON Jordan-128;Levi-128
OSBORN Arah-203;Eber-217;George-
47;Jacob-47-48-182;James-45-48;
Jonathan-148;Moses-36;Nicholas-

36;Solomon-48-166;William-45
OSMON Charles-34;Isaac-30;Jabez-
38-41(3)-42;John-183;Judier-41;
Samuel-30;Simon-33
OVERLIN John-224
OVERTON George-91;Joshua-71;Moses
48;Nathaniel-78;Susannah-36
OWENS Alexander-203;Andrew-134;
James-36-145-146-177;John-134-
135-145-199-201;Joseph-145;Mer-
cer-148;Owen-145(2)-146;Randolph
93;Robert-177-212;Samuel-36-148;
Thomas-19(2)-156-165;William-145
OZEE Michael-176

P see B, F
PACE Daniel-108-151;James-109-
134-138;John-128
PACKER George-125
PADEN Jacob-88-90
PADDOCK William-49
PADGETT Benedict-25-38-165-174-
175;Charles-174-175;George-25-38
James-175;John-174;William-25-
38(2)-174
PAGE William-104
PAINTER Aaron-168
PALMER Elijah-96;Henry-194;Horace
220;John-224;Mason-20(2);Parmen-
as-23;Richard-34
PANCAKE Jacob-230;Joseph-230;Pey-
ton-231;William-230
PANGBURN Walter-152
PARHAM Allen-185-190
PARKER Columbus-178;Frederick-109
George-215;Lorenzo-234;Sanford-
61;William-138-139-150-217
PARKINSON Hugh-66
PARKS Albert-200;Andrew-194;Ben-
jamin-204;George-200;Hugh-14;Ja-
mes-196-201-203;Joseph-33;Marra-
day-203;Parminter-209;Samuel-203
Stephen-194;William-201
PARRETT Richard-121
PARRIS George-136
PARRISH see Perisho;Abraham-196;
Eli-196
PARSONS Corydon-29;James-195-198;
Omy-29;William-28
PARVIN William-65
PARYWIRE Peter-76
PATE Allen-172;Benjamin-175
PATRICK Obadiah-43;William-195
PATRIDGE Patrick-38
PATTERSON A.-199;Arthur-98-196;
Gilbert-38;Greenberry-38;John-

118-207;Joseph-13;Martin-13(2);
Robert-73;William-38-115
PATTON George-9-16;James-87-88(2);
Samuel-194;Thomas-9-10;William-
PAUGH Hiram-193;Freeborn-148./189
PAUL Edmund-201;George-186-201;
Gilbert-200;William-53-200
PAULEY Abraham-193;Elijah-73;
Isaac-194
PAYNE Barnabas-167;Benjamin-219;
Jacob-201-216;John-172;Patrick-
56;Riley-167(2);Thomas-122-167-
201
PAYTON Elbert-167-178;Josephus-
178;Peter-178;
PEA Jacob-105;John-105
PEACHEE Benjamin-31;Henry-159;
James-17-30-34;Peary-10-41
PEARSON Eliphalet-143-148;Samuel-
49-138;William-75-77
PECK Barton-35-107;John-12-155;
Thomas-163
PEDIGO John-147(2)-149
PEED Richard-13-17
PEEK Cager-164-166;Hiram-166;Ja-
mes-170;John-23
PEERY see Perry;George-164;James-
PELIENZ Philip-99   164
PEMBERTON John-227;Reuben-53;
Thomas-227-228
PENDER Daniel-32
PENNINGER James-181;Jesse-176-181
PENNINGTON see Bennington;John-19;
Joseph-147-185-192(2);Samuel-185
PENNOR John-228
PENZWIRE Peter-76
PEIFER Hiram-153
PERCY see Piercy
PERISHAM John-205
PERISHO Joseph-199
PERKINS Abraham-30-32-40;Alfred-
29;Asbury-28-29-41;Benjamin-47;
Elisha-27-28-29(2)-32(2);James-
68;John-26-28-61-68;Mark-30;Reu-
ben-30;Robert-43;William-30-45-
47-144-145-146
PERRIN see Pierrin
PERRY see Peery;Nathaniel-234;
Samuel-159-160-161;William-21-102
PETERS John-148;Mary-195;William-
195
PETERSON Francis-36;Peter-21;
William-28-37
PETTAY Daniel-126(2);Francis-126
PETTYJOHN Daniel-111
PFEFFER see Pipher,Piper,Pepper;
Christian-166

PHARES see Ferris
PHELPS Francis-200;Gordon-206
PHILLIPS Alexander-54;Alfred-182;
Alvin-181;Andrew-52;Daniel-110-
129;David-118;Edmund-186;Edwin-
52-217;Elizabeth-190;Hannah-128;
James-53-118;John-46-53-103-119-
129-182-192;Lewis-128-131;Payton-
52;Peter-128-129;Pleasant-182;
Ramson-228;Robert-54;Roda-52;Sil-
as-46;Solomon-198-199;William-46-
53(2)-181-188-228
PHIPPS Benjamin-46-48-147-150;Ja-
mes-181;Jesse-47;John-150-171;Jo-
seph-167-172;Lewis-47
PICKLE Jacob-195
PIERCE see Piercy;Chauncey-91;
George-83(2);Henry-138;James-78-
138;John-150;Josiah-138-150;Nehe-
miah-54;Newton-138;Richard-117;
Warren-116;Washington-116
PIERCY Joseph-193-201
PIERRIN John-180
PIERSON see Pierrin,Pearson
PIETY James-118;Samuel-118;Thomas-
118;William-110
PILES Jacob-137
PILGRIM Henry-121
PINE William-151
PINKARD 120-Joseph
PINKNEY George-126
PINNEY Edward-64
PIPER Samuel-168
PIPHER see Pfeffer,Piper,Pepper;
Michael-161(2)
PIPPIN Michael-155
PITMAN Holland-136
PLOUGH Samuel-228
PLUCK John-27
PLUESS Jacob-138;John-128-129;
Joseph-128-131
PLUMMER Horace-219-230
POE Angus-207;Fielden-205-207;
Greenup-84;Jesse-220;William-206
POHLMEIER Frederick-113;Henry-113;
William-113(2)
POINDEXTER Christian-171(2)
POIK Charles-118;James-115-117;
William-118
POLLEY Absalom-199
POOL Anderson-177
POORMAN Jacob-104-106
POPE Harling-129
PORCH William-197
PORTER Calvin-15;David-168;Ezek-
iel-158-170;James-9;John-152;

Meshack-33-101;Samuel-162;Shad-
rack-101;William-45
POSEY John-216;Lane-232;Wade-212
POSTLETHWAIT Isaac-229;Jonathan-
211;Samuel-229;William-229
POTTER Absalom-60;Arnold-163;Ben-
jamin-149;Gideon-135;Josephus-
60;Lewis-135;Stephen-136;Thomas-
60-67;William-145
POTTS Samuel-20;William-31
POWELL Alexander-95-174;Eli-147;
Elijah-141;Ezekiel-232;James-95;
Jeremiah-51;John-95;Margaret-
155;William-141.   233
POWERS Samuel-232(2)-233;Simeon-/
POWNALL Isaac-180;Samuel-180
PRATER Jeremiah-14
PRATHER James-108
PRATT George-24-33-34-35-42-43-
44-49-51-52-59-66-212-215-223
PRENTISS John-16-156-158-165
PRESSEY Charles-97-103
PRESTON Azom-214;Shelton-149;
William-149-178
PRICE Amzi-53-54;Benjamin-96-97;
George-120;Henry-111(3);James-
88;John-89-178;Josiah-139;Morde-
cai-57;Stephen-77;William-54-96-
97
PRIDE Henry-211;Thomas-211;Wil-
liam-213;Wolsey-211-216
PRIDMORE Theodore-130
PRINCE Isham-186;John-143;Nathan-
iel-56;Presley-25-37-38
PRINGLE John-40-114
PRITCHETT Jeremiah-121;John-84-
86;William-121;Wright-83
PRIVETT Jacob-85
PROFFIT George-213
PRUCH John-221
PRUITT Daniel-182;J.-82;Joel-67
PRY John-23-25;Thomas-23;William-
24(2)
PUETT Amsted-203-209;Coleman-203-
206;William-209
PULSE George-141
PURCELL Adam-121(2);Andrew-52-98-
99-110;Daniel-137;Henry-136;Jon-
athan-100;William-72
PURDY Sarah-116
PURINGTON John-41-42
PURKEY Jacob-174
PURSER John-126
PUTHAM Caroline-122;Daniel-65-78-
121;Elijah-78;Hazael-64-78-93;
Henry-207-208;Reddin-93;Saml-121;
Wm.-82-209

QUACKENBUSH Albert-151;Peter-154
QUEEN James-172;Joseph-171;Rich-
ard-171;Thomas-164
QUIGLEY Joseph-30;Susannah-30
QUILLEN John-144;William-144
QUINCY see Guircy
QUINN John-126-127

RACHELS John-92
RACINE Henry-105
RADER John-202;Thomas-201
RAGAINS William-190
RAGLE John-47;Peter-36(2)
RAGSDALE Hezekiah-21;John-49;
Thomas-22
RAHM William-81
RAINBOLT Adam-147;Jesse-147;
Joseph-148
RAINEY Clement-27-166(2);George-
48-136-177-180;James-13-158-201
John-27-172;Johnson-155;Jonathan
158-166;Joseph-47-48-136-163(2)-
166;Matthew-27-227;Reuben-47-135
177;Robert-26(2);Valentine-164-
212;William-74
RAINS John-137;Jonathan-197;Wm-1
RALEIGH Richard-44
RALPH John-11
RALSTON James-82;Martha-80
RAMSEY Alfred-144;Francis-188;
John-100;William-122(2)
RAMSOUR Henry-29
RANEY see Riney,Rainey
RANSOM Isaac-108
RAPER Robert-35(2);Thomas-196
RAPP George-212
RATHBONE George-156
RATZE John-66
RAVELLET Francis-106;Louis-107
RAWLINGS Daniel-193;Elias-176;Fe-
lix-170-174;James-176-200;Joseph
137;Roderick-200-202-203;William
RAWLIS Henry-100(2)   208
RAY Daniel-207;Isaac-119;John-97-
125-133;Joseph-133(2);Nimrod-97
Squire-187;William-209(2)-210
RAYMOND David-131-201-206-210;
Jeremiah-20
RAZAR Daniel-47;Michael-47;Wm-48
REAVIS Alexander-65;Daniel-78-81-
86;Elias-75;Isham-65-67;Joseph-
65;Martin-67(2);Solomon-79-80;
Tabitha-62-65;William-60-61-62(
65(2)-67(2)-75-76-78-80-121-234
RECORDS Mary-180
RECTOR Isaac-168(2);Jesse-136;

John-127;Joseph-136(2)-137;
Levi-137-176-177
REDBURN Michael-56;William-56
REDDICK George-187;Hamilton-143
REDMAN Durham-83;Emily-177;Fer-
guson-110-111;John-88-157;Rob-
ert-84;William-88-95
REDNEY George-171
REED George-144-234;Isaac-68-69;
James-15-21-23-24(2)-28(2)-31(2)-
32(2)-33-234;John-144(2);Levi-
137;Nathan-35;Wm-80-81-162
REEDER Jacob-10;Joshua-91
REEL Aaron-96;Abraham-96-102-103;
David-96(2);Henry-52-85-96;Jac-
ob-96-103;James-26(2);John-97;
Joseph-85;Robert-97
REES Anthony-209;Thomas-33
REESINGER Daniel-114;David-30
REEVES Allen-112-114;Andrew-204;
Austin-196;Barnes-71-110;Edward-
166;John-196-203;Joseph-203;Jos-
hua-10;Lewis-43;Manasseh-108
REGAN Samuel-112
REGERSON Solomon-219
RENARD Daniel-205;Eli-167;Elias-
RENCH Philip-115   205
RENSHAW Thomas-198
REPP Jonathan-126
REYNOLDS see McReynolds;Abraham-
134-145;Benjamin-226;Charles-39;
Gabriel-167;J.L.-231;Isaac-64-
69;John-97-133;Joseph-65(3)-231;
Nathaniel-163;Richard-140;Thomas-
145-146-195;Washington-134;Wm-59
RHODES Lewis-212-219;William-212-
219;Willis-127
RHORER Christopher-194;John-221;
Joseph-222-229;Samuel-195.   142
RIBELIN David-136;Martin-136-141-/
RICE George-233;Jacob-154;Robert-
196;Washington-76;William-196
RICHARDS Gabriel-170;James-102;
Roland-71
RICHARDSON Ephraim-230;James-
181(2)-213;John-220;Joseph-132-
199;Richard-185;Wm-53-233
RICHARDVILLE Henry-106;John-
104(2)-106
RICHEY George-202;Jesse-46;John-
44-70-78;Sarah-46;Simpson-231
RICHISON Edward-167
RICKETTS John-234;William-114
RIDDLE William-200
RIDER William-147
RIDGE Benjamin-165-198-200-207;

Cornelius-28(2)-158-166;Isaac-
171;Levi-207
RIDGEWAY Benjamin-117
RIETZEL Joseph-93
RIGGINS James-134
RIGGS Aaron-124;Redden-124
RILEY Amos-164;Charles-9;Francis-
12-19;John-13-35-57-156(2)-162-
164-165-166;Luke-25;Michael-26;
Owen-17;Patrick-17-26-29;Terence-
9-14-15
RINEHART Caleb-151;John-162
RINGER Samuel-234
RIRDON John-9;Michael-9
RISINGER see Reesinger
RISLEY Charles-212;James-118;John-
102-229;Jonathan-219;Matthew-10;
Silas-216;William-96;Zachariah-10
RITEZEL Henry-209
RITTER George-194-201;Lazarus-51;
Moses-49-51;William-157
ROACH Isaac-181;William-45
ROARK Timothy-129
ROBB David-84-85-99;Edwin-227
ROBBINS Isaac-114-115-116;John-
114-115;Lewis-104;Martin-115;
Moses-115;Thomas-153;William-115
ROBERTS Archibald-122;Cornelius-
182;Daniel-219;Elias-57;Hiram-
178;James-160-176;John-138-149-
160-192;Joseph-70-71;Moses-176;
Silas-48;Thomas-68-178;Zach.-176
ROBERTSON Alexander-157;Asa-
119(3)-120(2);Edward-114;Freder-
ick-182;James-201;Jesse-47;John-
114;Michael-40-41-113;Moses-114;
Nathan-39-113-114
ROBINSON Abraham-84;Alfred-101-
108;Andrew-233;David-82;Elijah-
18(2)-35(2);Elizabeth-229;Henry-
87;Isham-84-94;James-50-174;John-
54-87-110;Joseph-46-50;Martin-94-
95;Michael-94(2)-114;Nicholas-94-
95;Richard-117;Samuel-68-97;Thom-
as-87;William-13-53-54-85-151;
Willis-209;Zedekiah-46;Zilpha-161
ROBLING John-219;Louis-227;Peter-
219;William-219-226;Wilson-219
ROBY Thomas-155
ROCHESTER John-139-142
ROCKWELL John-93
RODARMEL Abraham-21;Allen-101;
David-102;John-23
RODDICK George-29(2)-34;John-48;
Seth-17-29-34-35
RODENBURRY John-15

RODERICK Anna-98;John-98;Payton-98 S see Z
ROGERS Amos-22-25;Aquilla-193;
  Benjamin-194;Clayton-10-25-101;
  David-194-202;Elizabeth-146;Geo-
  rge-101;Henry-202;Isaac-193-197-
  198-199;James-194-198;Jonathan-
  194;Lewis-170(3);Samuel-202-205-
  206;Sarah-102;William-101
ROGERSON Solomon-211
ROLLMEYER Henry-92
ROLLAH Jacob-100
ROLLIS see Rawlin
ROOK Elijah-90
ROOT Charles-155
ROSBOROUGH Alexander-84;James-85;
  Joseph-94;Thomas-95
ROSE Charles-167-179-184;Jesse-93
ROSEBERRY William-205
ROSS John-34-36-136-137-138;Ran-
  dolph-189;William-195
ROSTER Daniel-108
ROUTT John-185-188-205;Valentine-
  29-32;William-31-32-53
ROWAN John-20
ROWE Robert-61;William-64
ROY see Faunt LeRoy;Leonard-149;
  Thomas-145;William-145
ROYAL Michael-26(2)
RUBLE David-116;Jesse-33
RUBY Spier-110
RUDYARD Isaiah-137;John-137;Jos-
  eph-137-177.   134
RUEBOTTOM Henry-45-46;Simon-131-/
RUGGLES Aaron-29;Nathaniel-158
RUMBLE Alexander-223;Samuel-223-
  226;William-223
RUMMER Daniel-41;Frederick-40;
  John-40
RUMPH Peter-174
RUMPLE Jacob-203
RUNGE Henry-92
RUNNIER George-173
RUPERT Michael-22
RUSH Azel-148;Clark-148;Dugan-
  192;Patrick-41
RUSSELL Abraham-58-122;Charles-
  211;Jeffery-127;John-211;Wm-211
RUST William-229
RUTHERFORD Ezekiel-152;Lloyd-157;
  Mark-152
RUTLEDGE-Ezekiel-84;James-117-
  119(2);Johnson-84-85;Wm-85-94
RUTTER John-71
RYALL George-213
RYAN Johanna-175;Michael-41;
  Richard-145

SADLER John-189(2)-193-198-199
SAIBURT John-81
SALMON Amos-163-174;Elijah-89;Hon-
  tage-89;William-16;Wilson-162
SAMPLE Thomas-34;William-21-39
SAMPSON Aaron-212;Aquilla-97;Jack-
  son-97-102;James-97;Jesse-96-102
SANDAGE William-48
SANDALL Christian-92
SANDERS see Landers,Souders;Benja-
  min-190;Elisha-197;Henry-197-198;
  James-168-172;John-125-177-205;
  Joseph-197(2);Leroy-205;Louis-
  173;Thomas-191
SANDERSON Robert-195
SANFORD Harriet-120
SANKLIN John-144
SAPP Clement-39
SARE see Sears;Mr.-206;Asbury-191;
  James-146;John-191;Lucian-192;
  Reuben-147;Samuel-150(2)
SARTOR George-110;John-110(2)
SATTERFIELD Samuel-26;Solomon-26-
  32;Wesley-25
SAVARNS Bryant-212-216;George-212;
  Silas-212
SAWYER Franklin-214-218-220-223;
  Milo-72
SAXON see Sexson
SAXTON Robert-77
SCALES John-233;Stephen-202(2);
  Thomas-9(2)
SCANDLING John-118
SCANTLIN James-69-80
SCARBROUGH Elijah-148
SCARLETT James-160
SCHELL Christian-220
SCHMIDT Adam-92
SCHMOLL Martin-65
SCHONK John-79
SCHOOLEY Henry-163-167;John-163;
  Reuben-162-163
SCHORSCH Peter-102
SCHRIETH Jacob-115
SCHWARTZ Frederick-115;John-115(2)
SCOGGAN Isaac-127
SCOTT David-185-188;Henry-148;Ja-
  mes-85-175;John-86-110-175-185-
  187-188;Jonathan-197;Joseph-84;
  Samuel-65-202-233;Smith-34;Thom-
  as-91-197-198;Vincent-162;William
  105-107-207(2)
SCRANTON Asher-149
SCRAPER George-213;Henry-211-213;
  Jasper-213;John-211-219-220

SCROGGINS John-44
SCUDDER Fenwick-22;Henry-11;John-
12-22-23(2)-24-25
SEABO Isaac-193
SEAIS John-38-163;Thomas-15-165;
William-38
SEAMAN James-72
SEARS see Saro;Andrew-141;Barton-
141;Benjamin-141;David-138-141-
188-194-196-205;Edward-141;Ezra-
139-141;Henry-141;Jacob-149-193-
206;Matthias-146-147;Michael-
147;Reuben-191;William-140
SEBRING Charles-221
SECHMAN Charles-99
SEE see Lee;George-195
SEIFRIET Mr.-29;Charles-29;Geo-32
SELBY John-222-223;Joshua-216;
Peter-224;Richard-220-221-224;
Zachariah-217;Zepheniah-218
SELGER Henry-115
SELLARS Abraham-120;Edward-141;
Henry-168;John-168-169;Levi-149;
Lewis-145
SEISOR Andrew-150-183;Milley-72
SENTENAY Lewis-150
SERGEANT Absalom-142-145-182;El-
isha-181;Joseph-140-142-181;
Thomas-172-182
SERVICE James-187
SEWELL John-160
SEXSON Joel-190;Lemuel-191
SHADLE Henry-121
SHAFER Anthony-94;Benjamin-227;
Charles-93-108-116;Elizabeth-93;
Henry-228;Levi-227;Wm-109-228
SHALLER Andrew-179
SHANER Catherine-96
SHANKLIN John-18-21
SHANKS John-22
SHANNER Charles-76
SHANNON Robert-79;Saml-55-65-66
SHARNST David-92
SHARP George-70-87-203(2)-210(3);
Harris-58-70;James-58(2)-70-87;
John-58;Micajah-88;Thomas-87;
William-58
SHARPLESS Thomas-180-181;Wm-181
SHARUM Harvey-25;James-163-172-
174;John-27;Thomas-184;Wm-175
SHARUND George-174
SHAUM John-31
SHAW Alfred-222-225;Elvis-218-
221-222;Hugh-221-222(3)-225;John-
154;Joseph-110;William-77-78
SHEA James-14(2);Michael-14(2)

SHEEKS George-146;John-130
SHELBURNE Augustin-209;Paschal-
208(2)-209
SHELDON Pardon-118
SHELL Truman-23
SHELMIRE Bedford-155;Jesse-158
SHENICK U.Frederick-23
SHEPARD George-165;Horace-118-120;
John-30(2)-32-33-35;Mary-31;Mil-
es-154-161;William-104
SHERIDAN Anthony-18
SHERMAN Mason-156-160-162-163-
171-174
SHERROW George-45-47;Lorenzo-46-48
SHERWOOD Marcus-83
SHERRY John-81;William-81
SHIELDS David-217;Henry-46;James-
46;John-160-167-170-206;Joseph-
56-122;John-46;Thomas-194;Wm-76-
188
SHIGLEY Joseph-228.
SHIPMAN James-198;John-185;Nicho-
las-190;Stephen-134-146;Thomas-
SHIPP Richard-193   189
SHIRCLIFF Mary-158;Robert-27;
Thomas-27
SHIRLEY Adam-170;Garrett-154;Geo-
rge-154;Henry-154(2);John-207;
Leeson-207;Richard-207
SHLATER Samuel-234(2)
SHIVELY Henry-39
SHOAF John-227
SHODY Benedict-35
SHOEMAKER see Slumaker;Moses-47
SHOLE Matthias-29
SHORT Alfred-149;Charles-139;Dod-
dridgo-139(2);Ezekiel-149;George-
195;Hansford-139;John-138(2)-139-
141-142-149(2);Martin-139;Milton-
150-177;Owens-139;Reuben-139;Sam-
uel-139(4);Thomas-138-139;Wesley-
139(4)-142
SHOTTS Frederick-15-28(2)-32-151-
152(3)-155-156-158(2);Matthias-
155-158
SHOULEE Michael-224
SHOUIS George-226;John-216-226
SHREVE Robert-105-106(2)
SHRYER Fetter-195;John-145
SHRYOCK Valentine-176
SHUCK George-210
SHUMALL Samuel-128
SHUTTER Jacob-183-184.   26
SIDELL George-78(2)-79-81;James-/
SIDES Henry-84;James-84;John-86
SIGHT see Like,Light;Russell-118
SILER see Sellars;Adam-130-137

SILLAVAN Andrew-82;Samuel-82
SILVER George-144
SIMMONS John-151-204;Michael-22;
Moses-151;Samuel-150
SIMON Isaac-228
SIMONSON Alfred-43-51;Isaiah-42;
John-43;Josiah-43;William-108
SIMPKINS William-47
SIMPSON Archibald-85-86;Arthur-
160;Bazil-225-228;Charles-129;
Demcy-176-178;Ephraim-88;Green-
berry-91;Hugh-74;Humphrey-228;
James-87;John-77-83-84-87;Levi-
176;Mary-234;Richard-87;Robert-
234;Solomon-74;Wm-74-77-88-233
SIMS Allen-207;Jackson-197;James-
177-179;John-135-162-167-177;
Nicholas-175-179-197;Starling+
135-177;William-177-207;Zachar-
iah-162-174-177
SINCLAIR John-119;William-172;
see St. Clair
SINCON Philip-16
SINGLETON Thomas-50
SINKS Salem-20
SIPES Clabourne-192;George-178-
187;Henry-192;William-179-192
SISCO Peter-100;William-100-171
SIZEMORE Isaac-177
SKAGGS Robert-123-126
SKAIN see Spain;John-108
SKEEN Henry-139
SKELTON Elias-75;James-62(2)-66;
John-72;Jacob-75(3)-76-77-80;Ja-
mes-75-87;John-75;Jonas-81;Ralph-
75;Robert-75(2)-79-81;William-
61-62-75-79;Zachariah-65
SKIDMORE James-68
SKINNER Alexander-187
SKOMP Henry-112(2)-113;Isaac-111-
112;John-112(2);Samuel-112(4)
SLAUGHTER Frederick-113;Moses-209-
210;Philip-113
SLAVIN Isaac-55-56;Robert-55
SLAYMAKER see Slumaker,Shoemaker
SLINKARD Daniel-112;Henry-112;
John-112;Moses-112(2)
SLOAN James-148;Mary-133;Richard-
57;Robert-68(2);Thomas-193
SLOPPER Joel-160
SLOTT James-100
SLUMAKER James-46
SLUSHER Eli-100;William-100-121
SMALL Benjamin-30;Jacob-102;
Thomas-97
SMALLWOOD Enoch-179

SMELTSER Paulser-48;Winfield-46
SMILEY Elizabeth-47-50;Jacob-49;
Jonathan-50;John-50
SMITH Adam-89;Alexander-191;Allen
39;Anderson-181-182;Andrew-70-71
Benjamin-141;Charles-127;Coleman
221;Daniel-81;David-89-90-91-202
Dudley-197;Edward-98-104;Elijah-
53;George-113-114-115-206-221;
Harrison-82-117-160;Henry-22-
221(2)-233;Hosea-216-223;Isaac-
85-101-166;James-18(2)-36-70-72-
86-161(2)-192-233;John-19-21-22-
82-86-101-114-115-141-147-149-
154-158-162(2)-165-179-183-187-
194-204-219;Jonas-176-177;Joseph
176-177;Martin-83-149;Matthew-
198;Nicholas-106-206(2);Nuttall-
66;Peter-90-91;Philip-58-199-206
Raphael-18-19;Robert-156;Samuel-
166-176-186-205;Sarah-141;Simon-
131-141-184;Thomas-80-104-122-
153-156-193-200-202-224;Warren-
220-229;Washington-207;Wiley-66;
William-18-24-31-84-161-186-189-
192-217;Willis-210;Wyett-65;
Zachariah-141-176-180
SMOCK Matthew-112
SMOTHERS John-199.   202
SMOYER Frederick-206(2);Lawrence-
SNAPP Elijah-117;Jacob-117;Wm-117
SNODDY Thomas-196
SNODGRASS Daniel-172;James-170-
173-179;Robert-9(2)
SNOW Isaac-110;Martin-190
SNYDER Abraham-40;Adam-218-227;
Daniel-218;David-33-51(2)-97-103
John-96;Richard-201;Samuel-33-96
103;William-166-202
SODA Peter-15-19;Philip-19
SOLIMAN George-92
SOLOMON Henry-17
SORGINS George-220;Jacob-220
SORGUS Michael-214
SOTE Henry-103-104
SOUTHERN Daniel-153-154;James-153
SOWDER see Lowder,Sanders;Caleb-
193;Henry-188;Joseph-193
SPAIN see Skain;Abraham-81-122;
Archibald-54;Macklin-70-80-81
SPAKE Daniel-218(2)
SPALDING Hillary-38;Ignatius-25;
John-38;Joseph-26-27;Peter-27-28
Thomas-38;William-172
SPARKS Daniel-29;George-174;Levi-
44;William-113-189

SPEAR Friend-12(2)-21;Harrison-
140;Henry-134;Jacob-78;James-78;
John-135;Richard-140-170;Robert-
74-76-234;Washington-140
SPEED Henry-127-131-132-140-150-
165-190-193-199
SPENCER Daniel-65;Hiram-161;Jos-
eph-154;Samuel-65;William-154
SPICELY William-134
SPINK Francis-35
SPORE Jacob-69
SPORTSMAN Hugh-84-86
SPRAGUE William-122
SPRINGGATE William-203
SPRINKLE Henry-119
SPROAT Benjamin-117;John-110-
117(3)-120(3)
SPROUL James-58;John-64(2)
SPURLING Samuel-123-128;Zachariah-
123;Zacheus-228
ST.CLAIR see Sinclair;Isaac-182
STAFFORD Christopher-28;James-10-
102(2);John-12;Matthew-112;Mich-
ael-20;Philip-103;Robert-199;
Trice-9-21   92
STALLINGS Moses-81;Reuben-81;Wm-/
STANDLEY Jacob-175;John-174;Wm-168
STANFIELD George-151;William-155
STANGER John-204
STANSBERRY Nathan-209;William-210
STAPLETON Edward-86;Joseph-86;
Joshua-63-64-67
STARK Franklin-148;Pleasant-166
STARNES James-204-205
STARR Abel-37
STASER Conrad-95;Frederick-93;
John-93-94
STATTES Albert-128;Peter-128
STEELE Andrew-76;David-221;Jack-
son-24;James-74-151-231;John-
37-75;Robert-62-63-74;Samuel-
150(2);Thomas-152;William-87
STEEN John-20-101;Richard-21;
Robert-56-57;Samuel-101
STEITING Simon-108
STEP Thomas-100
STEPHENS James-161-163-164(2)-165-
234;John-92-232;Joshua-75-76-79-
233-234;Nathan-228;Phineas-210;
Thomas-163
STEPHENSON Alexander-16;Dobson-
139;James-24(2);Peter-101(2);
Samuel-17-21;William-21-191
STERMER John-103
STERNS John-65
STERRETT Joseph-62;William-74

STEWART Abel-52-57;Charles-218;
David-142;Isaac-136(2);James-71-
72(2)-86-107;John-68-69-79-85(2)-
94-95-188-189;Levi-127;Luther-93;
Martin-234;Milton-143;Richard-
234;Samuel-39-41-55;Scoby-56-
58(2);Solomon-166(2);Thomas-
217(2);William-110-142-210
STIBBINS Eldad-42-43-50;George-24;
William-102.   /51/
STIGALL Henry-36-37
STILES see Stites;Johnson-209-210
STILLWELL Daniel-104;David-89;Geo-
rge-22-96;John-122;Niely-104;
Richard-122;William-88-90
STINE Elias-203;Enoch-210;Henry-
208-209;John-209;Paul-208
STINMAN Jeremiah-224
STIPP John-144;Michael-144
STITES see Stiles;Ann-174-175
STOCKTON Joseph-13-15
STOCKWELL Robert-77
STOGSDILL James-204;John-204;
William-204
STOKELY John-202
STONE Charity-148;Elias-10;Ellis-
193;Henry-211-225;Hiram-148;Jere-
miah-175;John-150;Mahlon-69;Ril-
ey-182;Silas-82;Thomas-87;Wm-39
STORK John-96(3)
STORM Alfred-147;James-186-188;
John-185-188-190-191-199   *
STORMONT David-57;James-63;Robert-
58-64-68-71;William-56-64
STORMS John-49; see Storm *
STOUT Daniel-201;Elihu-153;John-
STRAIN Polly-60   171
STRANGE Charles-26-38-174;Igna-
tius-174(2);James-37(2);John-37-
175;Joseph-175;Nancy-174;Philip-
37;William-171-174-175
STREAN Joseph-186
STREET see Stroot;Isaac-230;James-
STREIBY Joseph-104-106.   151
STRICKLAND Aaron-71;Daniel-79;Dav-
id-80;Elisha-77(2);Isaac-66-79;
James-77-79;Stephen-66(2)-67-77-
79;William-71
STRICTMOERDER Frederick-92
STRIKER Stephen-32
STRINGER Esek-22;John-21-25;Leon-
STRINGHAM Stephen-161.   /ard-22
STRIPE Henry-118
STROOT see Street;Anthony-152
STROUD William-108
STUBBLEFIELD John-215

STUCKEY Frederick-212;Jacob-215;
James-213;John-233;Martin-162;
Samuel-212;Upton-162
STULTZ Eli-182;George-144-180;Ma-
lissa-180;William-145-179-182
STUNKEL Frederick-92;Henry-92;
William-81
STURGIN Louis-123
SULLIVAN see Sillavan;Henry-53;
John-52;Joseph-140;Irvin-215-
217;Manoah-157;Thomas-53;William-
24-33-34-35-42-43-44-49-51-52(2)-
59-66-212-215-223
SUMEL Jacob-96
SUMMERS Ambrose-28;Andrew-32;Ben-
jamin-27;Charles-13-164;David-
153;Elijah-22-25;Franklin-45;Ja-
mes-12-13;John-13-32;Joseph-39-
42-94-166;Martin-215;Michael-24;
Richard-13;Rodolphus-13;Thomas-
13(2)-28;William-13-42-91
SUMMERVILLE John-180-181;Wm-181(2)
SUMMIT Christian-207-210;Jacob-
96;John-209
SUMNER Joseph-47;Philip-78;Thos-66
SUTHERLAND Alexander-136-150;
William-203
SUTPHEN Elias-52;James-52-99
SUTTON Benjamin-129;Ebenezer-98;
Ephraim-152;John-130-131;Josiah-
126;Rowland-14(2)-19(2);Samuel-
157;Silas-130;Sylvanus-156
SWAIN John-133
SWANEY see Sweeney
SWAYZE Alphas-172;John-172(3)
SWANN William-18
SWEENEY James-146-188;William-75
SWIFT Samuel-13
SWITZER John-185

T see D
TAHAN John-26;Michael-26
TALBOT Nathaniel-206
TAILEY Ellington-139
TANNER Michael-136
TARKINGTON Eli-189;Ellsberry-189;
Jesse-198-202;Pope-189;Sylvanus-
189-198
TARLETON Caleb-3Q
TARR John-195
TATE Andrew-207;Cary-49-50;Ed-
ward-50;John-23(2)-168-195;Nel-
son-126-159-170;Thomas-126;Wm-200
TATO David-229
TATUM Jonathan-147
TAYLOR see Traylor;Daniel-81-

100(2);David-70-79;Ephraim-76;
Henry-188;Isaac-79;Jacob-128-198
James-167-179-183;John-100-102-
163;Joseph-50-149-150-201-202-
205-229;Joshua-127-130;Mary-58(2)
Matthew-143;Robert-9-11(2)-16-
158-187-209;Samuel-150-167;Steph-
en-70;Tapley-209;Teckle-05;Wal-
ter-50;William-60-61-76-79-195
TEAGUE Edward-811-819;Francis-101
John-811-819;Lemuel-174;Michael-
191;Solomon-209;Thomas-134
TEFORTILAR George-12
TELLJOHANN see Katterjohn;Herman-
TENISON Martin-69.   232
TERRELL see Tewell,Duell,Ferrell;
Henry-126;James-58(2);John-126(2
160;Thomas-221;Walter-58-122;
William-123-125-157-160
TERRY Miles-60;Samuel-156;William
56-63-232
TEVENBAUGH Abraham-24-25-156-158;
George-97-117-118-213;Jacob-97-
102-103;Joseph-156;Nimrod-97-102
217;Riley-97;Solomon-96-97-102(2
TEWELL see Terrell,Duell;Charles-
164;Sarah-157
THACHER David-205;George-24-33-34
35-42-43-44-49-51-52-59-66-212-
215-223;Levi-194
THACKER Martin-101
THERIAC James-106
THOMAS Andrew-83-84;Benjamin-160-
163;David-84;Edmund-34-35;Eph-
raim-83;Fleming-213;Grandison-35
Isaac-92-220;James-82-97;John-91
220;Joshua-220;Lewis-214(3)-220-
221;Martha-214;Michael-220-222;
Orms-22-33-44;Solomon-35
THOMASON John-178;Nancy-128
THOMPSON Arthur-231;Harrison-230-
231;Mary-231;Robert-230;Samuel-
221-230;Greenup-83;Henry-54;John
35-54-72-107-202;Matthew-88-90;
Robert-98
THORN Asa-102;Charles-102;George-
101;Jacob-102;James-97(2)-103;
John-105;Joshua-102
THORNTON Joseph-70;Wm-69-136-205
THRASHER Elias-153;George-186
THRELKELD Moses-118
THROOP John-152
THURMAN Henry-84
TICHENOR David-119(2);John-119;
William-117
TIGERT William-43-114

TILLEY David-192
TILMAN Jonathan-232
TIMOTHY Felix-13
TIMFY see Jimpy
TINCHER Francis-130-131;George-
130-133;James-123-126-133;Sam-
uel-149;Stephen-133;Wm-149-150
TINDALE John-161(2)
TINN John-213
TINSLEY Milton-133;Ransom-133
TIREY John-129;Joseph-129;Thomas-
129;William-129(2)
TISDALE Haley-23-24(3);Renneson-
23;William-24-218-225-233
TISLOW Christopher-194;John-222;
Paul-211-216-217(2)-220
TODD Abbott-12;Andrew-193;Daniel-
139;Robert-212-215-217
TODDRILL John-190
TODRANK Casper-229
TOLBERT Henson-126
TOLIVER Allen-123;Andrew-125;
Charles-123;David-123;Franklin-
126;Jacob-123;James-179;Jesse-
123-124;John-123-124;William-
123-124-125-129-131
TOMKINS Reuben-203;Richard-82
TOMLINSON Henry-154;John-154;
-Samuel-45-135
TOMMY Amsted-40(2)-42;George-40;
Jacob-41;Josiah-40
TONGAST August-73;Emanuel-104
TOON Hillary-136;Lucian-183;Wm-183
TOTTEN Joseph-13
TOURTEILOT Abraham-216
TOUSEY Lucinda-99-106;Omer-99-107
TOWELL Jesse-141-142;John-131
TOWNSEND Amos-47-48;Erastus-55(3)-
65-67;James-122(2);John-47-48;
Milo-55(2);Susan-55
TOY John-20
TRABUE Ephraim-146
TRACY Patrick-35
TRANTER John-22
TRAVIS Daniel-194
TRAYLOR see Taylor;David-220;Jes-
se-211(2);John-225;Lewis-211;
Madison-220;Matthew-211;Thomas-
211(2)-220-224;William-23(2)
TRAYNOR Owen-13
TREADWAY Thomas-158
TREAKLE Thomas-26
TRENTHAM William-231
TRIBBLE Benjamin-194;George-85;
John-85-94;Thomas-80
TRIPPET Alexander-54;Caleb-55;
Waitman-54

TROGDON Isaac-145;Westard-145
TROVER Leonard-161
TROWBRIDGE Adole-108;Merrit-126
TRUEBLOOD Jesse-48;Josiah-128-132-
134;Mark-148;William-127-148
TRULOVE Michael-158;Wm-157-158
TRUITT Purnell-60
TRULOCK Thomas-100.   93
TRUMBULL Washington-155;William-/
TRUSDALE John-65-67-68-69(2)-234
TUBMAN John-233
TUCKER Daniel-78;John-9-32-185
TULLY James-17;Mark-134;Patrick-13
TUMEY Isaac-145
TUNING Thomas-34
TURMAN David-165;John-165
TURNER Elijah-94;James-53-208;
John-40-199-207;Owen-122;William-
9-10-38-40-46-74-159-163-164-169-
181-231-232-234
TURNEY Andrew-174;John-107;Sarah-
TURPIN Lewis-106;Wm-55(2).   106
TWEEDLE James-90-91
TYLER George-144;John-134;Patrick-
TYNER Stephen-115   144

ULM John-57
UNDERWOOD John-110;Robert-34
UNO Louis-106
UNWERFAHRT Louis-115
UPTON David-221-225;James-223
UTLEY James-61

V see F, P
VALES Lewis-47
VanBUSKIRK see Buskirk
VANCE Campbell-10-19-20;Joshua-110
VANDERHOOF Harvey-100-121
VANDERVOOT John-186
VANDIVER Elizabeth-160(2);Ichabod-
160;Madison-160;Nancy-160(2)
VANLANDINGHAM Thomas-69
VANMATER James-181;Joseph-45-46-
VANNOY Andrew-201   49
VanPRICE see Price
VanSANDT James-70
VANTREES Emanuel-34-35(2)-49
VAUDRY Joseph-98
VAUGHN Abel-92
VEALE James-22;William-23-24
VEATCH Asa-131-180;Jefferson-166
VERT Jacob-143;Milford-143;Nath-
aniel-142
VEST George-45;Littleberry-45;
William-176-205
VESTAL John-149

VICHE Henry-108-115
VICKERS Grandison-75;James-77;
  John-61;Stacy-75
VIGUS David-168
VLIET Corshon-173-175
VORIS Garret-183(2)
VOYLES Levi-229;Ransom-229

WADE Evan-39;Henry-147(2)
WADSWORTH John-37;Robert-126
WAGAMAN John-185;Joshua-185;
  Solomon-185
WAGGONER Abraham-149-150-176;Al-
  exander-140-181;Frederick-115-
  116-214;George-157;Henry-140(2)-
  160-176-180;Isaac-139-142;Jacob-
  140-177;James-181(2);Jeremiah-
  166;John-151-157-182;Jonathan-
  150;Michael-140(2);Noah-139;Rus-
  sell-178;Sally-177;Silas-181
WAGLEY Pierson-46
WAKELAND Samuel-230
WALDEN Abednigo-194;James-92;Jos-
  eph-90;Lewis-209-210;Robt-92(2)
WALDRIP James-156;John-154
WALK Jonathan-54
WALKER Catherine-233;Daniel-149;
  Eli-129;Elmore-190;George-188-
  190-201-233;Harris-138;Henry-26-
  162-163;Ignatius-32;James-163-
  164;John-17-26-42-59-62(2)-66-
  79-80(2)-157-233;Joseph-32-164-
  190;Robert-179;Thomas-160(2)-163-
  164-192;William-26-42-43;Zach-
  ariah-27
WALLACE Benjamin-214;Coleman-11-
  23;David-180;Franklin-70;George-
  216;Harrison-12;Henry-208;James-
  61-80;John-11-21-22-23-24(2)-62-
  70-177;Josiah-21-113;Nicholas-
  80;Thomas-80;Thompson-23;Wash-
  ington-82;Wesley-21-153;Wm-10-22
WALLEN Philip-228
WALLER George-29-35;John-92
WALLS see Wells;Adam-143;Andrew-
  192;Bartholomew-192;Elmina-101;
  William-101-108
WALROND James-88
WALTERS see Waters;D.-73-81-82;
  Daniel-72-79;Enoch-83;Isaac-79-
  85;James-79;Reuben-79-80-83;Rob-
  ert-206;Ruth-81;S.-73-81-82;Sea-
  man-73-79-81-82;Stephen-72-79
WALTON William-214
WAMPLER Adam-185;Andrew-208;David-
  208;Henry-200-202-203-206;Heze-

kiah-208;Jacob-210;Jefferson-204-
  208-210;Joel-109;Joseph-210
Martin-210
WARD Abner-46;Andrew-101-158;Dan-
  iel-21-22;Grandville-193-202;Ja-
  mes-71;Job-139;John-217;Jonathan-
  101;Joseph-225;Levin-214;Reuben-
  197;Rufus-200;Timothy-136-138;
  William-91
WARNER Jacob-96;Joseph-22-25-35-
  164-165;Martin-215;Philip-96
WARREN Eli-209;Hugh-209;Phillip-
  123-130
WARRICK Ellinder-83;Jacob-70-
  87(2)-88;John-68-69;Malachi-222;
  Montgomery-86
WARTH Harrison-52-99(2);John-99(2)
WASSON Joseph-88
WATERS see Walters;Israel-153;Ja-
  mes-72(2);Thomas-71-72-86;Wm-70-
WATHEN Nicholas-27.   72-90
WATKINS Jarret-52;William-95
WATSON Mr.-206;David-157;Edward-
  119;Joel-142;John-155-196-198;
  Lewis-113-169;Nelson-158;Thomas-
  221;Washington-155(2)
WATTERS see Walters,Waters
WATTS Asa-90(2);Elijah-195;George-
  60;Hugh-60-73;James-36;Thomas-59
WAY Anderson-124;Anthony-124;Eli-
  123-124;Hannah-154;William-154
WAYMON Kirtley-42
WEASE David-215-218-223;Job-102;
  John-97-215-225;Preston-96-102
WEAVER John-128-129-130;Richard-
  157;Wesley-130;Wiley-129;Wm-198
WEBB George-91;John-179;Wm-179
WEBER George-78;Solomon-16-32;
  William-14
WEBSTER Isaac-183;James-176-178-
  181;Jonathan-173;Lanford-46;Rich-
  ard-170-173;Sanford-183;Seth-168-
  173;Thomas-181;William-129-130;
  Wilson-47
WEED Zenas-84
WEEDMAN Jacob-215;Jonathan-219
WEEKS John-41;Patrick-41
WERNER Michael-93
WEIR John-205;Samuel-205
WEISS Henry-146
WELBORN Jesse-87
WELCH James-16;John-14;Wm-172-187
WELD Cornelius-149
WELLER George-66
WELLS see Walls;Abraham-88;Andrew-
  39-50;Charles-39-40;David-195;

-272-

Edward-87;John-112;Jonathan-
72;William-90
WELTON William-111
WENZEL John-16-158-165
WESNER Jacob-49-111
WEST Absalom-167;Andrew-227;Ja-
mes-84;Lewis-133;Littleberry-
197;Miles-131;Randolph-60-67;
Riley-76;William-224(2)
WESTFALL Abram-107;Calvin-88;Dan-
iel-134;Harvey-98;Hiram-88;Tho-
mas-52-98(2)-104
WHALEN John-34
WHALEY Bathsheba-214;Elijah-219
WHARTON John-196-197-198;Lawrence-
201;Stanfield-196
WHEATLEY John-24
WHEATON John-77
WHEELER Alexander-195;David-87;
Hardin-24;Henry-111-120;Horatio-
59-108-116;James-66-67-104;John-
78;Johnson-60-66(2);Payton-66;
Samuel-66-77-88(2)
WHISENAND Andrew-187;George-187-
200;Isaac-202;John-187(3)-198;
Jonathan-200;Nicholas-187-203-
209;William-188
WHITAKER William-180
WHITE Albert-229;Alvin-221;Anson-
55;Asa-157;Benjamin-120;Caleb-
210;Charles-217-222-229;Elias-
12-72-105;Ezekiel-81;Fenley-221;
Fielding-227;Francis-104-178;
Gilbert-15;Henry-216;Isaiah-190;
James-80-104-105-180;John-63-91-
187-190-191-193;Joshua-209;Levi-
148;Michael-14;Miles-161-173;
Neal-104;Samuel-10-23-24-71-132-
133;Seth-157;Stephen-128;Thomas-
178-219;Walker-131-132;Wm-128
WHITEHEAD Josiah-220;Solomon-217;
Wesley-227
WHITELY Robert-134(2)-135-137-
146;Stephen-177
WHITESIDES Joseph-63-67;William-15
WHITING Charles-84(2)
WHITMAN Asahel-229-231
WHITNEY Solomon-77
WHITSELL David-204;Jacob-204;Pet-
er-201;Robert-200
WHITSETT Benjamin-55-63;John-63-
67;Samuel-63-64
WHITTINGTON John-160
WHITTON John-132;Thomas-133
WHOOVER Isaac-129;Jacob-129
WIBLE Adam-168

WIDENER Adam-92
WIEFKING Henry-232
WIERLING Herman-105
WIGGINS Charles-88
WIGGS Alexander-221-229-230;John-
231;William-231
WILCOX Alonzo-169;Otis-107
WILDER Joshua-20
WILDMAN Jonas-159;Nimrod-170
WILES Andrew-101-107;Michael-26
WILEY Melville-30
WILHITE Franklin-40
WILKINS Andrew-120;Irvin-120;Ja-
mes-34-35-44;John-90-91;Wm-91
WILKINSON Isaiah-94;John-93;Wm-94-
WILKS Joseph-55;Willis-100.   95
WILLEMIN Hiram-33;John-20-33;
Levi-33
WILLIAMS see McWilliams;Aaron-183;
Andrew-131-169;Ann-14;Anthony-
111;Bartemius-131-166;Benjamin-
88-89-216-225;C.L.-14;D.-14;Dan-
iel-91;David-14;Diver-135;E.-14;
E.A.-14;Eleand-131;Eli-56-65-130;
F.D.-14;Garrett-131-141;George-
80-89-102;Henry-135-171-175;Is-
aac-91-92-131(2)-141-142;Jacob-
36;James-22-44-95-102-131;Jesse-
66;John-34-44-90-145-169-171;Jon-
athan-137-138;Joseph-33-44-71-91-
98-216;Martin-183;Moses-194;New-
ton-179;Patrick-143;Prior-131-
169;Richard-131-171;Robert-68;
S.-14;Samuel-79;Simon-95;Sterl-
ing-126;Thomas-14-27-69-79-80-
166-216;Thornton-95;Vincent-135-
171-184;Watson-17;William-31-38-
44-45-62-89;Zachariah-193
WILLIAMSON Aaron-111;Garrett-168;
John-113-212;Tucker-132
WILLIS Alexander-220;George-46;
Jackson-223;Jesse-51;John-223;
Louisa-51;Maxwell-224;Nancy-51;
Philip-220-223;Vincent-216-223;
Thomas-220;William-109
WILLOUGHBY Benjamin-195
WILIS William-68
WILLY Charles-102;Clement-89
WILMORE Joseph-11
WILSON Aaron-75-76;Abner-204;Alex-
ander-68-209;Allen-75-76-204;Ann-
62;Broker-148;David-74-77-103-
136-233;Dillard-147(2);Ellen-62;
Emsley-193;Ephraim-18-21-22-32-
33;Francis-15;Gabriel-102;
George-47-183;James-61-62-64-94-
154;

Jesse-40;John-28-46-47-75-84-102-
194-197;Jordan-147;Joseph-26-73;
Joshua-89;Leroy-46-47-48;Maxwell-
227;Peter-10;Peyton-141;Riley-
187-208;Robert-64;Squire-183;
Thomas-17-21-192-202-233;Walter-
67-68-217;William-30-62-64-83-
176-198-200-210-233;Willis-103-
104;Zachous-75-105
WINFIELD John-46;Rosana-46
WINGATE George-232;John-20
WININGER John-151;Samuel-151
WINGFIELD see Winfield
WINKELMANN Jacob-93./*WINEMILLER:
WINSOR George-155-161.Coonrod-119;
WINSTANDLEY John-153. Henry-120(3);
WIRE John-75-76-80.   James-119;
WIRTH see Warth.   Thomas-119.
WISE Abraham-17-22(2)-151-152;
Adam-16-17;Augustus-163;Henry-
116-120;John-12-17-28-96-99-121-
154-156-161-212;Morgan-17(2);
Samuel-28-111-120-154-156-161;
William-28-111-154-156-157-161
WISELY Frederick-186
WISMORE William-186.   217
WITHERS Isaac-189;Thomas-215-216/
WITHERSPOON James-70;John-83;Mos-
es-82;William-57-70-82
WITHROW John-81-82-92-93(2);Rich-
son-93;William-93
WITT Booker-196
WITTINGHILL James-233;Lurinda-233
WITTMAN Pierre-92
WOLF Benjamin-119-120;Jacob-117-
119(2);John-104-117;Solomon-
119(2);Vance-119-120
WOLFKILL John-78
WOLFINGTON McKinsey-155
WOLTINGMIRE Ernest-115
WOLVERTON John-156
WONZER Ephraim-58-72
WOOD see Woody;Alselm-129;Archi-
bald-139-140-142-149-189-192-
197-203-206*210;David-70-81-82;
Dickson-78;Emsley-199-207;Hamil-
ton-78;Hugh-78;Isaac-68-69-82;
James-65-66-76-78(3)-161-164-
165(3)-175-202;John-68-75-79-83-
129-130-166-201;Johnston-116;Jo-
nas-39;Joseph-65-69(2)-81-85;
Mary-31;Patrick-76;Richard-34-
35-107;Robert-127-137(2)-168;
Samuel-69(2)-75;Vincent-65-67;
William-34-35-62-66-69-78-107;
Zachariah-30;Zebedee-129-130
*Archibald-209

WOODALL Joel-139
WOODEN Amos-118;Jonathan-37;
Solomon-185-186;Stephen-36
WOODHOUSE Henry-122;Wm-121-122
WOODREW see Woodry;Isaac-228
WOODRUFF John-175;Moses-37-134-
135(3)-136-175
WOODRUM William-141-142
WOODRY see Woodrew;Henry-220;Pet-
er-220;Joseph-220
WOODWARD Bartlett-185;Elzey-191;
James-48;Julius-210;Silas-186-
188;Simpson-48
WOODY Elias-172;Henry-131-140;Mo-
ses-39;Sarah-141
WOOLSEY Eldredge-232;George-232;
Temple-232;William0230-232
WOOTEN James-192
WORKMAN Jeremiah-123;John-123-189
Robert-159
WORLEY Hiram-205
WORTH see Warth
WRIGHT Absalom-196;David-182-190;
Elijah-191;Hiram-97;James-189-
190-193-203;Jesse-186-193(2);
John-82-83-94-225;Jonathan-37-83;
Josiah-196;Peter-192;Preston-191;
Richard-193(2);Wiley-34-35;Wil-
liam-216-218-219.   96
WYANT George-107;Henry-103;James/
WYATT Benjamin-223-225;Emanuel-
224;Franklin-223;George-220;Jere-
miah-234;William-220
WYCOFF Jacob-20
WYMORE William-191
WYNNE Michael-26

Y see J
YALE Colin-142
YEAGER Elijah-94(2);George-94;
Jeremiah-71;Joel-94;Joseph-71;
Miles-53;Moses-94;Nicholas-82-86
YEATS Charles-164
YELCHEHERS Stephen-155
YIERLING Barbara-78
YODER Emanuel-207;George-200;Hen-
ry-201;Jacob-199
YORK Ezekiel-33;Jeremiah-208;John
46(2)-47;Joshua-160;Pleasant-
204;Solomon-47(2)
YOST see Jost
YOUNG Abraham-190;Daniel-226;Hen-
ry-111;Jacob-223-226;John-111;

Jonathan-77;Joseph-47(2);Josh-
 ua-226;Josiah-227-Peter-228;
 Sparling-52(2);Thomas-18
YOUNT Margaret-105;Michael-50;
 Peter-39
YOUTT William-104

Z see S
ZEIGLER George-192
ZELIFF David-43
ZIKE Jacob-146
ZIMMERMAN Daniel-55;John-54-55
ZINKS Daniel-205-206
ZUMWALT John-144

www.ingramcontent.com/pod-product-compliance
Lightning Source LLC
Chambersburg PA
CBHW020454030426
42337CB00011B/118